AF539660

PRO DIGITAL PORTRAIT LIGHTING

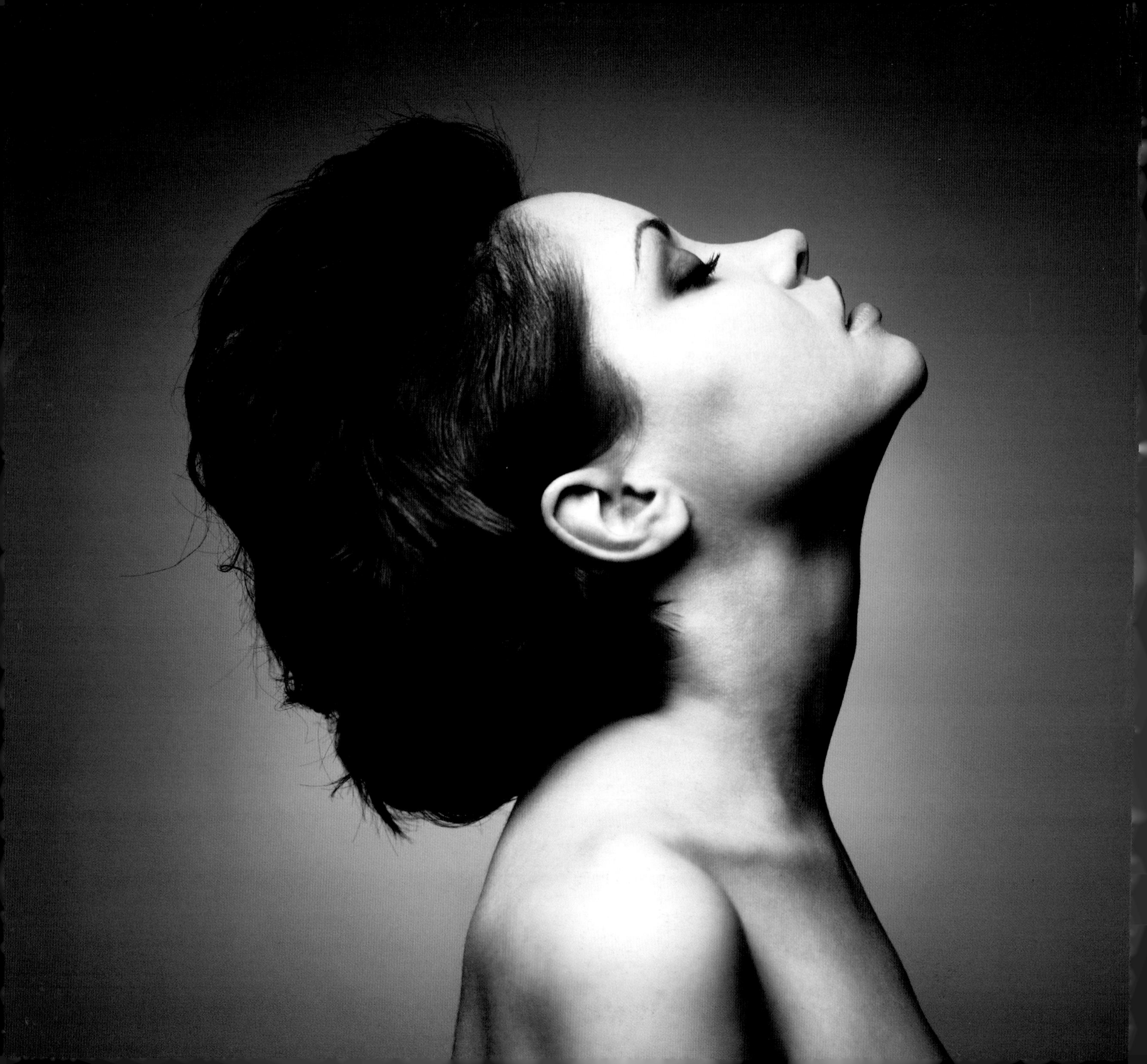

PRO DIGITAL PORTRAIT LIGHTING

THE DEFINITIVE REFERENCE TO LIGHTING SETUPS

Peter Hince

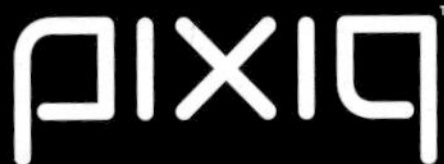

An Imprint of Sterling Publishing Co., Inc.
New York

Pro Digital Portrait Lighting

Library of Congress Cataloging-in-Publication Data
Hince, Peter.
Pro digital portrait lighting : the definitive reference to lighting setups / Peter Hince. -- 1st ed.
p. cm.
Includes bibliographical references and index.
ISBN 978-1-60059-784-8 (alk. paper)
1. Portrait photography--Lighting. I. Title. II. Title: Professional digital portrait lighting.
TR575.H56 2011
778.9'2--dc22
2010032942

10 9 8 7 6 5 4 3 2 1
First Edition
Published by Pixiq
An Imprint of Sterling Publishing Co., Inc.
387 Park Avenue South, New York, N.Y. 10016

This book was conceived, designed, and produced by:
ILEX, 210 High Street, Lewes, BN7 2NS, United Kingdom

Publisher Alastair Campbell
Creative Director Peter Bridgewater
Associate Publisher Adam Juniper
Managing Editor Natalia Price-Cabrera
Senior Designer James Hollywell
Designer Simon Goggin
Photographer Peter Hince
Color Origination Ivy Press Reprographics

Distributed in Canada by Sterling Publishing,
c/o Canadian Manda Group, 165 Dufferin Street
Toronto, Ontario, Canada M6K 3H6

If you have questions or comments about this book, please contact:
Pixiq, 67 Broadway, Asheville, NC 28801
(828) 253-0467

Manufactured in China

ISBN: 978-1-60059-784-8

For information about custom editions, special sales, premium and corporate purchases, please contact Sterling Special Sales Department at 800-805-5489 or specialsales@sterlingpub.com. For information about desk and examination copies available to college and university professors, requests must be submitted to academic@sterlingpublishing.com.

Key
L1 = Light 1
L2 = Light 2
H = Horizontal
V = Vertical
R = Reflector
C = Camera

CONTENTS

INTRODUCTION

Of all the many genres of photography, portraiture is perhaps the most enduring, and certainly the longest standing. From its very earliest exponents right through to this moment, people all around the world have felt the urge to pick up their cameras and photograph other people around them.

Initially, the photograph took the place of a painted portrait, with much of the excitement coming from the newly born process itself—a mechanical and chemical operation that revealed people as they truly were, rather than relying on the interpretive skills of a painter. As a result, wealthy individuals would commission photographers to produce first daguerrotypes, and later, ambrotypes (among many other print types) of themselves, their families, and the people they knew and cared for, as much to show their wealth as to have the photograph itself.

It was not until 1859, when André Adolphe-Eugène Disdéri patented his *carte de visite* (or "visiting card"), that the photographic portrait truly revolutionized—and arguably replaced—the classical painted portrait. For the first time, photographers could set up a commercial studio and invite "the public" to enter and have their picture taken, before leaving with a modestly priced, small-format albumen print that they could show and share with their friends and family.

This tradition continues today and the widespread popularity of digital cameras has done nothing but make portrait photography easier, cheaper, and more accessible than ever before. Whether it's a formal family portrait, a candid snapshot of a loved one, or even a portrait that someone has commissioned, it seems that photographers are still obsessed with picturing people—and why not? Even the most humble snap can tell us so much about the person it shows; what they look like, how they dress, an insight into their personality, or even a piece of their soul according to some.

However, there's an unmistakable difference between a simple snapshot and a crafted, posed photograph taken in a studio. This isn't just down to the skills of the photographer in choosing the right camera, lens, aperture, shutter speed, or any of the other technical settings, it is also about how the portrait is lit. All photography needs light, but portraiture requires a mastery of lighting if it is to be achieved at the highest level. It is through the careful placement and control of light that truly great portraits are made, and with this book as a reference, you can begin your journey to follow in this historic photographic tradition.

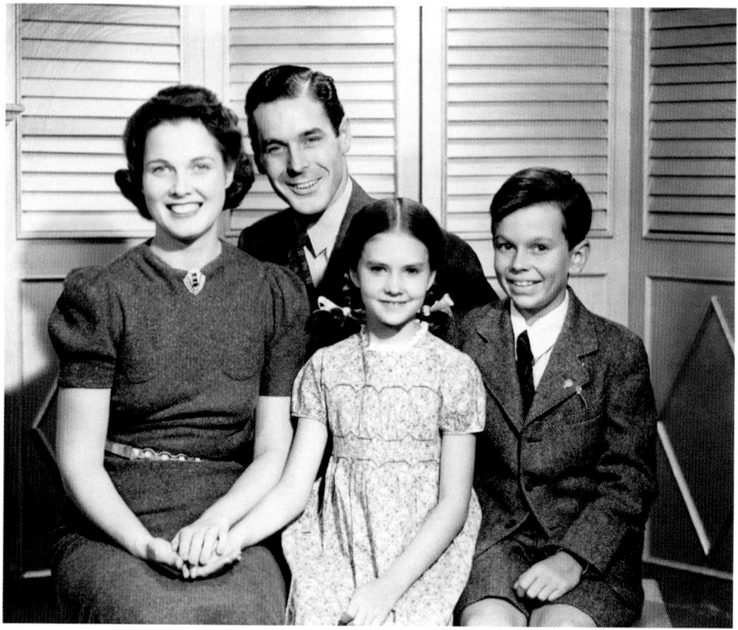

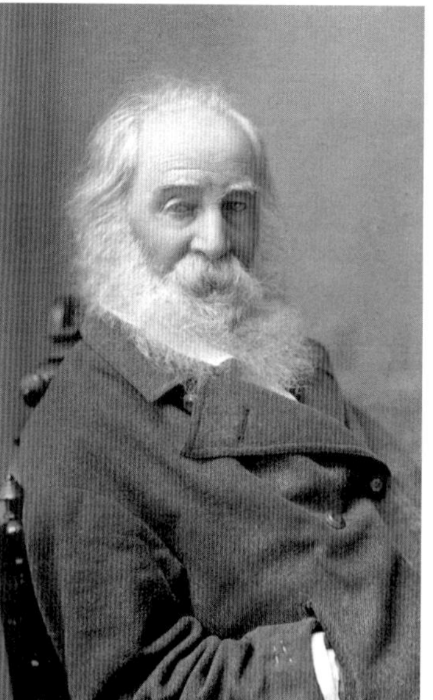

Since photography was invented, people have been taking portraits, whether it's formal studies of noted figures of the time, such as American poet Walt Whitman (left), or formal family photographs (above). These traditions continue today, although advertising, fashion, and countless magazines have also created a demand for more creative people-pictures (right). Regardless of the subject, what they all have in common is the need for light—without it, photography simply isn't possible.

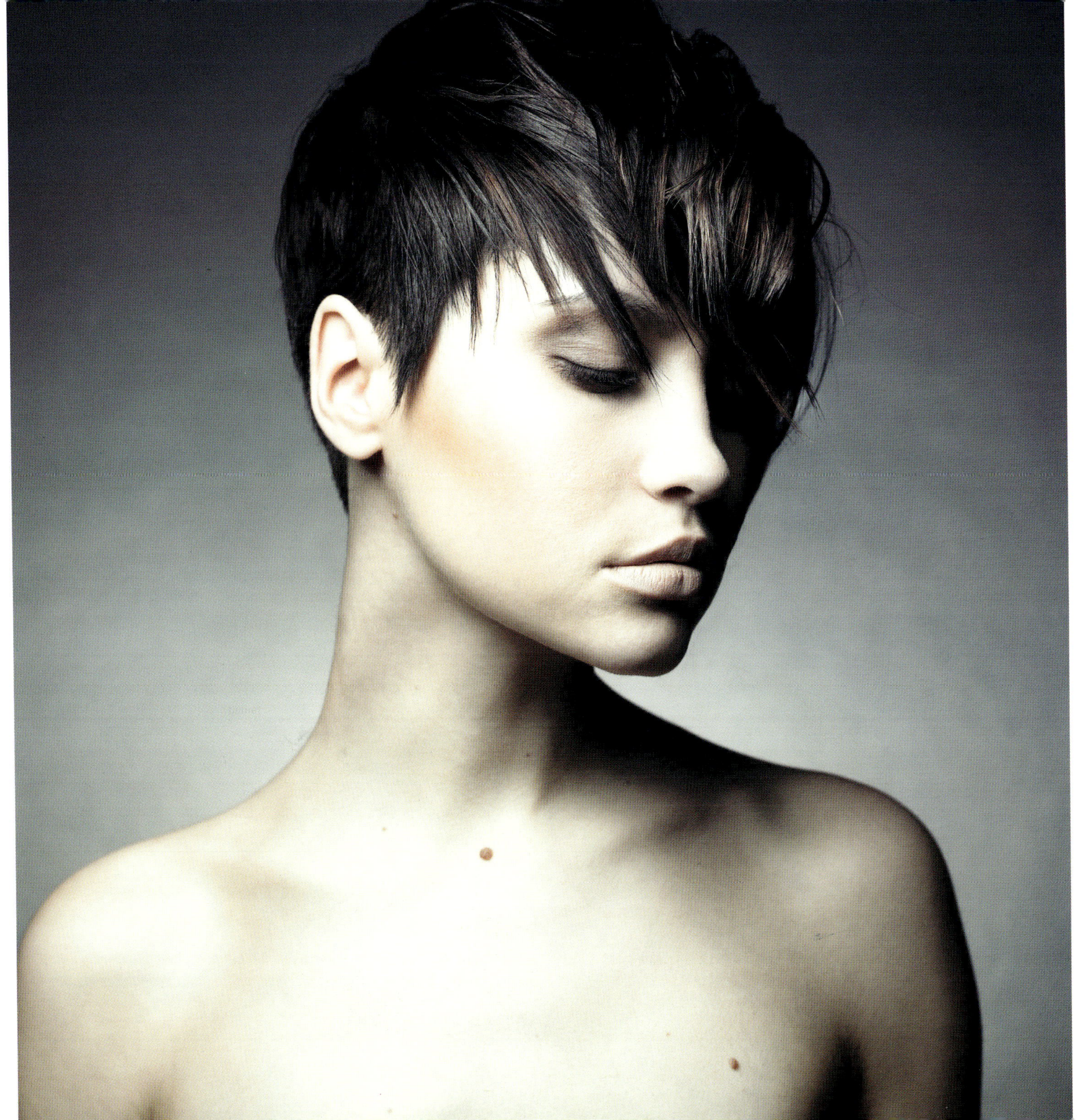

HOW TO USE THIS BOOK

This book consists of over one hundred lighting setups that you can refer to for your portrait photography. Each setup has been given a double-page spread, so whether you are working in the studio or on location, all the information you need is available to you at a glance. Before you start, however, it is worth taking a little time to familiarize yourself with exactly what information appears on the pages, and where.

Here you will see how many lights were used and their position. Where an angle is given in degrees, this is in relation to the camera position.

This graphic shows the position of the lights in relation to the model. Shown from above, the model is in the center, with the position of the lights marked on the outer ring.

The three-dimensional illustration shows you precisely where each of the lights is positioned, as well as the model and the camera. You can also see which light modifiers or accessories were used.

Accompanying each lighting reference is text highlighting the key elements of the setup, its potential uses, and handy hints on where and when it could work best.

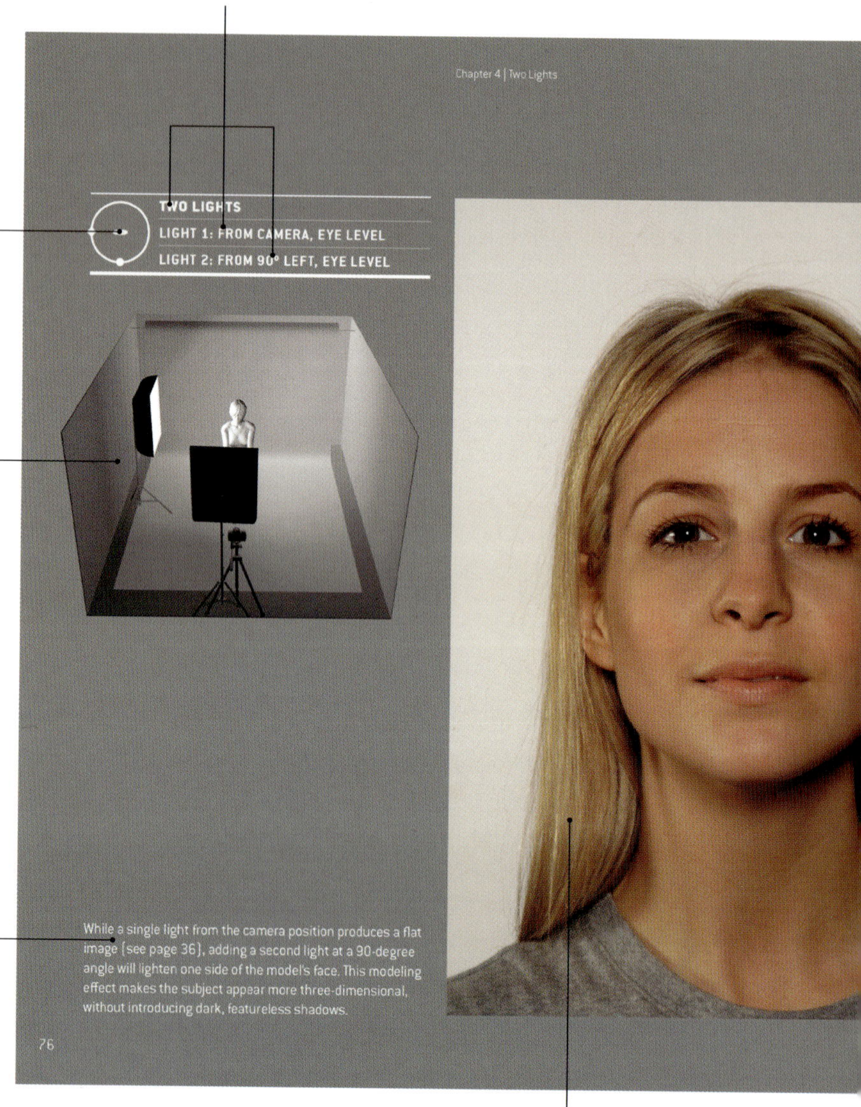

A large reference shot for each setup allows you to see clearly what effect you get from the lighting.

Different skin types can have a profound effect on the lighting, so reference images of models with different skin tones are shown.

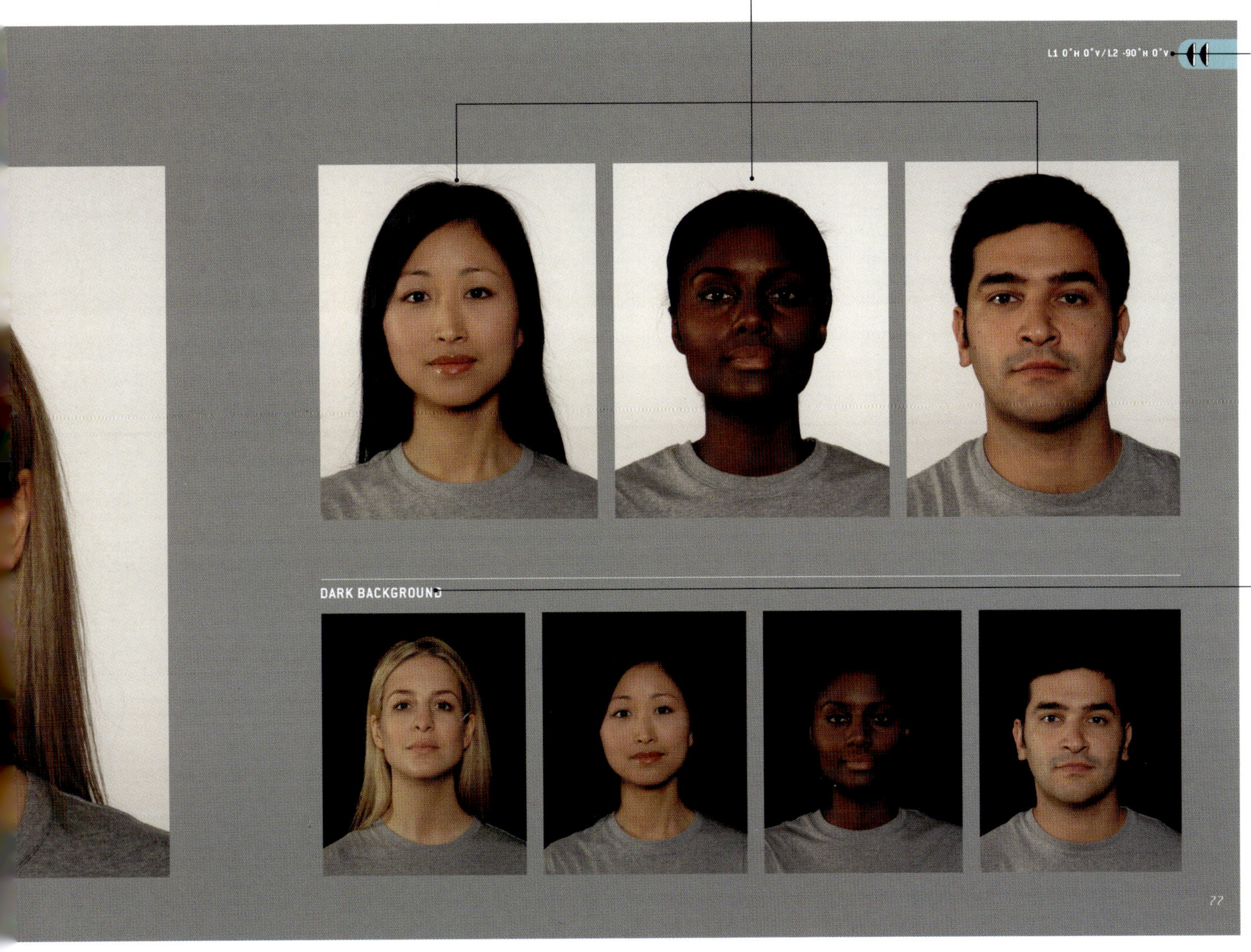

At the top corner of every setup is an at-a-glance guide to the lighting used, showing the angle of the lights both horizontally (H) and vertically (V). In this example, two lights were employed, one at 0°, and the other at a -90° angle to the camera. Both were set at eye level (0° vertical).

While the color of a model's skin can affect the appearance of a particular lighting setup, so can the color of the background. To show the differences, all of the reference images have been shot against both a light and a dark background.

LIGHTING: THE OPTIONS

Today, there is a bewildering array of lighting options available to portrait photographers, from tungsten- and fluorescent-based continuous lighting through to the many and varied designs of short-duration flash. Historically, continuous lighting has a much longer association with portrait photography than flash, simply because it has been around for many more years.

Perhaps the most iconic examples of continuous lighting for portraiture come from the golden era of Hollywood cinema. From the mid-1920s, when the "movie star" was arguably born, an army of photographers were recruited to photograph the cinematic celebrities of the day—from glamorous screen sirens such as Greta Garbo and Marilyn Monroe, to the brooding figures of Marlon Brando and Humphrey Bogart. Although the photographic treatment of male and female subjects differed—typically soft and diffuse for her, and hard-edged for him—what these celebrity portraits all had in common was their reliance on continuous lighting.

However, the popularity of continuous lighting—in this instance the incandescent, or tungsten lamps used in movie-making—was soon replaced by an enthusiasm for flash. With its daylight color balance, high power, and short duration, flash was far better suited to photographers working with color film; the camera didn't need to be filtered, and shooting with a mix of both flash and ambient daylight was straightforward. Flash also ran much cooler than tungsten lights, which was an important consideration for photographers working in the confines of a studio, where a number of tungsten lamps could quickly heat a room to temperatures that were unbearable for both the photographer and their model.

Yet while there were quite obvious practical reasons behind the widespread move from continuous lighting to flash when everyone shot on film, in the digital age many of the arguments are now moot—in-camera white-balance control overcomes many of the concerns about filtration on the lens or the lights, while cool-running continuous lighting systems resolve any issues about comfort. Over the following pages we'll take a look at the lighting options that are currently available and their benefits—and shortcomings—for portrait photography.

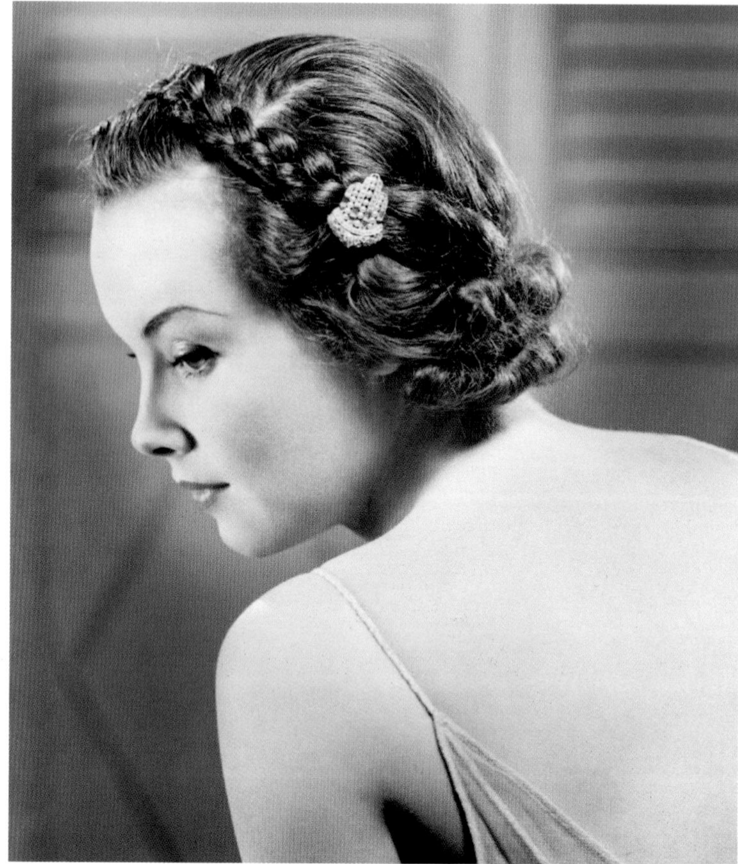

ABOVE:
Continuous lighting and black-and-white pictures became synonymous with Hollywood cinema of the 1920s until the late 1950s.

RENTING LIGHTS

Although professional photographic lighting equipment tends to come at a high price, there are studios and dedicated photographic rental centers all around the world that will hire lights on a daily—or even hourly—basis, whether you're interested in flash, incandescent, or even modern movie-style HMI lighting equipment. The advantage of this is you're only ever paying for the equipment when you want to use it, and the rental costs are a fraction of the purchase price. In addition, should something go wrong with the lights you're using, you won't be the one left picking up the repair bill or even dealing with the repair process.

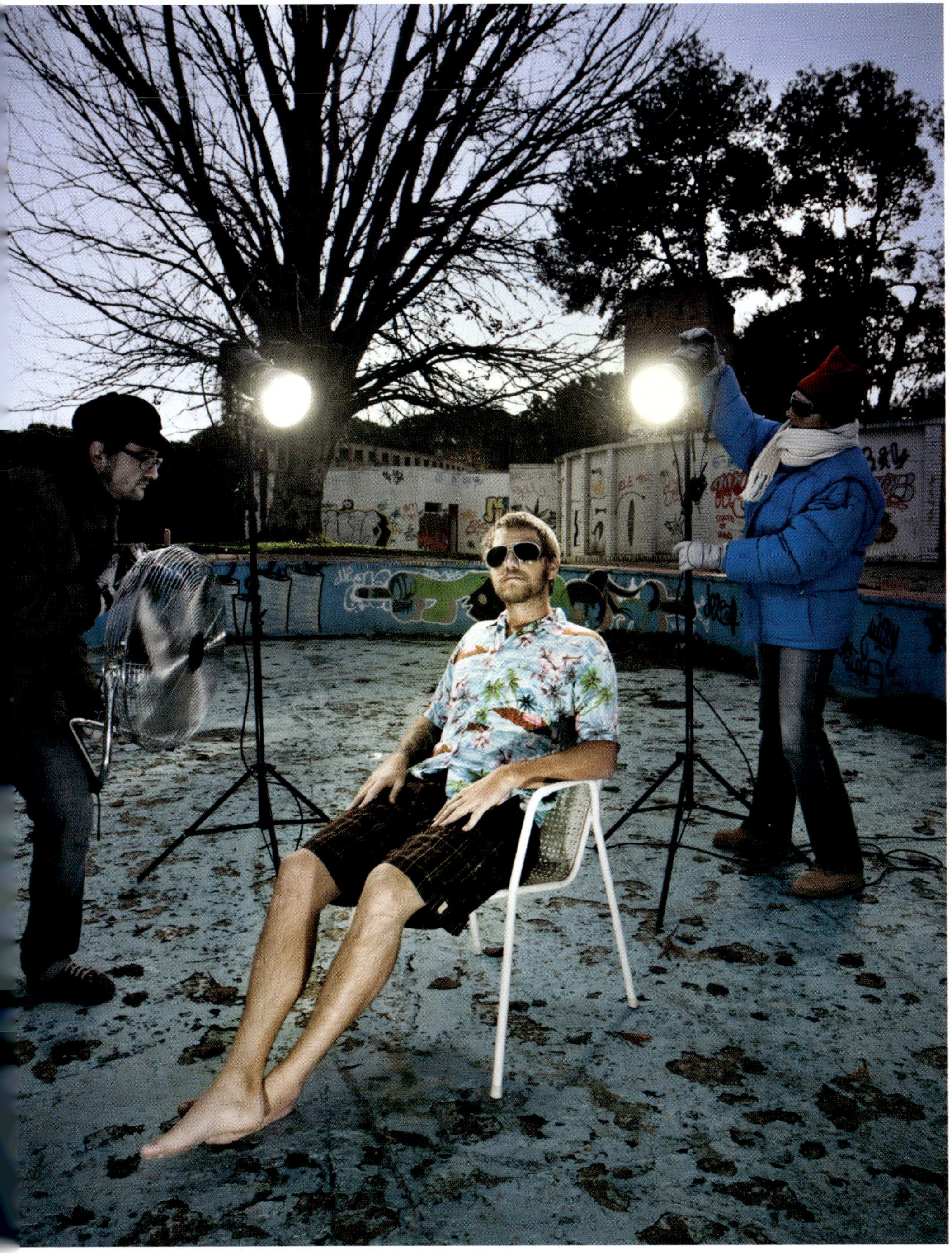

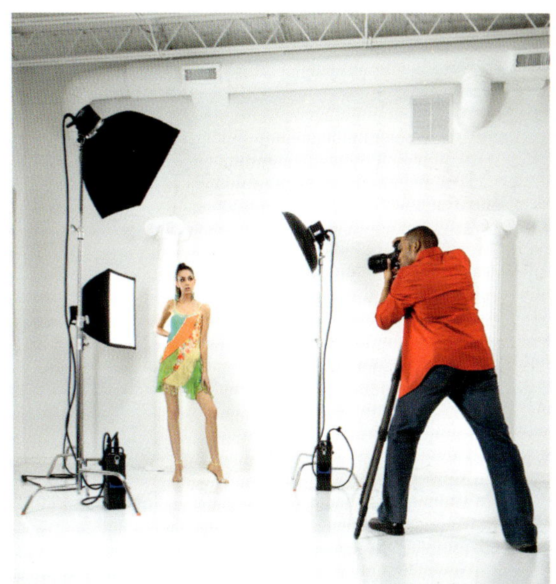

ABOVE:
Most studio photographers use flash to light their shots, and many will choose strobes that attach to power packs.

LEFT:
If you plan to take your lights on location, you need to look for a lighting kit that's both compact and portable.

BELOW:
The modeling bulb helps preview the effect of the flash. Here you can see the modeling bulb in the center of the flash head and the flash tube partly encircling it.

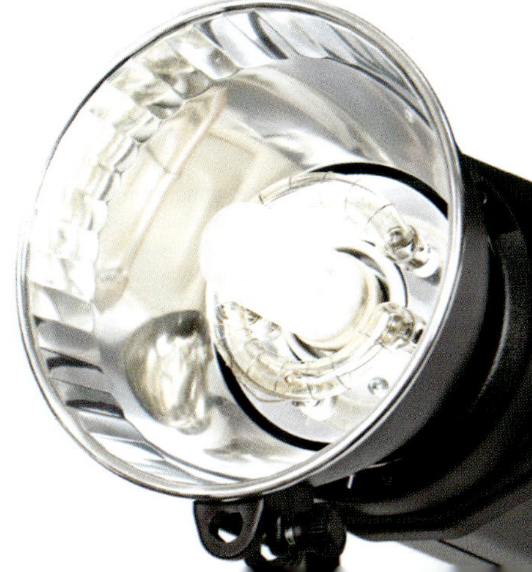

FLASH LIGHTING: POWER PACKS

For the majority of portrait photographers, flash is the light of choice: all of the reference shots in this book were taken using studio flash units. The reasons for its popularity are fairly straightforward: flash produces a brief burst of high-power light that allows relatively fast shutter speeds to be used, without generating an excessive amount of heat. Moreover, the output of a flash can be controlled electronically, so you can simply increase or decrease the power to regulate the amount of light falling on your subject, rather than moving your lights closer to your subject or further away. Add a wide range of light-modifying accessories that are available from the established brands and third-party manufacturers, and it's easy to see just how versatile studio flash lighting can be.

Although there is a number of companies that make studio flash equipment, when it comes to the lights themselves, there are only two options for photographers; monolights (which we will look at on the following pages), and flash systems that use an auxiliary power pack to control the flash heads.

At its most basic, power-pack lighting systems consist of two components—a "pack" that generates power for the flash, and a flash "head" that can be plugged into it. Packs come in a range of powers, measured in watts per second (w/s), which is the input power to the pack. Depending on the make and model you choose, you'll likely be able to plug more than one head into a single pack and they will all share the power between them. For example, if you had a single flash plugged into a 2400w/s pack, firing it at full power would nominally give you a 2400w/s flash, while plugging two flash heads into the pack and splitting the power equally between them would give you a 1200w/s output from each. Some packs allow you to independently set the amount of power sent to each light for greater control over the power distribution.

The advantage of a pack-based system is that the control of all your lights is in one place—the pack—so you can adjust all the lights you are using from a single point. Because the flash heads aren't controlling the power themselves, this makes them simpler in design and construction, which in turn means they cost less to buy than monolights. However, the main disadvantage with this type of lighting system is that without the power pack your lights won't work, so should the pack breakdown mid-shoot you may have no other option than to abandon your shoot.

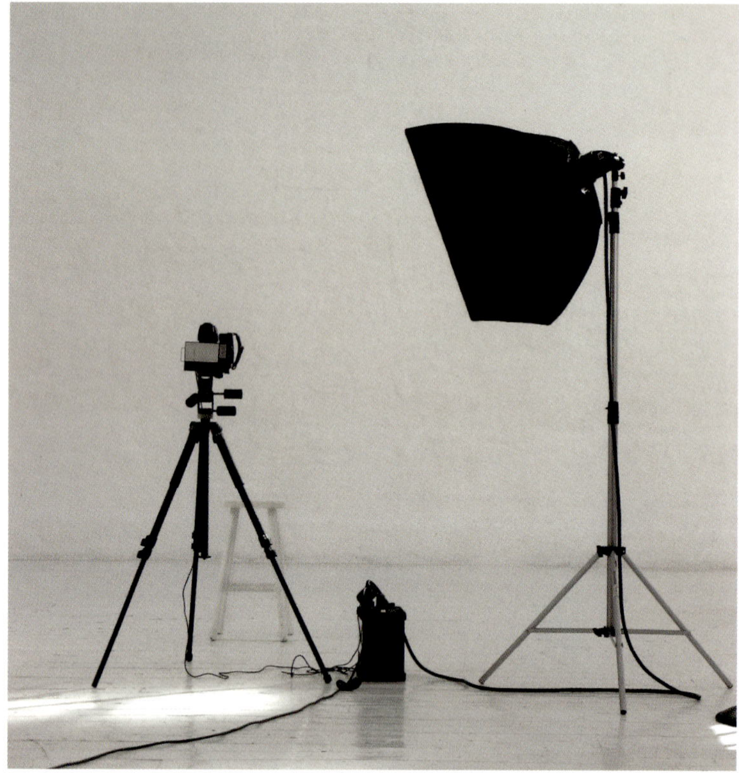

ABOVE:
In a studio, a pack-and-head based flash system provides the photographer with a single control point over all of the flashes.

BELOW:
A power pack contains all the controls for the flash heads that are plugged into it, from the power output to the modeling light controls.

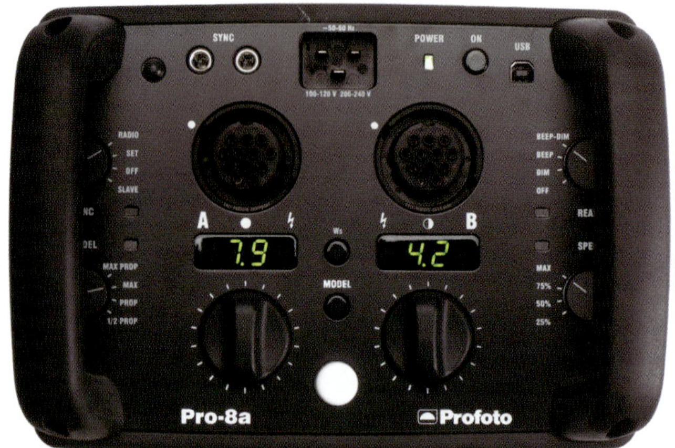

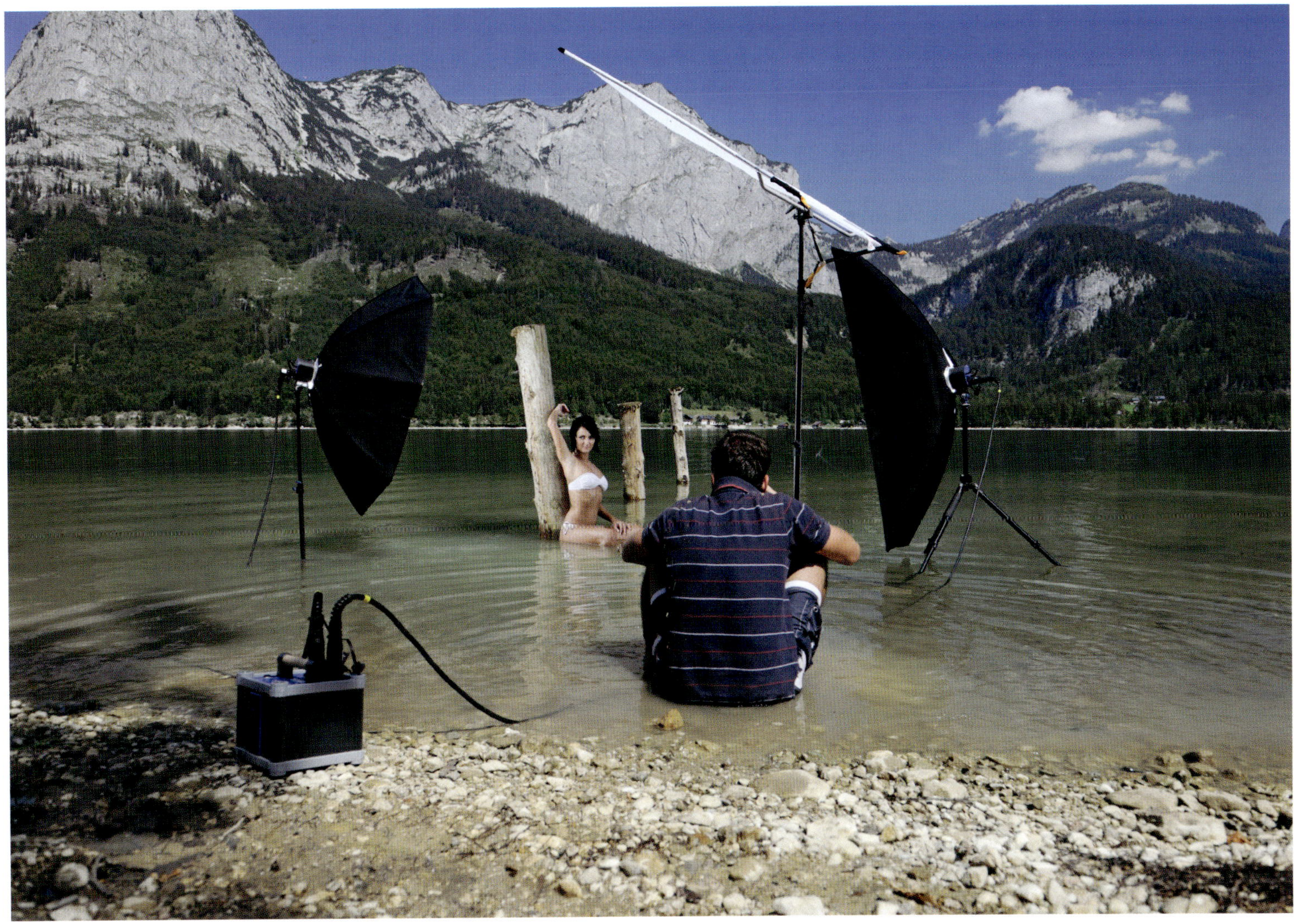

ABOVE:
Battery packs allow you to use the same flash heads in the studio or on location where there isn't access to an AC outlet.

PROS/CONS

+ High power outputs available.
Battery-powered packs available for location shooting.
Flash heads cheaper than monolights.
Wide range of accessories available.

– If the power pack breaks down, the flashes won't work.
Tied in to one manufacturer—packs and heads from different companies are generally not interchangeable.

FLASH LIGHTING: MONOLIGHTS

The alternative to pack-and-head lighting systems is monolights, which are the preferred choice for many portrait photographers, especially those that find themselves shooting on location—at their subject's house, for example. As with pack-based systems, the power of a monolight is measured in watts per second (this is again the input power and not necessarily the output measurement), but the key difference is that all of the flash controls—and the technology needed to make them work—is built into the flash itself. So while a flash head that is designed to be plugged into a pack may have nothing more than an on/off switch, a monolight will typically bristle with dials and switches that allow you to adjust the power of the light, switch the modeling light on or off, activate an optical slave cell, and so on.

While this may sound complicated, having all of these controls on the flash head itself actually makes monolights slightly easier to use than packs and heads because it is easier to see precisely how each flash is set up. A further advantage with monolights is their compact size. Monolights are often not that much larger than a flash head designed to be used with a pack, but as you don't need an auxiliary power pack they don't take up as much space. You are also not as restricted when it comes to positioning monolights as you don't have to worry about their leads all reaching the same pack—all you need is an electrical outlet to plug them into.

The only real downside to monolights is their cost. Having all of the flash's features built in to the head makes them more expensive than a flash that runs off a power pack, although as each head is a self-contained unit, you don't need to invest in a power pack, which balances things out to a certain extent. That said, repairs can be more expensive if a monolight breaks down, which can (and will) happen given there are so many components involved. Taking a "spare" head on a shoot is definitely advisable unless you can go back and reshoot on another day.

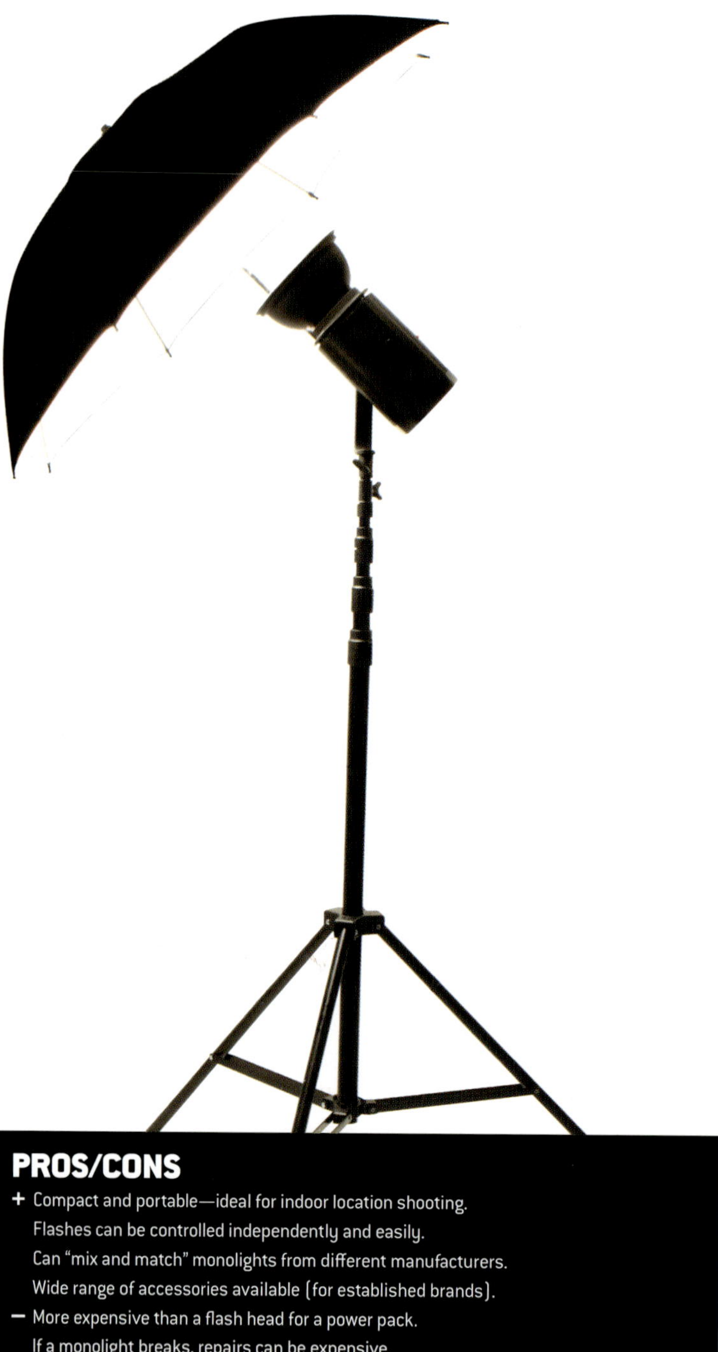

RIGHT:
Monolights are great for shooting on location when you want to avoid leads trailing to and from a power pack.

PROS/CONS

\+ Compact and portable—ideal for indoor location shooting.
Flashes can be controlled independently and easily.
Can "mix and match" monolights from different manufacturers.
Wide range of accessories available (for established brands).

– More expensive than a flash head for a power pack.
If a monolight breaks, repairs can be expensive.

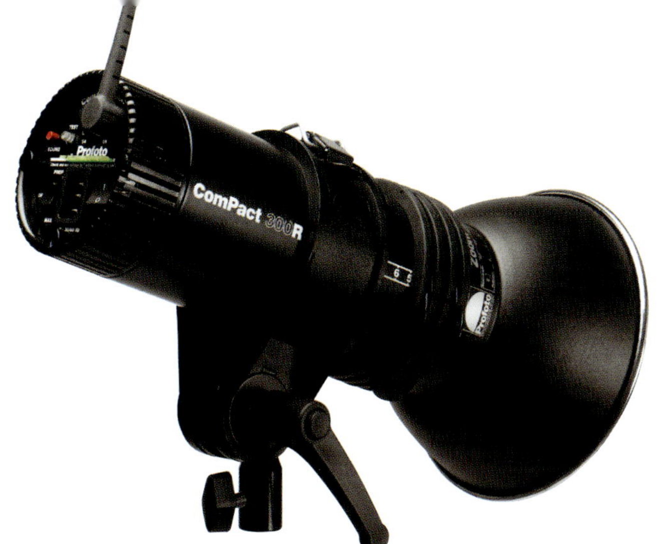

ABOVE:
A monolight contains all the controls for the flash in the head itself, making it easy to check how each flash is set.

BELOW:
Monolights are just as versatile as pack-and-head flashes, allowing the same range of accessories to be fitted to control your lighting.

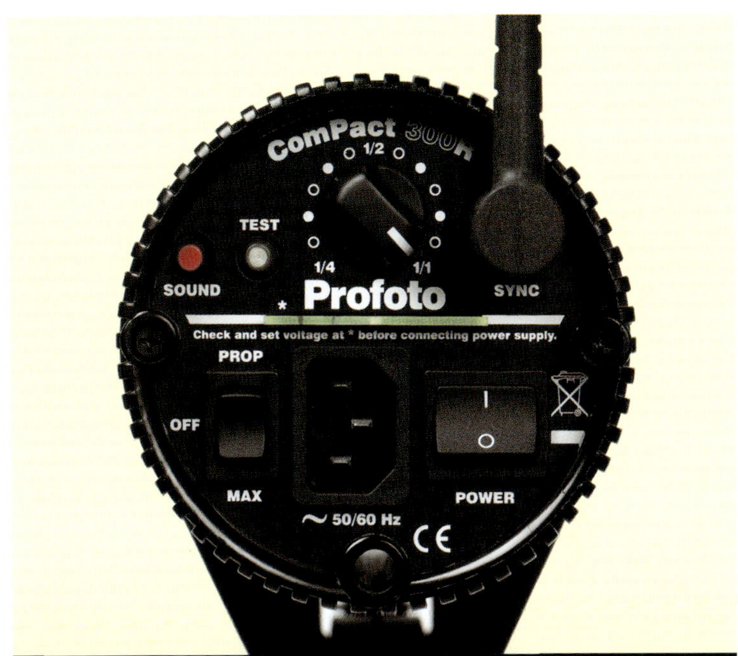

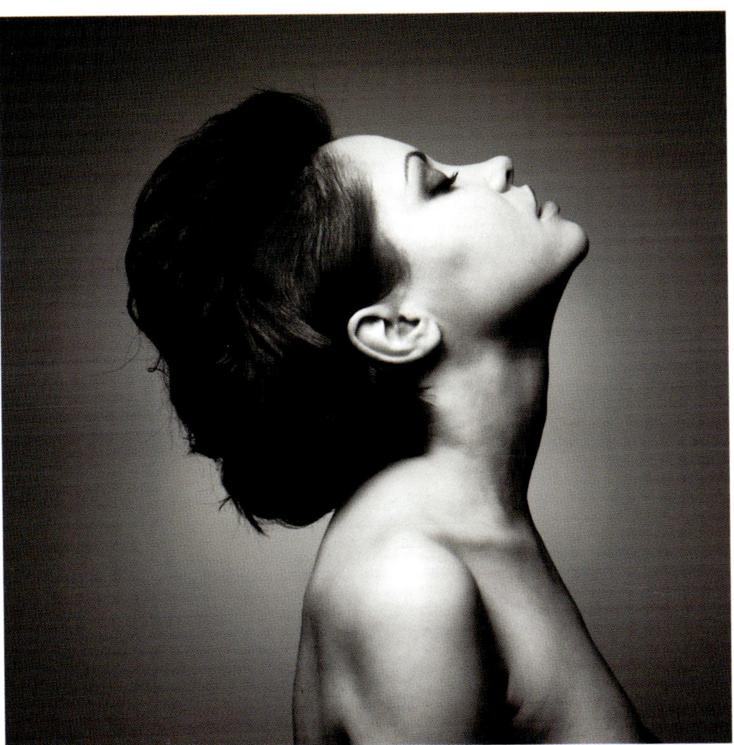

KEY MONOLIGHT FEATURES

Generally, the more you spend on a monolight, the wider the range of features it will have, and the more sophisticated they will be. Here's what to look for:

POWER CONTROL:
Having the ability to adjust the power of a light across a wide range will allow you to experiment more with your lighting setups without having to move your lights. Some monolights offer settings from full to 1/32 power.

MODELING LIGHT:
A modeling light will help you see the effect the flash will have on your subject, but to get the most accurate preview the modeling light should be proportional to the flash power. If you're working outdoors, brighter modeling bulbs are best.

SLAVE CELL:
A monolight's optical slave cell should be sensitive enough to work in daylight and it should also work when it isn't receiving the light from another flash directly. Some lights have built-in radio receivers that don't suffer from this problem and offer photographers a more sophisticated solution.

RECYCLING TIME:
The more powerful the flash, the longer it will take to recycle the charge before it is ready to fire again, but some flashes are faster than others—useful if you like to shoot at a fast pace.

CONTINUOUS LIGHTING: INCANDESCENT

Continuous lighting may have a longer association with portrait photography than flash, but for most professional photographers it is no longer their first choice. The main reason for this is because flash is more versatile. Unlike a flash unit, a photographer has very little control over continuous lights such as incandescent lamps, as the power is largely determined by the strength of the bulb and the lamp's distance from the subject. The warm tungsten glow is also a far cry from the color temperature of daylight, meaning the lights have to be filtered if you want to use them in daylight and match the color temperatures of both lightsources.

However, perhaps the least desirable trait of incandescent lighting is the amount of heat they generate—it isn't for nothing that these lamps are often referred to as "hot lights." Because incandescent lamps work by heating a tungsten filament to produce light, they naturally create a large amount of heat, which can become particularly unpleasant for all involved if several lamps are used at once in a fairly small studio.

It isn't just the photographer and their model that suffer from the heat; the accessories fitted to the lights will suffer too. Because of the high temperature generated by even a relatively "weak" 800-watt bulb, incandescent lights require specialist heat-resistant softboxes, which cost more than their flash counterparts. Any sort of reflector dish that might stifle the flow of air—such as a snoot—is also not a good idea as it can cause the lamp to overheat, and possibly explode.

Having said all that, incandescent lights do have one major advantage over flash—what you see is what you get. Unlike flash lighting, which generally requires trial exposures to see how the lighting looks, when you're using a continuous light source the effect of any light can be seen "live" on the subject and, if it isn't falling where you want it to, it's easy to identify and fix the problem. Because of this, continuous lights are great for those starting out in portrait photography who don't have an in-depth knowledge of flash. The low purchase price of incandescent photo lights also means you don't have to commit yourself to spending a lot of money if you simply want to give it a go.

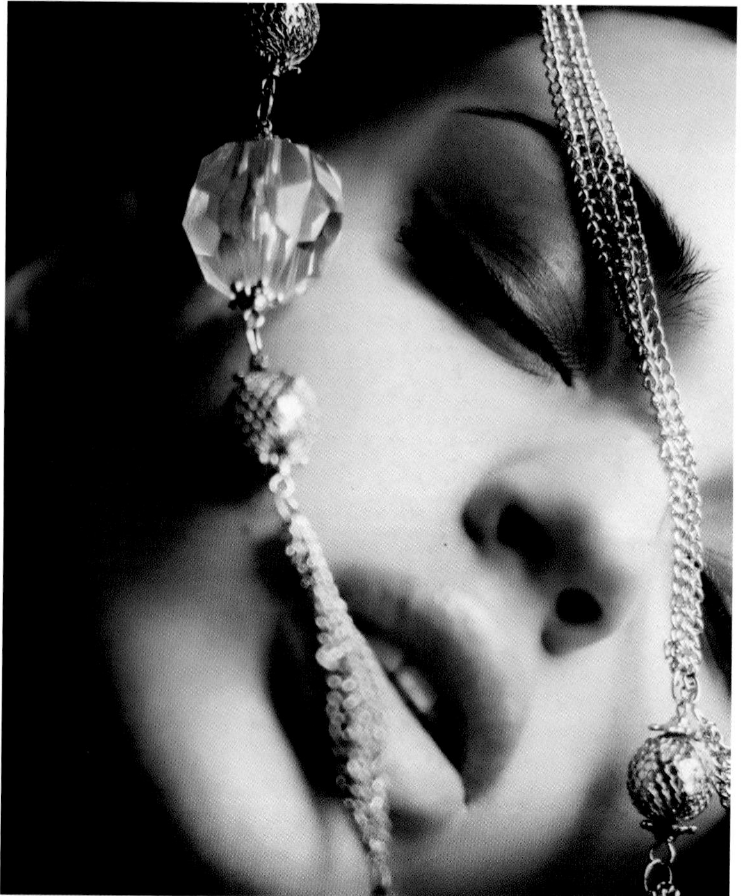

ABOVE:
One of the biggest advantages of continuous lighting over flash is the ability to see the precise effect your lights are having.

COLOR TEMPERATURE

Unlike the other lights shown here, incandescent lighting has a much warmer color temperature than daylight—3200K (degrees Kelvin) compared to the 5500–5600K of daylight. This is more of an issue with film-based photography than it is with digital, as you can simply set your camera's white balance to incandescent, but you'll still need to use blue gels over the lights if you want to match their color temperature to daylight.

BELOW:
Continuous incandescent lights come in a wide range of shapes, styles, and sizes, including the ubiquitous 800-watt workhorse shown here.

RIGHT:
Black-and-white "film noir" style portraits have a close connection with continuous lighting that harks back to their cinematic origins.

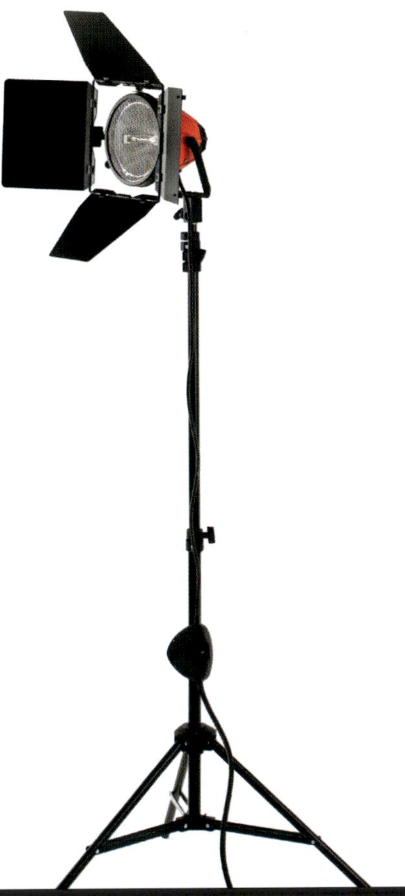

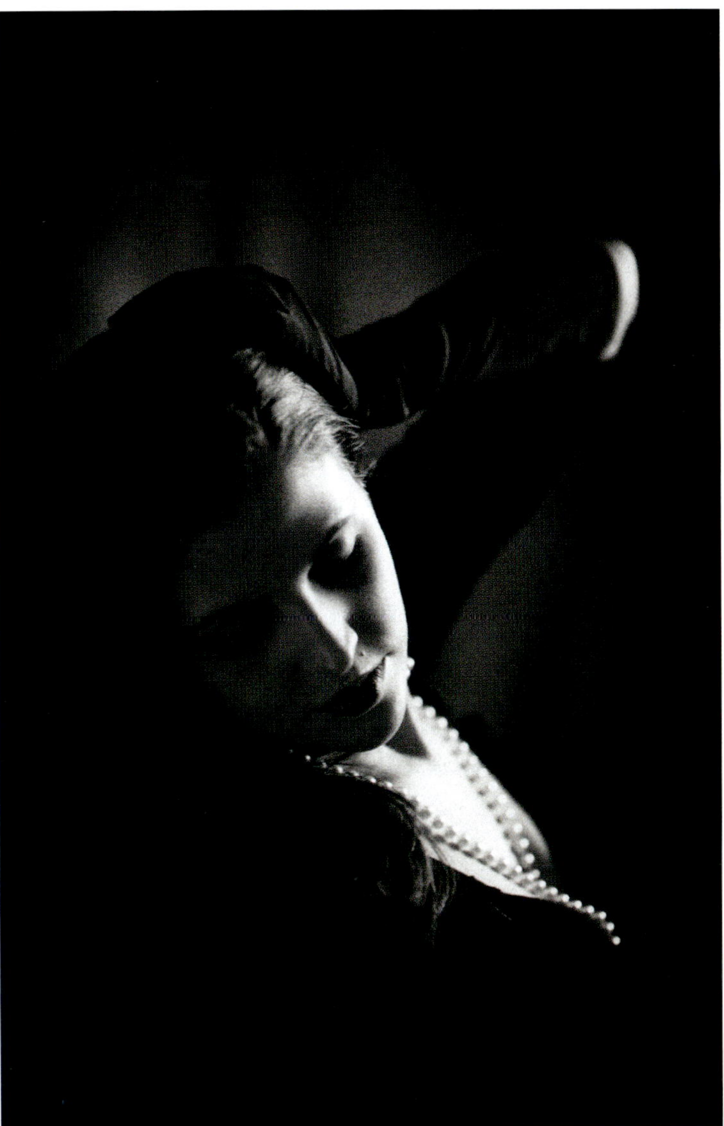

INCANDESCENT SAFETY TIPS

To avoid any hot light disasters, observe the following:

- Take regular breaks and switch off the lights to allow them to cool.
- Never leave incandescent lamps unattended when they're switched on.
- Use dichroic filters to convert the tungsten light to daylight, rather than acetate gels—dichroic filters will better withstand the high temperatures.
- Never try to make your own lighting accessories. A card snoot may work on a flash, but on a hot light it's a potential fire hazard.
- Only use accessories designed specifically for incandescent lighting. The softboxes might cost more, but that's because they're heat resistant.

PROS/CONS

\+ Very easy to use—what you see is what you get.
Low cost.

– Produce a lot of heat.
Need to use gels to balance them with daylight.
Limited range of accessories.

CONTINUOUS LIGHTING: HMI

An abbreviation of Hydrargyrum Medium-arc Iodide, HMI lighting became a popular alternative to flash in digital photography's infancy, especially with high-end advertising and fashion photographers. The problem for pioneering photographers using digital backs on their medium- or large-format cameras was that the early digital backs "scanned" an image, rather than making a momentary, split-second exposure. This meant a continuous light source was needed, and the answer was HMI lighting—a technology already established in movie and television production.

One of the main reasons HMI works so well for photographic work is that it operates at a color temperature of 5600K, so it mixes readily with daylight. In addition, HMI lights use an arc lamp that consumes far less power than an incandescent lamp, and runs at a much cooler temperature—an important consideration when multiple lights are needed in the confines of a studio.

However, while HMIs are still used widely in the movie and television industries, their use in stills photography has declined. Today, cheaper continuous lighting alternatives have been developed, and the "scanning" digital camera backs that once made continuous lighting a necessity have largely been updated, at least when it comes to portrait photography.

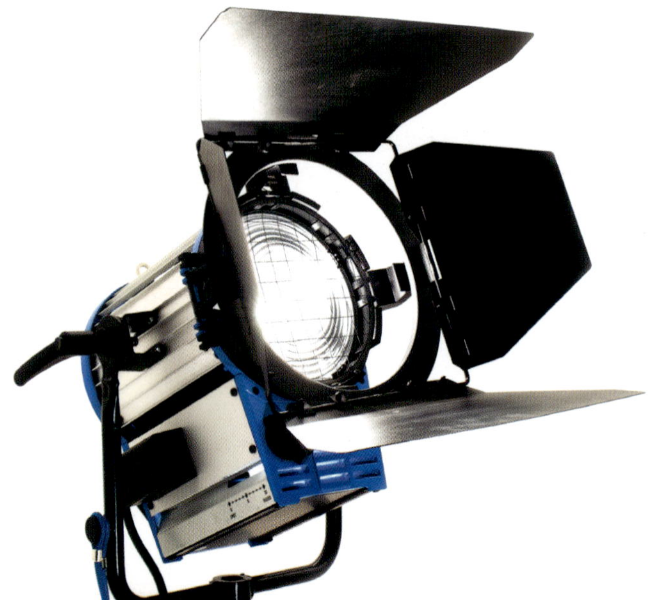

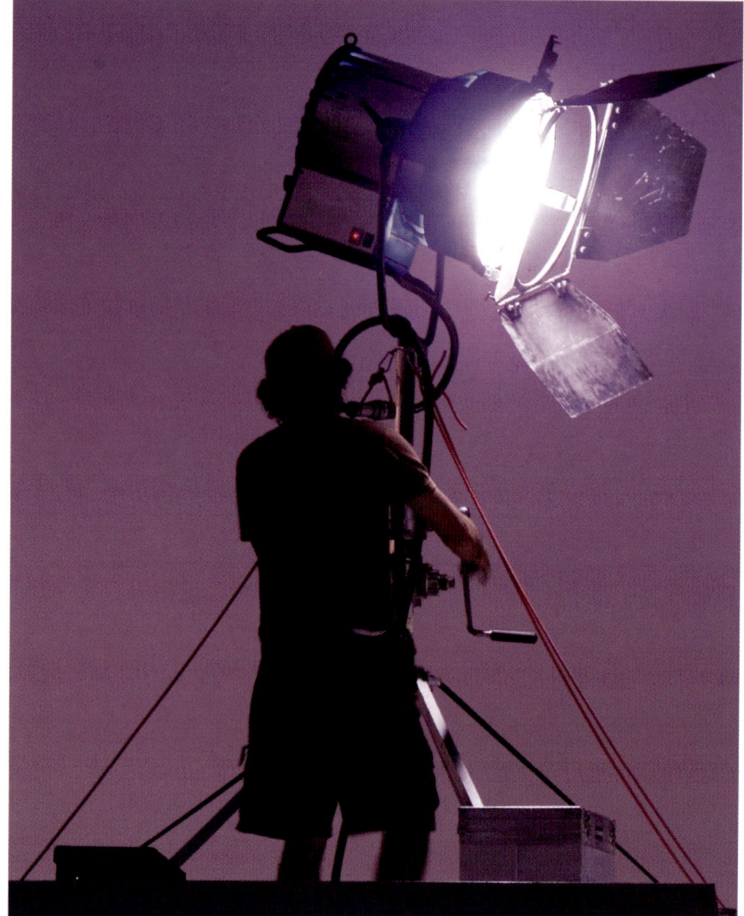

LEFT:
HMI lights burn at a color temperature that matches daylight, without the heat of incandescent lighting.

ABOVE:
High-power HMI lighting is more closely associated with the movie and television industries than photography.

PROS/CONS

+ Cool running.
  Daylight balanced.
  Generally exceptional build quality.
– VERY expensive.
  Lack of accessories for stills photography.
  Require a bulky "ballast" pack to ignite and regulate the electrical arc.

CONTINUOUS LIGHTING: FLUORESCENT

Fluorescent studio lighting is a relatively recent addition to the continuous lighting options available to photographers and it largely falls into two distinct groups: high-end, professional fluorescent lighting equipment (from manufacturers such as Kino Flo and Balcar), and "prosumer" lights that are becoming ever more prevalent in photo stores and on Internet auction sites. It's the latter that we'll focus on here as the typically low purchase price potentially makes them the most appealing option for portrait photography.

Many of the prosumer fluorescent lighting kits you'll see use a variation of a screw-fit, "daylight balanced" fluorescent bulb, with numerous bulbs housed in a single lamp to increase the brightness of the light. Regardless of the number of bulbs used, the temperature of the lights remains cool when they're turned on, especially compared to incandescent lamps. However, with a nominal color temperature of around 5000K, many of these lights aren't quite a true match for the accepted temperature of daylight (5500–5600K). Although they aren't far off (and the disparity can be overcome with a custom white balance setting on your camera), if you wanted to mix them with daylight or flash the difference would show.

It's also worth considering what accessories are available for the lights. As we'll see on pages 22–25, accessories that modify the light will give you greater versatility in what you can achieve in your portrait photography, but only a few manufacturers produce lighting accessories for their fluorescent lamps. Unless you're careful, you could easily find yourself with a couple of low-cost lights that restrict your creativity..

PROS/CONS

+ Cool running.
  Low cost.
– Not necessarily daylight balanced.
  Limited accessories.
  Some models suffer from poor build quality.

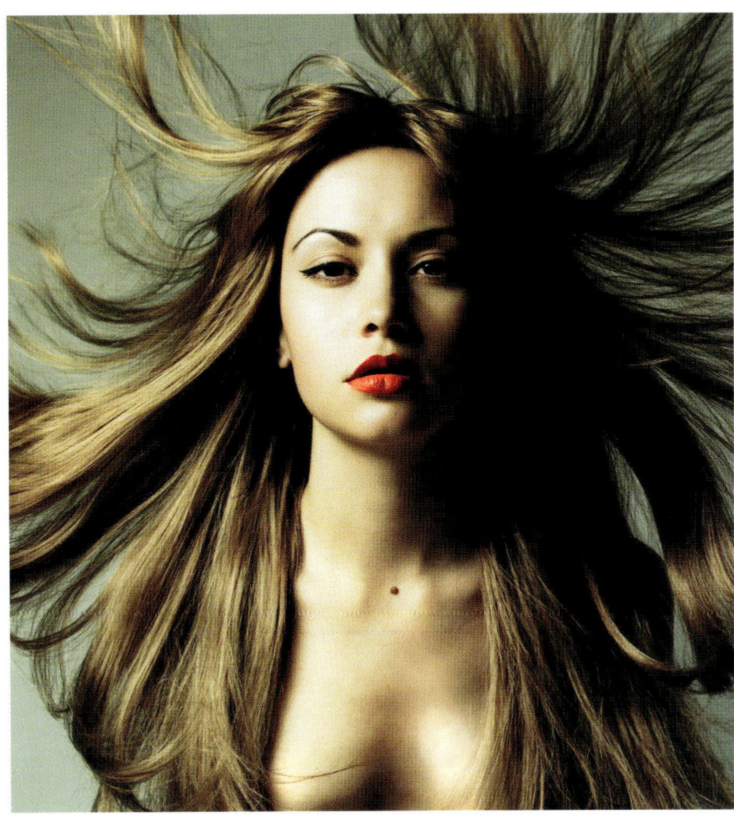

ABOVE:
Cool-running, continuous fluorescent lighting is becoming an increasingly popular option for digital portrait photographers.

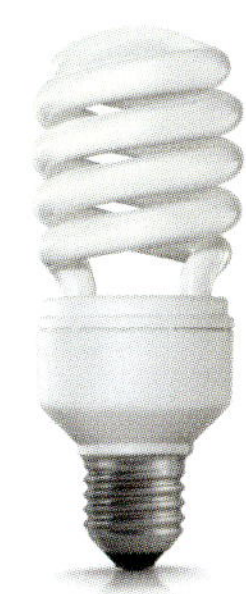

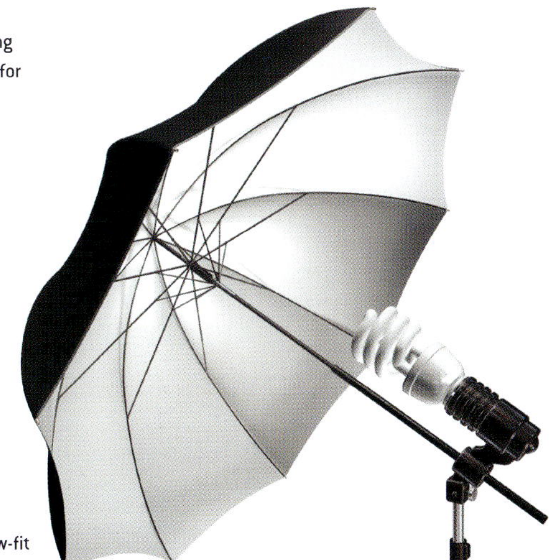

ABOVE & RIGHT:
Most low-cost fluorescent lights use a screw-fit bulb that has a nominal color temperature that matches daylight.

RINGFLASH

Initially designed and used in the slightly less glamorous fields of medical, dental, and forensic photography, the humble ringflash looked set to spend its days taking pictures outside the world of "mainstream" image-making. However, in the late 1990s its potential as a creative tool was picked up by some of the world's cutting-edge fashion and portrait photographers, with such luminaries as Nick Knight and David LaChapelle seizing upon it as a then alternative form of lighting. Now, a whole generation of portrait photographers have grown up with the visual signature of the ringflash, and what was once a radical look has become relatively commonplace.

What makes a ringflash so distinctive is the way it works. Unlike a regular flash, a ringflash circles the camera lens, which means it casts a virtually shadowless light from the viewpoint of the lens—the only shadows tend to be an equally-sized shadow "halo" around the subject if they are close to the background. Its shadowless quality also means that a ringflash is ideal if you want to provide an overall fill in a portrait to lighten hard shadows, as it won't cast any further shadows of its own. A side-effect of all this is a perfectly circular catchlight reflected in the subject's eyes which, assuming the eyes can be seen, is guaranteed thanks to the flash's proximity to the lens.

As a result of its popularity, most flash manufacturers now have a ringflash in their lineup that can be hooked up to a power pack, while some companies, such as AlienBees, have gone as far as producing the ringflash equivalent of a monolight—their ABR800 is a self-contained ringflash offering a five-stop power range (full to 1/32 power). If this is more than your budget can manage, there are also countless adaptors for regular hotshoe-mounted flashes that claim to create a ringflash effect by directing the flash into a circular reflector that sits around the camera's lens. Alternatively, the Internet has plenty of plans for making your own ringflash adaptors (just search for "DIY ringflash adaptor") which is a great way of getting the distinctive look, without paying the distinctively high ringflash price.

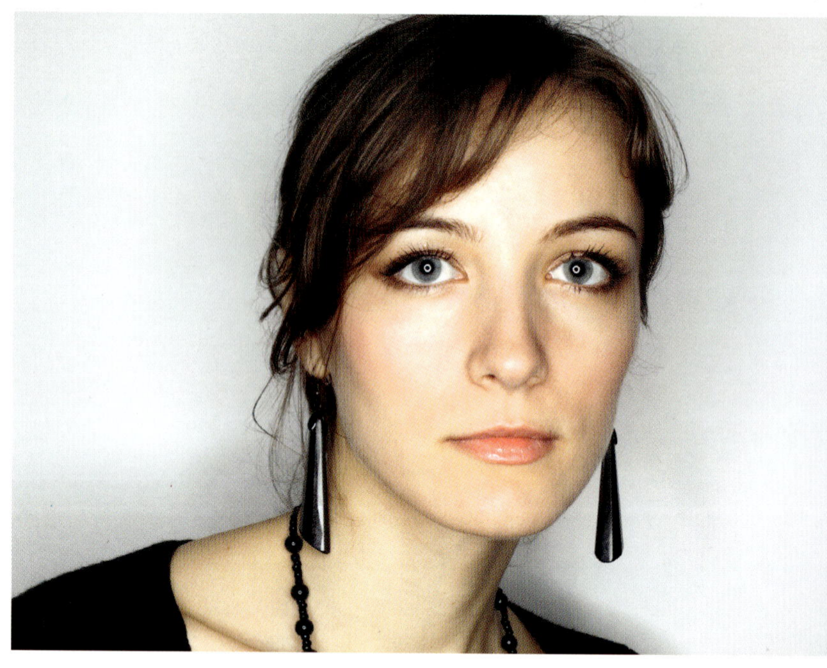

ABOVE:
Although a ringflash produces relatively few shadows on the subject, if they are close to the background, you are likely to see a shadow "halo" around them.

RIGHT:
Because a ringflash is a circular light source, you can readily identify a portrait taken with this type of light due to the catchlights in the eyes.

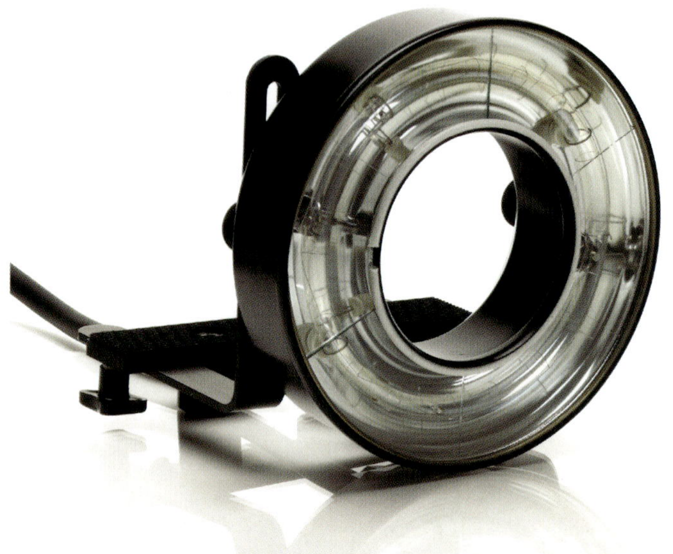

RIGHT:
With a ringflash such as this, the camera mounts on the platform behind the flash, with the lens pointing through the center.

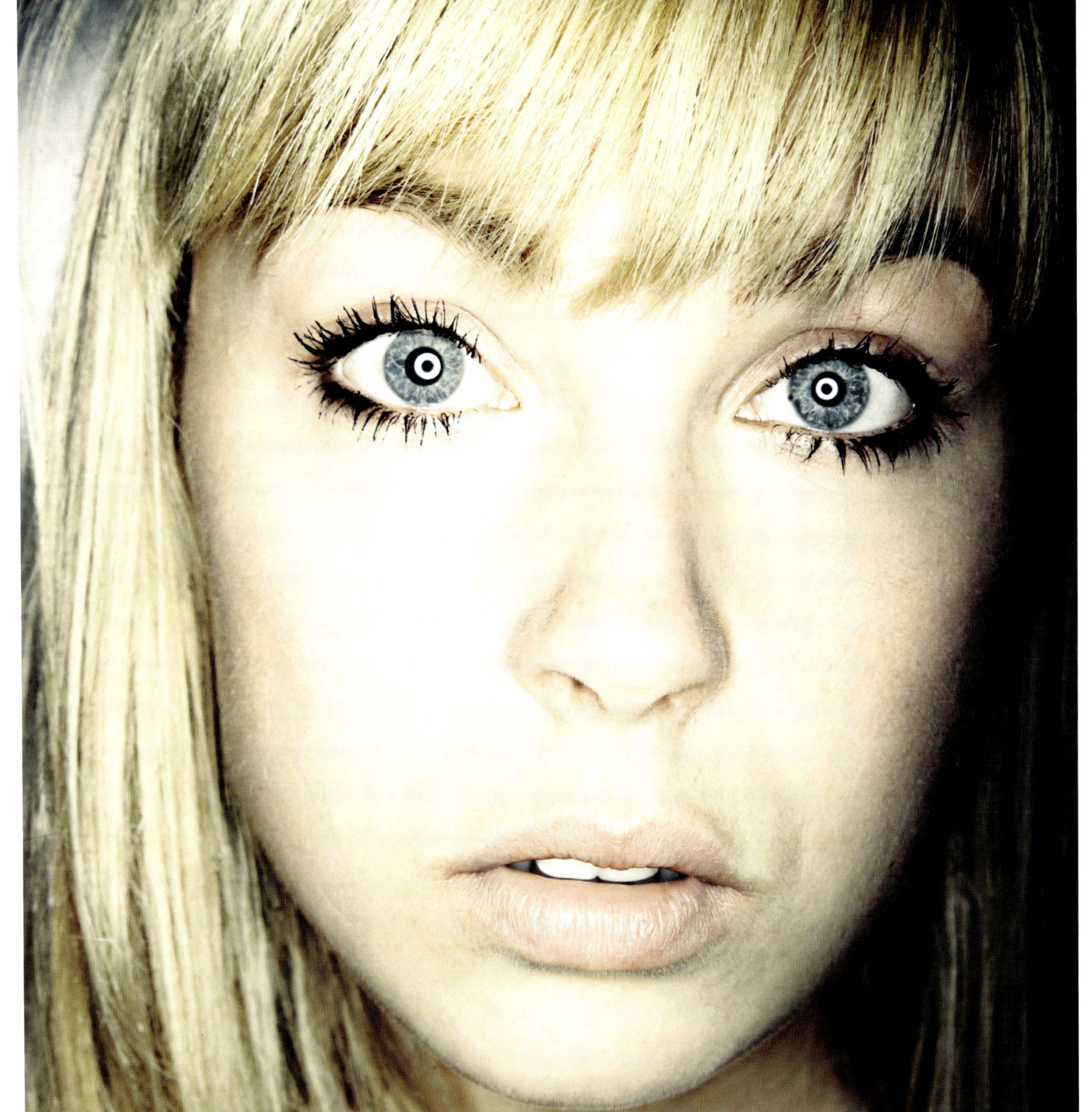

LIGHTING ACCESSORIES

Although the lights themselves form the backbone of a portrait lighting kit, the accessories that you use on them are just as important. These are the tools that will help you control and regulate the light, making it hard and direct for atmospheric high-contrast shots, or softening it for a more romantic, gentler look to your images. Which of these accessories you will need, or will want to use, depends on the type of portrait you are looking to create and—to a certain extent—the lighting system you have invested in: not all manufacturers provide a full range of accessories for all of their lighting systems, so consider this when you buy your portrait equipment.

LIGHT STANDS

The majority of lights designed for studio photography are offered as a set, comprised of a light and a stand, and it's almost always worth taking this option if it's available. Even if you already own a few light stands, when you get one as part of a set it tends to be cheaper than buying it on its own and for portrait photography you can never have too many. While you might not think you need it now, if another stand breaks you'll have a spare, and light stands are always useful for supporting a reflector or a flag, or to mount a hotshoe flash on if you need to.

However, while these general purpose stands are good for most situations, there are times when you need something more specialist—a floor stand that lets you put a light at ground level (to shine up at a backdrop, for example), or a taller, sturdier stand that will let you raise your light much higher.

For studio-based portraiture, you might also want to consider investing in a boom arm. This will give you much greater flexibility when it comes to positioning a light, including the option to place it directly above the subject without the stand appearing in shot. But be sure to mount a boom on a sturdy stand—if the stand's too flimsy it can easily topple over and damage your light or, worse, come crashing down on you or your model.

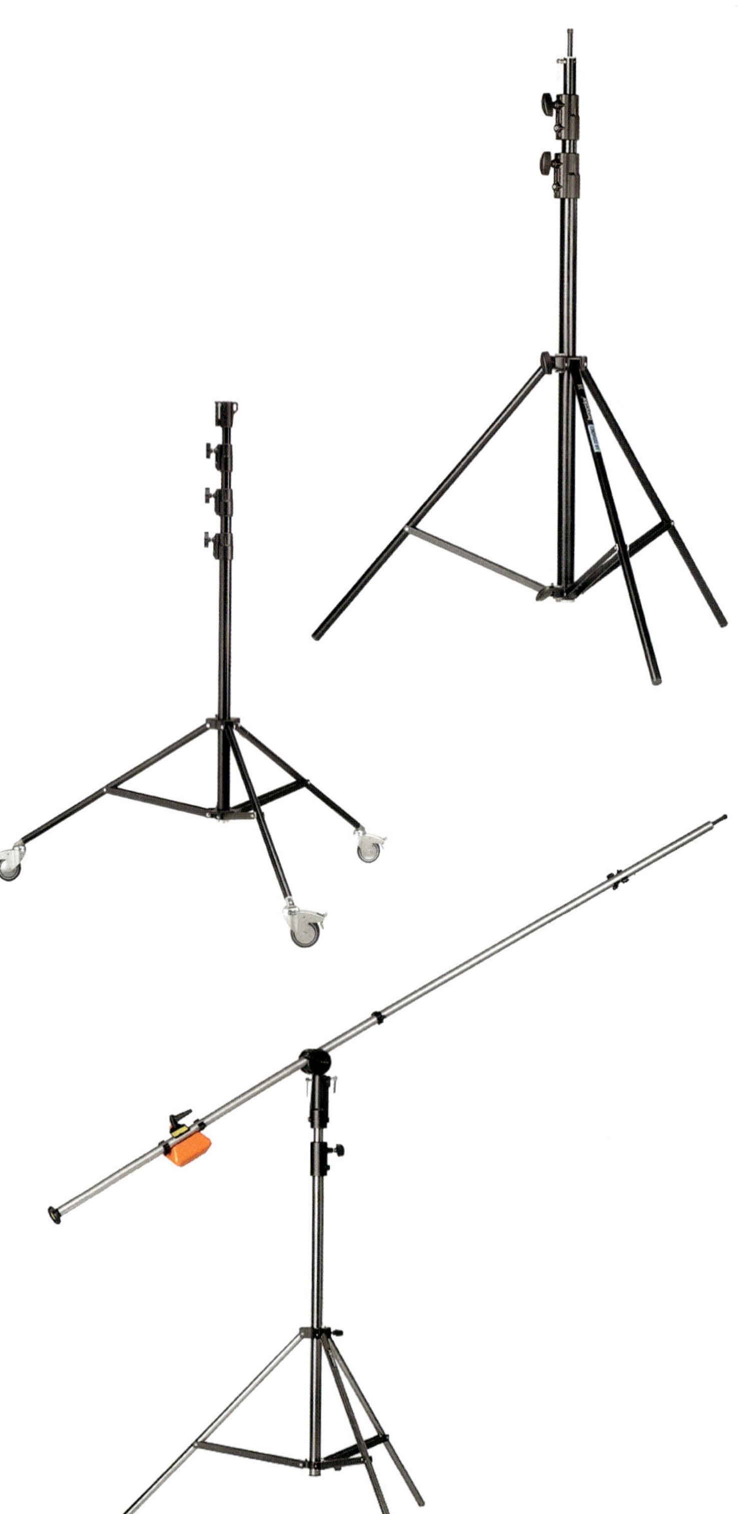

REFLECTOR DISHES

Whether you use continuous lighting or flash, controlling the direction of the light helps maximize its output and prevent stray light spilling out and potentially creating flare if it hits your camera's lens. The easiest way of doing this is to fit a basic reflector dish to your light, and the majority of flash units will come with one of these "spill-kill" dishes as standard.

A basic spill-kill isn't the only type of reflector dish, though, and there are myriad different sizes and shapes available. Each is designed to modulate the light in a different way, from relatively shallow, large diameter dishes that will allow a wide spread of light, to deep, tulip-shaped reflectors that will restrict the pool of light to a more confined area.

SOFTBOX

Softboxes are the staple of portrait photography, creating a soft, diffuse light that helps prevent deep shadows being cast across the subject. Typically, a softbox will be used as the main, or key light, to provide the overall illumination, with additional lights picking out smaller areas of the subject.

Softboxes are available in a wide variety of shapes and sizes, from small squares to gigantic octagons (known as octaboxes), and the larger the surface area and the deeper the softbox, the softer the light it will produce. Removable internal diffusers known as baffles will soften the light further, as will a softbox that has a white interior, rather than a silver one. In terms of "must have" lighting accessories for portraits, a softbox should be near the top of your list.

UMBRELLA

Synonymous with studio portraits, umbrellas—or "brollies" as they're more commonly known—are often used as a simple means of softening a light. Just as you might bounce a flash off a wall or ceiling to diffuse it and prevent it looking too hard, so a brolly works in a similar fashion—the light is aimed away from the subject and into a reflective brolly that bounces the light back. As the light is reflected, it is spread, becoming softer.

Brollies are generally available in a number of sizes, with larger brollies having an increased softening effect that can be further controlled by moving them closer to, or further from the flash head. Different colored brollies provide subtly different results, with white being the standard for portrait photography. Silver brollies reflect more light (useful if your flash isn't particularly powerful), while gold brollies have a subtle warming effect on an image, although most photographers now adjust the color digitally, rather than with the light.

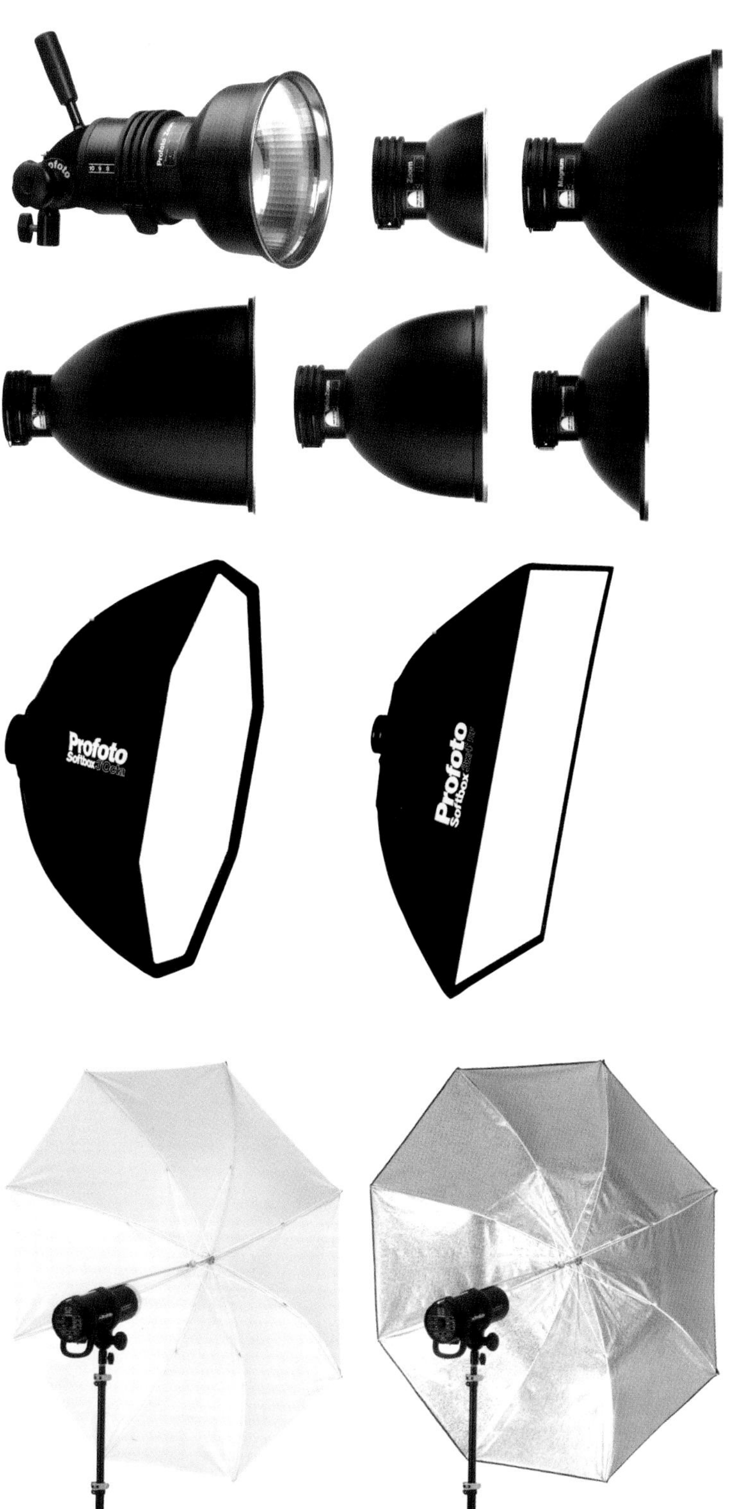

BEAUTY DISH

A beauty dish is a variation on a standard reflector dish and is particularly useful for portrait work. Unlike a standard reflector that simply funnels the light, a beauty dish has a reflective plate at the front that sits in front of the light. As a result, the light bounces off the plate and back into the wide-diameter reflector dish before it is reflected onto the subject. Because the light is being "bounced" onto the subject, rather than striking them directly, it is diffused, making it softer—hence "beauty" dish, as it is ideal for helping create smooth, shadow-free skintones.

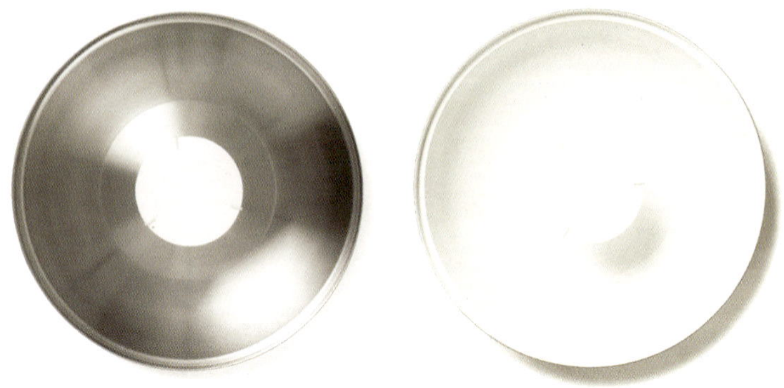

A beauty dish with a white reflector bowl will soften the light more than a silver-coated dish, and larger diameter dishes also soften the light more than smaller ones. Some also come with a "bonnet"—a fine gauze or mesh panel that can be fitted across the front of the dish for added diffusion.

SNOOT

Conical in shape, a snoot has one very specific purpose—to narrow down the light so that it's concentrated on a small area. For portrait photography snoots are particularly effective in lighting just the face, for example, or used from a high angle behind the subject as a hair light. As you will see later in this book, a snooted light, used in conjunction with a softbox can create a wide range of looks and the two together can create an incredibly versatile lighting combination.

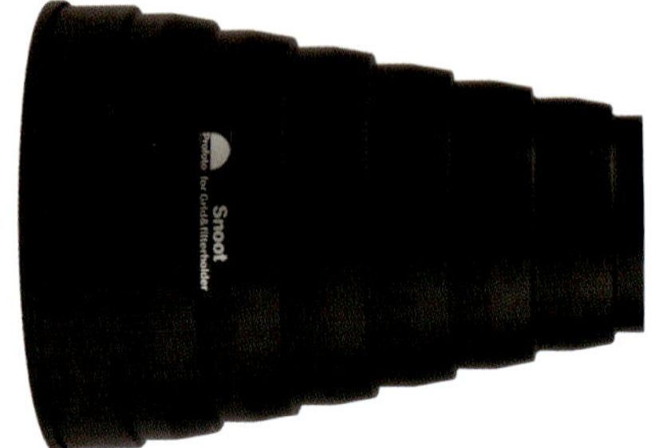

FRESNEL / SPOT

Although not used as often as a snoot, a fresnel lens or spot attachment (or even a dedicated spotlight) can be used to concentrate a very small amount of light on a specific part of your subject. With a narrow enough spot you can literally illuminate a single eye on your model for creative effect, or use a slightly broader spot to lighten the face slightly. The advantage of a spot over a snoot is that the spot can usually be controlled more accurately, so you can make the pool of light broader, or tighter, without moving the lamp itself. In addition, you can adjust the focus of the spot to regulate the hardness of the edge of the light—from a distinctly crisp edge to one that is a little softer. Spotlights can also be used to project shapes and shadows onto a background, a classic example being to create a window-like shadow that gives the impression that light is coming in through an out-of-shot window, even if you're shooting in a windowless studio.

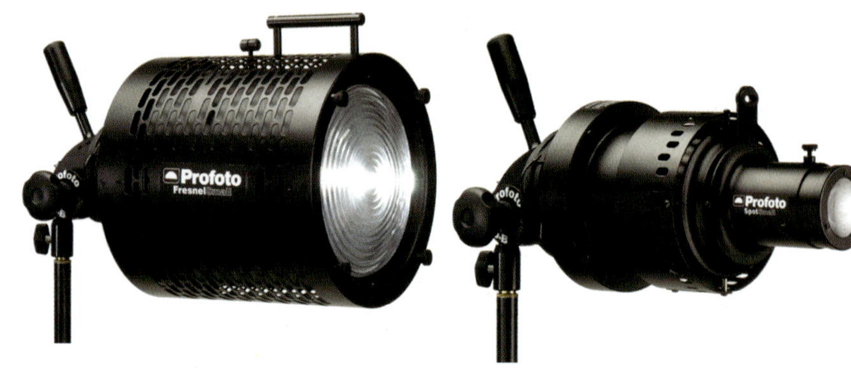

GRIDS

Grids, or honeycombs, fit into the front of a reflector dish where their honeycomb-like structure channels the light in a straight line, preventing it from spreading so that it appears more direct. The deeper or more densely packed the grid, the greater the channeling effect, which reduces the chance of it spilling into other areas and helps concentrate the light pool on a specific part of the image.

BARNDOORS AND FLAGS

Barndoors are more commonly found on continuous lights than flash heads, and are used to control where the light falls. By opening or closing the "doors" you can effectively prevent the light from falling on areas where it isn't wanted—either on the subject, or to stop it hitting the camera and creating flare.

However, although barndoors aren't used that often with flash units, flags are commonly used in the studio to perform a similar role. Often nothing more than a thick piece of card, a flag can be any size and shape, and its sole purpose is to sit somewhere in front of the light to stop it reaching a certain area of the subject or set. Attaching flags to spare lighting stands will give you increased versatility when it comes to positioning them.

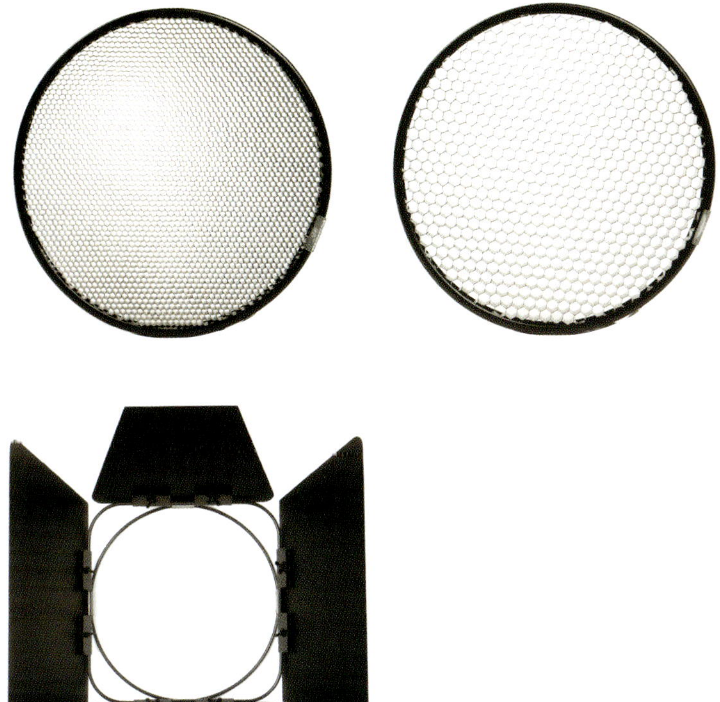

REFLECTORS

As well as accessories that are physically attached to your lights to modulate the light, one of the most useful tools for a portrait photographer is a reflector. This can be little more than a sheet of white card, but what it will do is help you fill in shadows by bouncing light back onto the subject. There are numerous reflectors available to buy, in an array of colors and finishes, but the Lastolite-style of pop-up reflectors are perhaps the most well known. Aim for a reflector with a diameter of at least three feet (one meter) for head-and-shoulders portraits, or larger if you intend to shoot full-length portraits. Some reflectors are double sided, so you can pick a white/gold reflector that can also be used to warm an image slightly, or white/silver that will provide you with two different "strengths" of reflective surface.

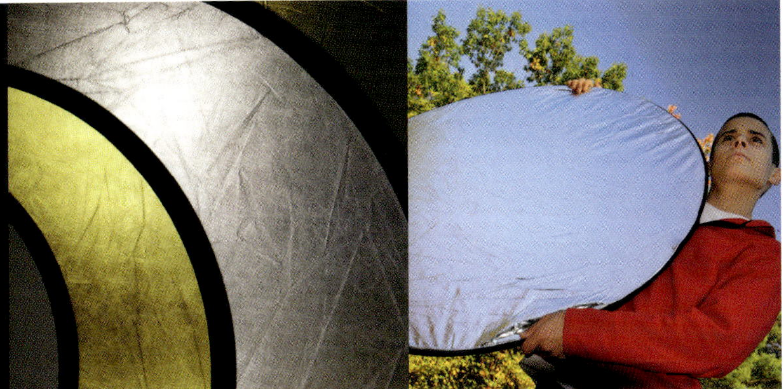

LENSES FOR PORTRAITS

Although a lot of people still talk about "portrait lenses" as if there's only a single lens that can be used for people pictures, the truth is there's no such thing. Some focal lengths may be more widely regarded as suitable for portraits than others, but trying to specify a single lens is a futile exercise—there are occasions when a wide angle might be just what you need to create a certain look to a portrait and other times when a much longer telephoto gives the right result. All that really matters is that you pick the right lens (or focal length) for the image you're looking to create.

ZOOM LENSES

As a general rule, zoom lenses fall into one of two categories—low cost or pro spec—with plenty to separate the two, not least their relative prices. Starting with the budget option, anyone with a digital SLR will have access to a wide range of lenses, and both camera and lens manufacturers keep adding to this list on an annual basis. Typically, a low-cost zoom will have a fairly small maximum aperture of ƒ/4–ƒ/5.6, which isn't always enough when you want a really shallow depth of field that throws the background out of focus.

Conversely, pro-spec zooms will have a maximum aperture of ƒ/2.8 on lenses containing focal lengths up to 200mm, and if you want to work with shallow focus this is really what you need to be looking for. In addition, professional lenses are likely to contain more lens elements (the glass in the lens), which are there for one simple reason—to maximize image quality. However, this does come with a considerably higher price tag.

Regardless of the amount of money you spend on your lens, for portrait photography the one thing all zoom lenses gives you is flexibility when it comes to fine tuning your composition, allowing you to zoom in or out, or change the focal length quite dramatically for a totally different look to your portraits without interrupting the flow of the shoot to change lenses.

When it comes to choosing a zoom, a 70–200mm ƒ/2.8 zoom is a great starting point as it allows you to keep a comfortable distance between you and your subject, while enabling you to switch between tight head-and-shoulder shots at the telephoto end of the lens and looser compositions when you zoom out. A lens that features image stabilization or vibration reduction is also a good idea if you like to shoot handheld—nothing's worse than a great shot that loses its edge through slight camera shake.

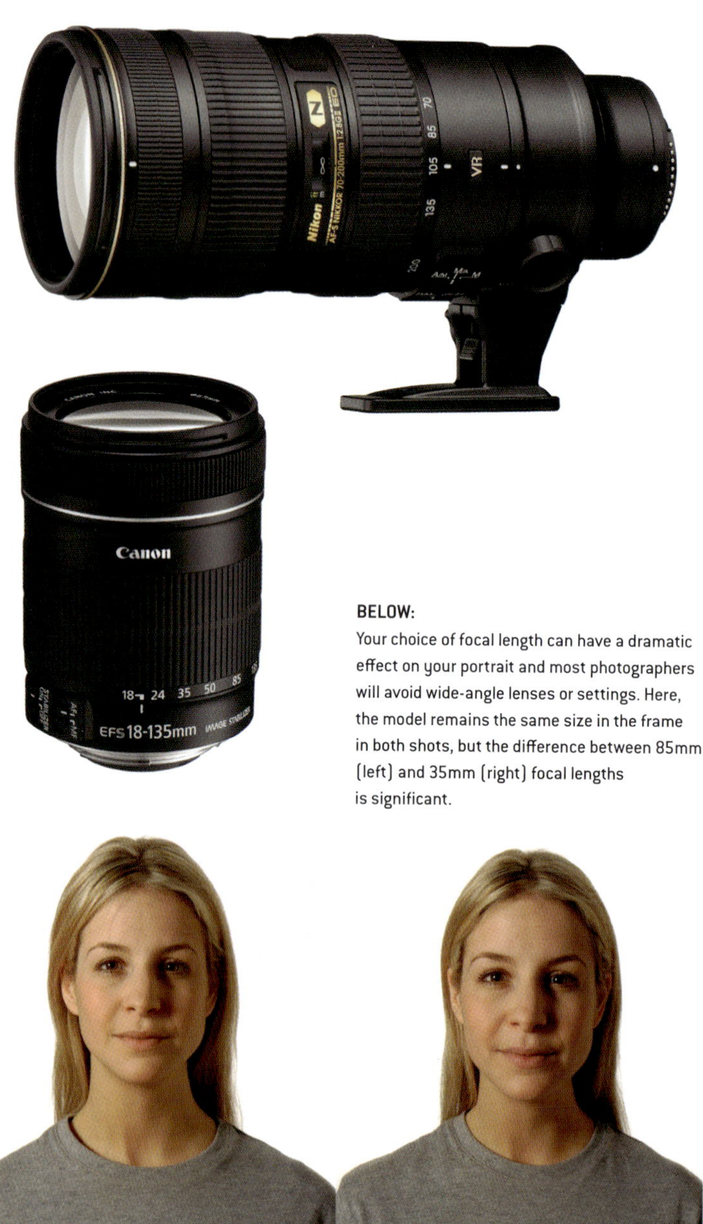

BELOW:
Your choice of focal length can have a dramatic effect on your portrait and most photographers will avoid wide-angle lenses or settings. Here, the model remains the same size in the frame in both shots, but the difference between 85mm (left) and 35mm (right) focal lengths is significant.

PRIME LENSES

While a prime, or fixed focal length lens may not offer you the same versatility in terms of multiple focal lengths, this doesn't mean they're no use for portraits—before zoom lenses they were the only option and there were some stunning portraits taken. In fact, a number of portrait specialists still rely almost exclusively on prime lenses for posed shots because fixed focal lengths have a number of advantages over zooms.

For a start, prime lenses generally have wider maximum apertures than zooms, even when compared to pro-spec ones. Most manufacturers have a 50mm $f/1.8$ prime lens in their line-up, and the fast maximum aperture makes them ideally suited to shooting in low light, or for producing shots with a minimal depth of field—a portrait that has the subject's eyes sharply focused, while the tips of their nose and ears aren't, for example, will really draw the viewer's attention and this is something that you can only do with a wide aperture lens.

At the same time, prime lenses don't make the same demands on lens designers as a zoom. Rather than try and combat various distortions and aberrations across a wide range of focal lengths, the designers only have to resolve a single set of issues, which is much easier to achieve. As a result, a prime lens will often outperform a zoom lens that contains the equivalent focal length, resulting in higher image quality.

Perhaps most appealing to photographers on a budget is that you can have both of these things—an ultra-wide aperture and high image quality—without spending a whole stack of cash as a 50mm $f/1.8$ lens from most manufacturers will typically cost around $150 or less. This is a great starting point for portrait photography, especially if you're using a digital with an APS or FourThirds sensor. On cameras such as these, the effective focal length will be increased to around 75–80mm depending on the sensor size (100mm on a FourThirds camera), which is perfect for general portrait work. The mild telephoto effect will compress your subject slightly (which is always flattering), while maintaining a comfortable working distance.

If you're using a full-frame sensor, a fast, 50mm prime is still a valid choice for portraits, although many pros would opt for an 85mm focal length instead, just so they don't have to get quite as close to their subject for frame-filling head-and-shoulder shots. The price of these is significantly higher, though.

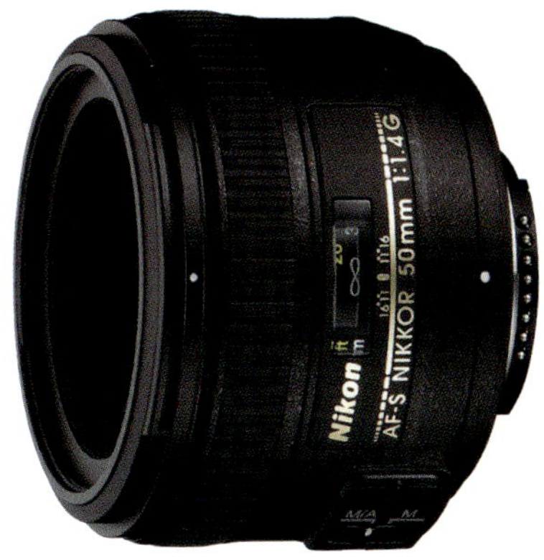

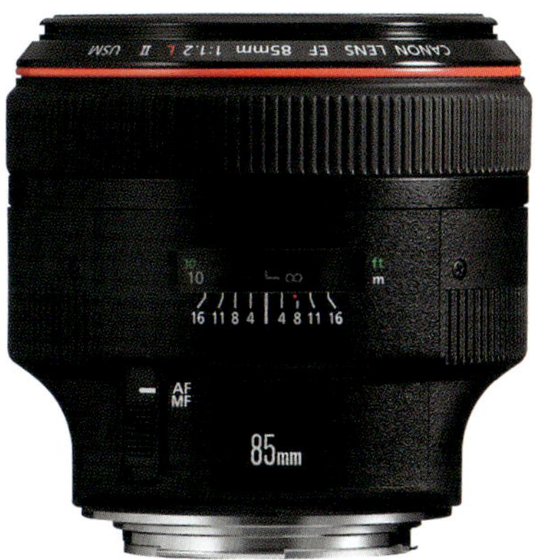

MANUAL 50MM

Although most manufacturers have an autofocus 50mm prime lens in their current catalog, if you really want to try a prime "on the cheap," then why not consider a 50mm manual focus lens? Once the standard lens for 35mm SLRs, there are thousands of these lenses around and you can pick them up for next to nothing in yard sales and Internet auctions. Like their modern-day counterparts they benefit from wide maximum apertures and high optical quality, although the reliance on manual focusing and, in some cases manual metering, may not be for everyone.

CHAPTER 1
SINGLE LIGHT

A single light is the basic building block for portrait photographs. Used on its own it is capable of producing a variety of distinct "looks," depending on the position of the model, the angle of the light, and whether the light is used on its own or in conjunction with a reflector.

On its own, a single light typically produces hard-edged, contrasty results as the light emphasizes textures such as wrinkles and hair. This is better suited to stark "character studies" of male figures than it is to flattering female portraits, although it can be just as effective in creating distinct low-key style images, as we will see.

For greater versatility with a single light, the simplest solution is to use a reflector to bounce the light back into the subject and lighten areas that would otherwise be in deep shadow. A white reflector (or a piece of card) will provide a general fill, or you can get a little more creative: silver reflectors will reflect more light and create a crisper fill than white, while gold reflectors will have a warming effect that is well suited to female models.

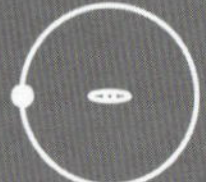

ONE SOFTBOX

LIGHT 1: FROM 90° LEFT, EYE LEVEL

LIGHT 2: NONE

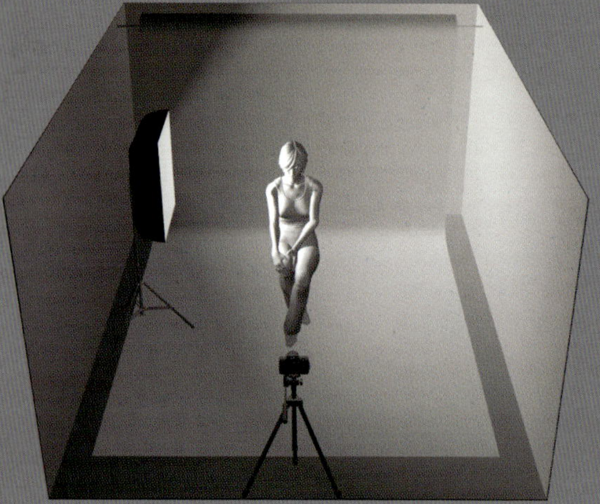

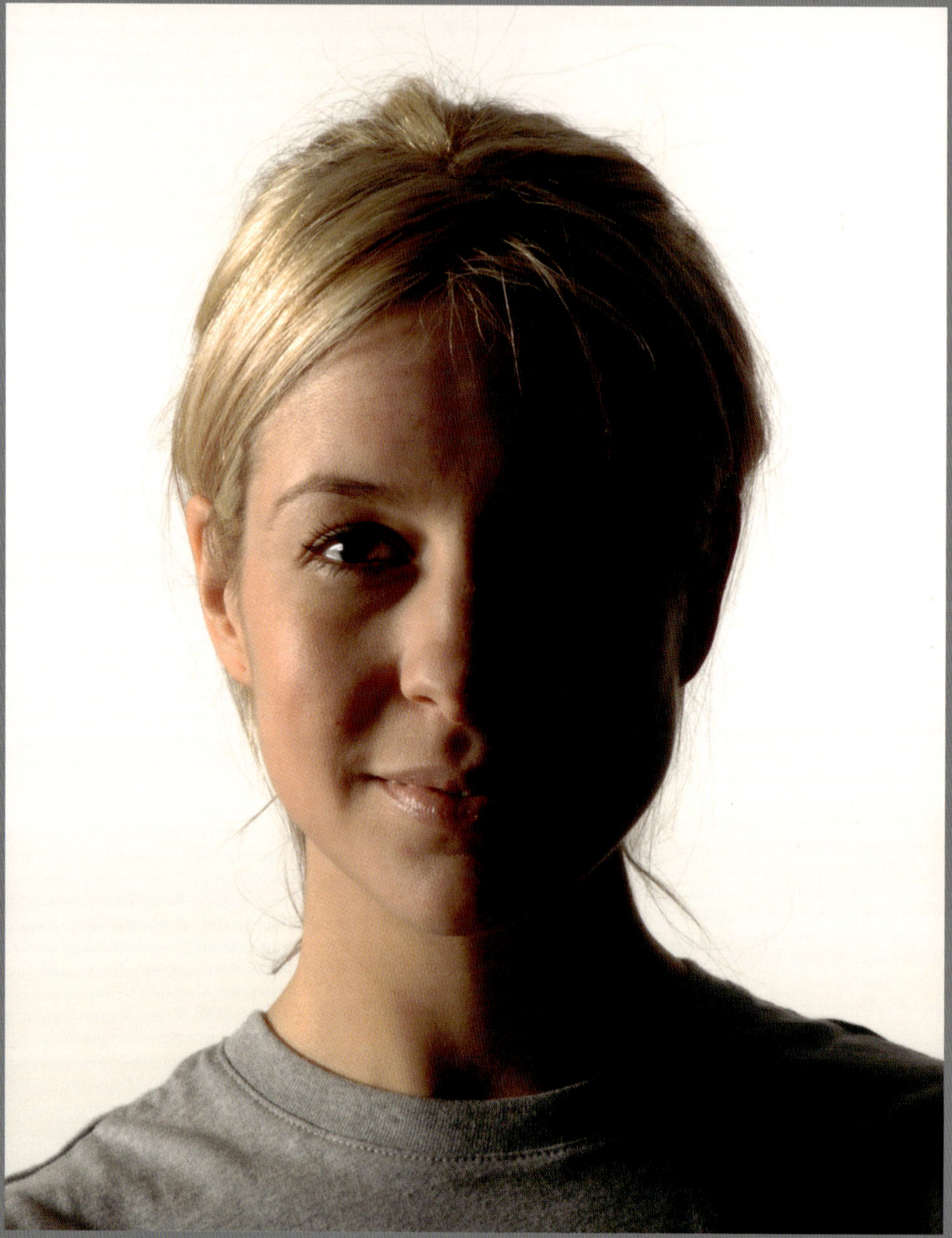

A single light at a 90-degree angle to the subject will illuminate one half of the model's face, but the opposite side will be cast in deep shadow. For a more revealing portrait, consider using a reflector opposite the light to lighten the shadow areas.

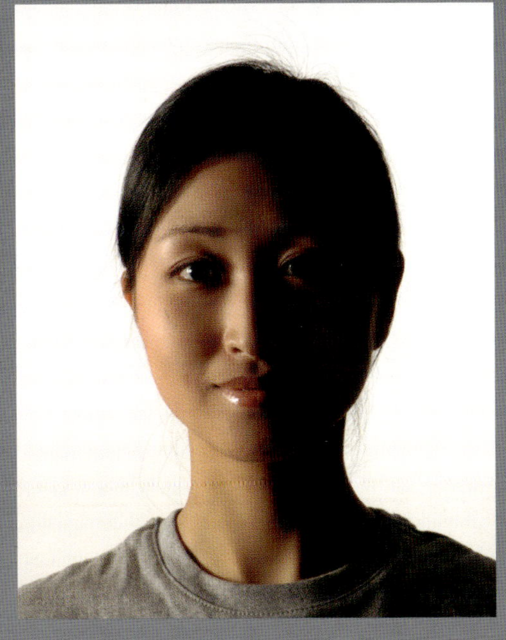
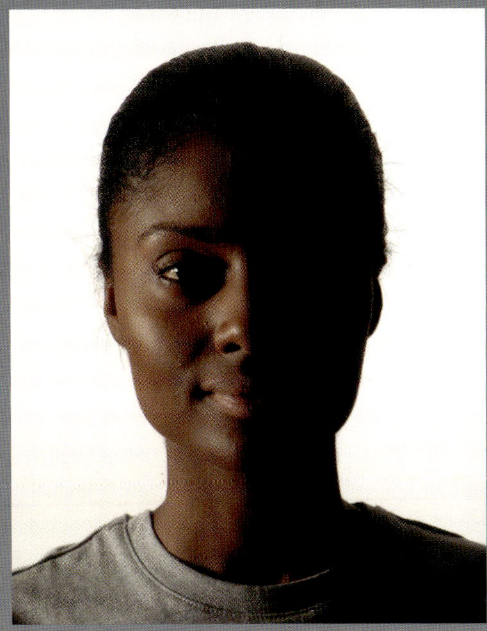
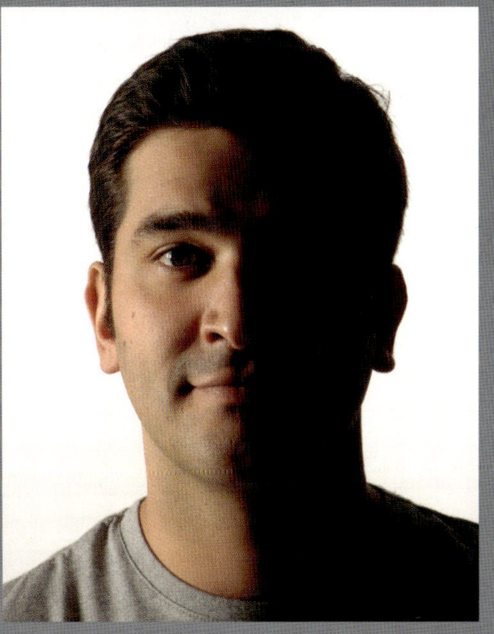

DARK BACKGROUND

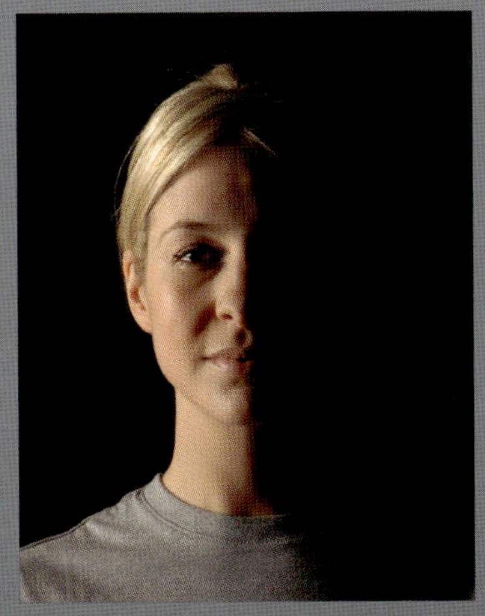
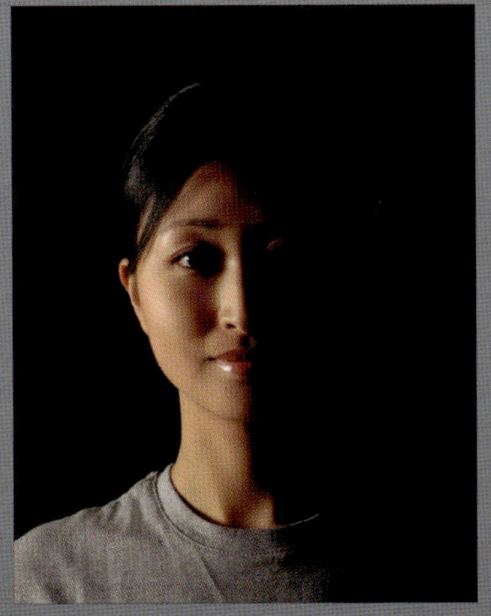
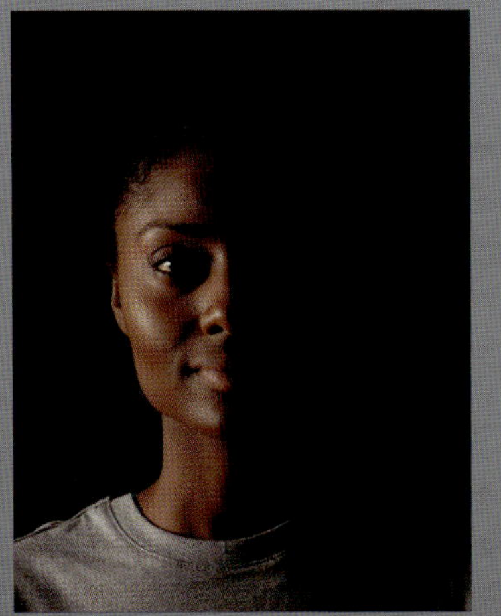
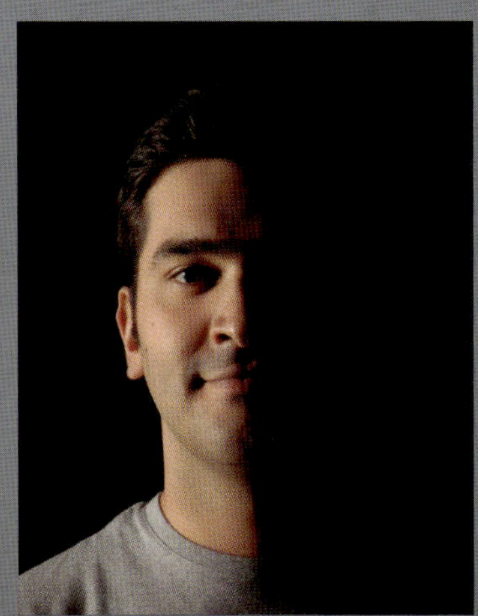

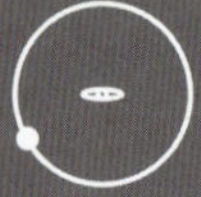

ONE SOFTBOX

LIGHT 1: FROM 60° LEFT, EYE LEVEL

LIGHT 2: NONE

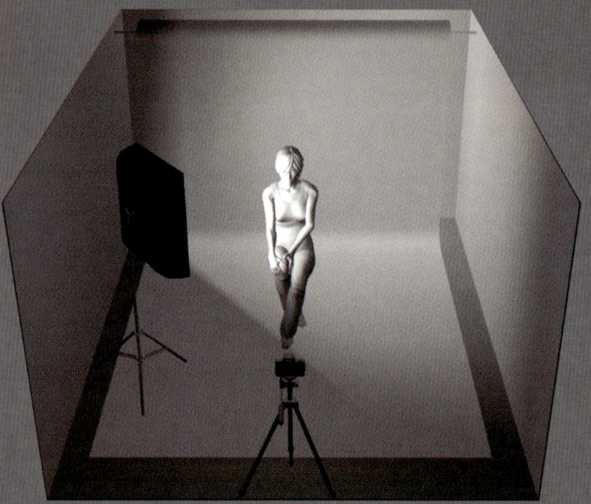

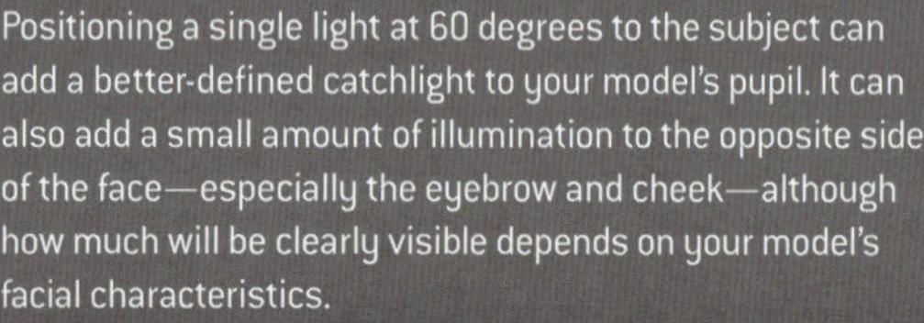

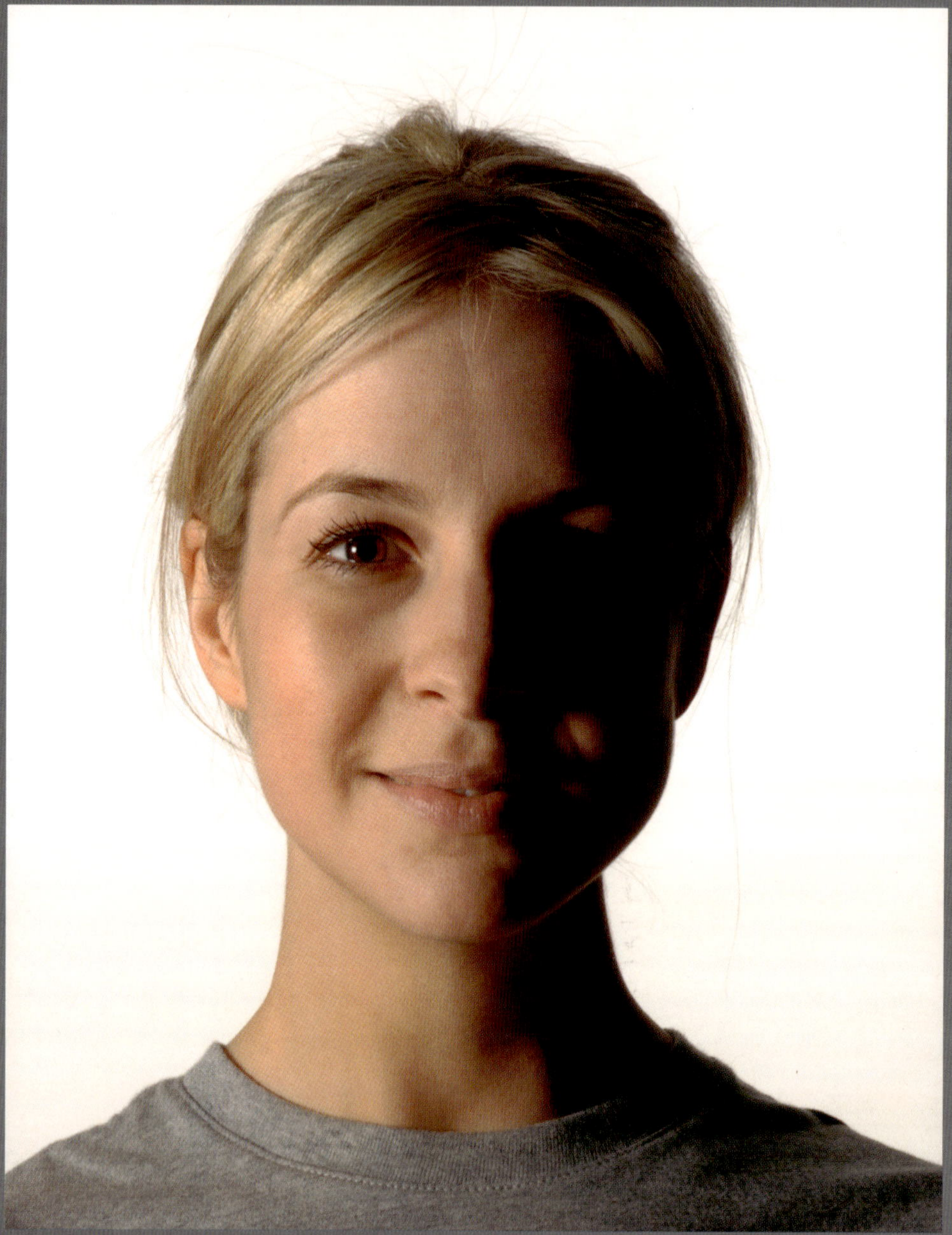

Positioning a single light at 60 degrees to the subject can add a better-defined catchlight to your model's pupil. It can also add a small amount of illumination to the opposite side of the face—especially the eyebrow and cheek—although how much will be clearly visible depends on your model's facial characteristics.

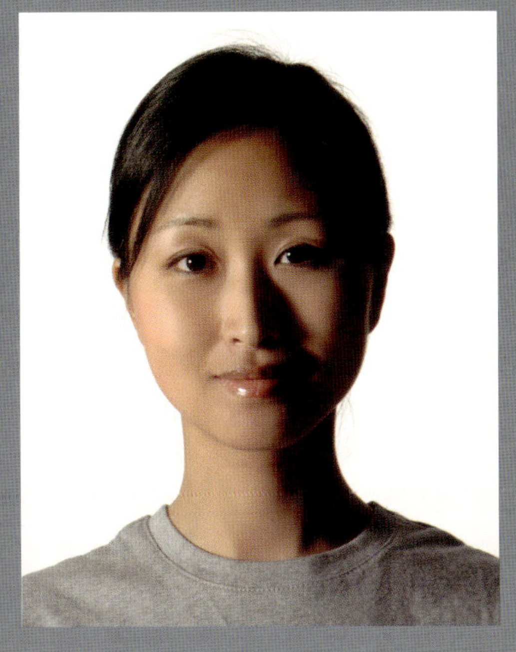

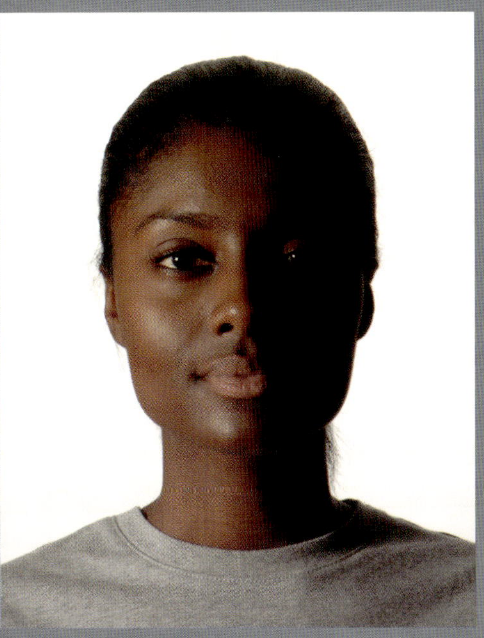

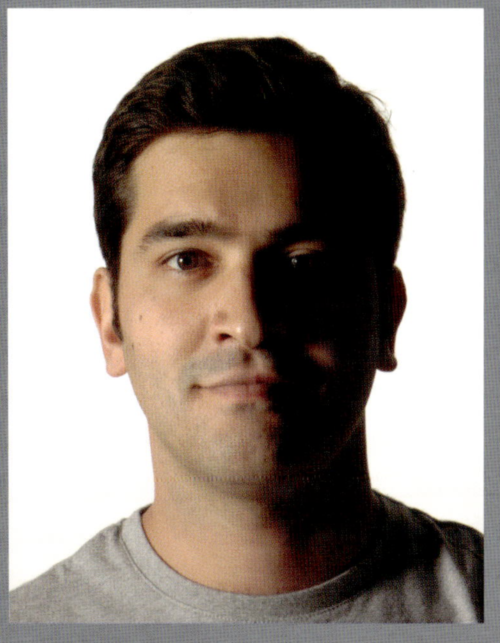

DARK BACKGROUND

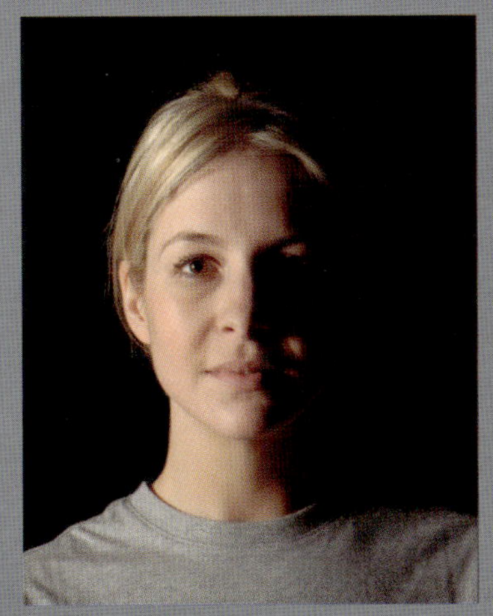

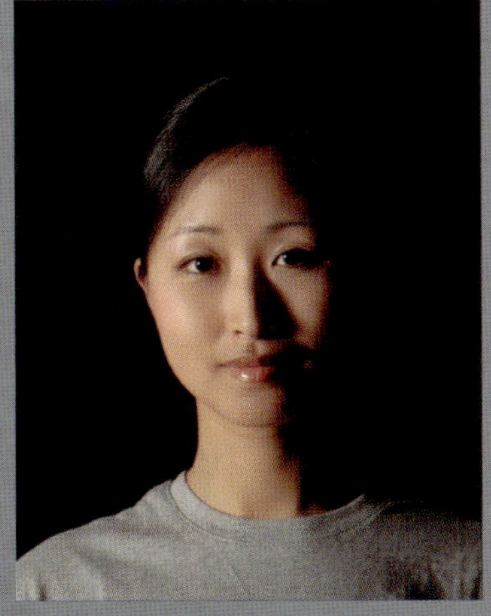

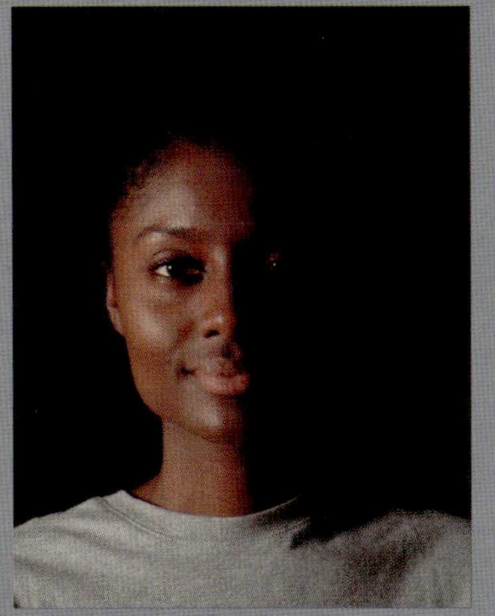

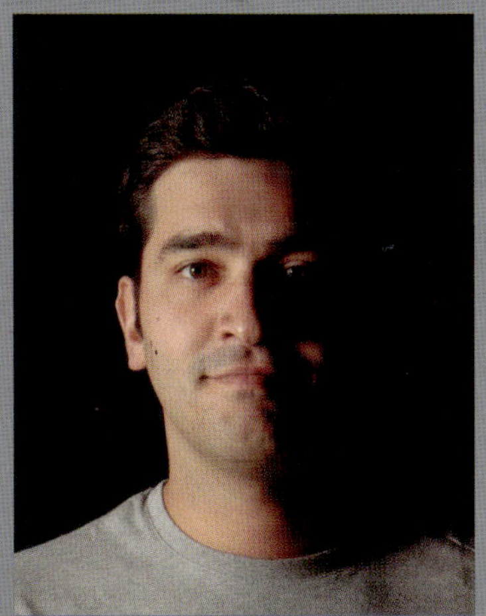

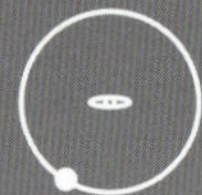

ONE SOFTBOX

LIGHT 1: FROM 30° LEFT, EYE LEVEL

LIGHT 2: NONE

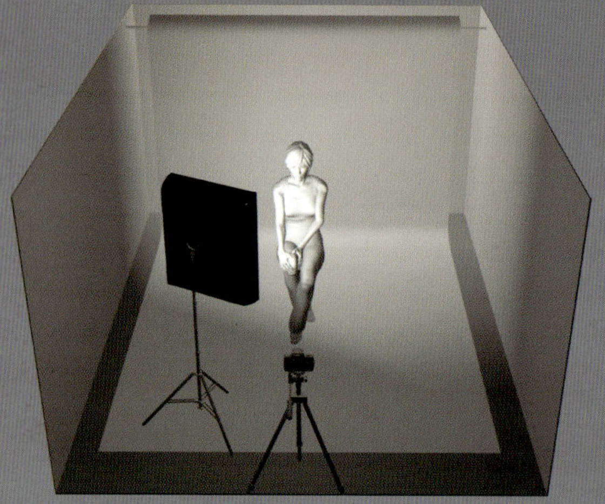

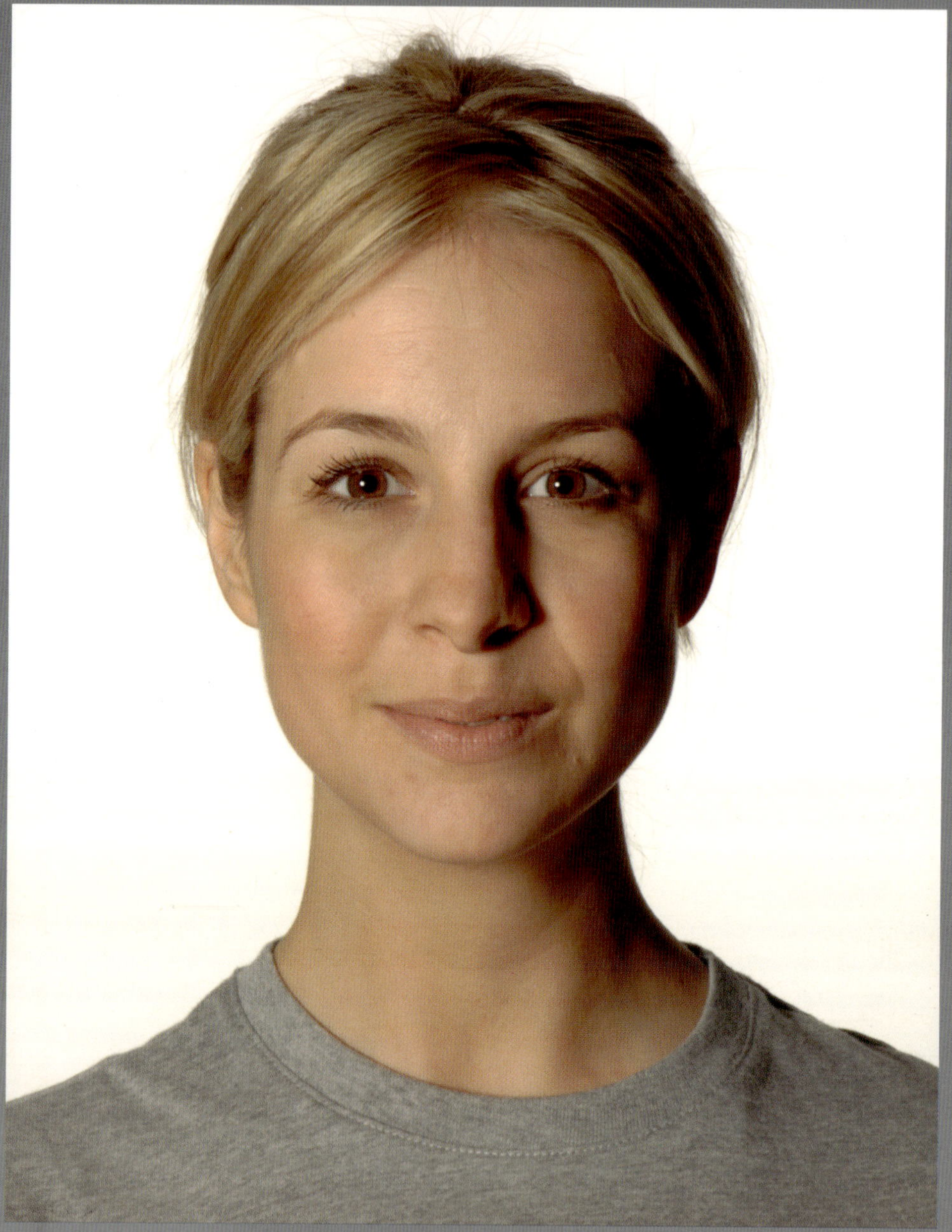

As the light is moved closer to the camera axis, more of the model's face is revealed—both eyes are now distinct, and both contain catchlights. The shadows that remain on the side opposite the light will be dark, but can be lifted easily with a reflector to reduce the contrast.

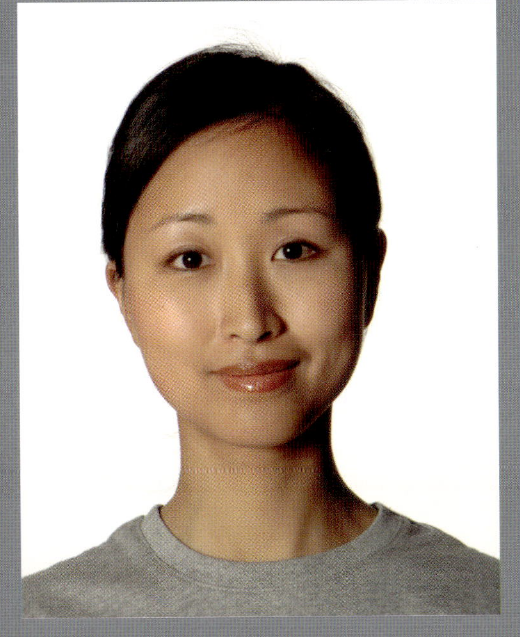

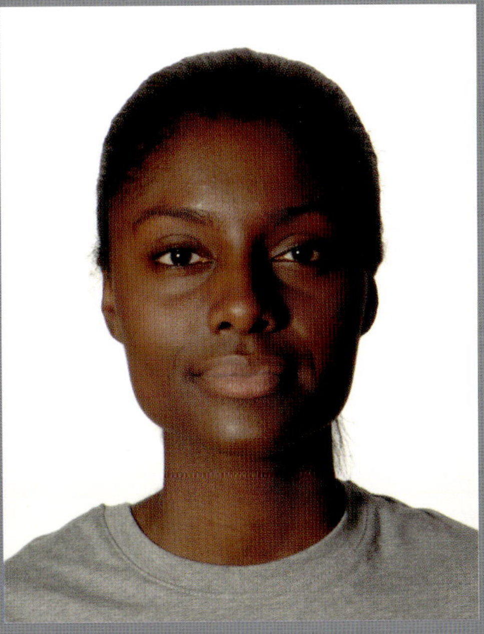

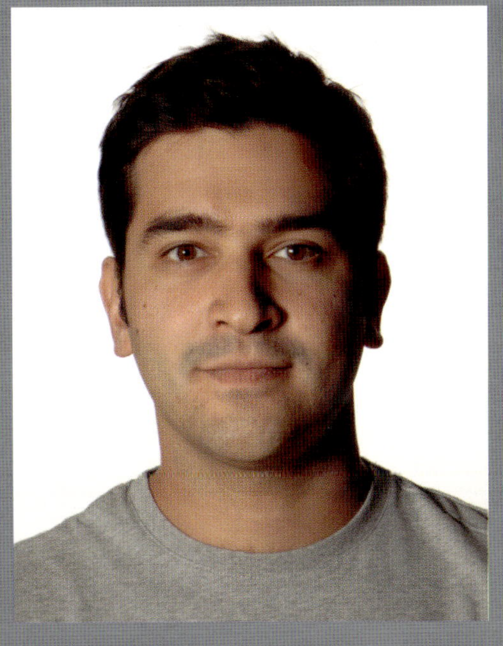

DARK BACKGROUND

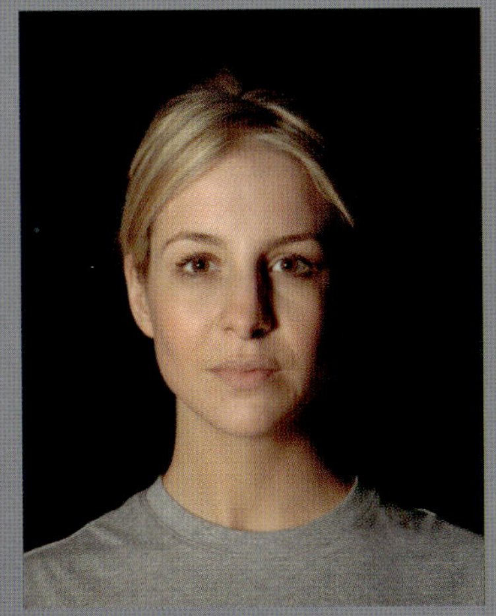

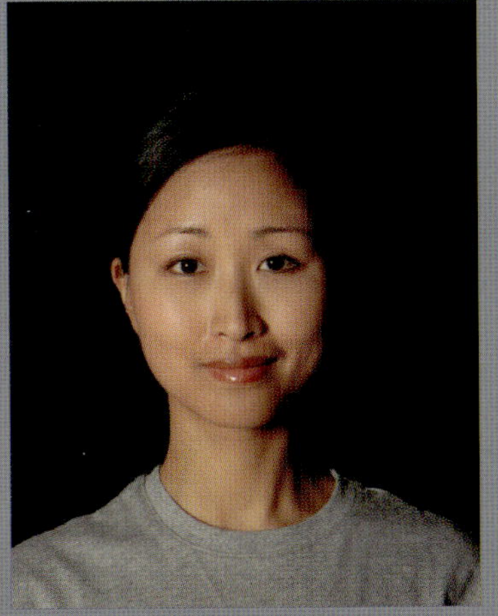

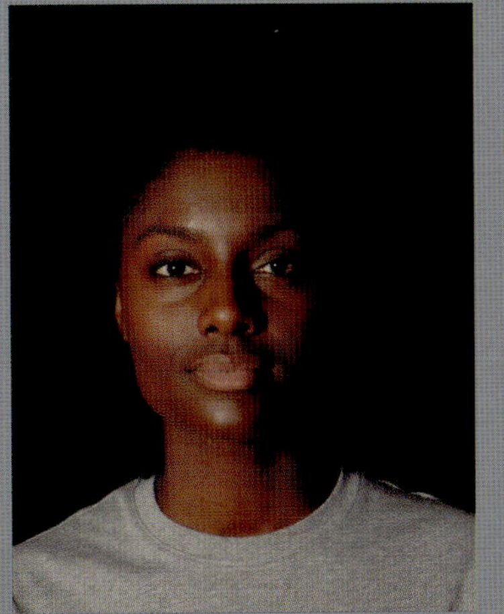

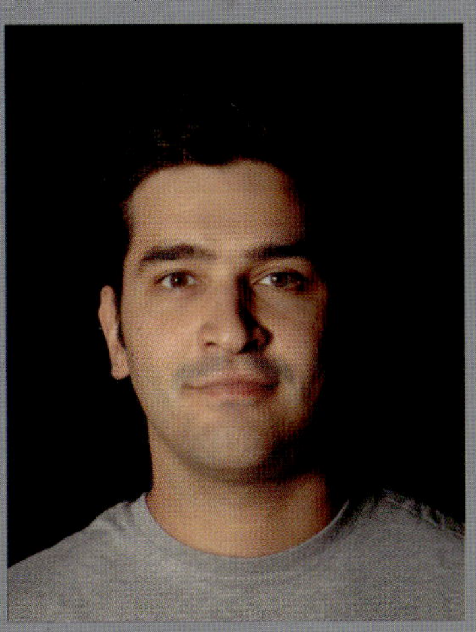

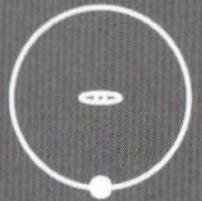

ONE SOFTBOX

LIGHT 1: FROM CAMERA, EYE LEVEL

LIGHT 2: NONE

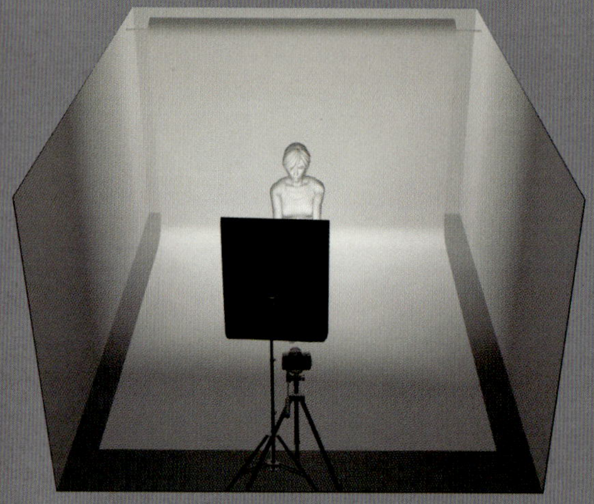

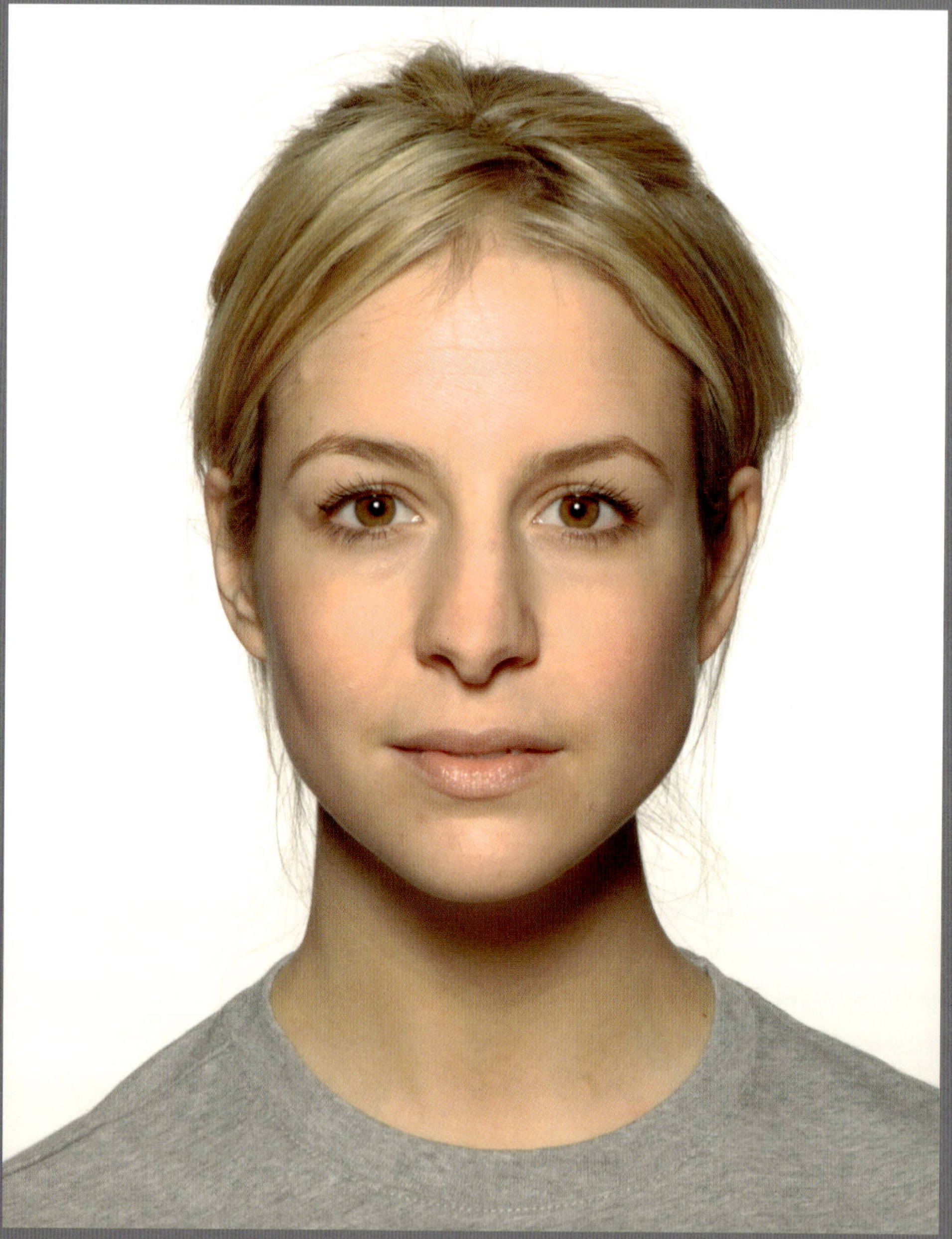

When the light and camera are both pointing at the subject from the same position, the lighting is evenly balanced across the face, minimizing any shadow areas. This has the effect of "flattening" the face—without shadows to "model" the face, the image has a two-dimensional feel to it.

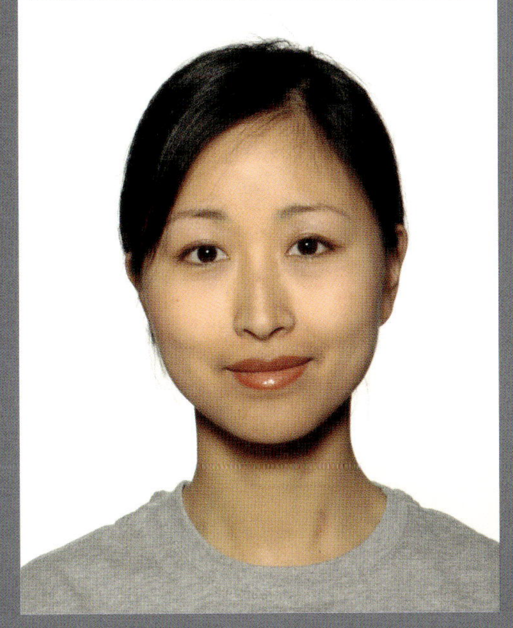
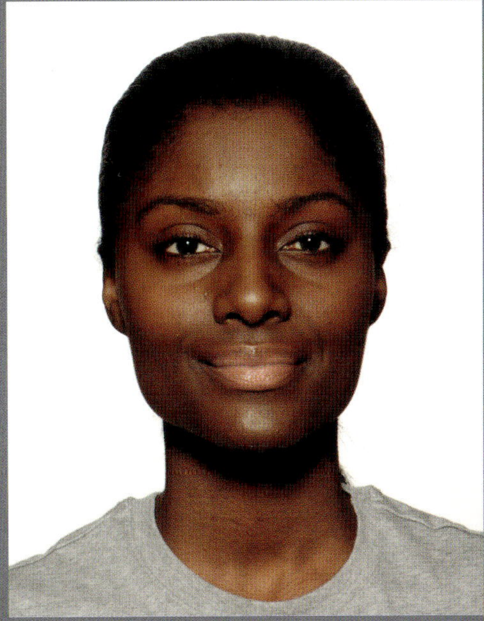
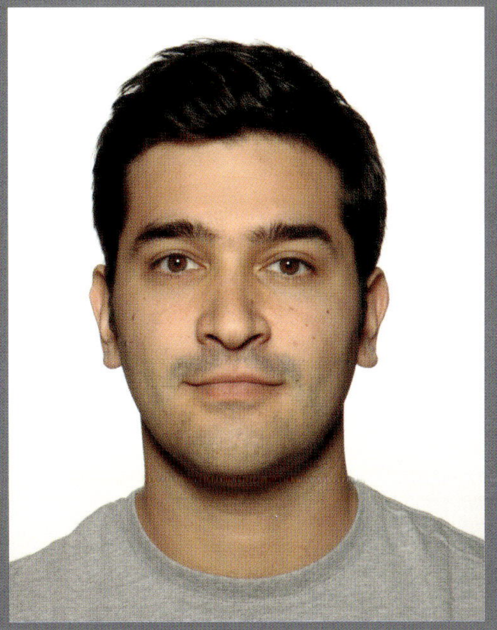

DARK BACKGROUND

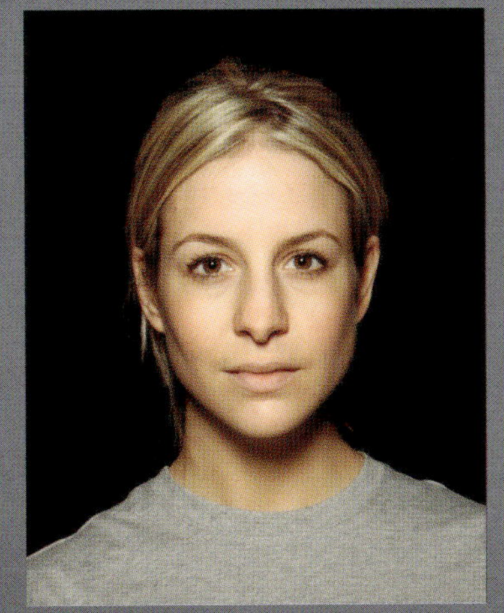
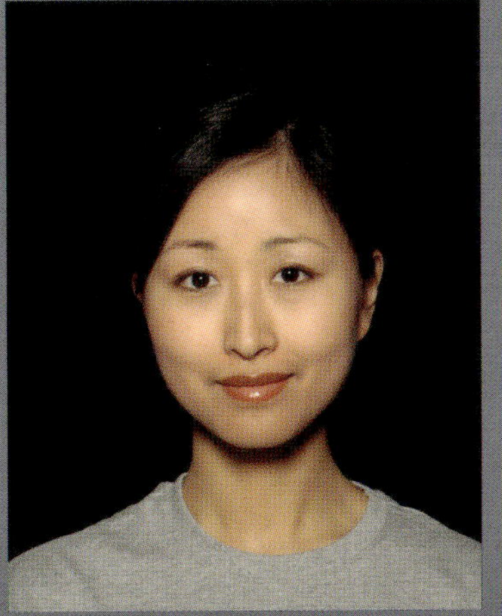
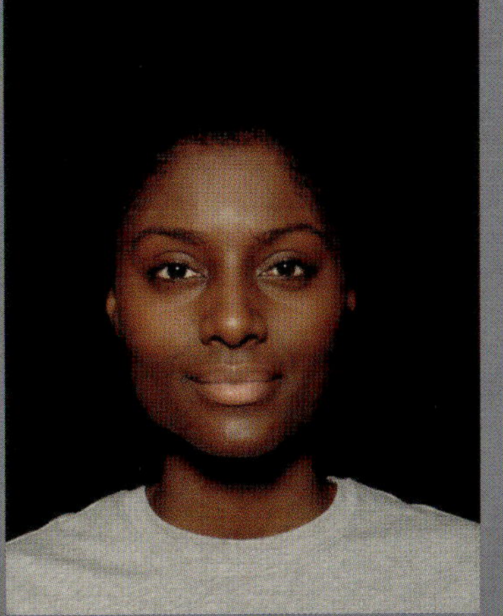
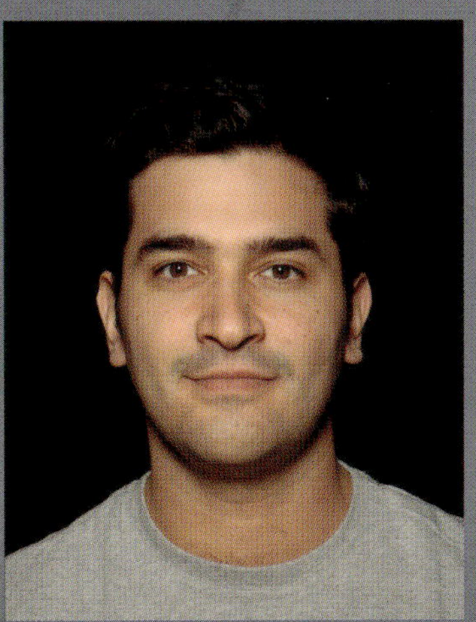

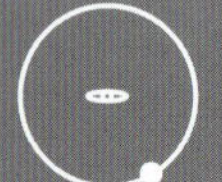

ONE SOFTBOX

LIGHT 1: FROM 30° RIGHT, EYE LEVEL

LIGHT 2: NONE

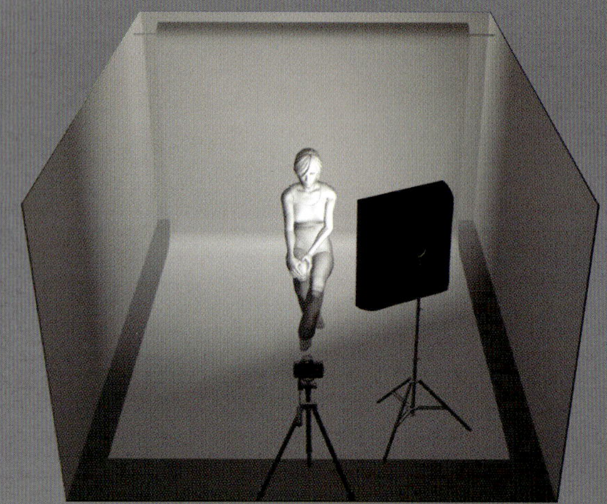

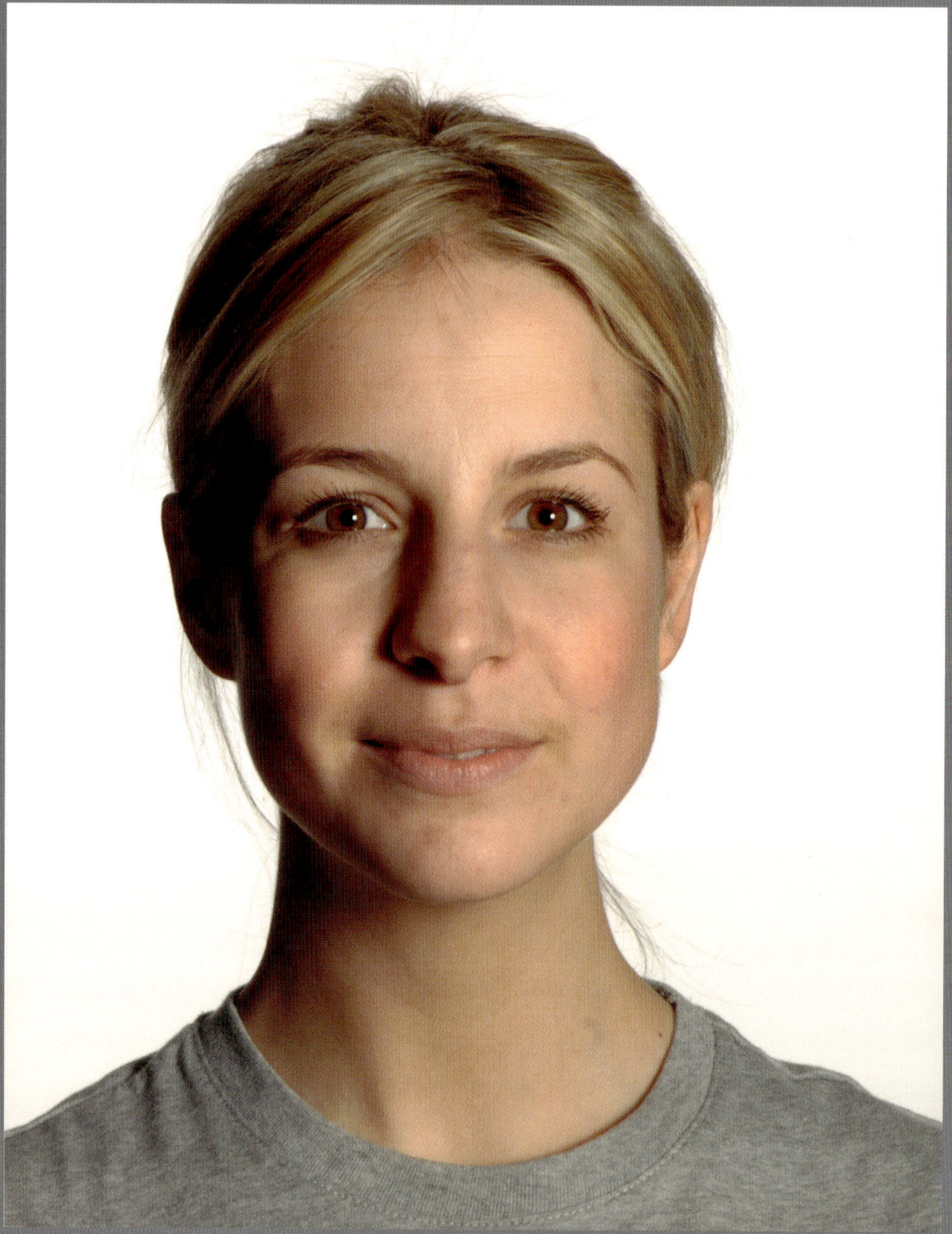

Compared to the full-frontal lighting on the previous page, moving the light slightly to one side of the camera axis—even by as little as 30 degrees—adds a shadow to the side of the nose and face that enhances the three-dimensional appearance of the subject.

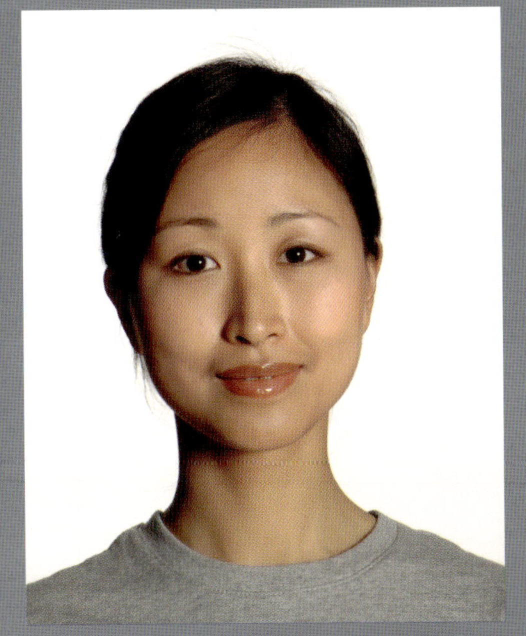

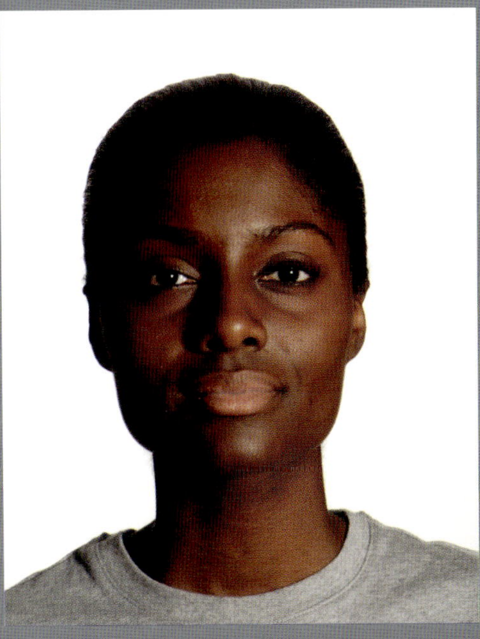

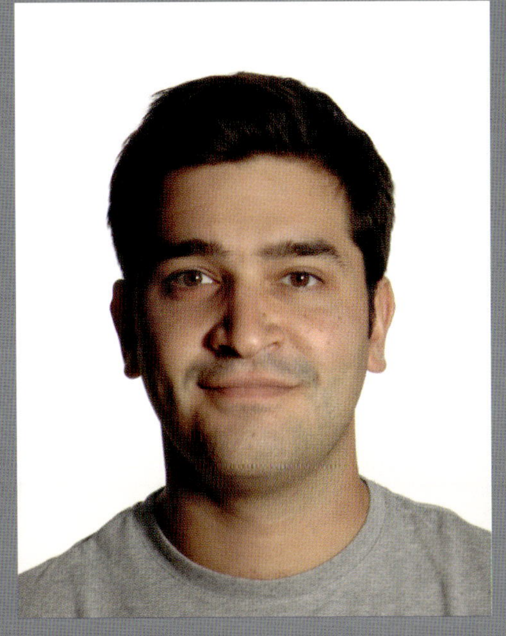

DARK BACKGROUND

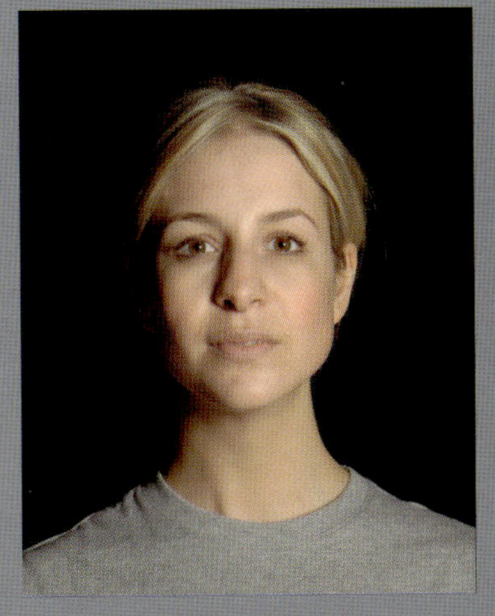

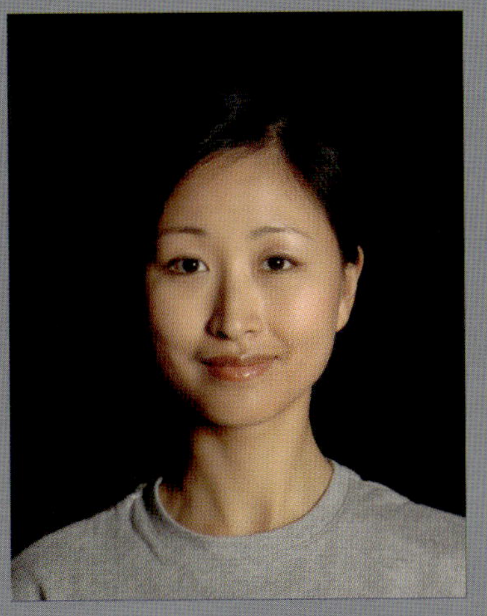

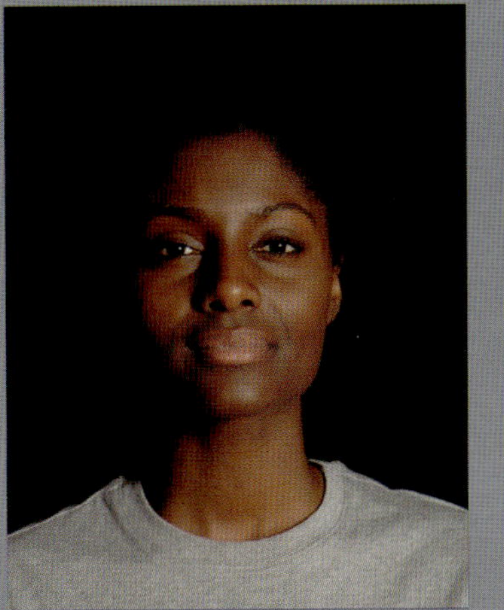

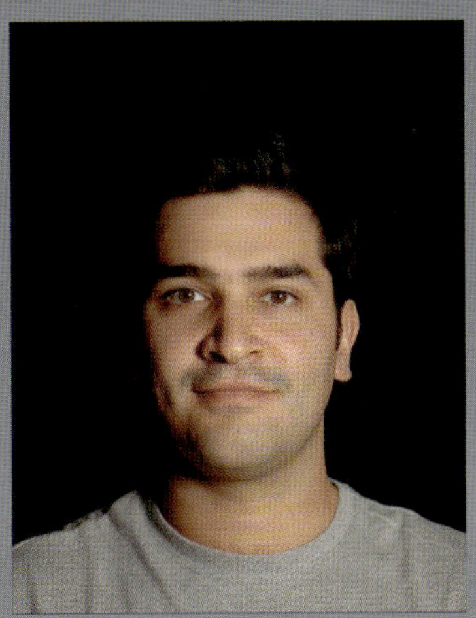

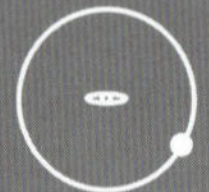

ONE SOFTBOX

LIGHT 1: FROM 60° RIGHT, EYE LEVEL

LIGHT 2: NONE

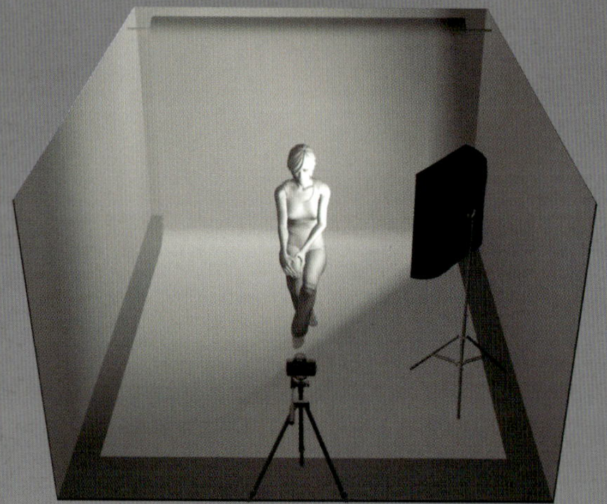

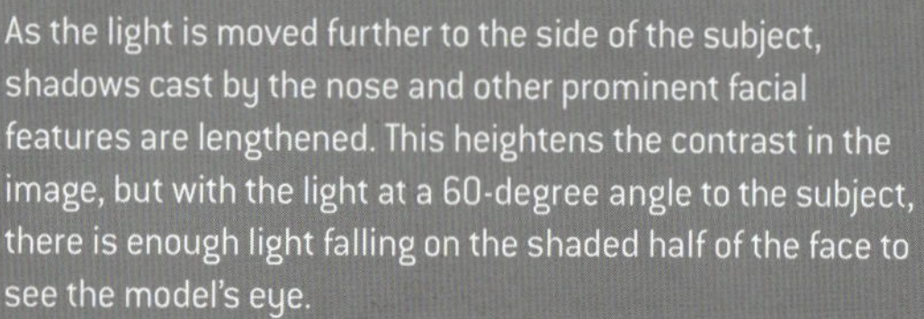

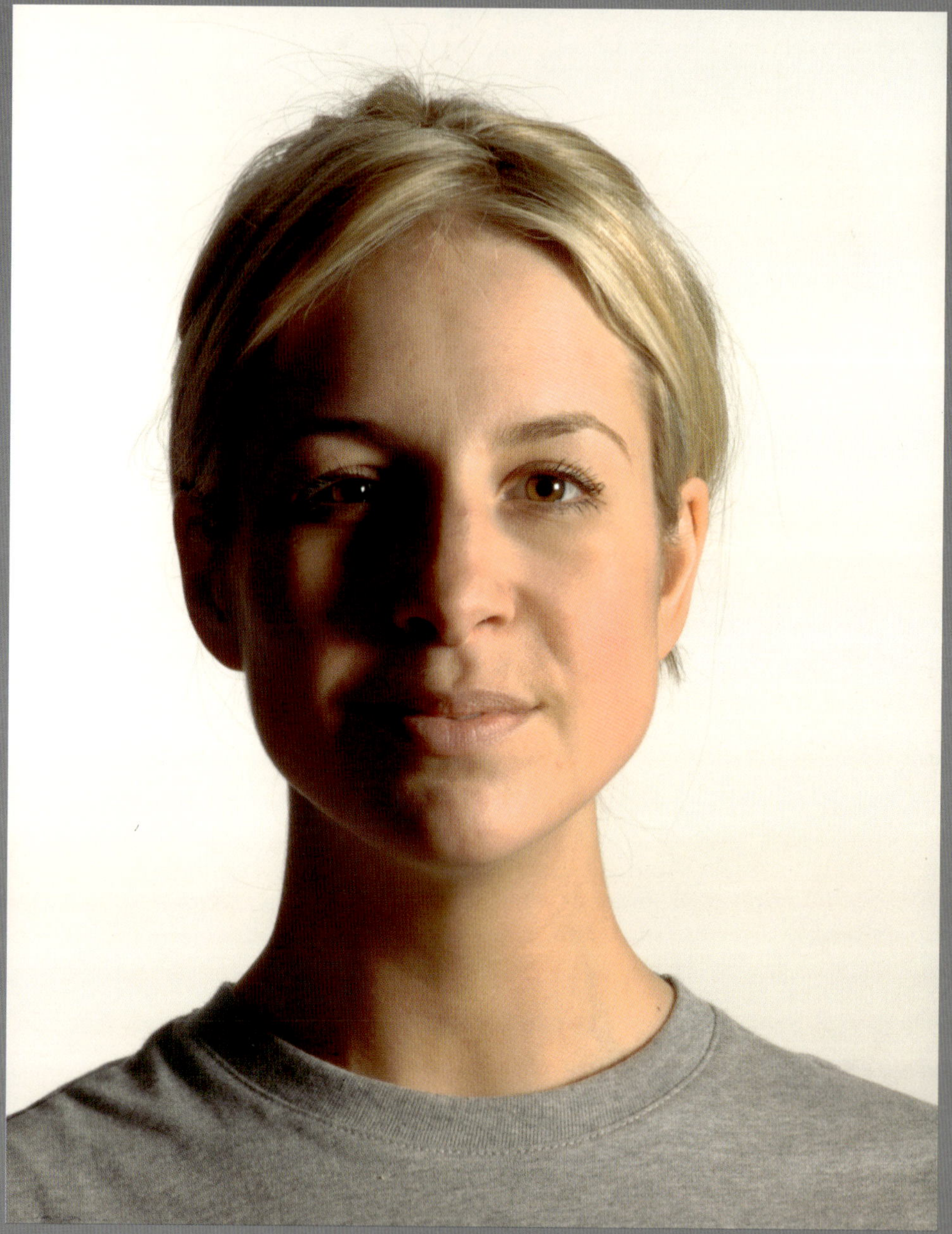

As the light is moved further to the side of the subject, shadows cast by the nose and other prominent facial features are lengthened. This heightens the contrast in the image, but with the light at a 60-degree angle to the subject, there is enough light falling on the shaded half of the face to see the model's eye.

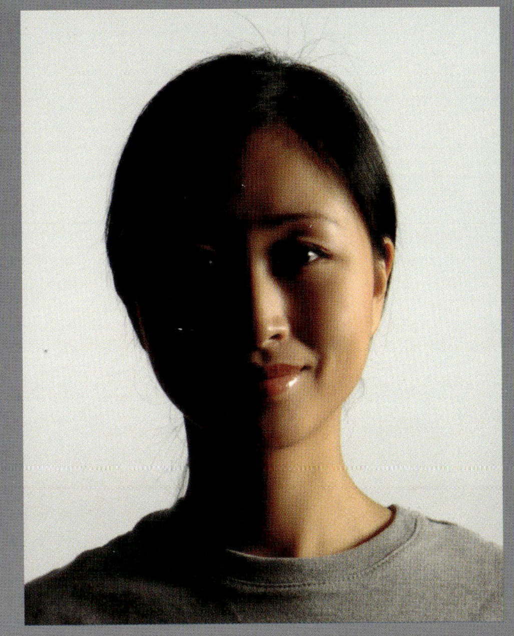
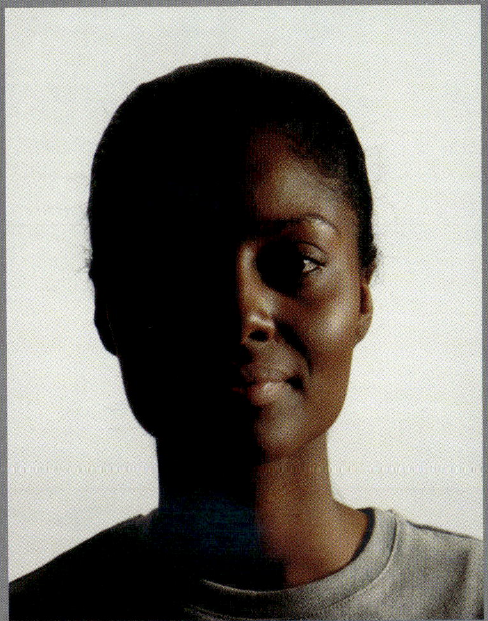
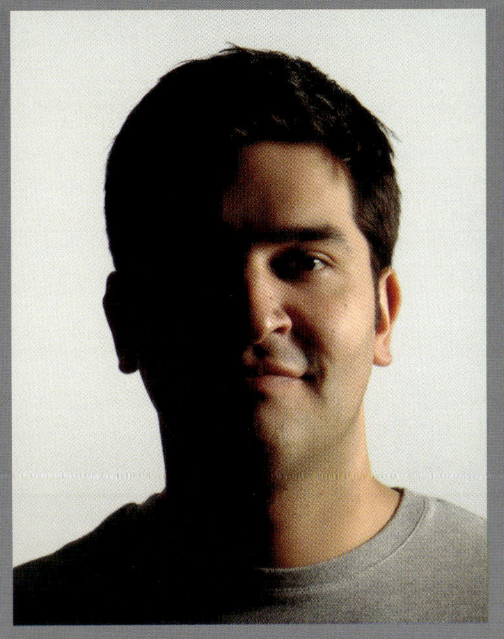

DARK BACKGROUND

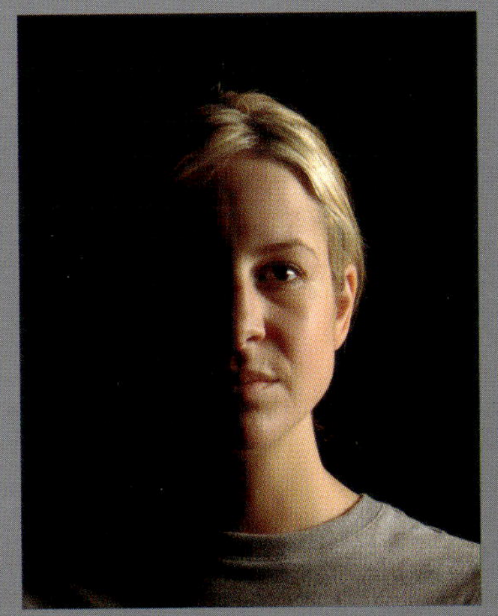
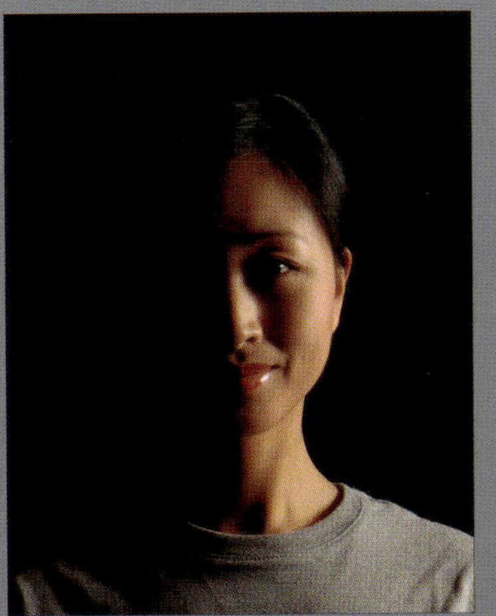
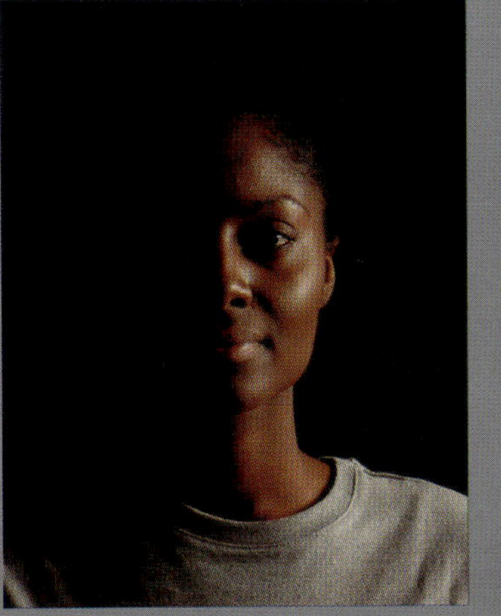
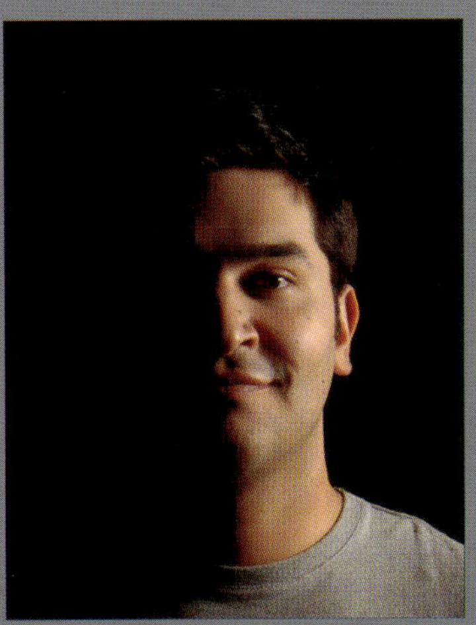

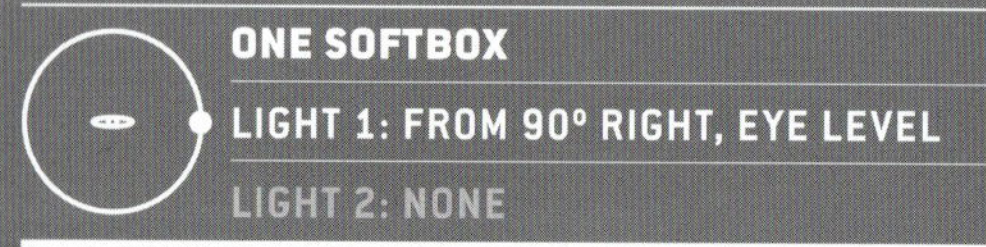

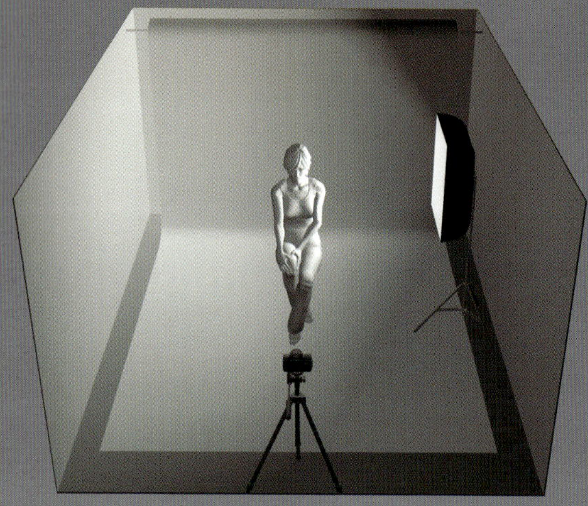

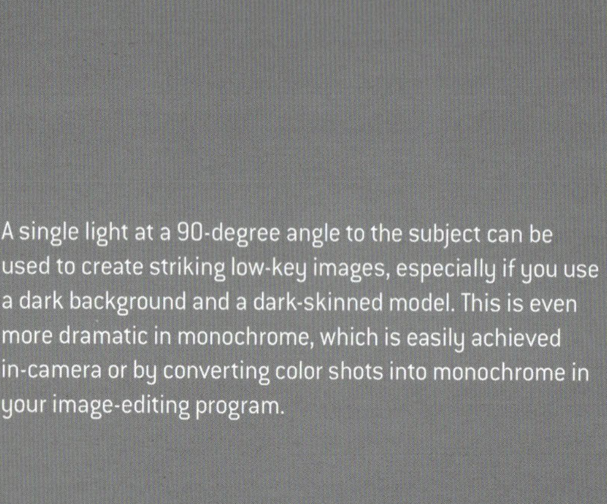

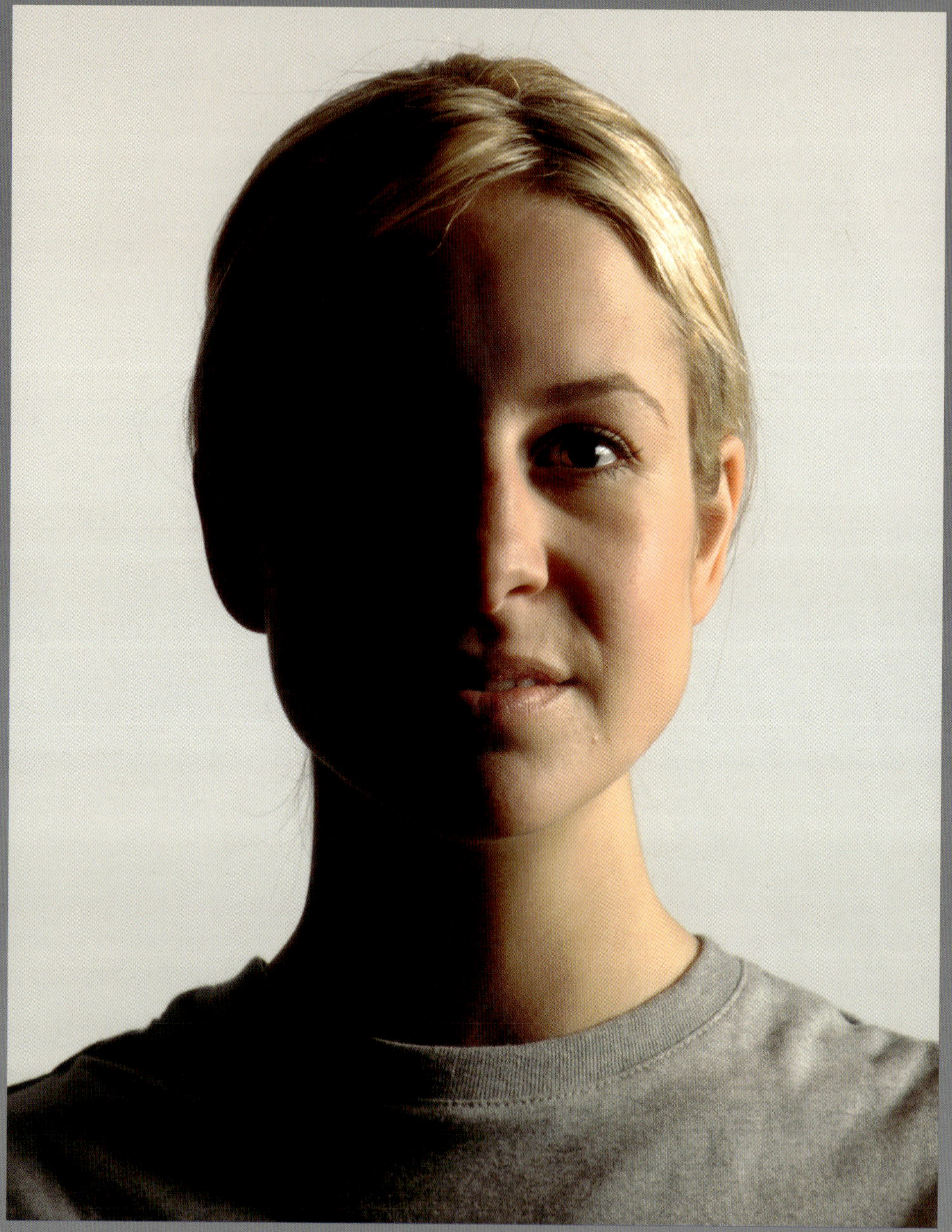

A single light at a 90-degree angle to the subject can be used to create striking low-key images, especially if you use a dark background and a dark-skinned model. This is even more dramatic in monochrome, which is easily achieved in-camera or by converting color shots into monochrome in your image-editing program.

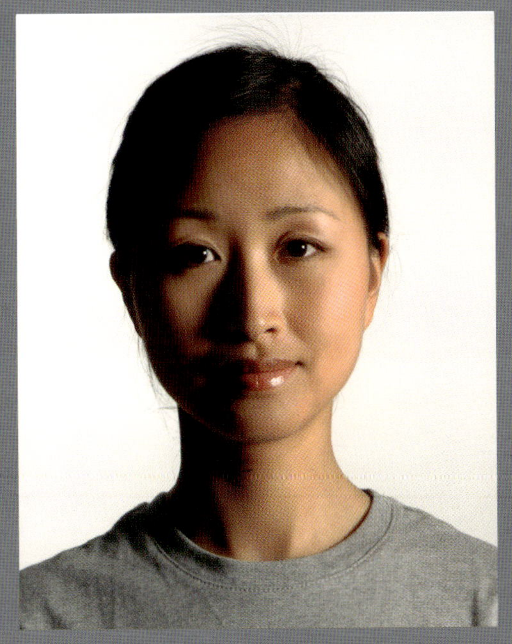

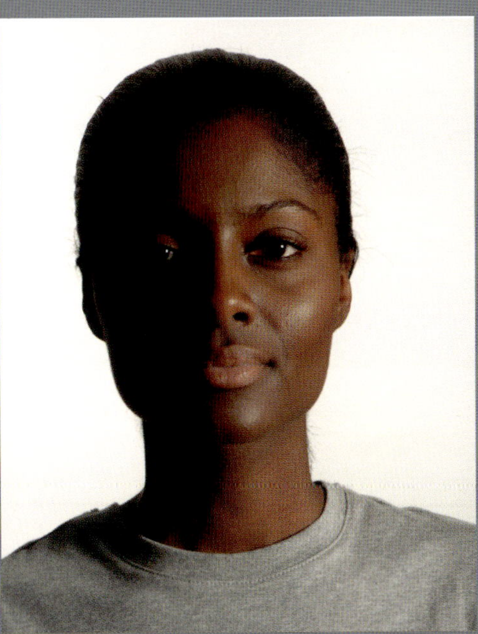

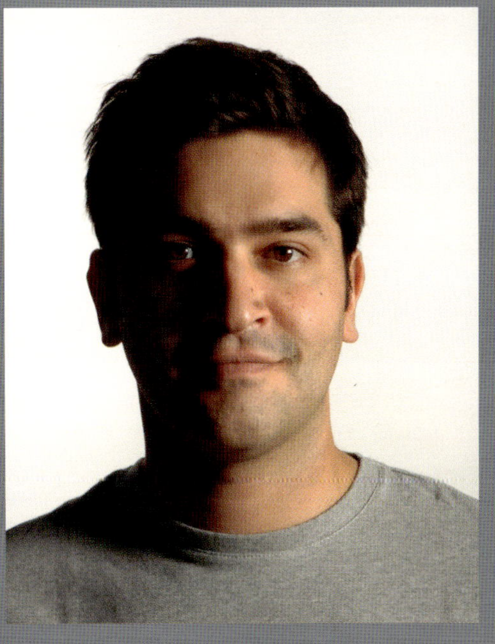

DARK BACKGROUND

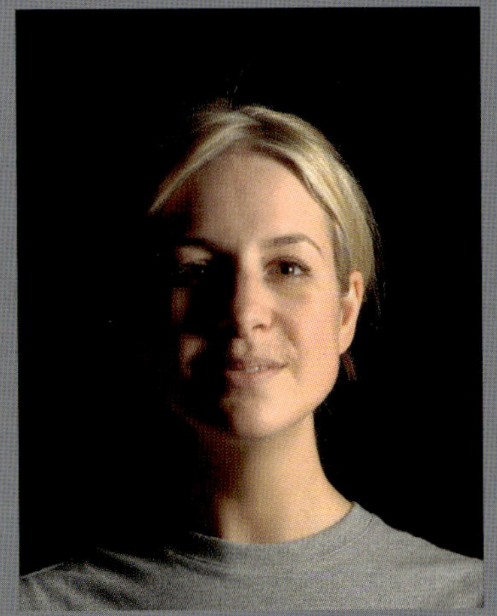

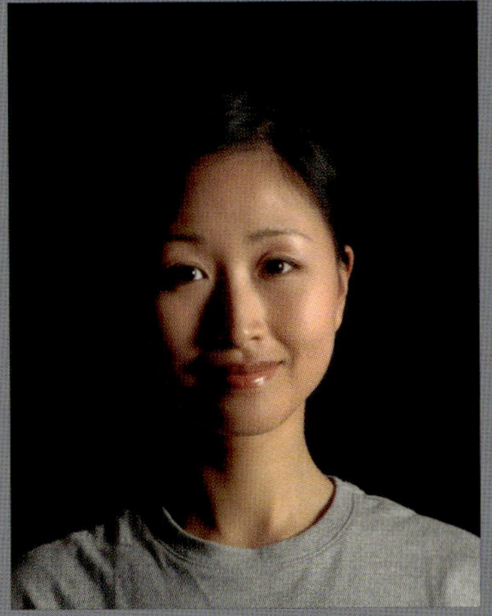

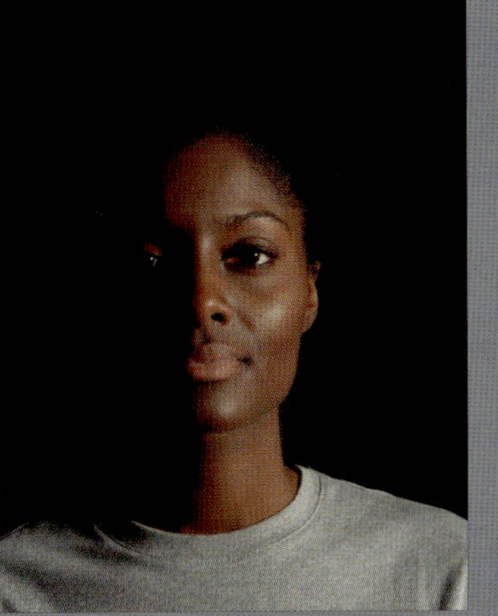

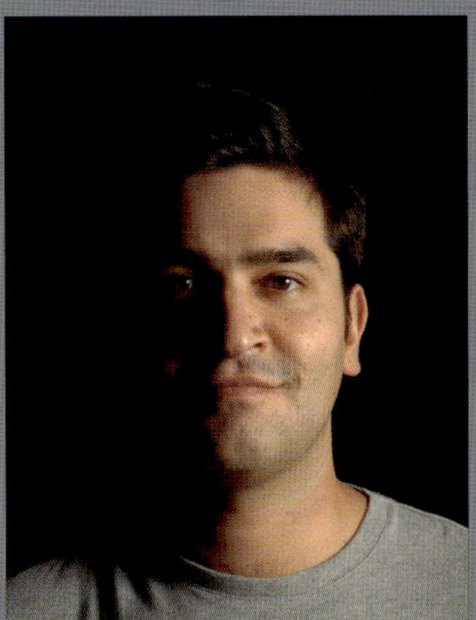

CHAPTER 2

HALF PROFILE, SINGLE LIGHT

Although a single light can produce a range of styles when your subject is photographed face on, there is a limit to how much you can do. A light set at 60 degrees to the left of the camera will produce a similar result to a light set at 60 degrees to the right, for example—the only difference is which side of your subject's face the shadows fall on. However, turning your model slightly is a very quick way of broadening your creative opportunities, as we'll see on the following pages.

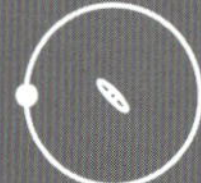

ONE SOFTBOX

LIGHT 1: FROM 90° LEFT, EYE LEVEL

LIGHT 2: NONE

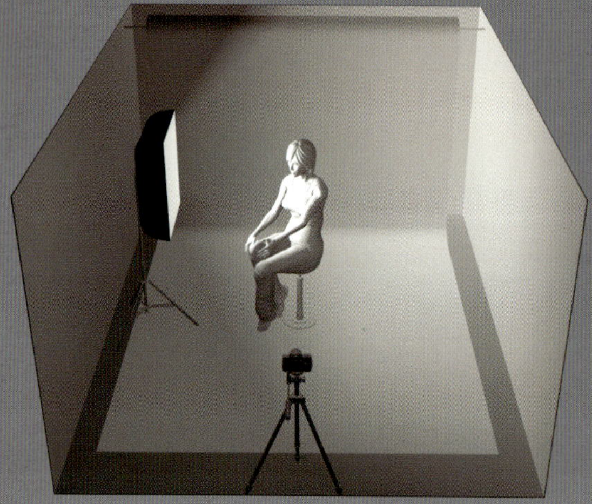

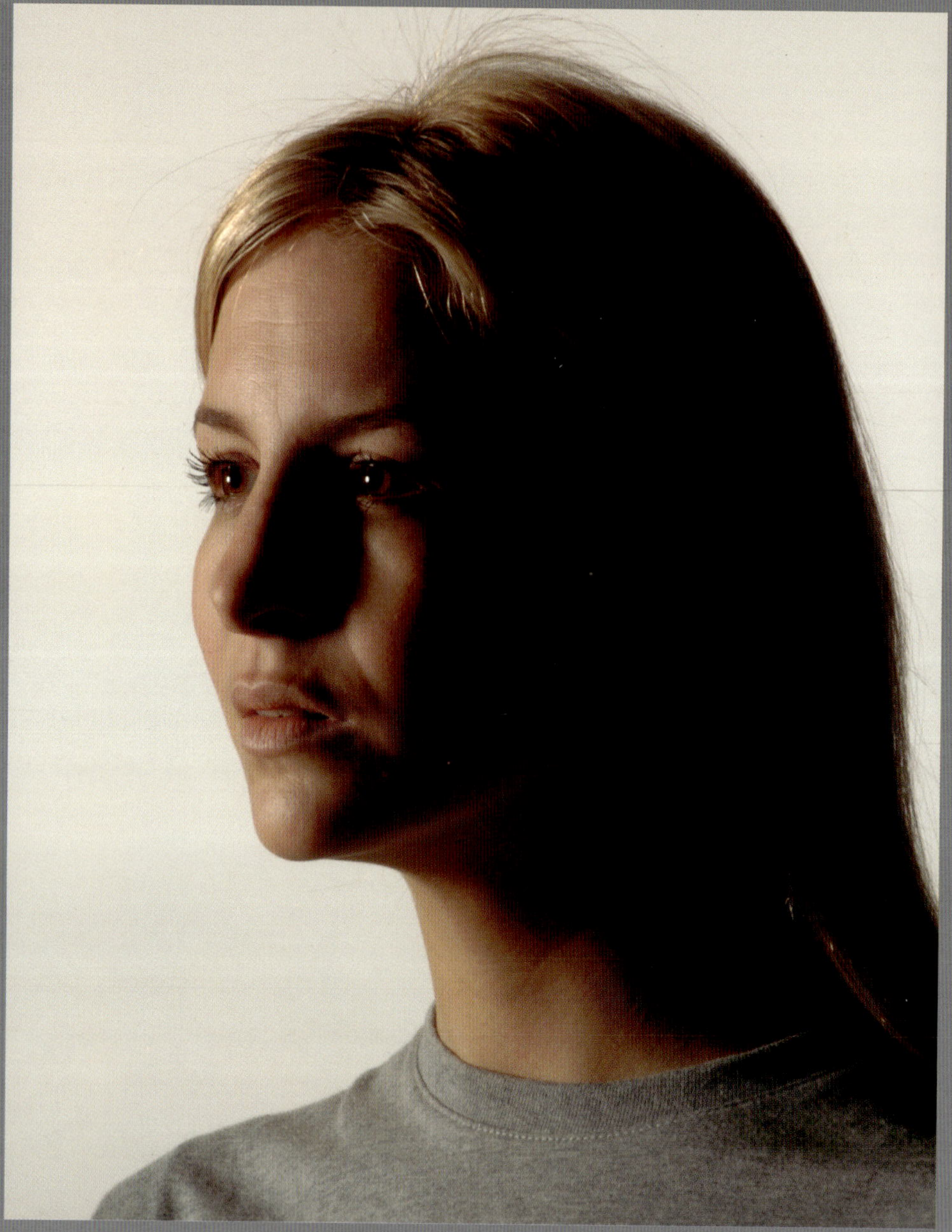

While aiming a light at a face-on subject from a 90-degree angle can create a striking low-key portrait, if the model turns slightly, the effect becomes more dramatic. The shaded side of the face may dominate the frame, but both eyes can be seen and the catchlights in them help draw attention to them.

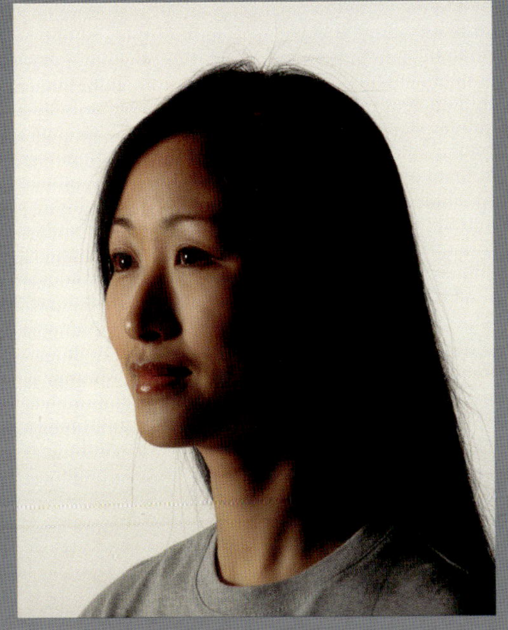

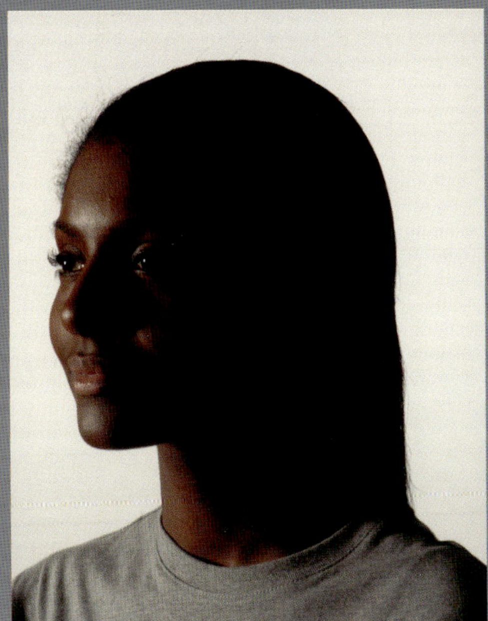

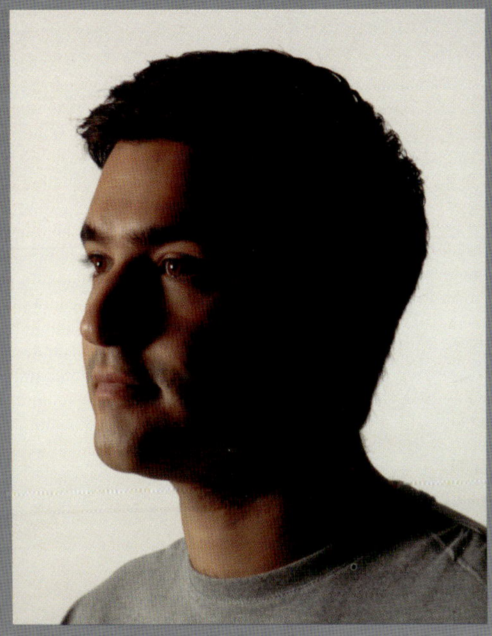

DARK BACKGROUND

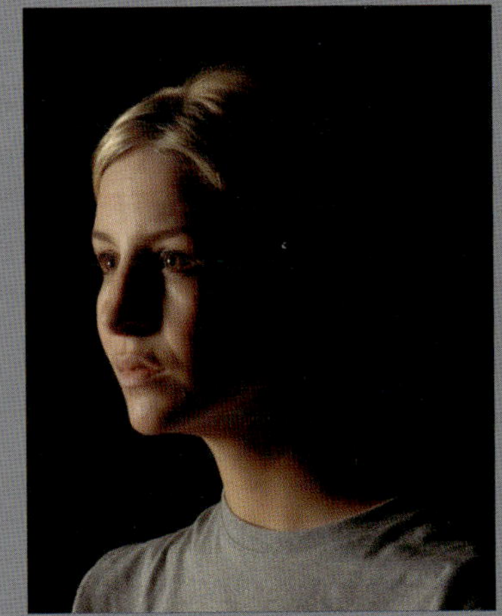

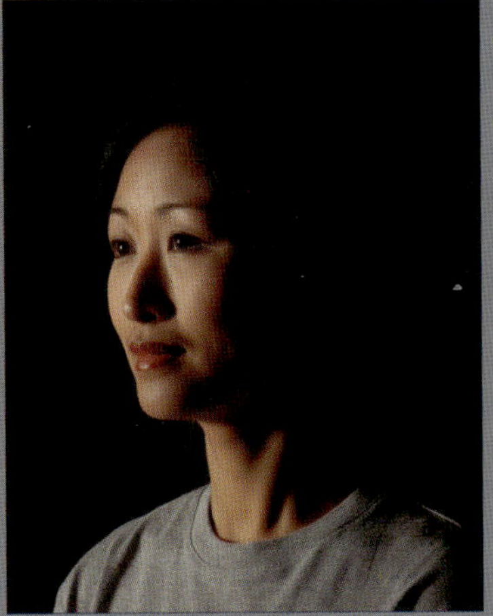

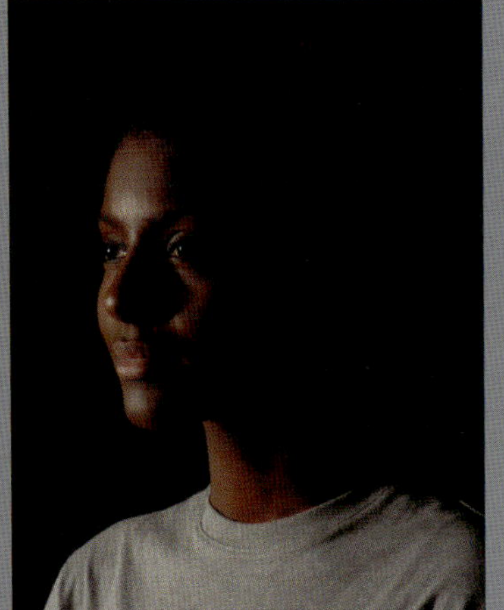

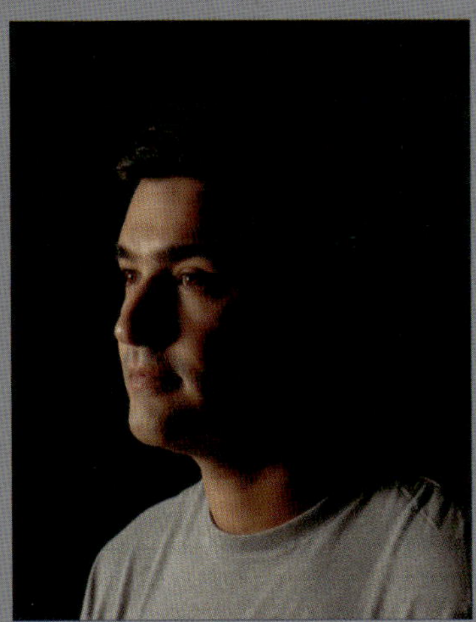

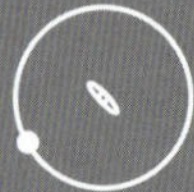

ONE SOFTBOX

LIGHT 1: FROM 60° LEFT, EYE LEVEL

LIGHT 2: NONE

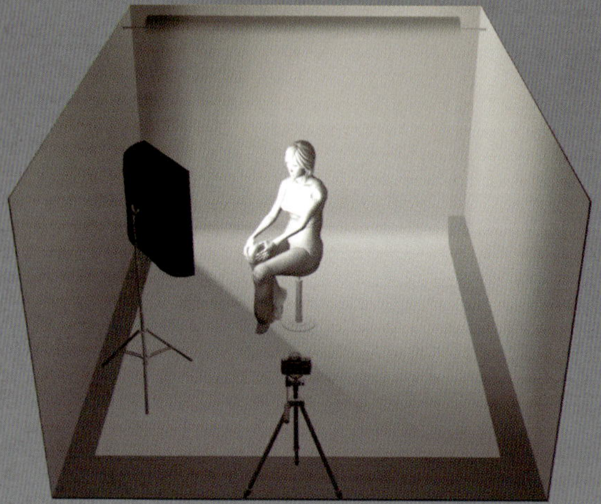

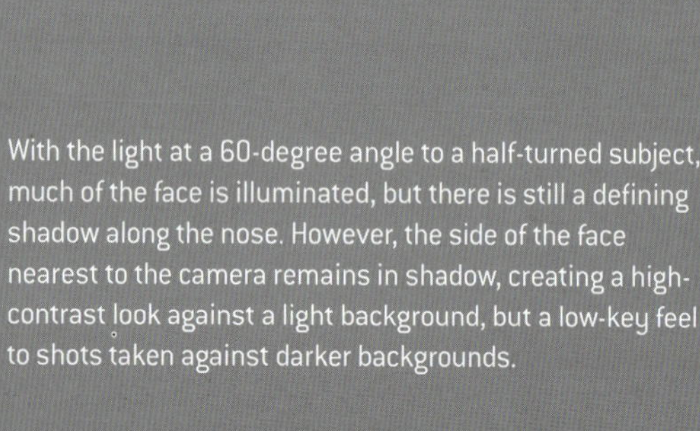

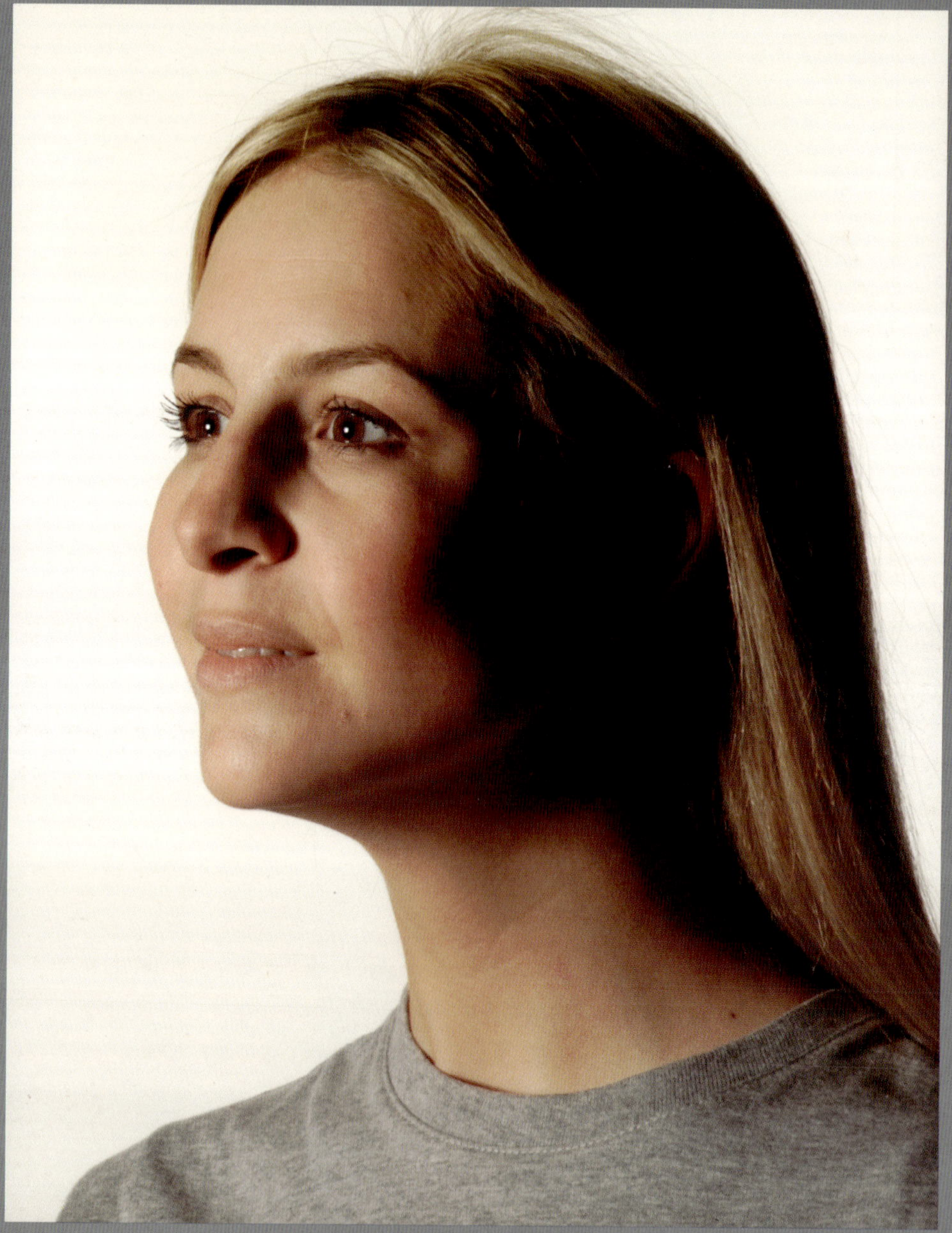

With the light at a 60-degree angle to a half-turned subject, much of the face is illuminated, but there is still a defining shadow along the nose. However, the side of the face nearest to the camera remains in shadow, creating a high-contrast look against a light background, but a low-key feel to shots taken against darker backgrounds.

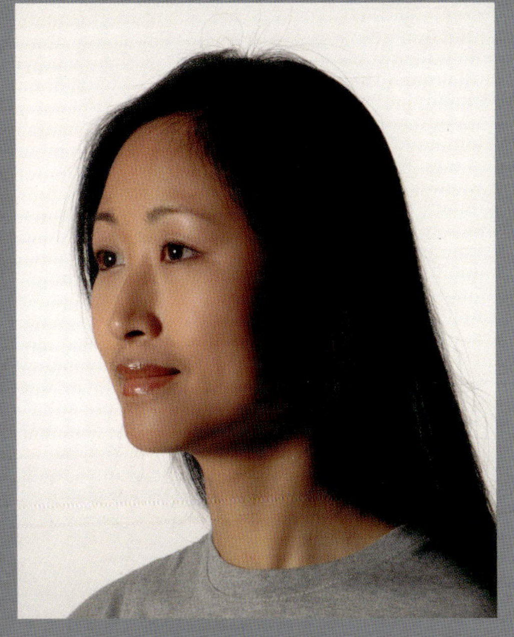

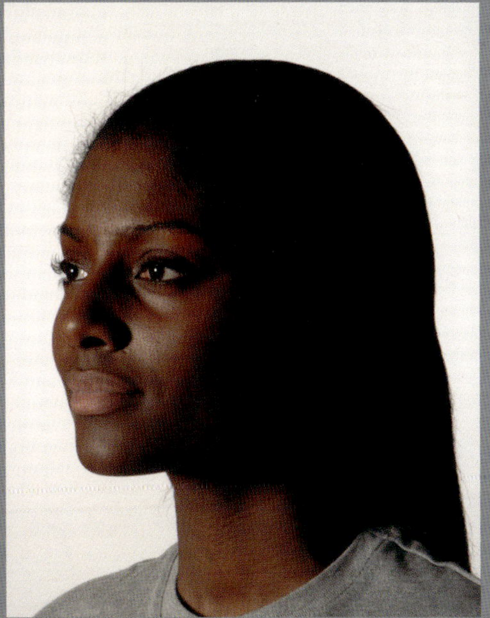

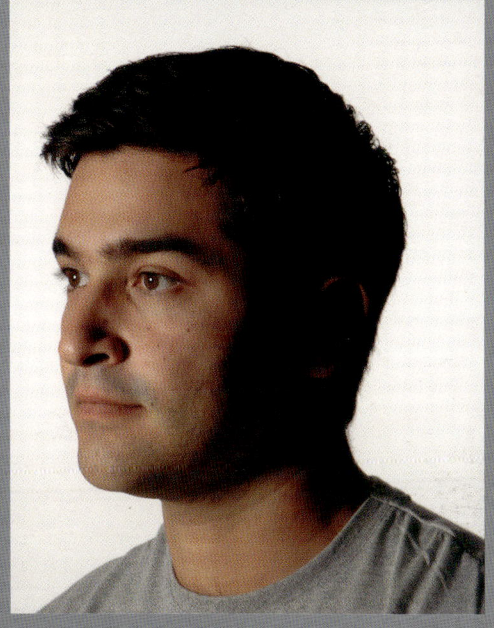

DARK BACKGROUND

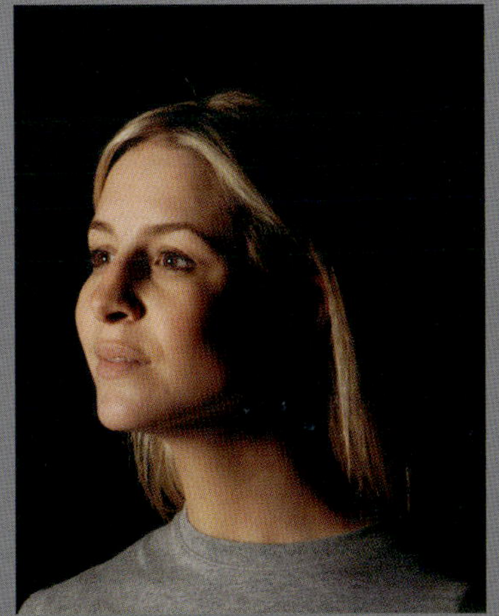

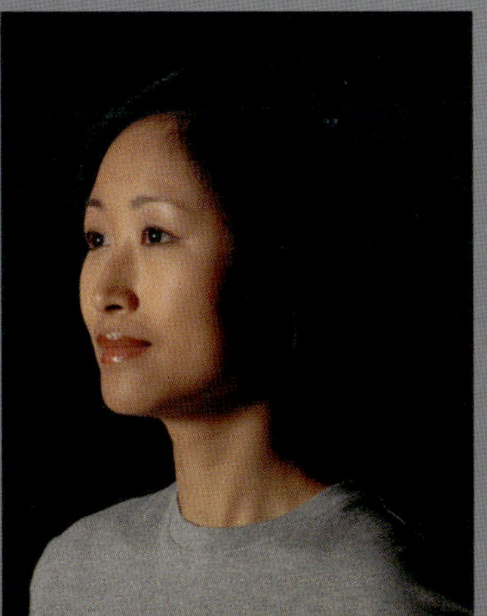

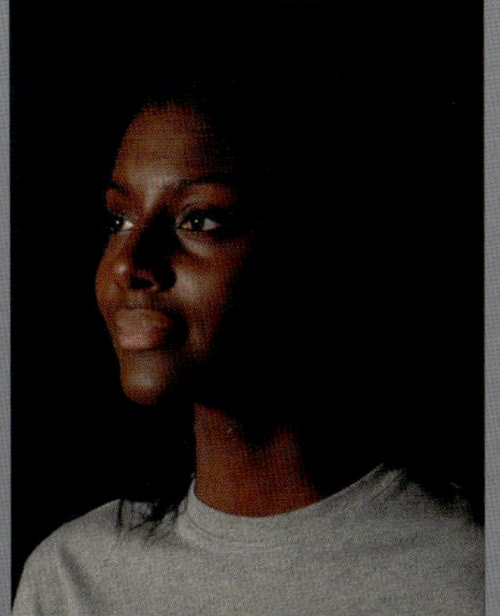

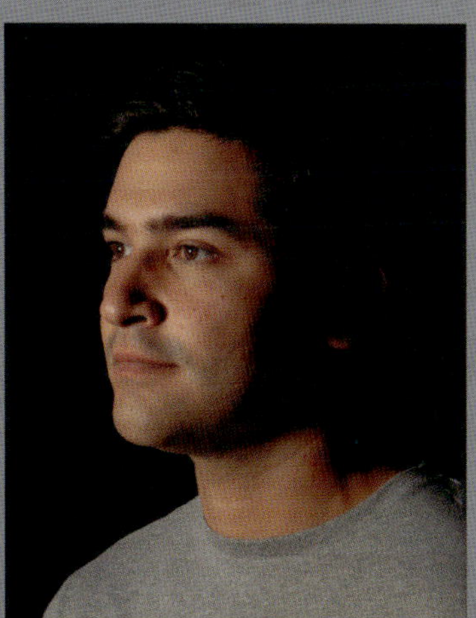

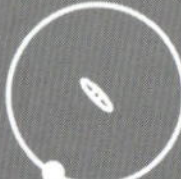

ONE SOFTBOX

LIGHT 1: FROM 30° LEFT, EYE LEVEL

LIGHT 2: NONE

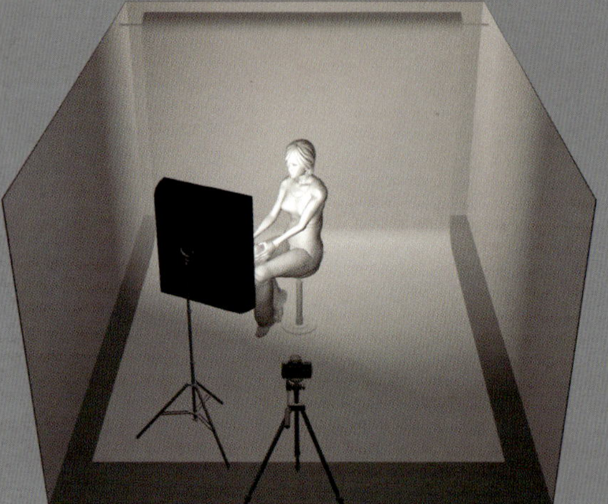

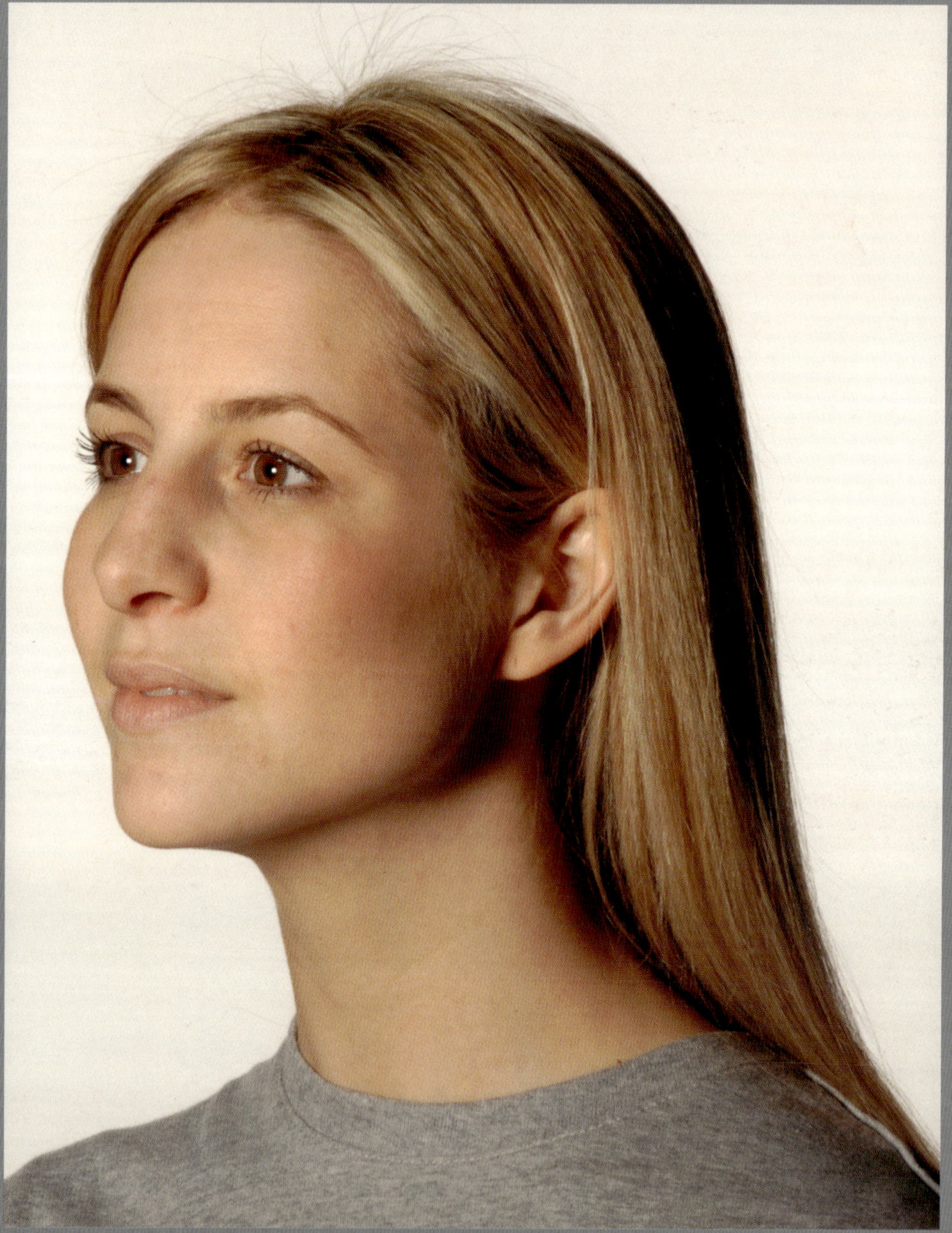

At a 30-degree angle to the subject, the light will strike the side of the model's face that is nearest to the camera. Although this reduces the shadows and reveals detail, the light falling on the front of the subject dominates slightly, so there is still some soft modeling to the figure.

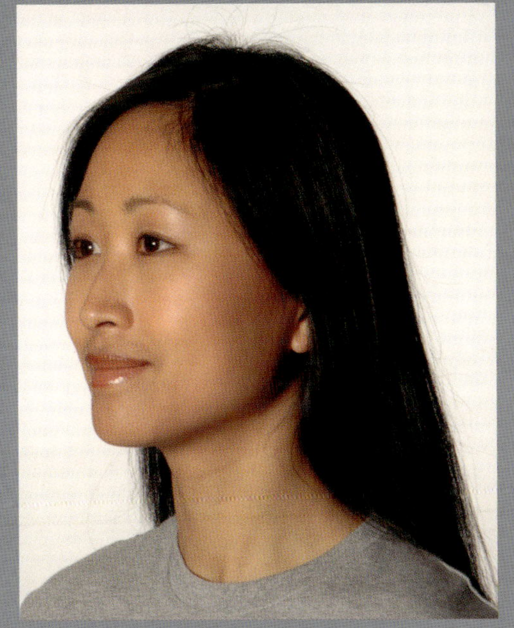
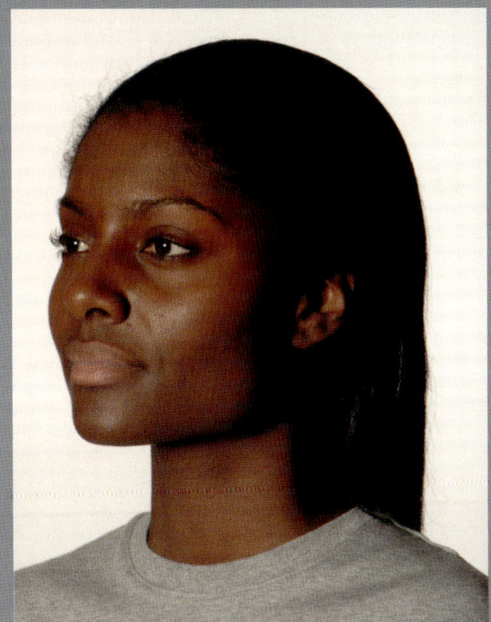
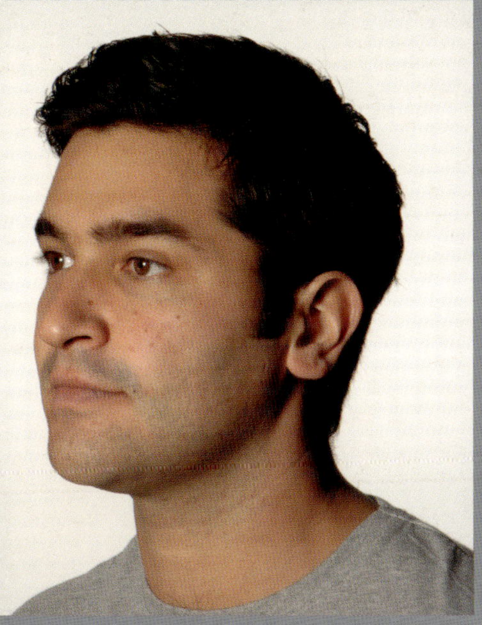

DARK BACKGROUND

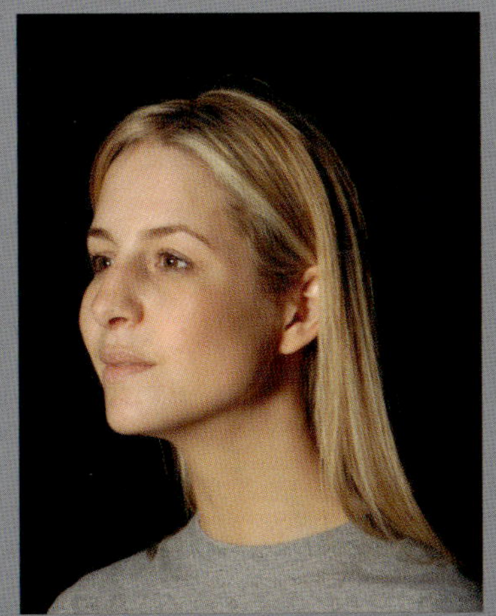
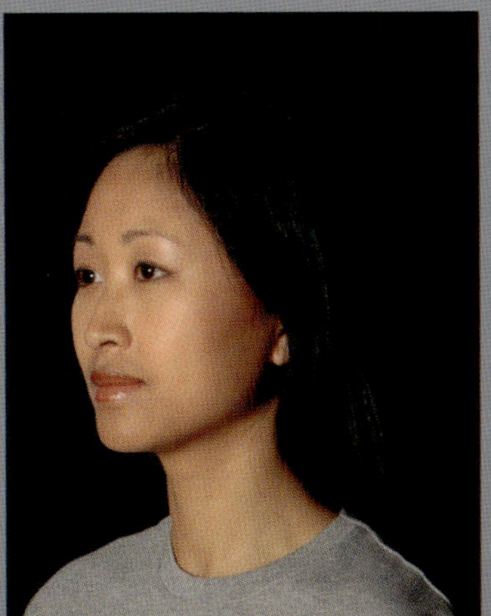
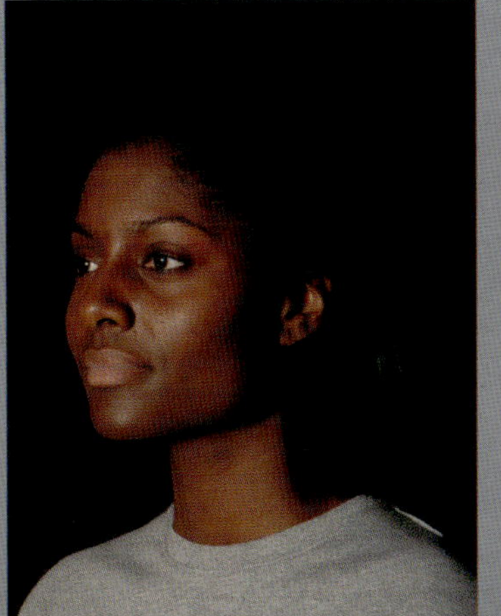
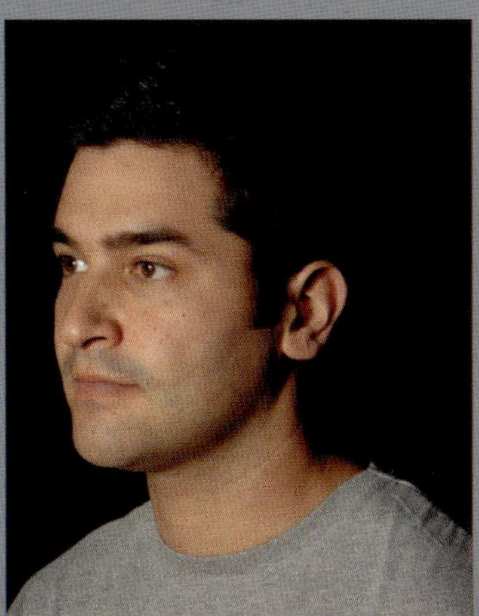

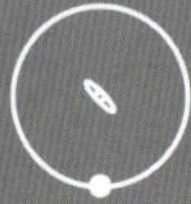

ONE SOFTBOX

LIGHT 1: FROM CAMERA, EYE LEVEL

LIGHT 2: NONE

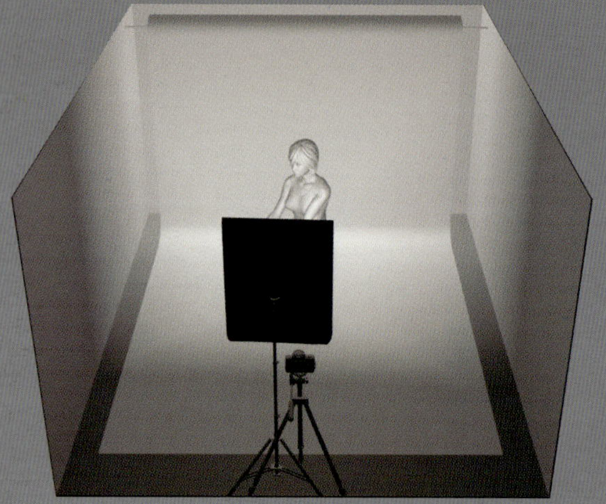

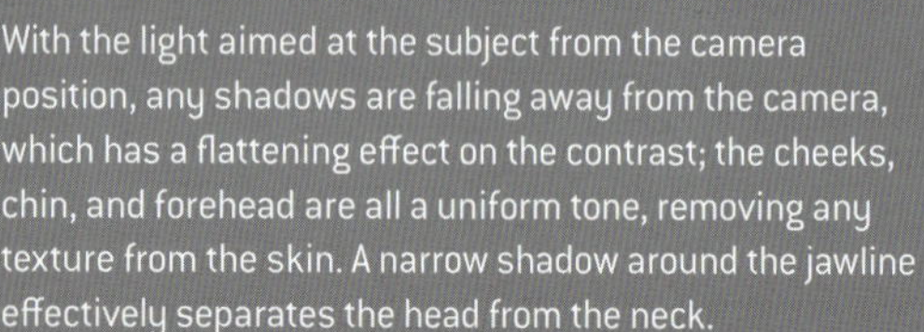

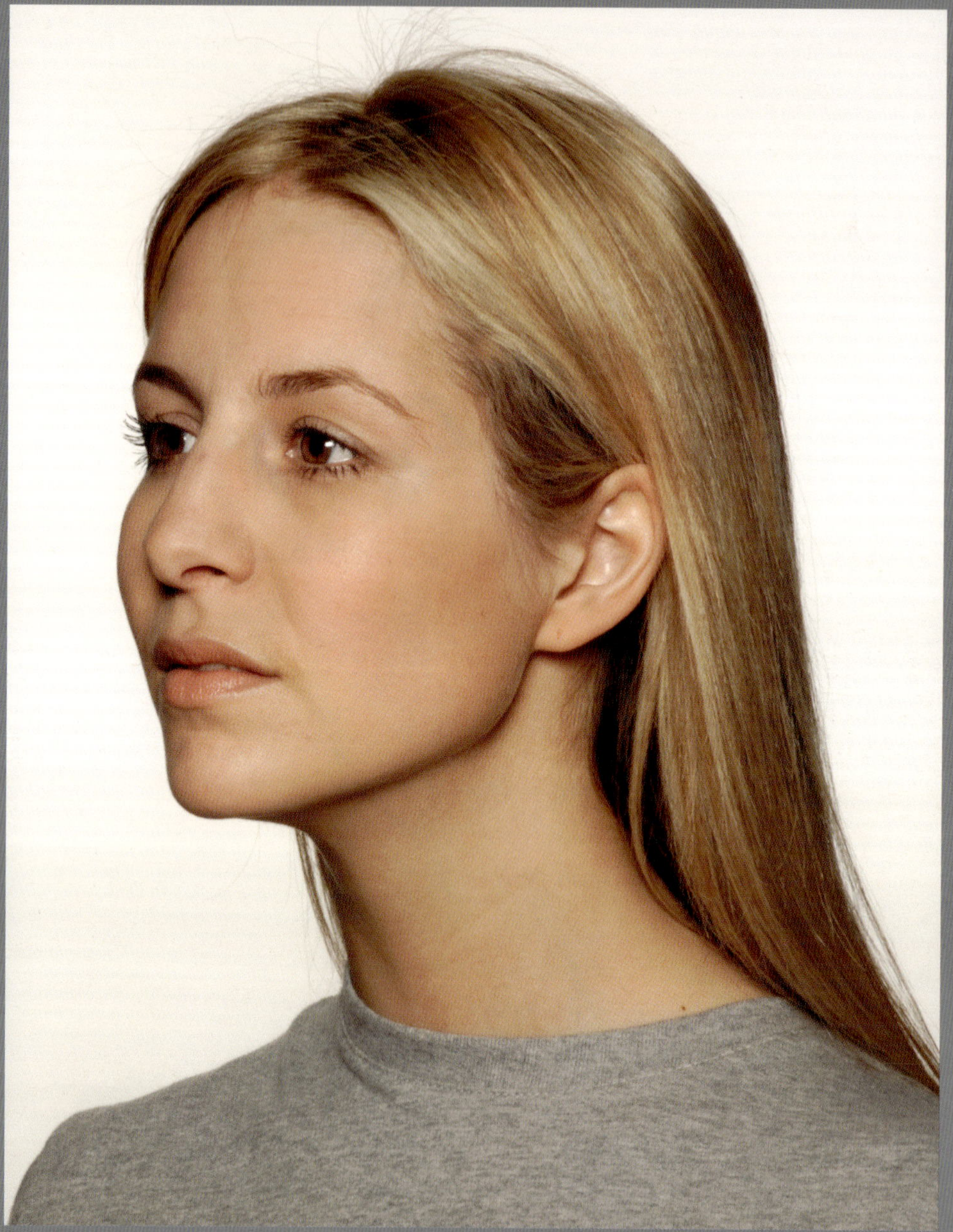

With the light aimed at the subject from the camera position, any shadows are falling away from the camera, which has a flattening effect on the contrast; the cheeks, chin, and forehead are all a uniform tone, removing any texture from the skin. A narrow shadow around the jawline effectively separates the head from the neck.

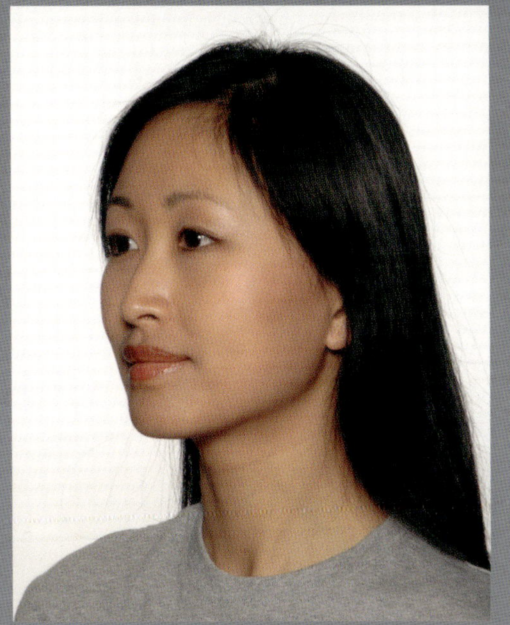
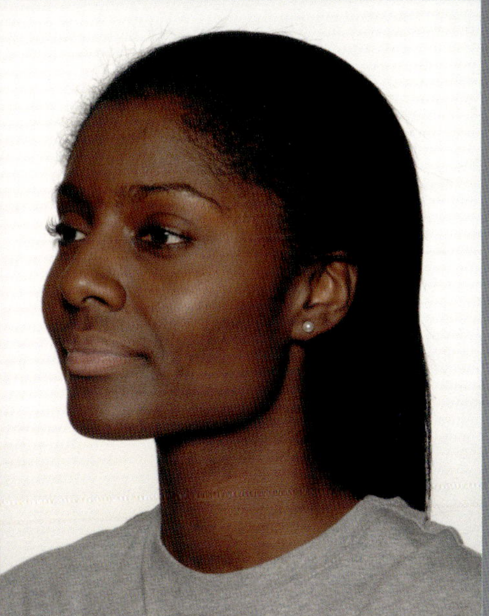
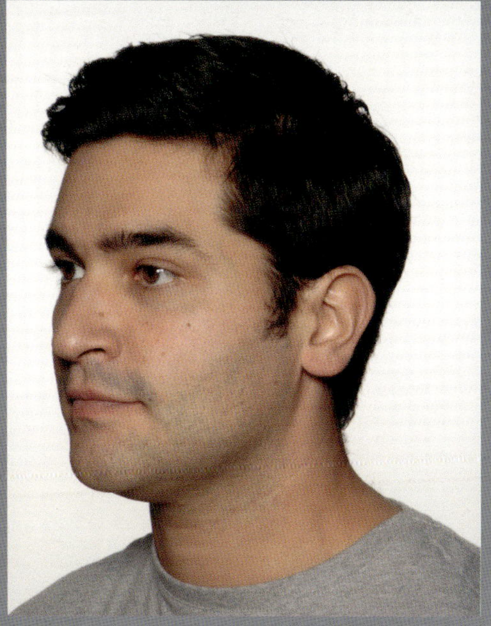

DARK BACKGROUND

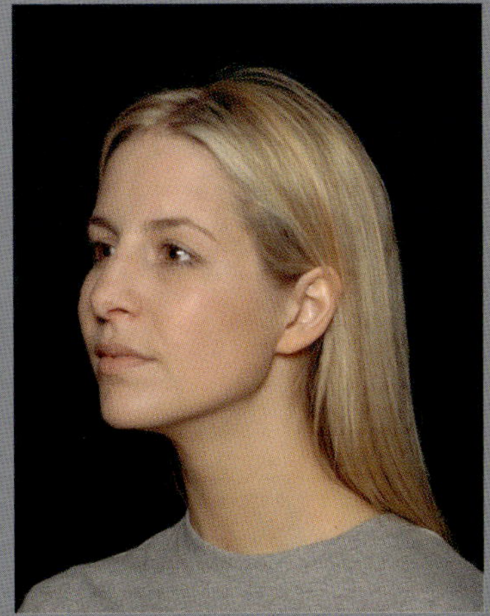
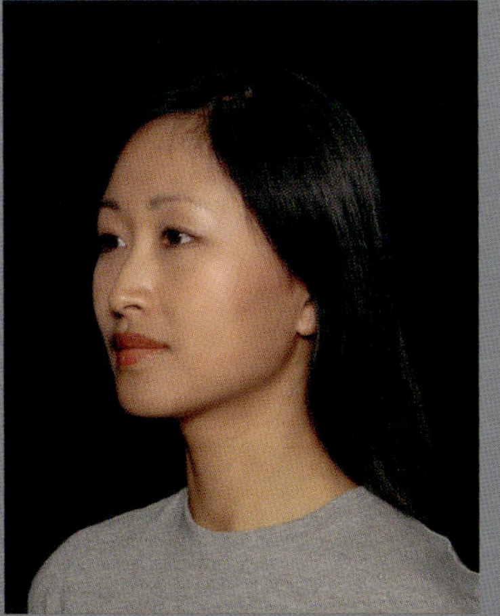
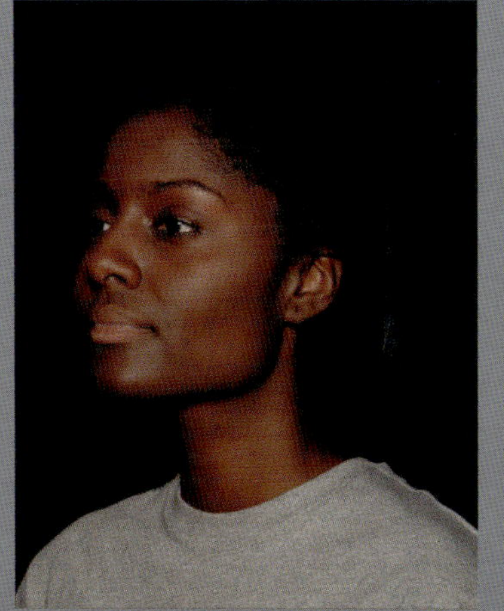
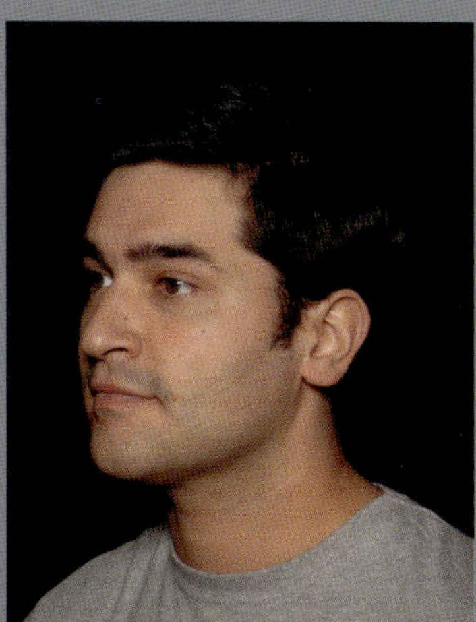

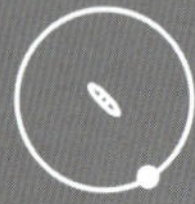

ONE SOFTBOX

LIGHT 1: FROM 30° RIGHT, EYE LEVEL

LIGHT 2: NONE

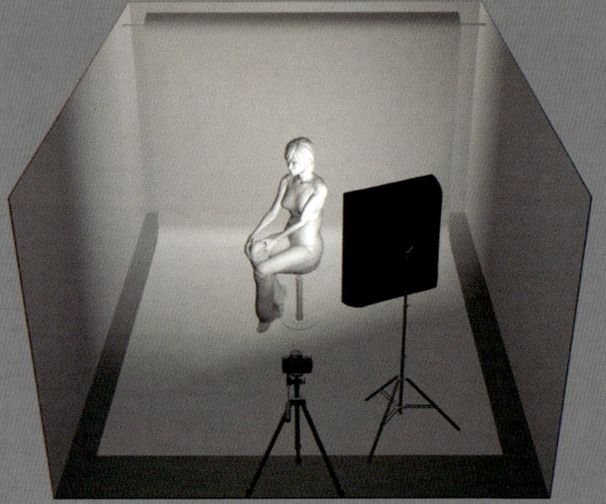

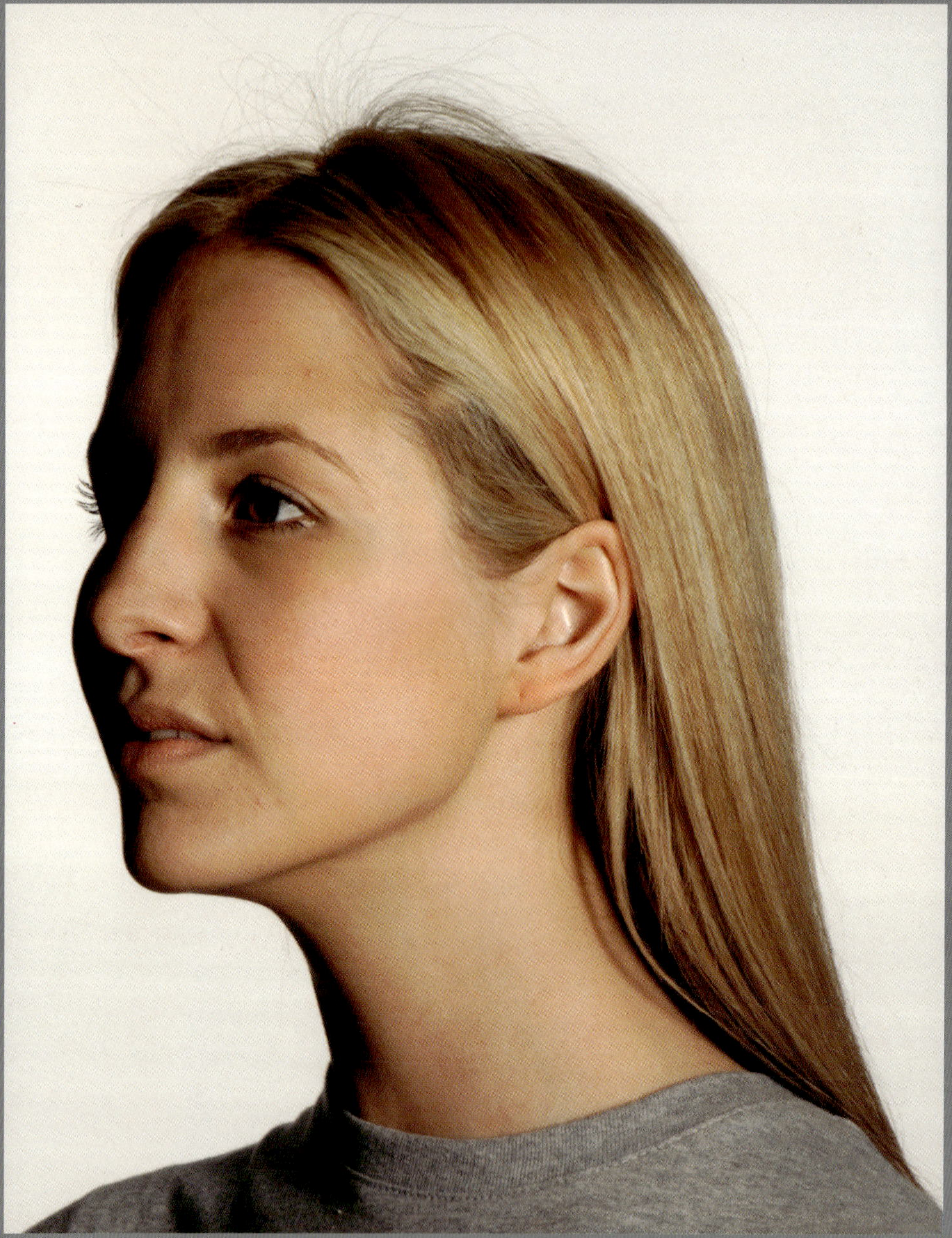

As the light moves around toward the back of the subject, the side of the face and neck that is furthest from the camera starts to fall into shadow. It is also notable that any catchlights are lost from the eyes, which can have a “deadening” effect on a portrait.

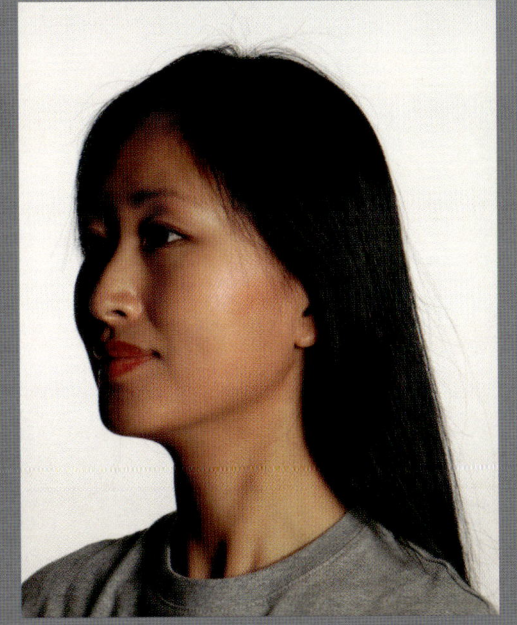
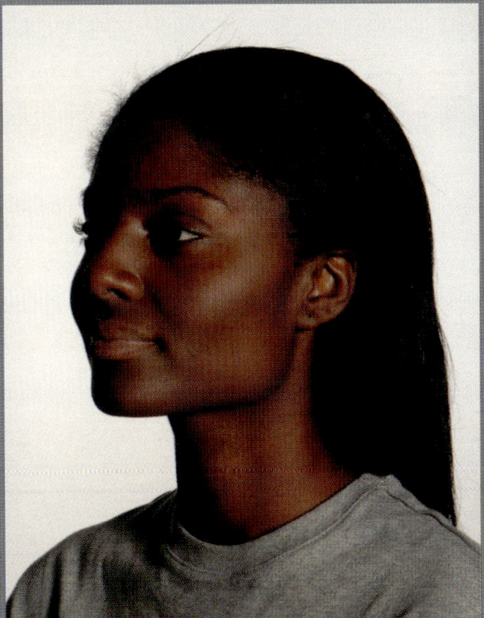
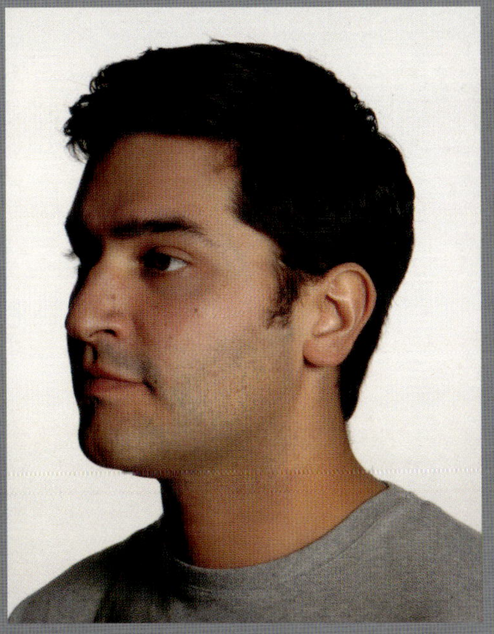

DARK BACKGROUND

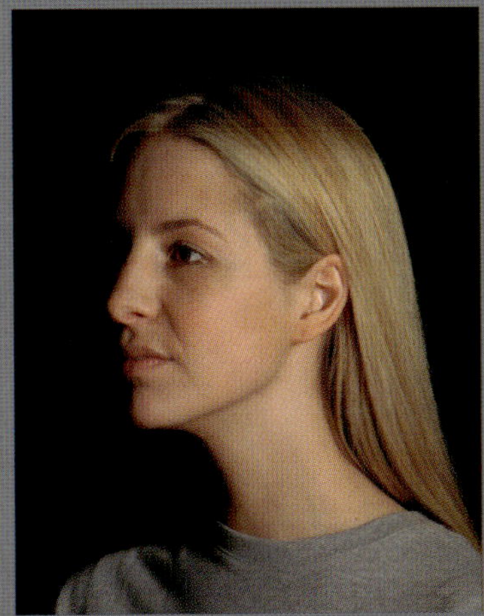
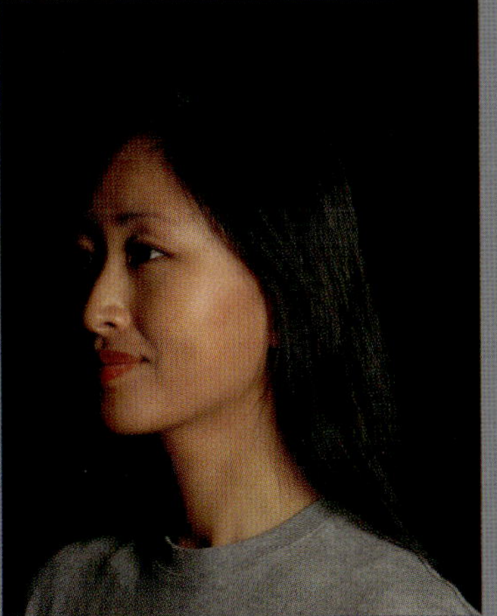
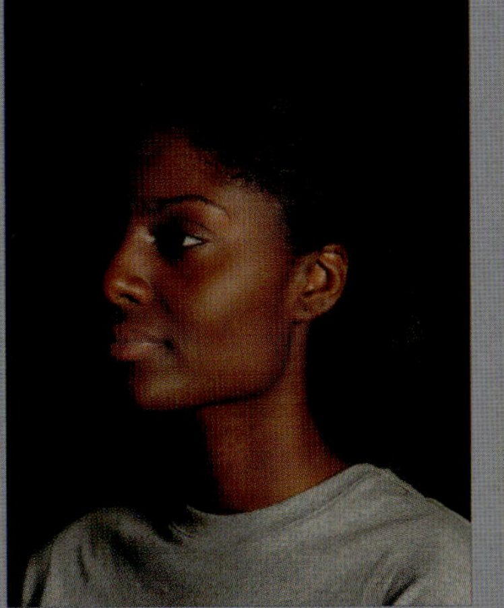
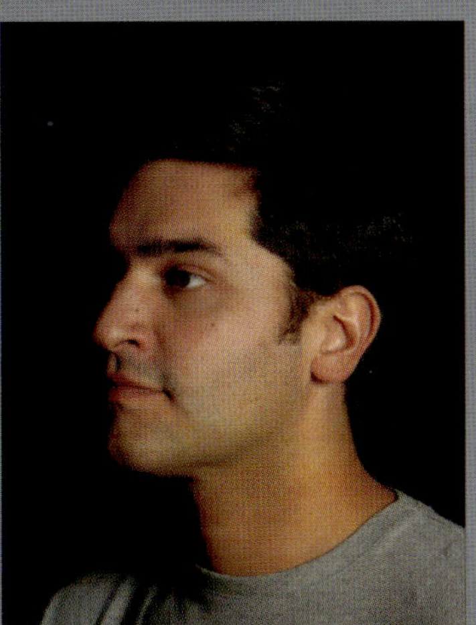

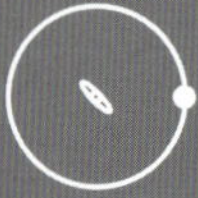

ONE SOFTBOX

LIGHT 1: FROM 90° RIGHT, EYE LEVEL

LIGHT 2: NONE

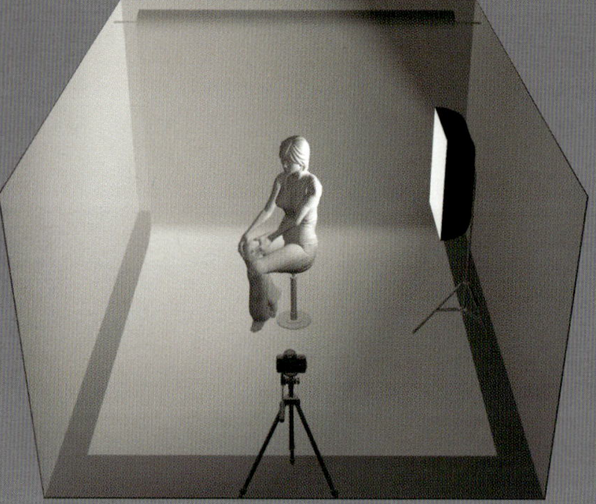

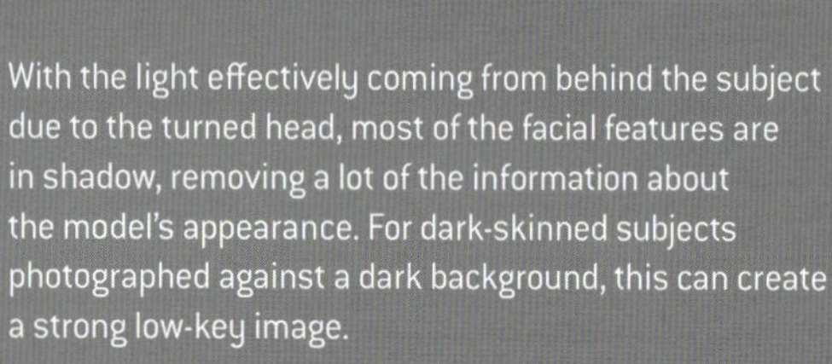

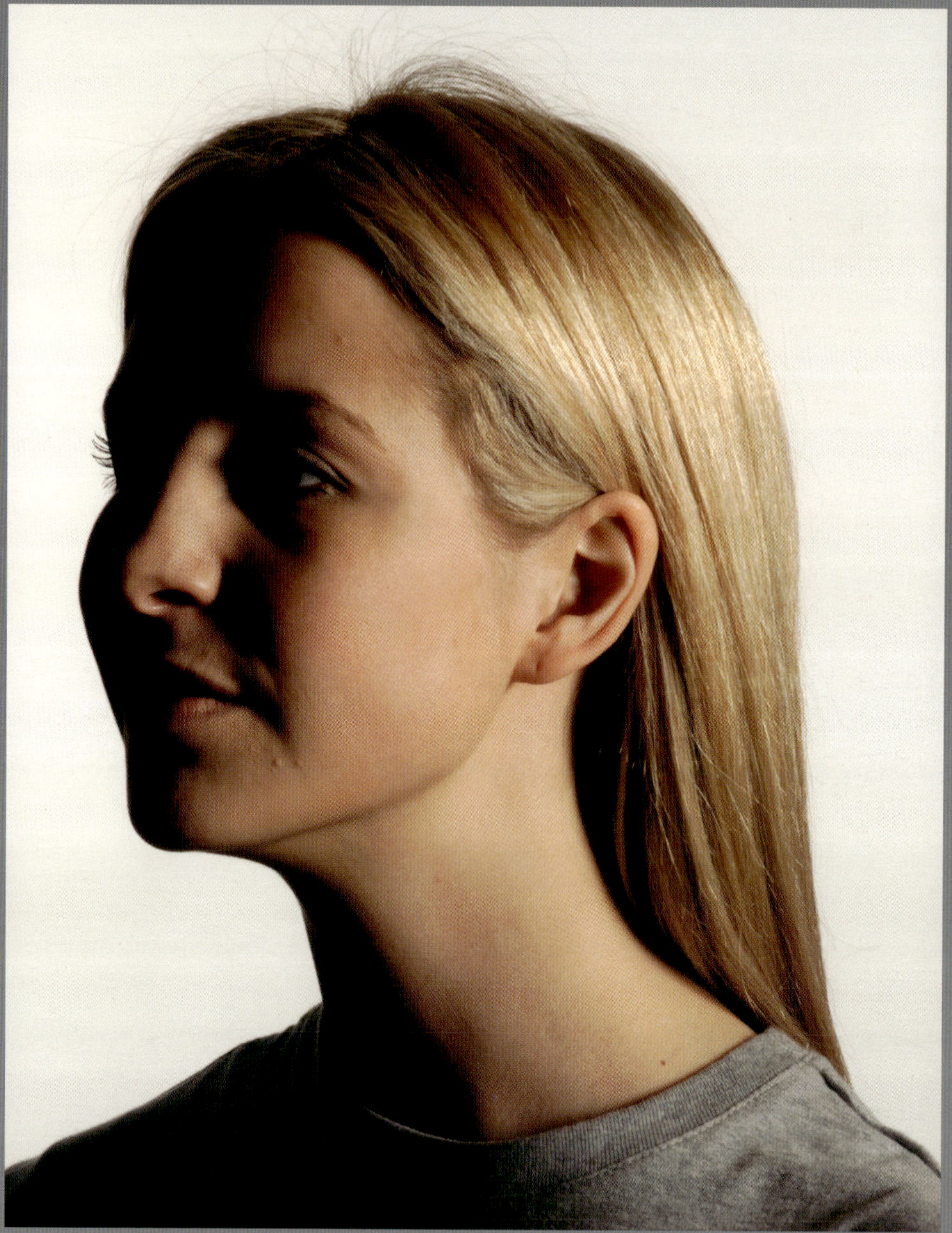

With the light effectively coming from behind the subject due to the turned head, most of the facial features are in shadow, removing a lot of the information about the model's appearance. For dark-skinned subjects photographed against a dark background, this can create a strong low-key image.

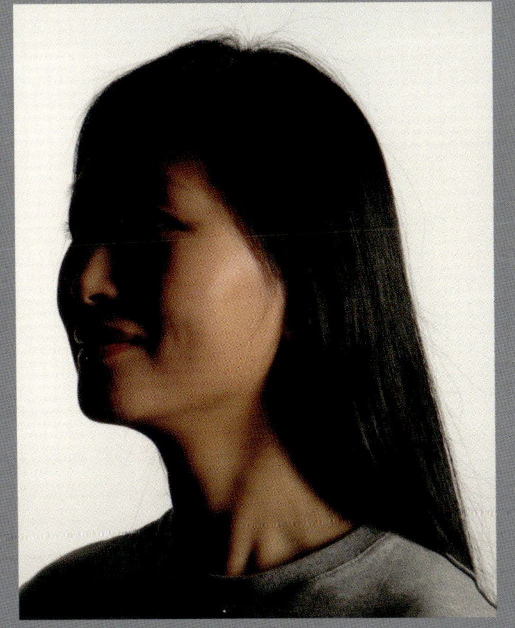

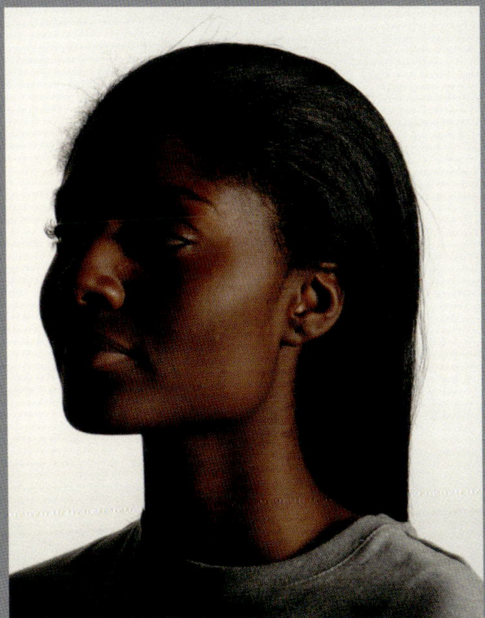

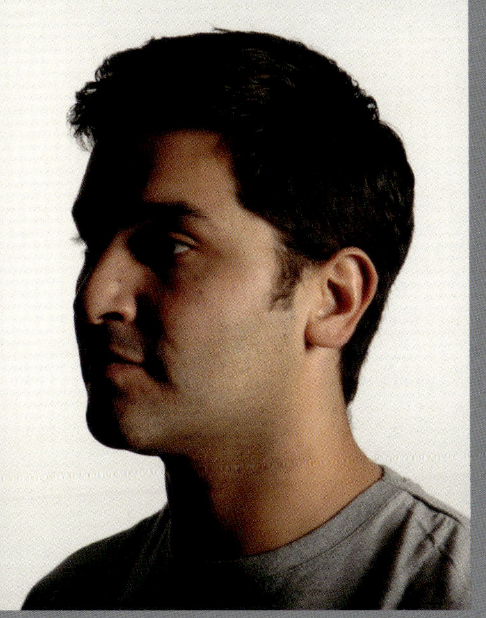

DARK BACKGROUND

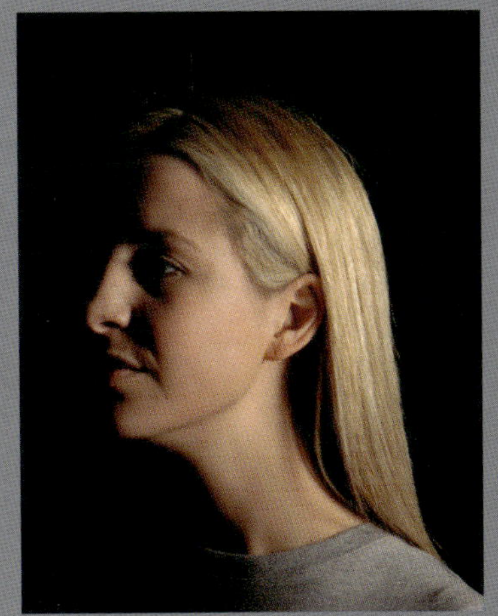

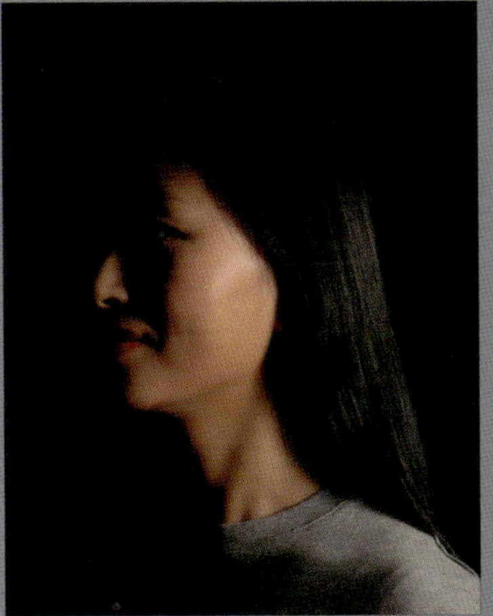

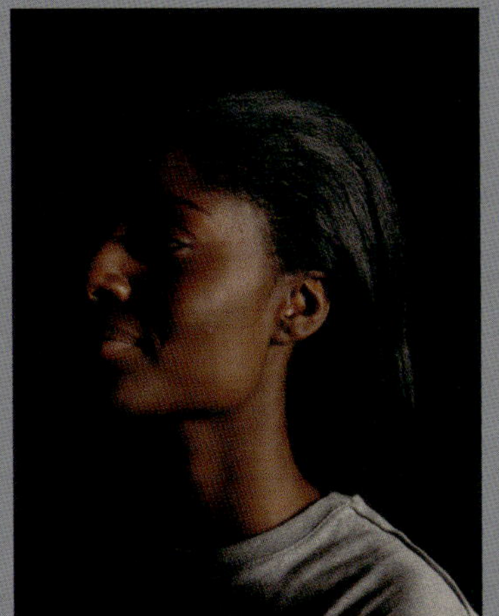

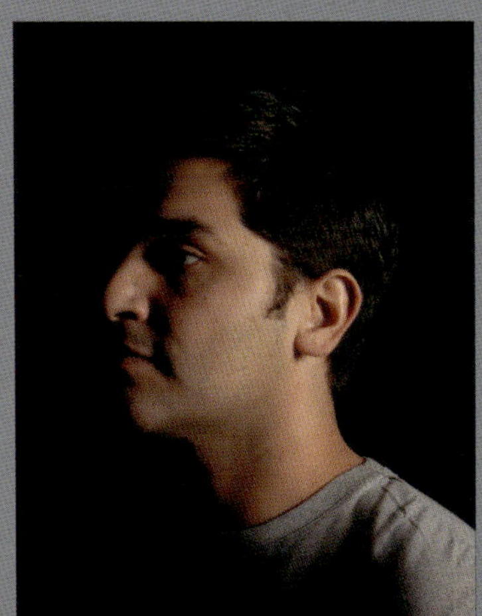

CHAPTER 3

PROFILE, SINGLE LIGHT

Photographing your model in profile may not produce a "true" picture of what they look like, but in conjunction with a single light it's still possible to create eye-catching images. Perhaps the most striking effect to consider here is low-key shots that rely on a dark background and heavy, featureless shadow areas punctuated by selective lighter tones that pick out the subject. Low-key images such as these work well in color, but can really come to life in monochrome, so consider converting your pictures to black and white once they've been shot.

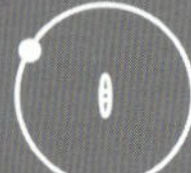

ONE SOFTBOX

LIGHT 1: FROM 120° LEFT, EYE LEVEL

LIGHT 2: NONE

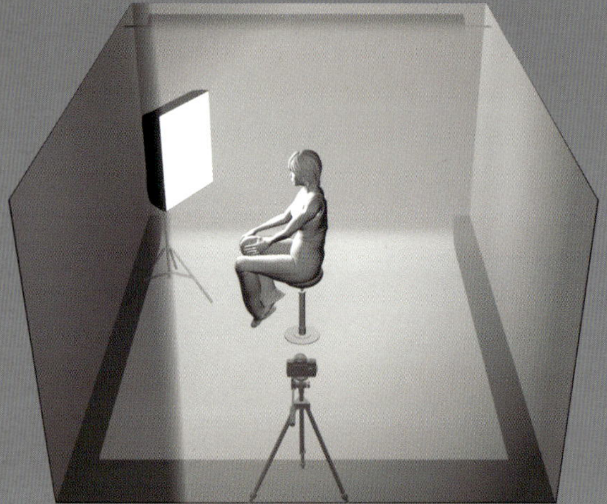

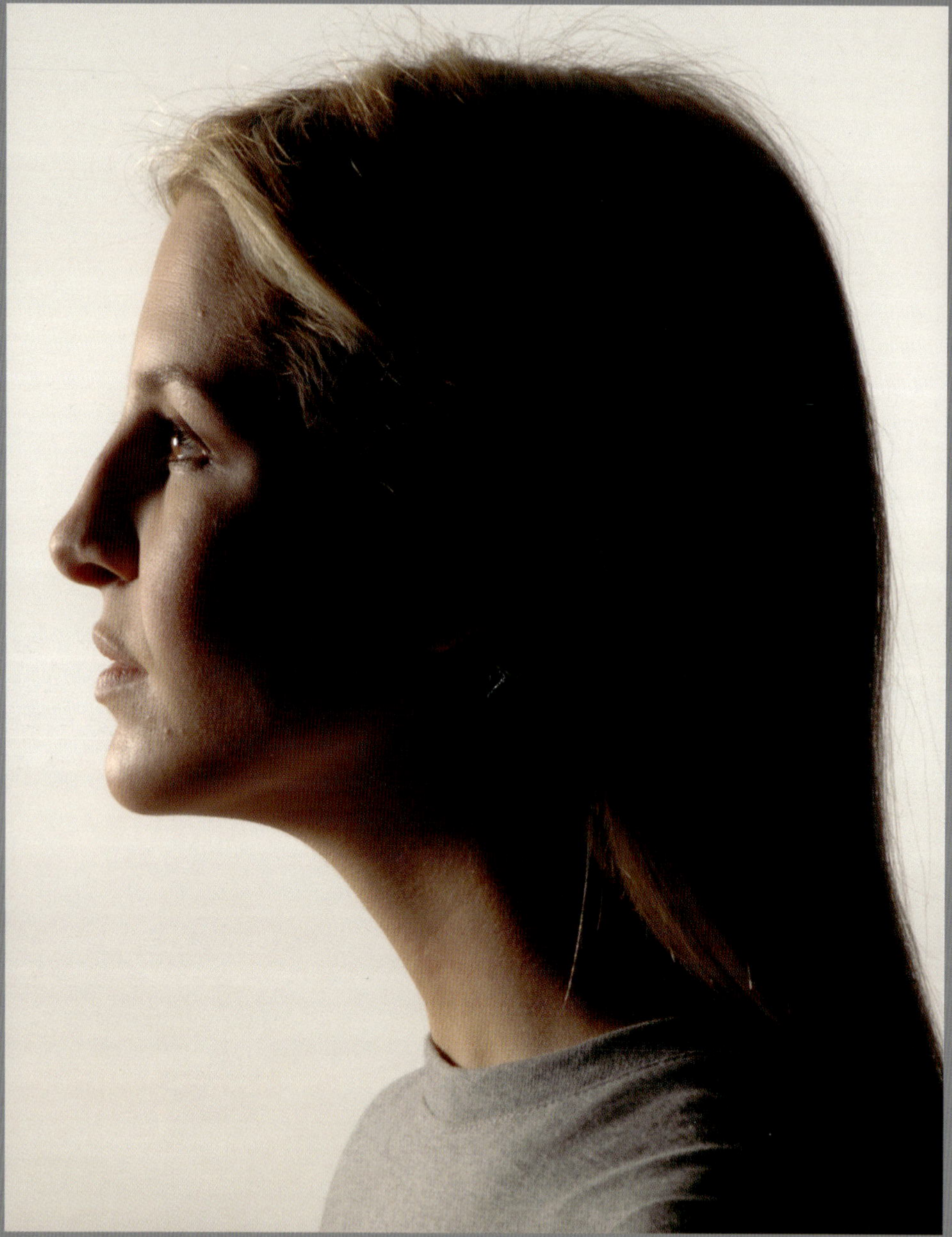

Positioning a single light slightly behind the subject produces a strong back-lit effect. Although much of the model's face will be in deep shadow, catchlights remain in the eye that can be seen by the camera. Against a dark background, the contrast between the lit areas of the face and the shadows makes the subject stand out.

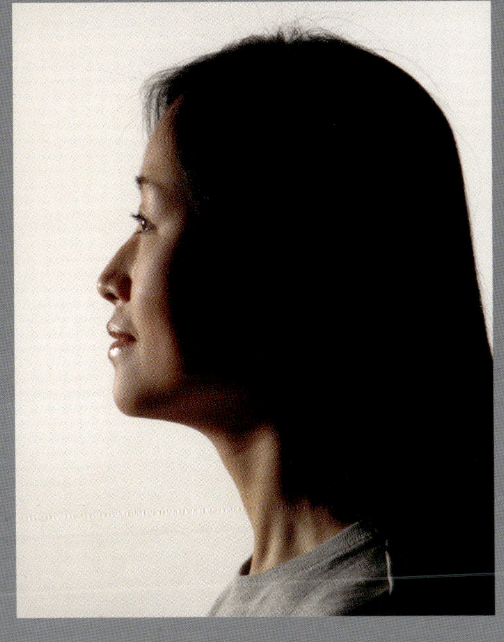

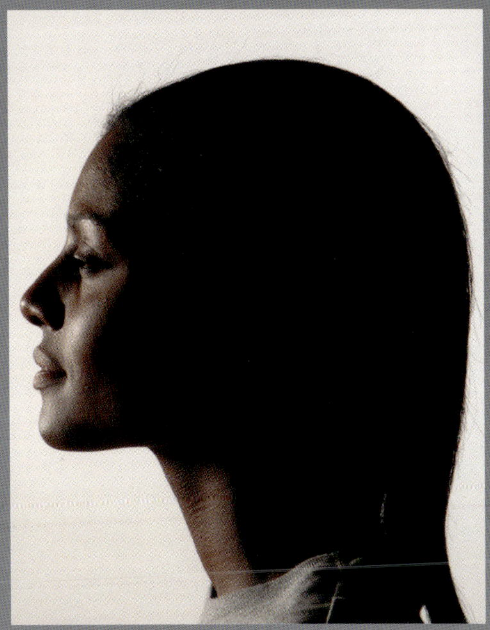

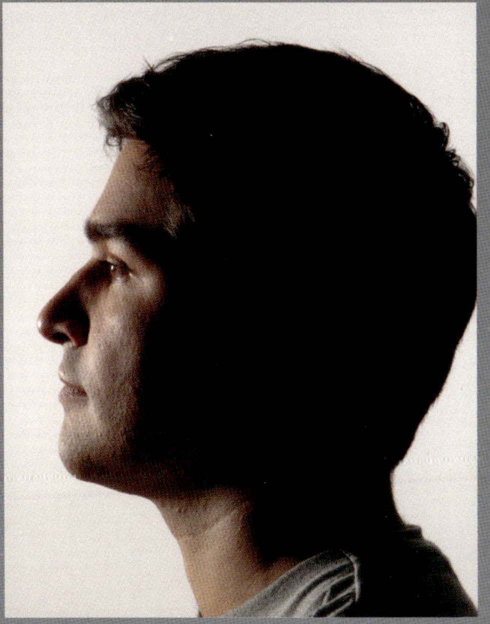

DARK BACKGROUND

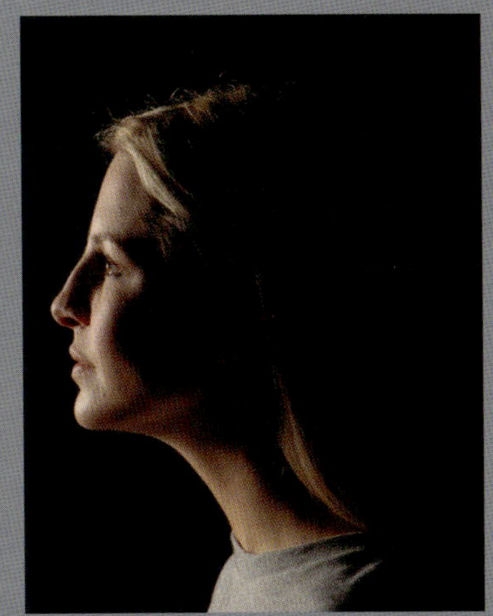

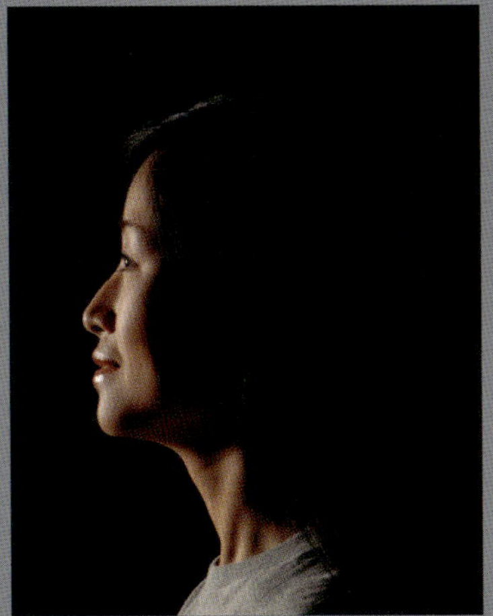

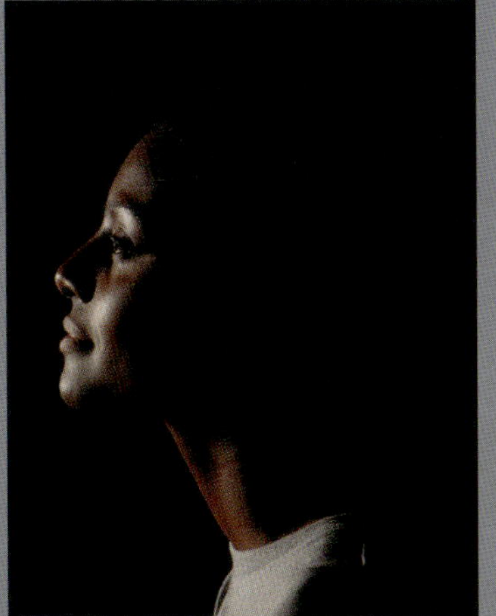

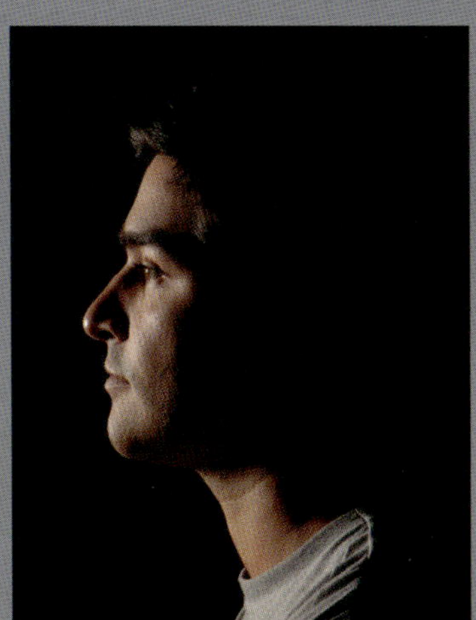

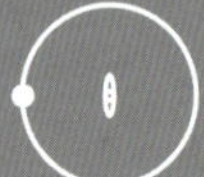

ONE SOFTBOX

LIGHT 1: FROM 90° LEFT, EYE LEVEL

LIGHT 2: NONE

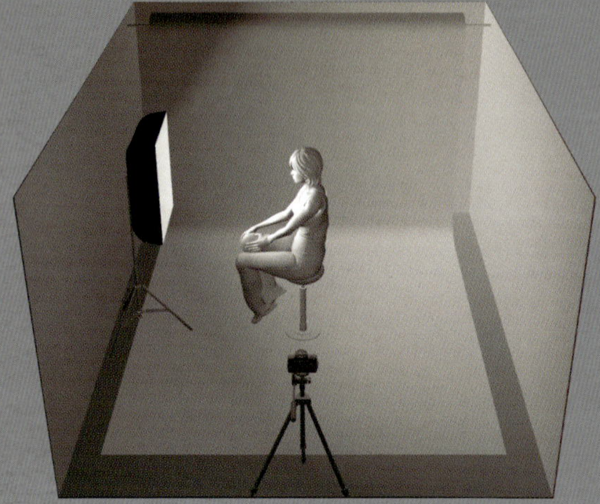

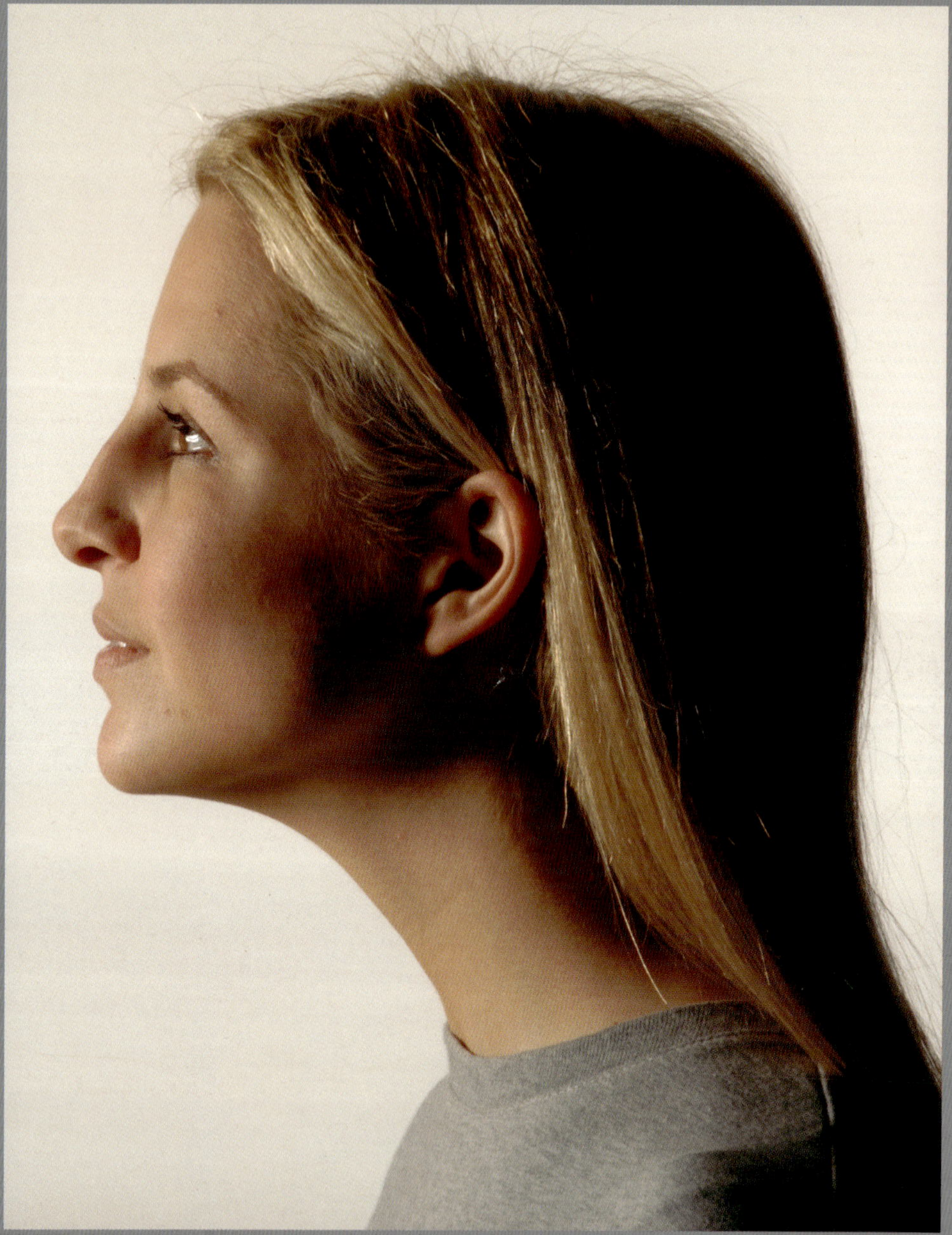

With the light facing the subject—both at a 90-degree angle to the camera—much of the subject is in shadow, although key features such as the eye (with catchlights) and the ear are picked out. Adding a reflector on the opposite side of the subject could bring out more detail in the hair if that was also important to the portrait.

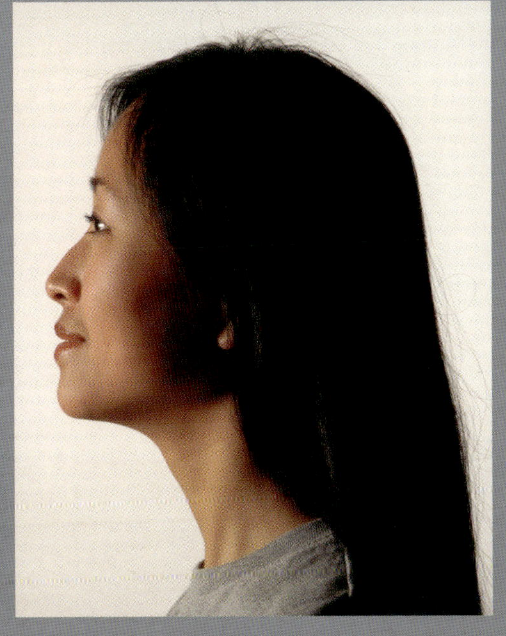
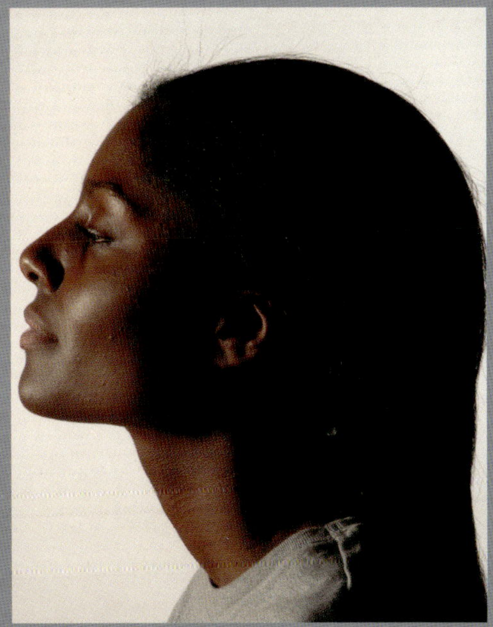
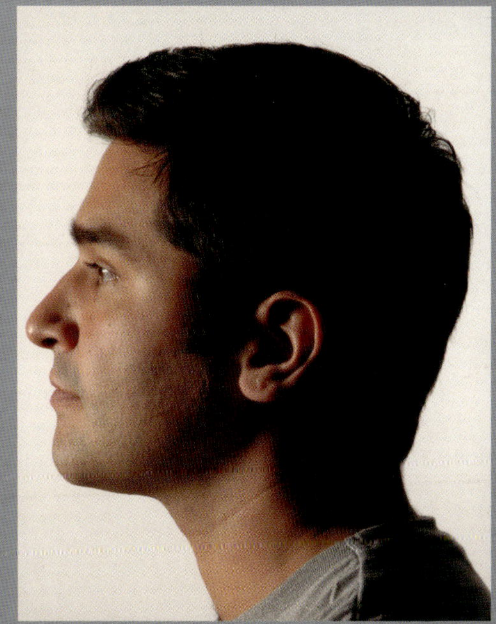

DARK BACKGROUND

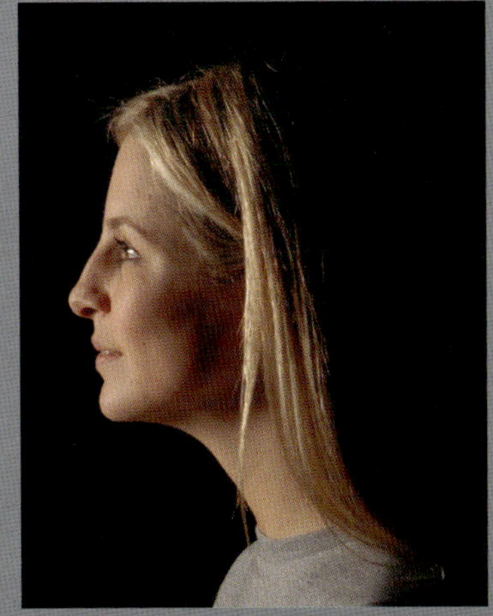
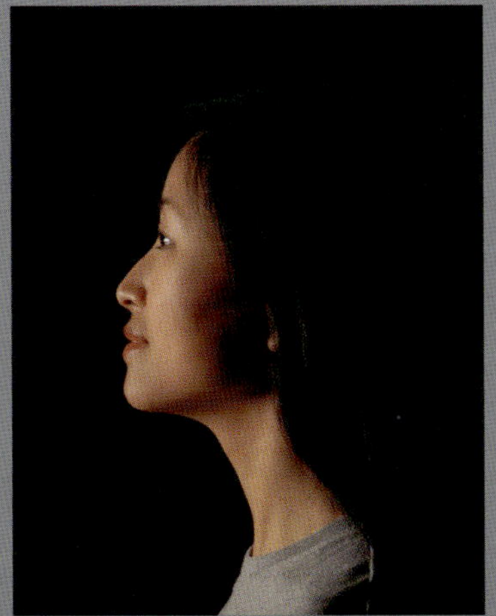
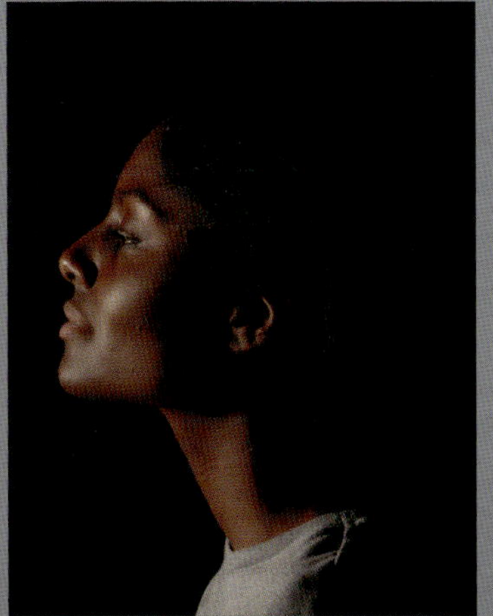
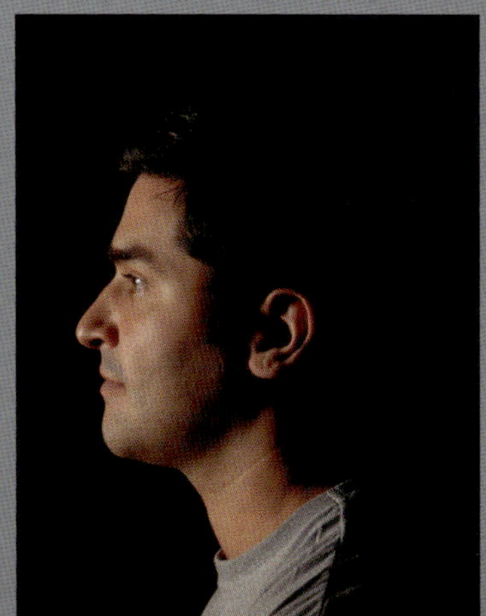

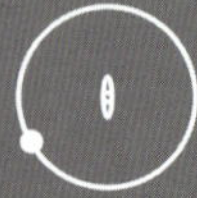

ONE SOFTBOX

LIGHT 1: FROM 60° LEFT, EYE LEVEL

LIGHT 2: NONE

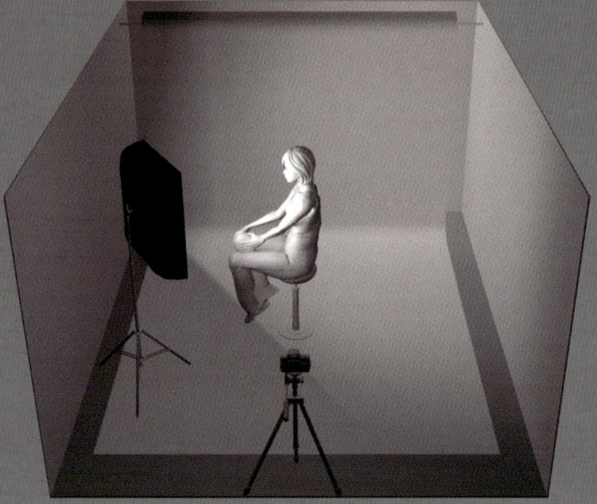

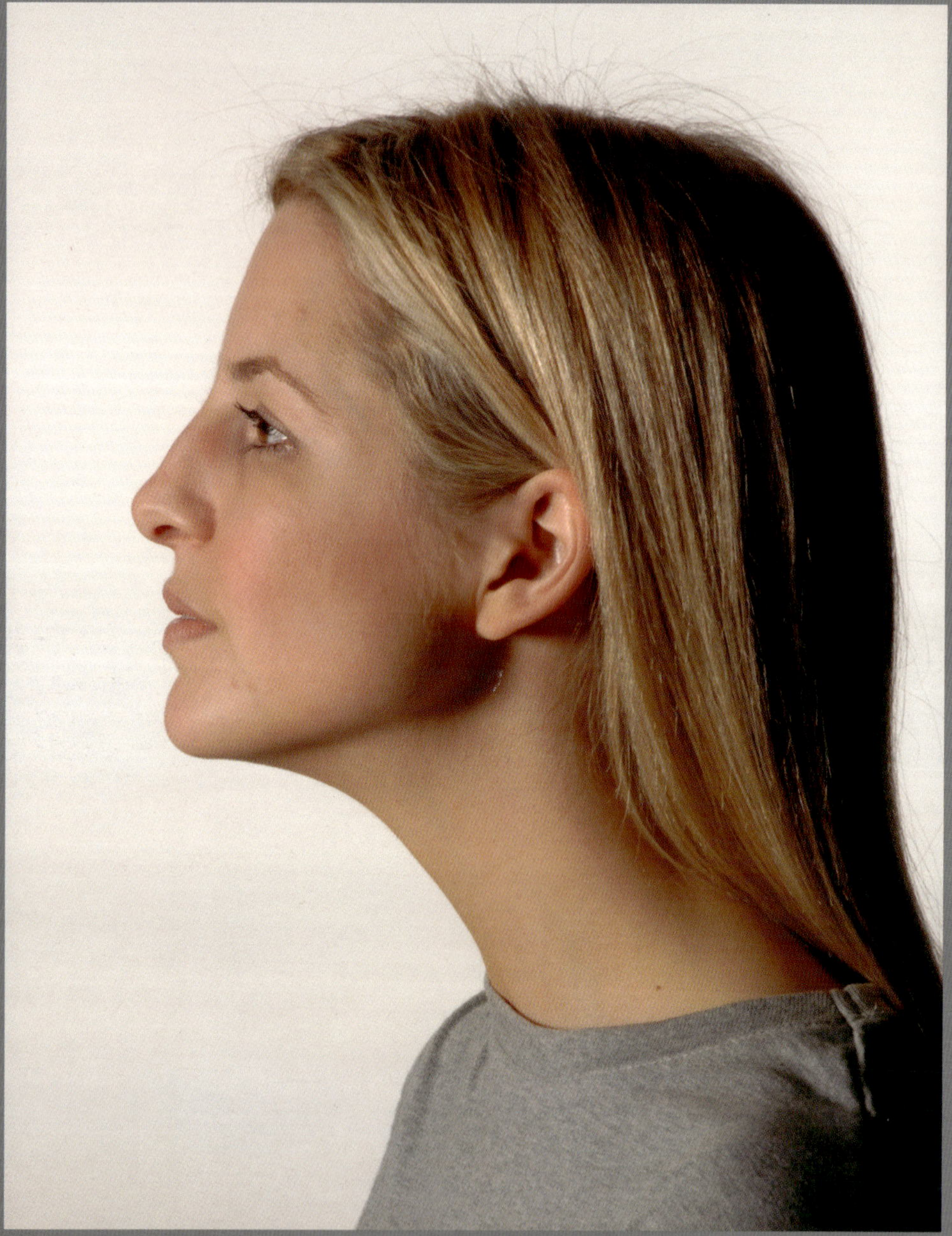

With the subject in profile and the light at a 60-degree angle, the majority of the model's face is evenly lit. With few shadows, there's minimal suggestion of texture, which gives a flat appearance to the skin, although contrast is increased in the hair toward the back of the subject.

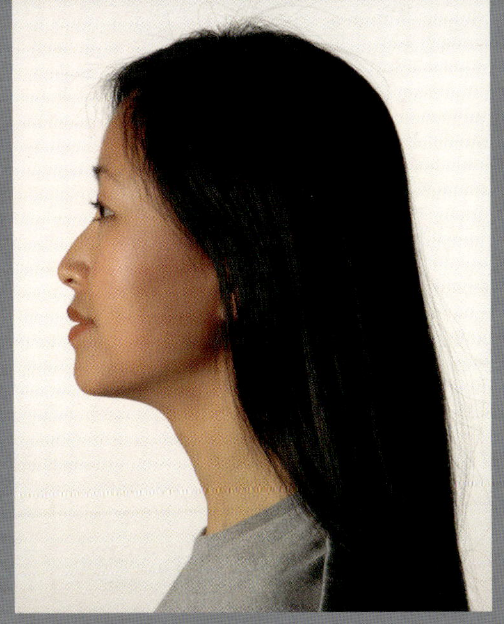

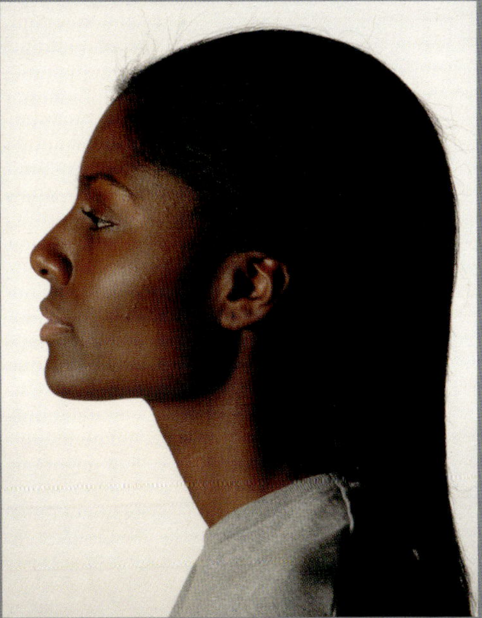

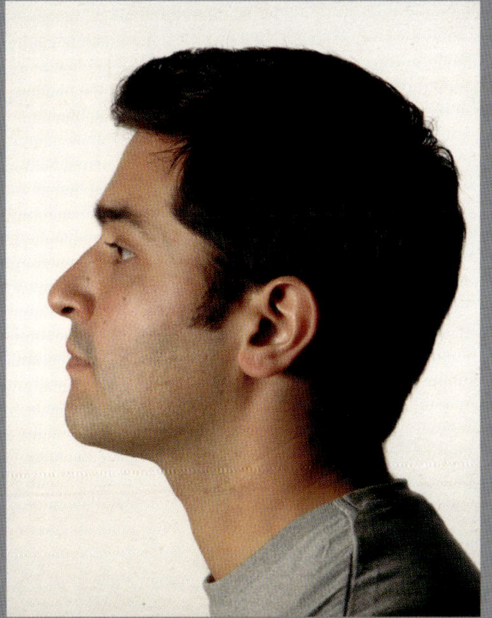

DARK BACKGROUND

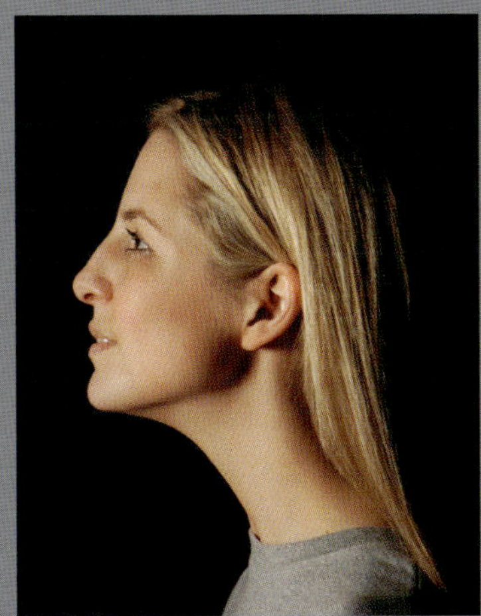

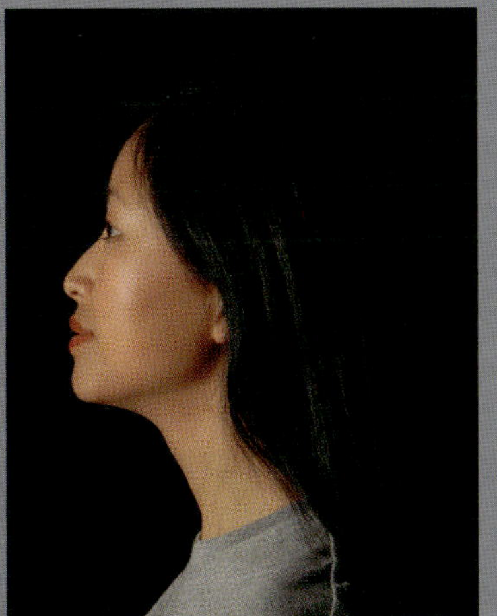

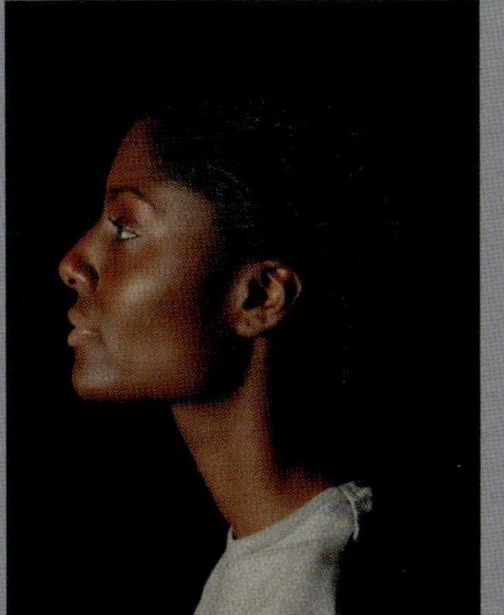

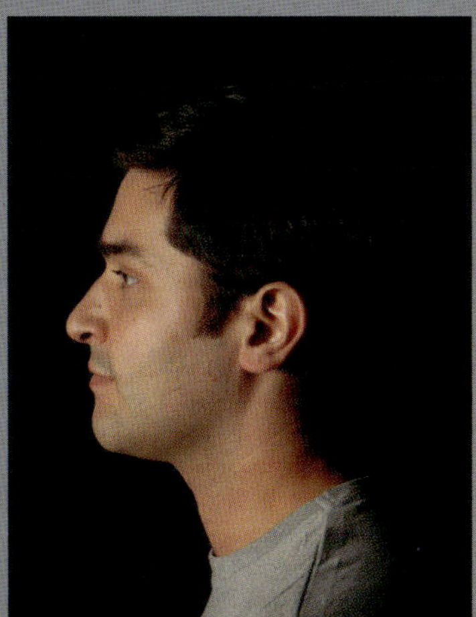

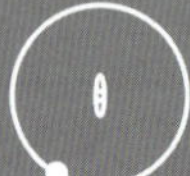

ONE SOFTBOX

LIGHT 1: FROM 30° LEFT, EYE LEVEL

LIGHT 2: NONE

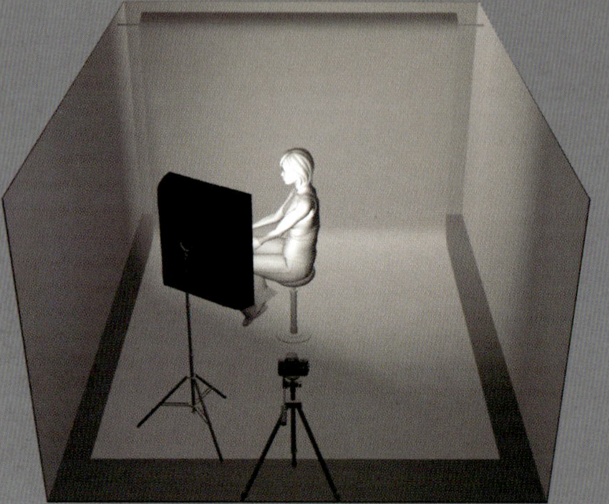

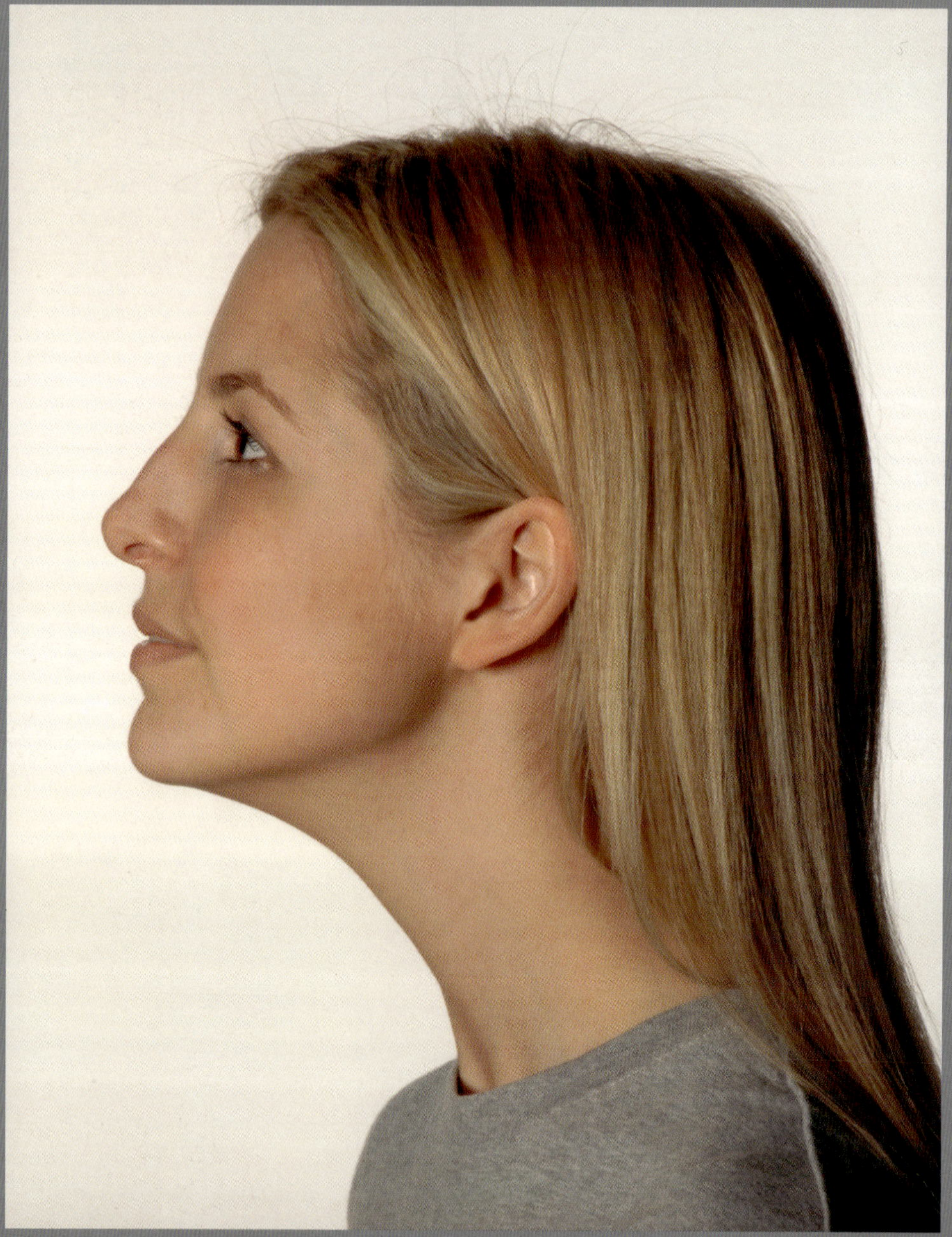

As the light moves further toward the camera axis, the light becomes more even on both the model's face and hair, with the lack of contrast reducing any sense of texture in the skin and making it appear smooth. Note that any catchlight in the visible eye is lost.

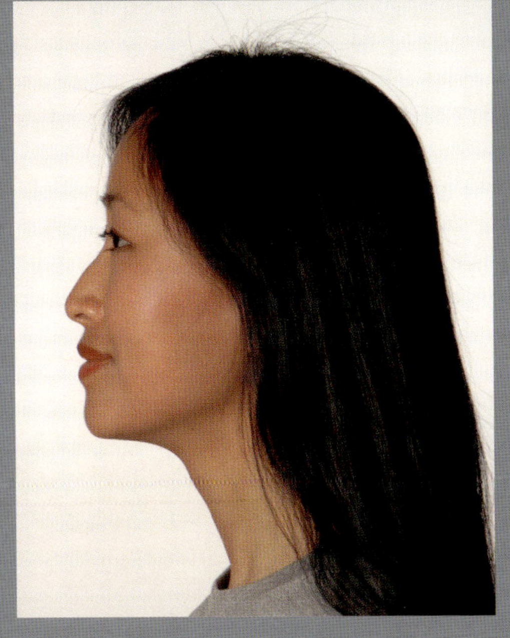

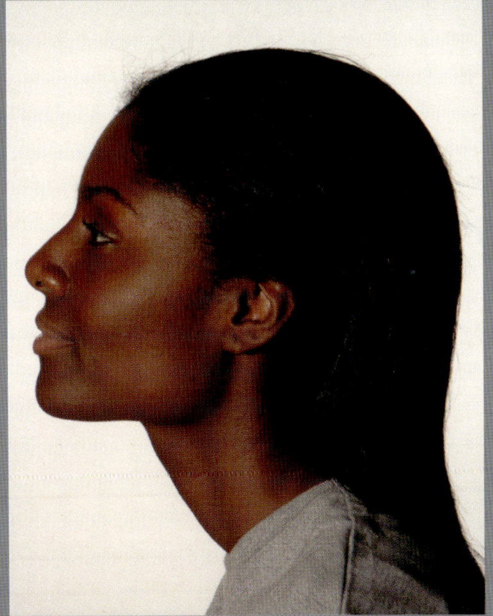

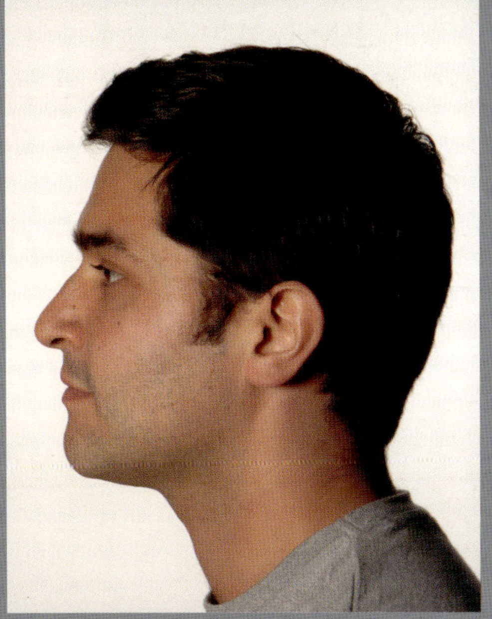

DARK BACKGROUND

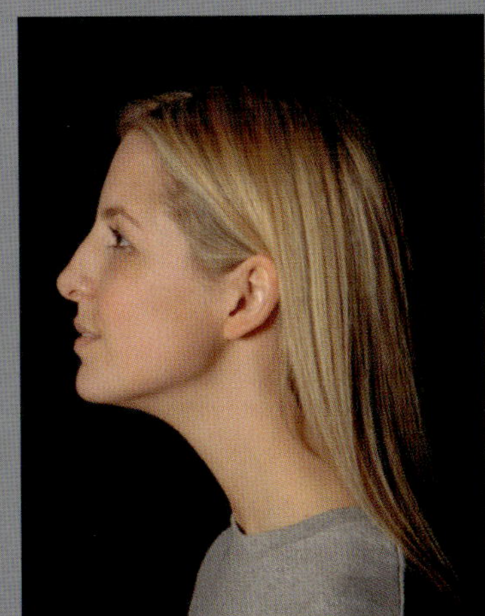

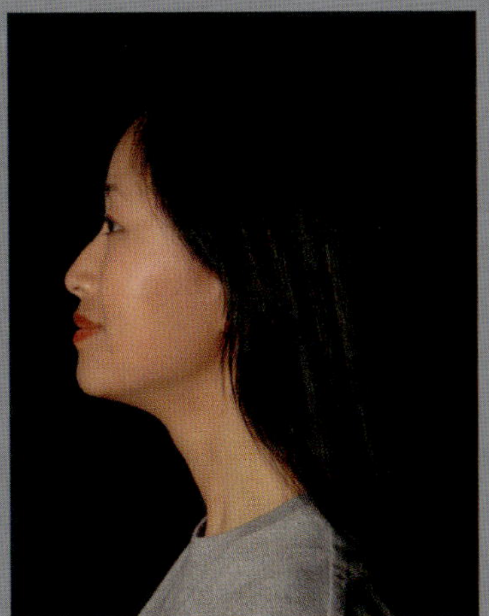

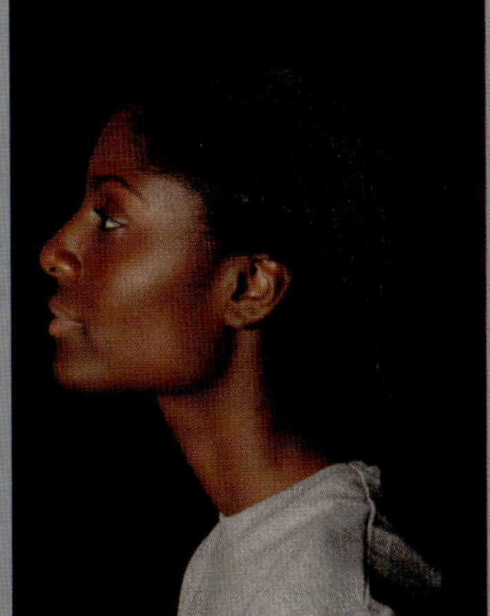

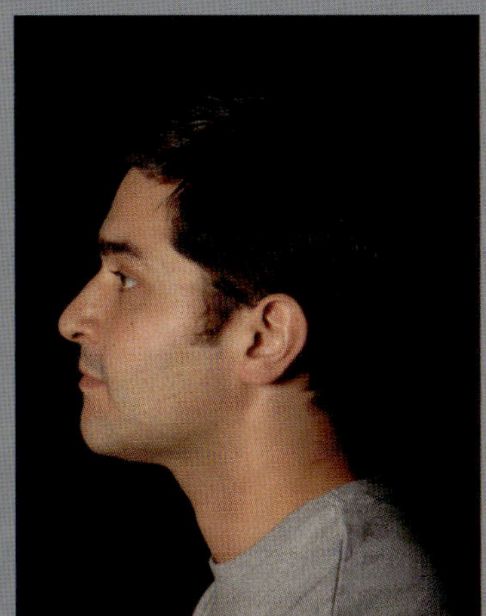

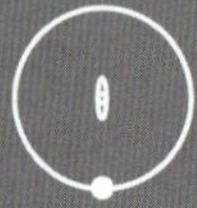

ONE SOFTBOX

LIGHT 1: FROM CAMERA, EYE LEVEL

LIGHT 2: NONE

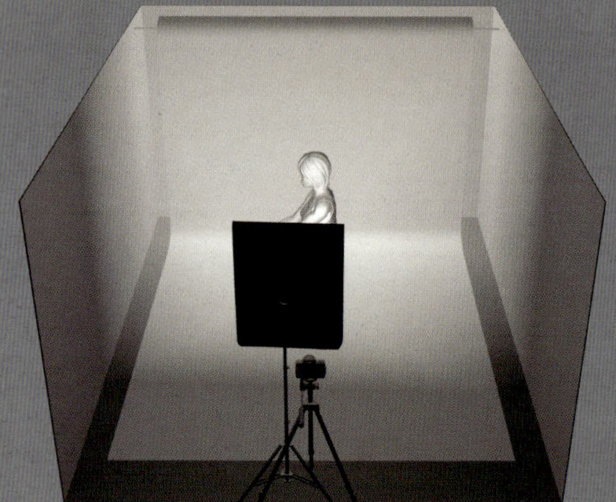

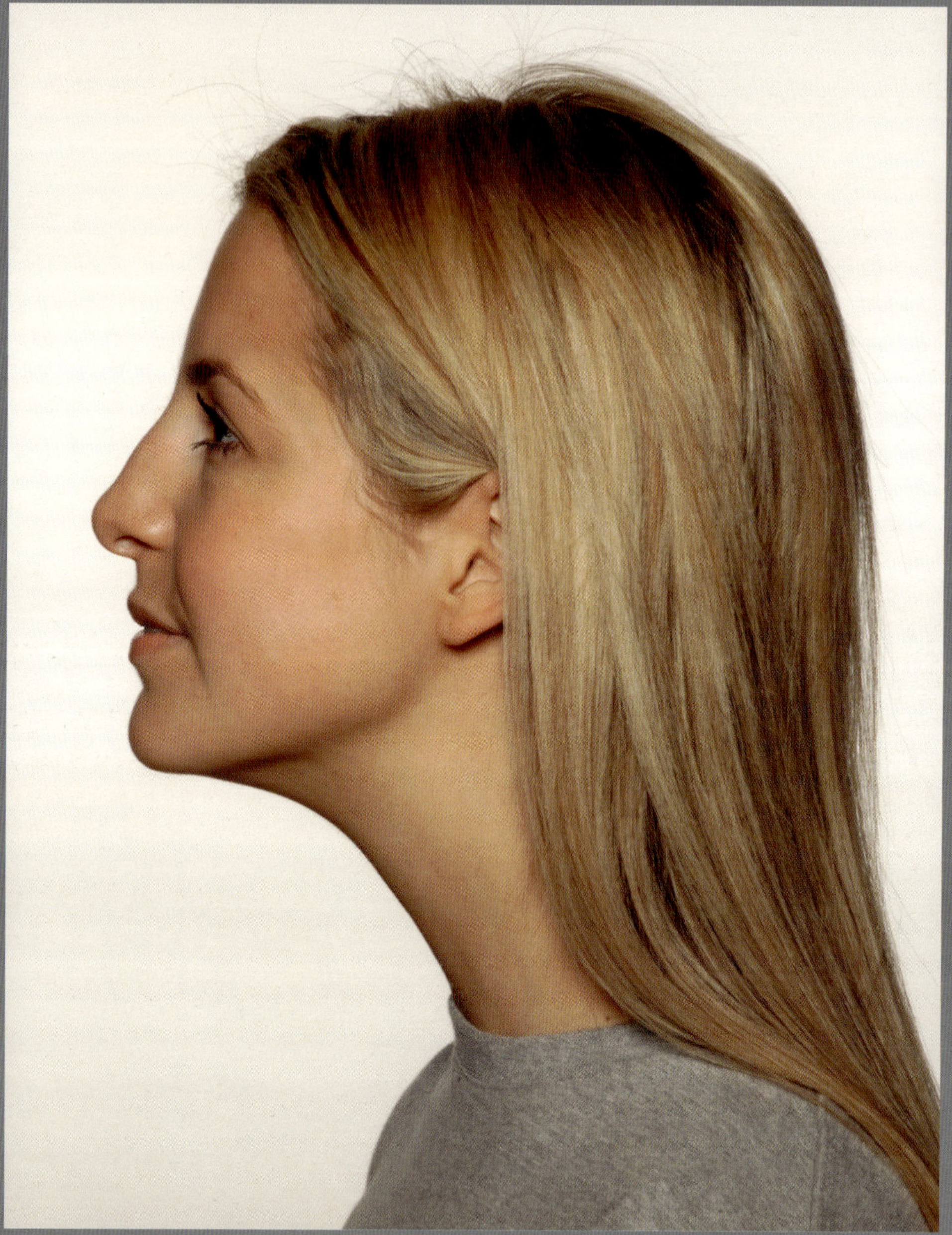

With both the light and the camera pointing from the same direction, a soft shadow surrounds the model. Against a light color, this helps lift the subject from the background, although the effect is lost when the model is shot against a darker background.

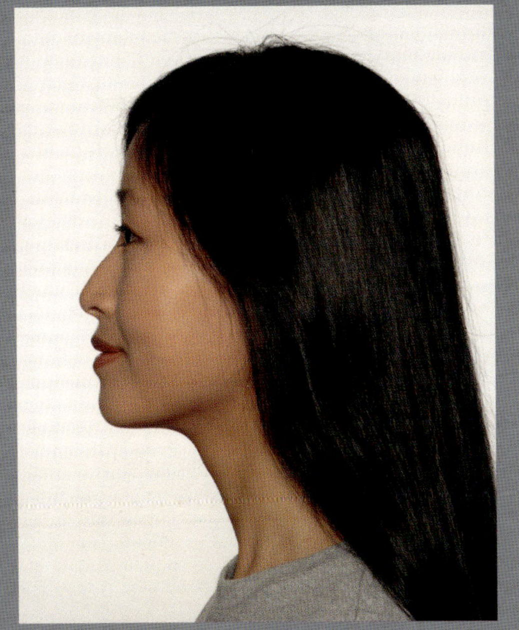
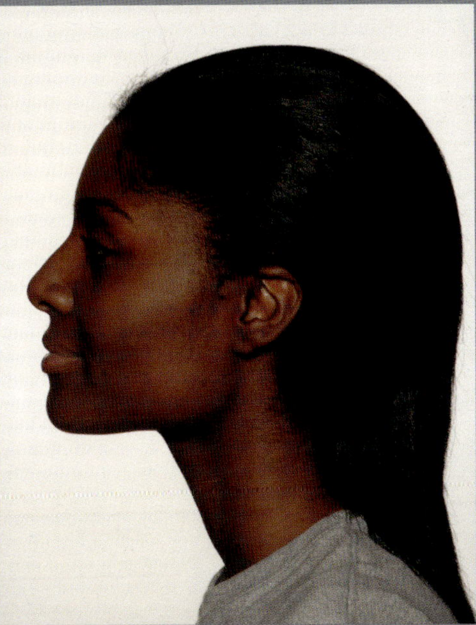
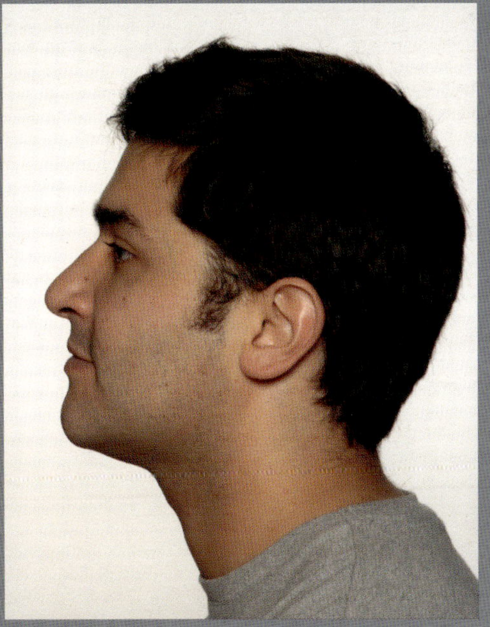

DARK BACKGROUND

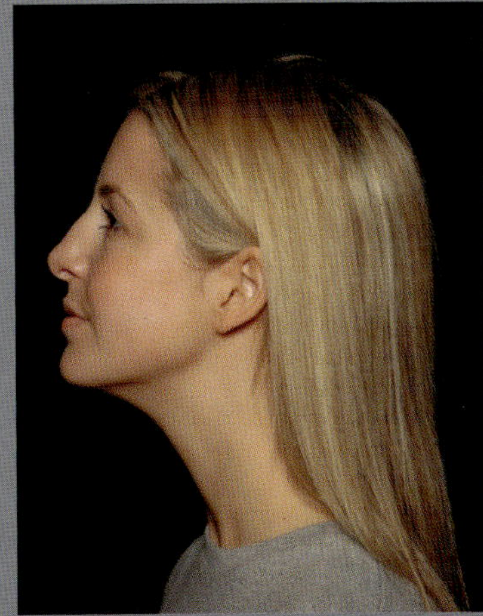
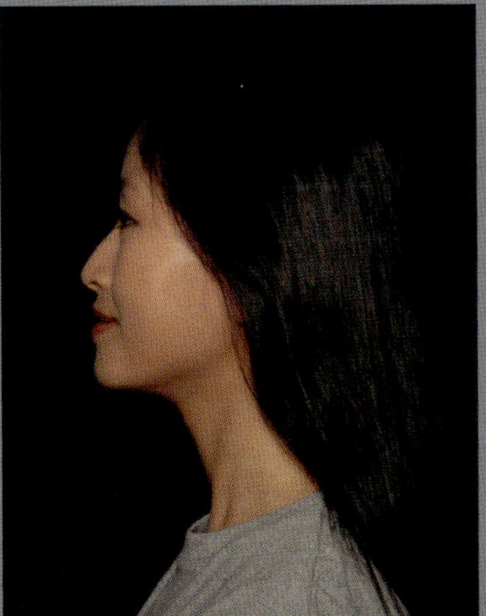
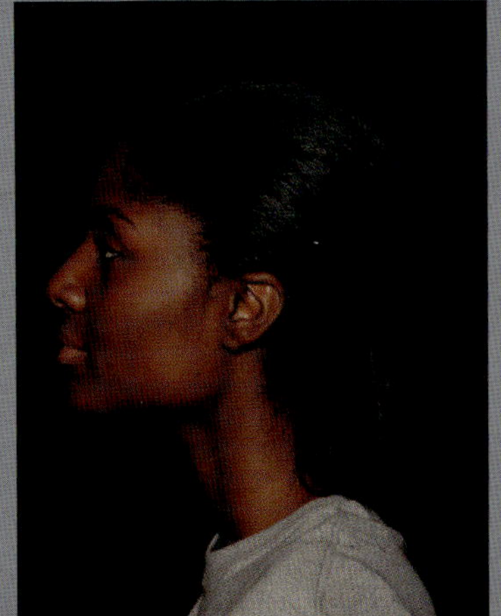
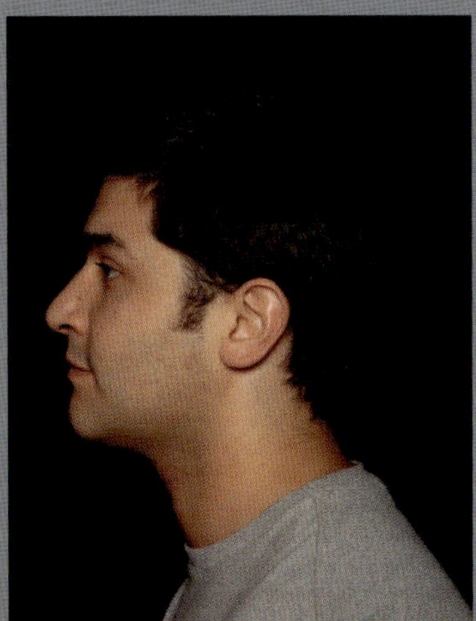

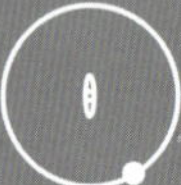

ONE SOFTBOX

LIGHT 1: FROM 30° RIGHT, EYE LEVEL

LIGHT 2: NONE

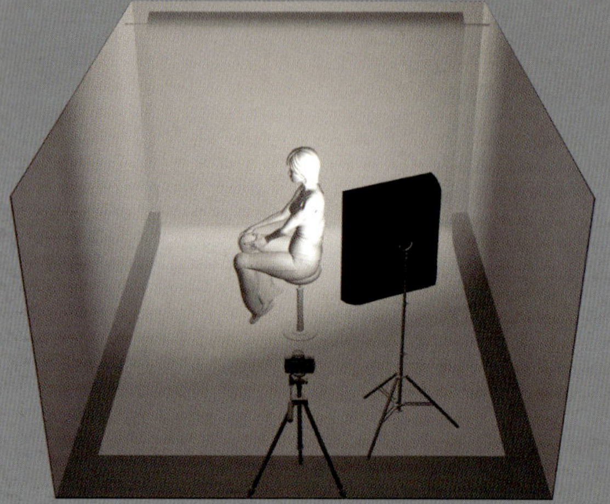

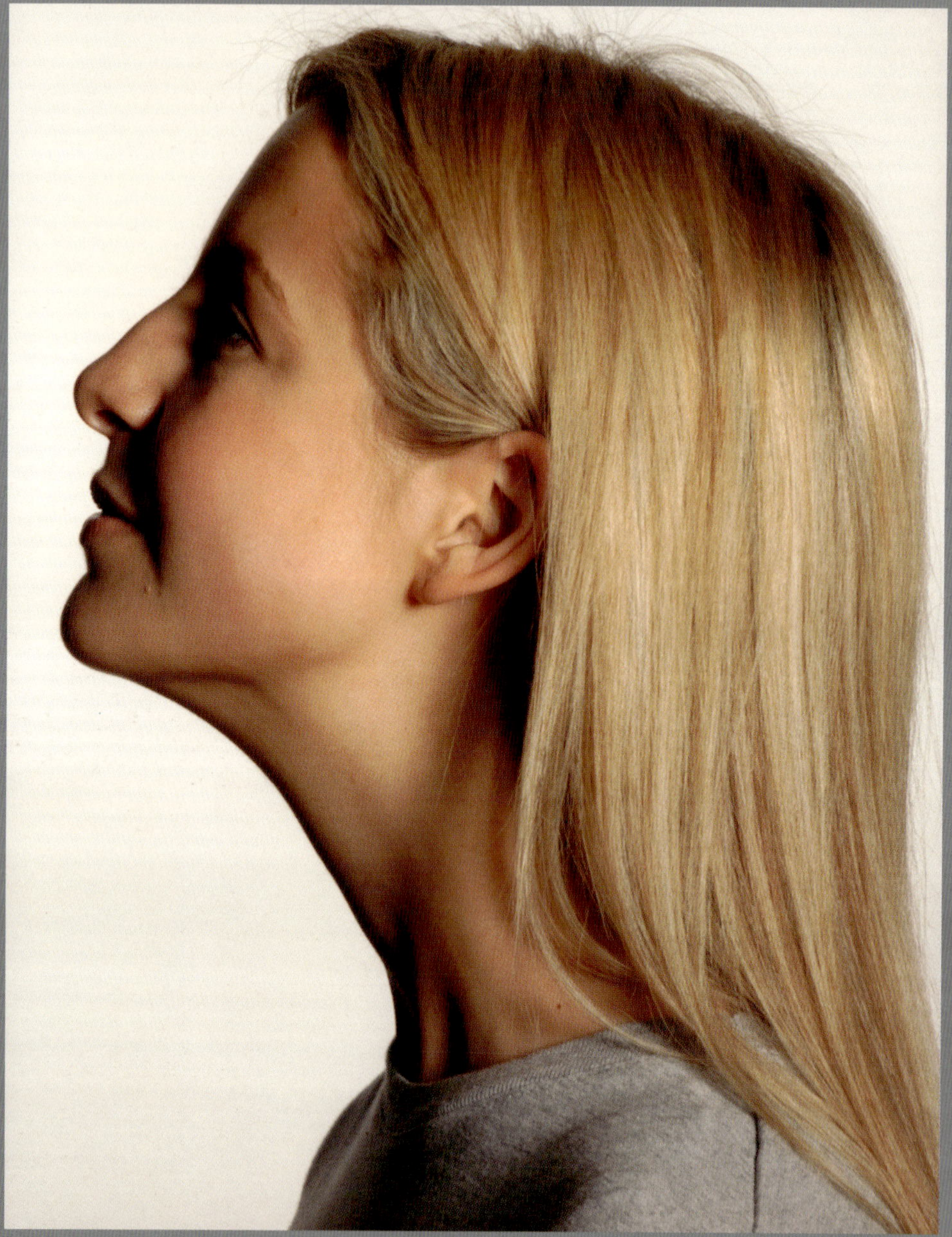

With a single light positioned at camera right, the illumination falls mainly on the subject's hair, rather than the face. What light there is on the face creates a strong shadow at the front of the cheek, that extends to partially conceal the subject's eye.

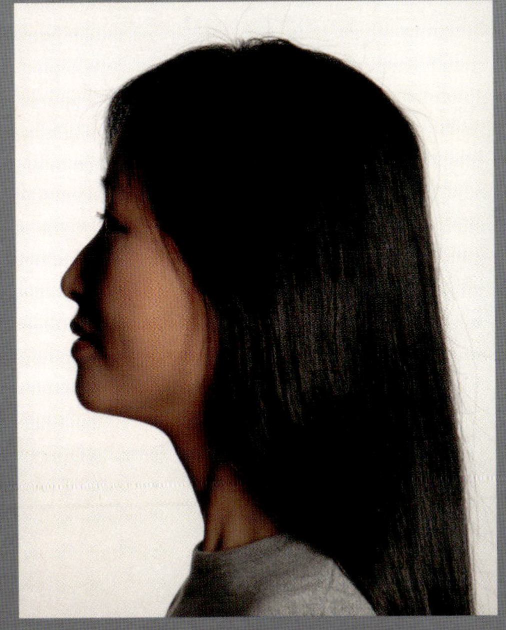
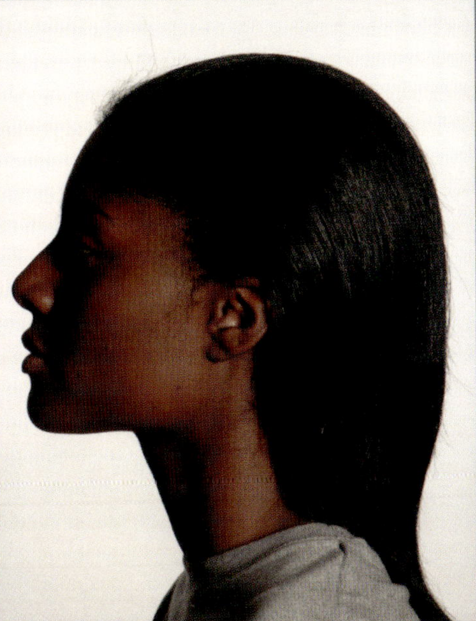
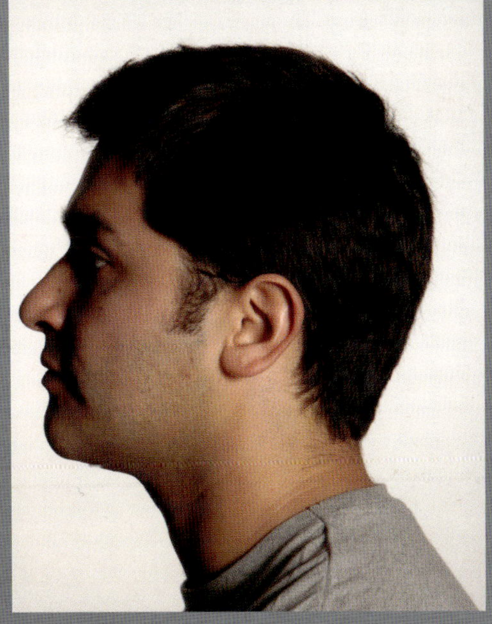

DARK BACKGROUND

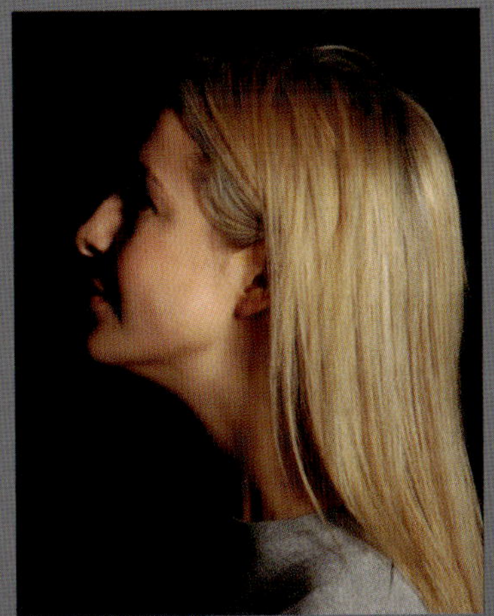
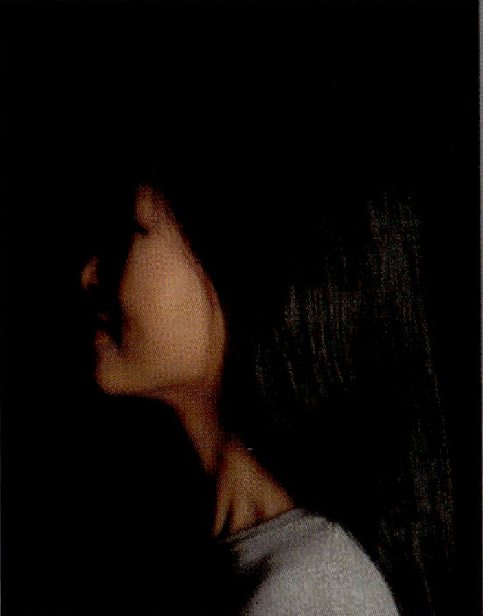
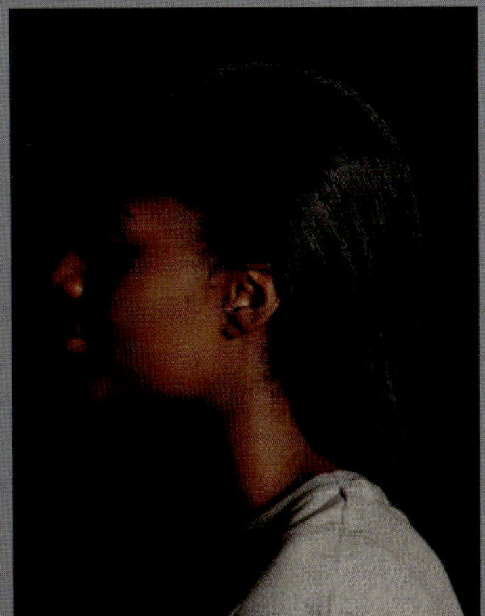
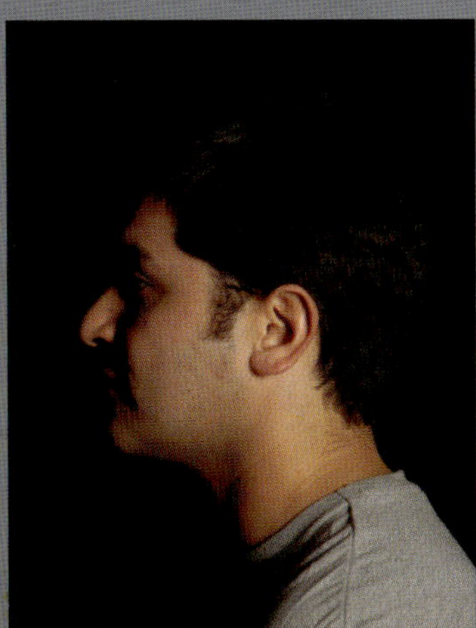

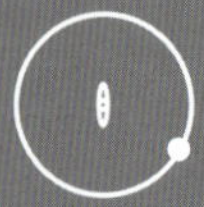

ONE SOFTBOX

LIGHT 1: FROM 60° RIGHT, EYE LEVEL

LIGHT 2: NONE

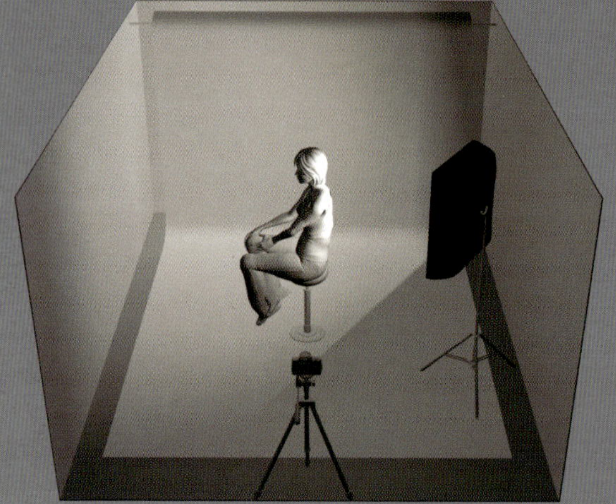

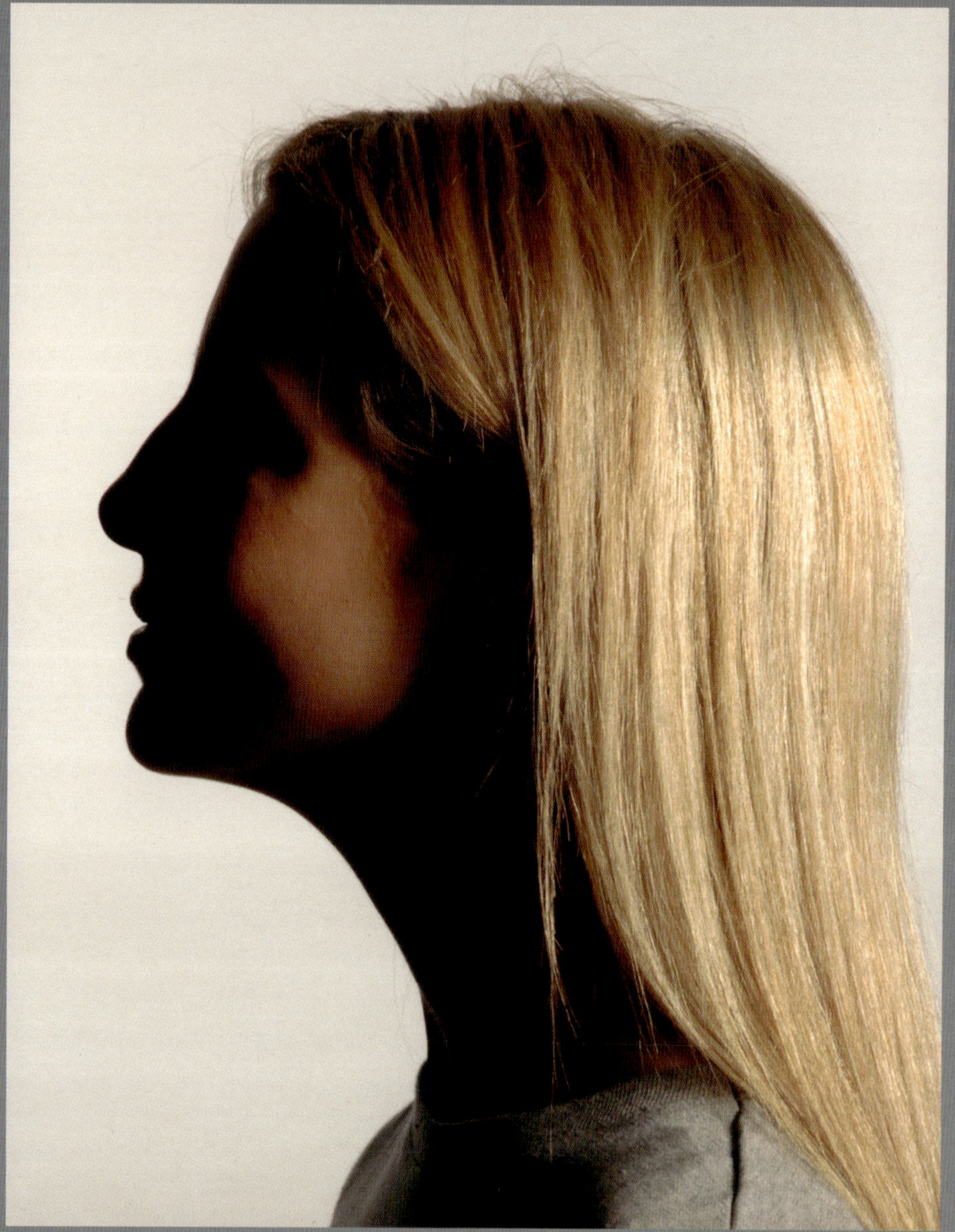

With the light striking the subject at a 60-degree angle from opposite the face, the profile falls into semi-silhouette and all of the facial features are lost. Against a light background, this creates a striking contrast, but against a dark background only the model's hair, ear, and cheek are visible.

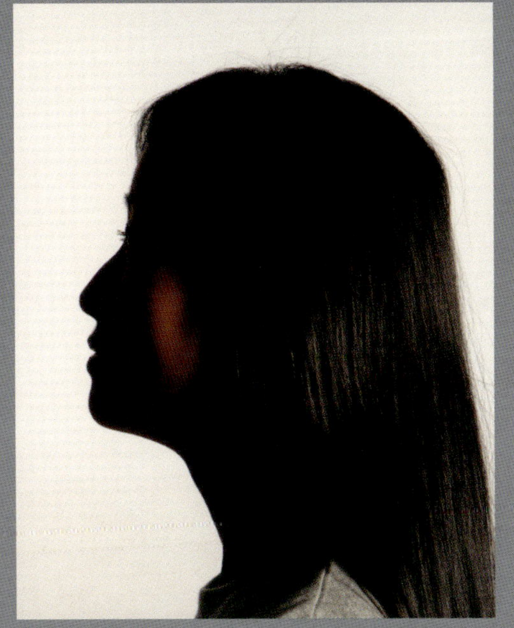
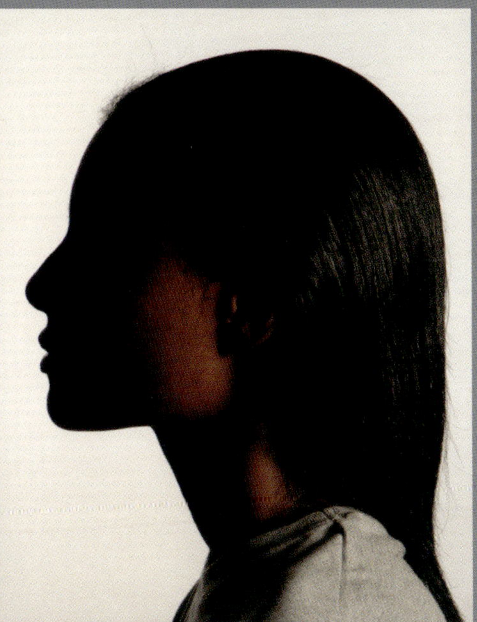
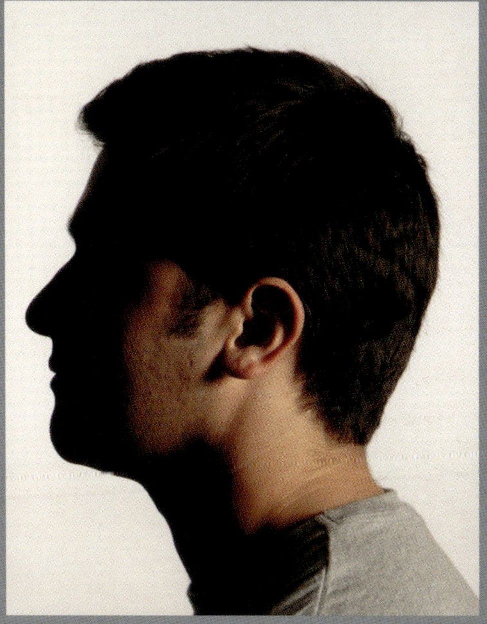

DARK BACKGROUND

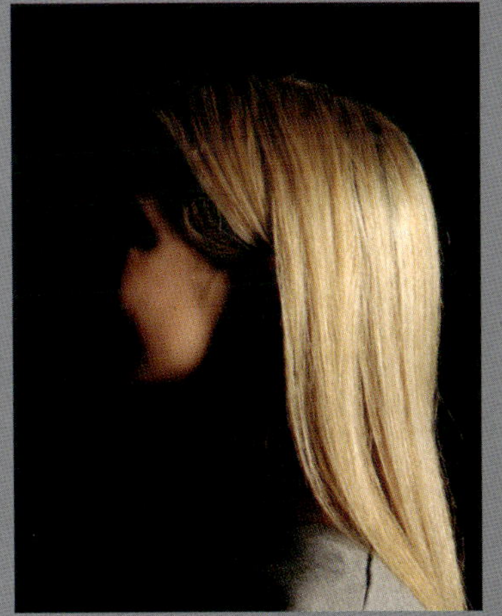
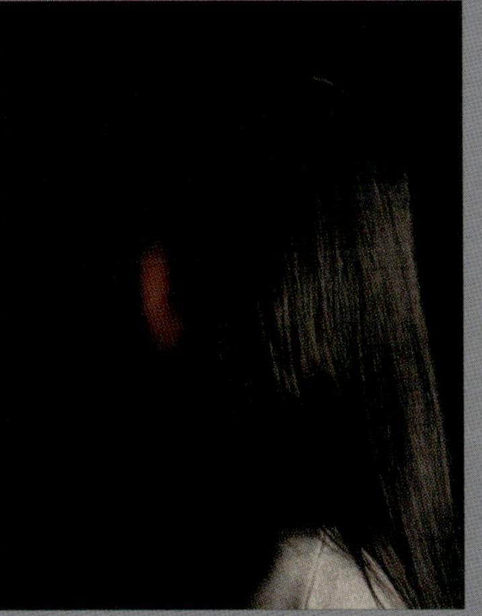
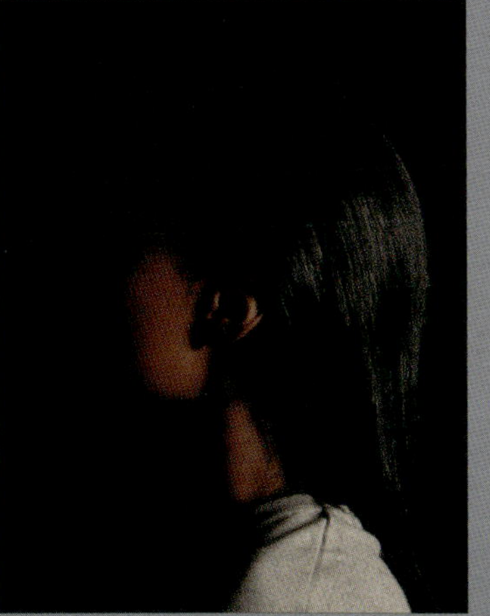
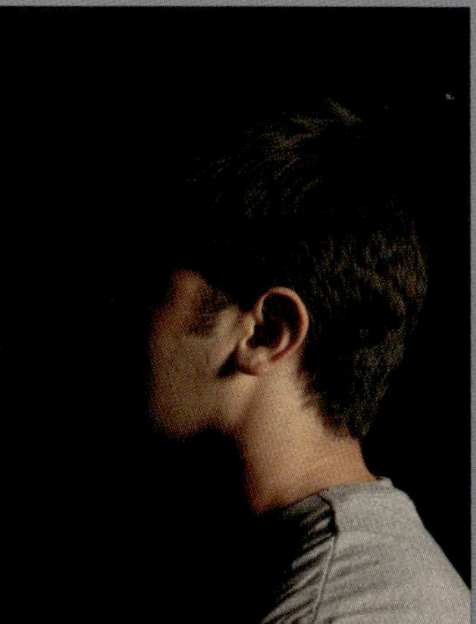

CHAPTER 4
TWO LIGHTS

While a single light can be used to create dramatic portraits, there are limits to how much you can do with it. This is why the majority of portrait photographers will use two or more lights when setting up a portrait; one light may be the basic building block, but two lights are the cornerstone of most portraits.

With two lights at your disposal, you open up a whole world of lighting opportunities, from where you position the two lights in relation to one another and the subject, through to how much light each one provides—are they going to be throwing equal amounts of light onto your subject, or is one going to be having a stronger effect than the other, for example?

If you're serious about shooting portraits—perhaps even on a professional or semi-professional basis—this should be considered the minimum number of lights you need, and over the following pages we will see how two lights form the foundation of a highly versatile—and often portable—portrait lighting solution.

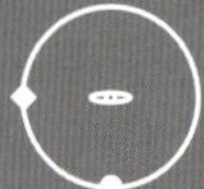

TWO LIGHTS

LIGHT 1: FROM CAMERA, EYE LEVEL

LIGHT 2: FROM 90° LEFT, EYE LEVEL

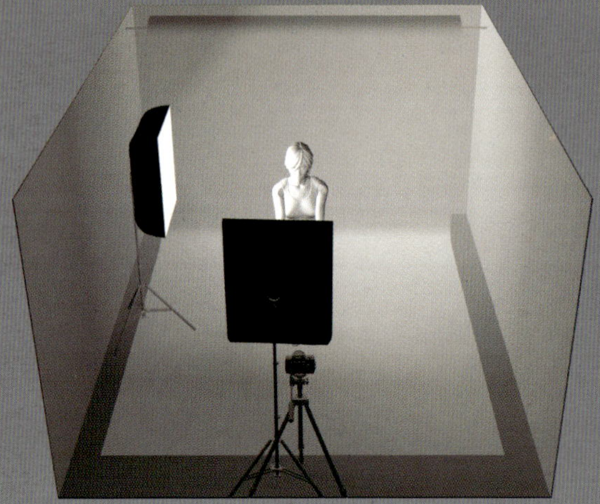

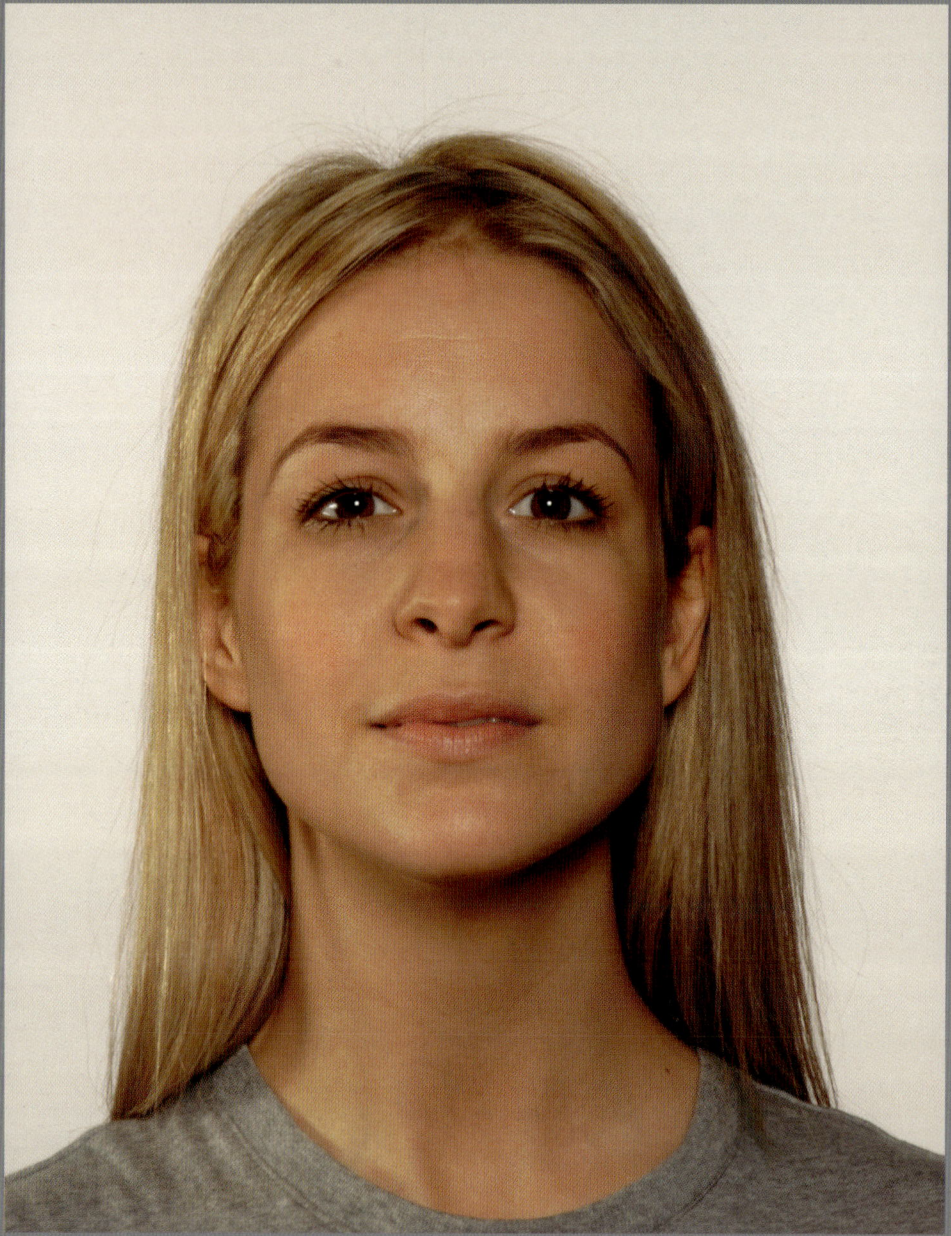

While a single light from the camera position produces a flat image (see page 36), adding a second light at a 90-degree angle will lighten one side of the model's face. This modeling effect makes the subject appear more three-dimensional, without introducing dark, featureless shadows.

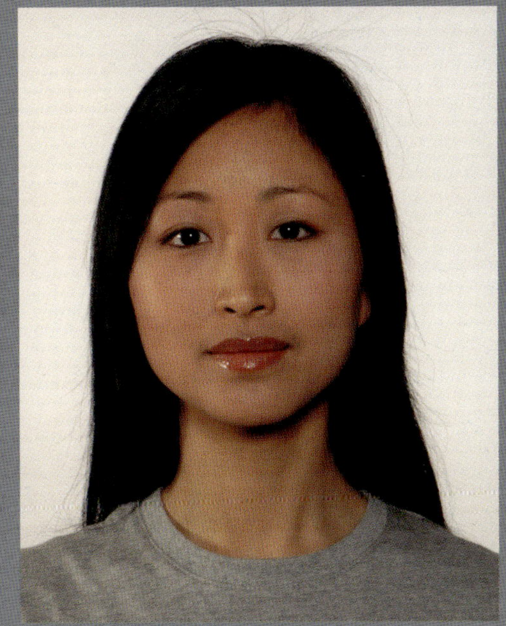
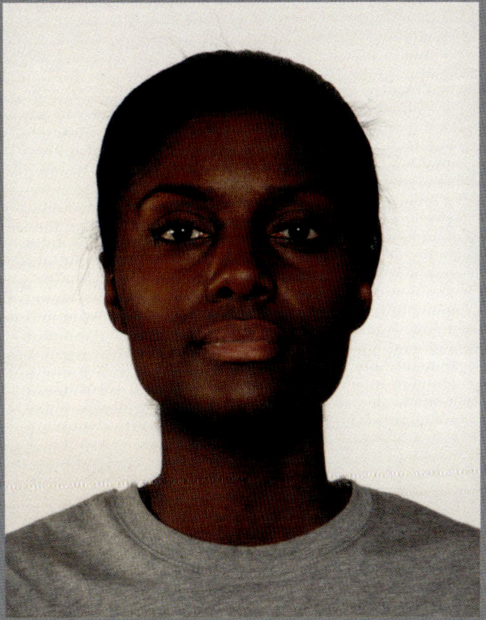
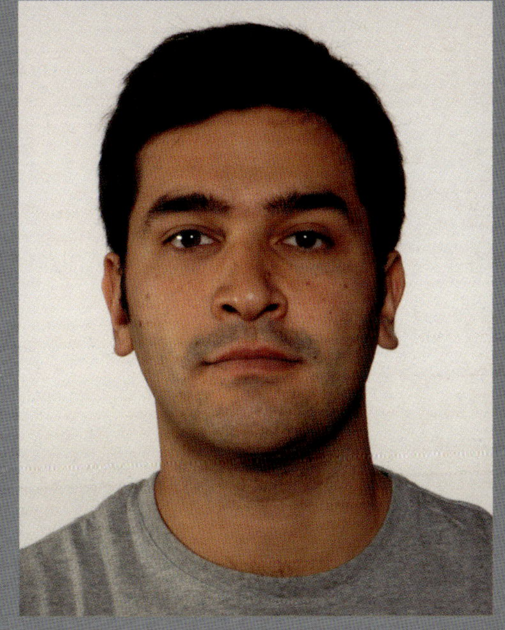

DARK BACKGROUND

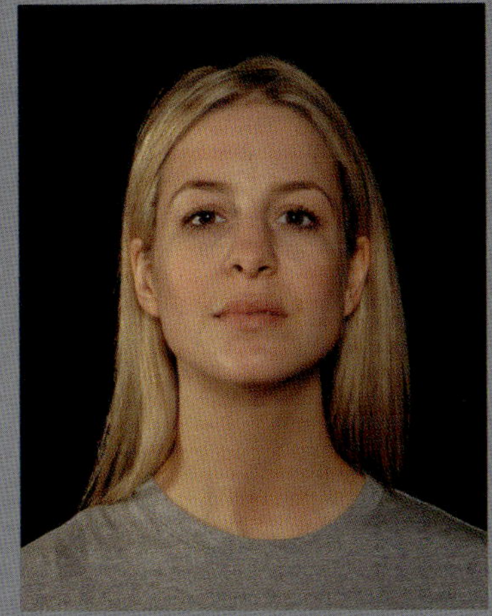
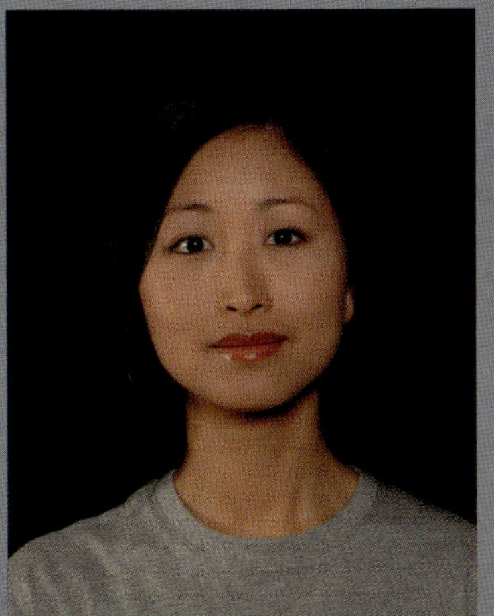
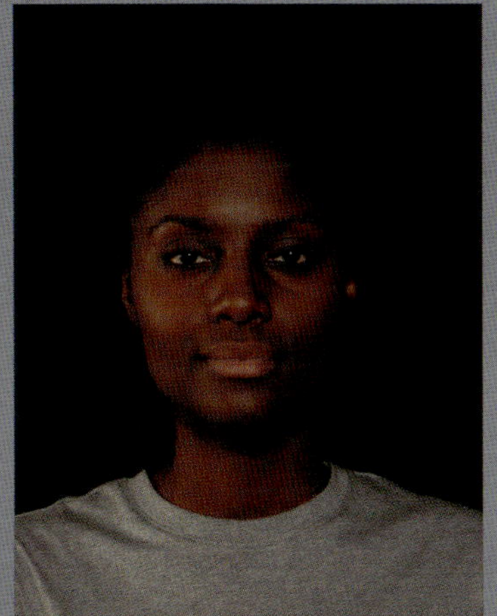
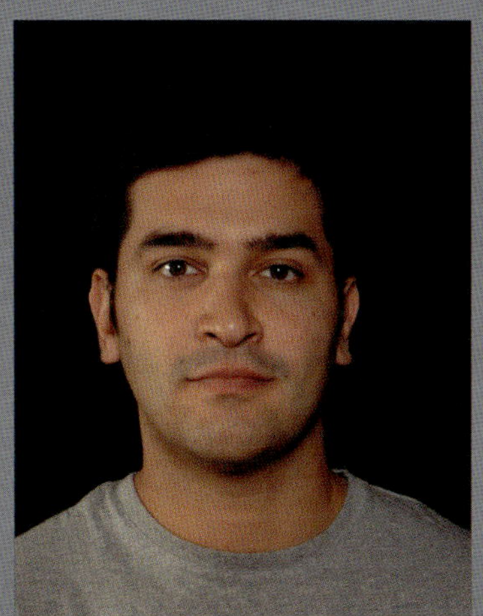

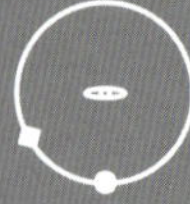

TWO LIGHTS

LIGHT 1: FROM CAMERA, EYE LEVEL

LIGHT 2: FROM 60° LEFT, EYE LEVEL

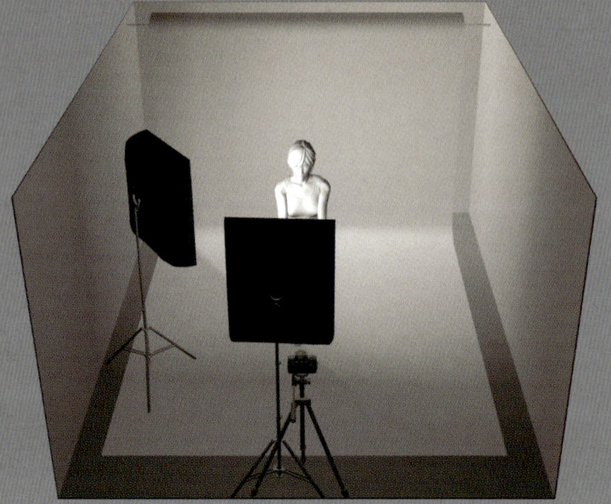

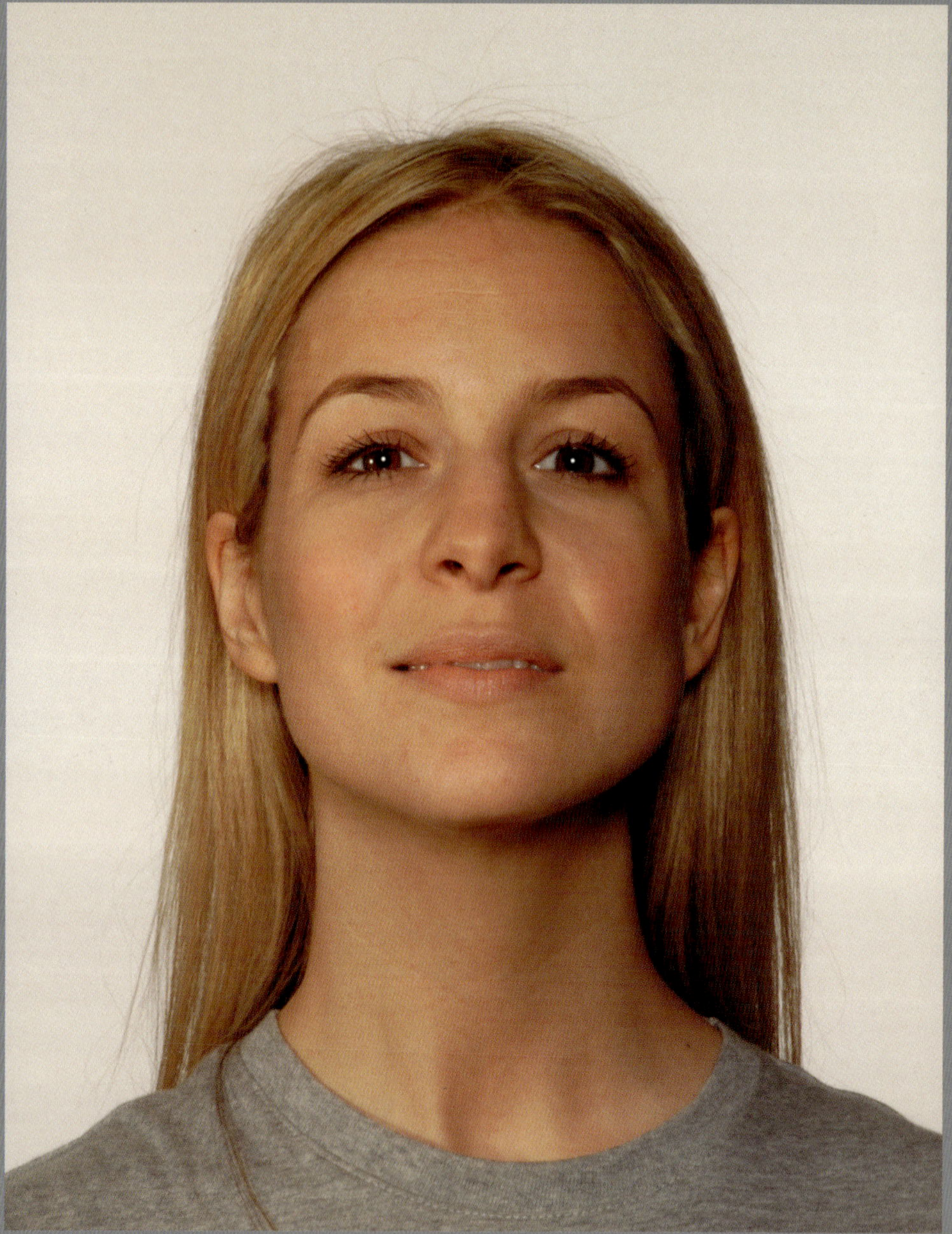

With a second light pointing at the subject at a 60-degree angle, the shadows to the side of the face are minimal, but noticeable enough to model the face. However, with dark-haired subjects there is little separation between the hair and a dark background; the two areas merge into one.

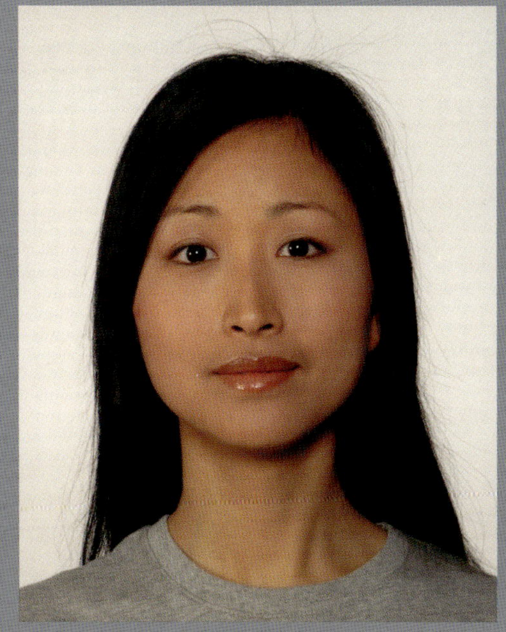

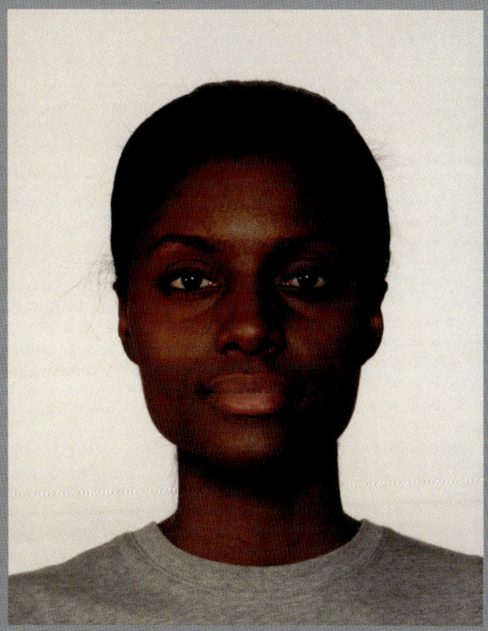

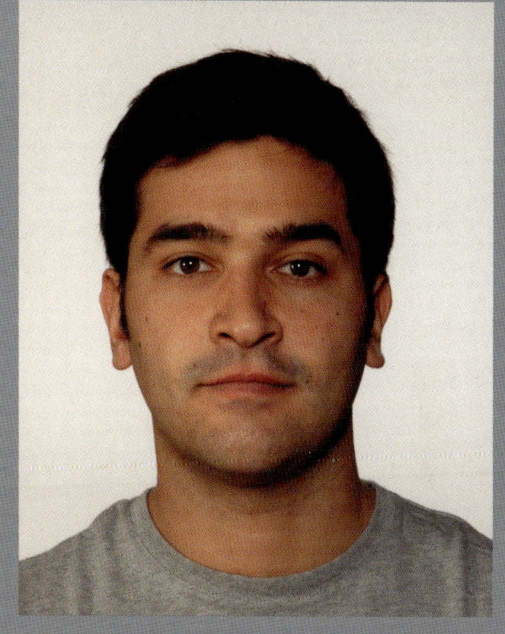

DARK BACKGROUND

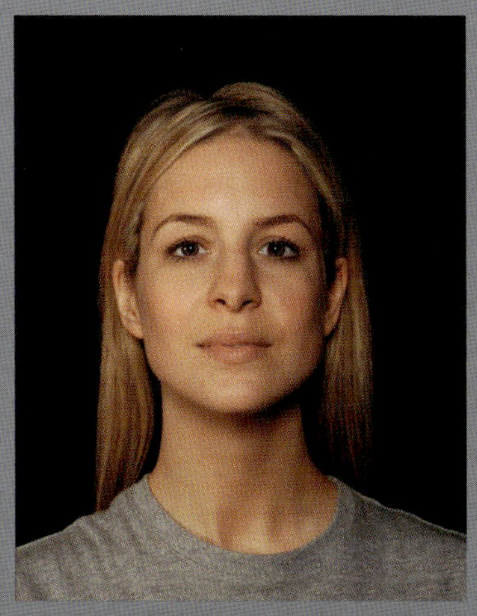

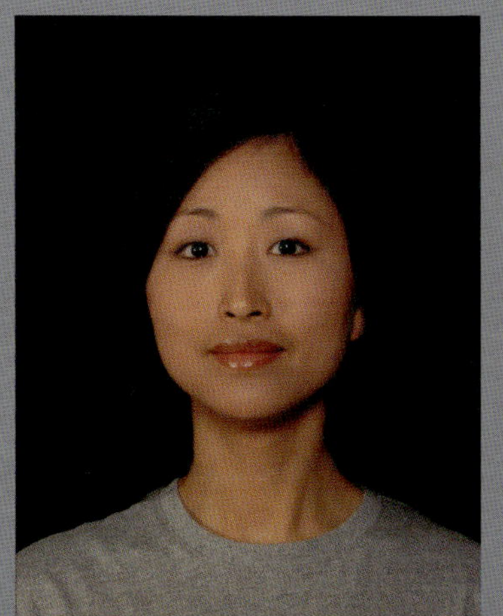

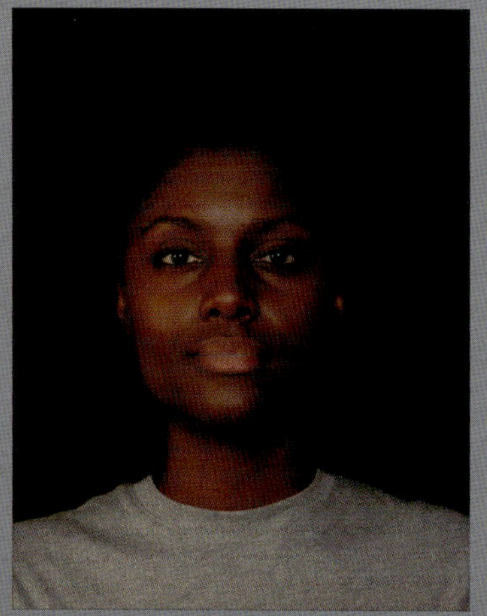

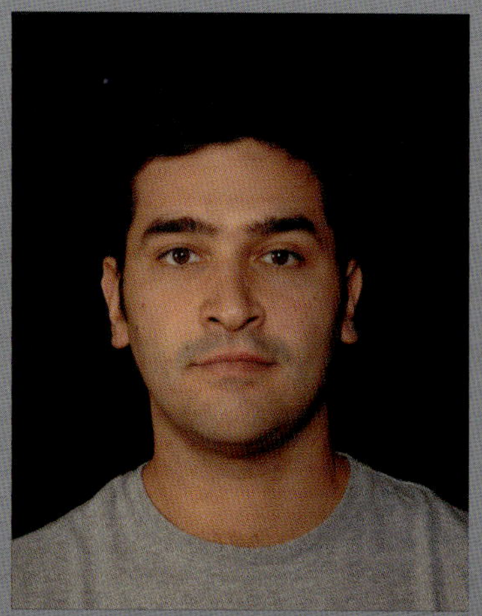

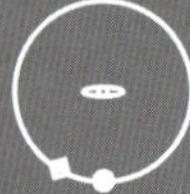

TWO LIGHTS

LIGHT 1: FROM CAMERA, EYE LEVEL

LIGHT 2: FROM 30° LEFT, EYE LEVEL

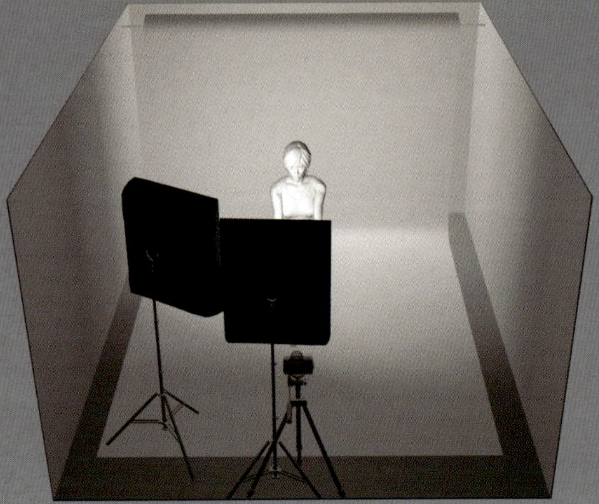

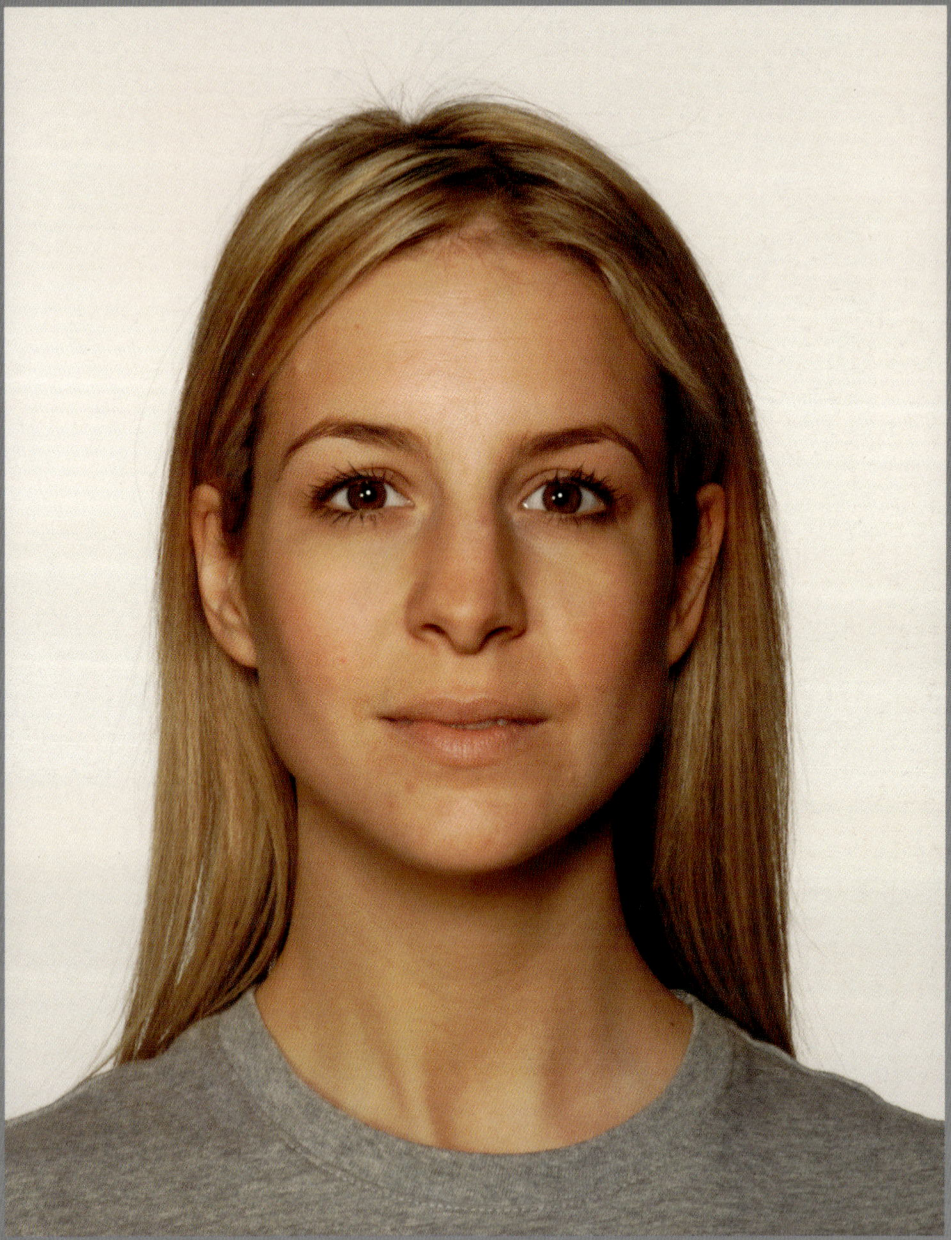

Here, a second light is positioned close to the light on the camera axis. With both lights so near the camera, the face is evenly lit, with the additional light creating a slight, defining shadow along one side of the face.

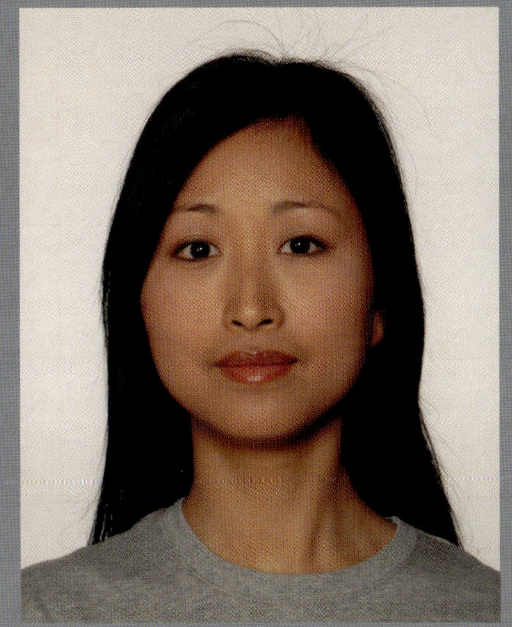
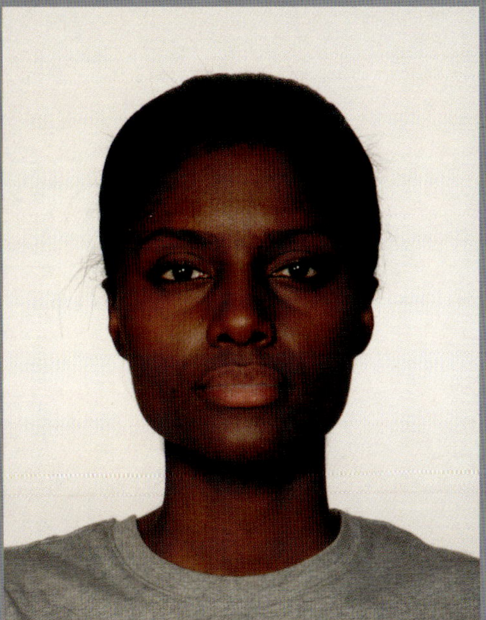
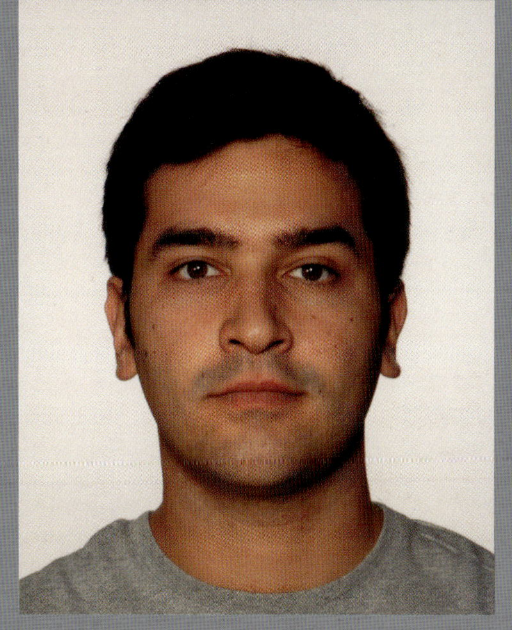

DARK BACKGROUND

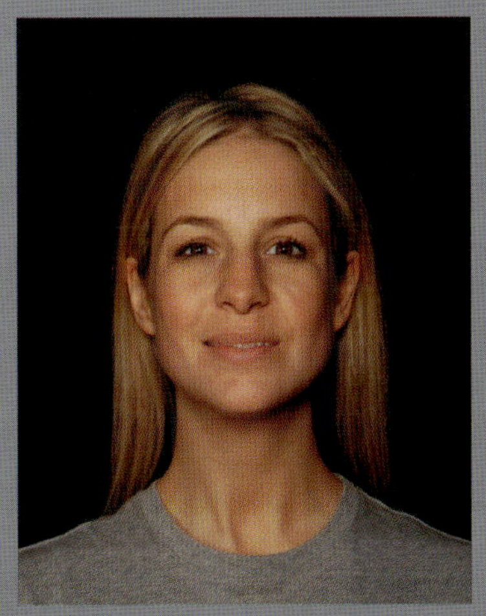
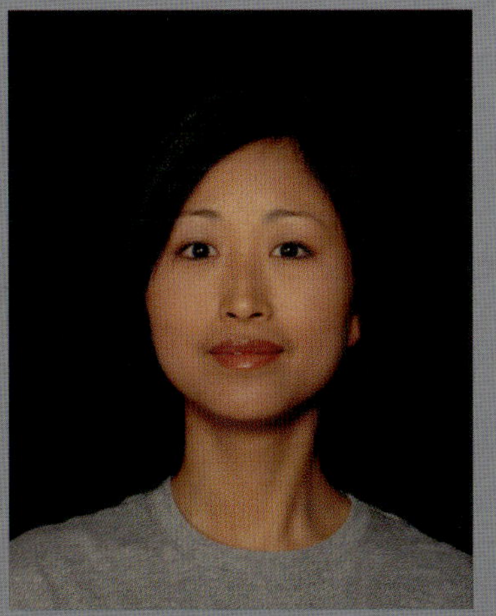
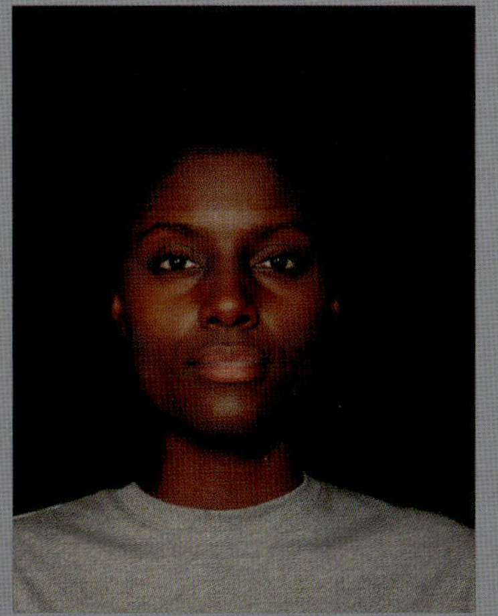
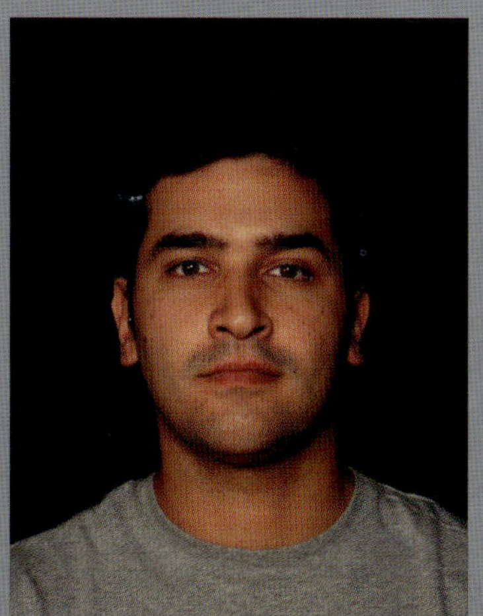

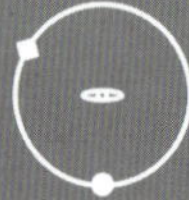

TWO LIGHTS

LIGHT 1: FROM CAMERA, EYE LEVEL

LIGHT 2: FROM 120° LEFT, EYE LEVEL

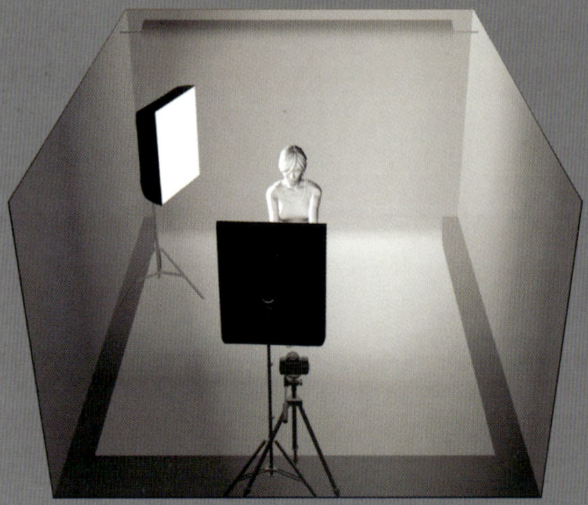

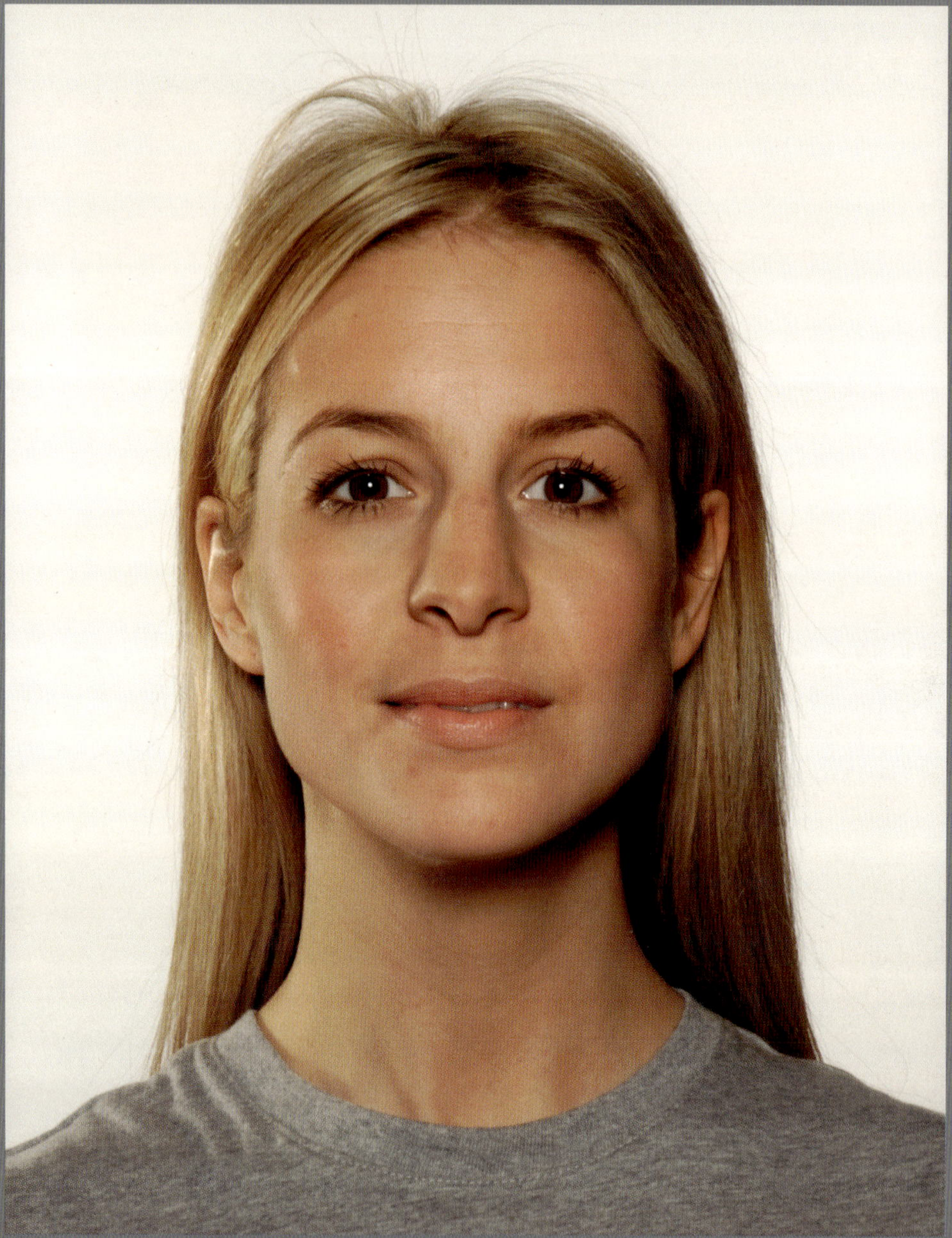

With one light illuminating the model from the camera axis and a second positioned just behind the subject, you start to get a slight "rim-light" effect from the light behind. This can help separate dark hair from a dark background, although it will only do this on one side of the subject.

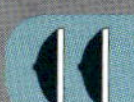

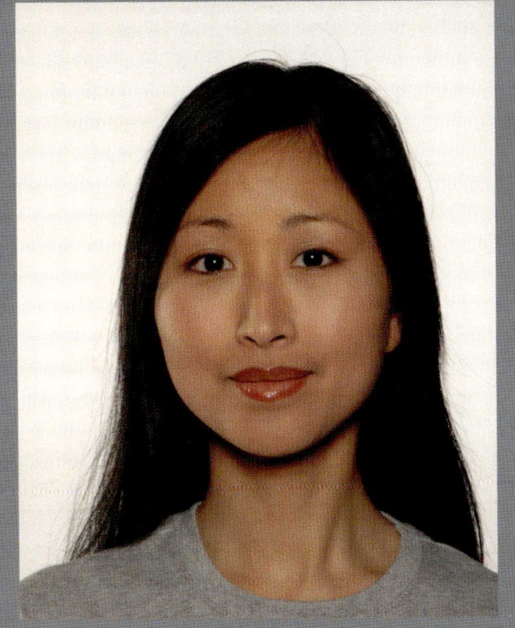

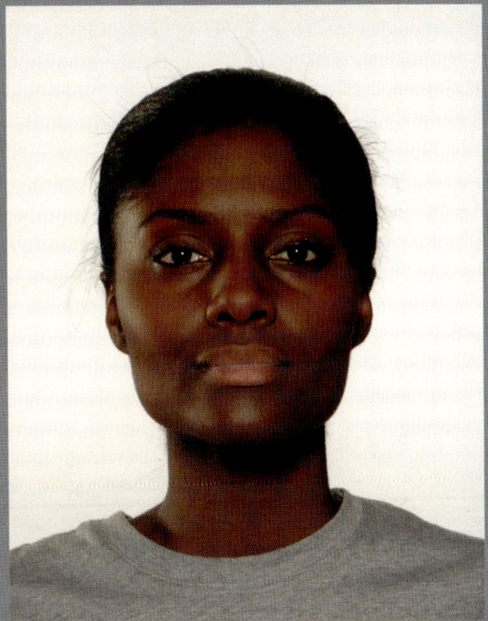

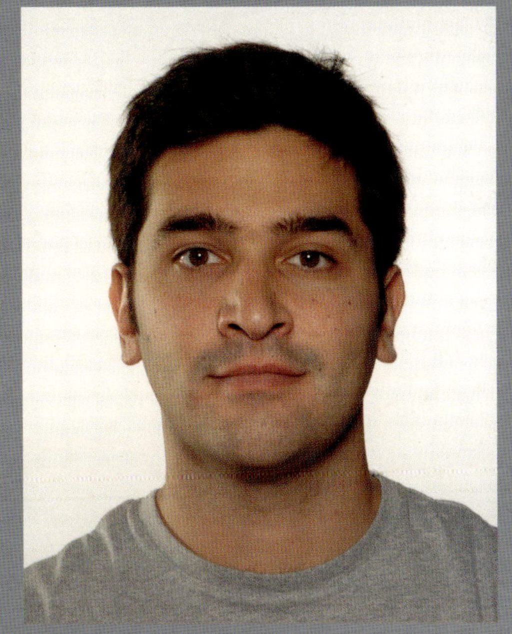

DARK BACKGROUND

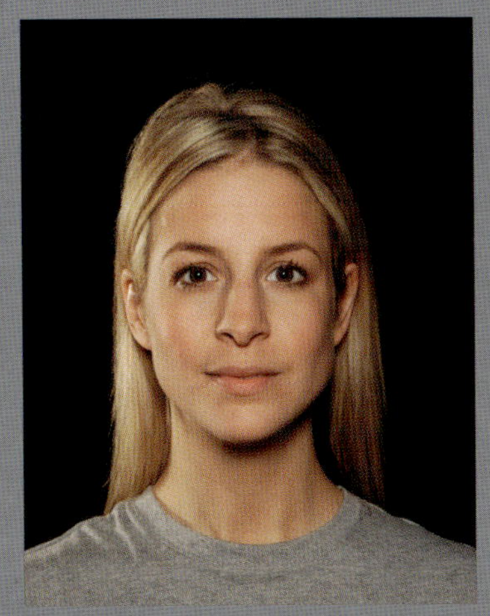

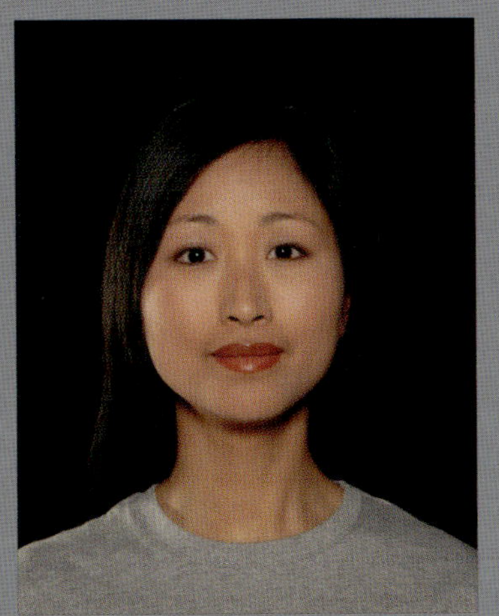

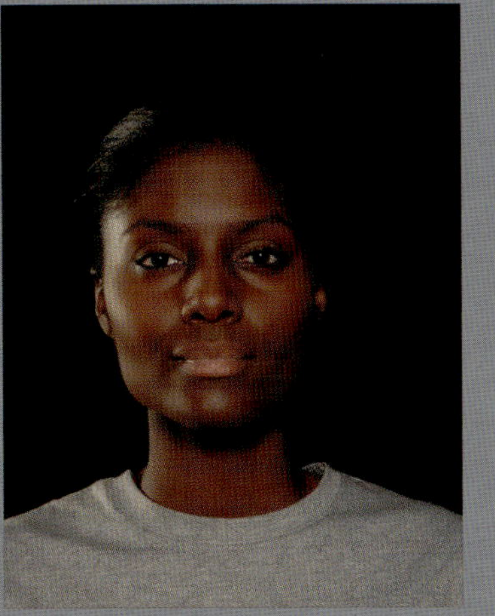

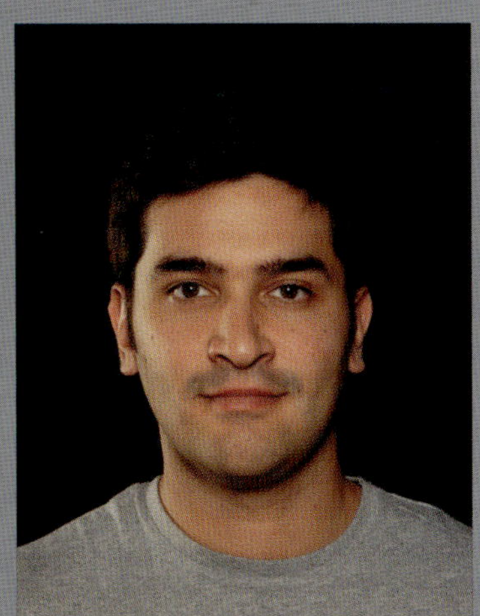

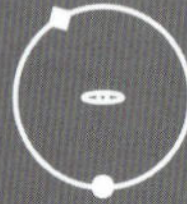

TWO LIGHTS

LIGHT 1: FROM CAMERA, EYE LEVEL

LIGHT 2: FROM 150° LEFT, EYE LEVEL

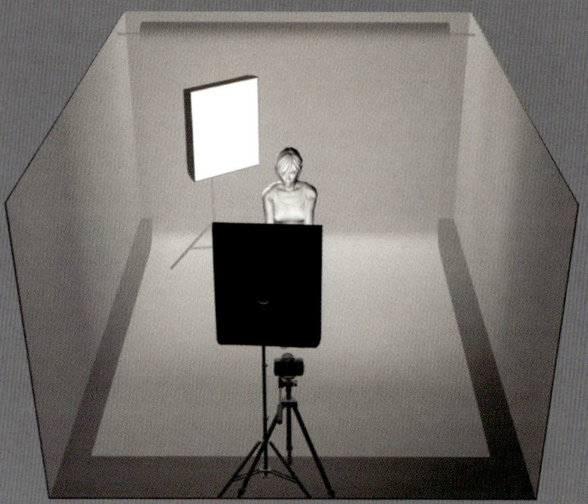

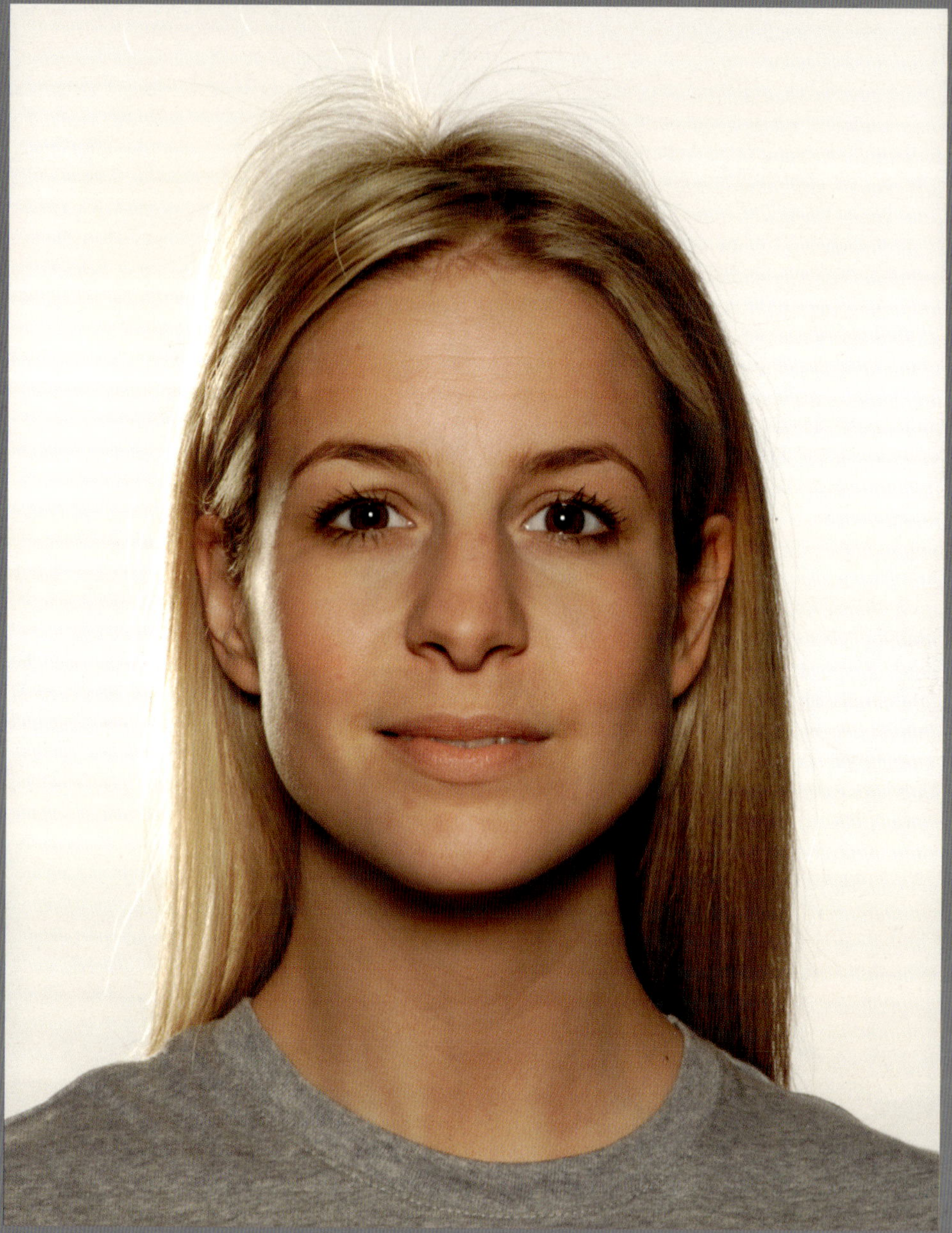

As the second light is moved further behind the subject, the rim-light effect is strengthened and a more distinct highlight can be seen around one side of the model's hair. The main light falling on the subject is now coming solely from the front, so the lighting on the face is uniform.

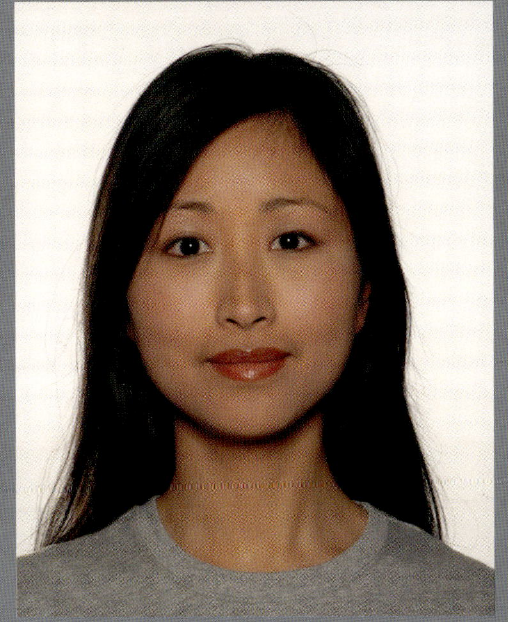

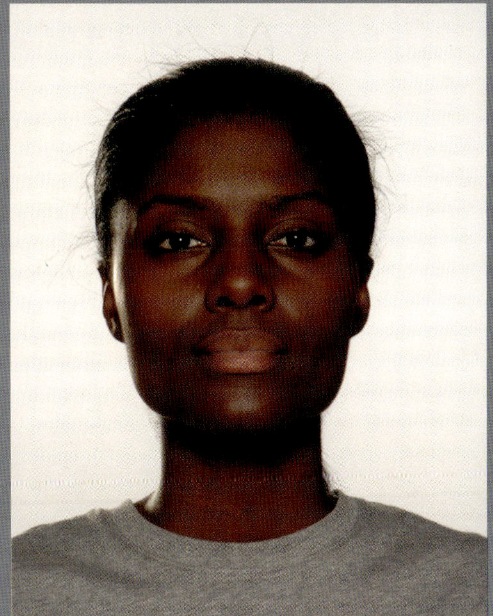

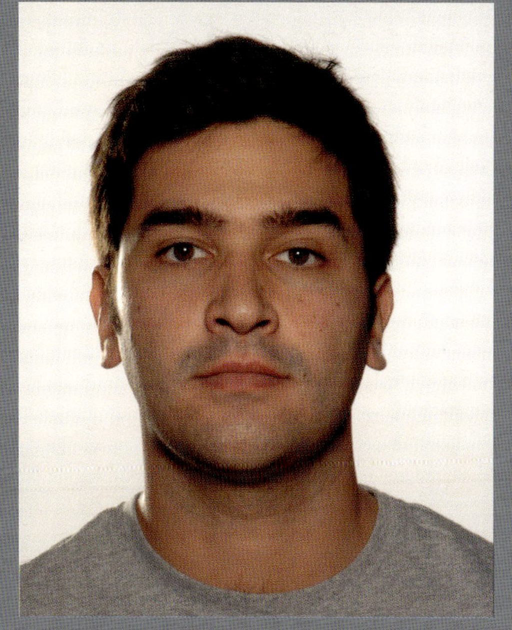

DARK BACKGROUND

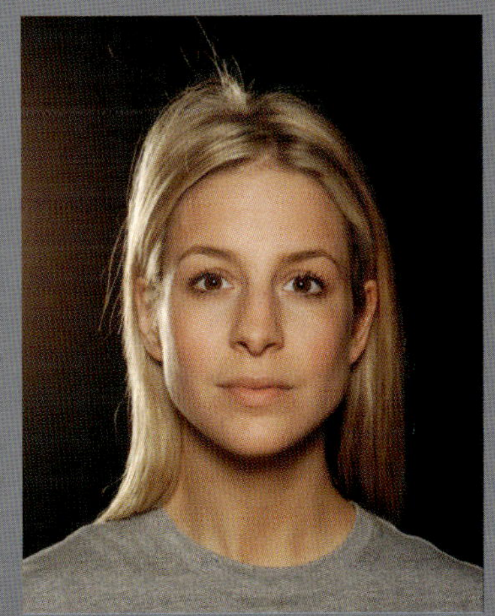

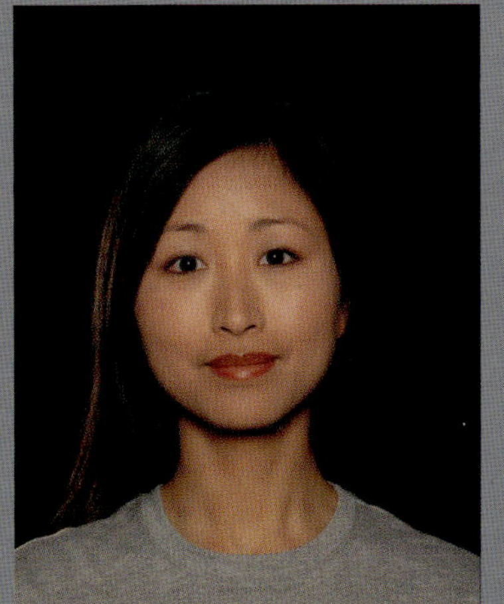

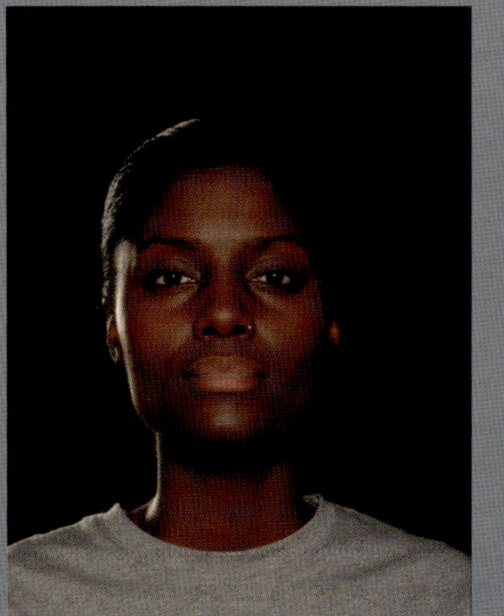

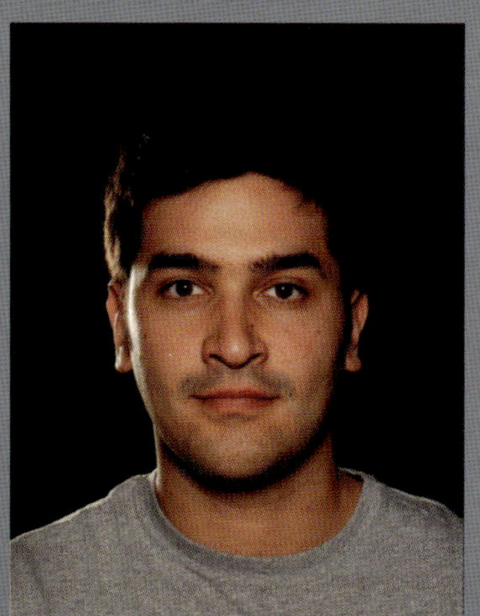

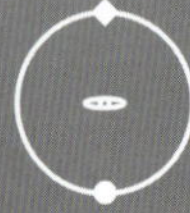

TWO LIGHTS

LIGHT 1: FROM CAMERA, EYE LEVEL

LIGHT 2: FROM 180° LEFT, EYE LEVEL

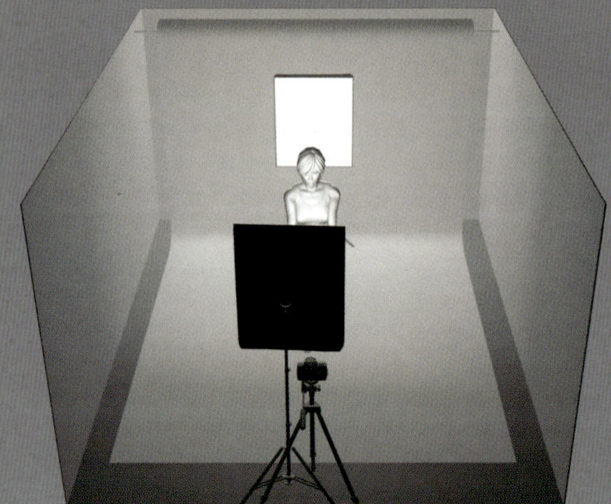

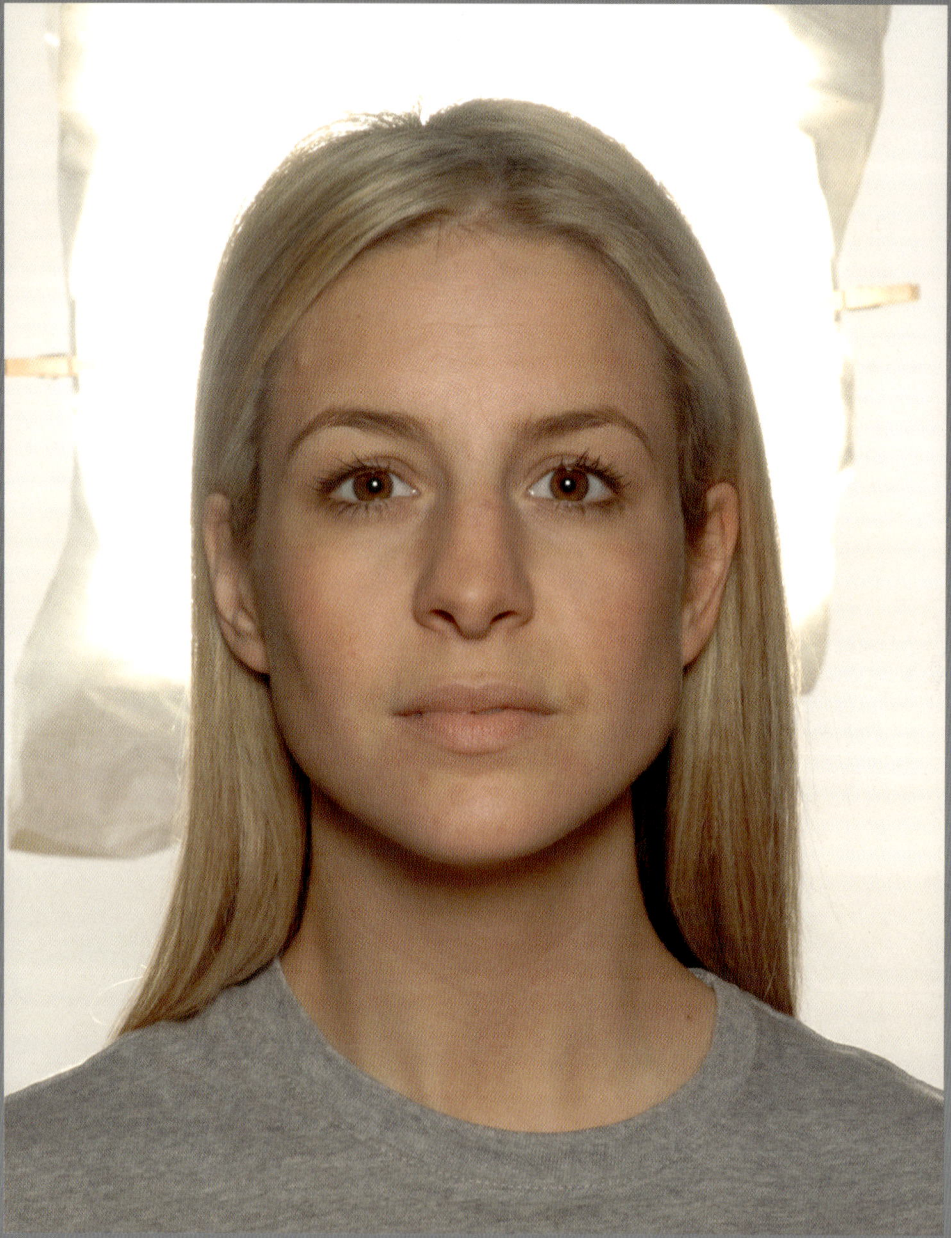

Although unconventional, positioning a light behind your subject so that it's pointing at the camera (and appears in shot), can create interesting results. The overall effect is of low contrast due to the backlight introducing low-level flare as it hits the camera's lens.

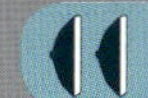

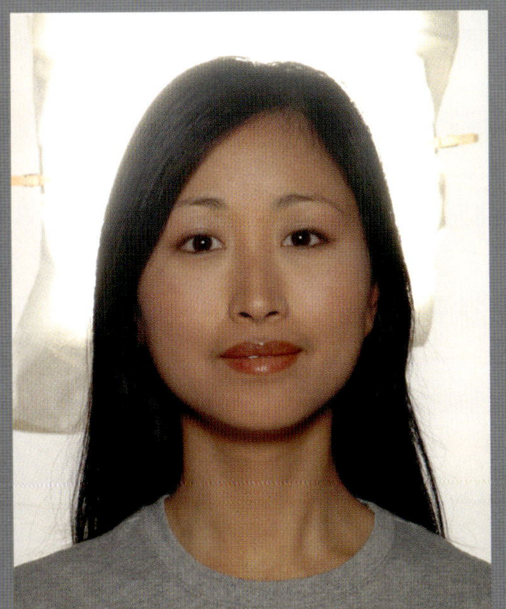

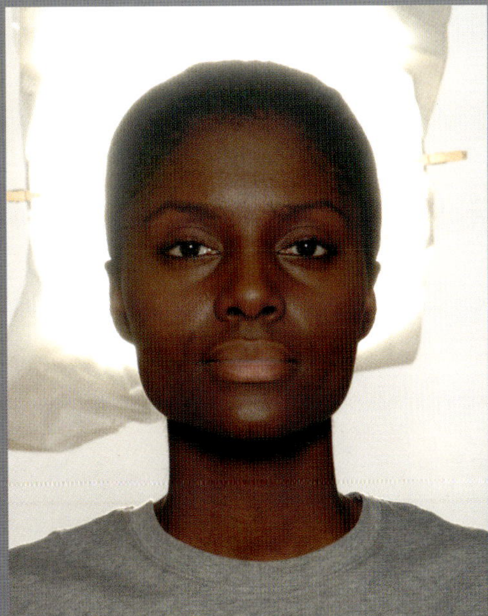

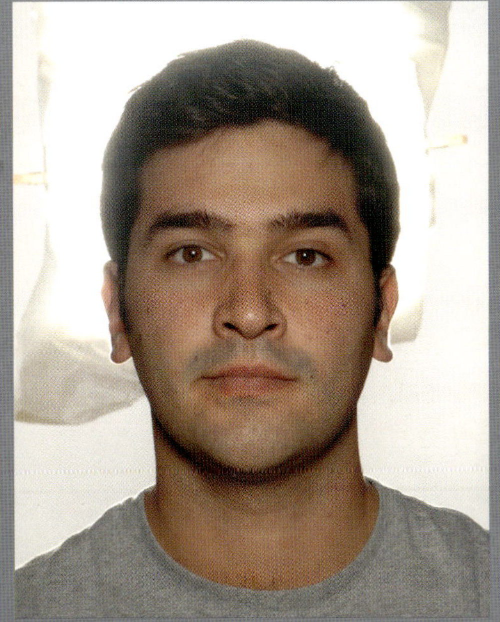

DARK BACKGROUND

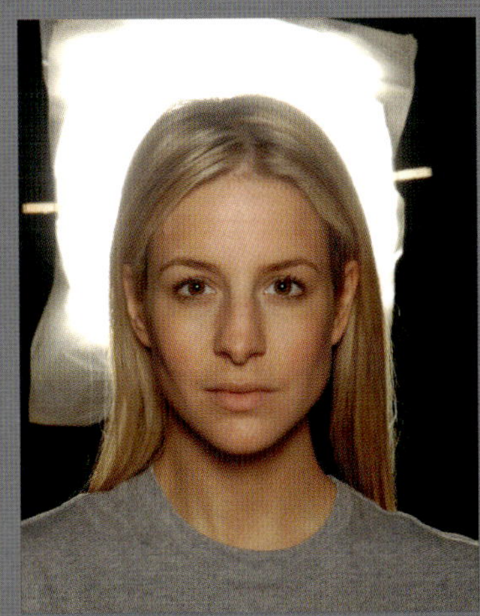

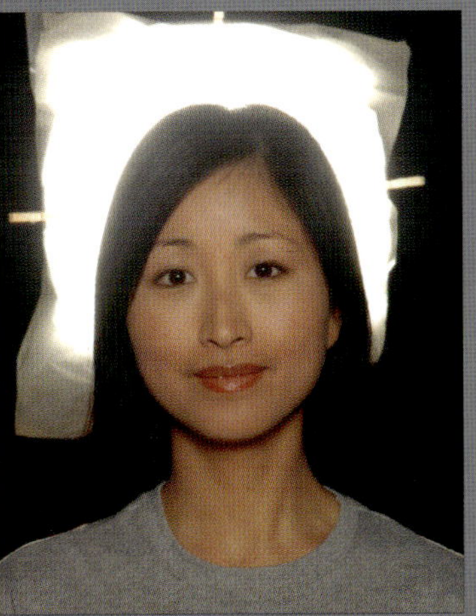

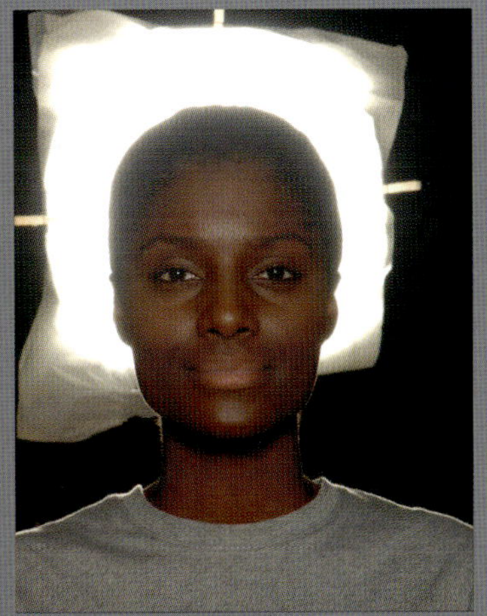

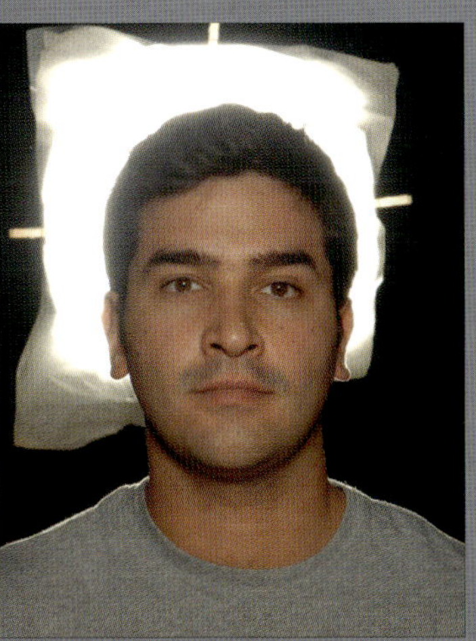

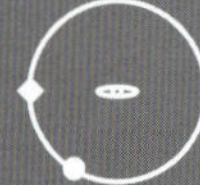

TWO LIGHTS

LIGHT 1: FROM 30° LEFT, EYE LEVEL

LIGHT 2: FROM 90° LEFT, EYE LEVEL

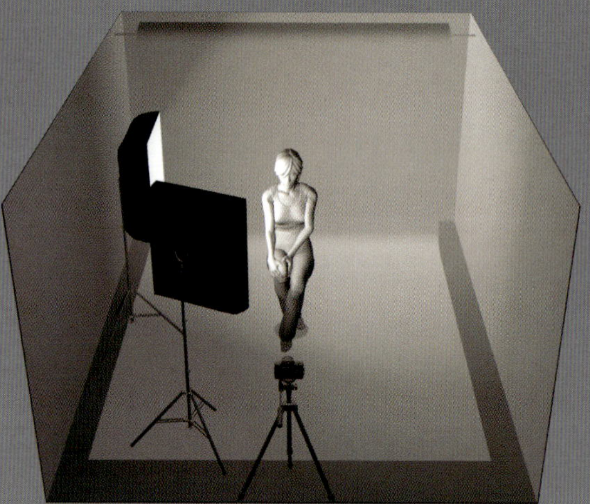

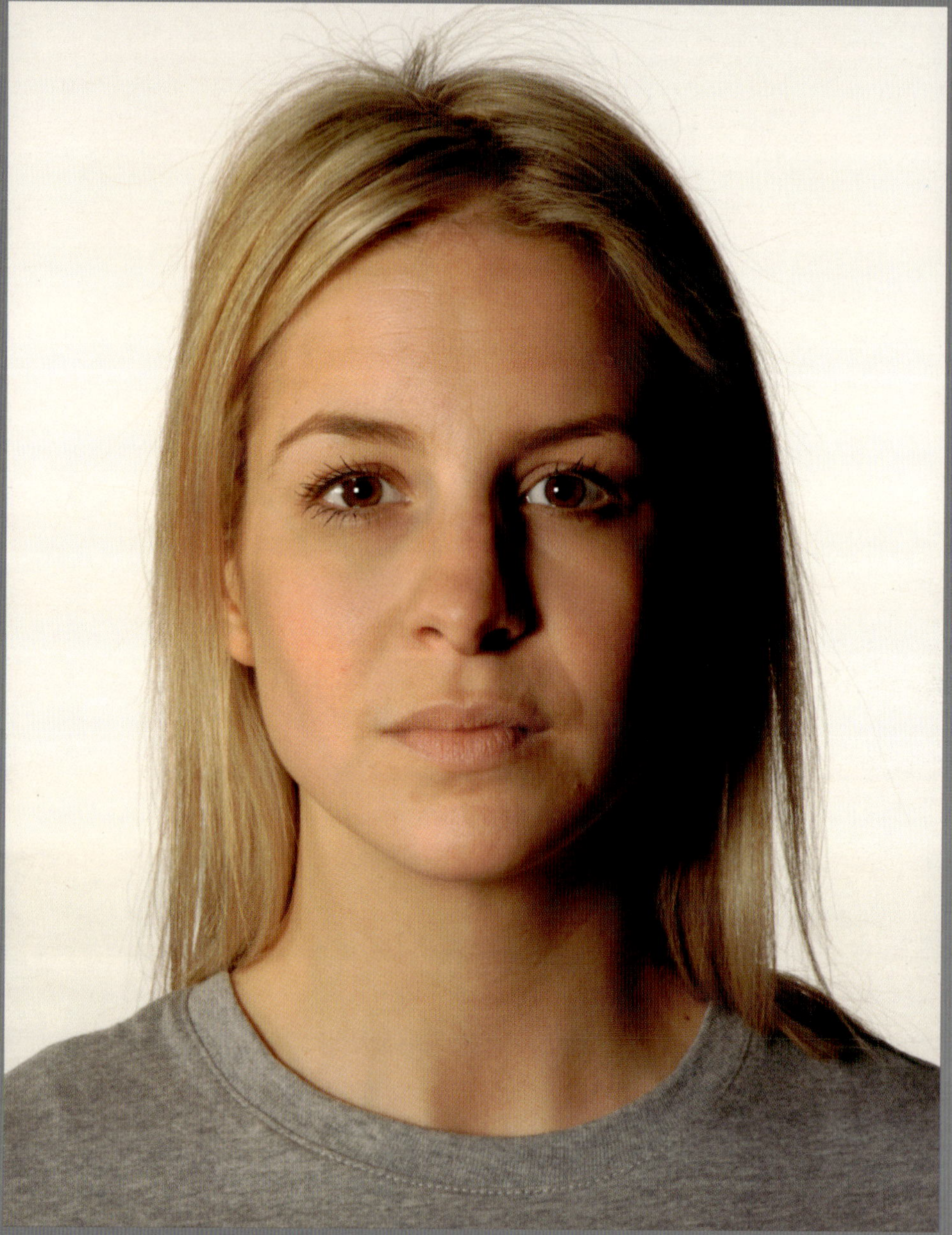

There's no reason why you have to have one of your lights aimed at your subject from the camera position. Here, they have both been moved off-axis. One light, at a 90-degree angle, lights one side of the face, while the other (at a 30-degree angle) prevents the opposite side of the face from falling into total shadow.

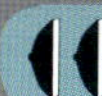

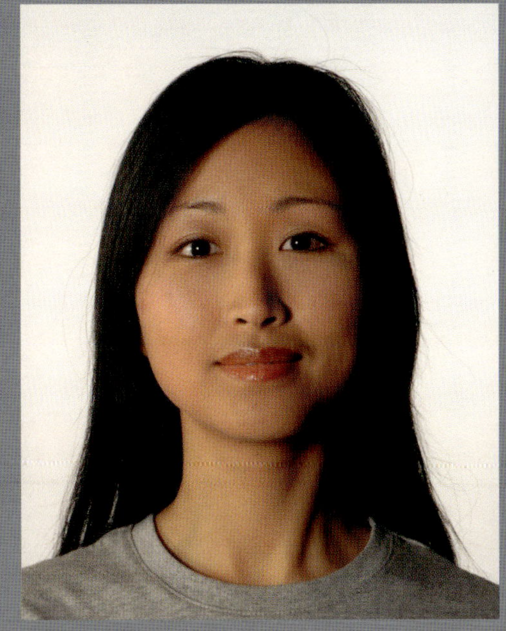

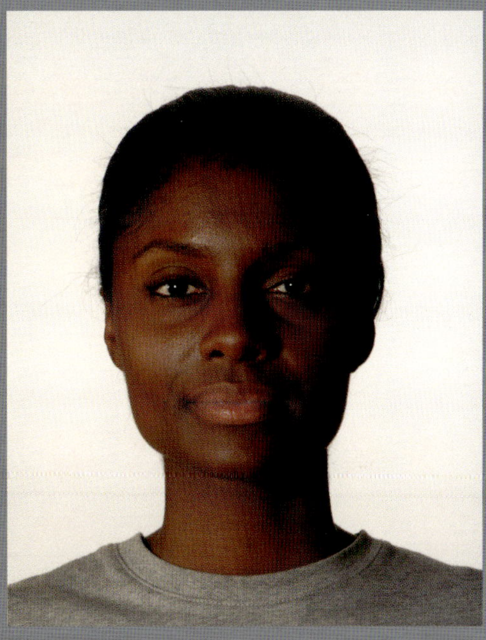

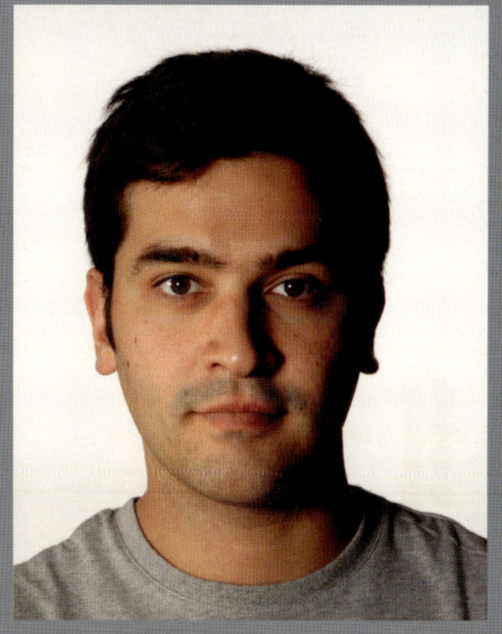

DARK BACKGROUND

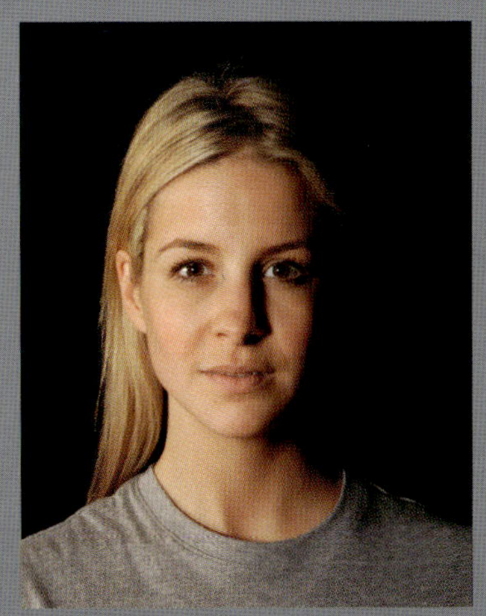

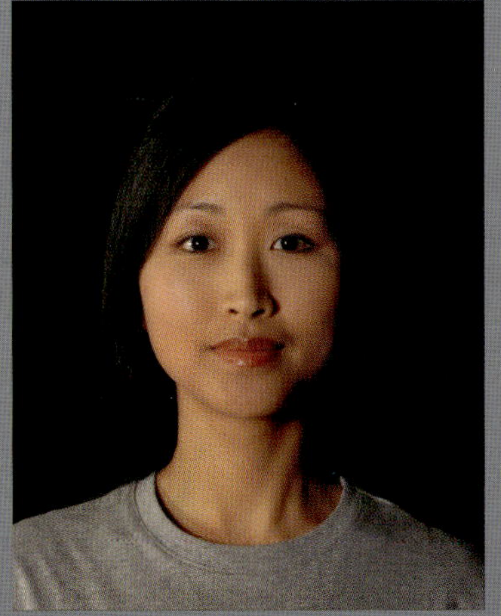

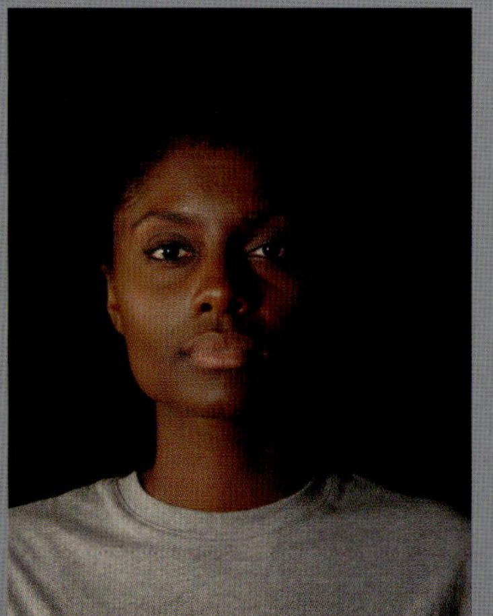

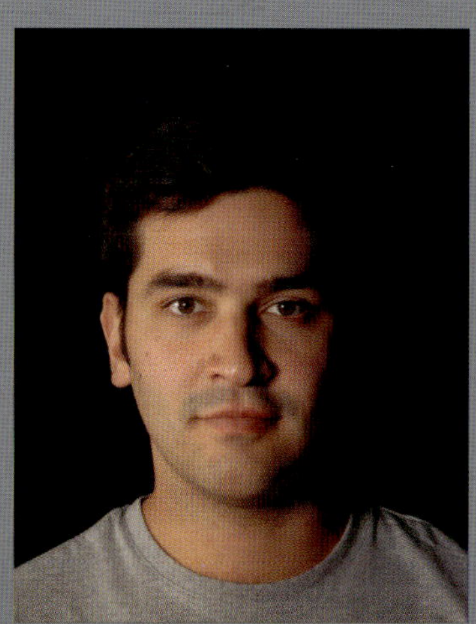

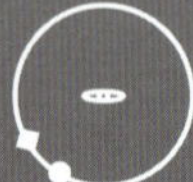

TWO LIGHTS

LIGHT 1: FROM 30° LEFT, EYE LEVEL

LIGHT 2: FROM 60° LEFT, EYE LEVEL

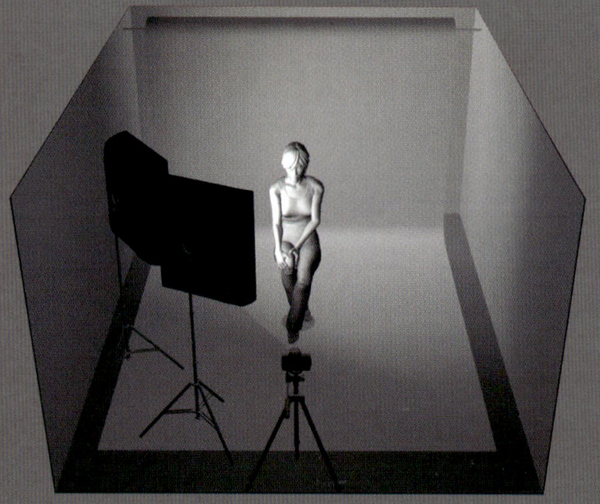

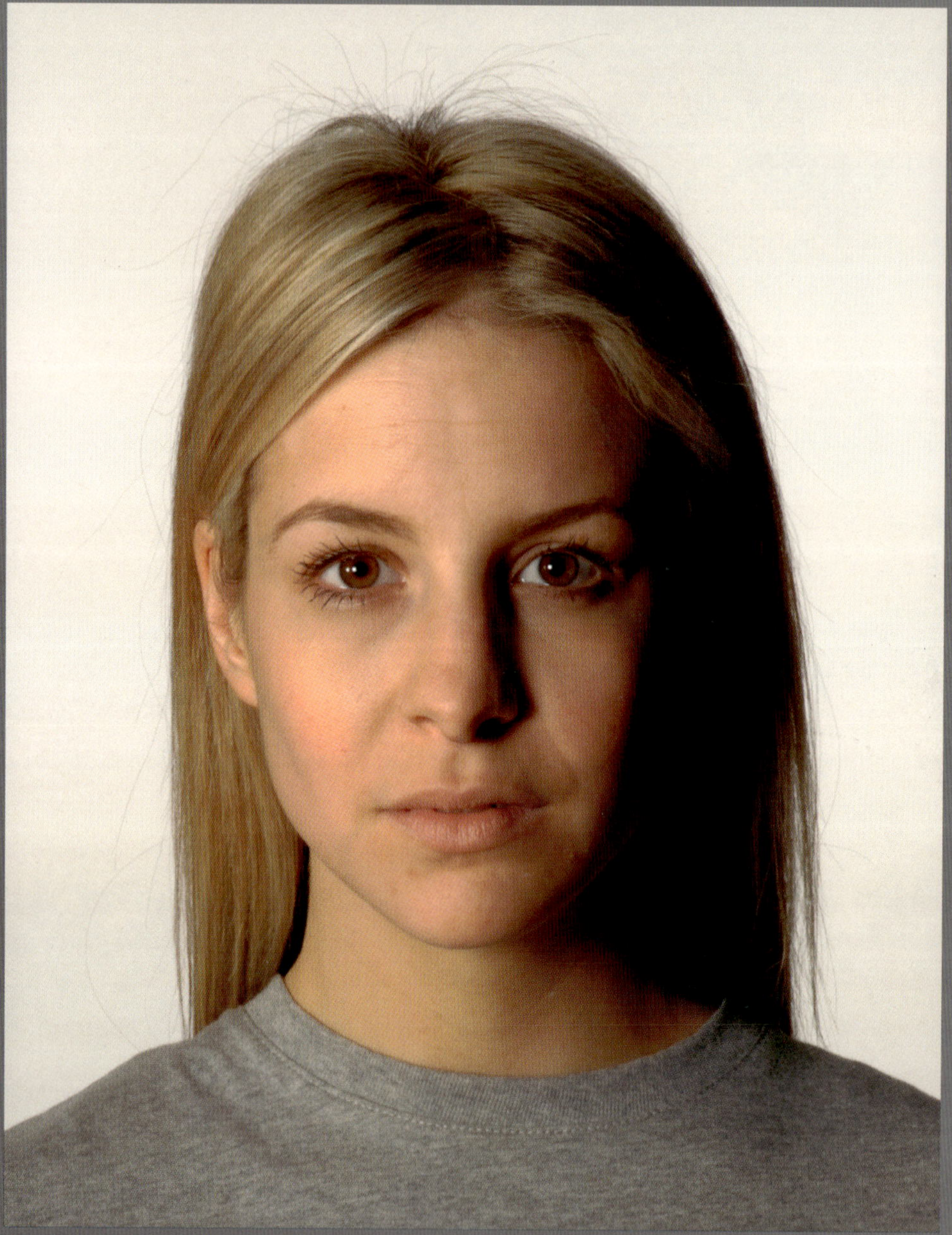

Positioning the two lights close to each other, but still on the same side of the subject, reduces the contrast in the hair and helps to smooth the areas of skin that are lit. At the same time, there are hard shadows that define the nose and prevent the image looking overly flat.

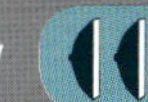

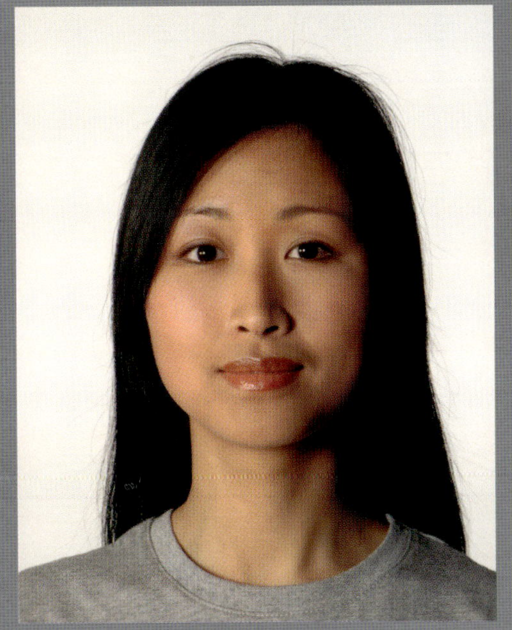

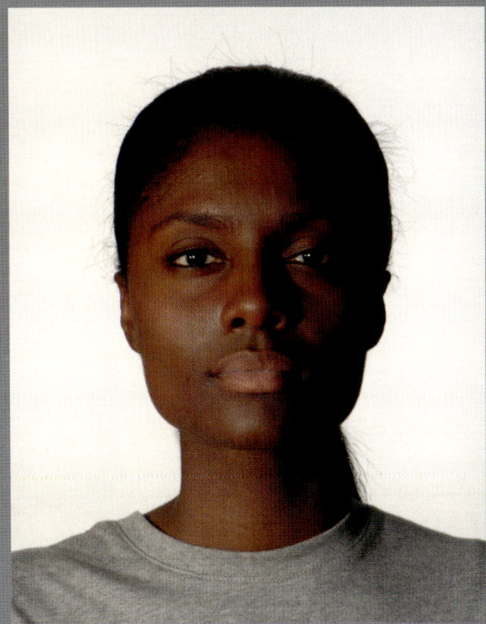

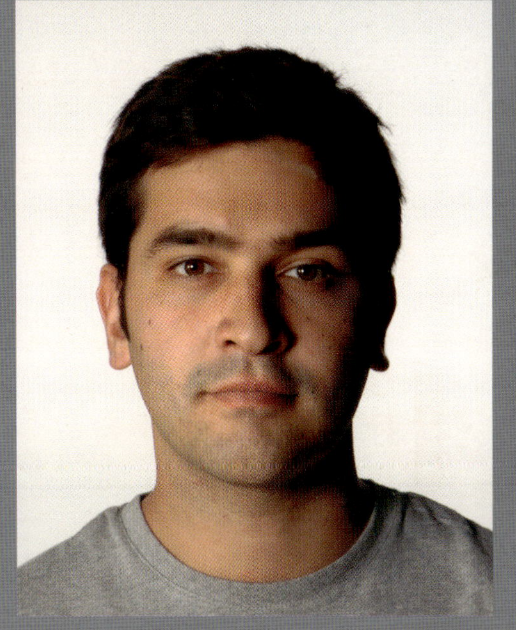

DARK BACKGROUND

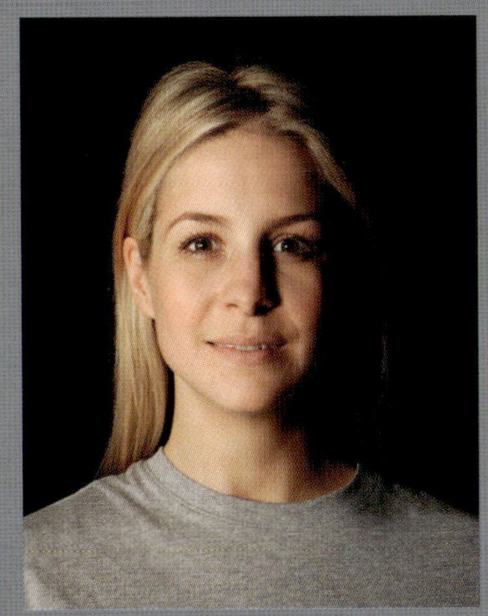

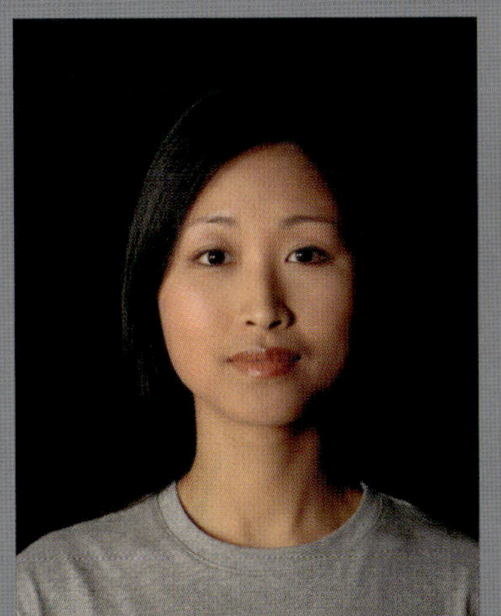

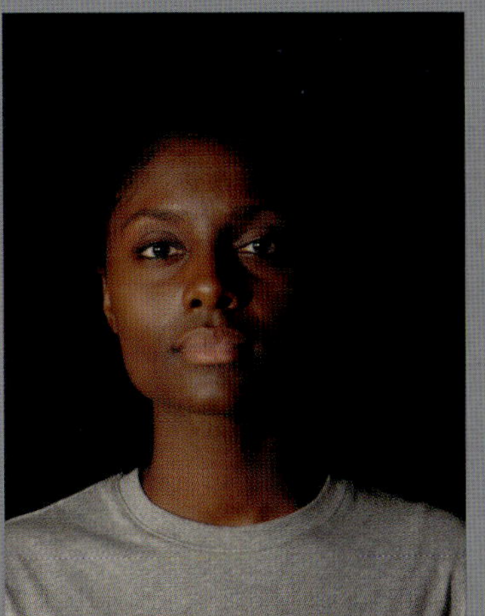

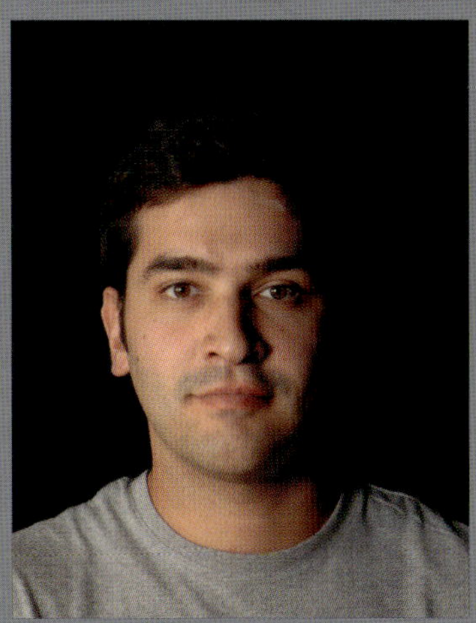

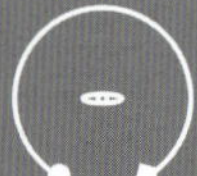

TWO LIGHTS

LIGHT 1: FROM 30° LEFT, EYE LEVEL

LIGHT 2: FROM 30° RIGHT, EYE LEVEL

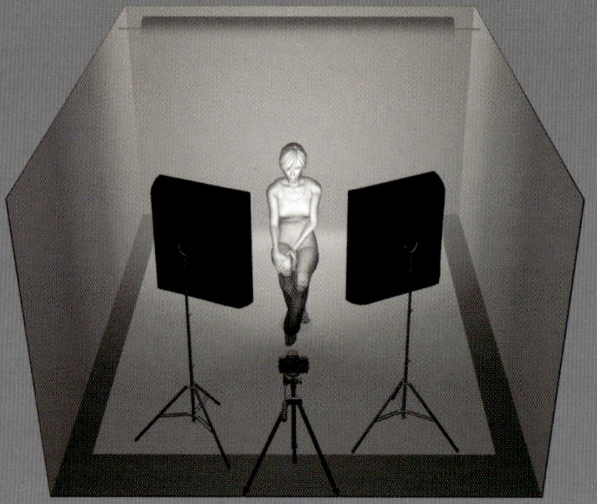

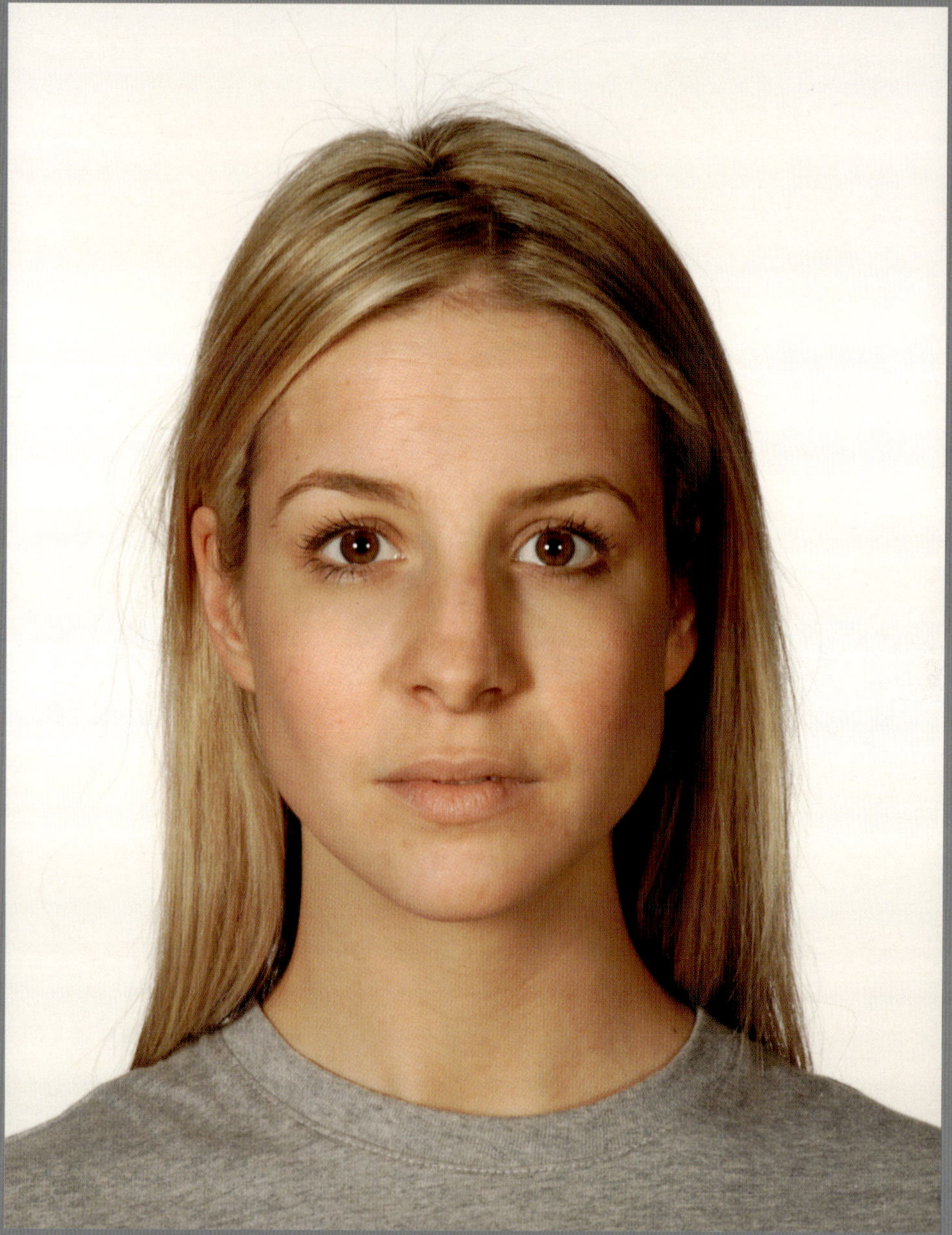

Lighting a subject with a light from either side will create a flat image unless one of the lights is stronger than the other. In this example, the light at the left of the camera is brighter than the one at the right, creating a distinct modeling effect. If your lights don't let you change their power output, simply moving one closer to the subject and the other further away will achieve a similar result.

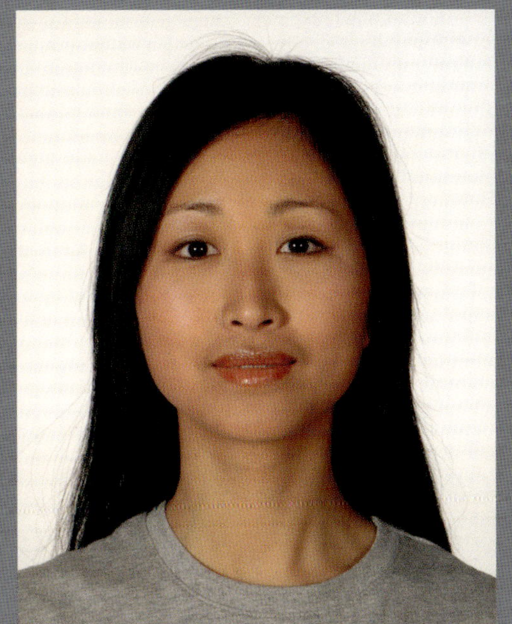
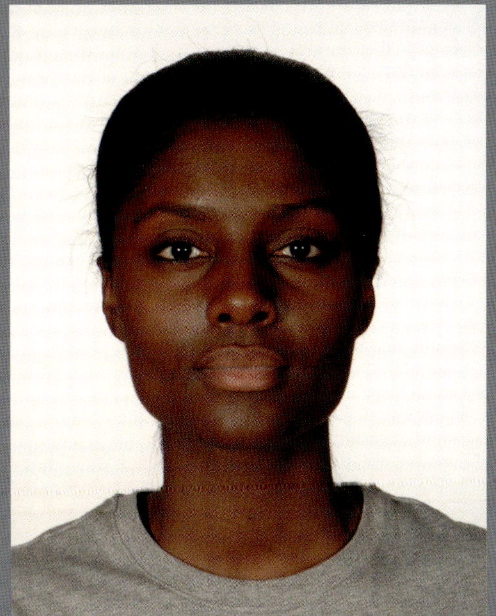
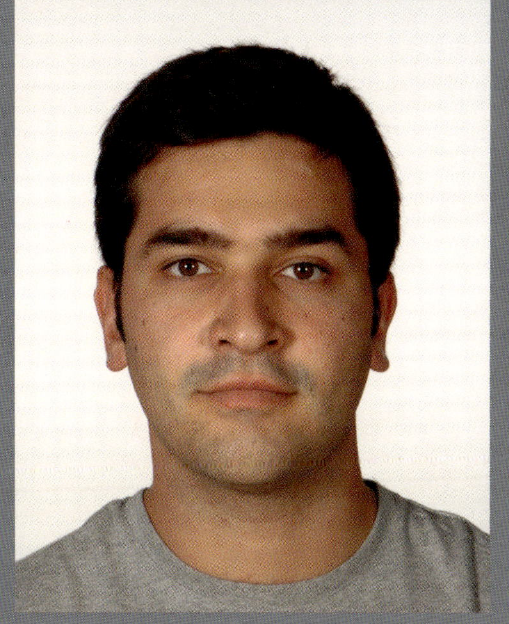

DARK BACKGROUND

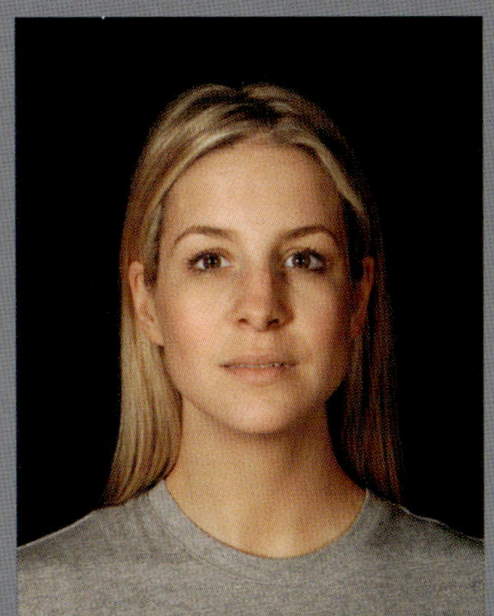
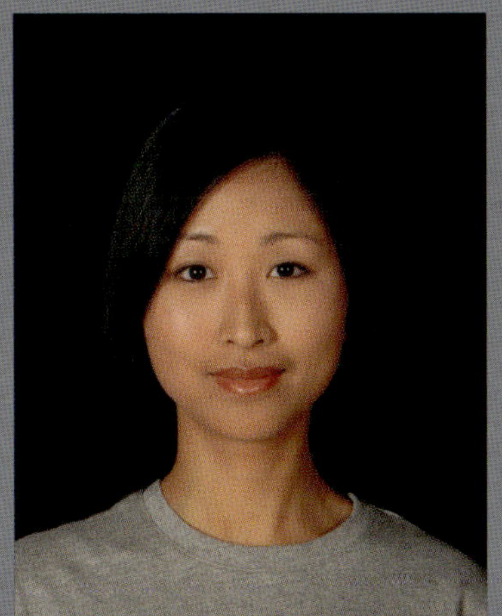
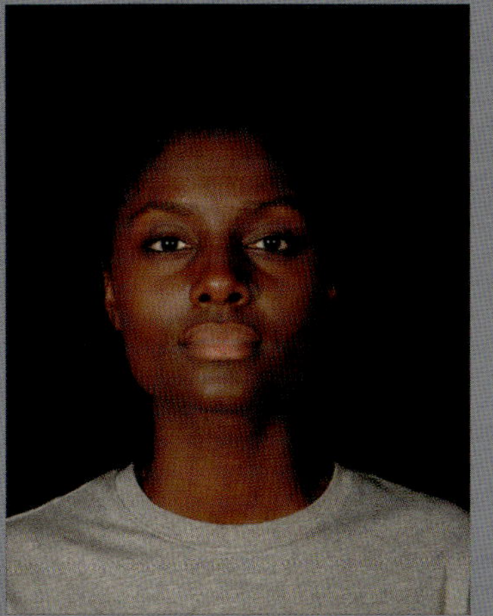
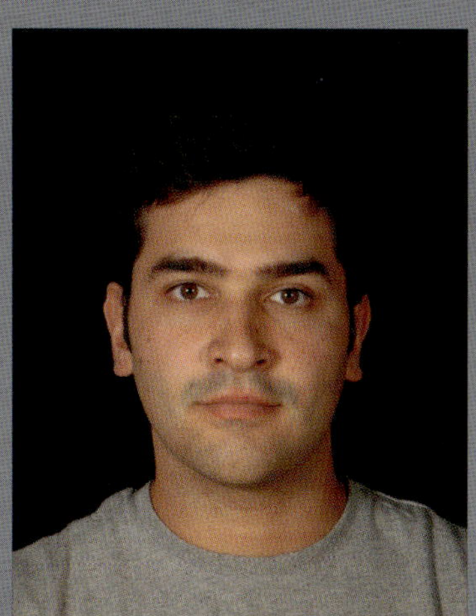

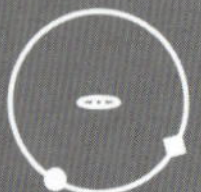

TWO LIGHTS

LIGHT 1: FROM 30° LEFT, EYE LEVEL

LIGHT 2: FROM 60° RIGHT, EYE LEVEL

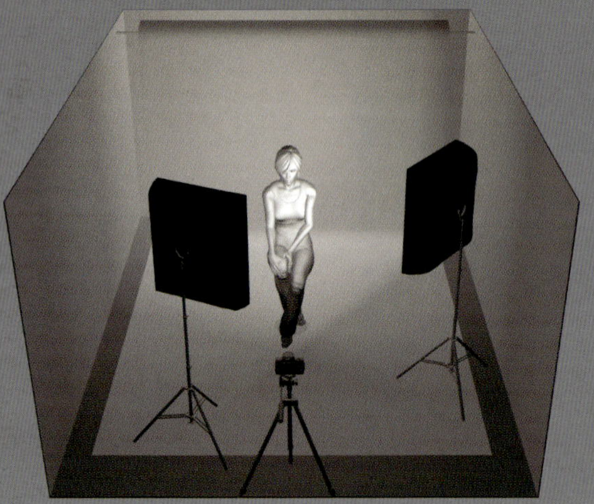

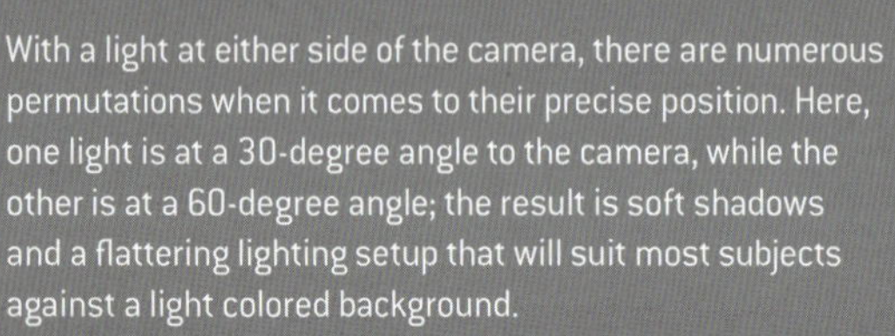

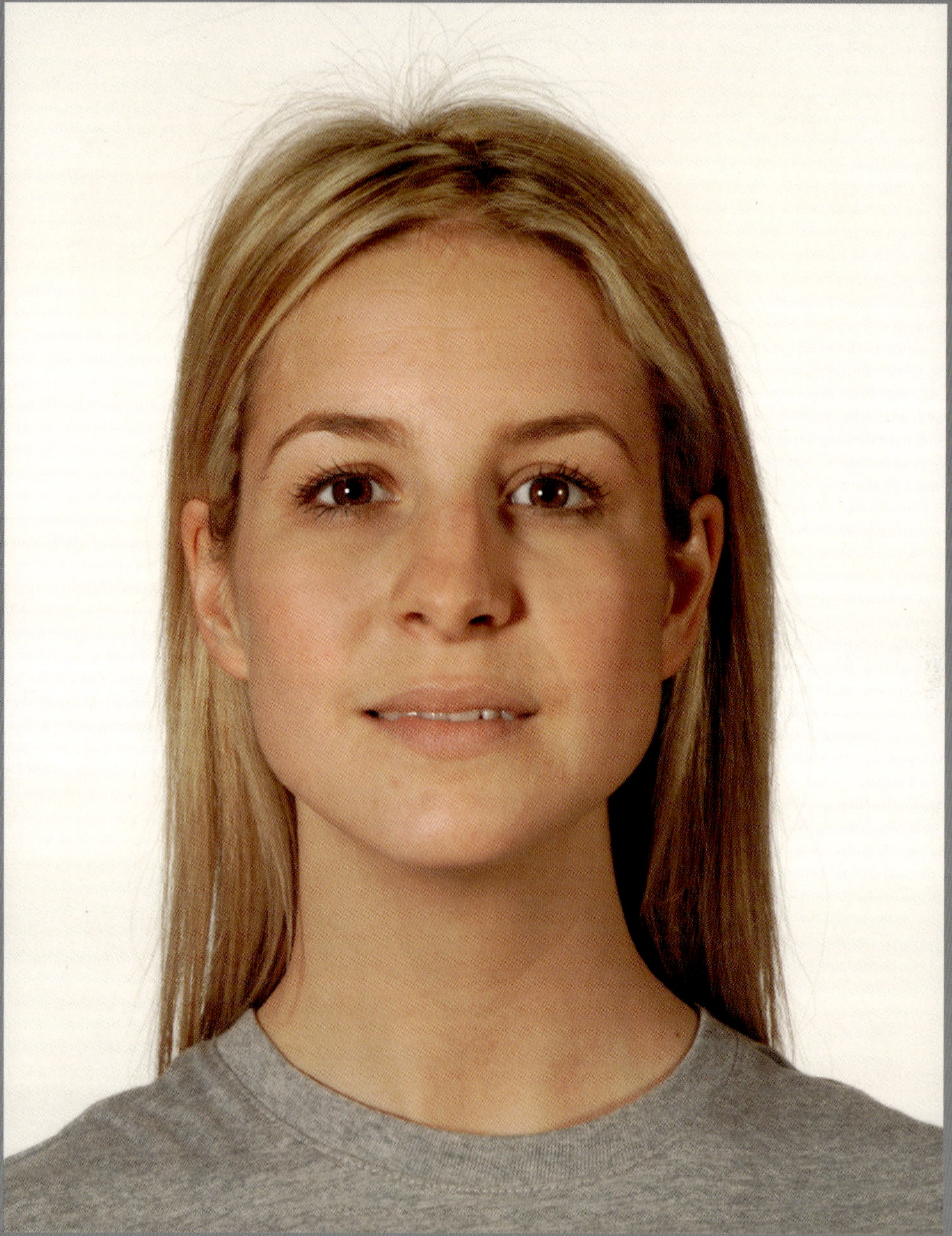

With a light at either side of the camera, there are numerous permutations when it comes to their precise position. Here, one light is at a 30-degree angle to the camera, while the other is at a 60-degree angle; the result is soft shadows and a flattering lighting setup that will suit most subjects against a light colored background.

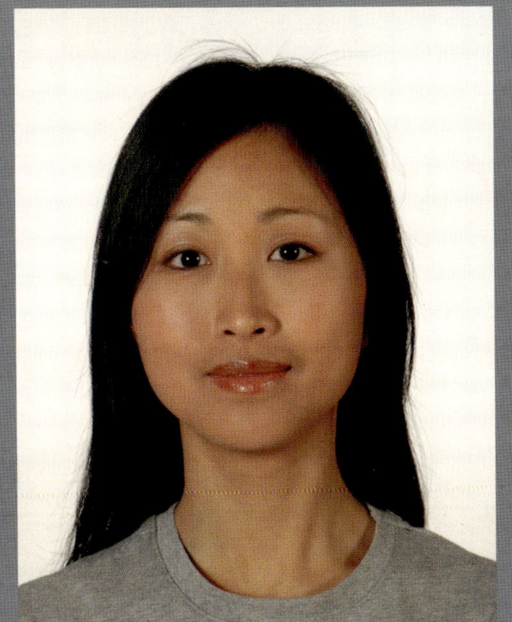
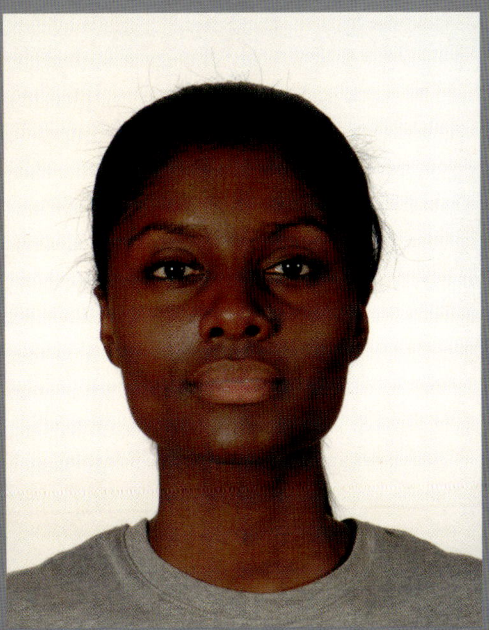
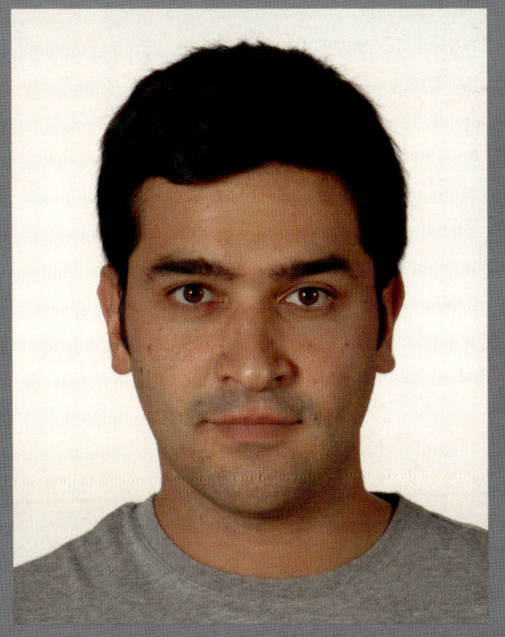

DARK BACKGROUND

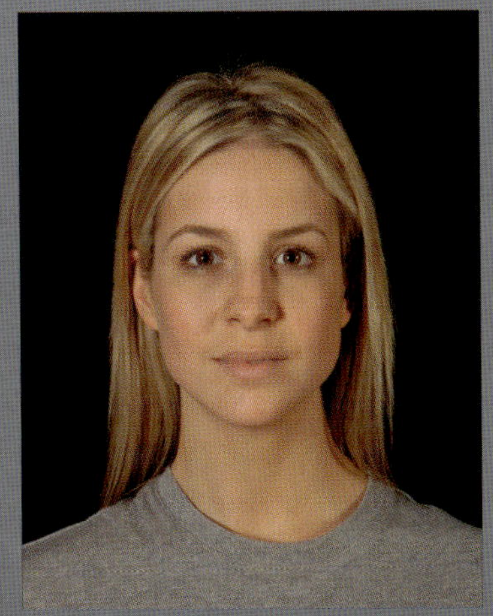
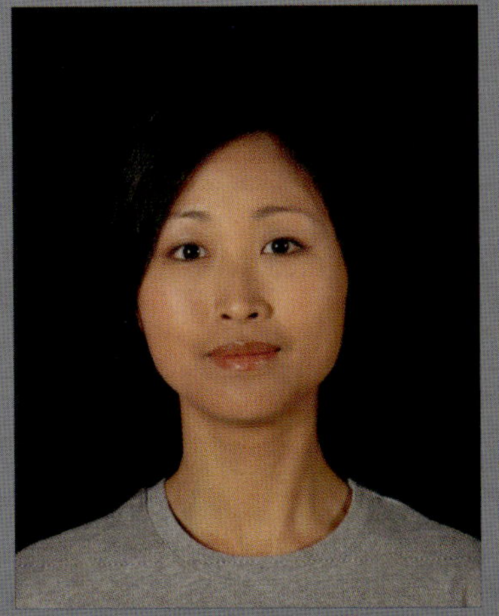
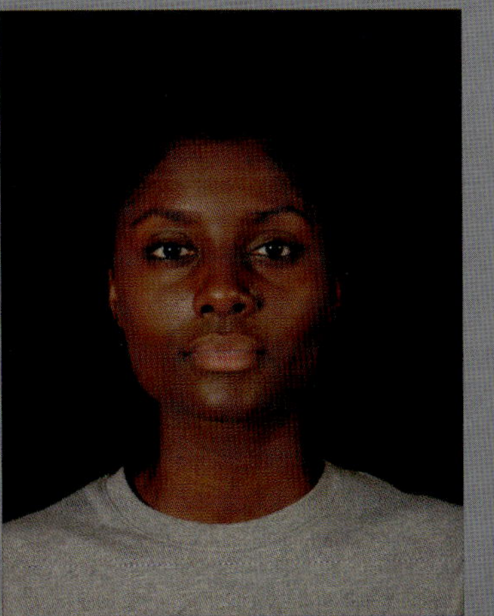
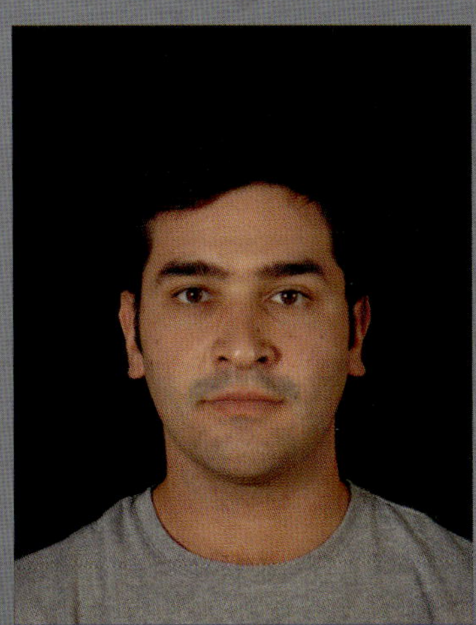

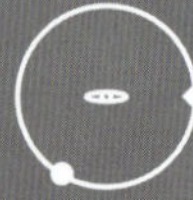

TWO LIGHTS

LIGHT 1: FROM 30° LEFT, EYE LEVEL

LIGHT 2: FROM 90° RIGHT, EYE LEVEL

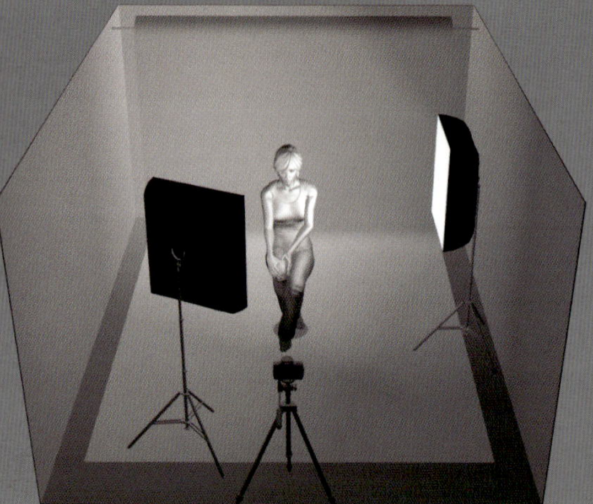

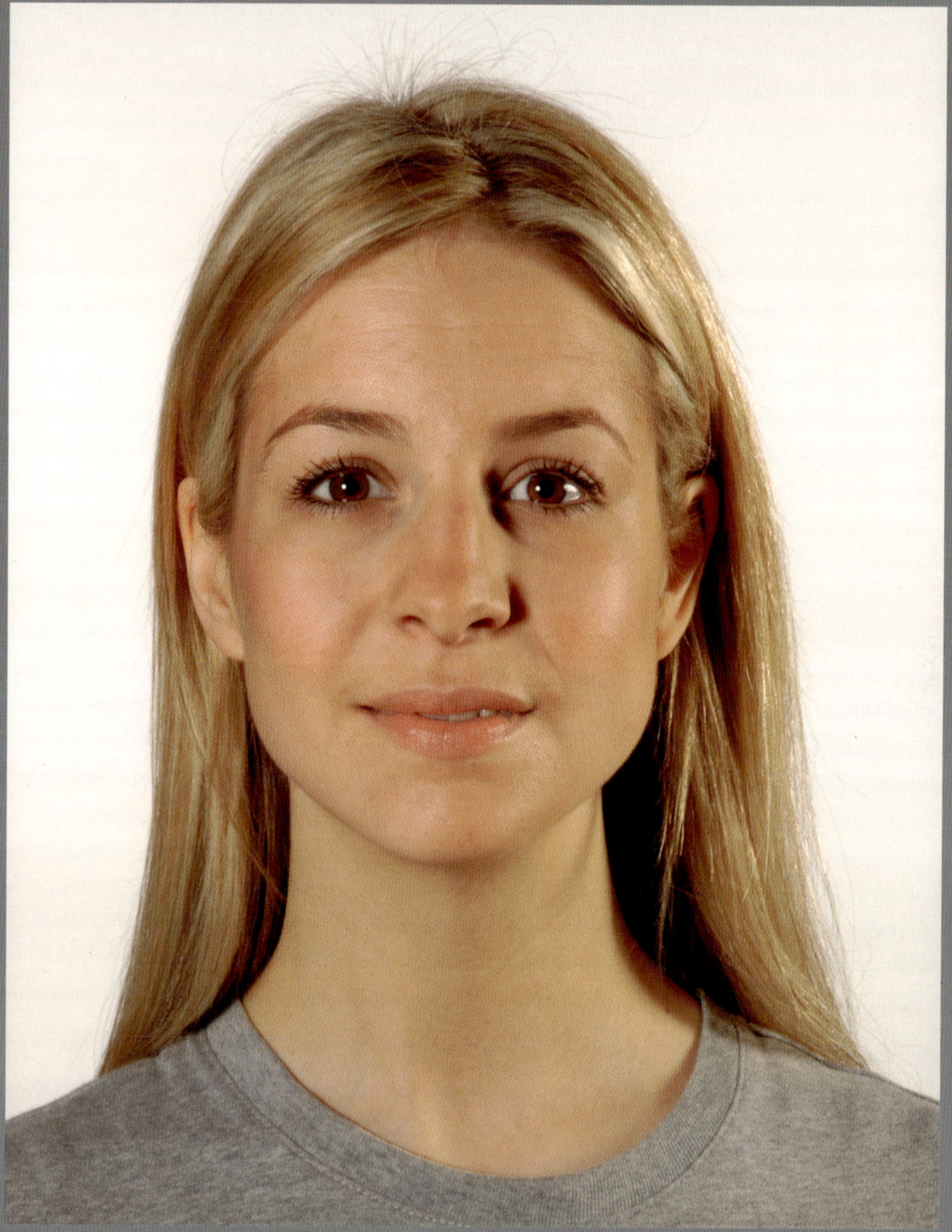

Keeping one light at a 30-degree angle to the camera, but moving the second to a 90-degree angle on the opposite side creates an unusual broken shadow along the subject's nose, as well as a light, narrow shadow down the center of the model's face.

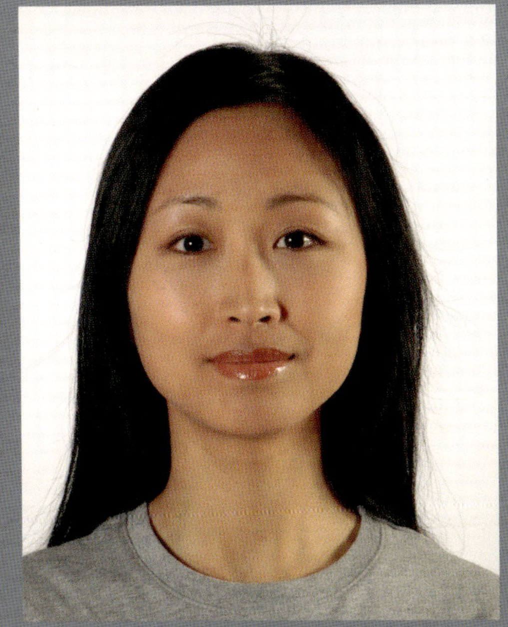

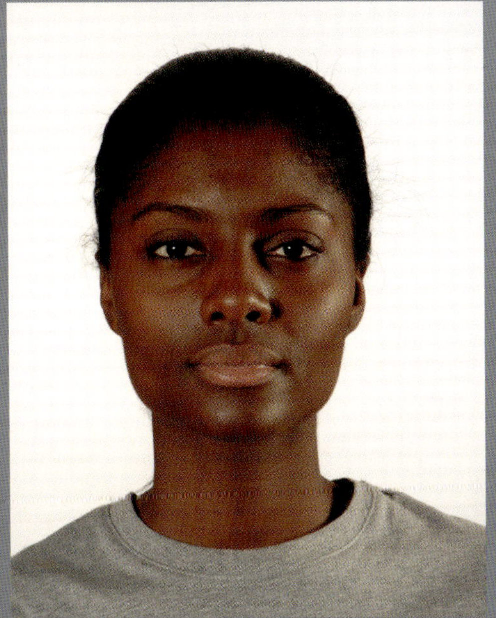

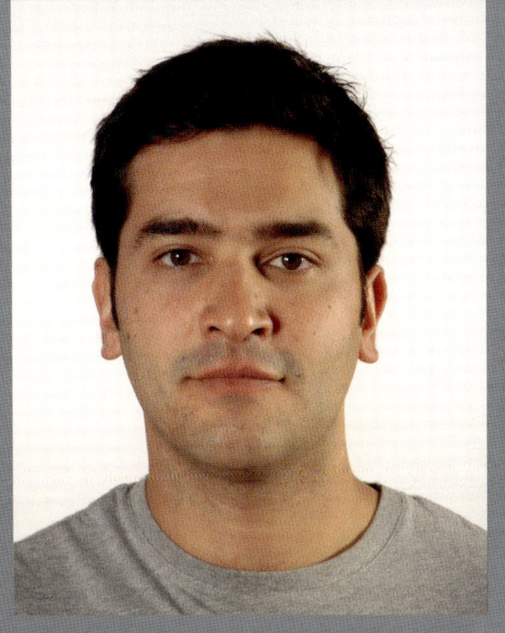

DARK BACKGROUND

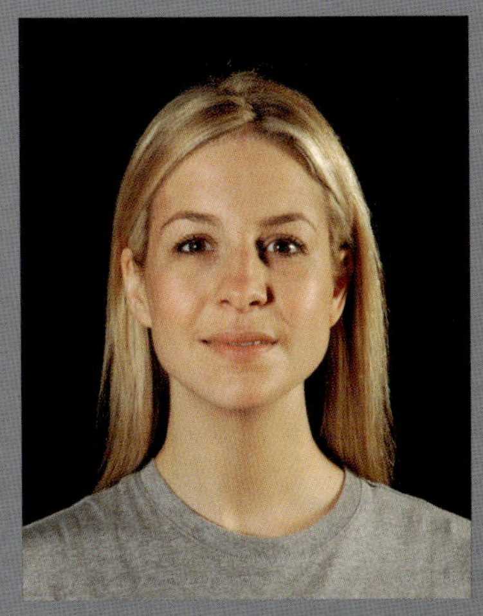

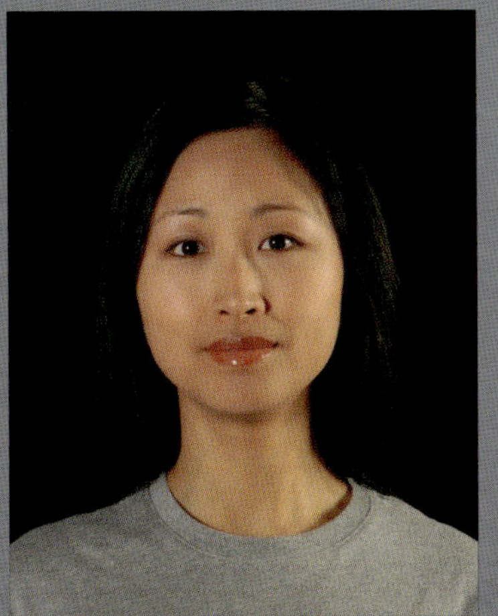

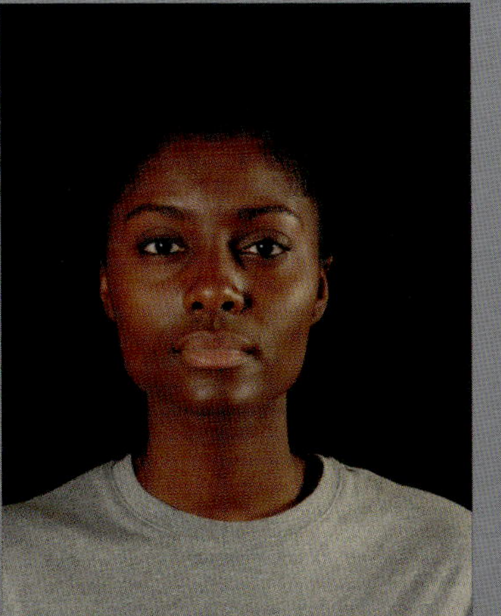

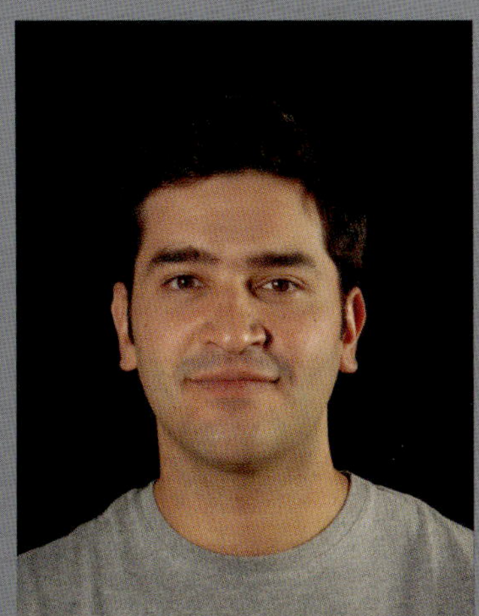

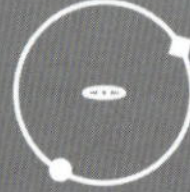

TWO LIGHTS

LIGHT 1: FROM 30° LEFT, EYE LEVEL

LIGHT 2: FROM 120° RIGHT, EYE LEVEL

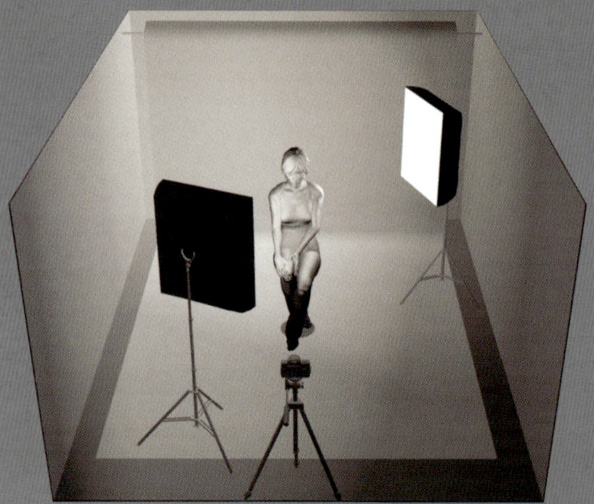

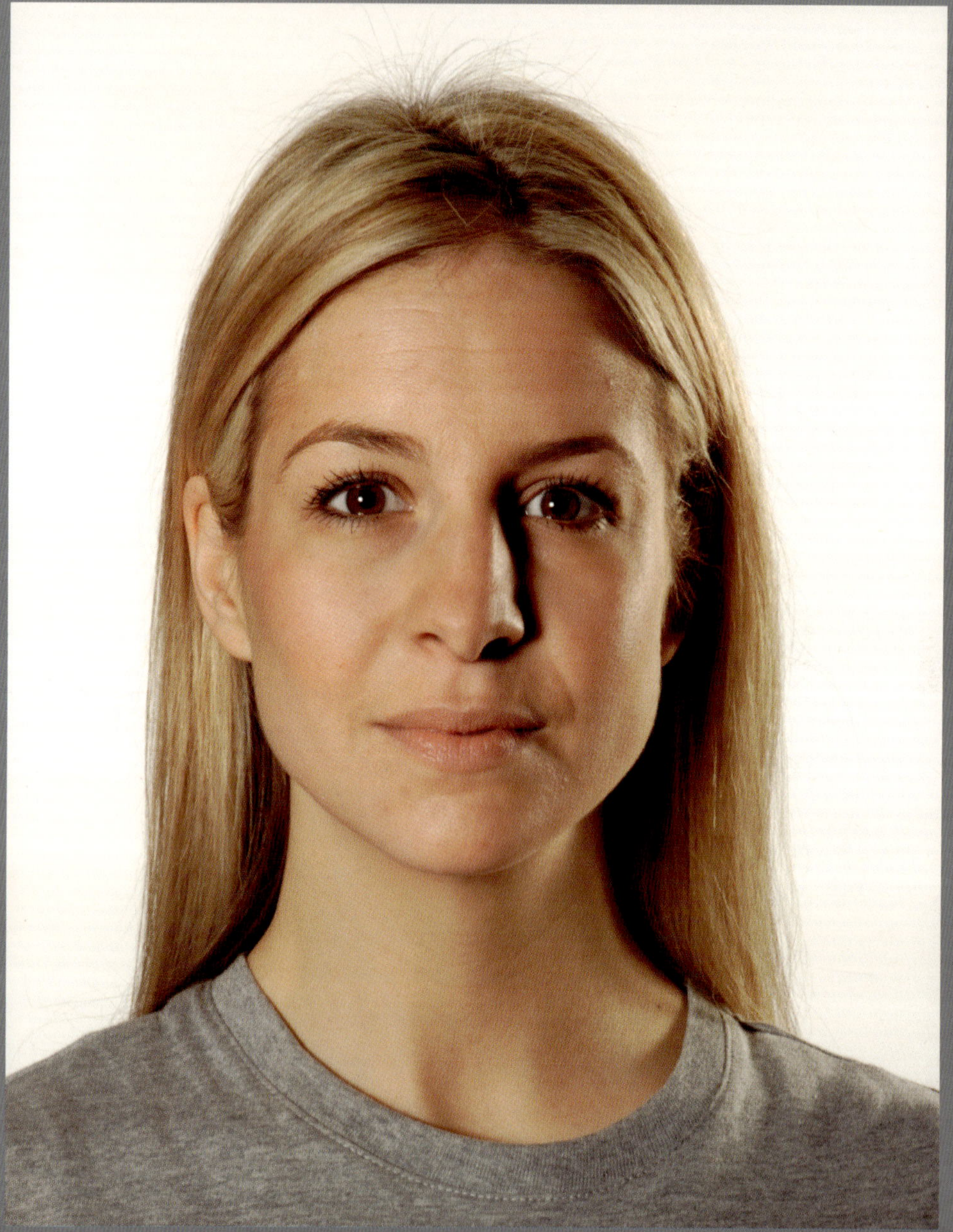

A light close to the camera axis provides the main lighting for the subject, with a second light—positioned slightly behind the model and on the opposite side—creating the backlighting that is necessary to help a dark-haired subject stand out from a dark background.

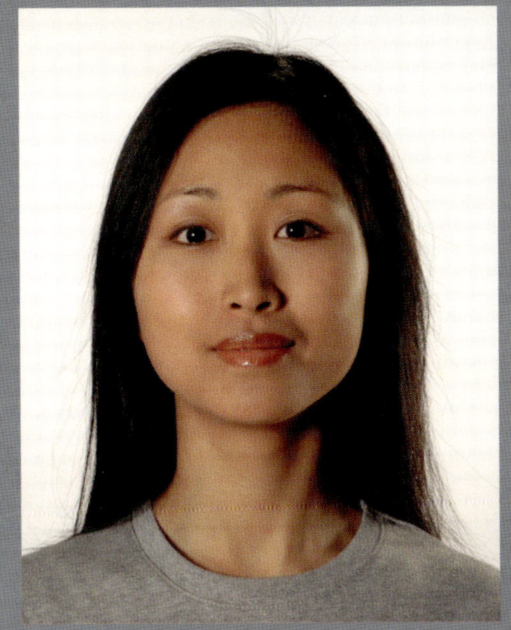
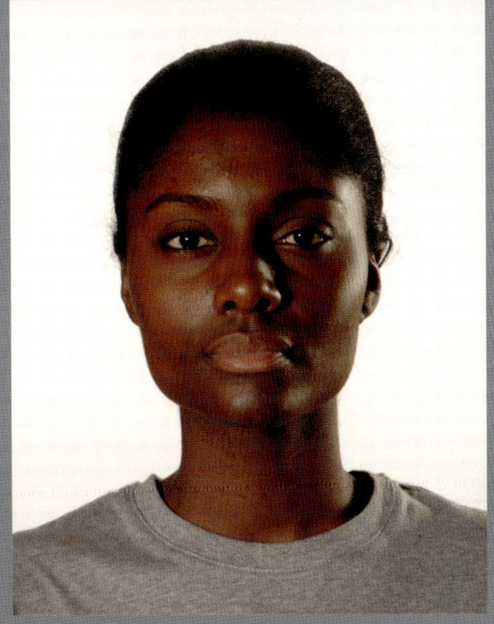
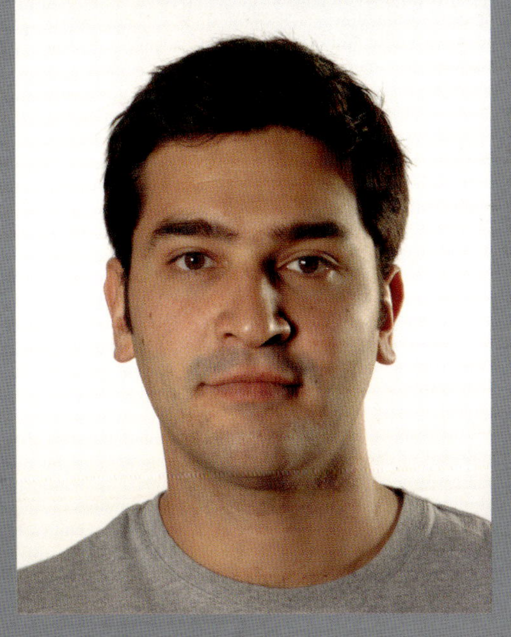

DARK BACKGROUND

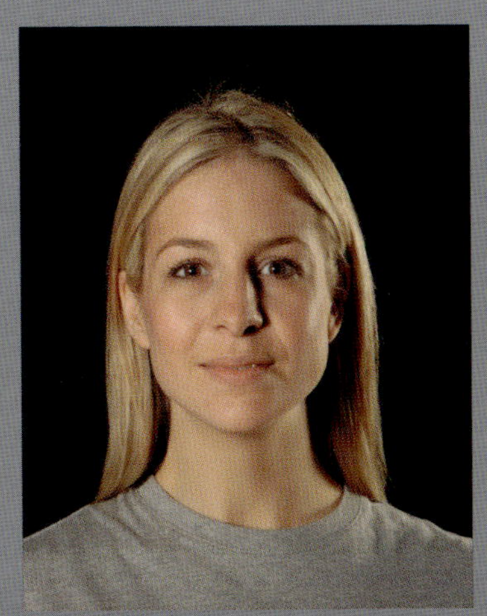
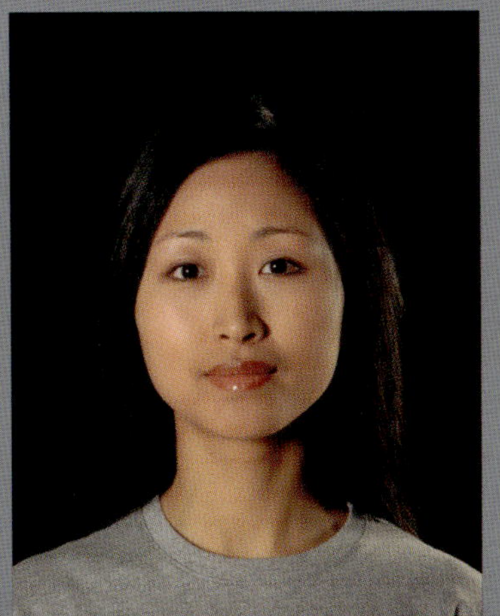
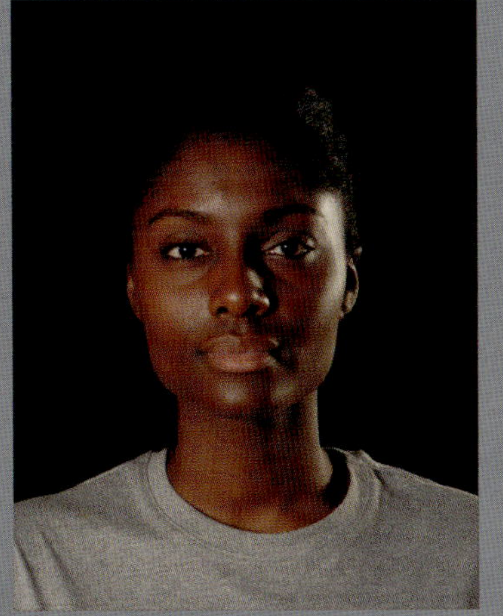
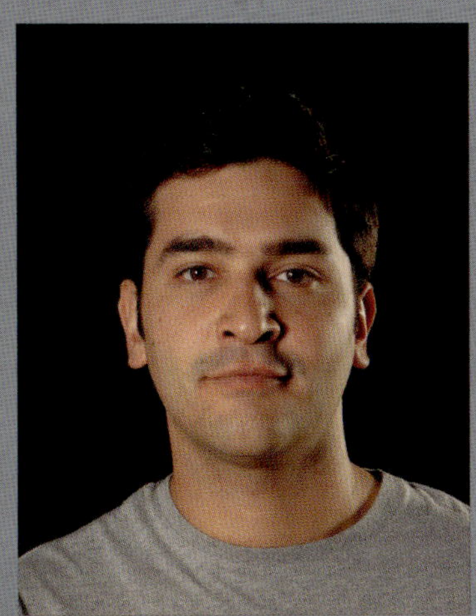

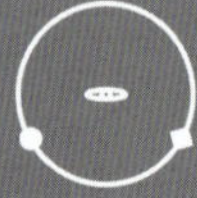

TWO LIGHTS

LIGHT 1: FROM 60° LEFT, EYE LEVEL

LIGHT 2: FROM 60° RIGHT, EYE LEVEL

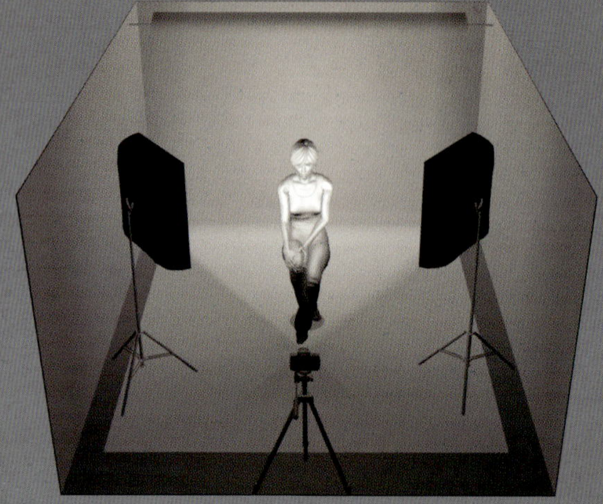

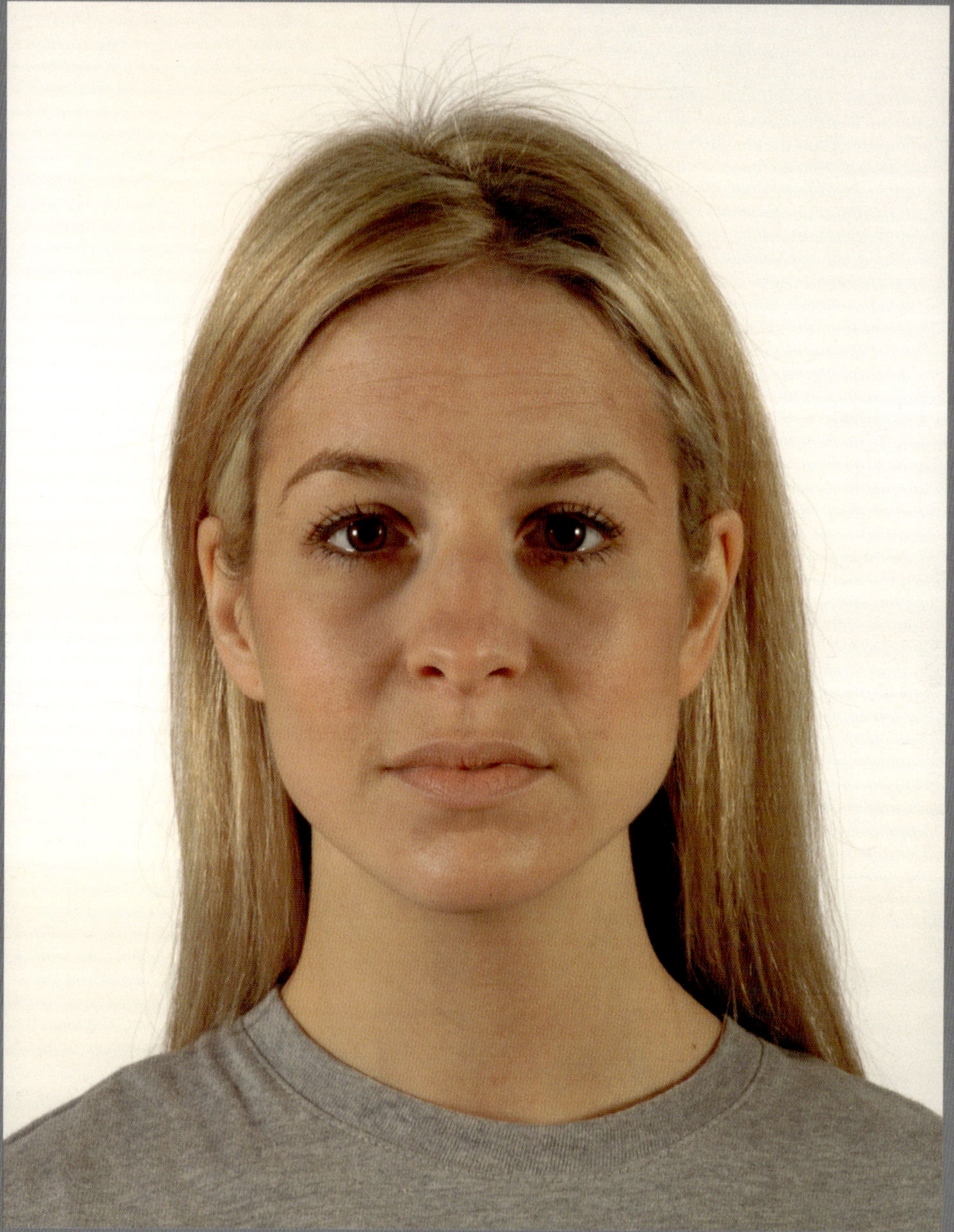

Here, a pair of lights are aimed at the subject from an identical angle, either side of the camera. At an angle of 60 degrees, they are lighting the subject from the side, more than they are from the front, creating matching shadows on either side of the face for a symmetrically balanced portrait.

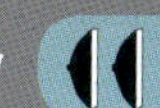

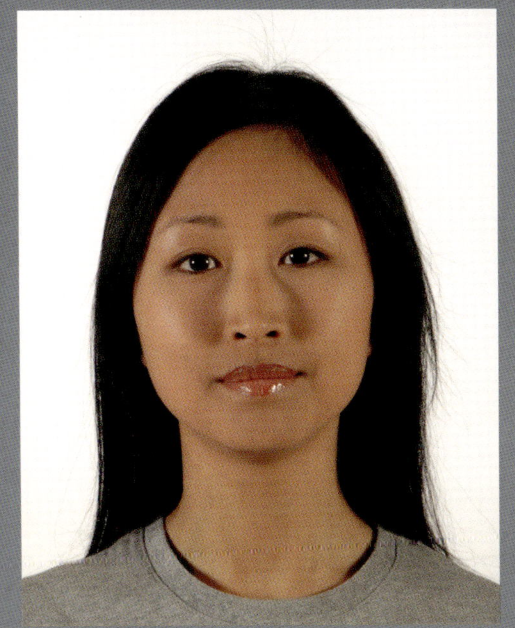

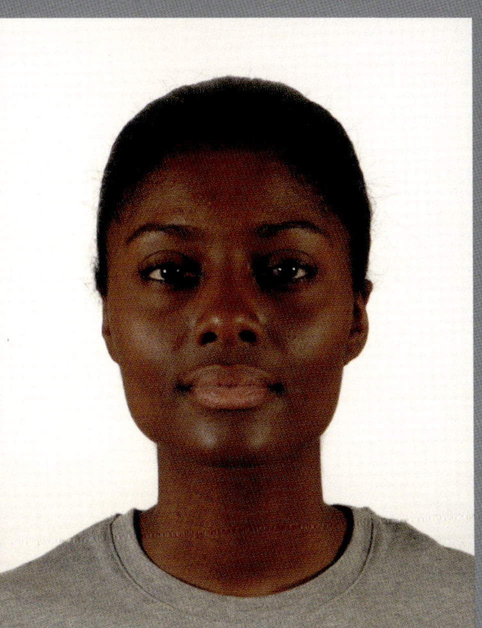

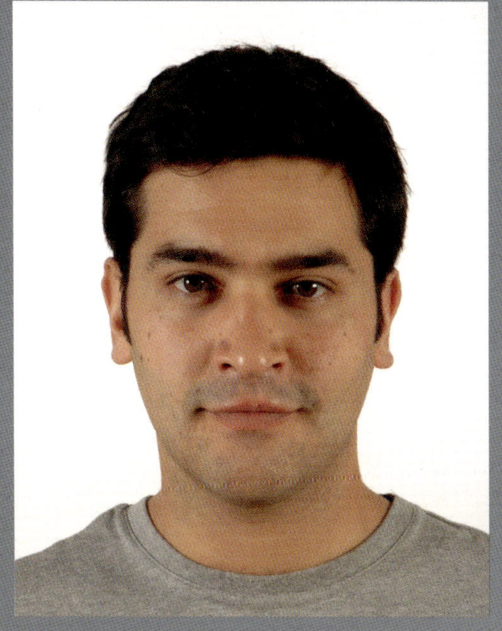

DARK BACKGROUND

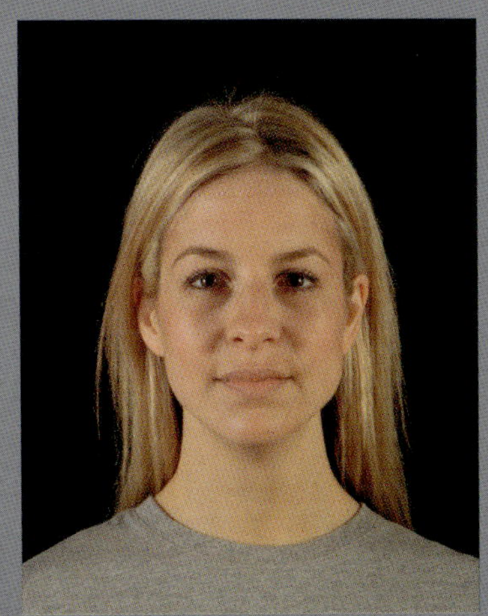

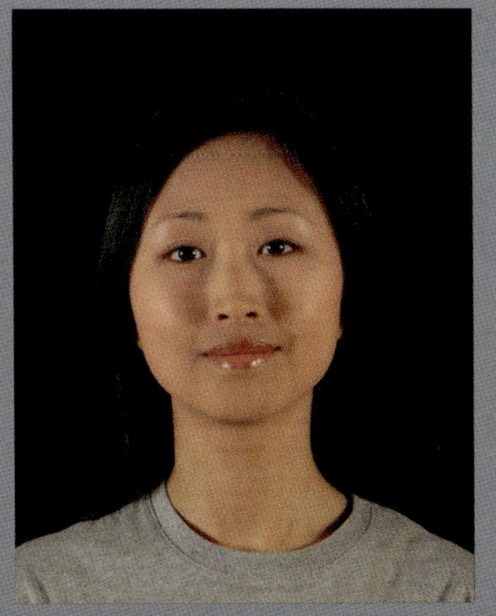

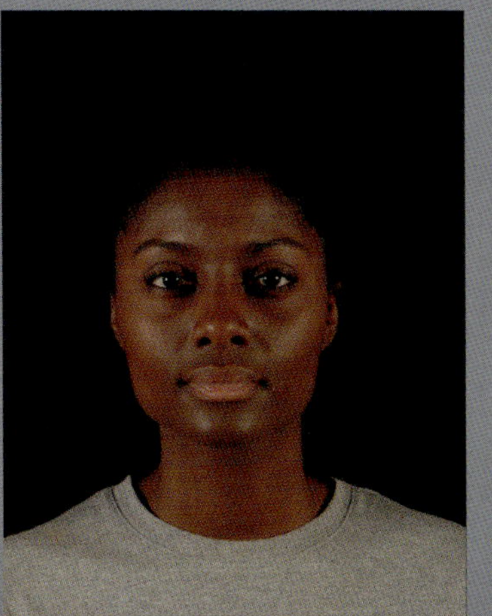

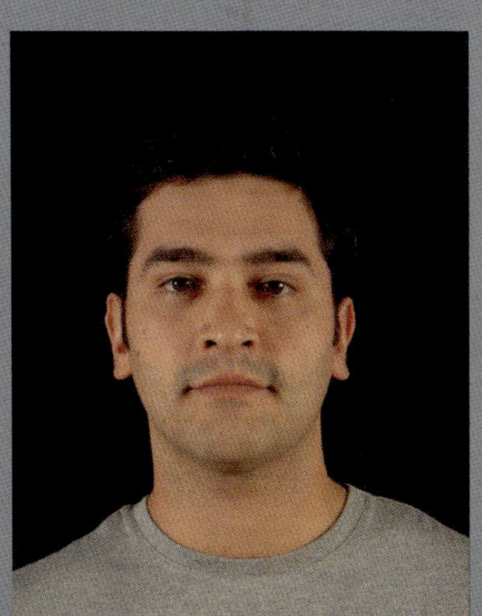

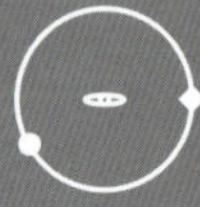

TWO LIGHTS

LIGHT 1: FROM 60° LEFT, EYE LEVEL

LIGHT 2: FROM 90° RIGHT, EYE LEVEL

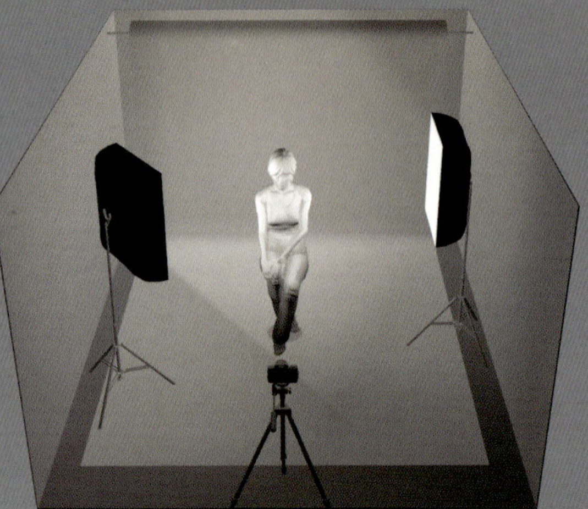

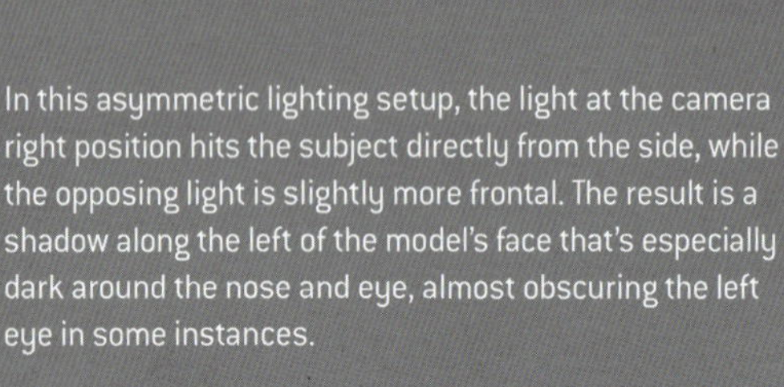

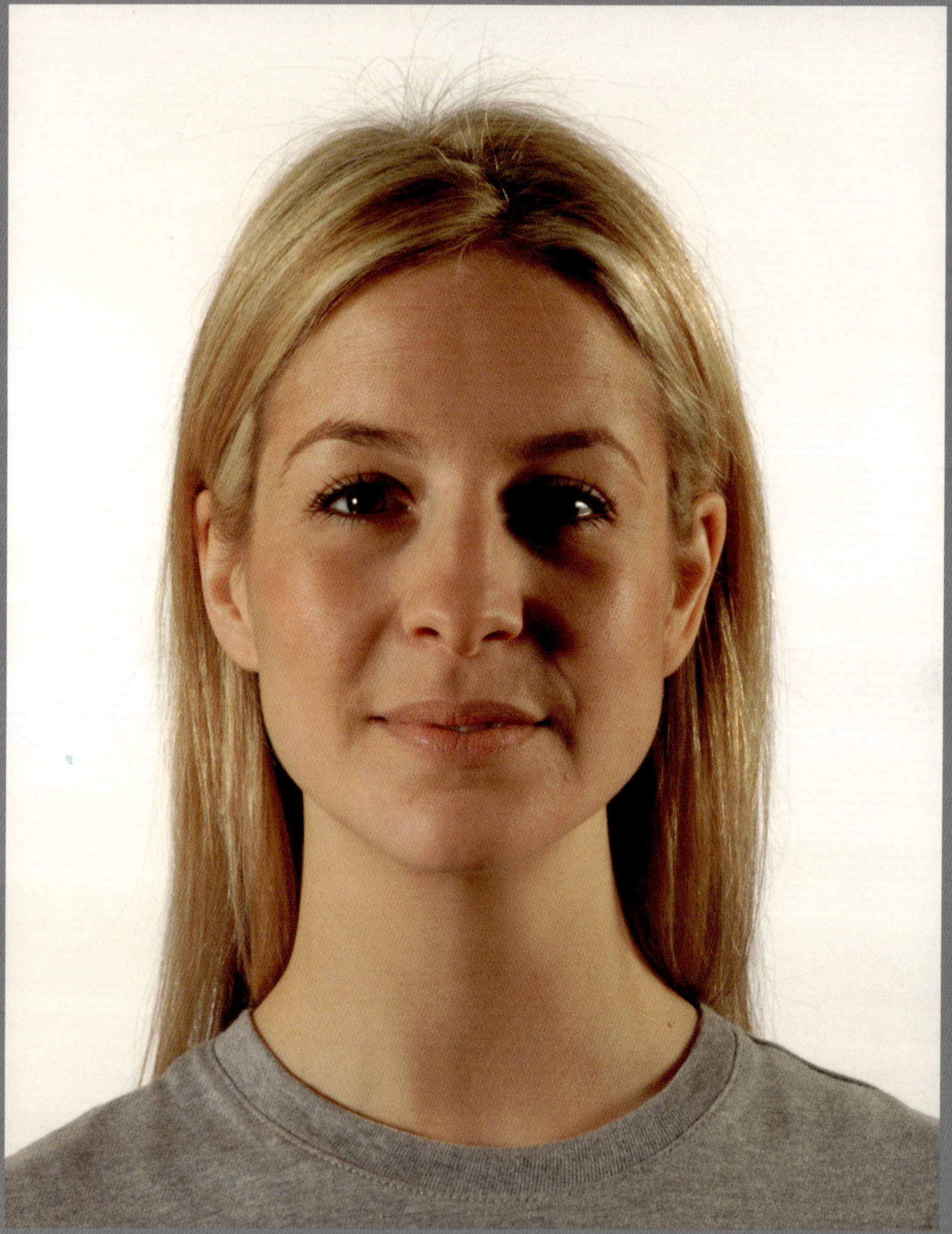

In this asymmetric lighting setup, the light at the camera right position hits the subject directly from the side, while the opposing light is slightly more frontal. The result is a shadow along the left of the model's face that's especially dark around the nose and eye, almost obscuring the left eye in some instances.

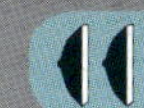

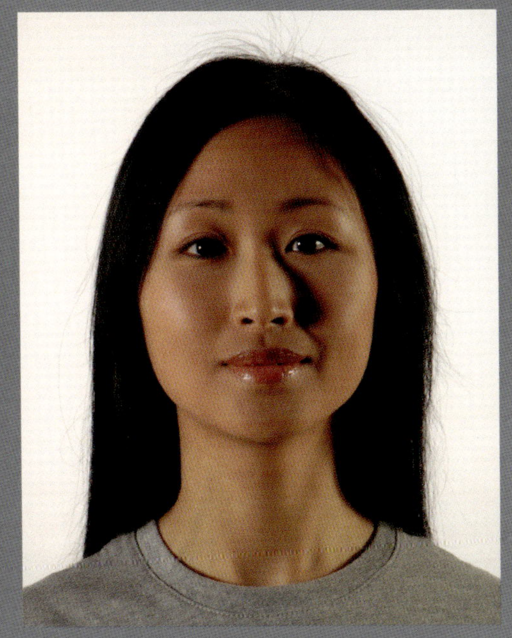

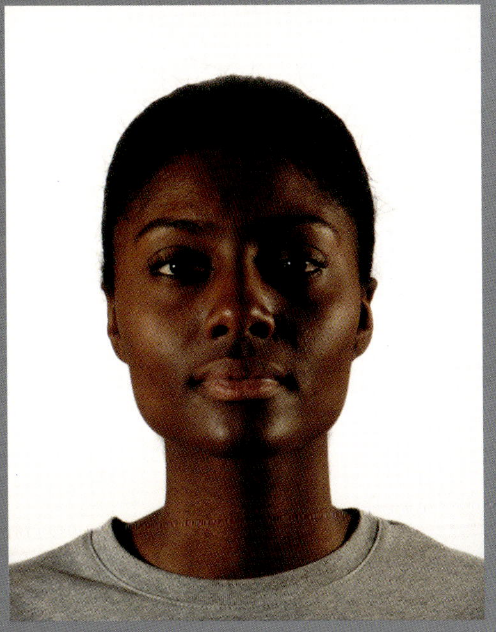

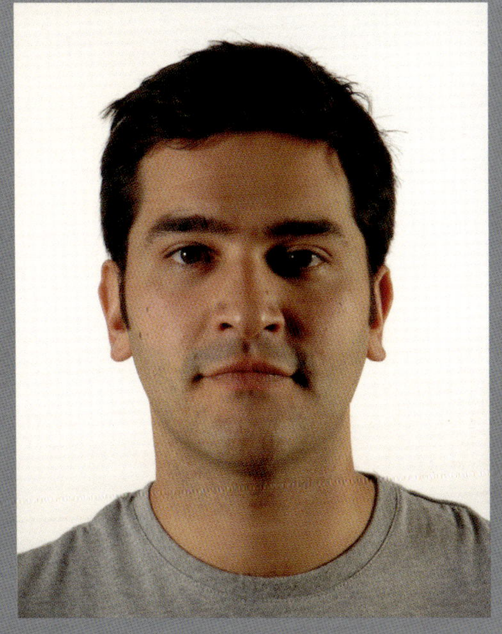

DARK BACKGROUND

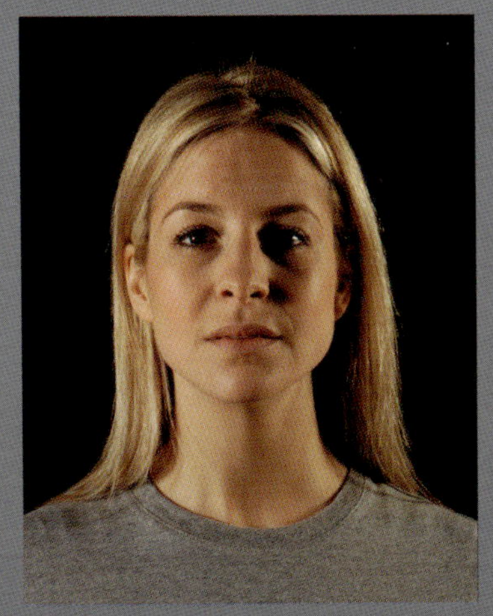

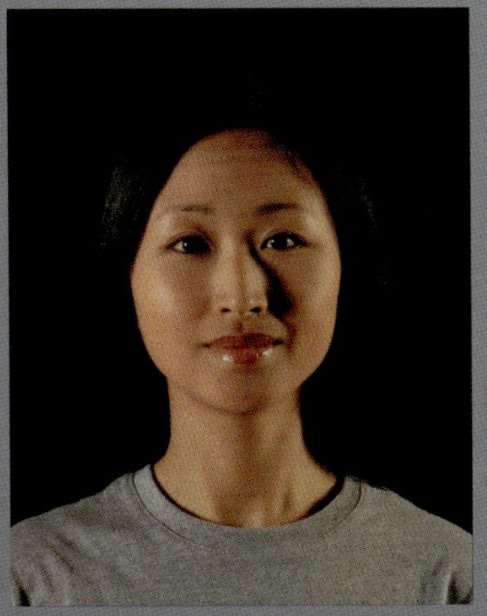

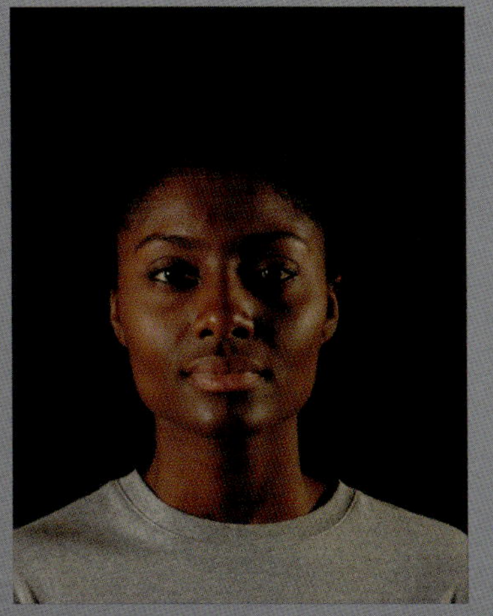

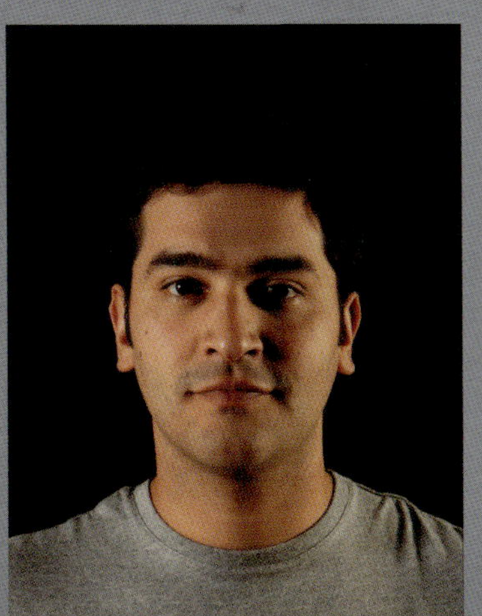

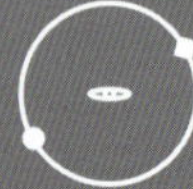

TWO LIGHTS

LIGHT 1: FROM 60° LEFT, EYE LEVEL

LIGHT 2: FROM 120° RIGHT, EYE LEVEL

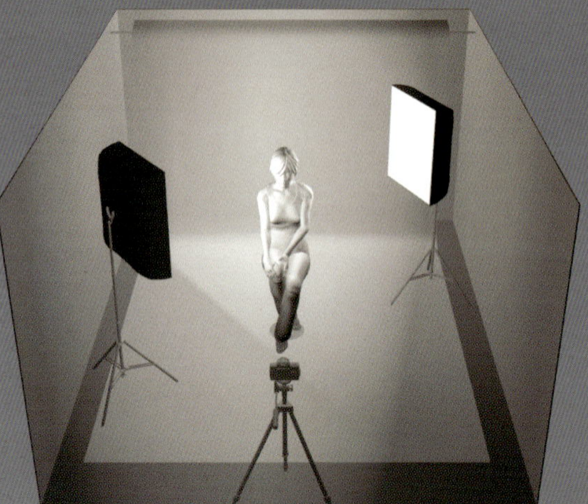

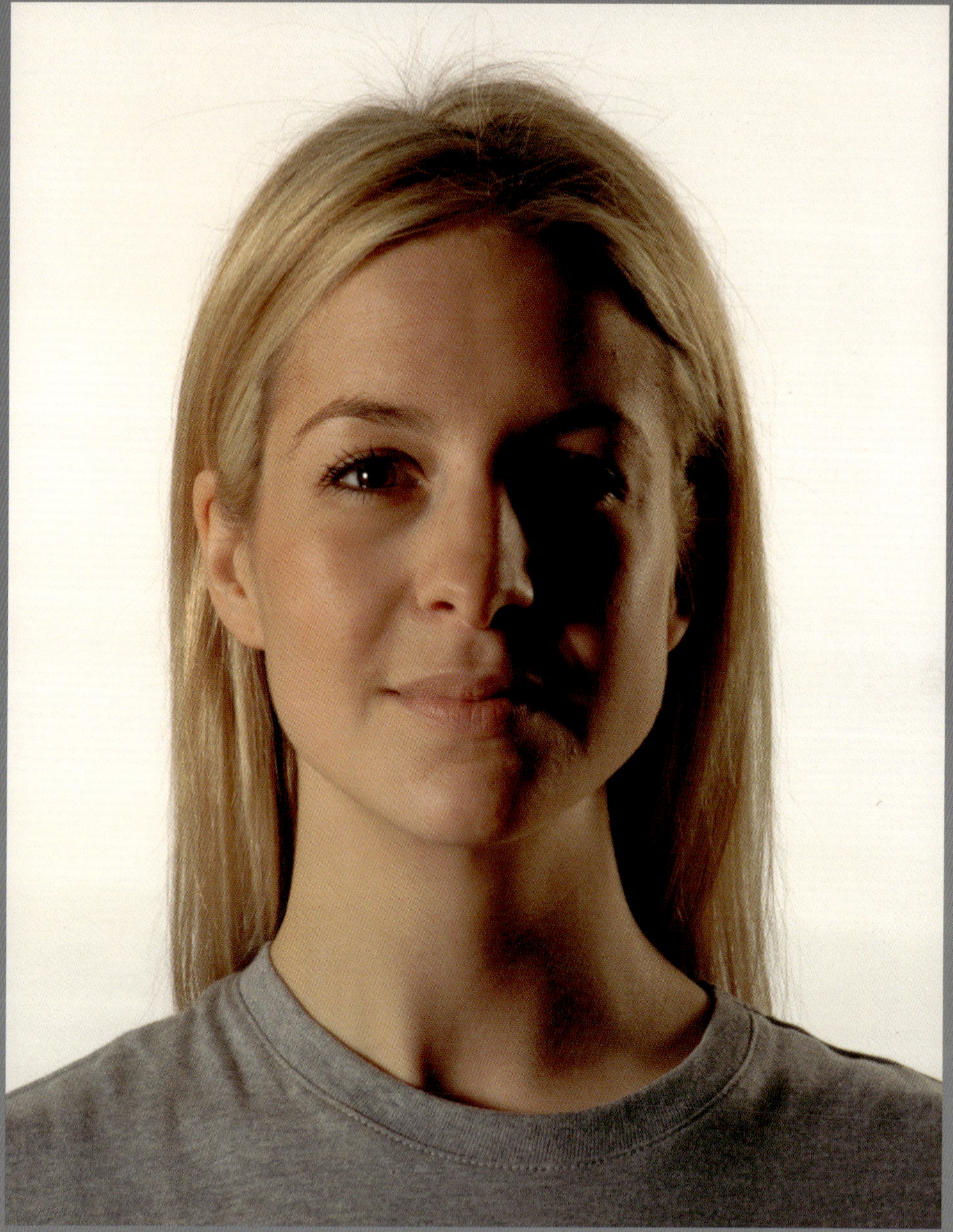

A variation on the previous setup, the light at the camera right position has been moved behind the subject. While the right side of the model's face remains softly lit, the left side of the face is now much higher in contrast—the shadows are darker and the eye is easily concealed as a result.

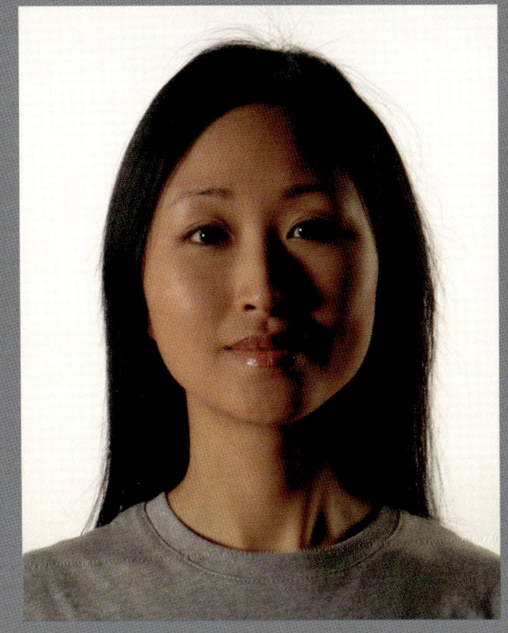
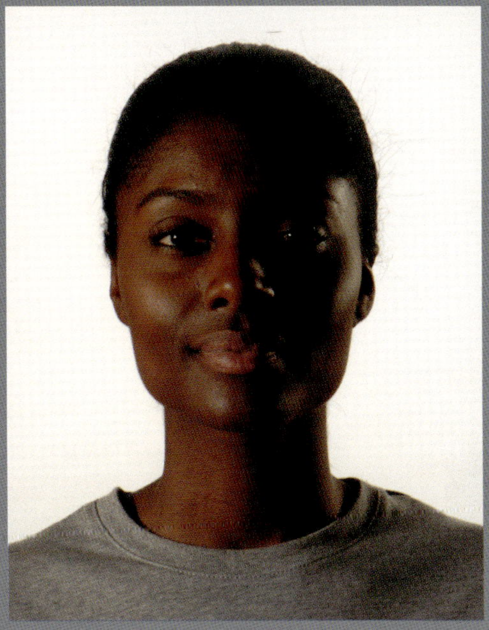
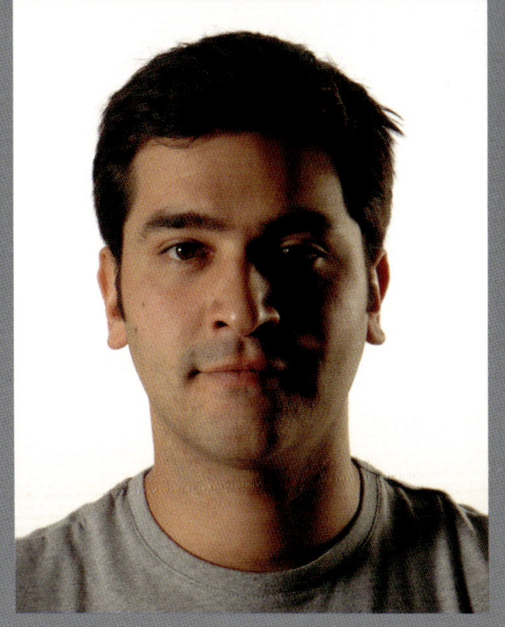

DARK BACKGROUND

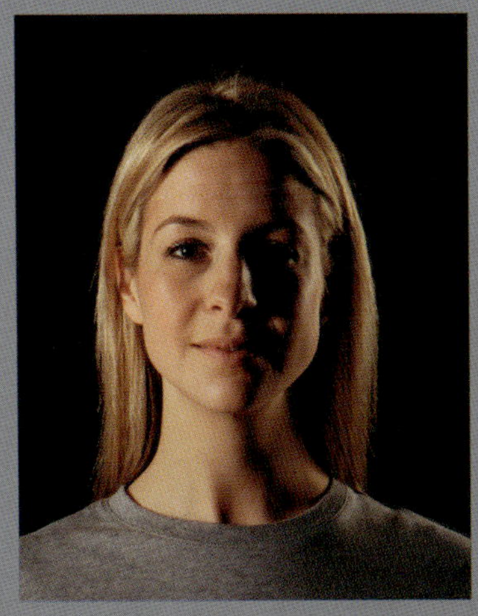
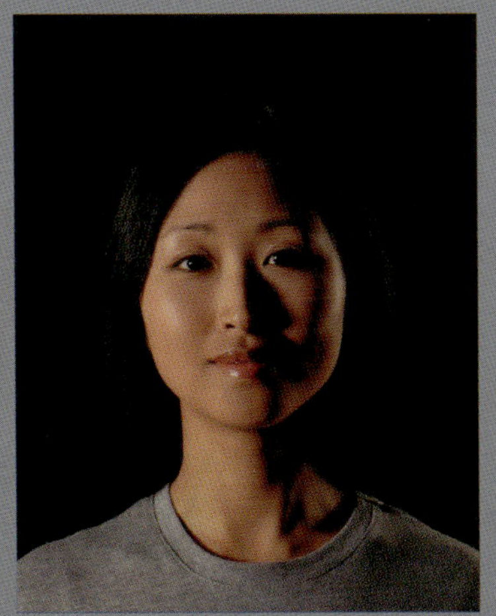
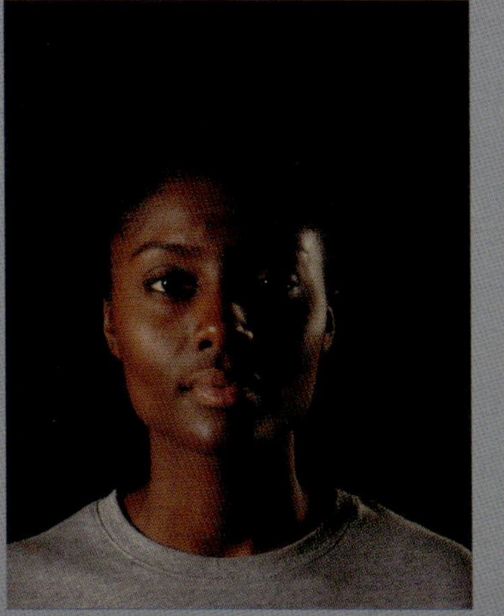
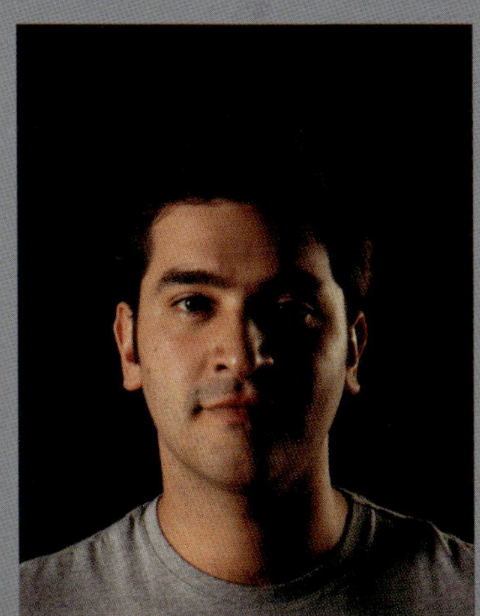

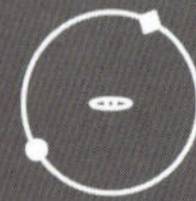

TWO LIGHTS

LIGHT 1: FROM 60° LEFT, EYE LEVEL

LIGHT 2: FROM 150° RIGHT, EYE LEVEL

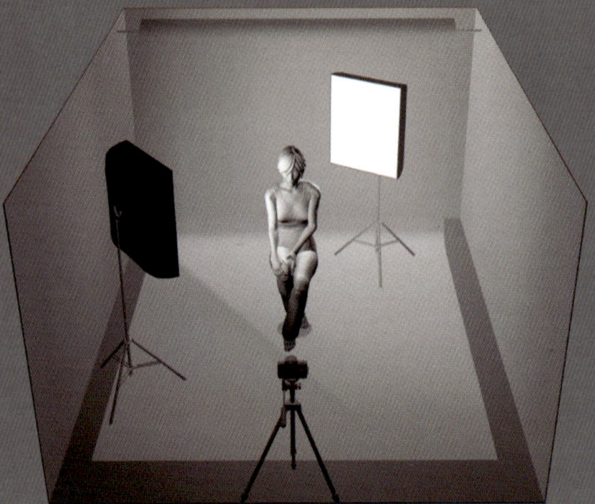

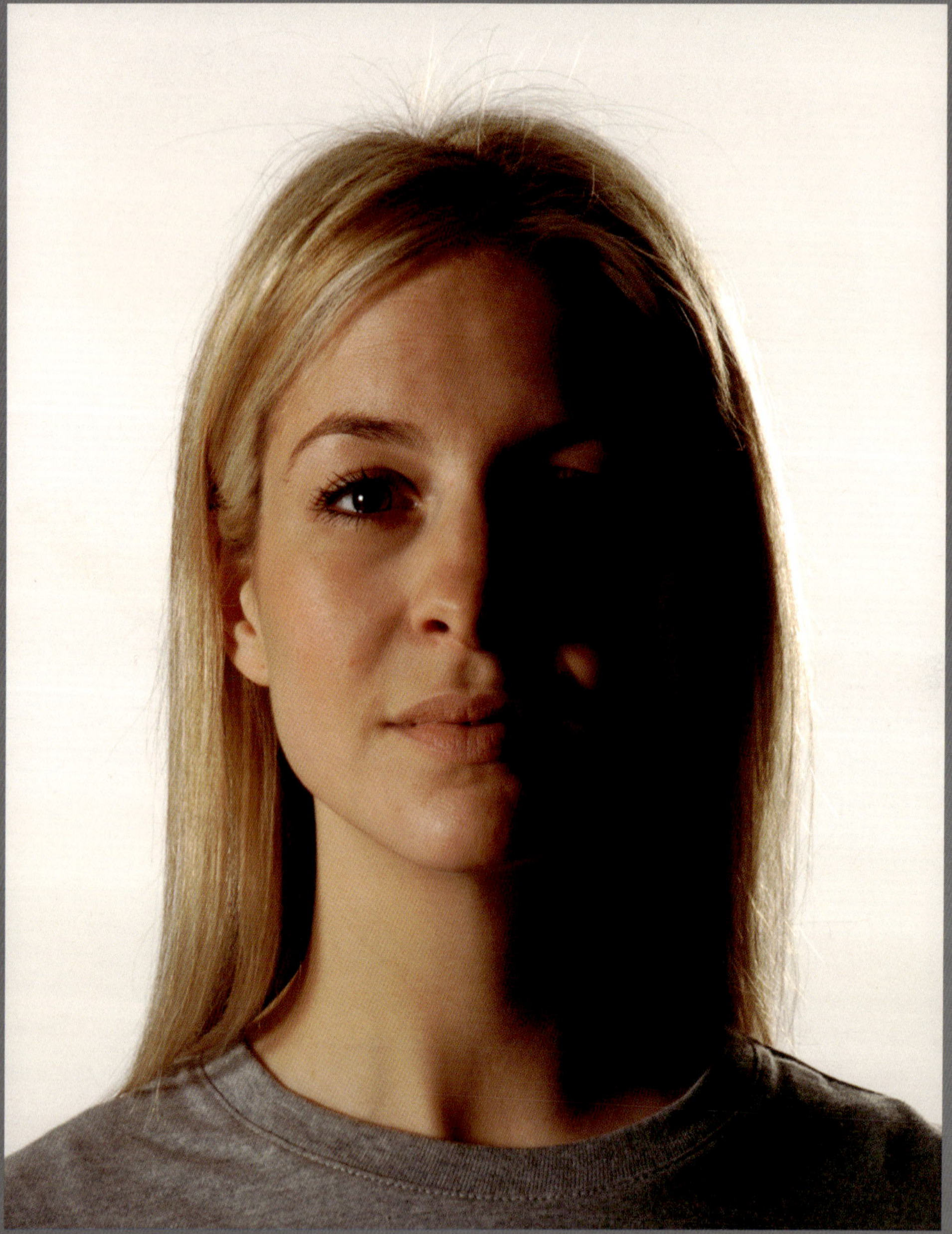

As the second light is moved further behind the subject, the left side of the model's face is in almost total shadow. At the same time, though, the backlighting effect is more powerful, creating a strong highlight around the hair that makes the subject stand out against a dark background.

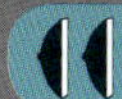

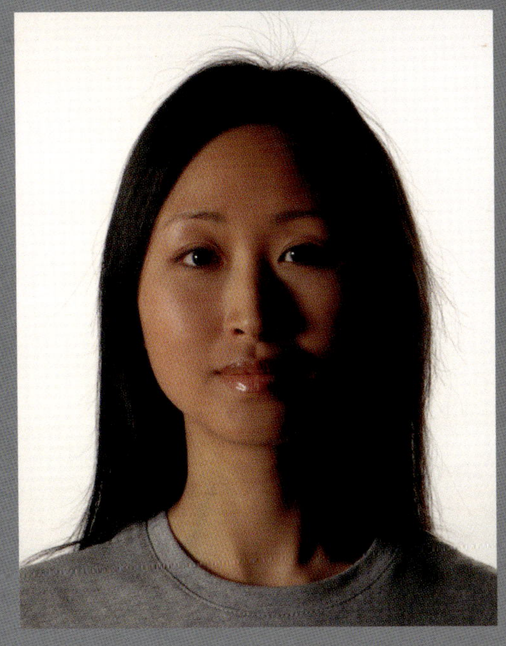

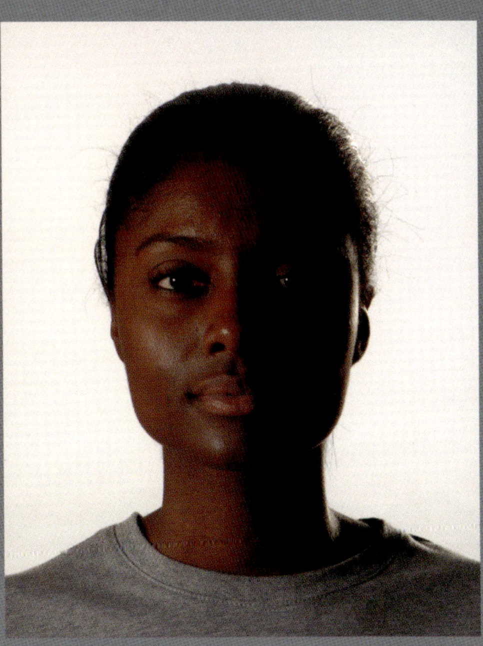

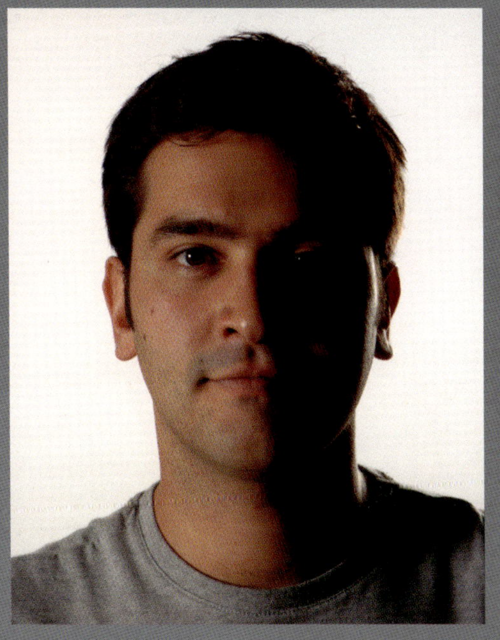

DARK BACKGROUND

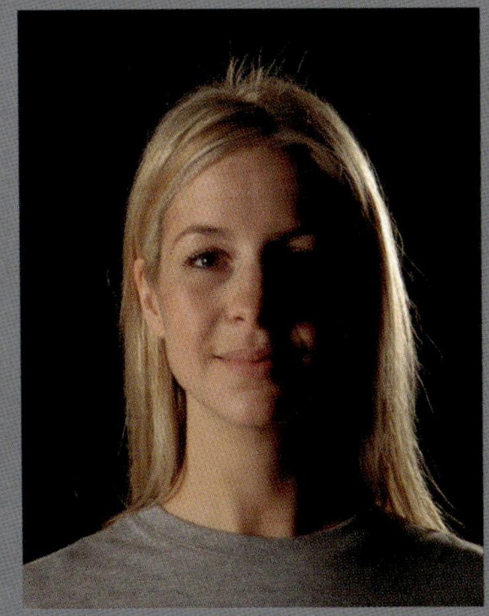

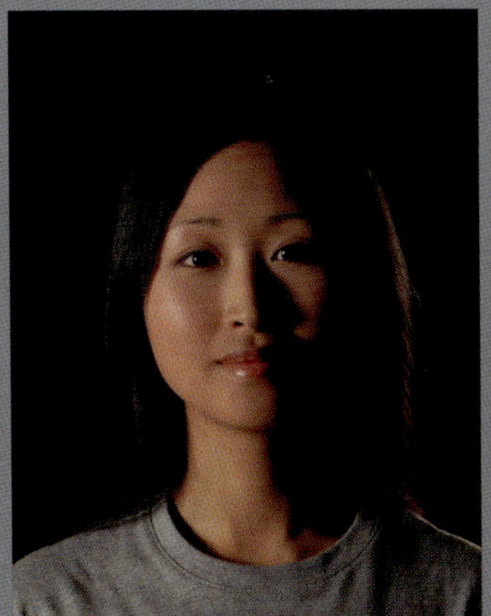

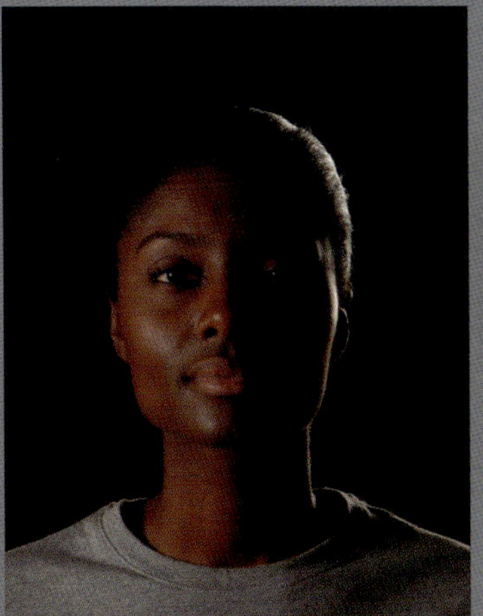

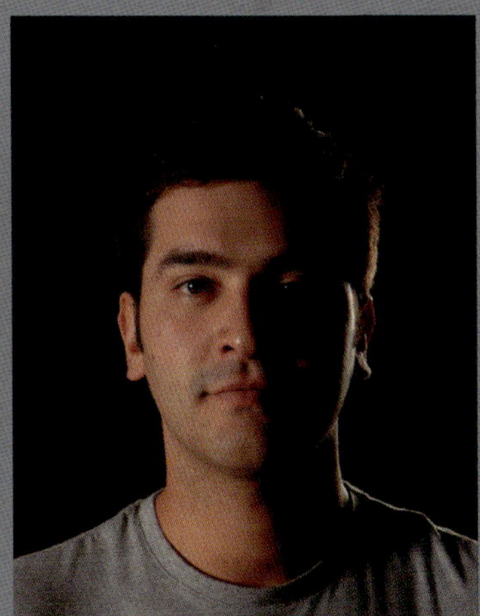

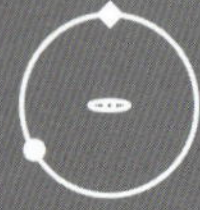

TWO LIGHTS

LIGHT 1: FROM 60° LEFT, EYE LEVEL

LIGHT 2: FROM 180° RIGHT, EYE LEVEL

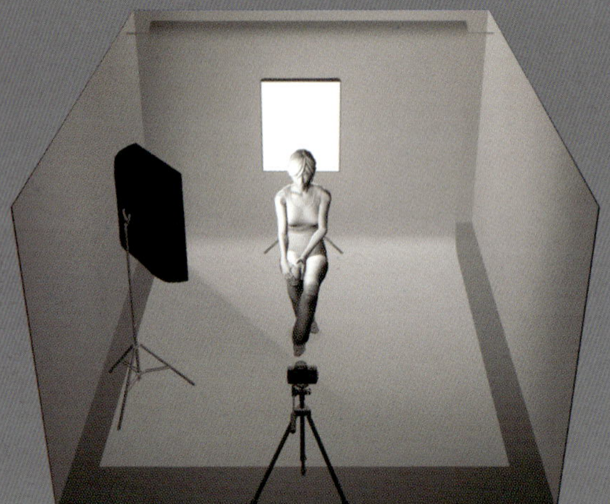

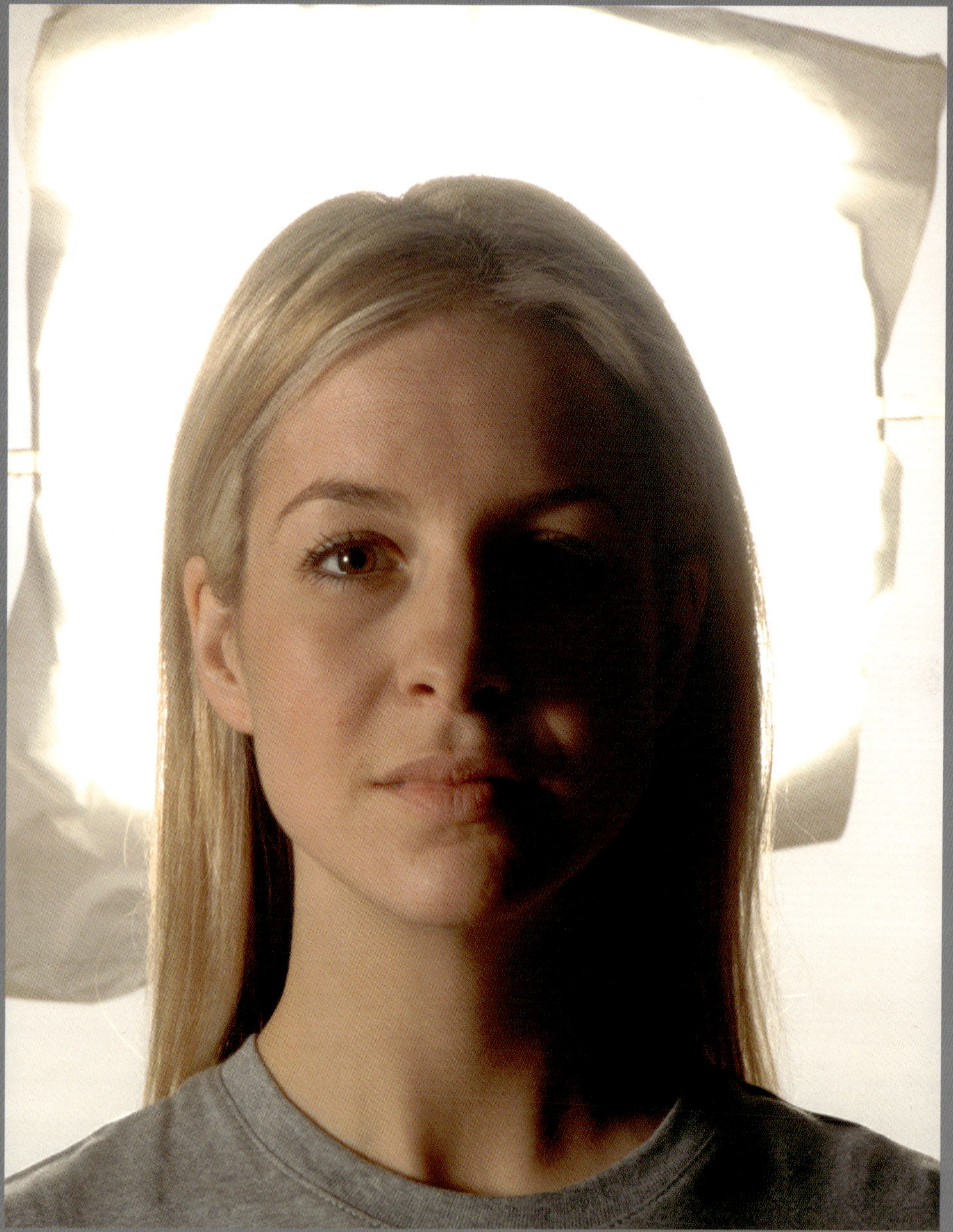

Positioning a light behind your subject—in this case aimed directly toward the camera—will almost certainly lower the contrast of the shot as the light hits the lens. However, if you direct a second light at the subject from the side, you can complement the diffuse backlight with a hard side light.

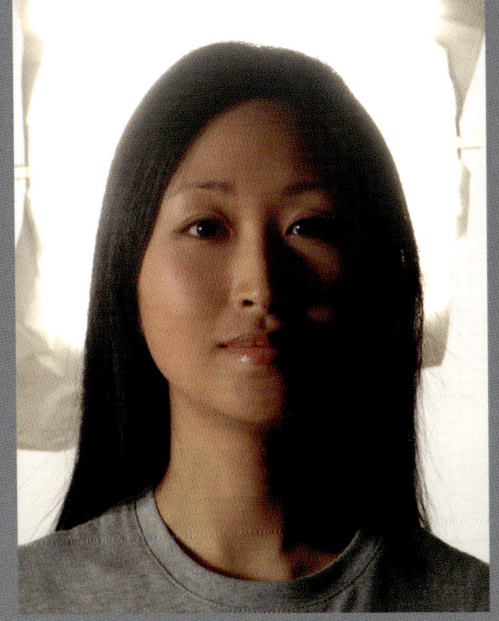
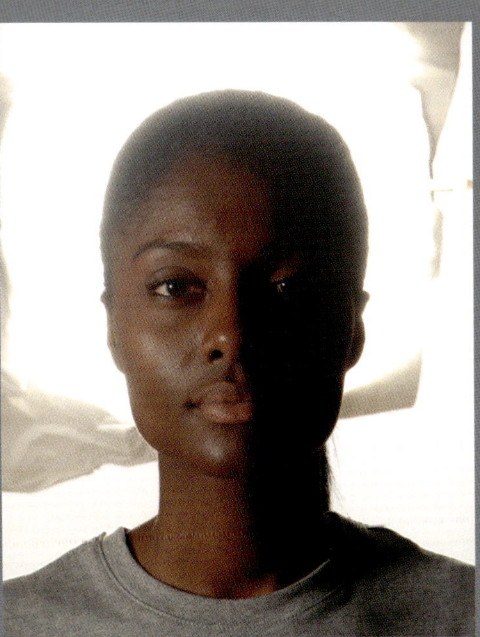
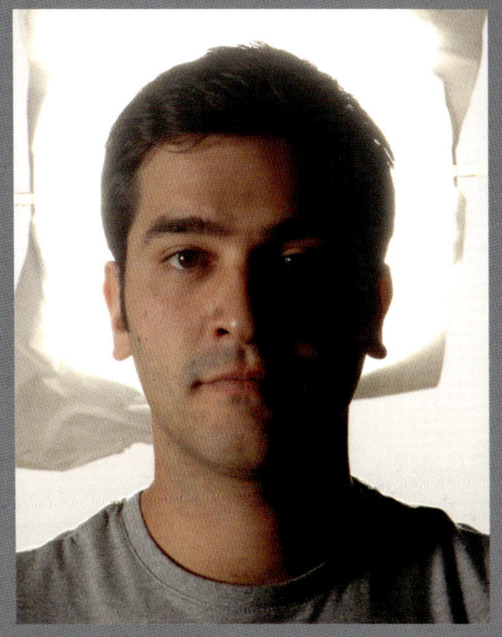

DARK BACKGROUND

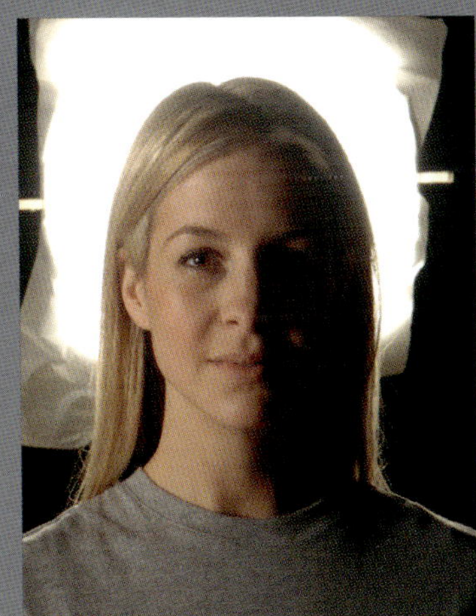
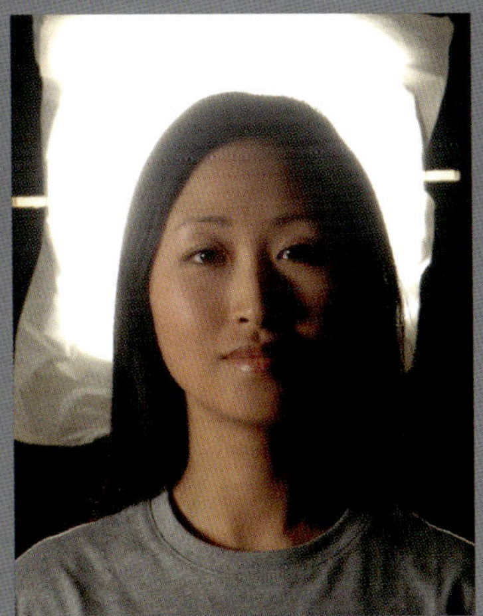
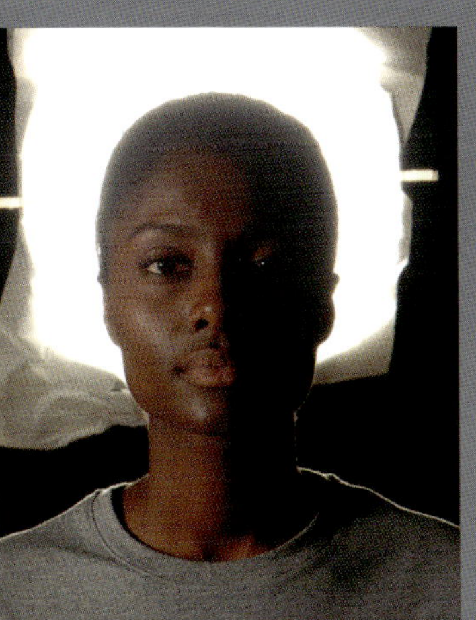
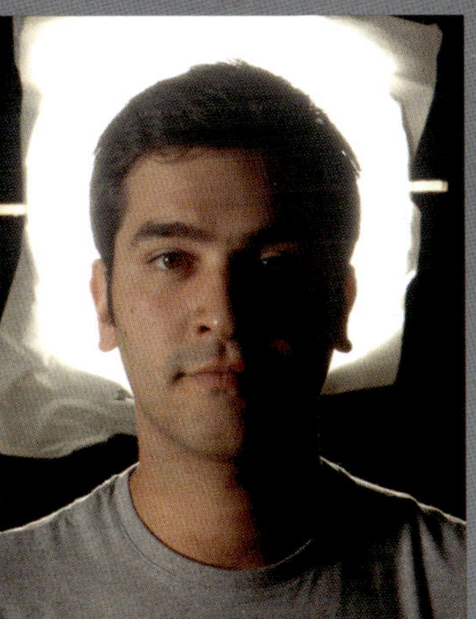

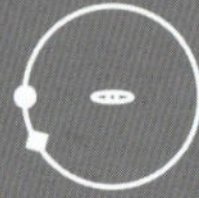

TWO LIGHTS

LIGHT 1: FROM 90° LEFT, EYE LEVEL

LIGHT 2: FROM 60° LEFT, EYE LEVEL

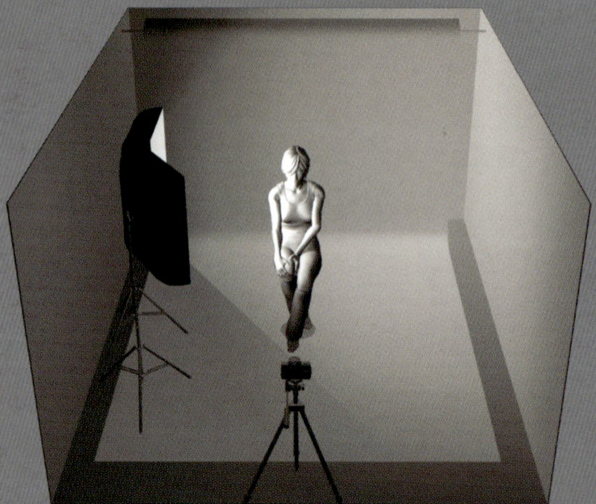

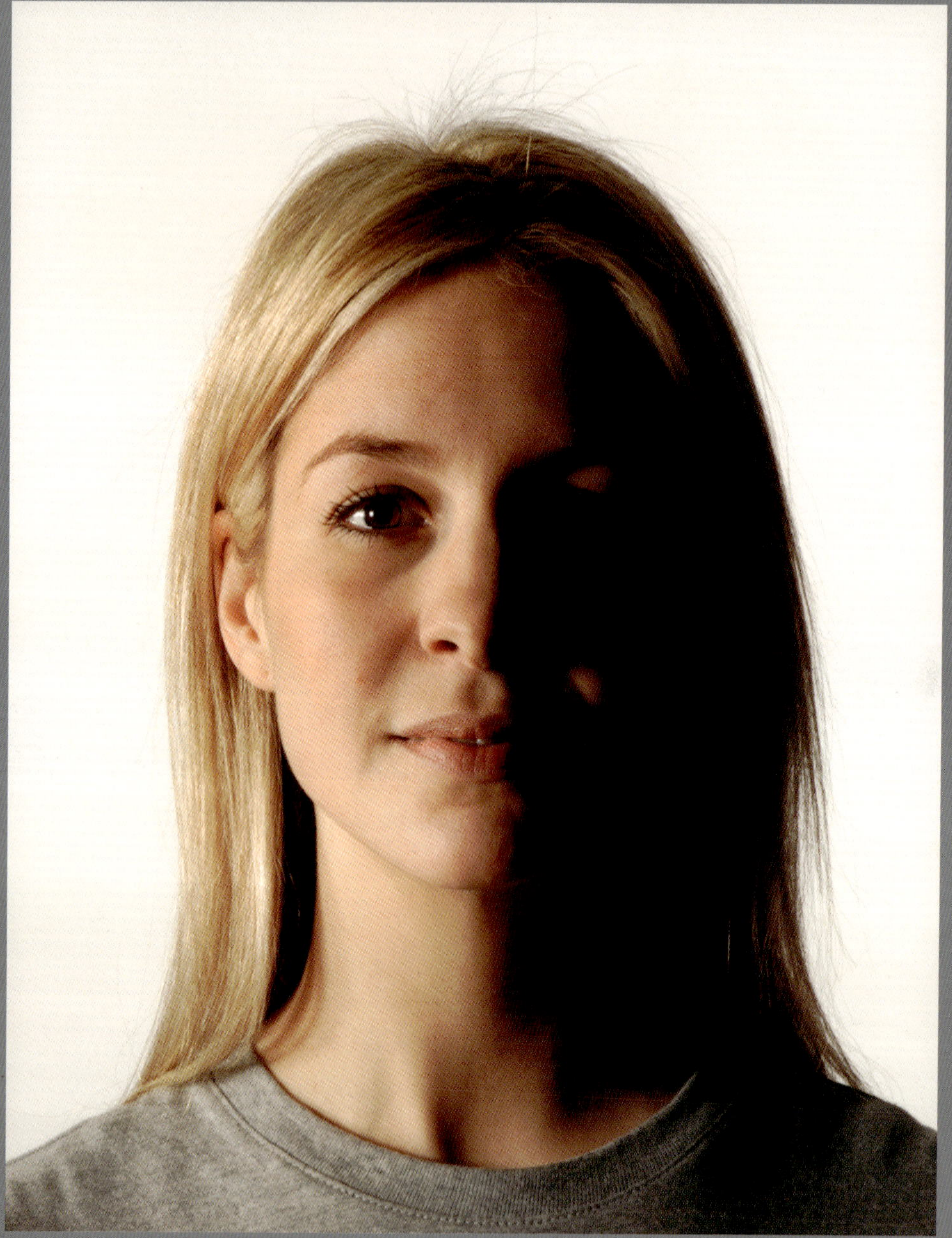

A single light at 90-degrees to the subject would throw one side of the model's face into deep shadow, but introducing a second light from a slightly more frontal position—perhaps at a reduced power setting—will help fill in the shadows and draw out a little extra detail.

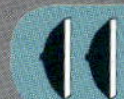

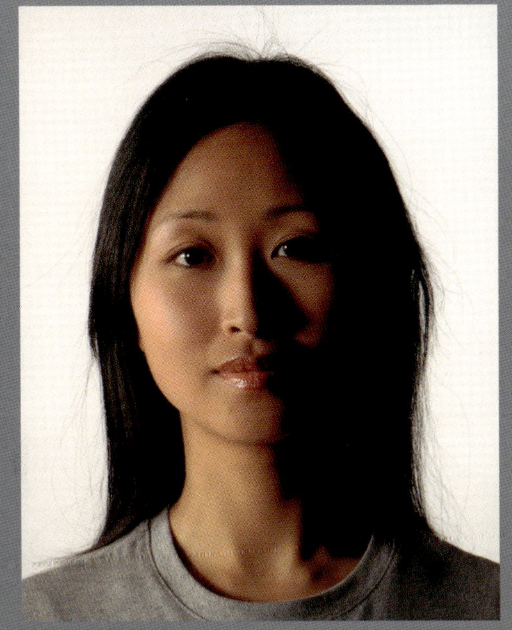

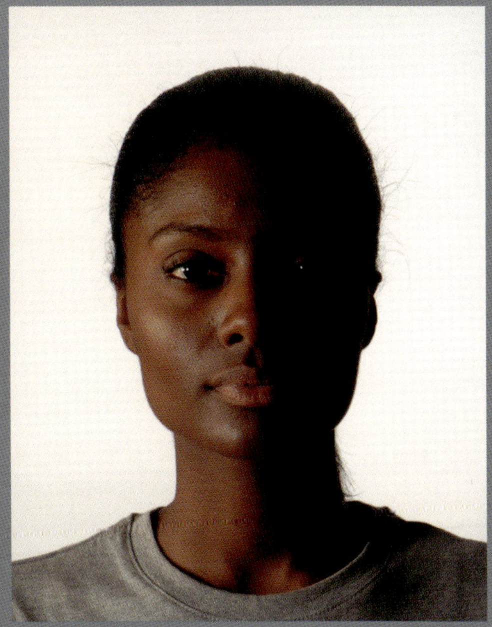

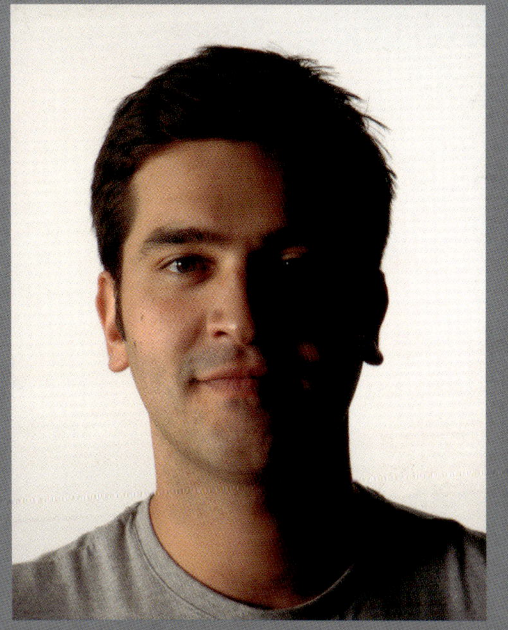

DARK BACKGROUND

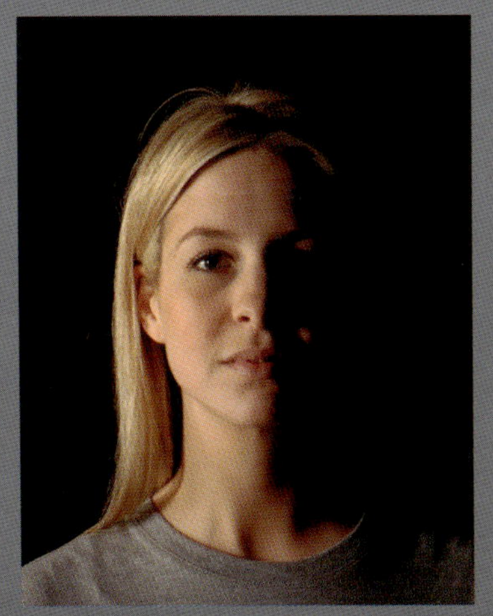

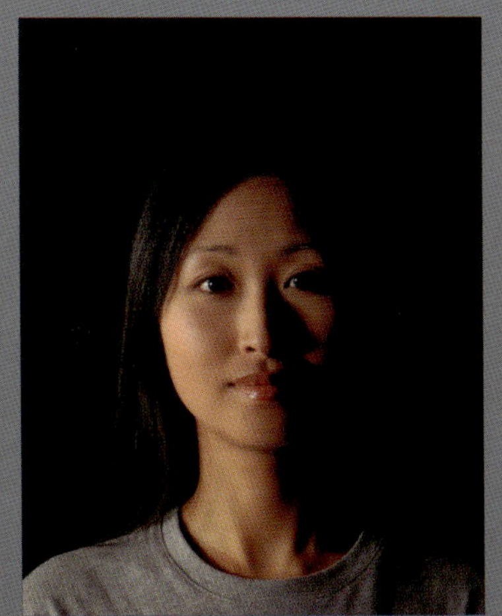

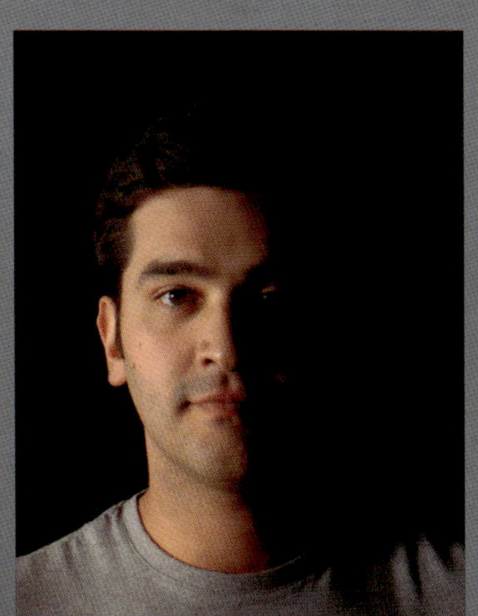

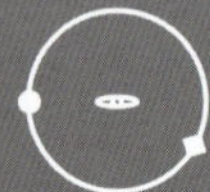

TWO LIGHTS

LIGHT 1: FROM 90° LEFT, EYE LEVEL

LIGHT 2: FROM 60° RIGHT, EYE LEVEL

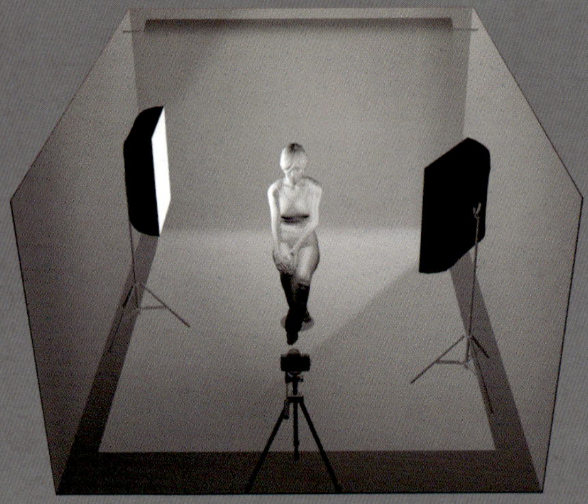

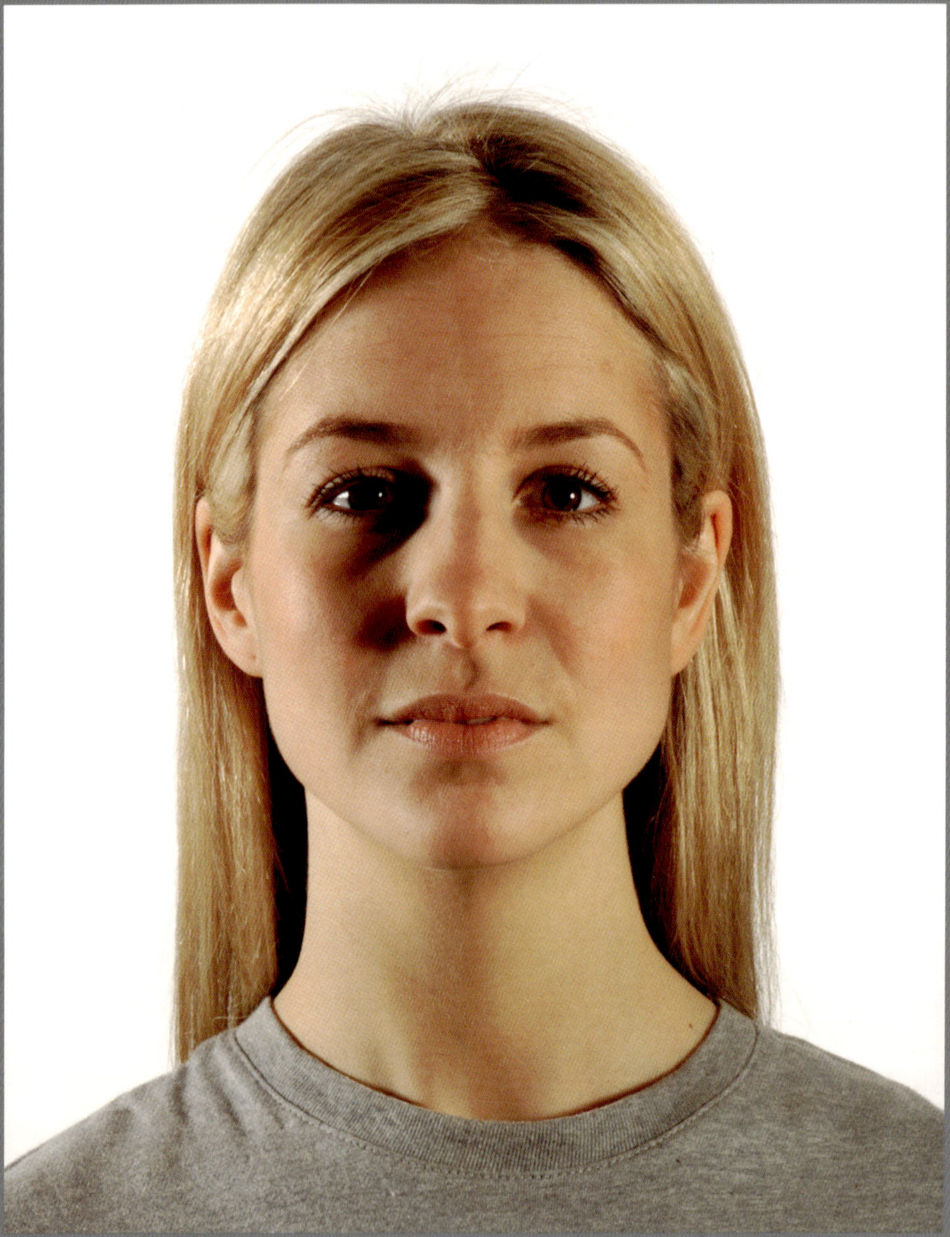

Keeping one light at a 90-degree angle to the camera, as in the previous setup, but moving the second light to the opposing side (at a 60-degree angle) gives a pleasing result: The whole of the subject can be seen, there are catchlights in both eyes, and even dark-haired subjects aren't lost against a dark background.

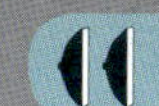

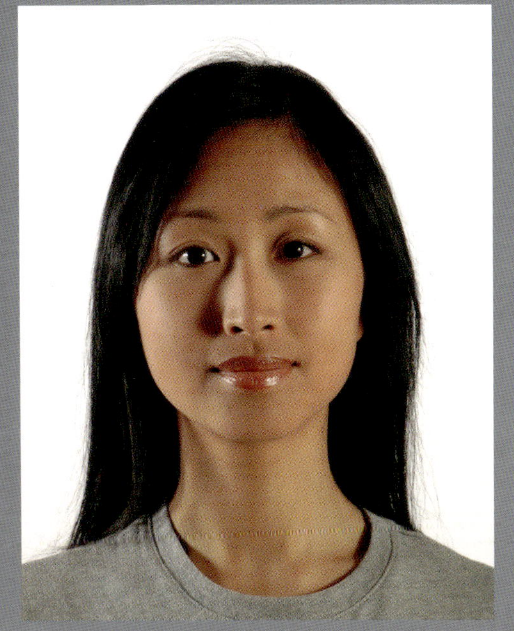

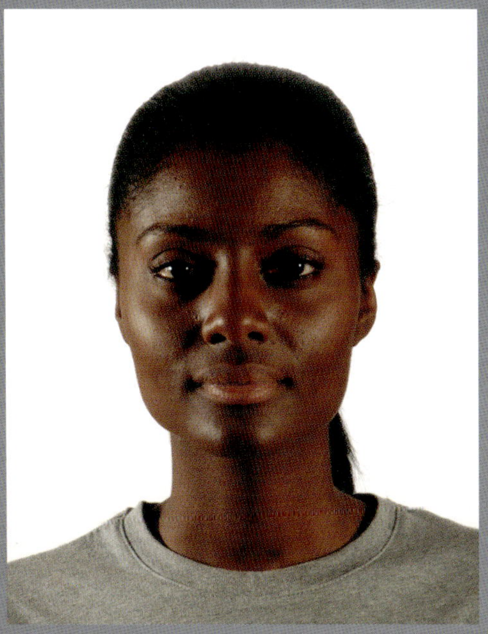

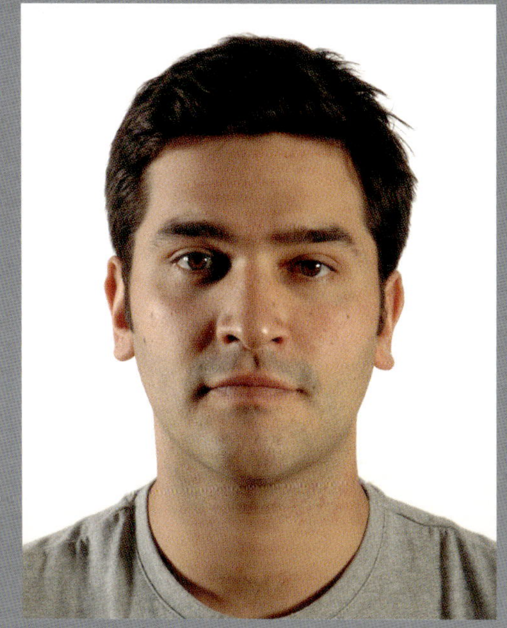

DARK BACKGROUND

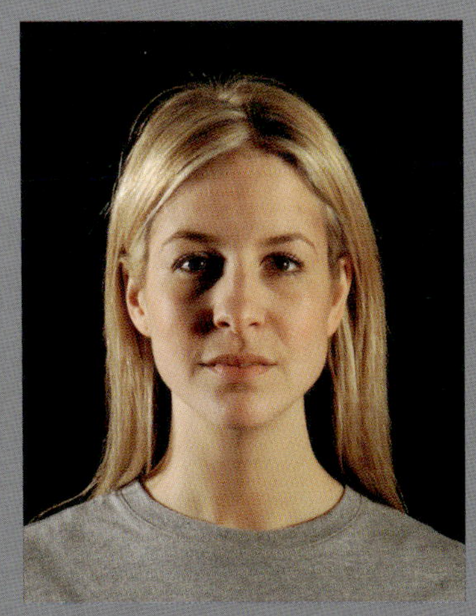

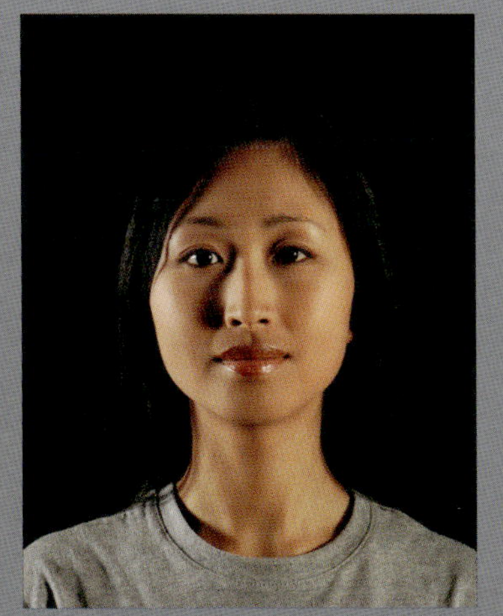

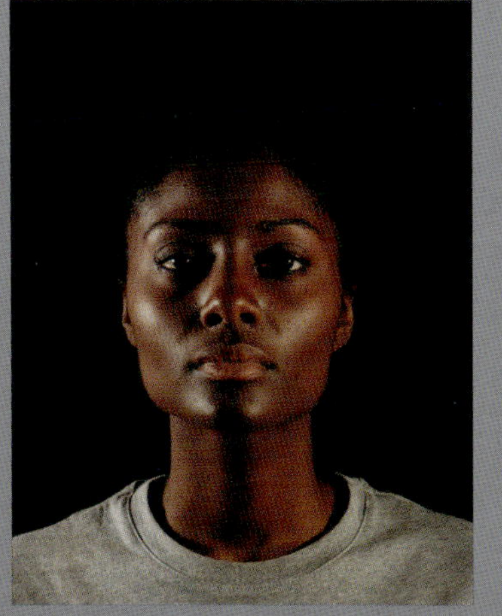

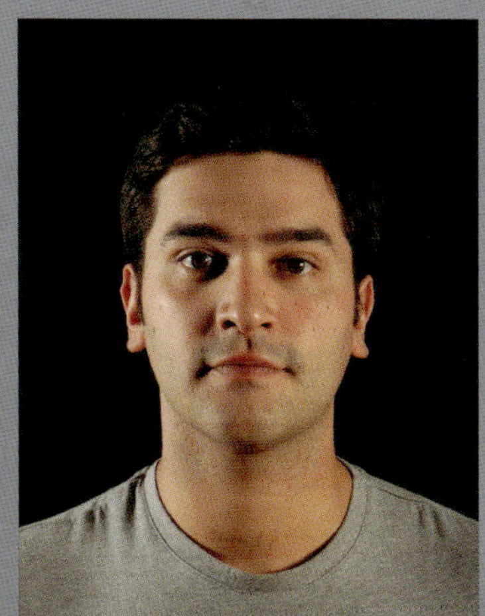

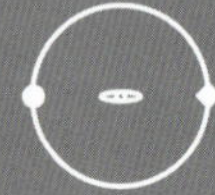

TWO LIGHTS

LIGHT 1: FROM 90° LEFT, EYE LEVEL

LIGHT 2: FROM 90° RIGHT, EYE LEVEL

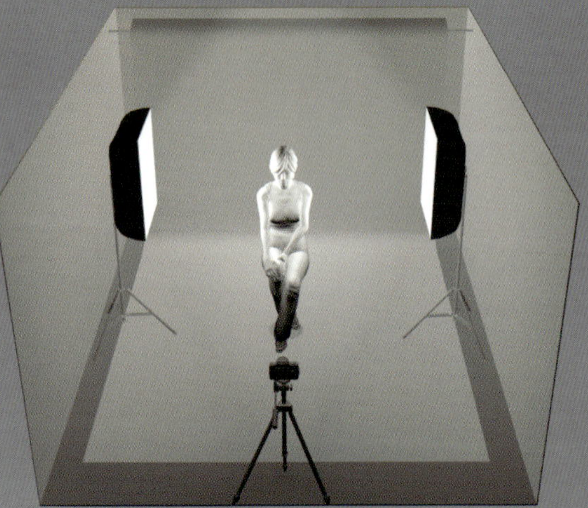

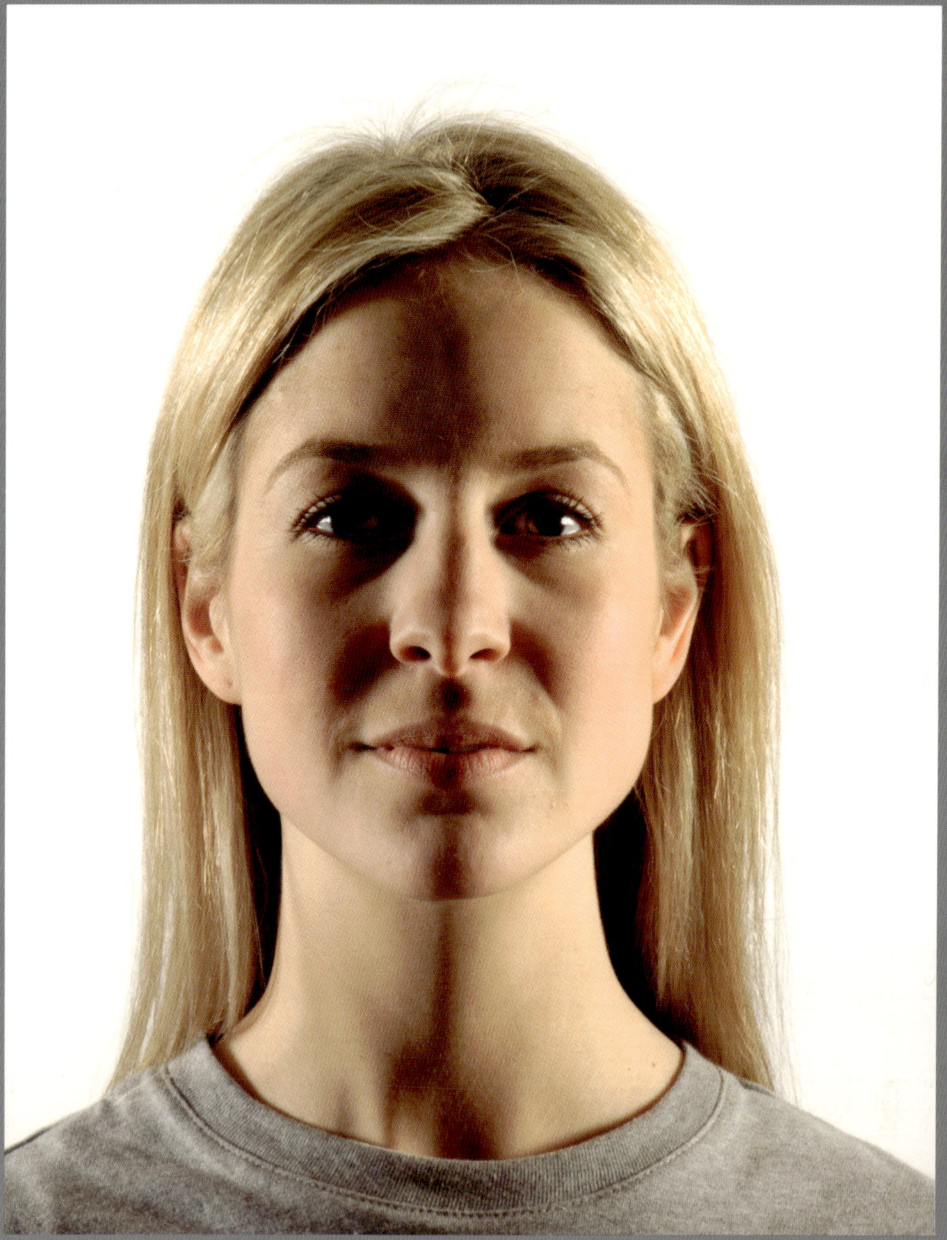

In this perfectly symmetrical lighting setup, both lights are at 90 degrees to the camera, effectively aiming at each of the model's ears. The result isn't particularly flattering, but it is dramatic, with symmetrical shadows running down the center of the subject's face.

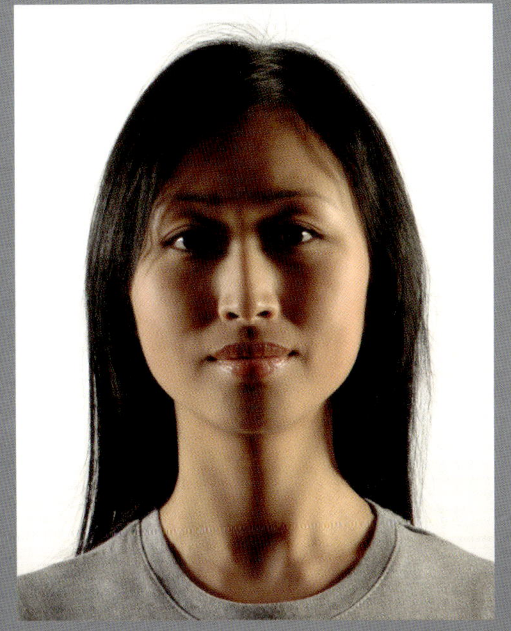

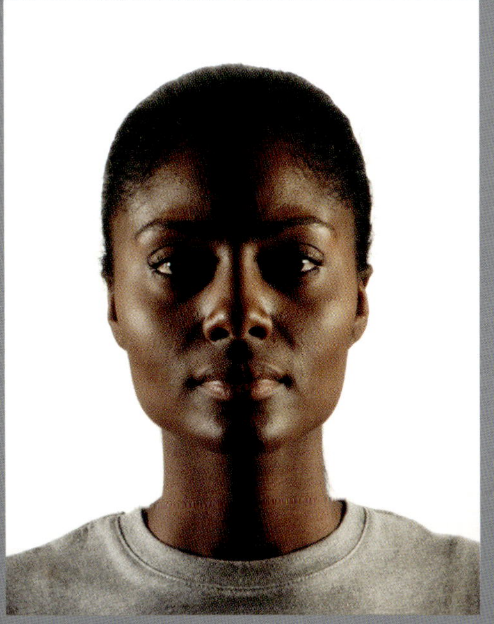

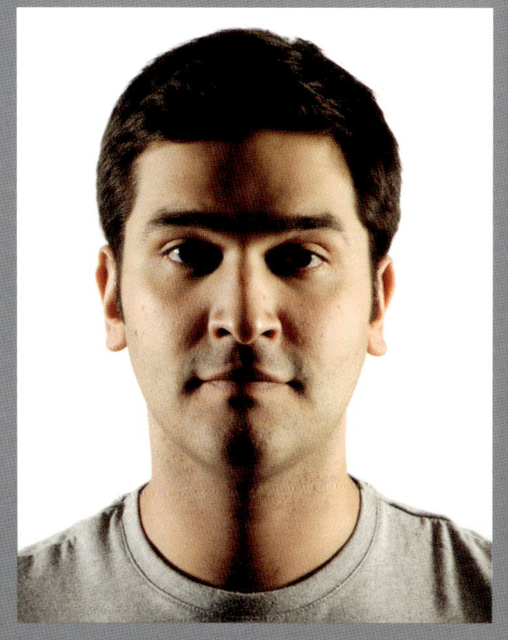

DARK BACKGROUND

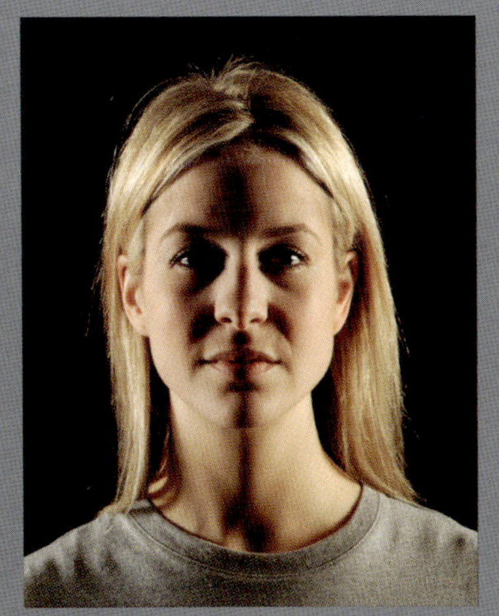

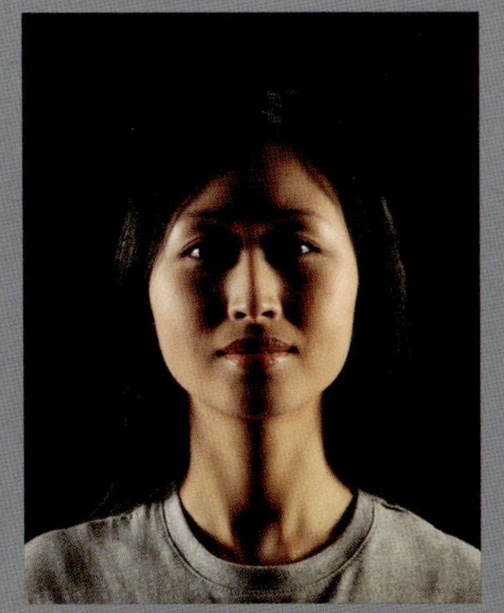

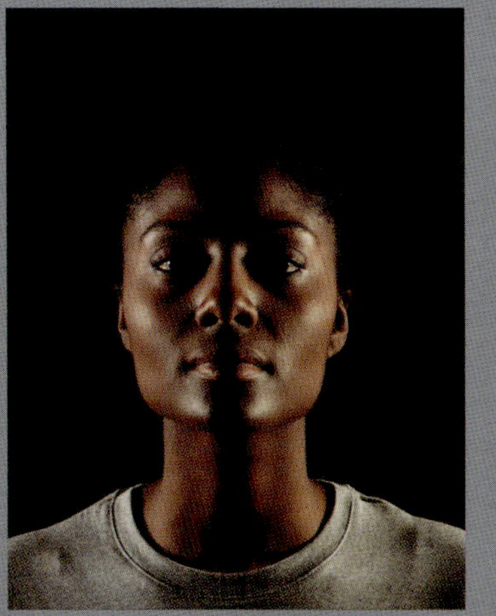

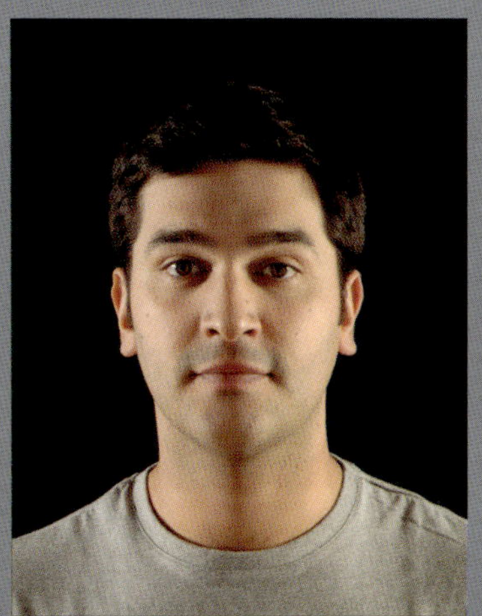

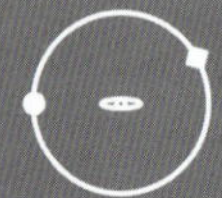

TWO LIGHTS

LIGHT 1: FROM 90° LEFT, EYE LEVEL

LIGHT 2: FROM 120° RIGHT, EYE LEVEL

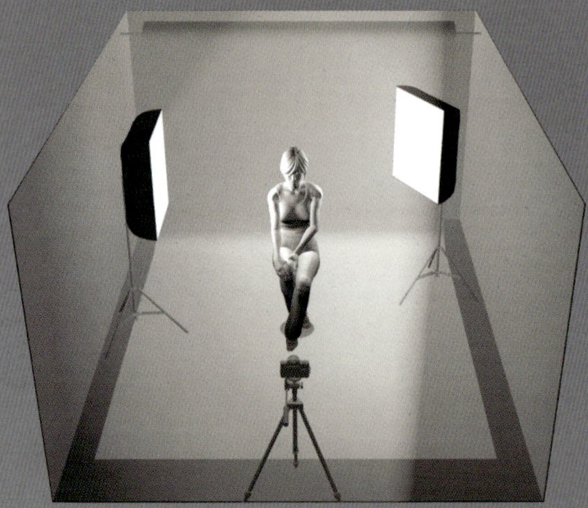

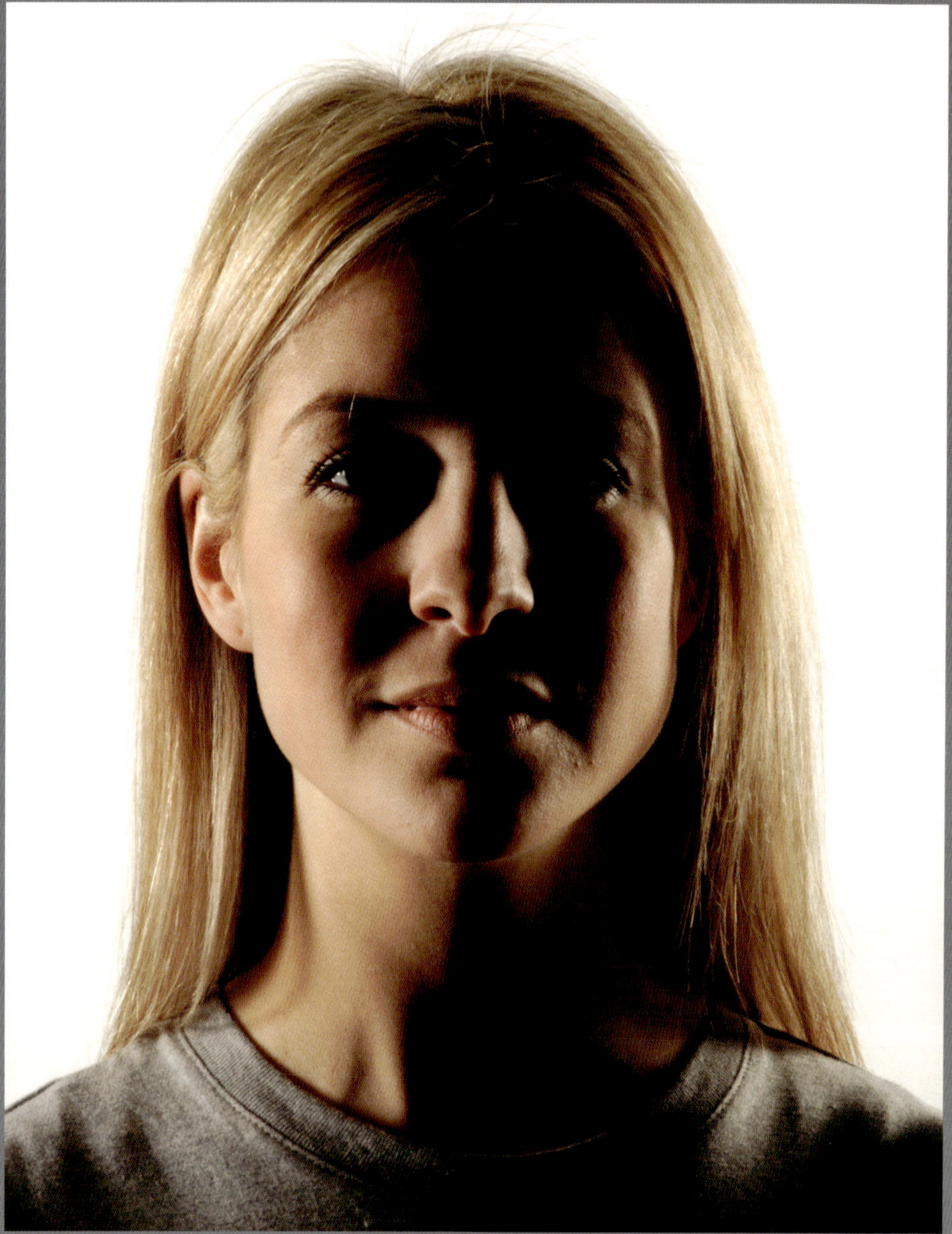

With one light at 90 degrees to the camera, and a second positioned slightly behind the subject on the opposite side, a high contrast result is guaranteed. However, the angle of the lights means that you aren't guaranteed a catchlight in your subject's eyes, and you certainly won't get a catchlight in both of them.

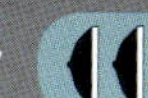

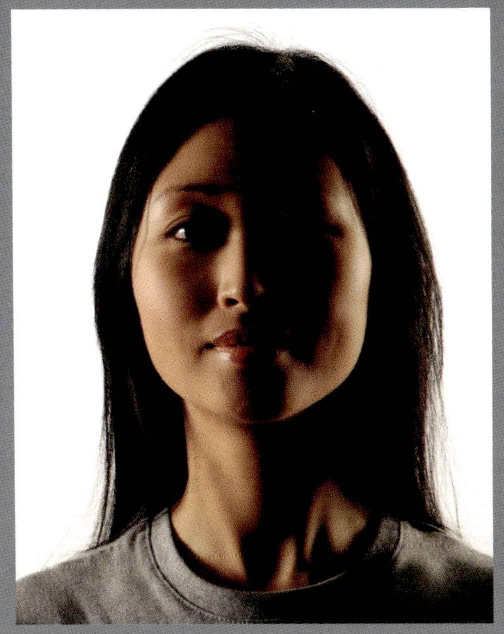

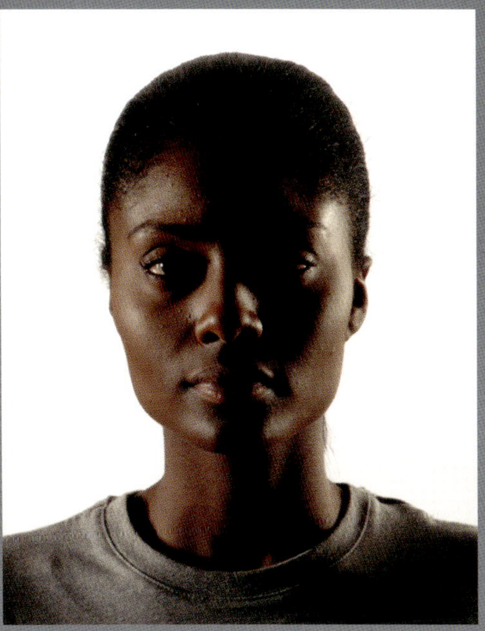

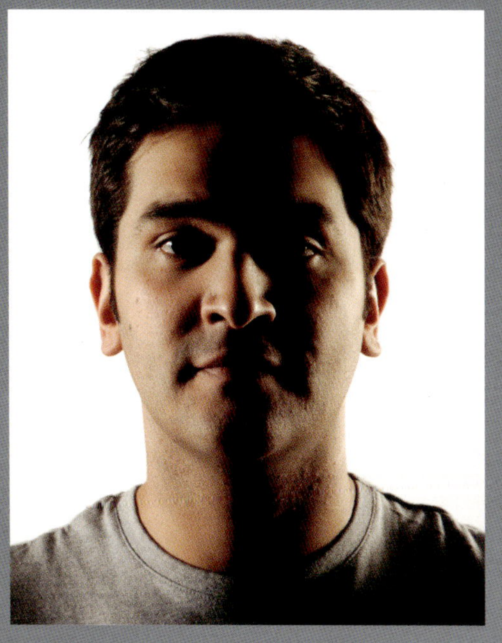

DARK BACKGROUND

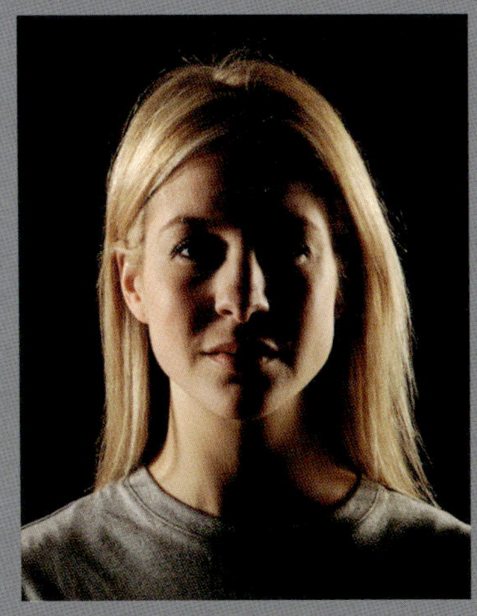

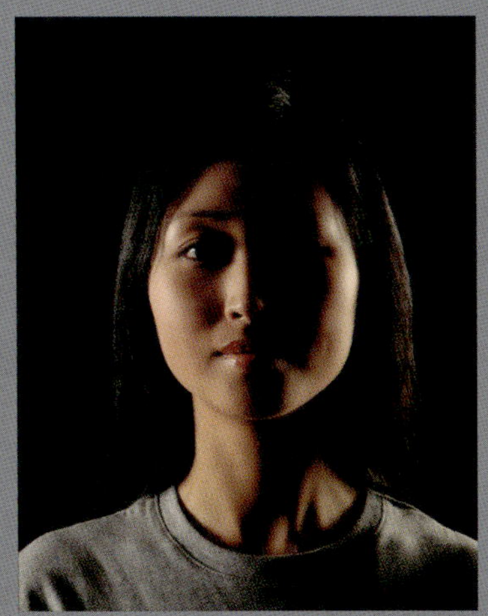

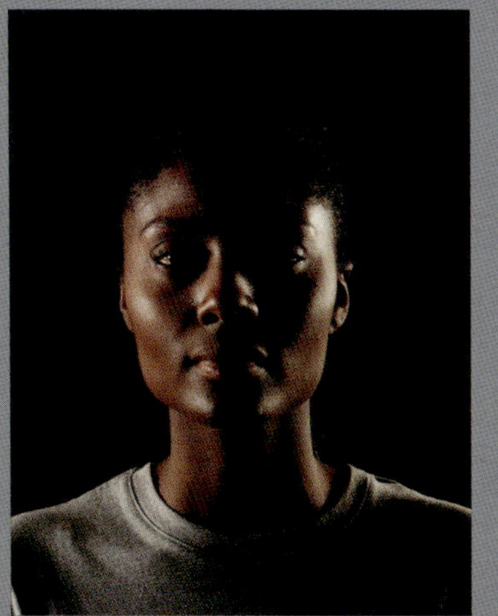

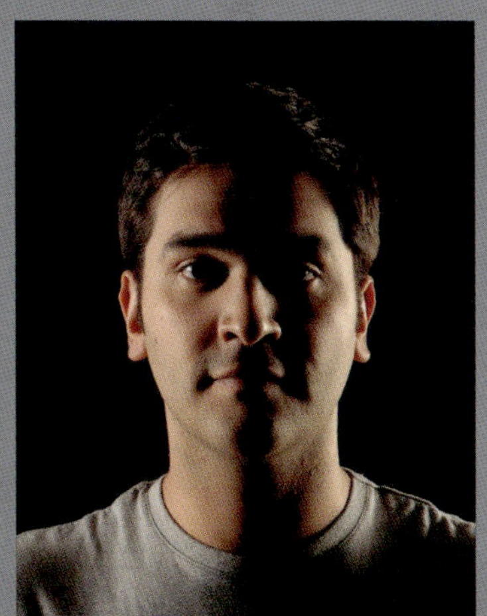

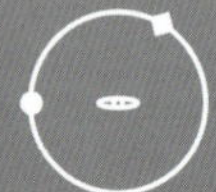

TWO LIGHTS

LIGHT 1: FROM 90° LEFT, EYE LEVEL

LIGHT 2: FROM 150° RIGHT, EYE LEVEL

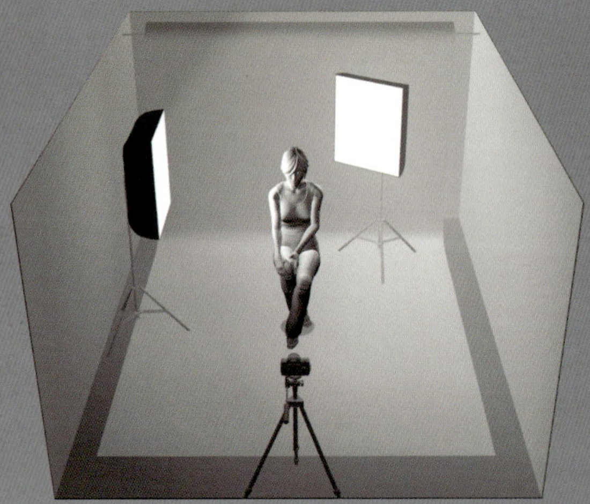

With the first light remaining at a 90-degree angle, and the second light moving further behind the subject, the shadows on the left side of the model's face are intensified. However, the backlight adds a strong, narrow highlight to both the face and hair, preventing the side of the face from being totally shaded.

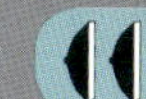

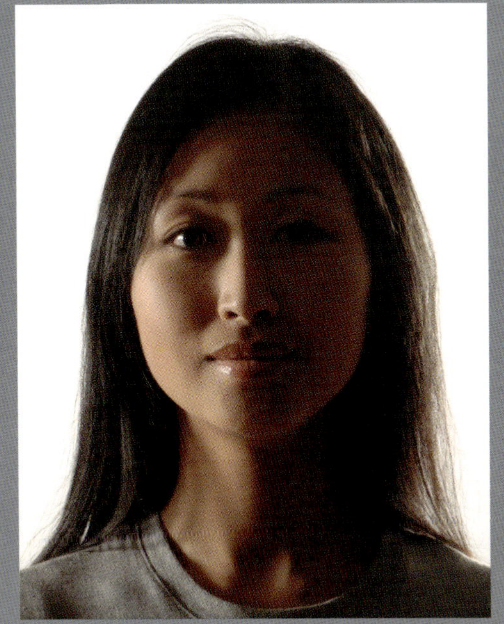

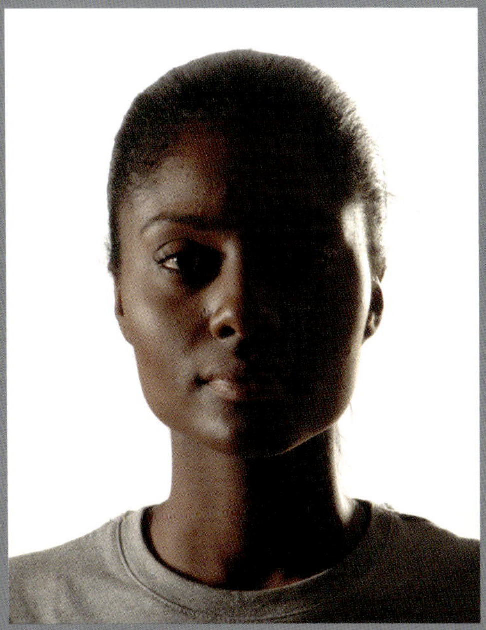

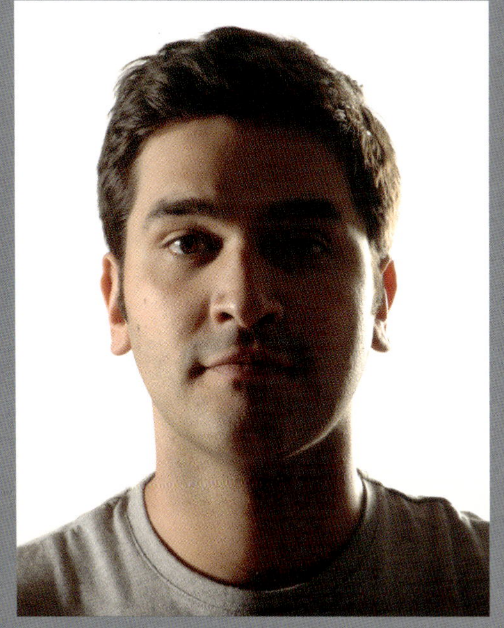

DARK BACKGROUND

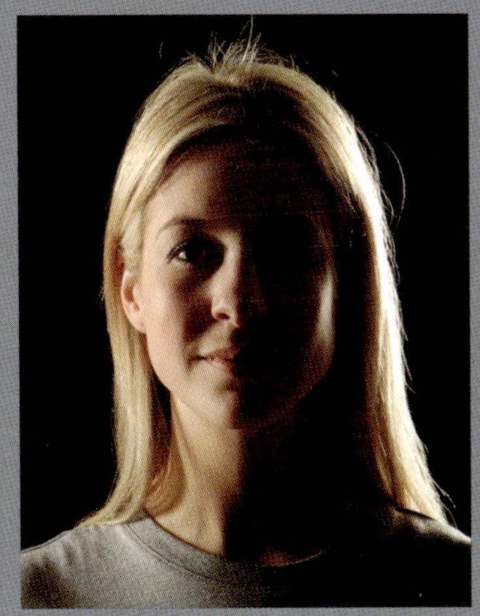

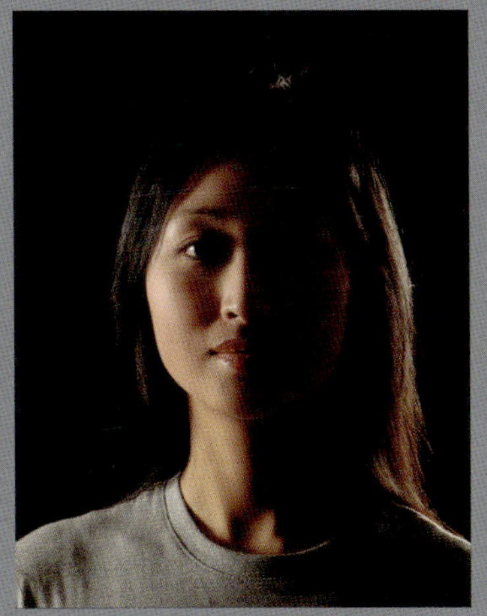

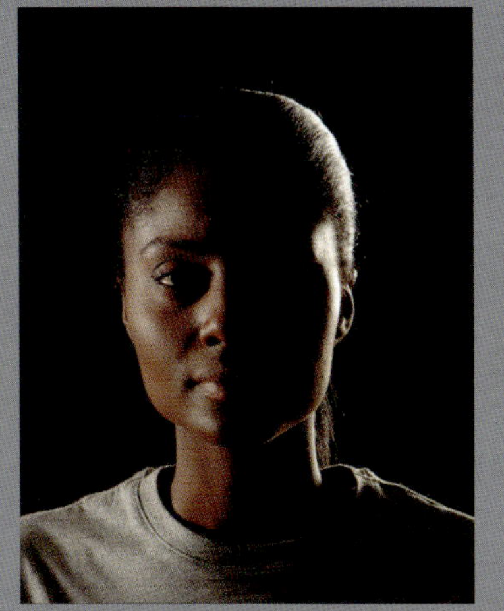

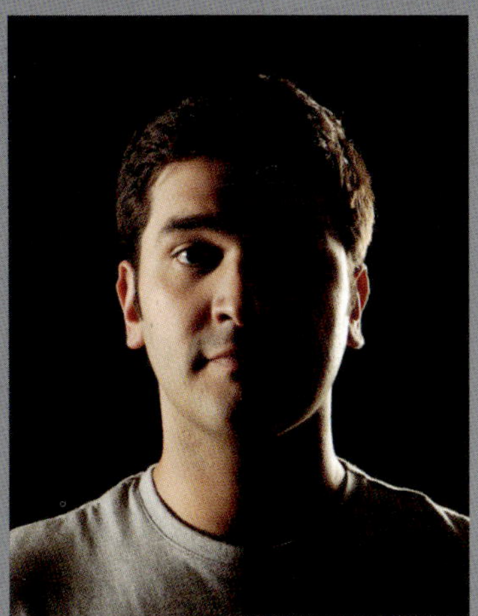

CHAPTER 5

UMBRELLA LIGHTING FROM ABOVE

So far, you have seen the potential for using one or two lights, in various configurations, to create a basic portrait lighting setup. Each of these setups will work equally well whether you're using professional studio flash units, hotshoe flashes that you've taken off-camera, or a constant light source such as incandescent or fluorescent lamps.

However, in each setup the light has been targeted directly on the subject, and this can often result in hard shadows on the opposite side to the light, especially if you are just using a single lamp. If you are looking for a high-contrast look to your image, this can work well, but if this isn't what you are setting out to achieve and you don't want to (or can't) use an additional light or reflector, then you need some other way of softening the light.

As we will see on the following pages, one way of doing this is to "bounce" light onto your subject, using a reflective umbrella to spread the light and make it more diffuse. With care, shadows can be softened, even with a single lamp.

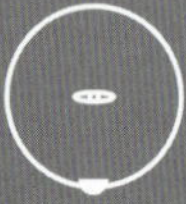

UMBRELLA

LIGHT 1: FROM 0°, 45° ABOVE

LIGHT 2: NONE

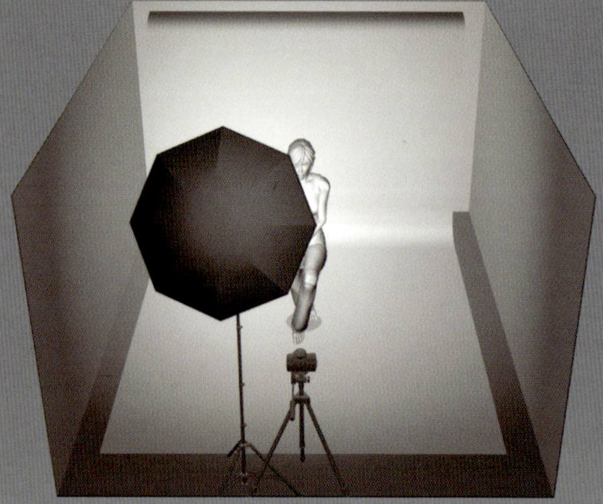

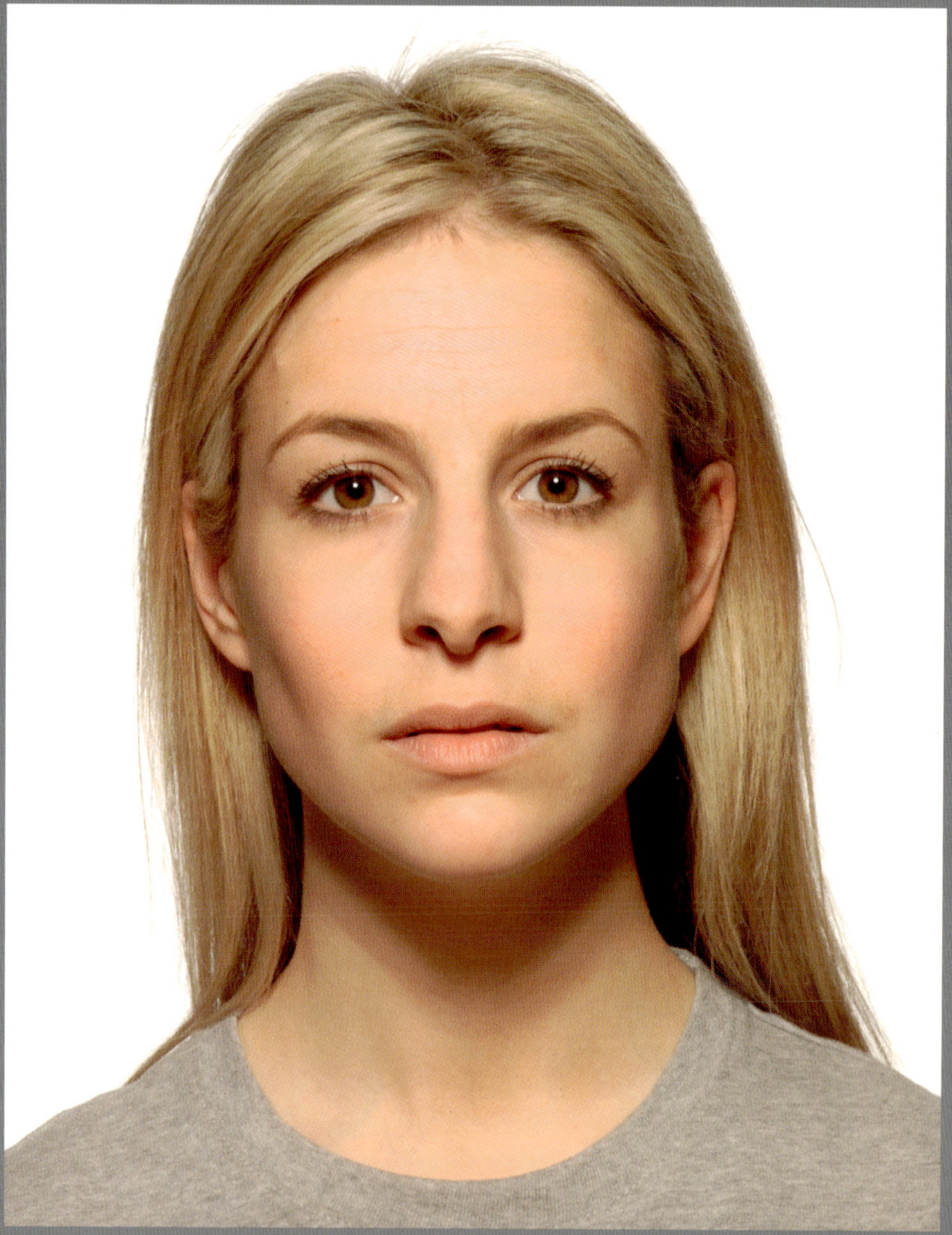

Positioning a single light above the camera, with an umbrella fitted, will produce an even light on the model's face, regardless of their skin tone. The majority of the shadows cast by the light are soft, although there may be a small, dense shadow beneath the nose. How noticeable this is will depend on your subject's facial characteristics.

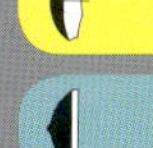

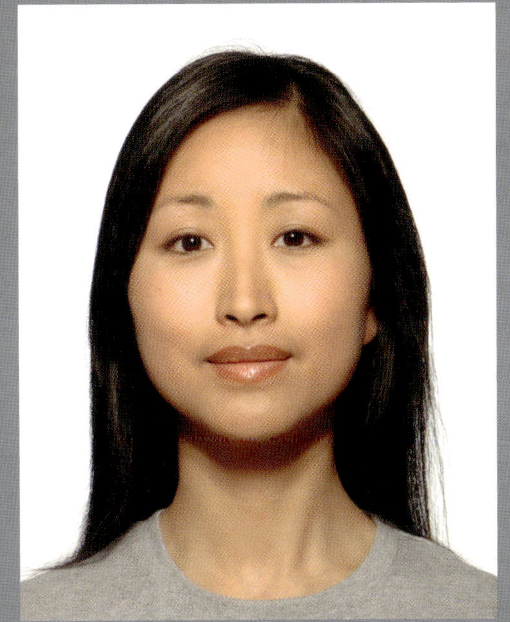

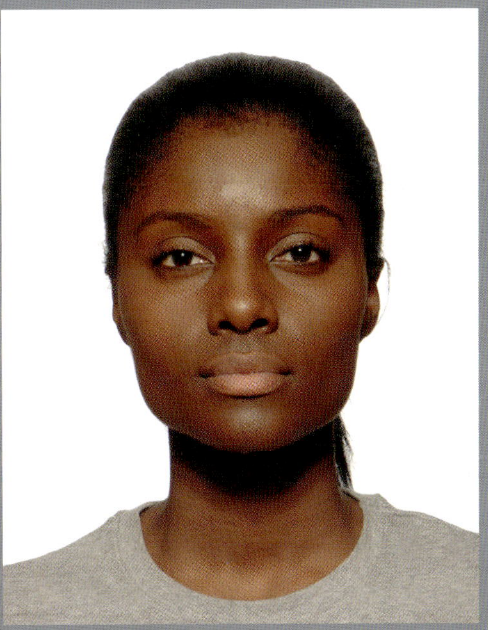

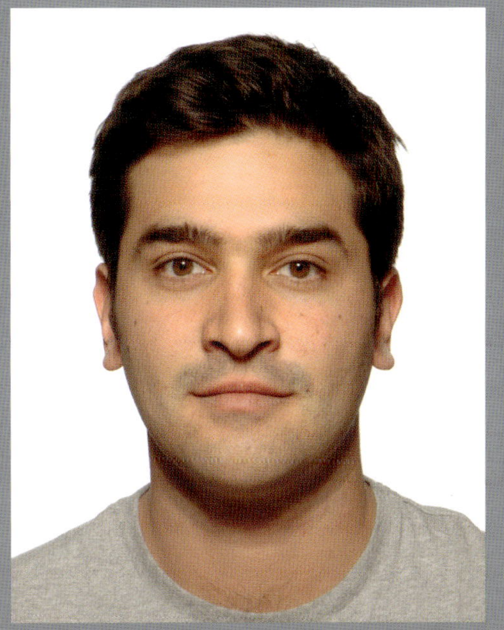

DARK BACKGROUND

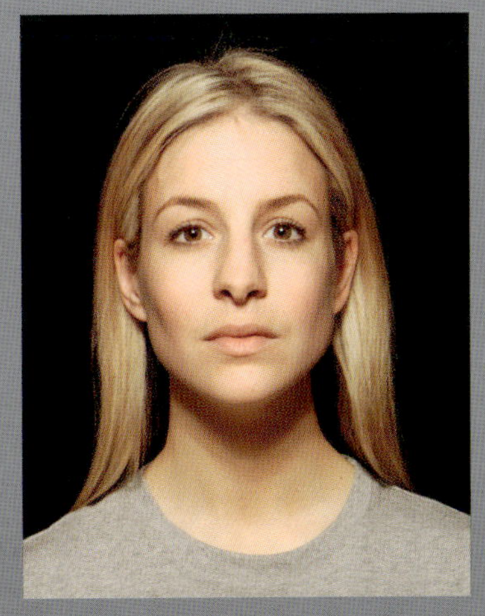

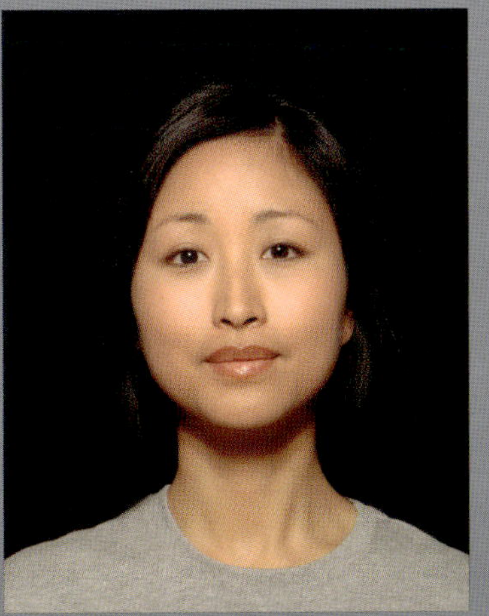

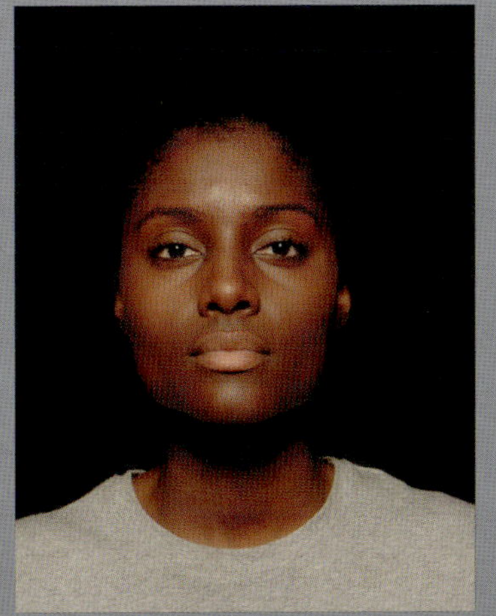

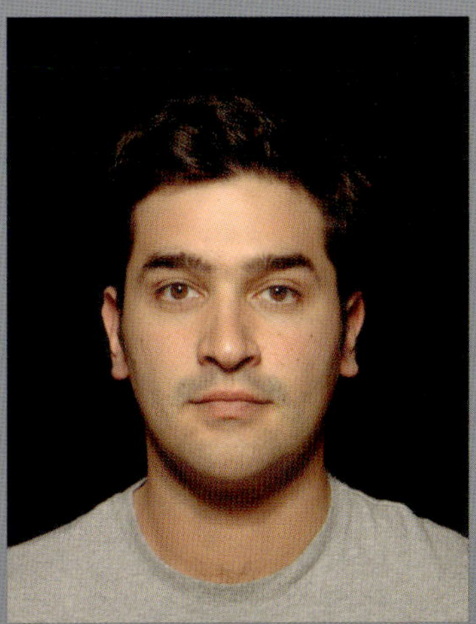

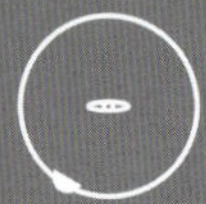

UMBRELLA

LIGHT 1: FROM 30° LEFT, 45° ABOVE

LIGHT 2: NONE

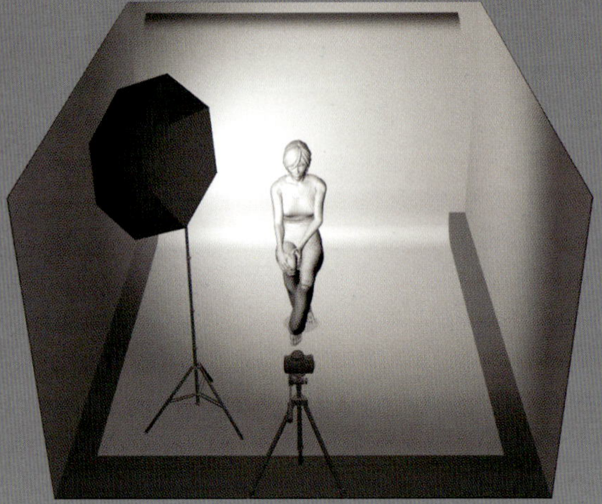

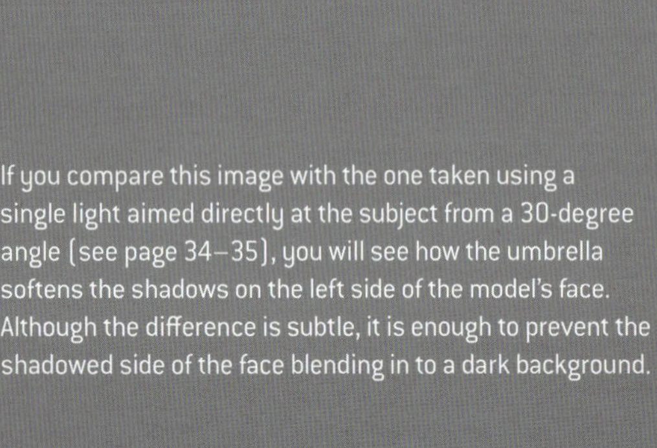

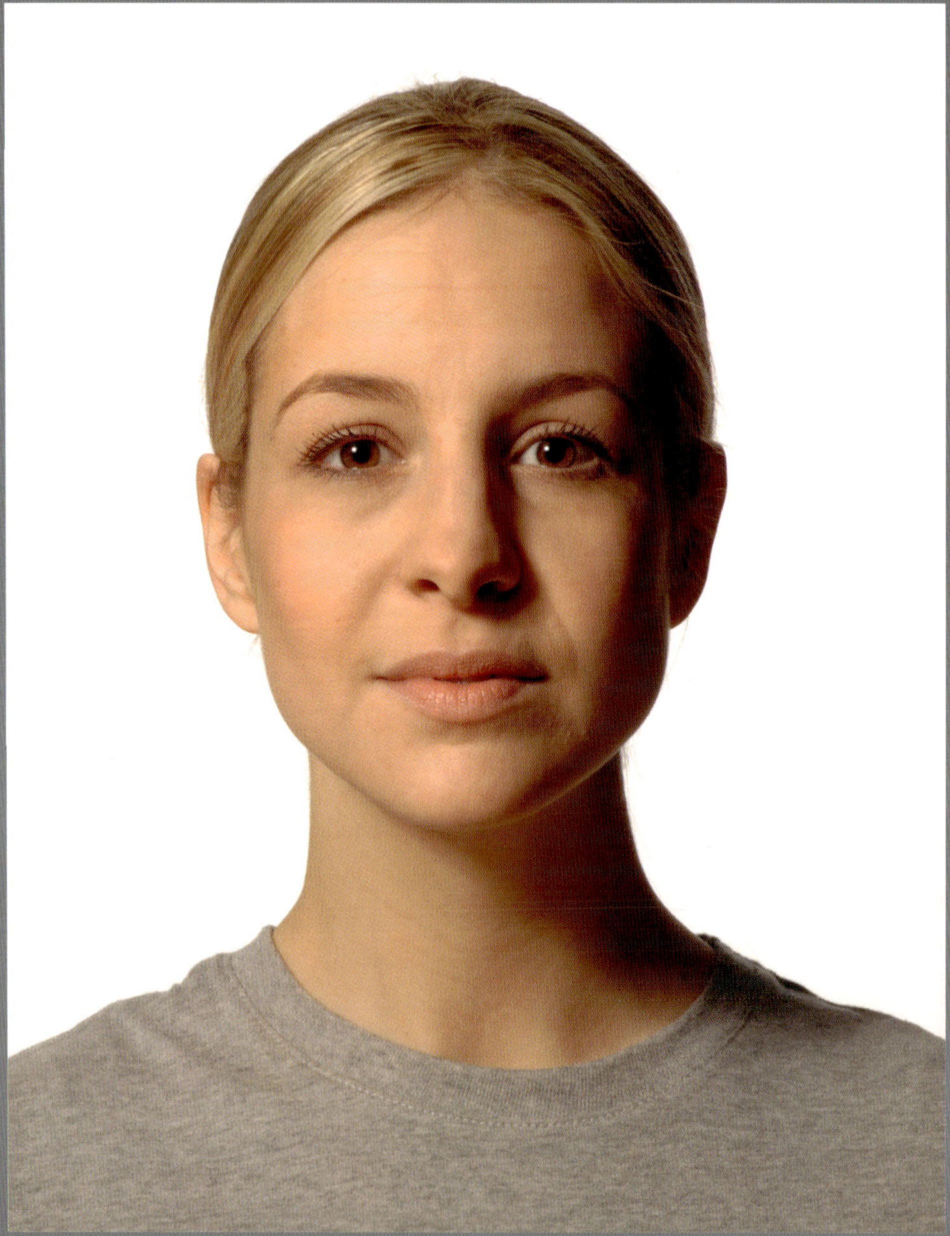

If you compare this image with the one taken using a single light aimed directly at the subject from a 30-degree angle (see page 34–35), you will see how the umbrella softens the shadows on the left side of the model's face. Although the difference is subtle, it is enough to prevent the shadowed side of the face blending in to a dark background.

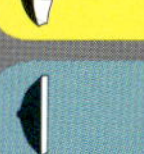

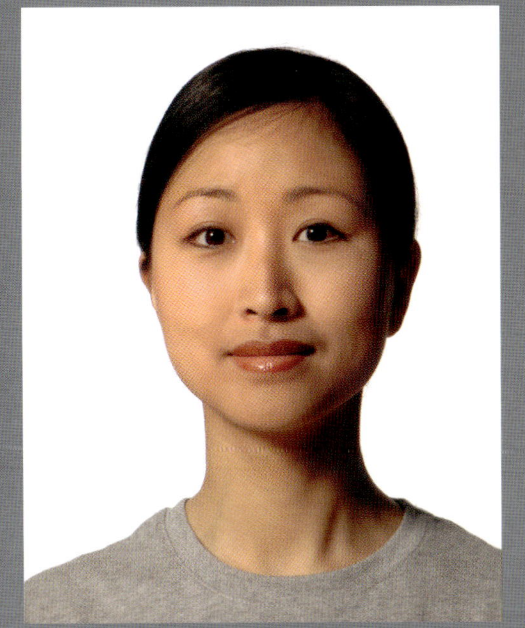

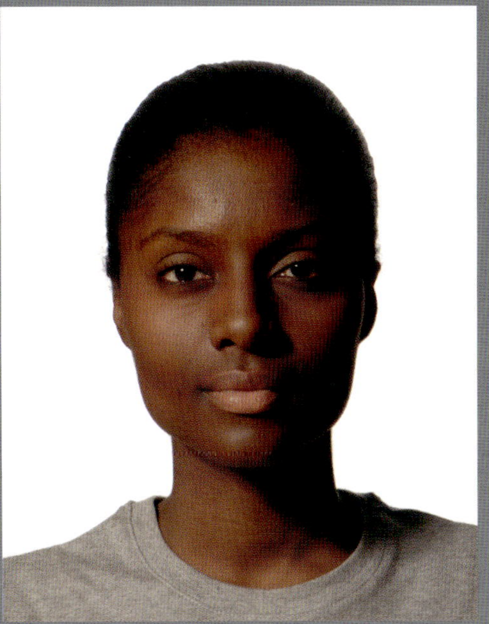

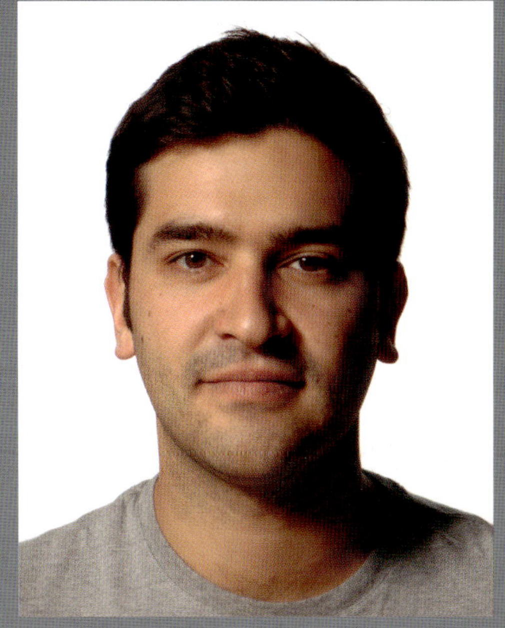

DARK BACKGROUND

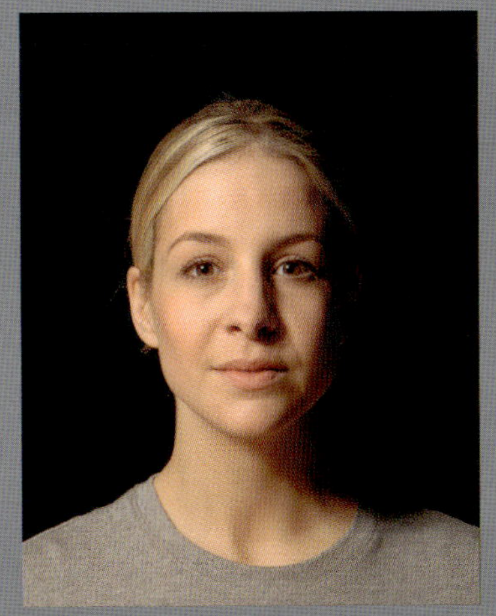

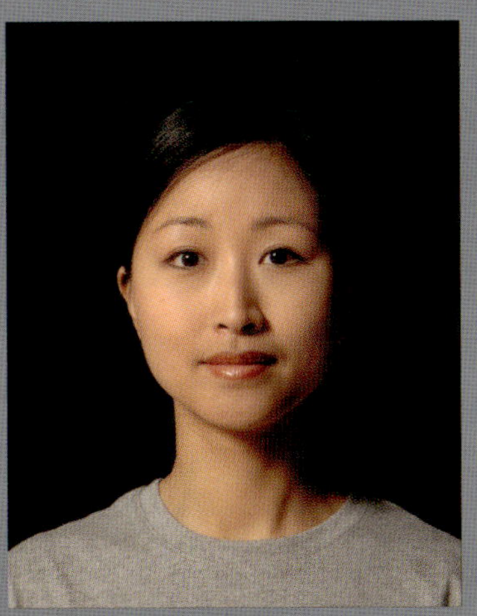

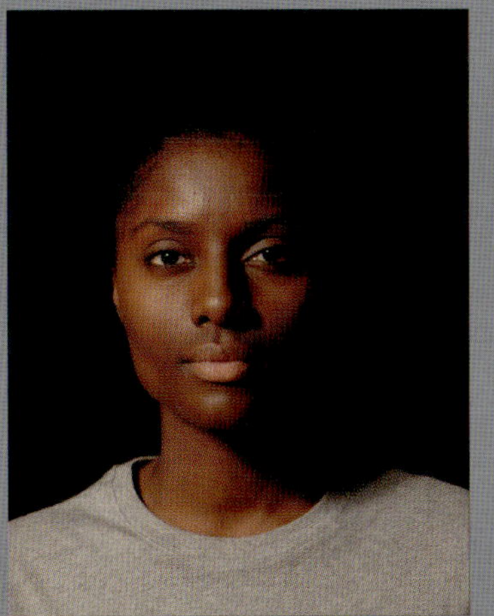

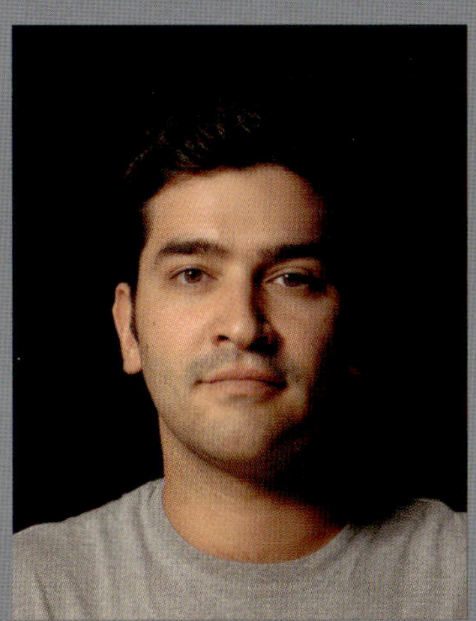

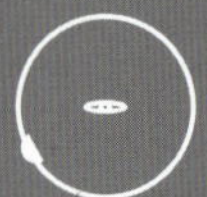

UMBRELLA

LIGHT 1: FROM 60° LEFT, 45° ABOVE

LIGHT 2: NONE

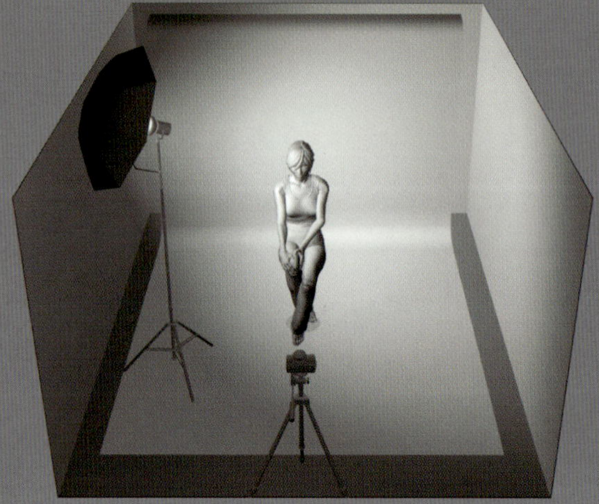

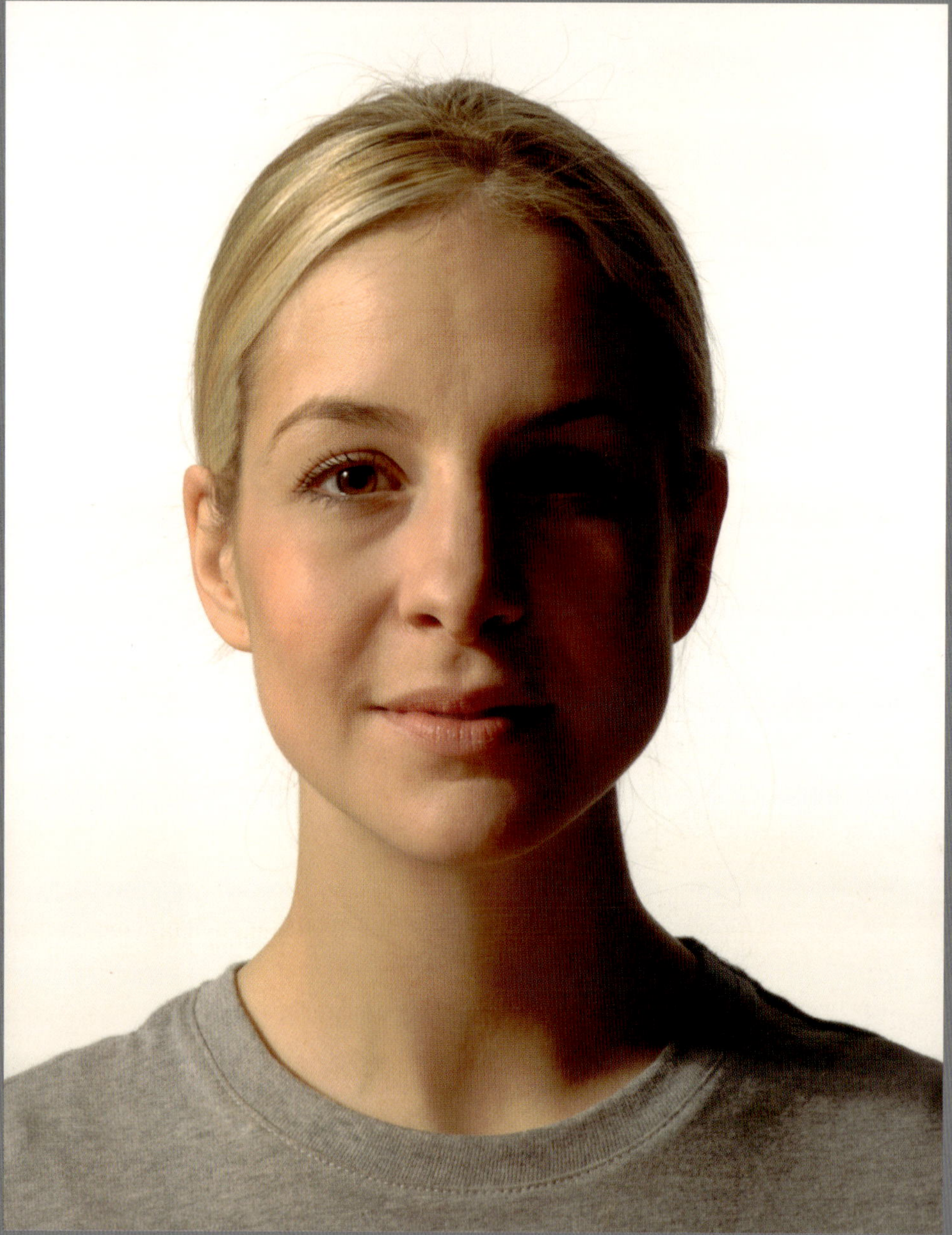

Increasing the height of your light in relation to your subject helps highlight the hair. It will also change the position of the catchlight in the model's eye. Compare the catchlight when the light is at a 60-degree angle raised above the subject, to the position of the catchlight on pages 32–33 when the light is at eye level.

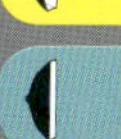

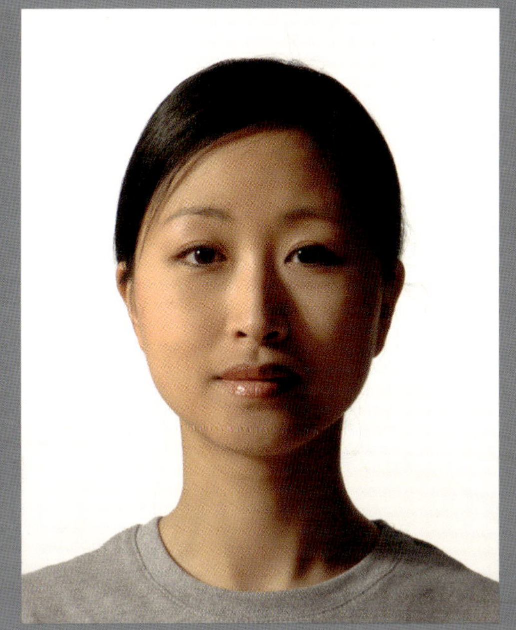

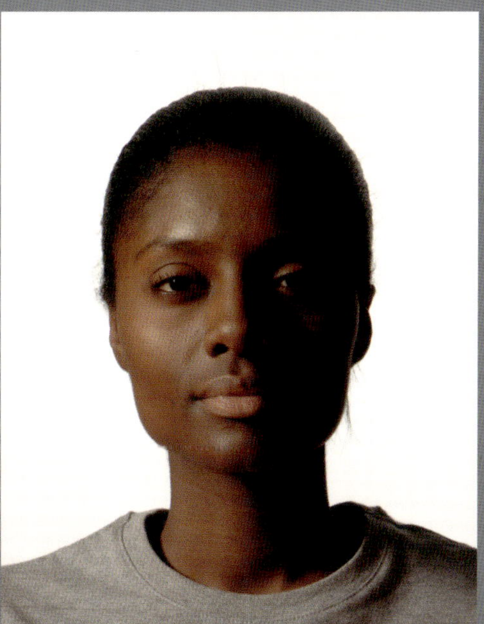

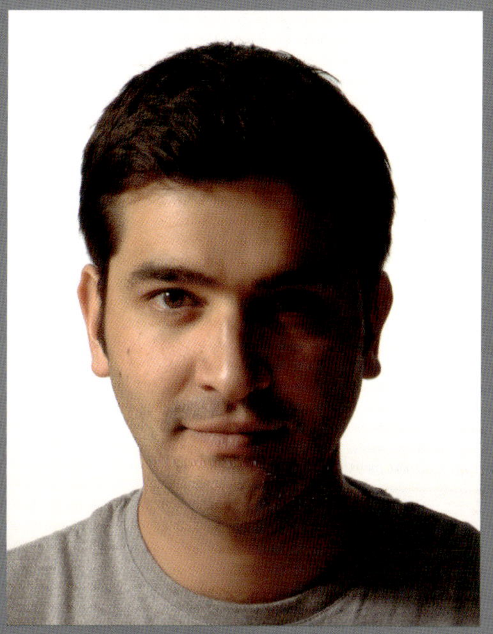

DARK BACKGROUND

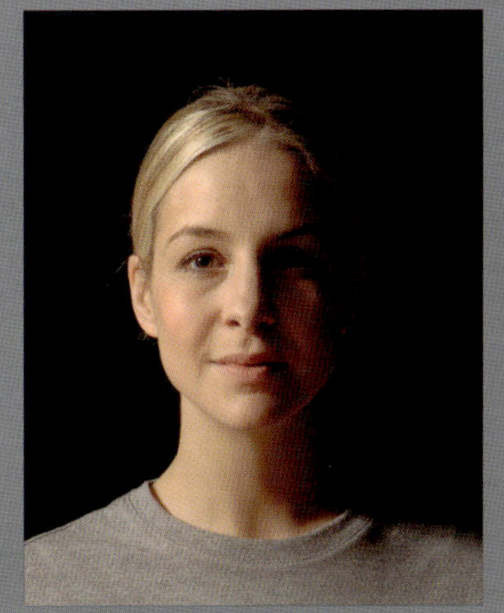

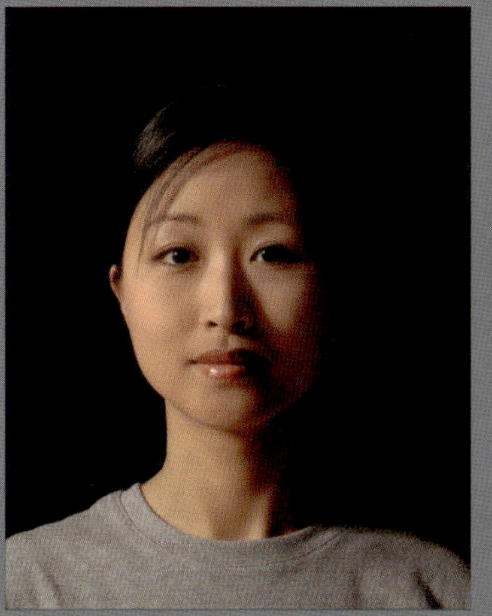

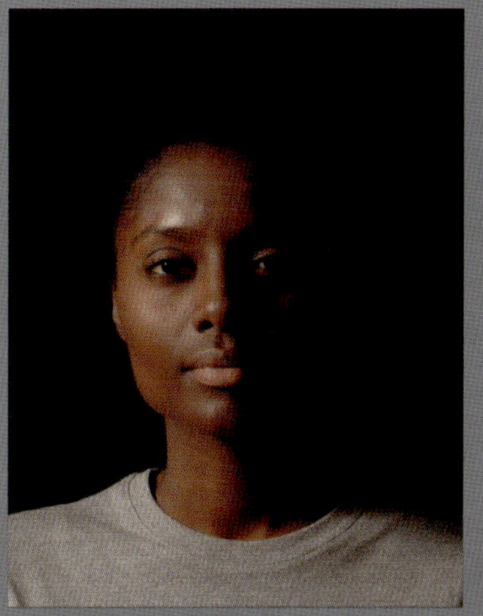

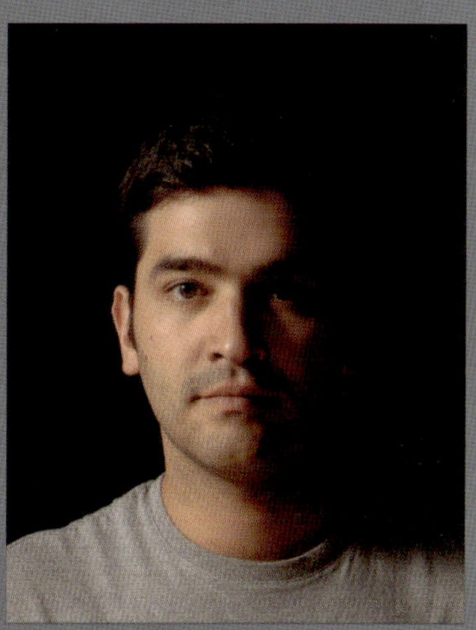

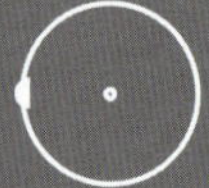

UMBRELLA

LIGHT 1: FROM 90° LEFT, 45° ABOVE

LIGHT 2: NONE

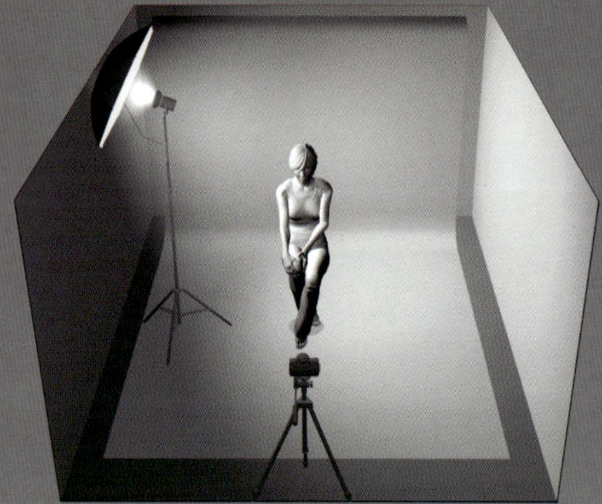

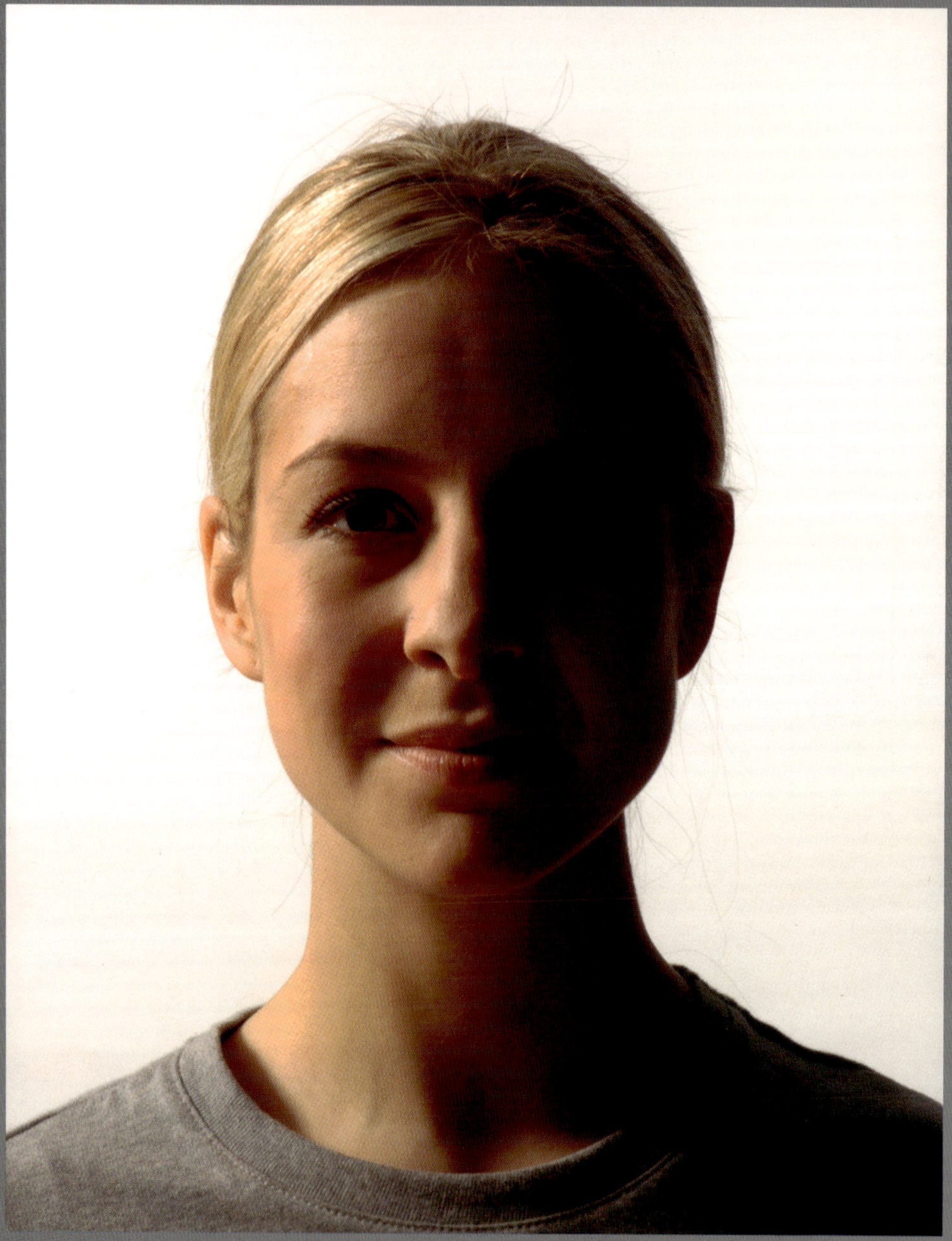

Setting a direct light at a 90-degree angle to your model is a surefire way to create a striking half-light, half-dark effect on their face (see pages 30–31). However, when you use an umbrella to bounce the light back onto the subject, the shaded side of the face retains a small amount of detail.

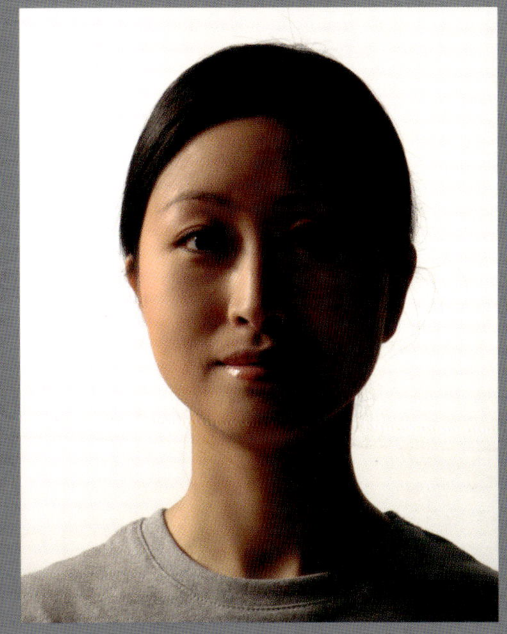

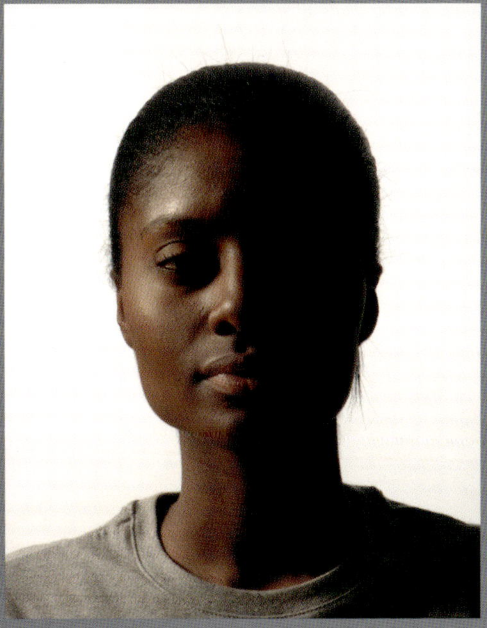

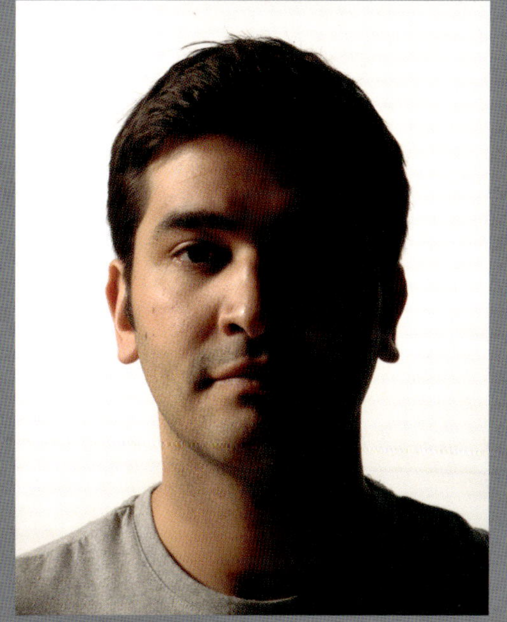

DARK BACKGROUND

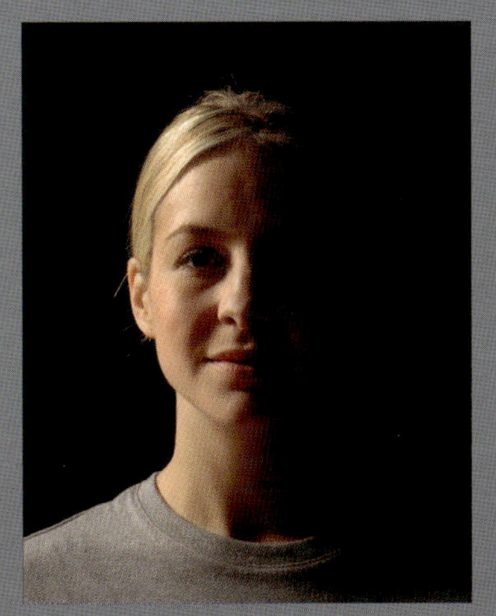

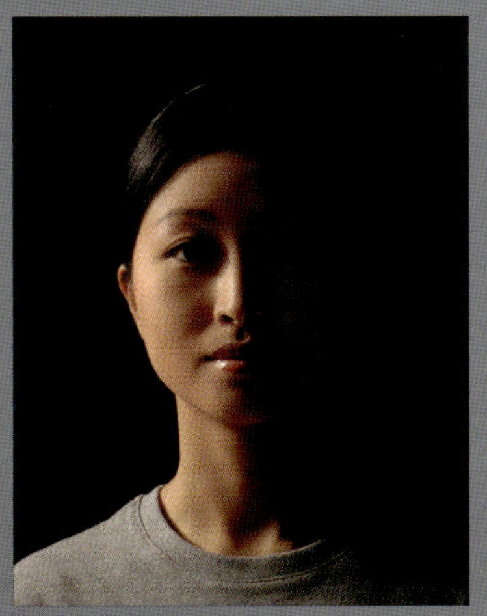

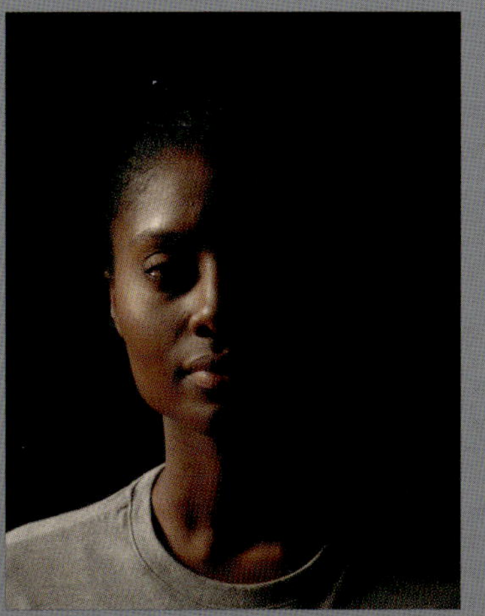

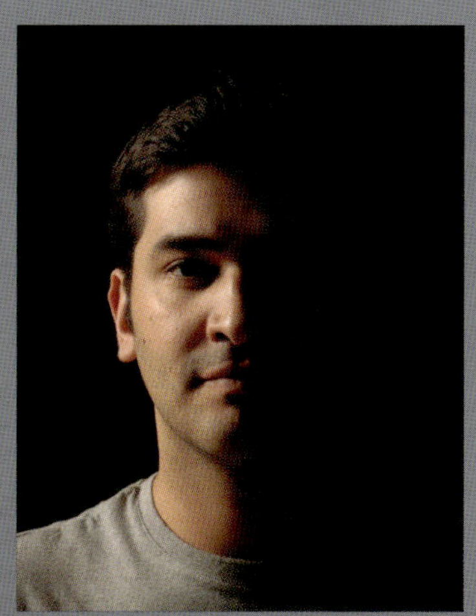

CHAPTER 6

SNOOT ANGLED DOWN

An umbrella is just one of many accessories that you can use on flash units and some incandescent lamps to modify or regulate the pattern and position of the light. While an umbrella has the effect of softening the light by spreading it as it is bounced into, and back from, the umbrella's reflective surface, so a snoot has the opposite effect.

Little more than a metal cone that's attached to the front of a lamp, a snoot narrows the beam of light to help target it on a specific area. A snooted light is nearly always aimed directly at the subject to make the most of the effect, and they are particularly useful for creating a hair light—positioned behind the model, with the lamp pointing in the direction of the camera, the snoot helps prevent any stray light hitting the lens and creating flare. Snoots can also be used to good effect to light a small area of a background, helping lift the subject from their surroundings.

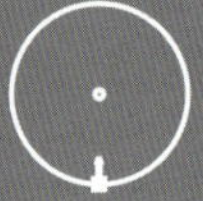

SNOOT

LIGHT 1: FROM 0°, 30° ANGLED DOWN

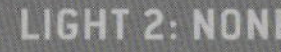

LIGHT 2: NONE

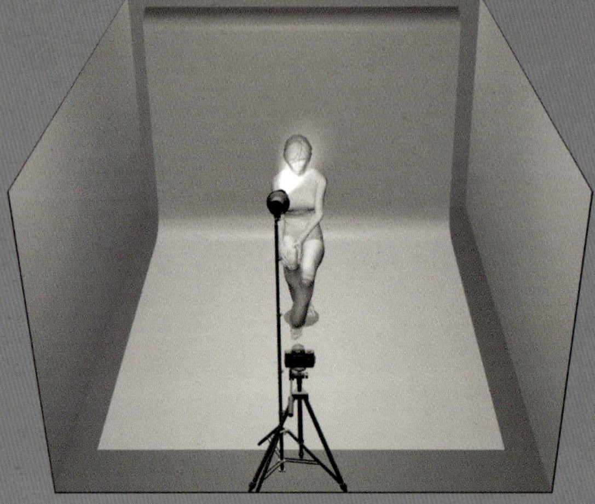

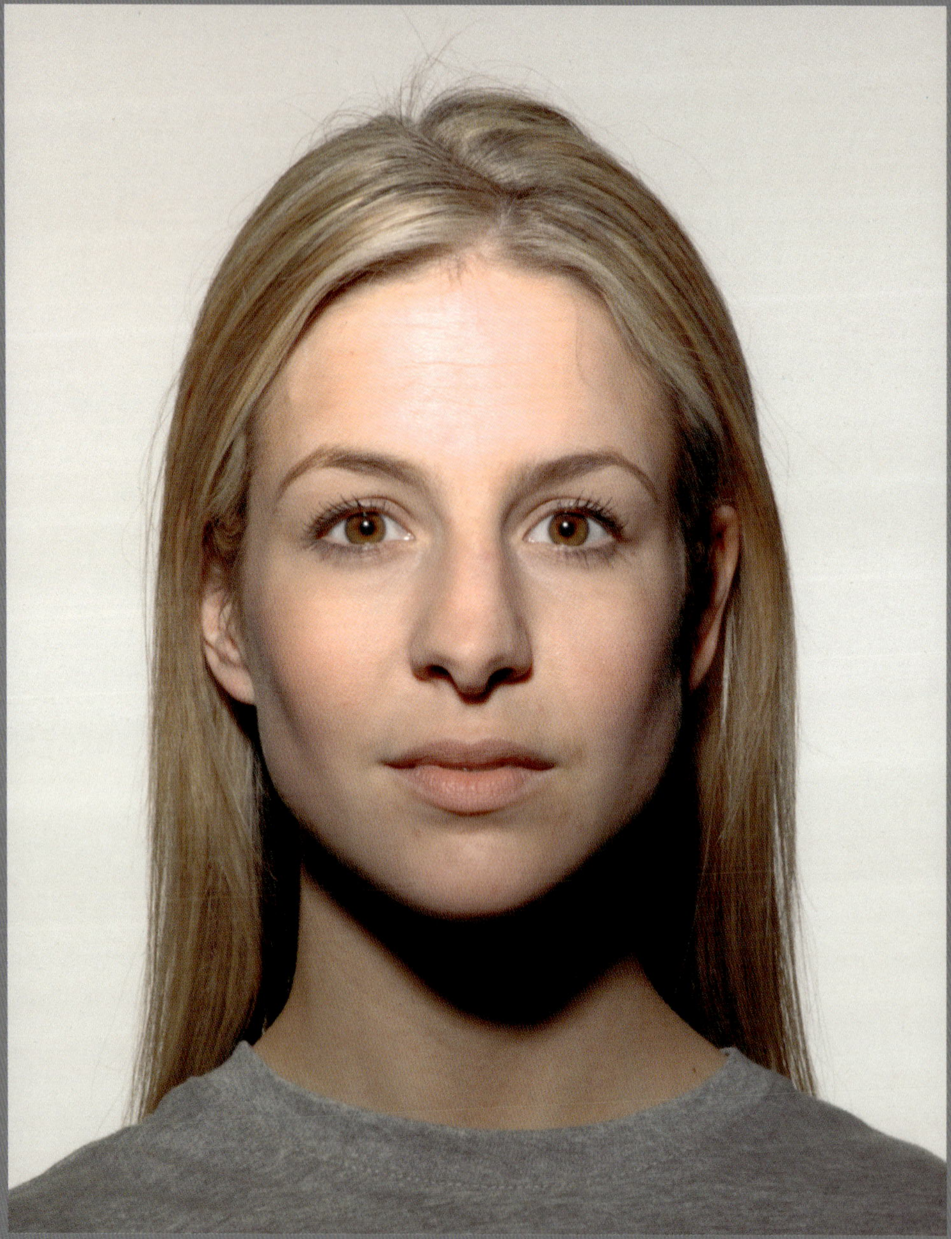

There is an immediate difference between the effects of a snoot and an umbrella if you compare these shots to those on pages 122–123. Both sets of images were taken with the camera and light in the same position, but here a snoot was used instead of an umbrella. Note also the effect on the dark background as the light spills beyond the subject.

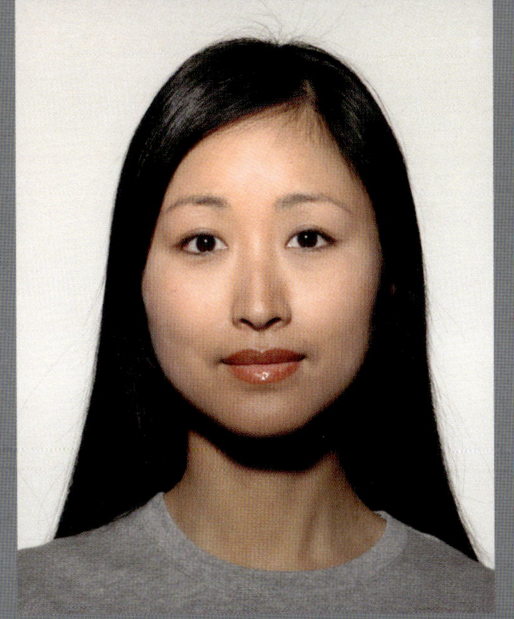
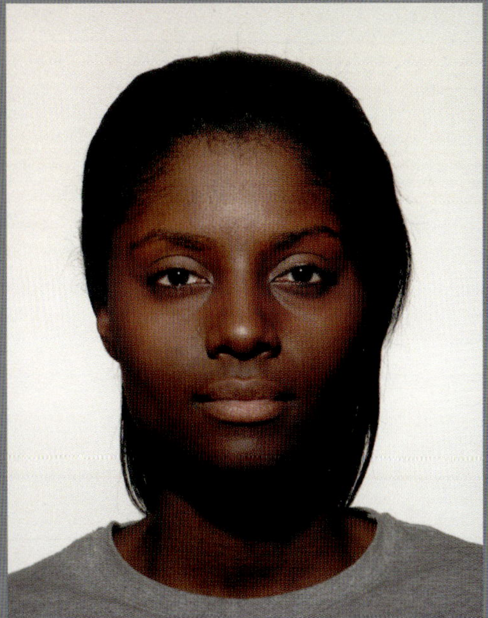
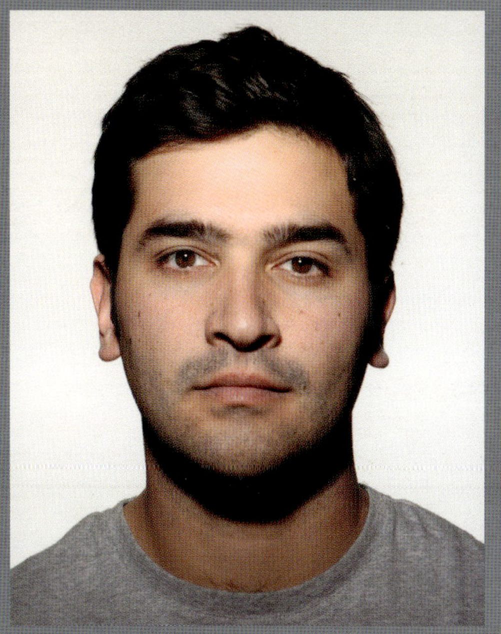

DARK BACKGROUND

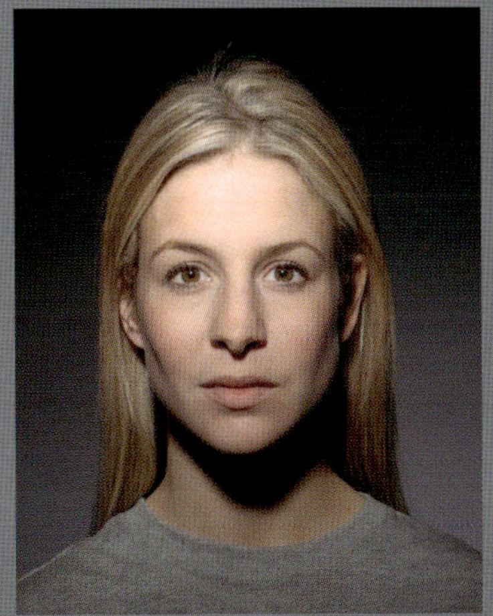
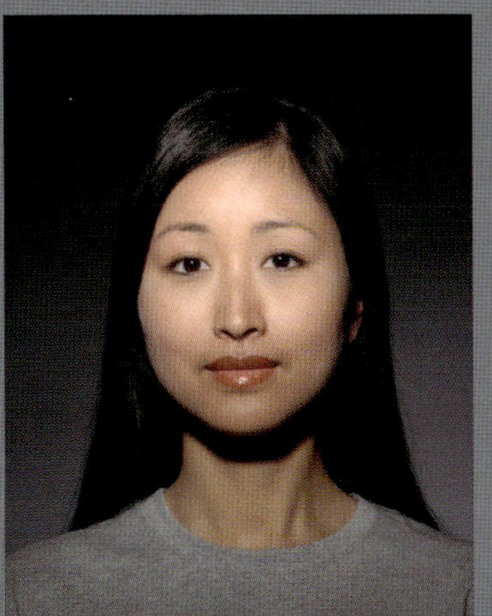
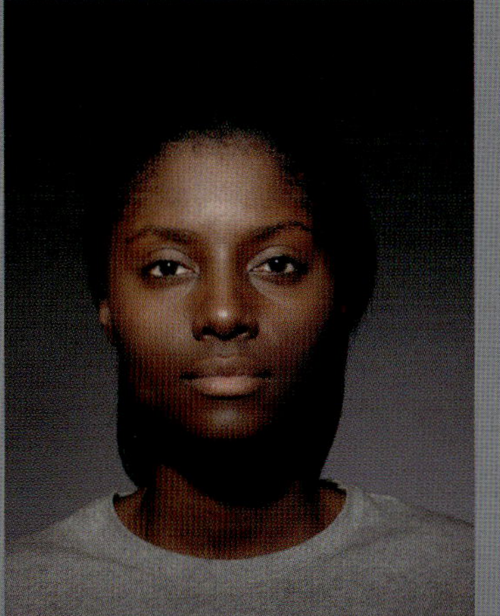
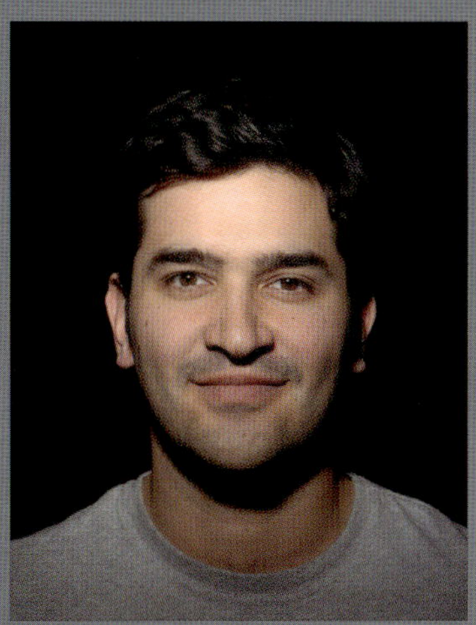

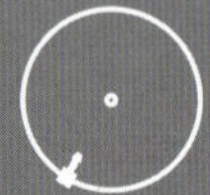

SNOOT

LIGHT 1: 30º LEFT, 30º ANGLED DOWN

LIGHT 2: NONE

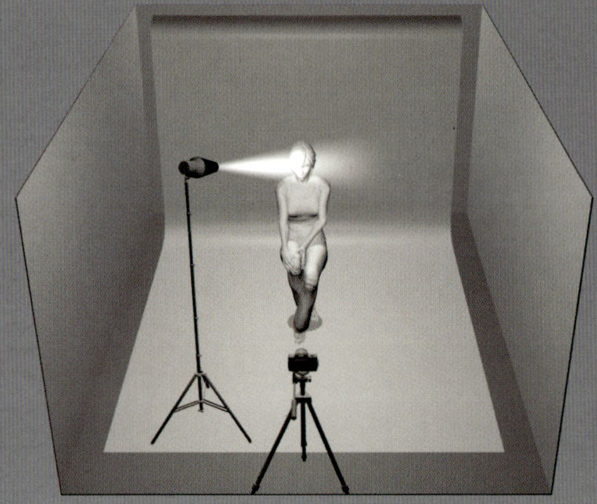

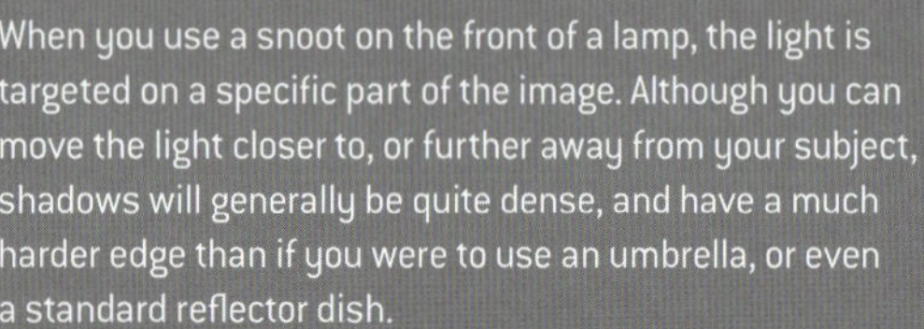

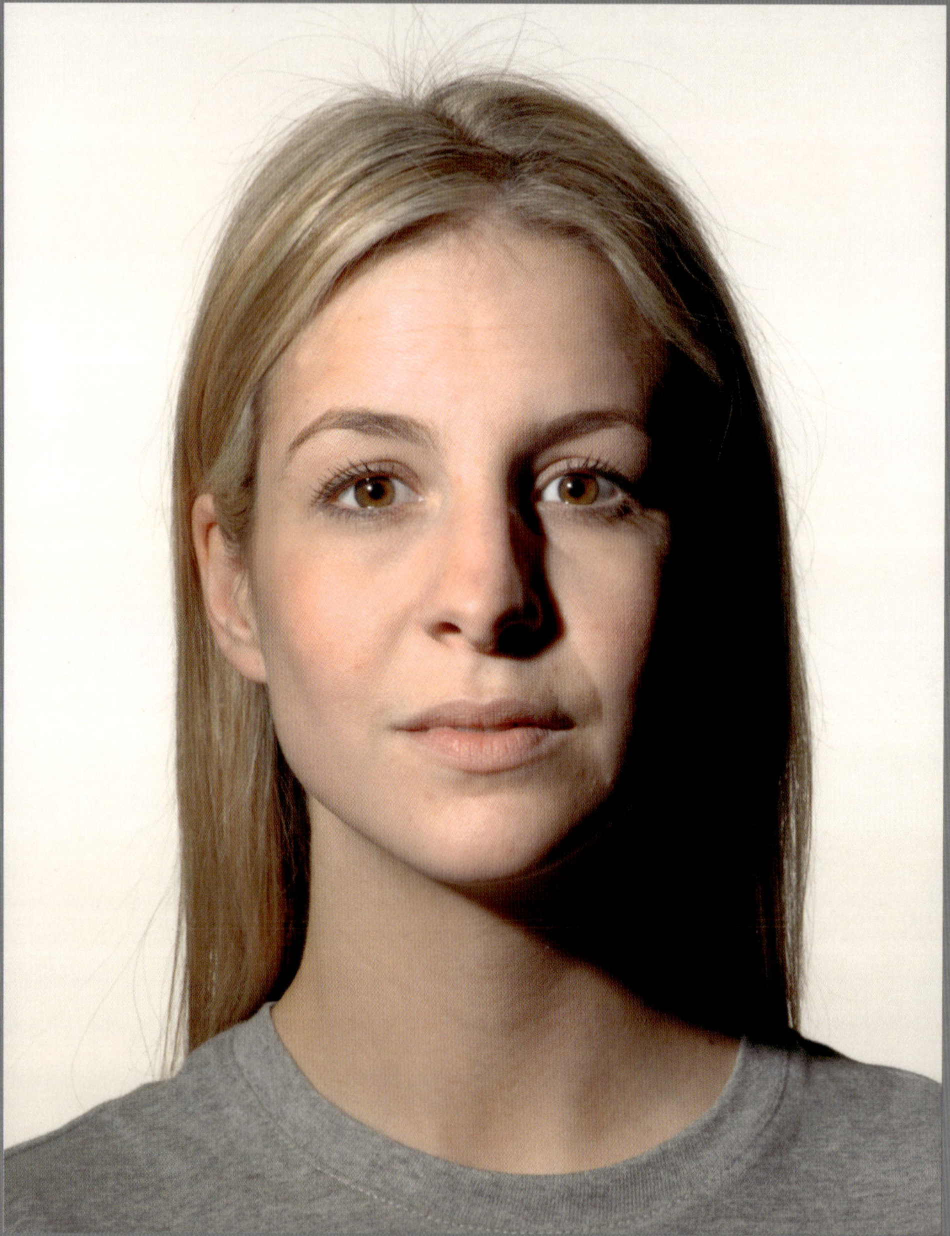

When you use a snoot on the front of a lamp, the light is targeted on a specific part of the image. Although you can move the light closer to, or further away from your subject, shadows will generally be quite dense, and have a much harder edge than if you were to use an umbrella, or even a standard reflector dish.

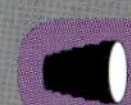

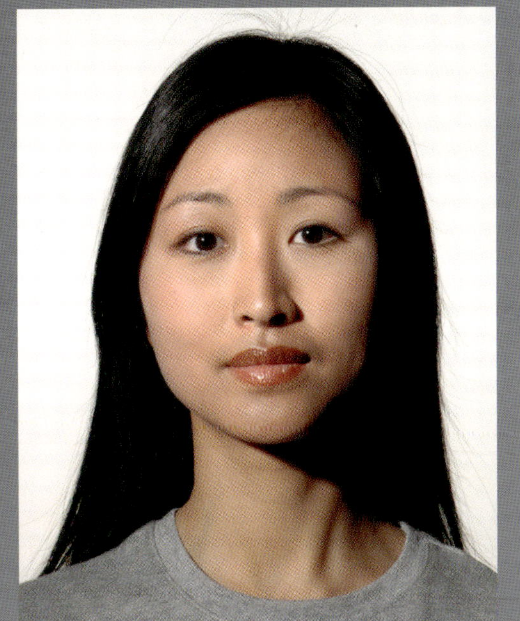

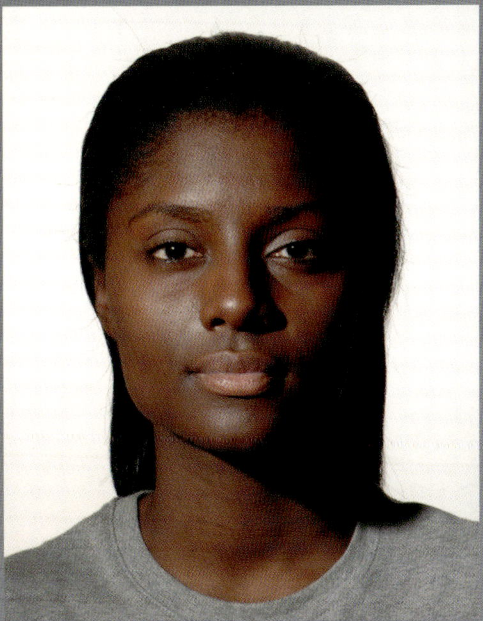

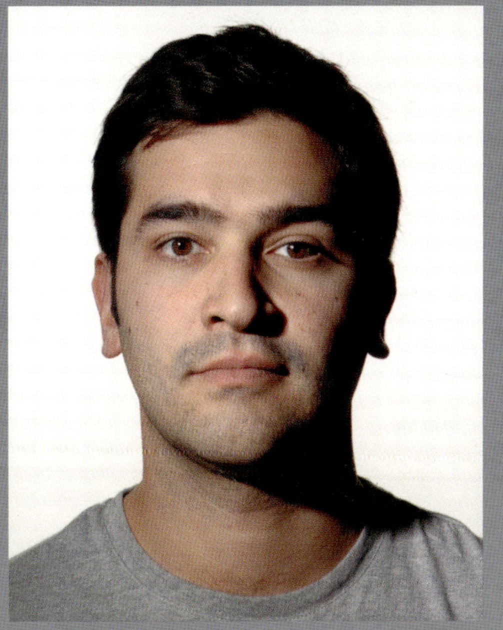

DARK BACKGROUND

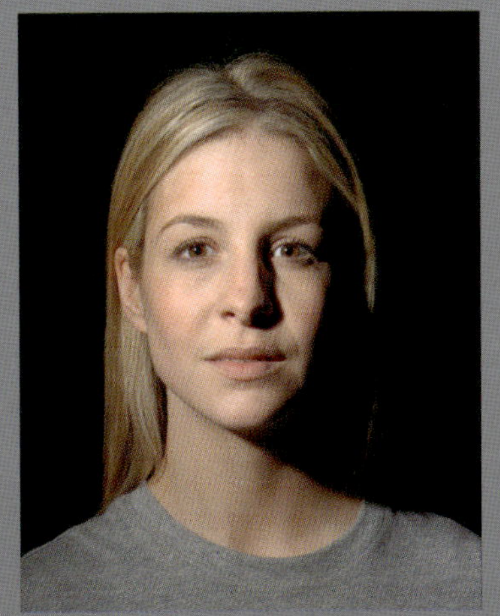

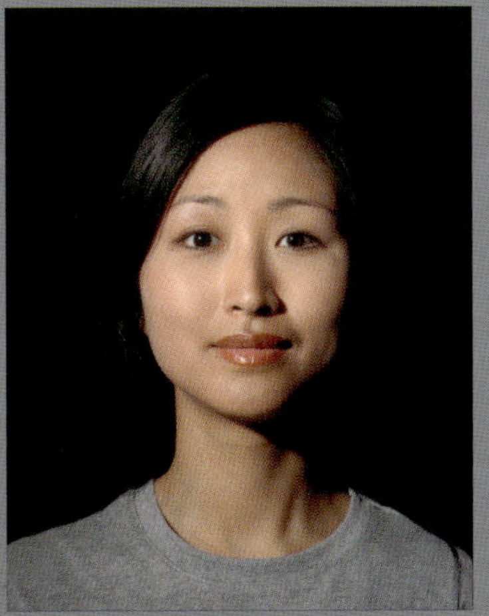

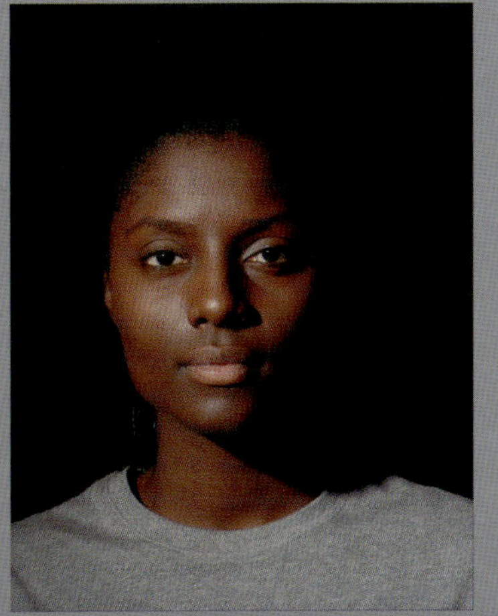

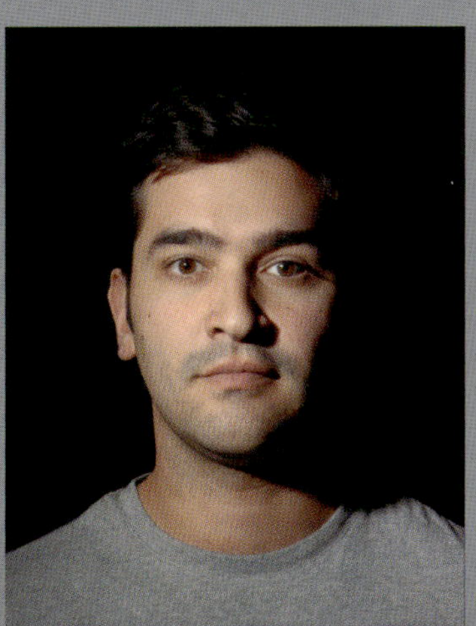

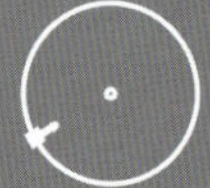

SNOOT

LIGHT 1: 60° LEFT, 30° ANGLED DOWN

LIGHT 2: NONE

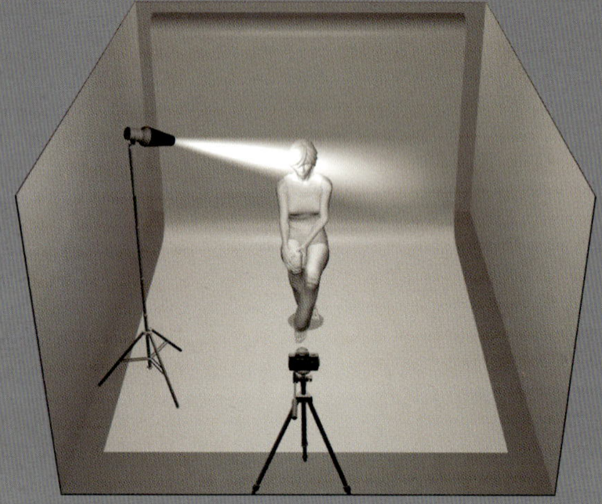

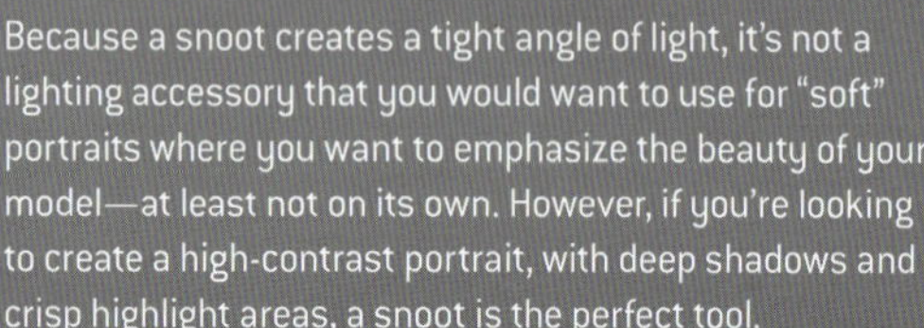

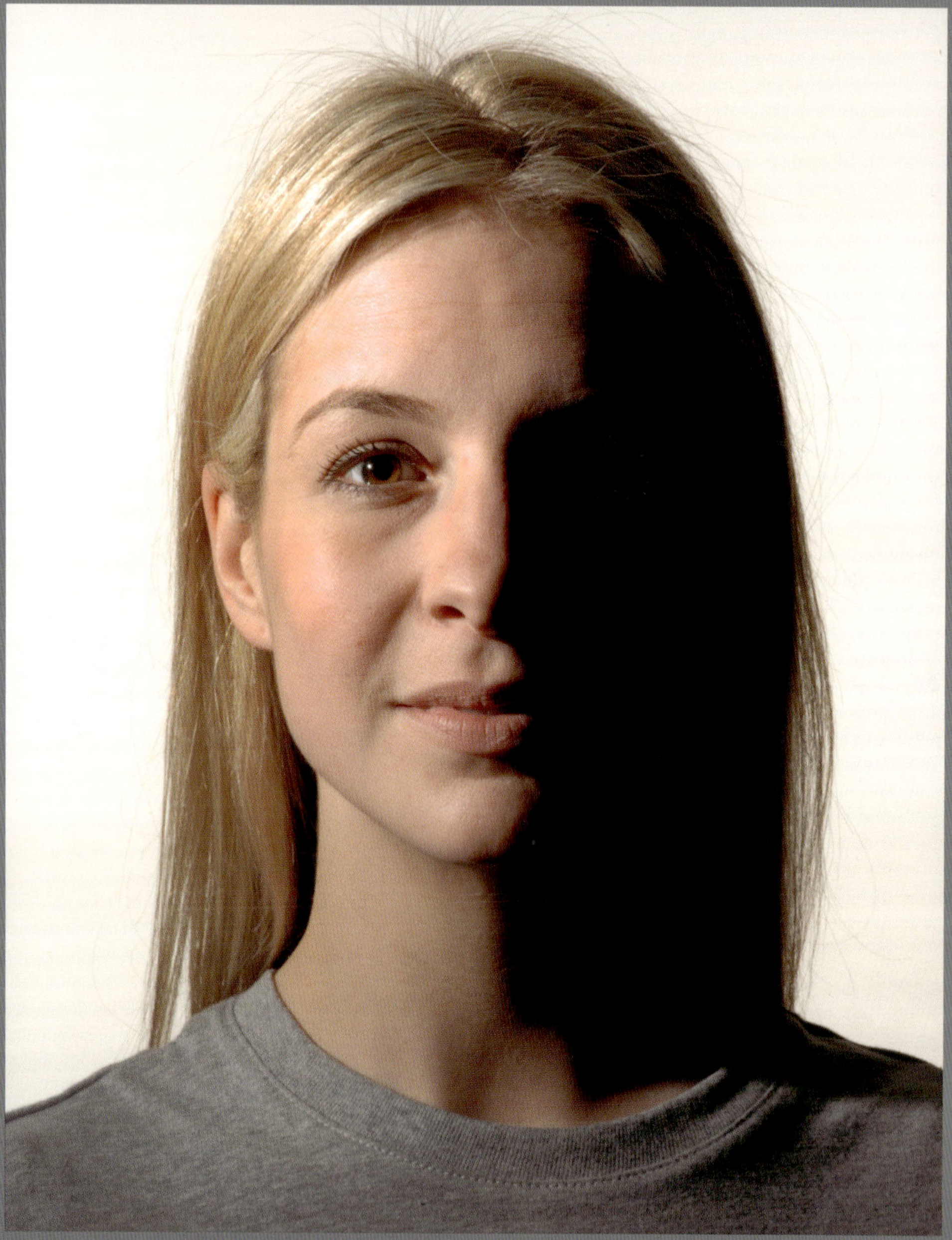

Because a snoot creates a tight angle of light, it's not a lighting accessory that you would want to use for "soft" portraits where you want to emphasize the beauty of your model—at least not on its own. However, if you're looking to create a high-contrast portrait, with deep shadows and crisp highlight areas, a snoot is the perfect tool.

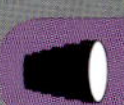

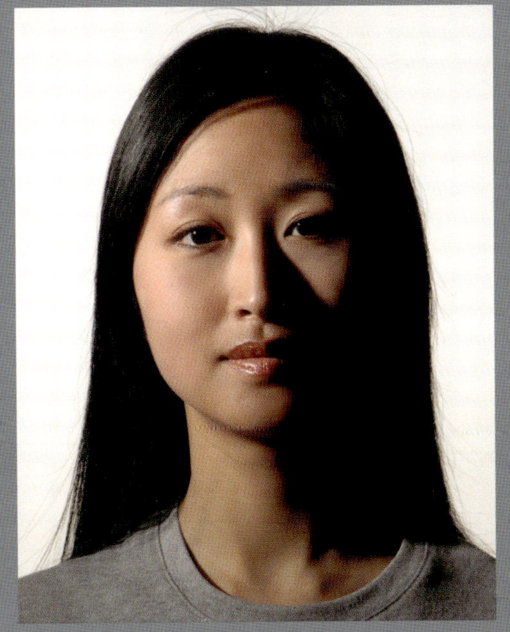

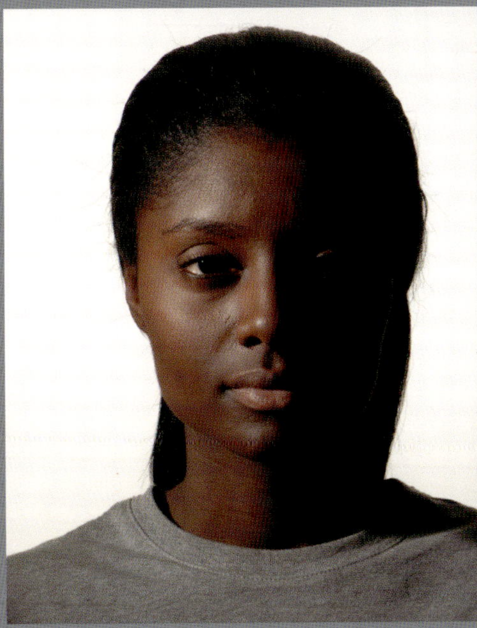

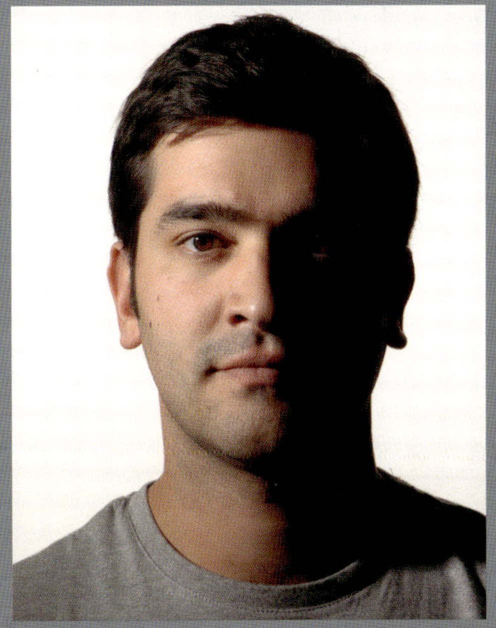

DARK BACKGROUND

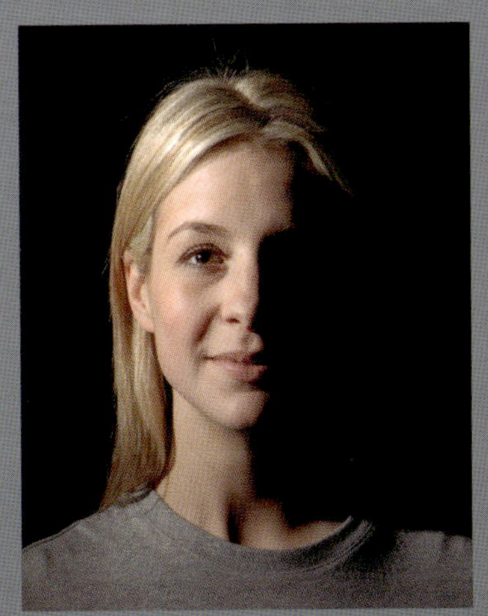

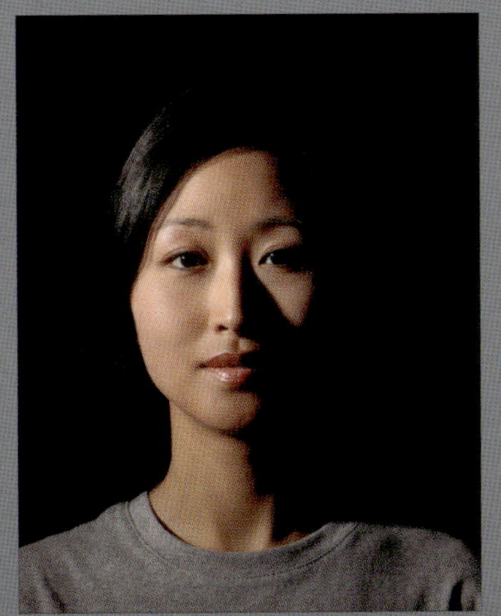

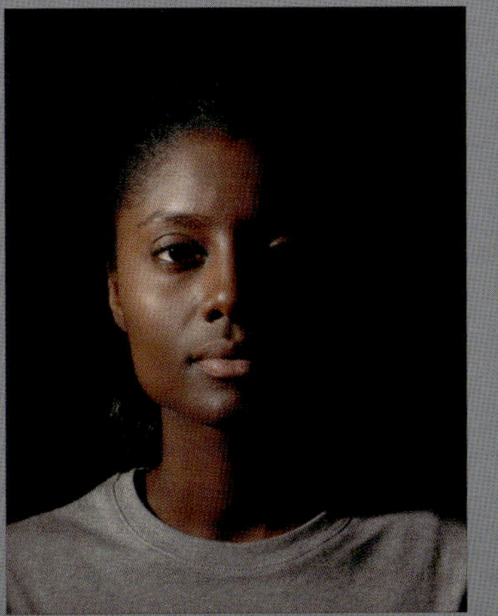

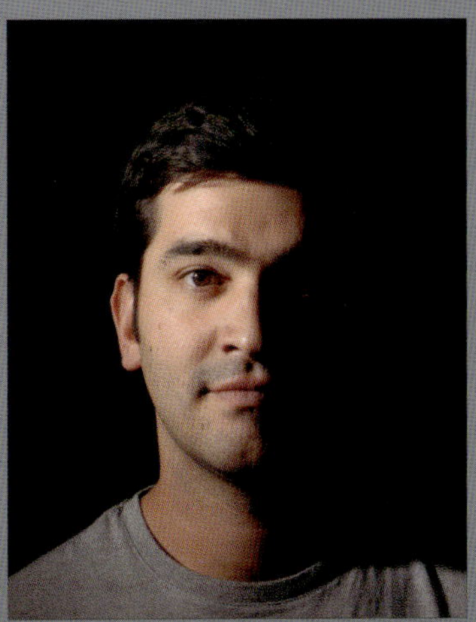

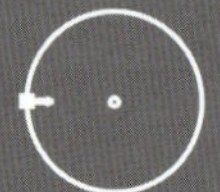

SNOOT

LIGHT 1: 90° LEFT, 30° ANGLED DOWN

LIGHT 2: NONE

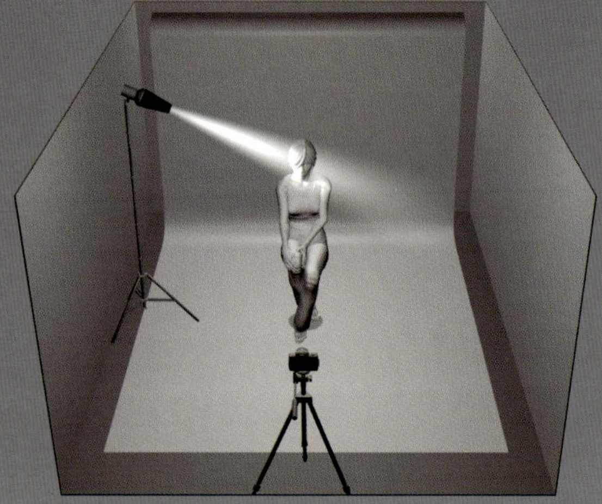

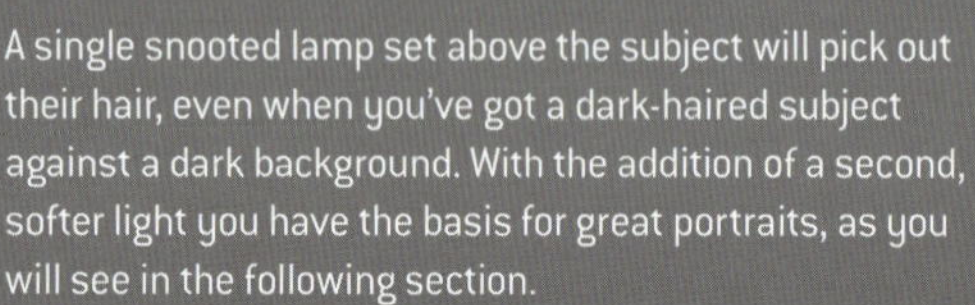

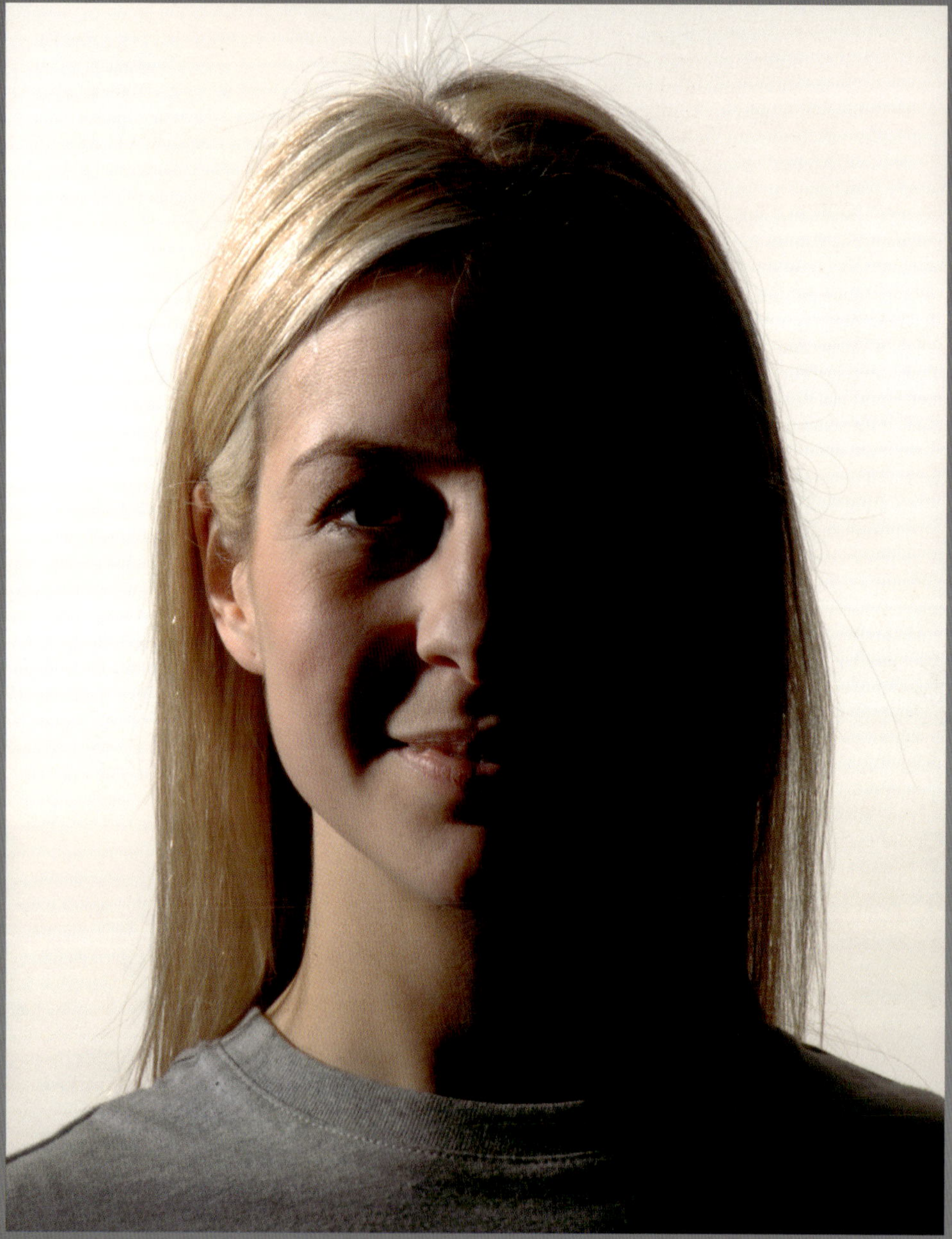

A single snooted lamp set above the subject will pick out their hair, even when you've got a dark-haired subject against a dark background. With the addition of a second, softer light you have the basis for great portraits, as you will see in the following section.

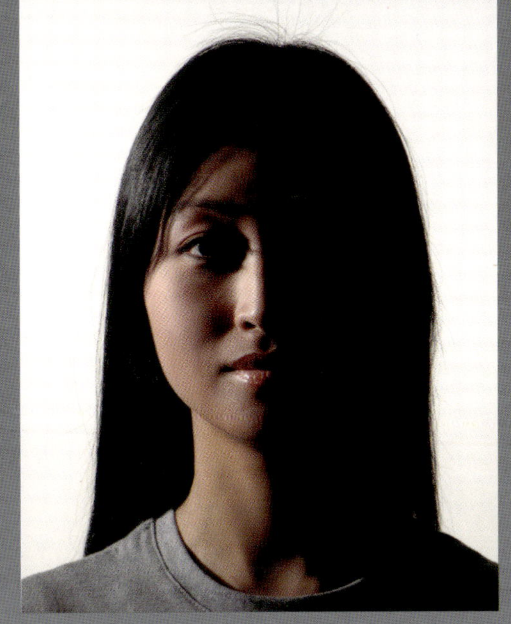
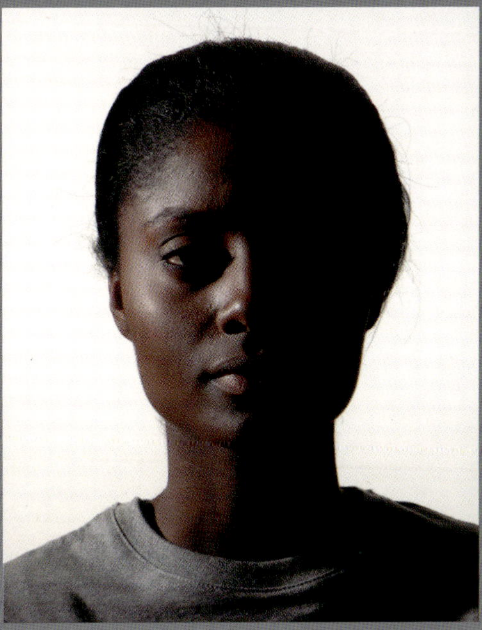
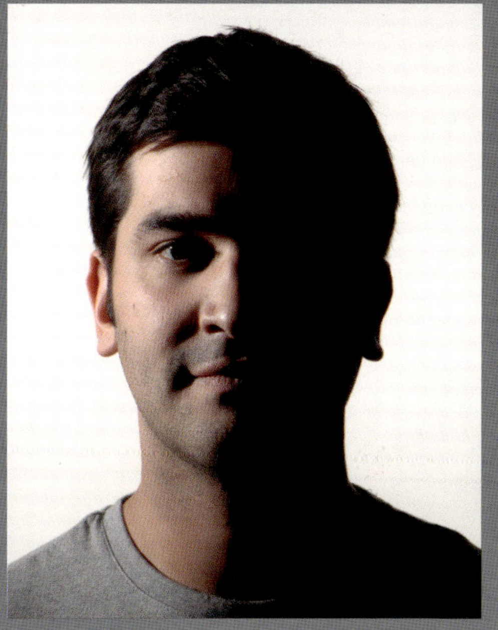

DARK BACKGROUND

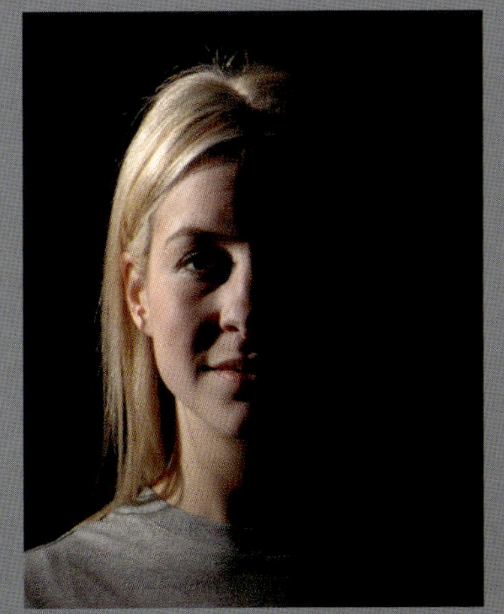

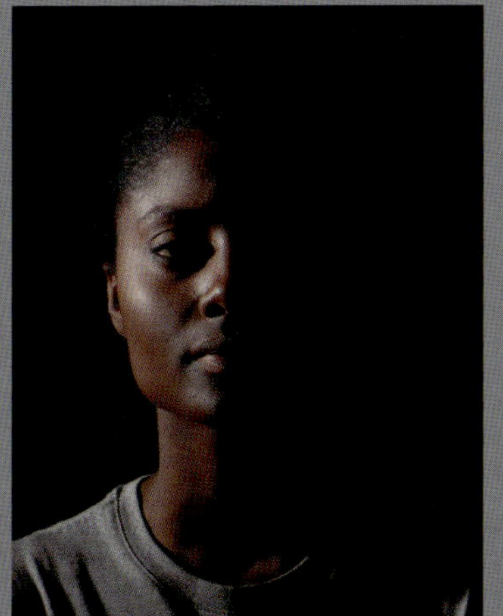
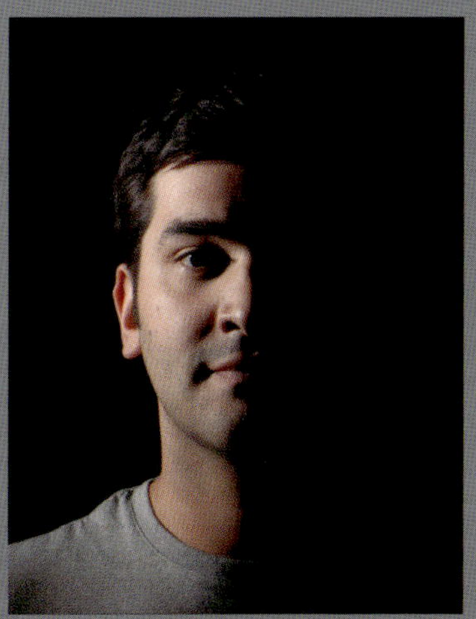

CHAPTER 7

SOFTBOX & SNOOT

A snooted light may not be the best choice for portrait photography when you use it on its own, but when you combine its narrowed beam of light with the soft-light capabilities of a softbox, you've got yourself a very versatile two-light setup.

The softbox works in a similar way to a large window, flooding the subject with a diffuse light. What shadows it creates are light and soft edged, which is particularly flattering when your subject has folds or creases in their skin that you want to disguise.

However, add a snooted lamp to the setup and you have the best of both worlds—the soft, shadow-filling light from the softbox that provides you with your overall illumination, plus the direct, targeted beam from the snooted lamp that can be used to subtly add contrast. Together, these two lights can be used to create a wide range of looks in your portrait photography.

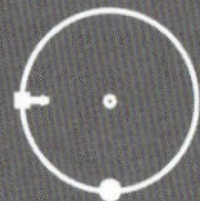

SOFTBOX & SNOOT

LIGHT 1 (SOFTBOX): FROM 0°

LIGHT 2 (SNOOT): FROM 90° LEFT

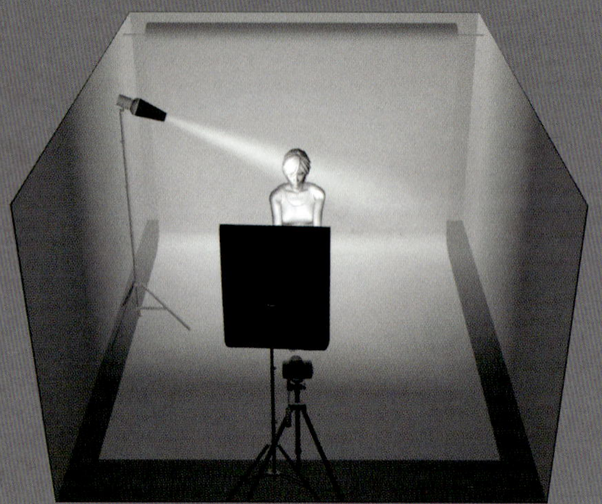

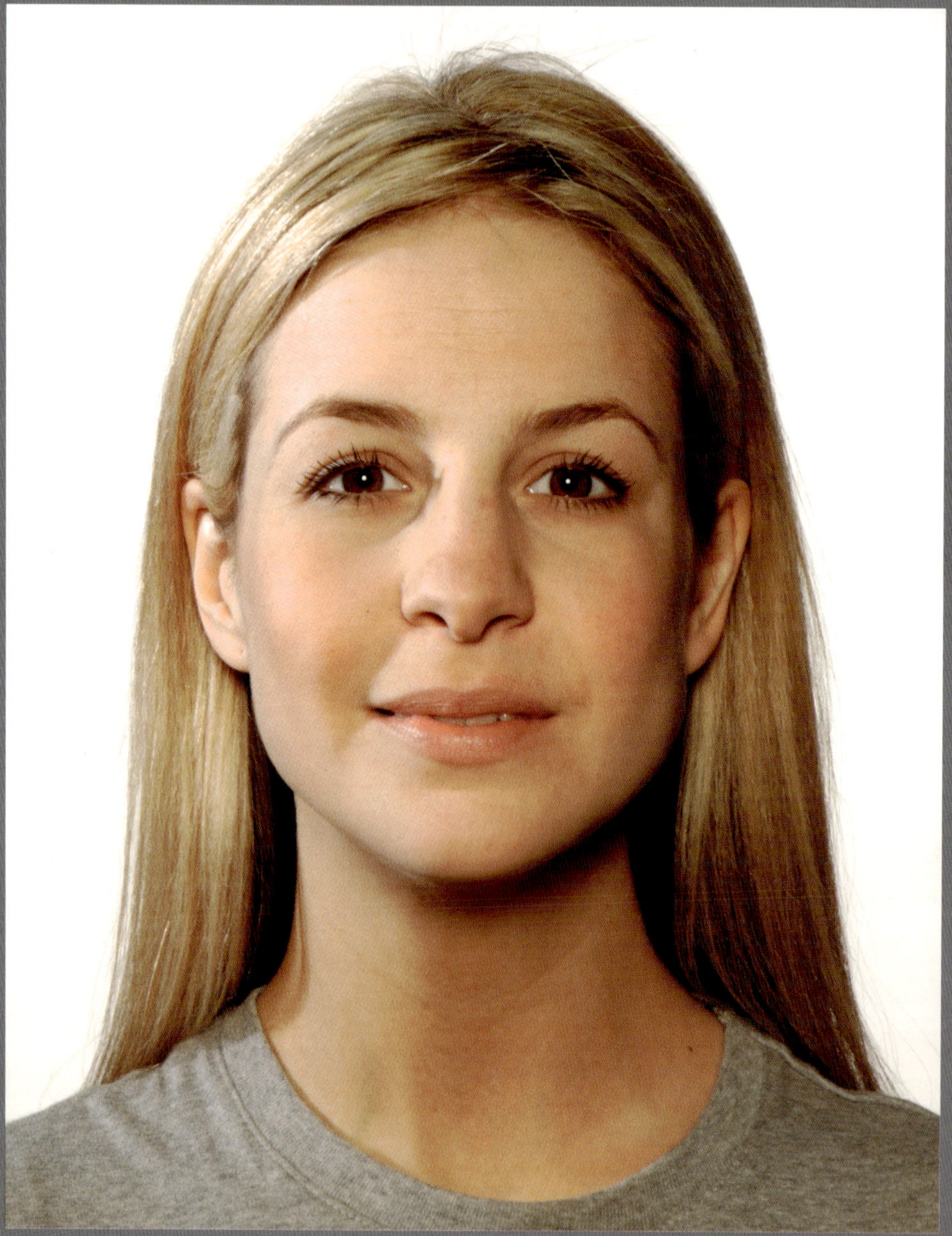

Used face-on to the subject, the softbox produces a flattering, diffuse light that creates strong catchlights in the subject's eyes, but without introducing any deep shadow areas. Adding a snoot lifts the right side of the model's face, preventing the portrait from looking overly flat.

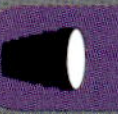

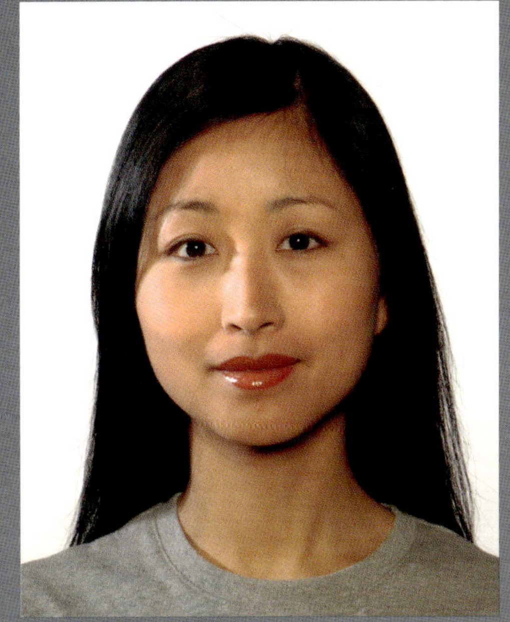

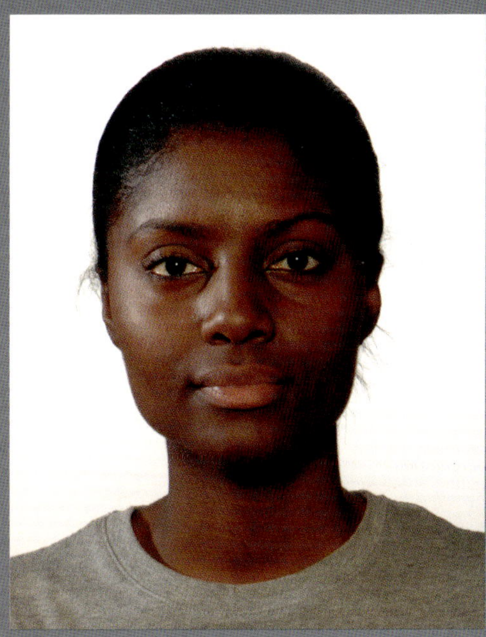

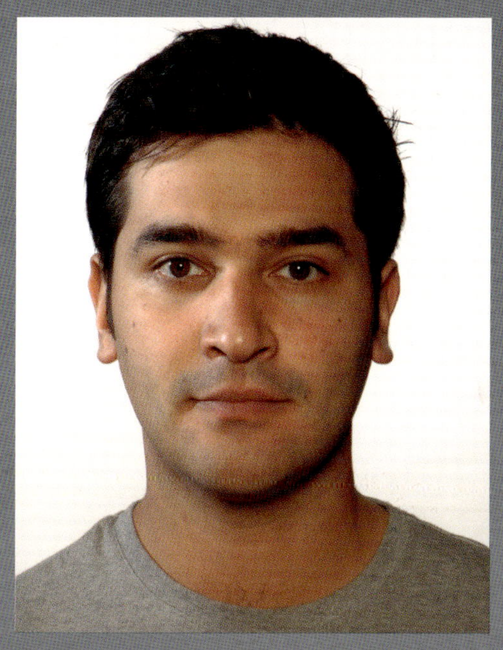

DARK BACKGROUND

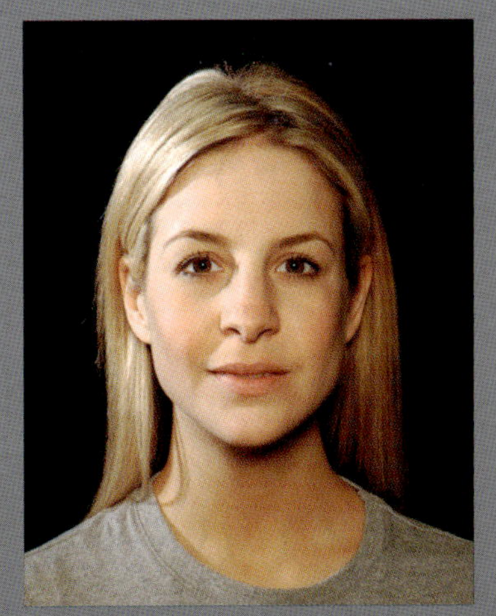

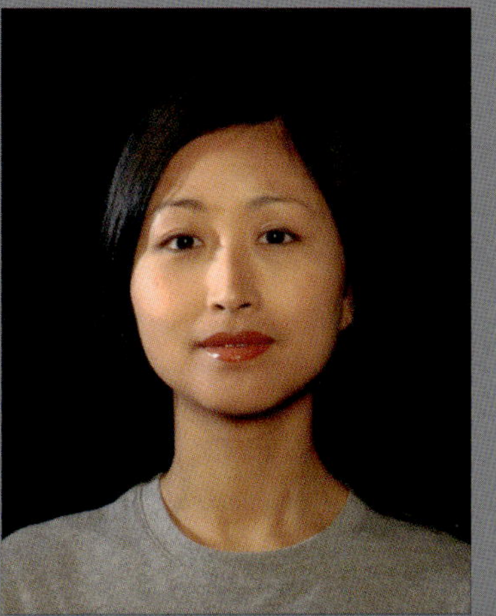

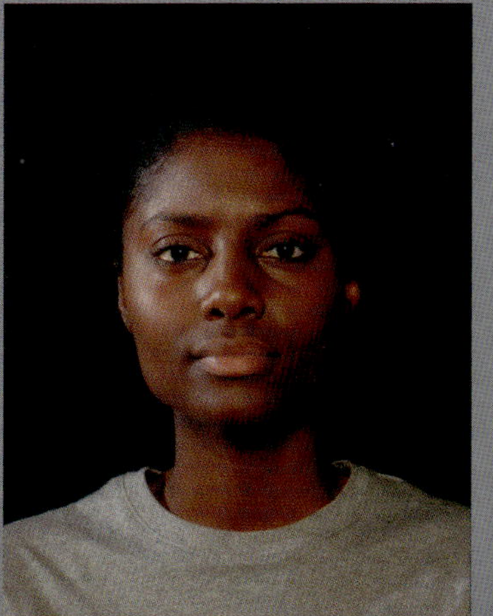

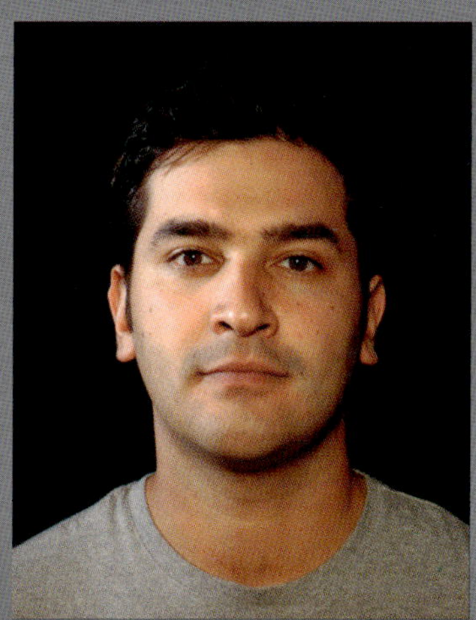

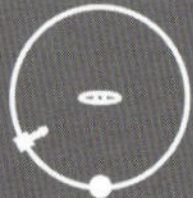

SOFTBOX & SNOOT

LIGHT 1 (SOFTBOX): FROM 0°

LIGHT 2 (SNOOT): FROM 60° LEFT

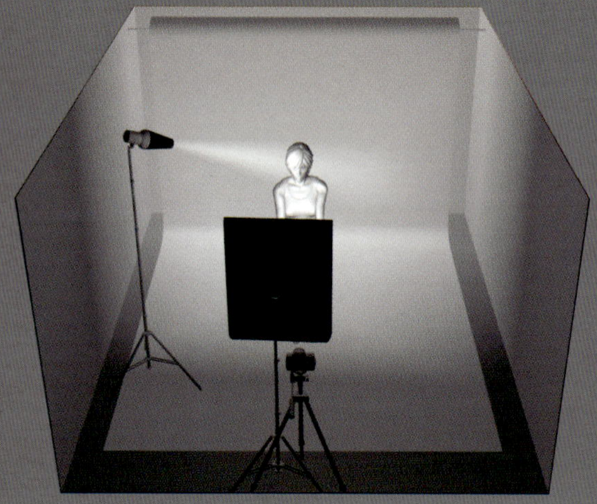

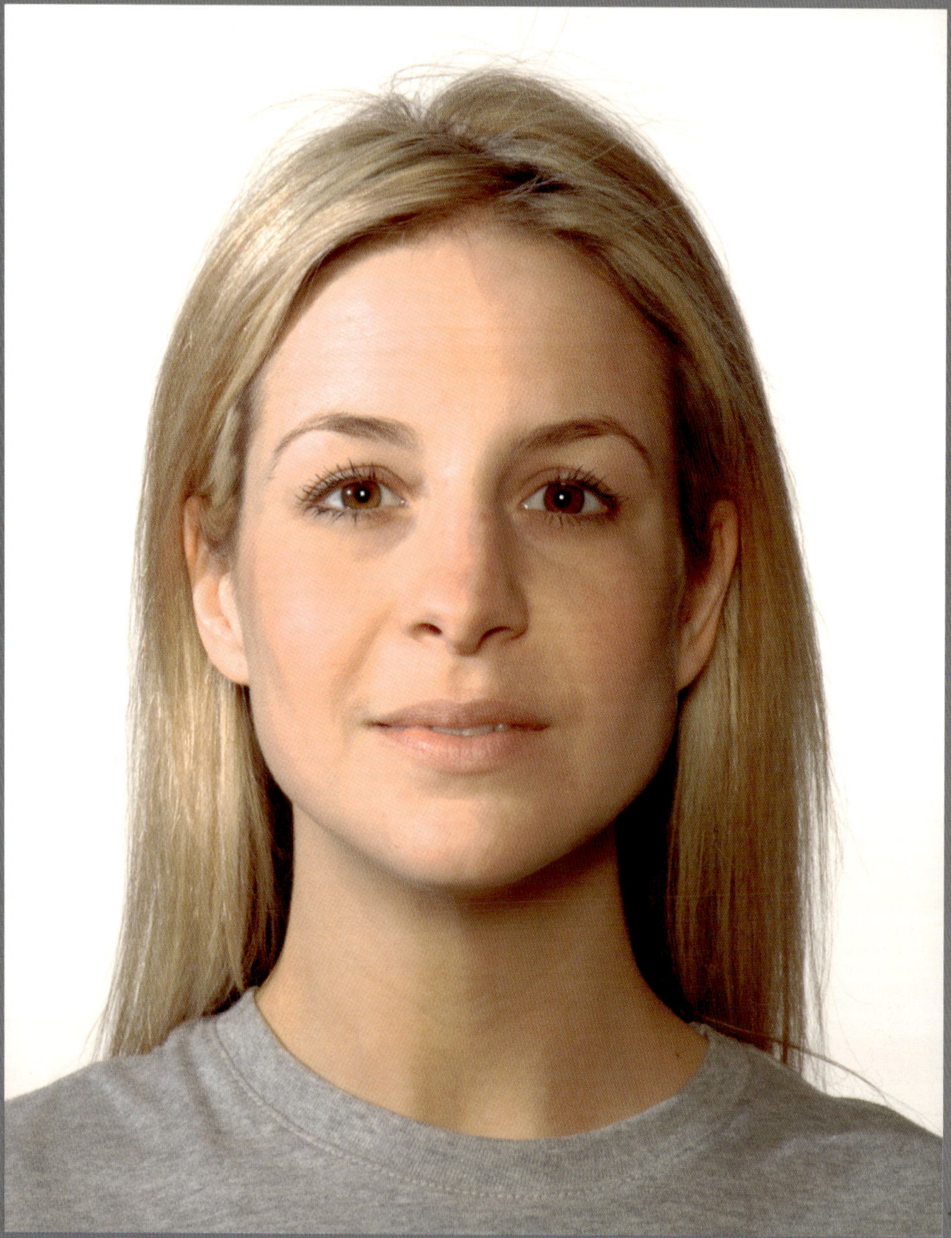

With the softbox remaining in the same position as the previous shots, the snoot has been moved round so that it is closer to the camera axis. As a result, the left side of the model's face is now lighter, and the portrait is slightly flatter. Overall, it is slightly less three dimensional.

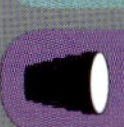

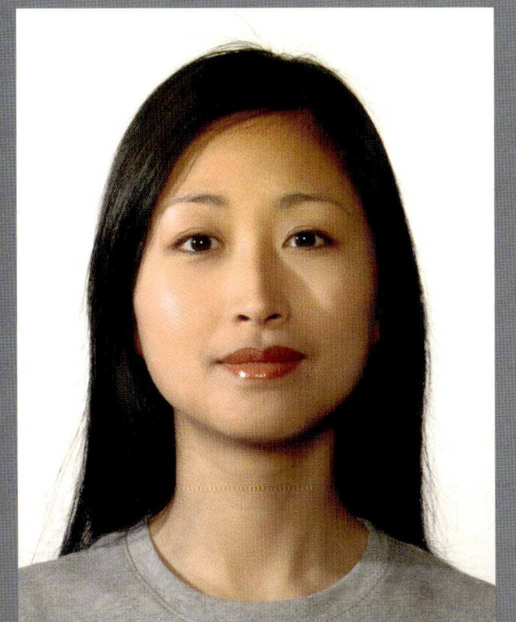

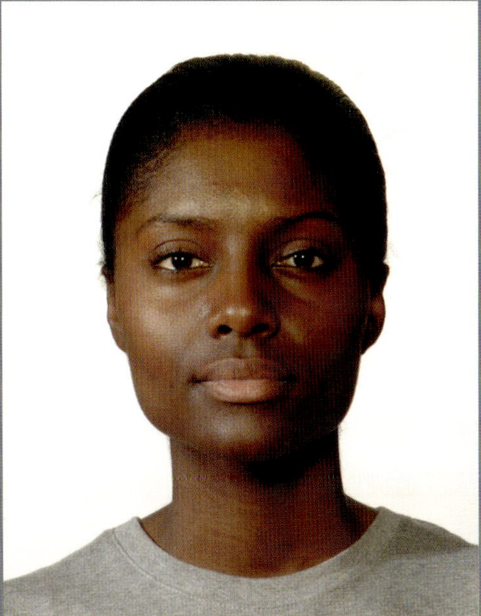

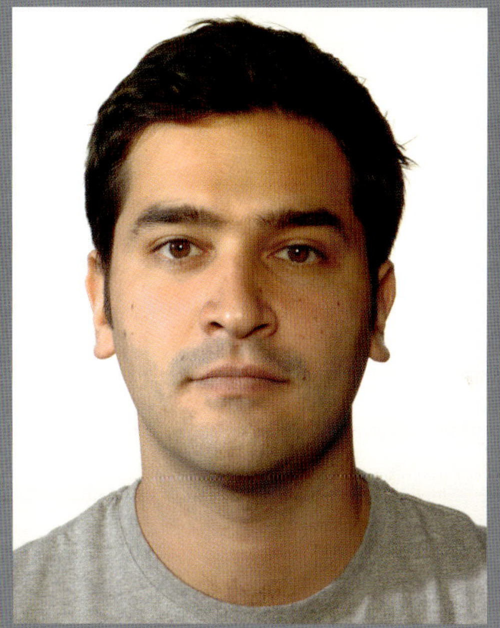

DARK BACKGROUND

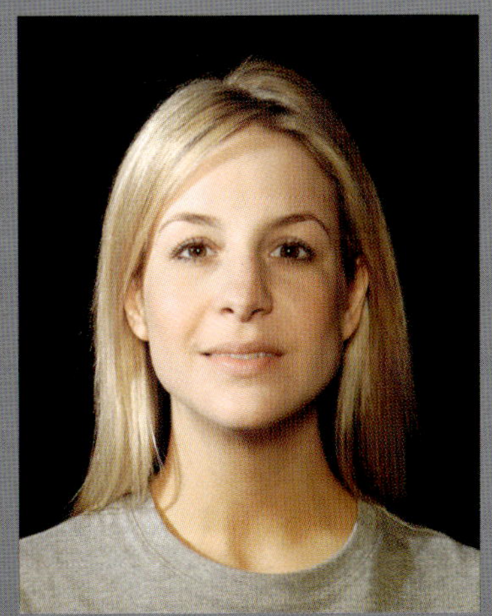

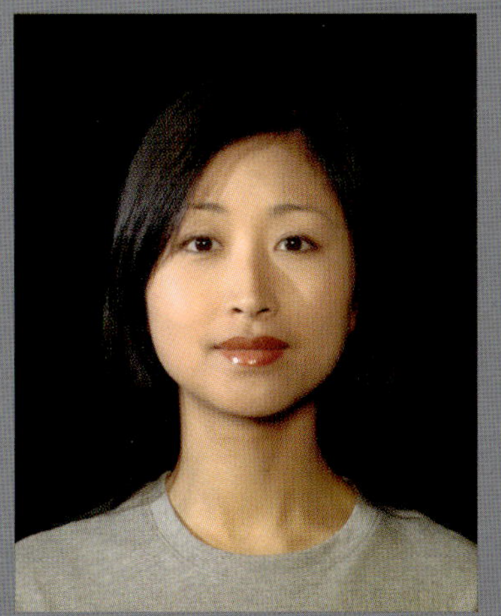

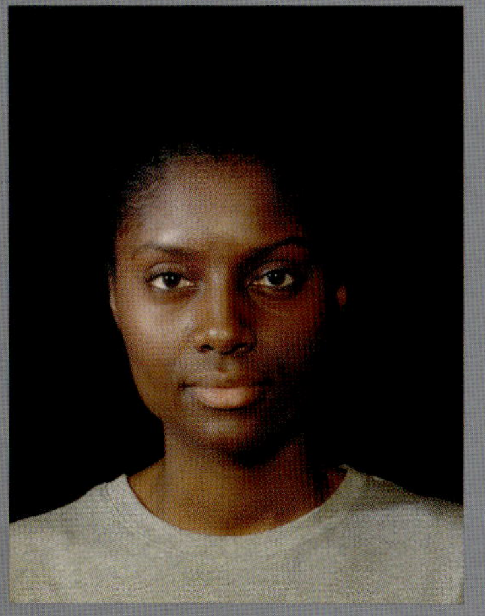

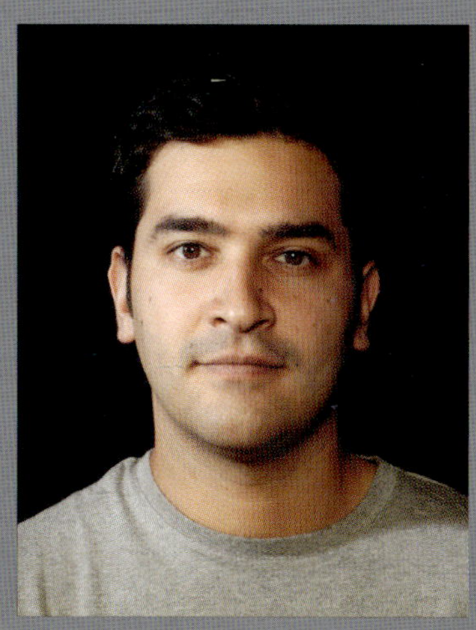

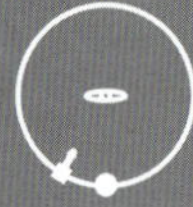

SOFTBOX & SNOOT

LIGHT 1 (SOFTBOX): FROM 0°

LIGHT 2 (SNOOT): FROM 30° LEFT

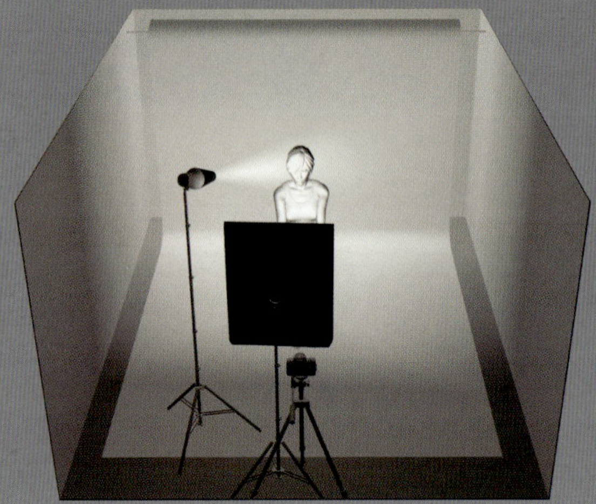

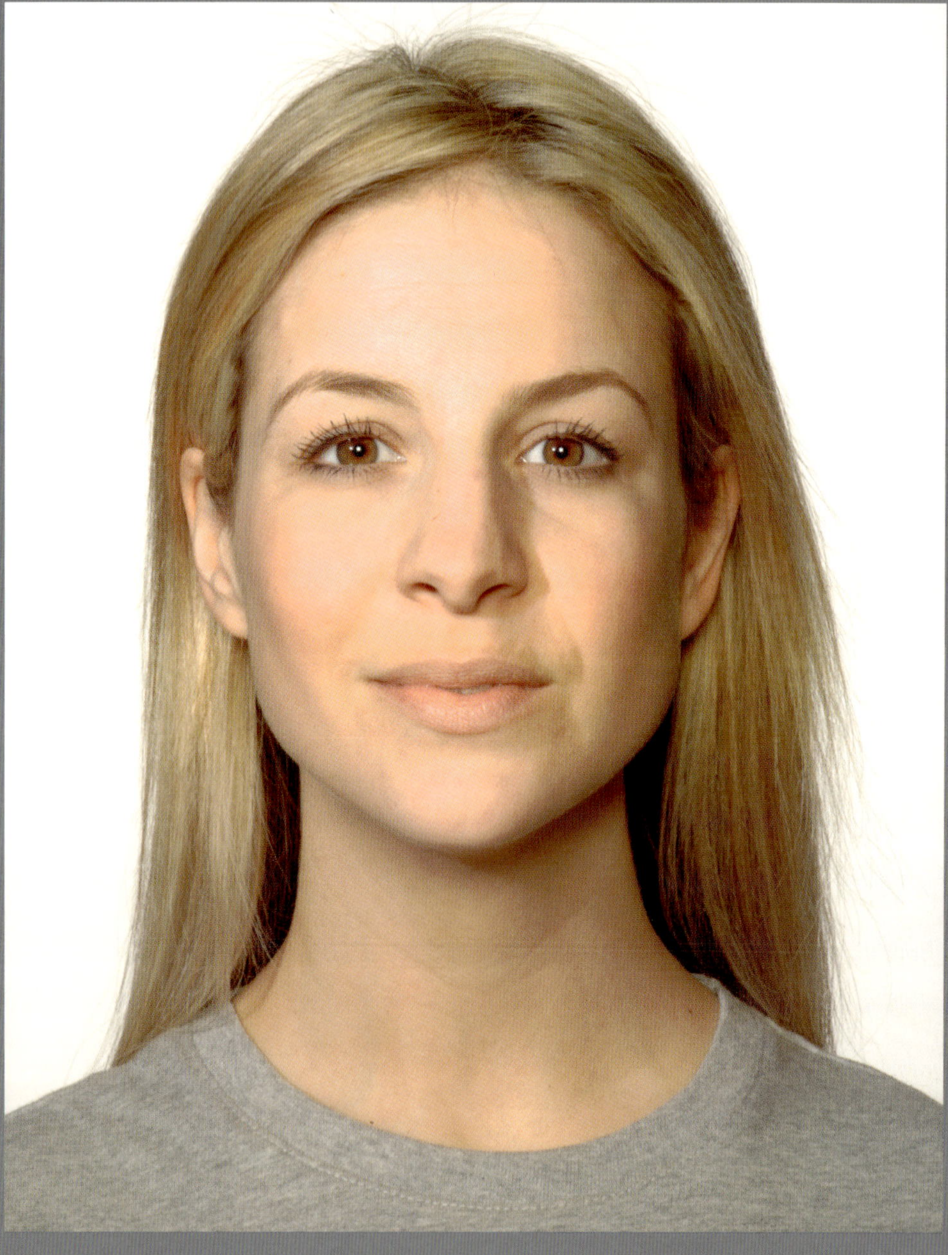

The snooted lamp is now only 30 degrees away from the softbox, so both lights are striking the subject from a similar angle. Shading to the left side of the model's face is minimal, although soft shadows remain along the nose and the edge of the face, providing a subtle modeling effect.

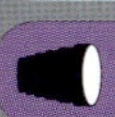

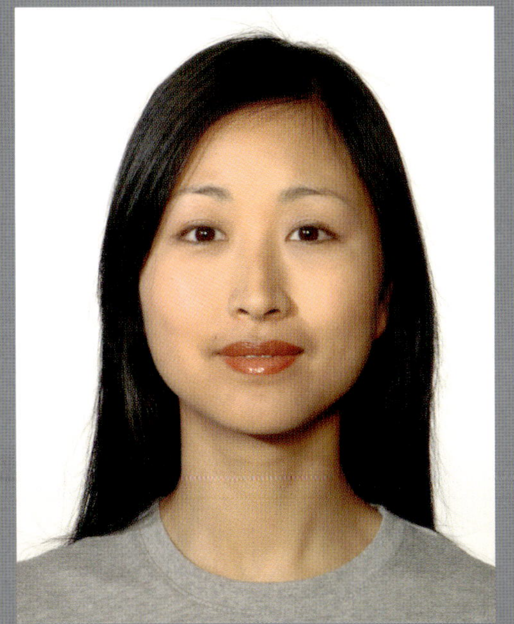

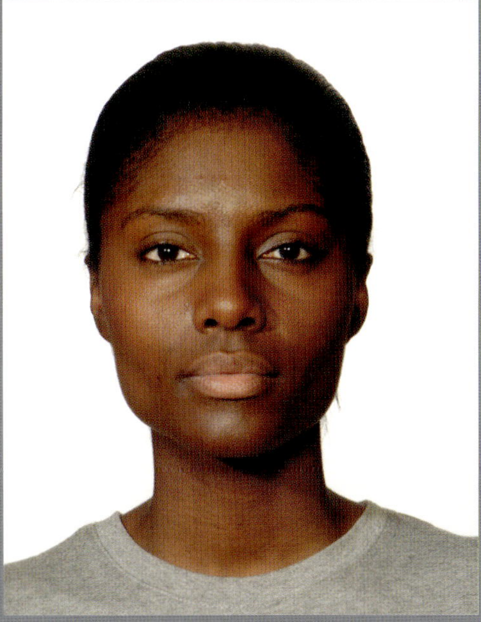

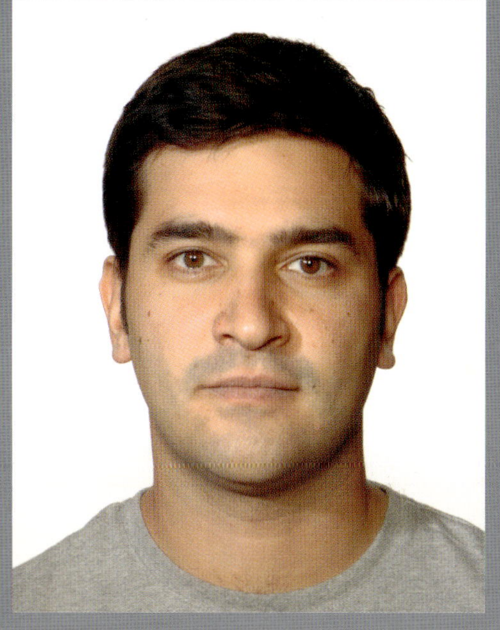

DARK BACKGROUND

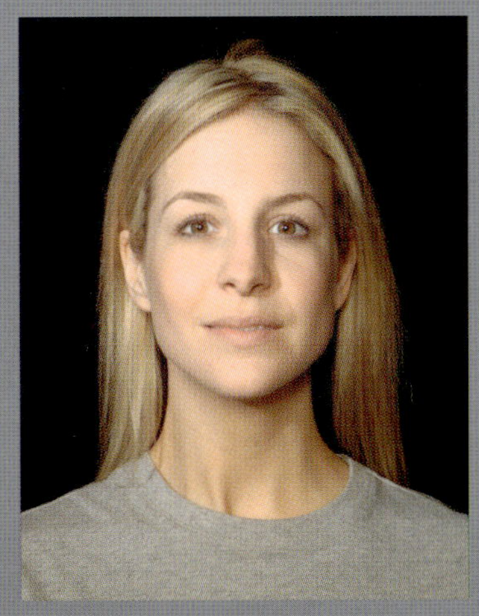

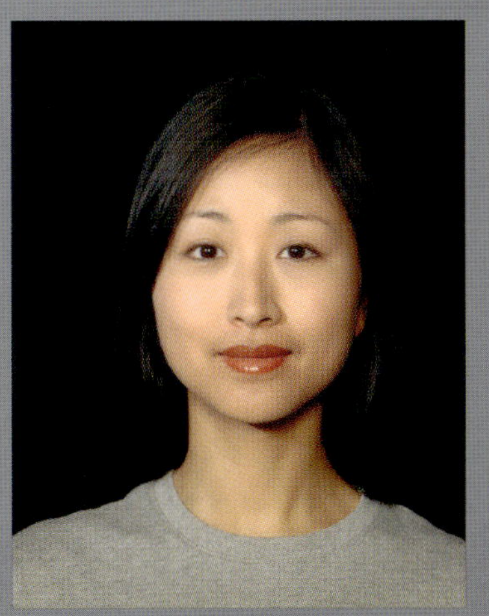

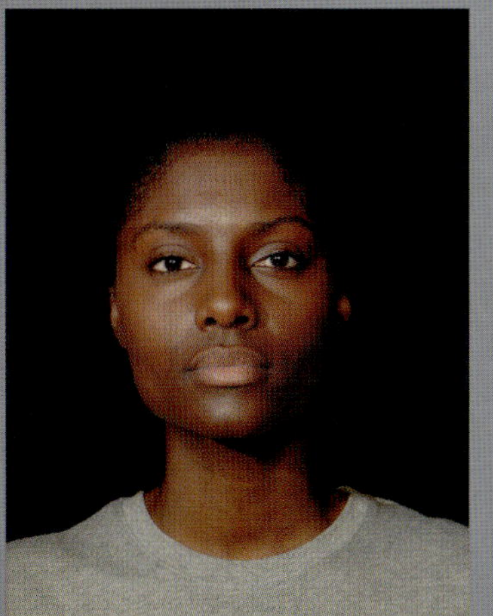

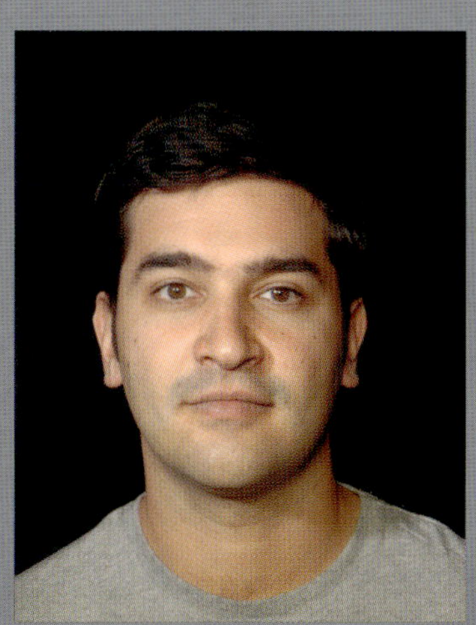

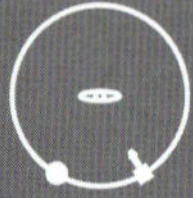

SOFTBOX & SNOOT

LIGHT 1 (SOFTBOX): FROM 30° LEFT

LIGHT 2 (SNOOT): FROM 30° RIGHT

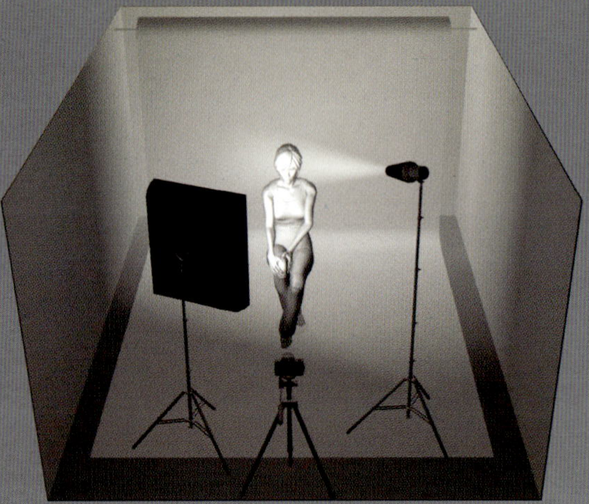

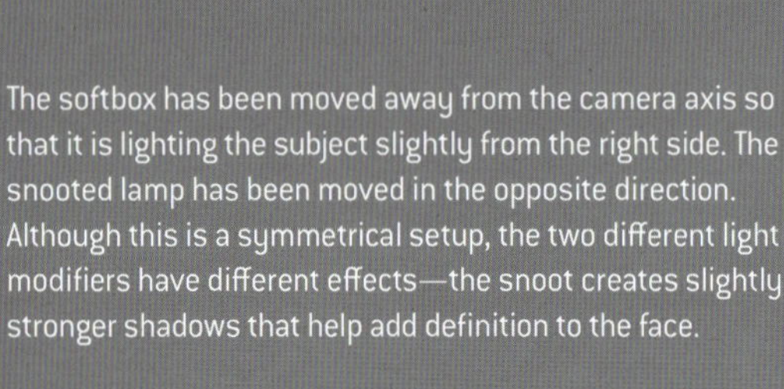

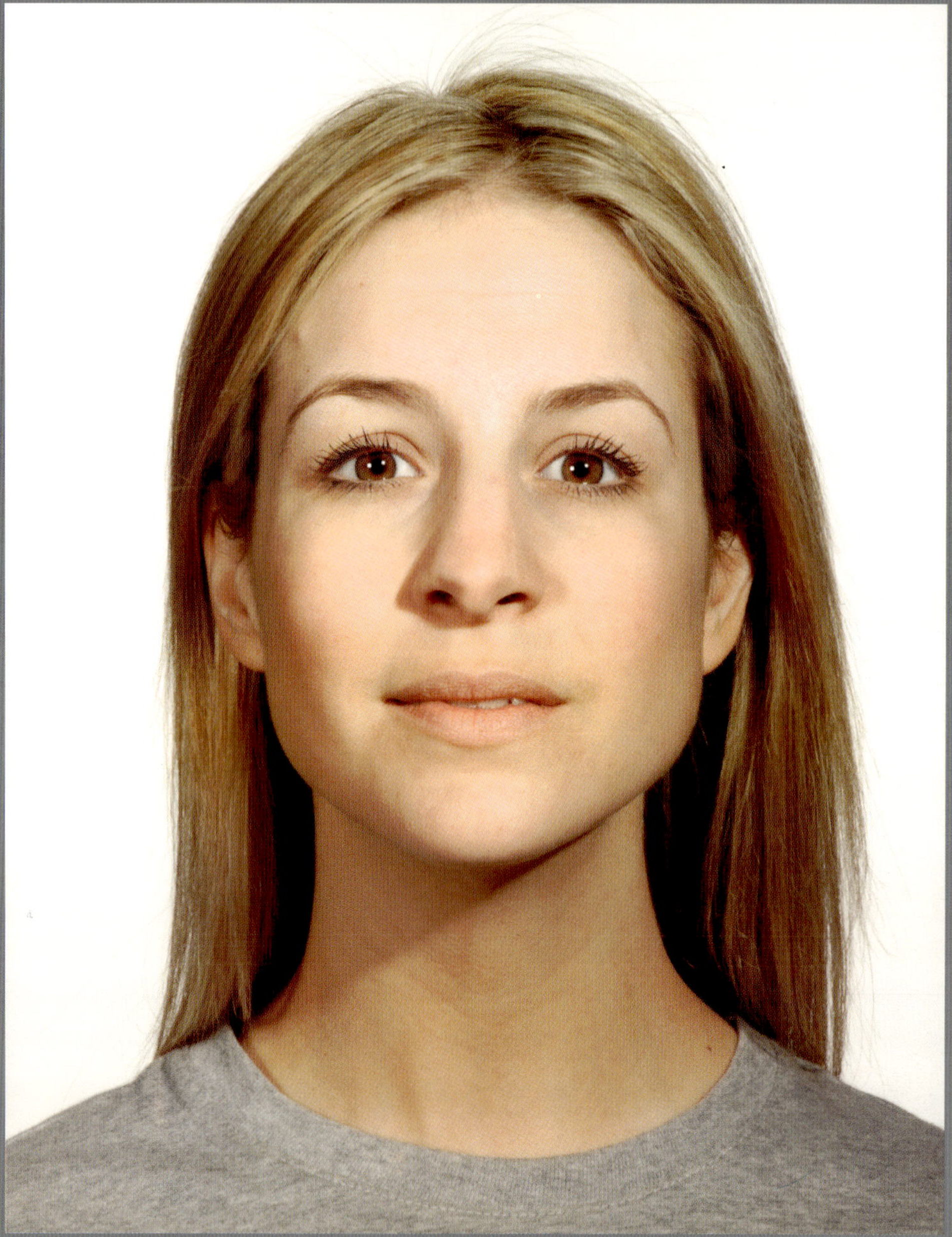

The softbox has been moved away from the camera axis so that it is lighting the subject slightly from the right side. The snooted lamp has been moved in the opposite direction. Although this is a symmetrical setup, the two different light modifiers have different effects—the snoot creates slightly stronger shadows that help add definition to the face.

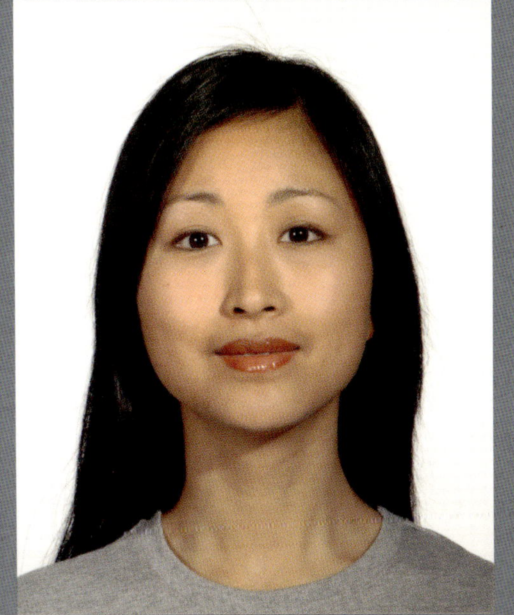
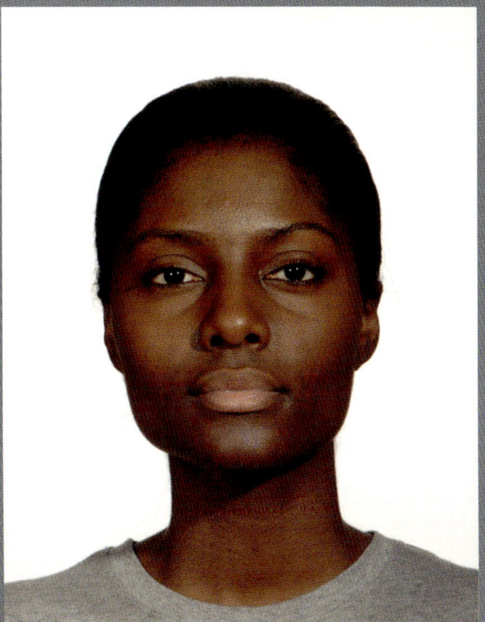
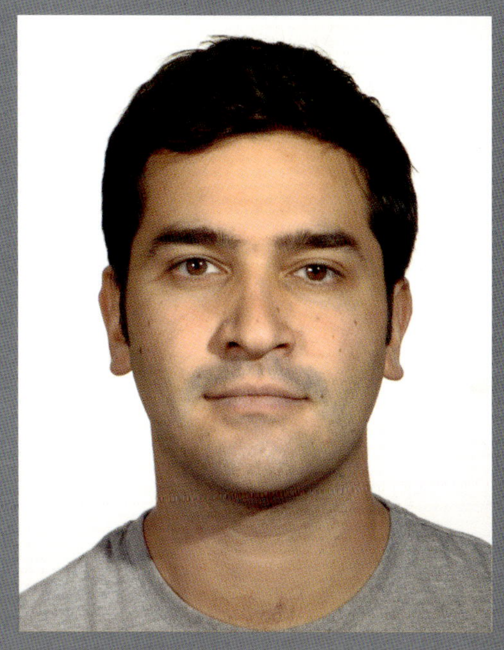

DARK BACKGROUND

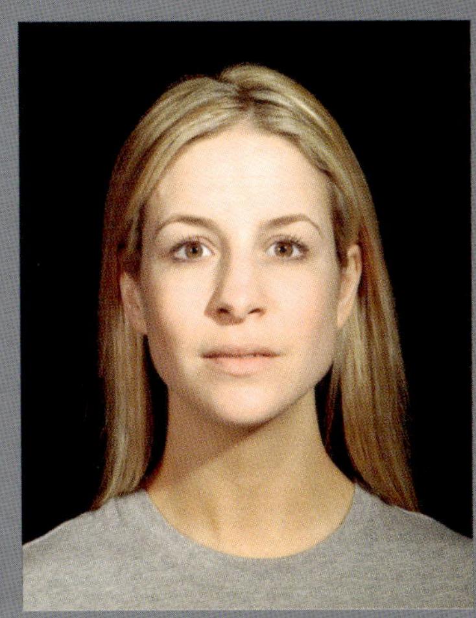
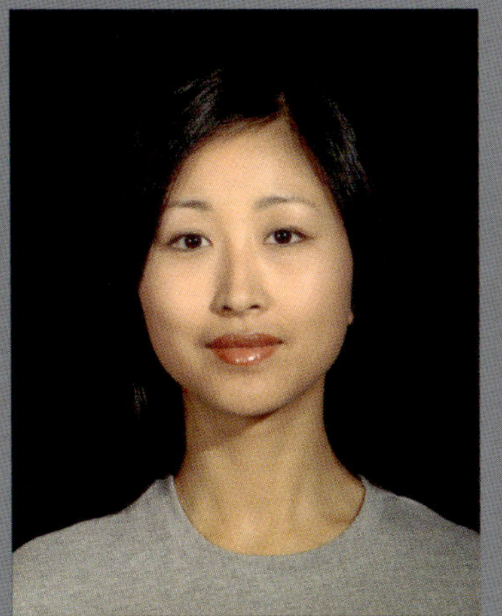
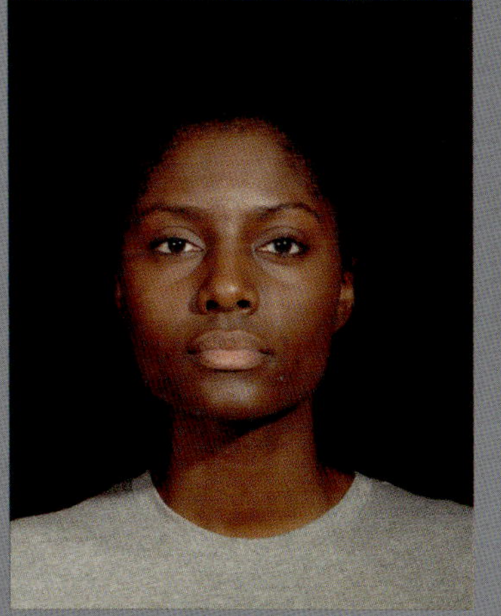
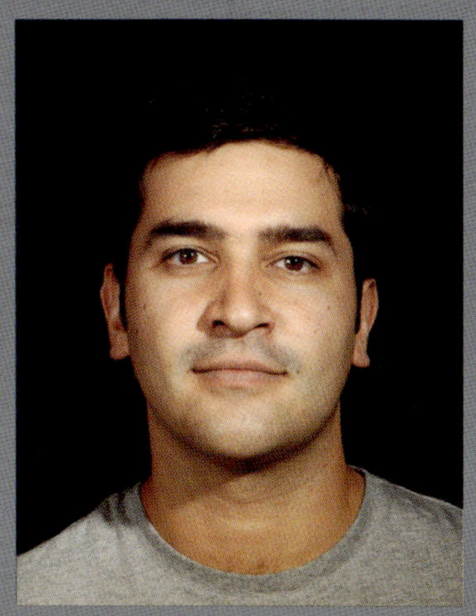

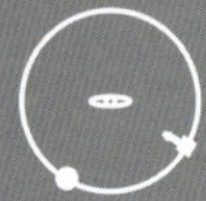

SOFTBOX & SNOOT

LIGHT 1 (SOFTBOX): FROM 30° LEFT

LIGHT 2 (SNOOT): FROM 60° RIGHT

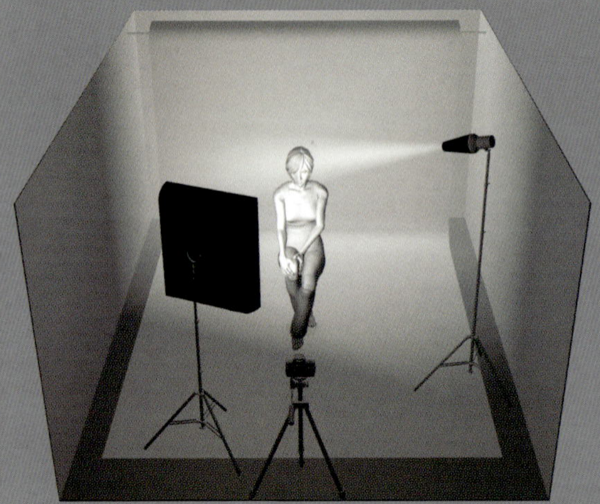

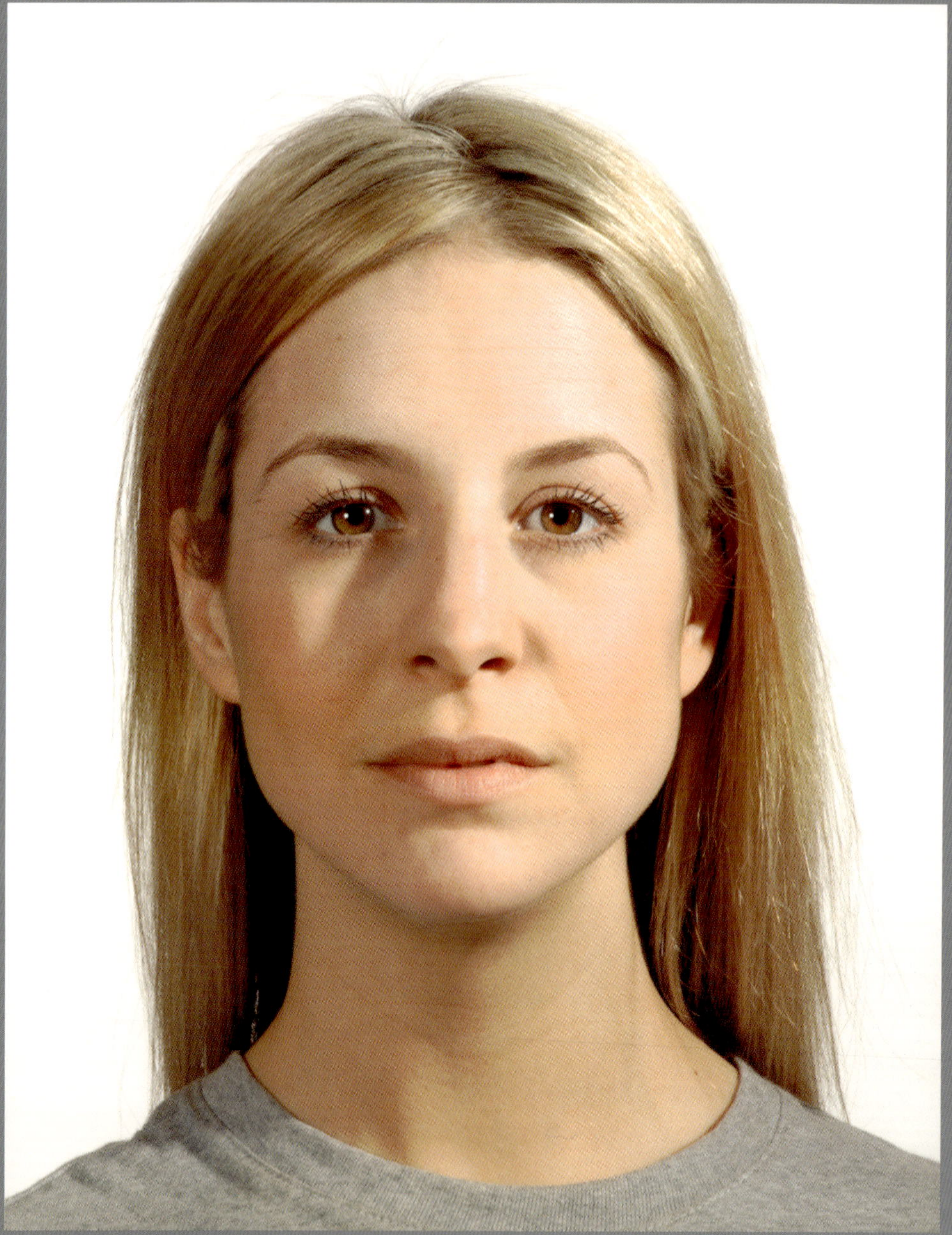

As the snooted light moves further to the right of the camera, the shadows on the opposite side of the subject's face are strengthened. This is especially noticeable along the nose, where—depending on the model's facial structure—a small "triangle" of light may appear beneath the right eye.

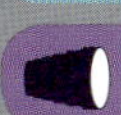

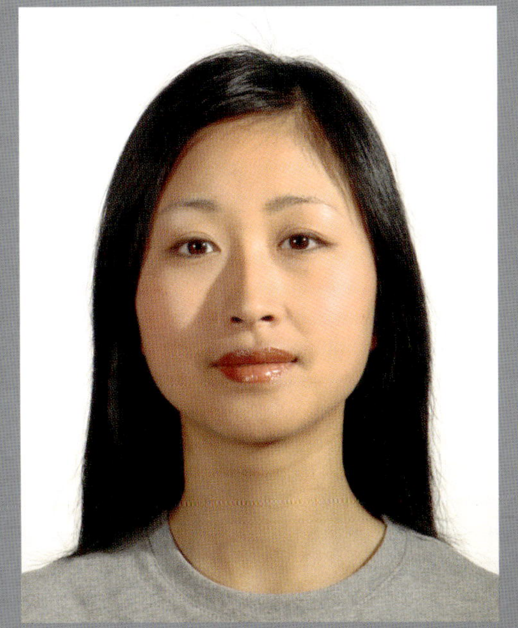

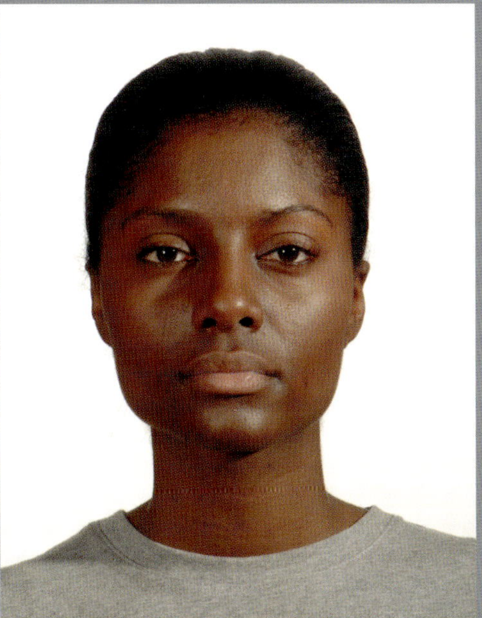

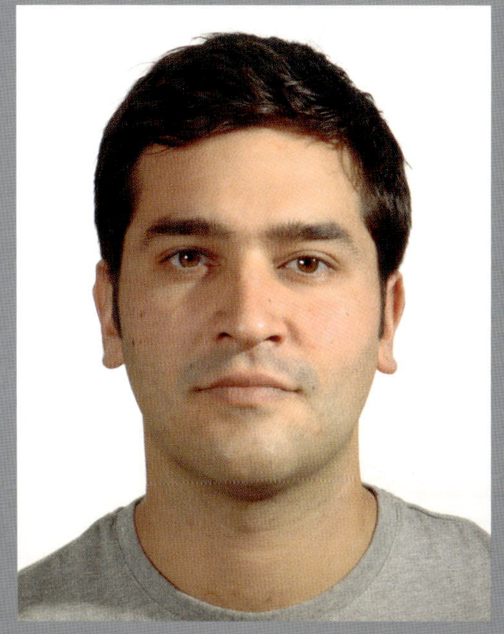

DARK BACKGROUND

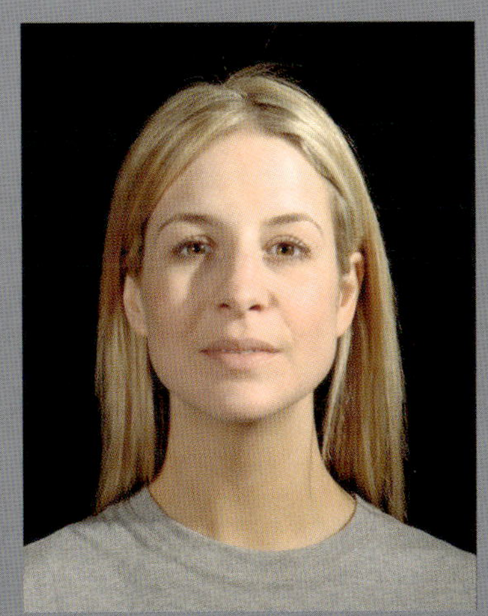

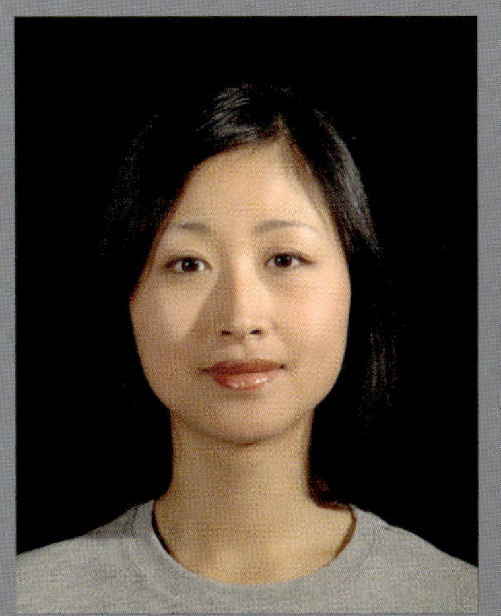

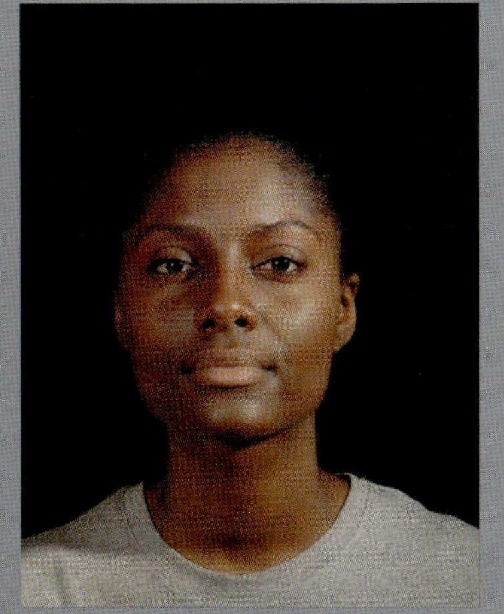

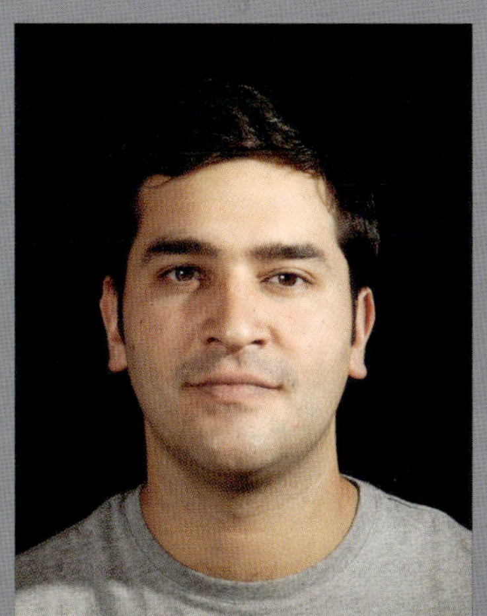

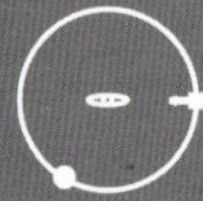

SOFTBOX & SNOOT

LIGHT 1 (SOFTBOX): FROM 30° LEFT

LIGHT 2 (SNOOT): FROM 90° RIGHT

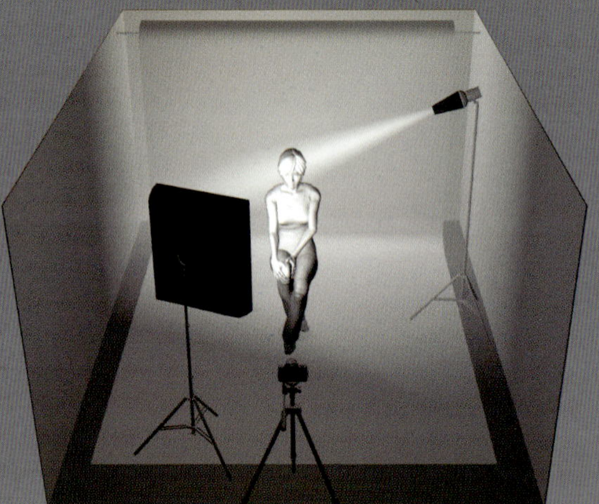

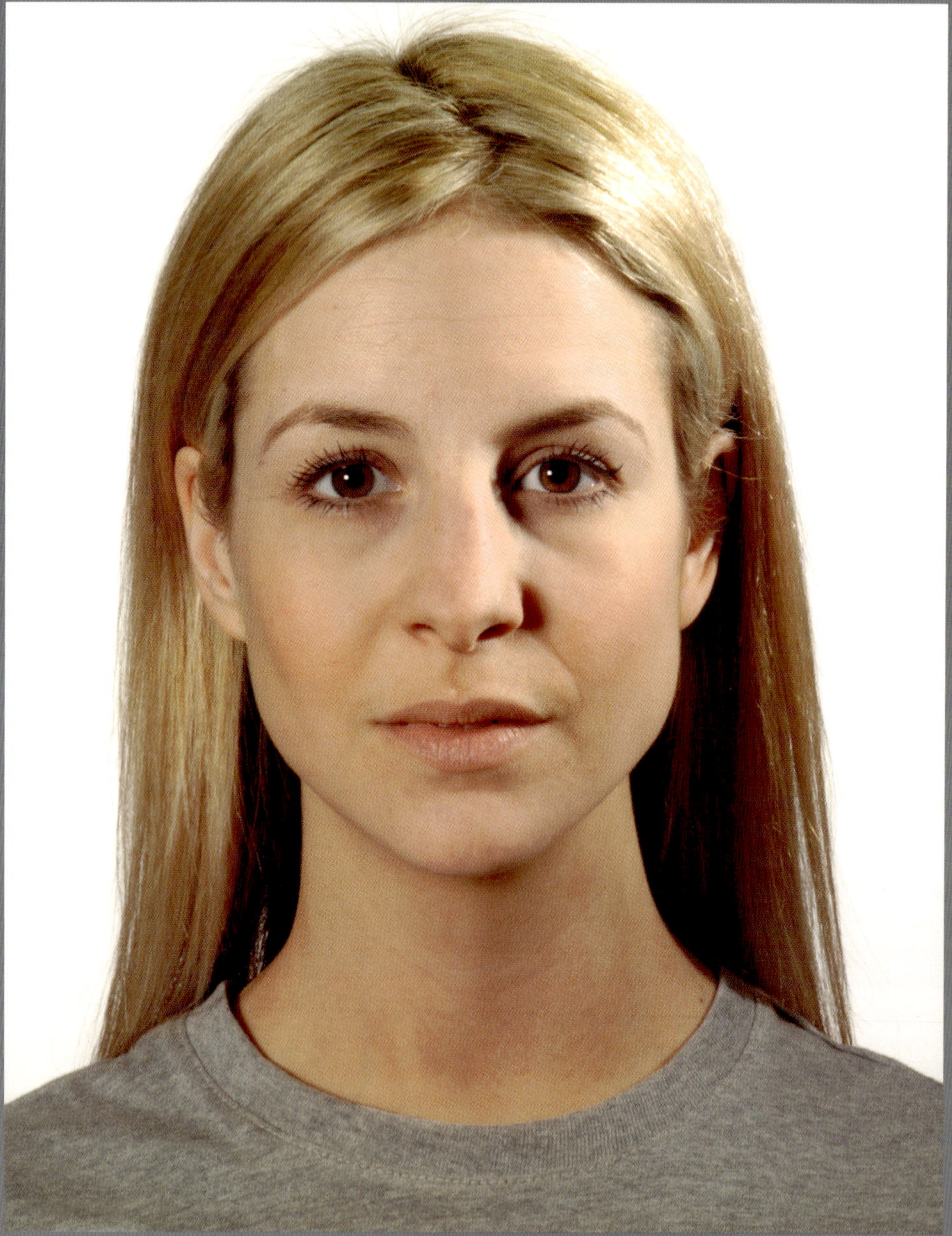

With the snoot at a 90-degree angle to the camera, the softbox provides much of the lighting to the face, with the snoot highlighting the hair. However, although the softbox is now the main, or "key" light, the snooted lamp adds a couple of small shadows to the left of the subject's nose.

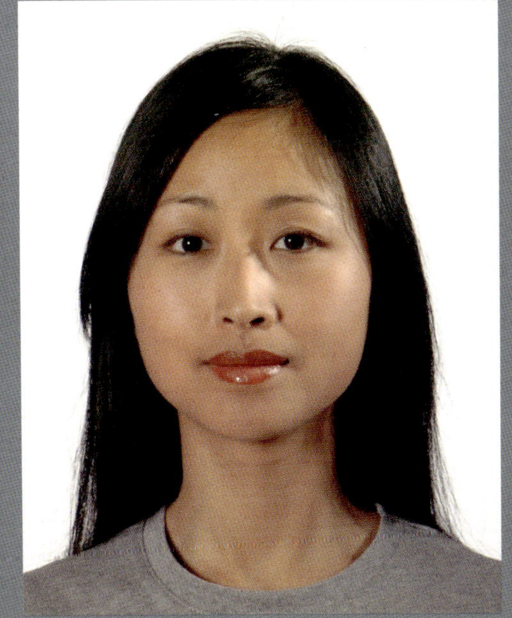

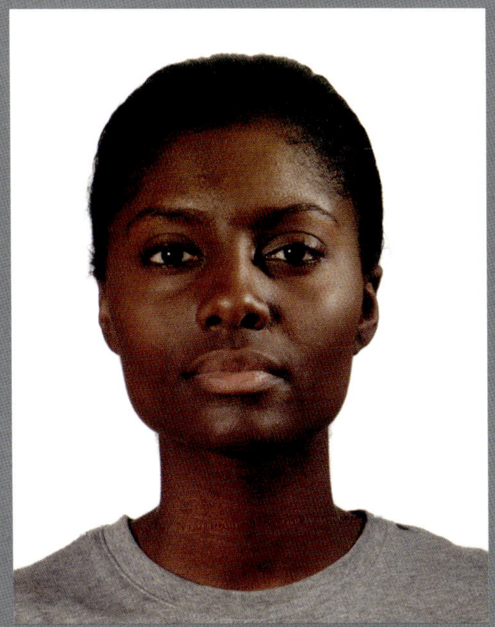

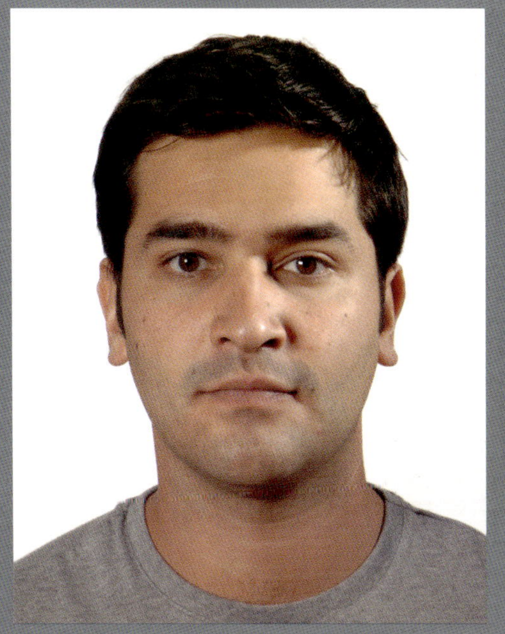

DARK BACKGROUND

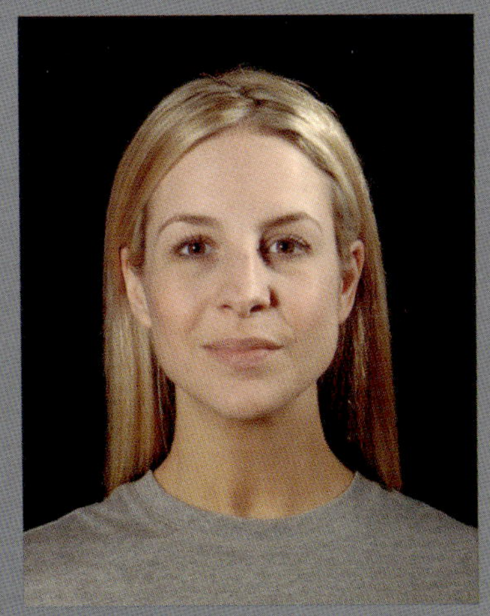

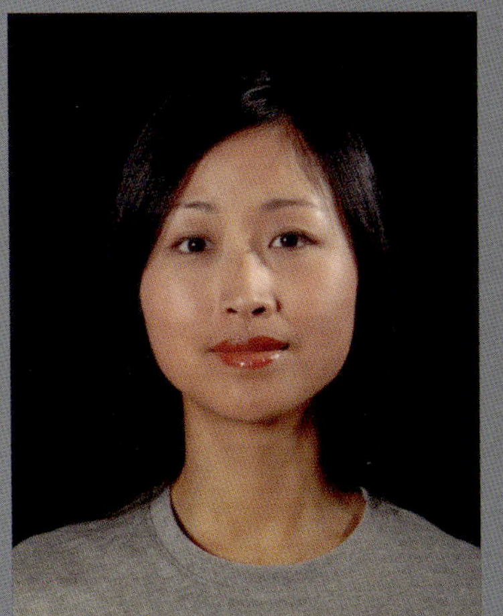

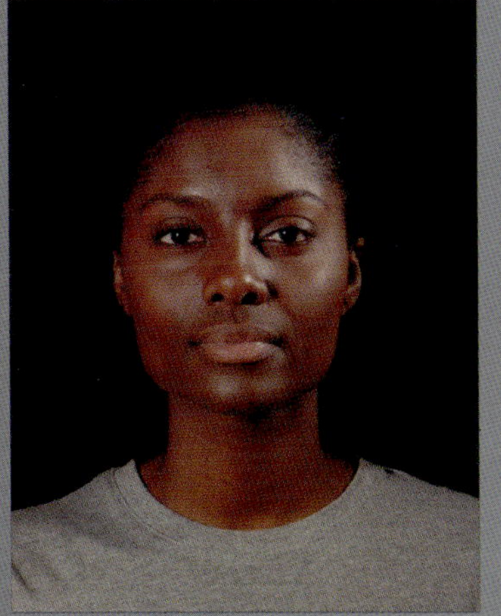

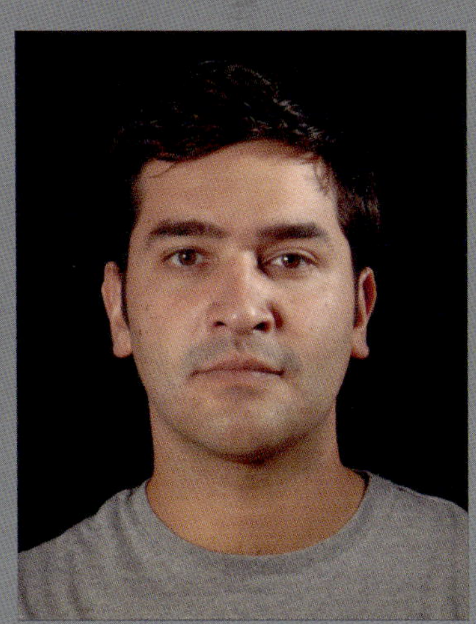

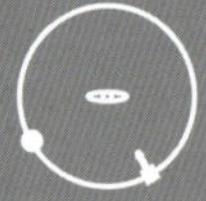

SOFTBOX & SNOOT

LIGHT 1 (SOFTBOX): FROM 60° LEFT

LIGHT 2 (SNOOT): FROM 30° RIGHT

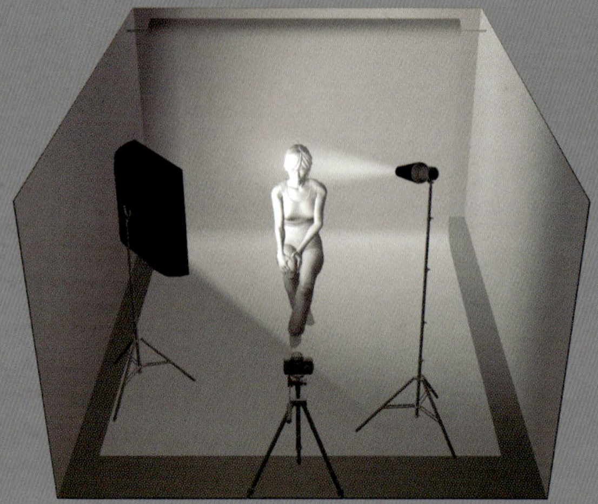

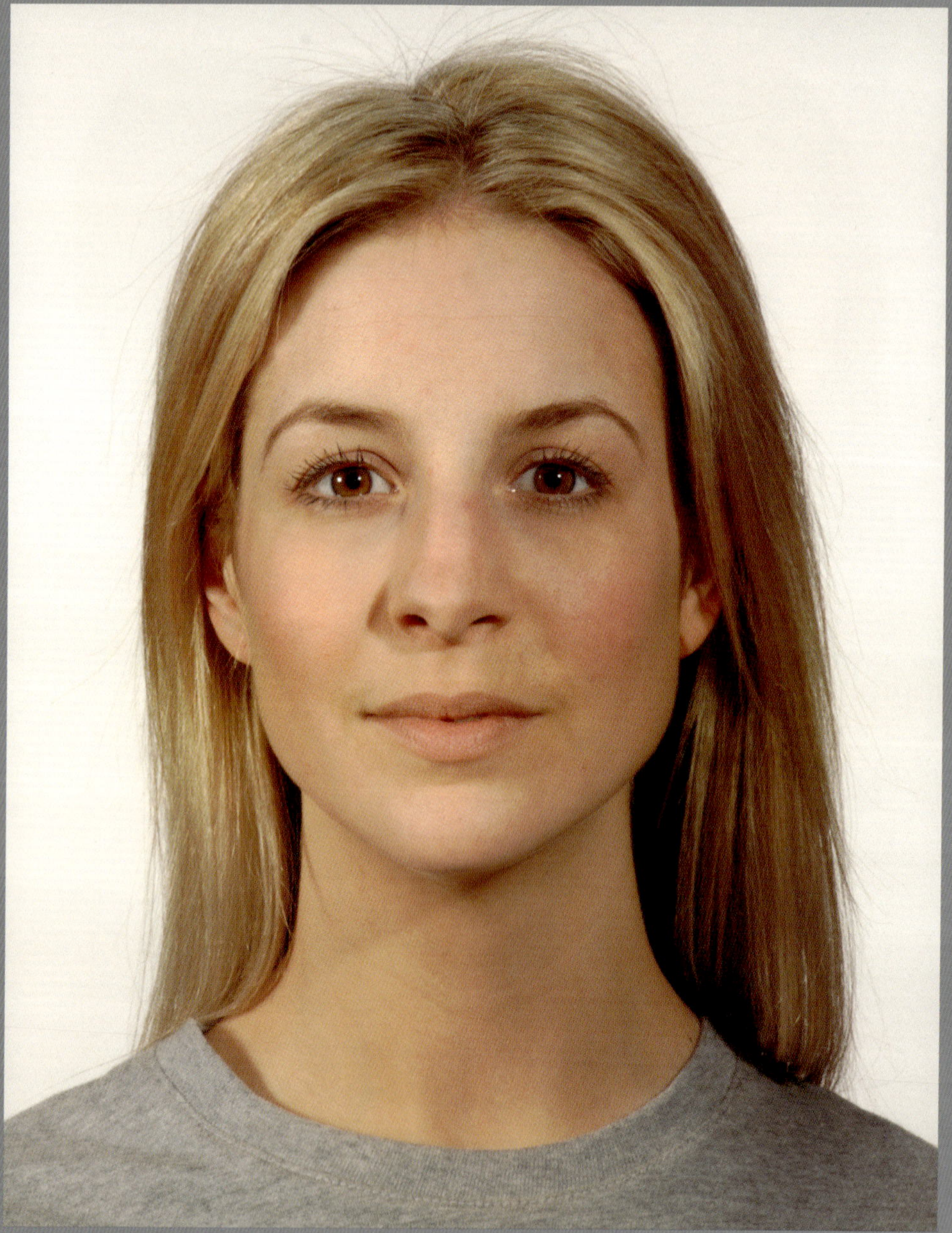

Here, the softbox has been moved further to the left of the camera, but it is still providing the overall illumination of the subject. The effect of the snoot is less obvious, and its usual dark shadows are largely filled in by the softbox.

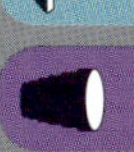

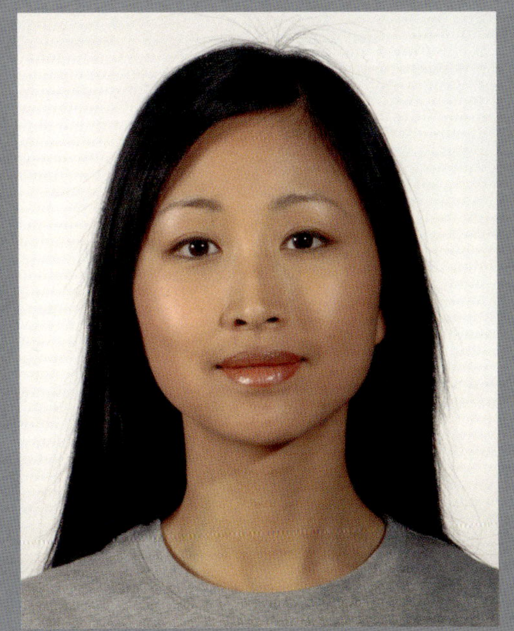

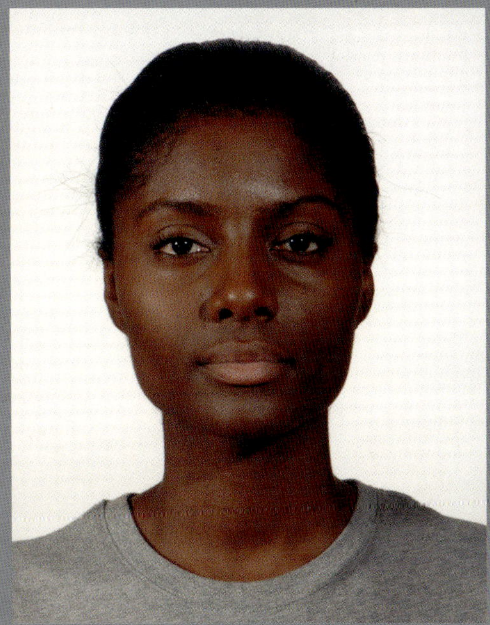

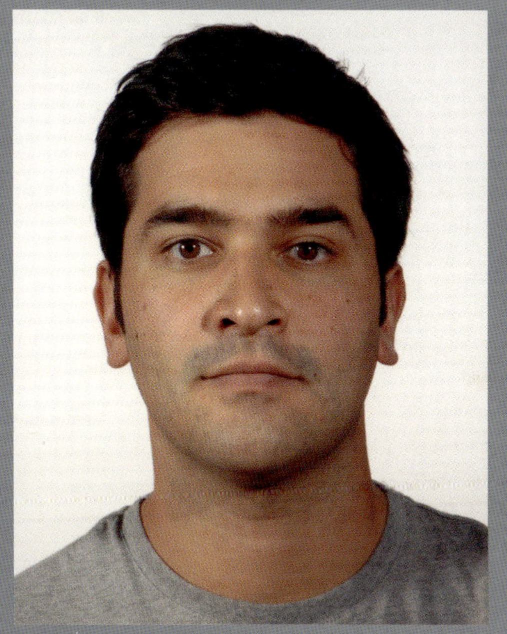

DARK BACKGROUND

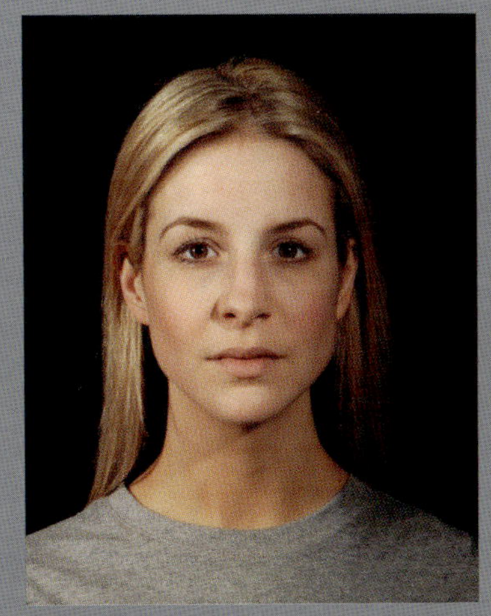

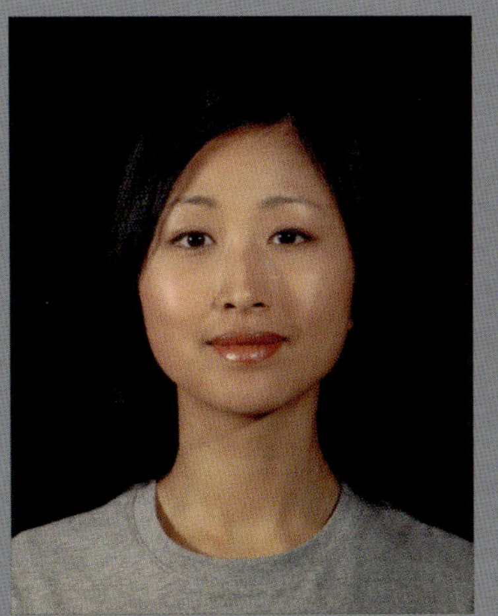

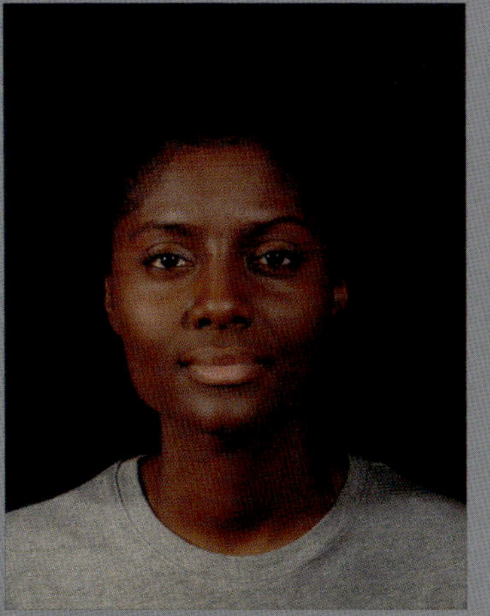

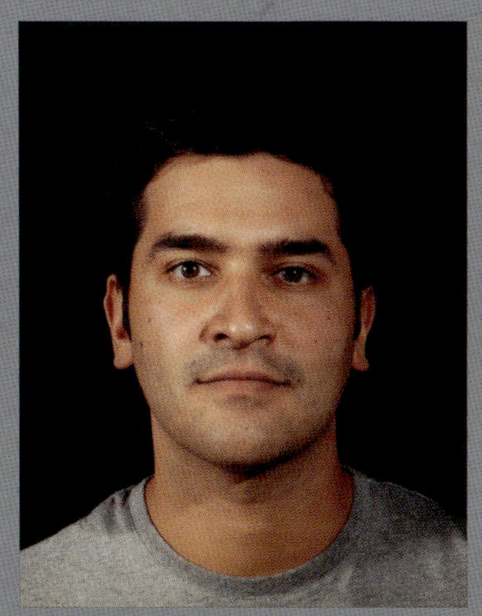

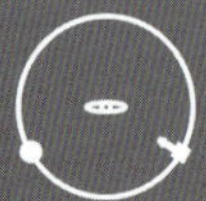

SOFTBOX & SNOOT

LIGHT 1 (SOFTBOX): FROM 60° LEFT

LIGHT 2 (SNOOT): FROM 60° RIGHT

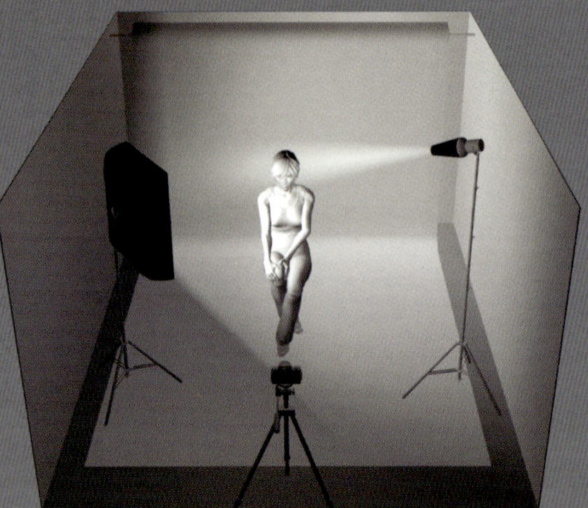

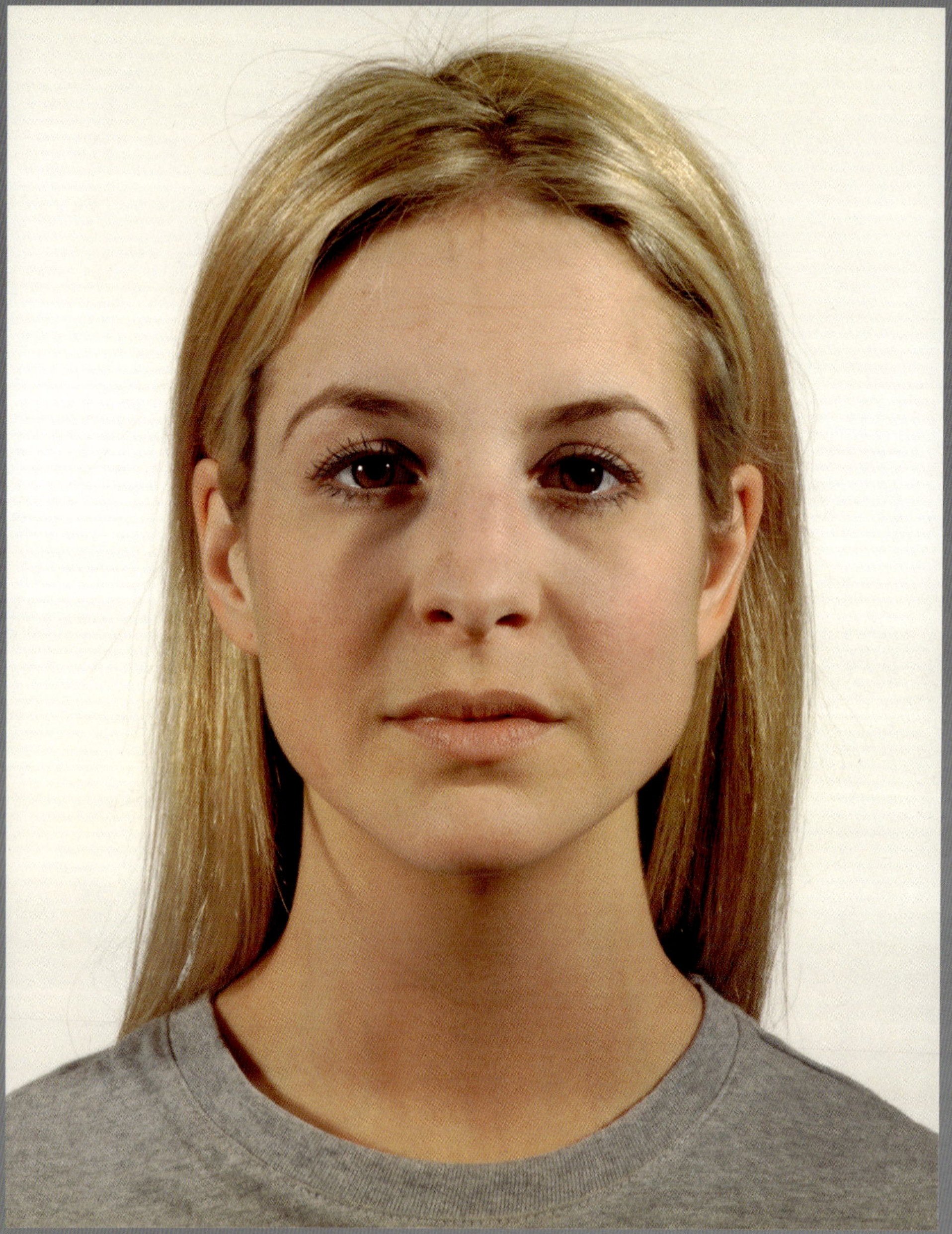

This symmetrical setup sees the softbox and snoot aimed at the subject from the same angle, on opposite sides of the camera. With both lights positioned at 60 degrees to the camera, the result is very low in contrast, and the lack of distinct shadow areas creates a flat portrait.

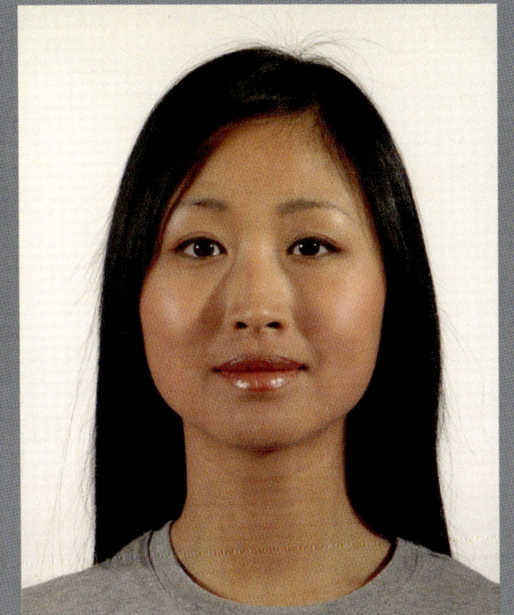

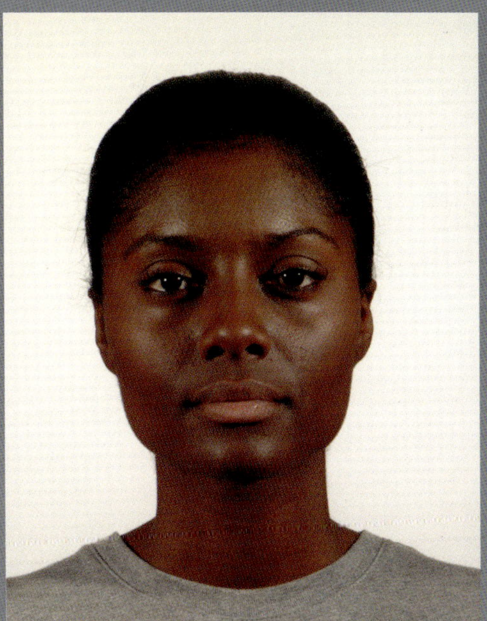

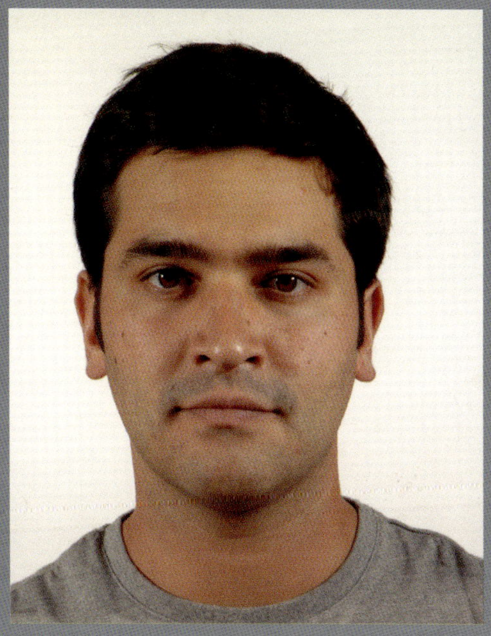

DARK BACKGROUND

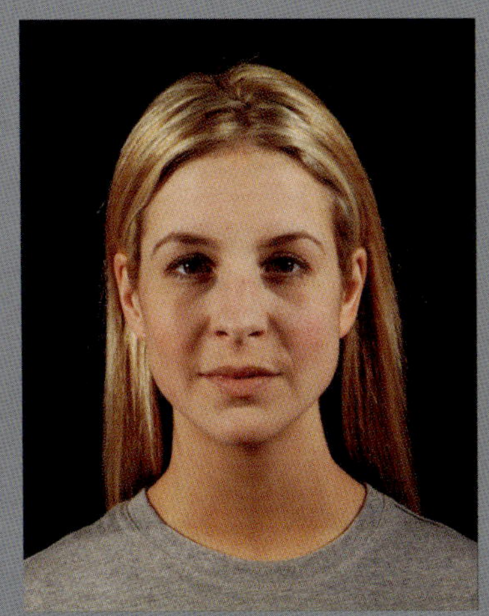

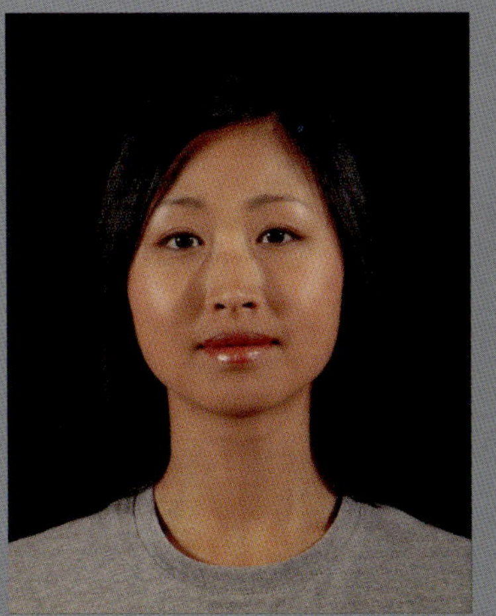

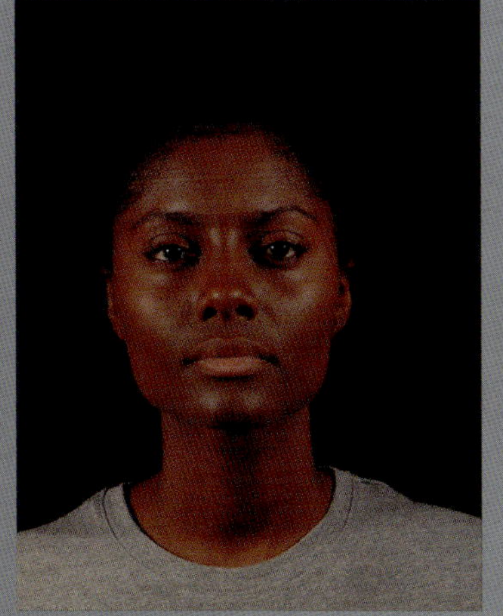

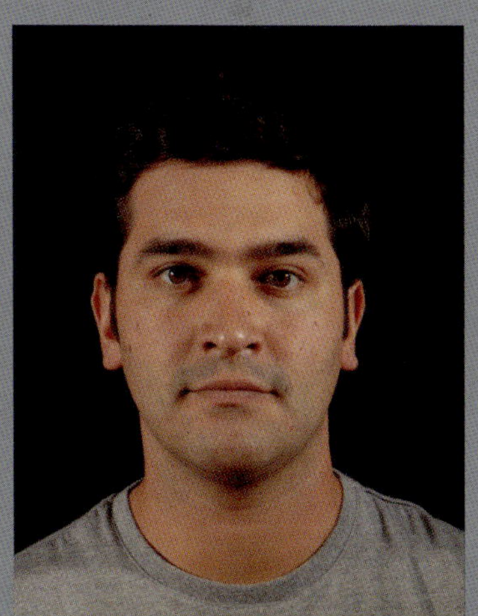

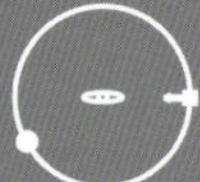

SOFTBOX & SNOOT

LIGHT 1 (SOFTBOX): FROM 60° LEFT

LIGHT 2 (SNOOT): FROM 90° RIGHT

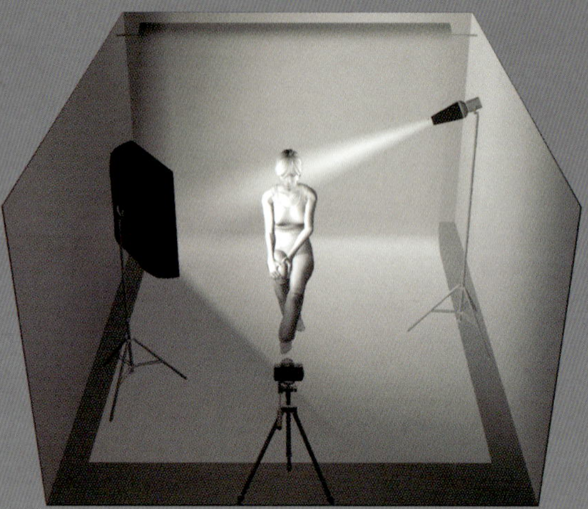

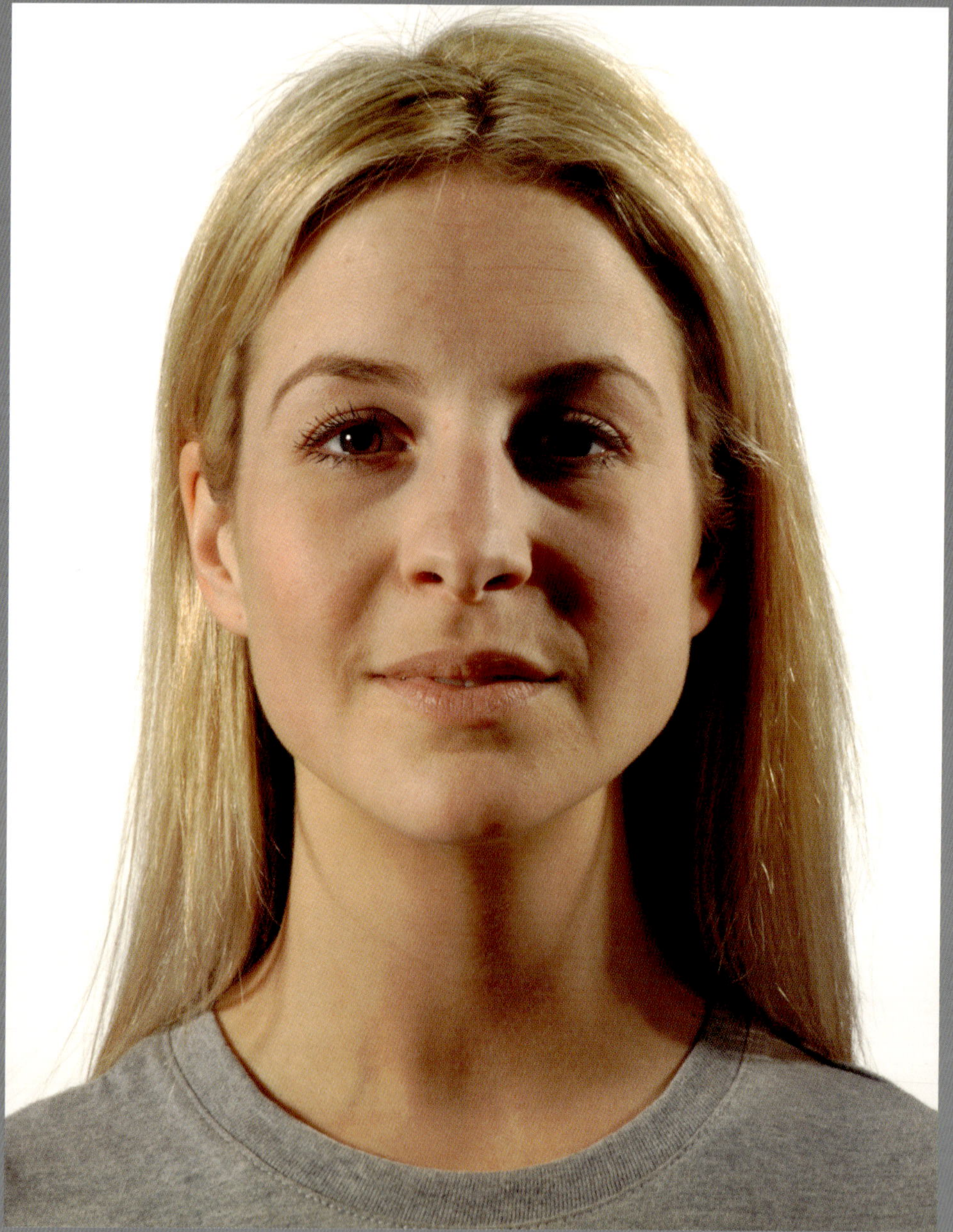

With the softbox aimed at the subject from a 60-degree angle, and the snooted light coming from the opposite side at a 90-degree angle, dark shadows can appear around your model's eye-socket and nose. The size, shape, and intensity of these will depend on their facial features.

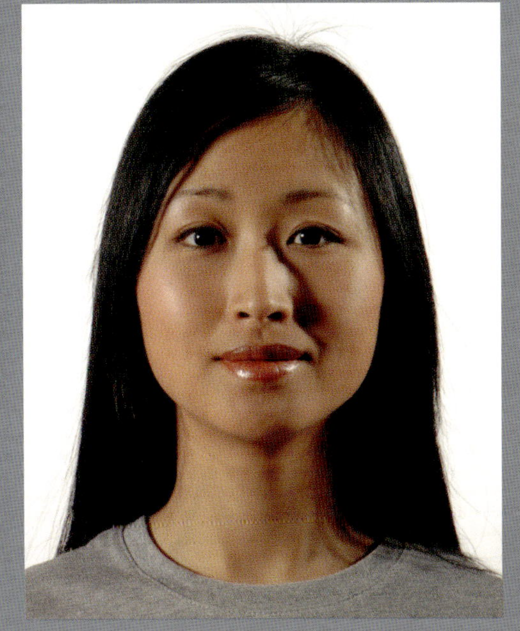
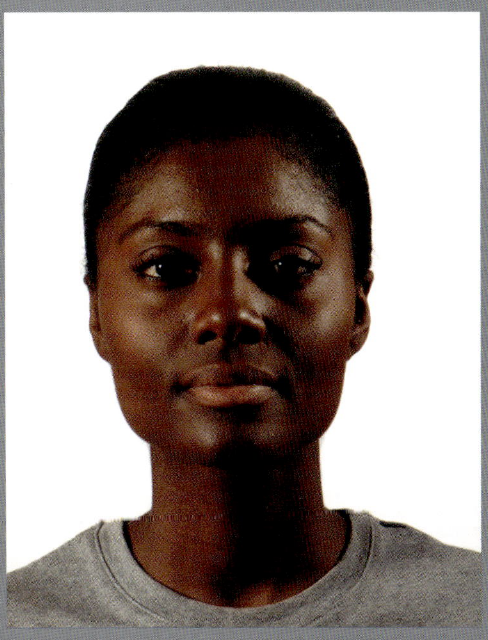
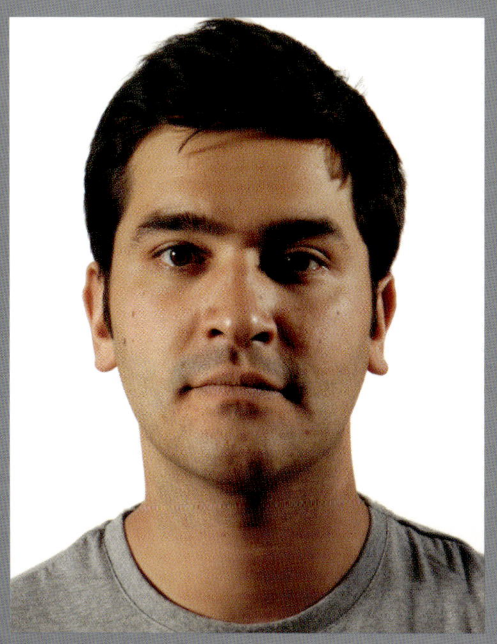

DARK BACKGROUND

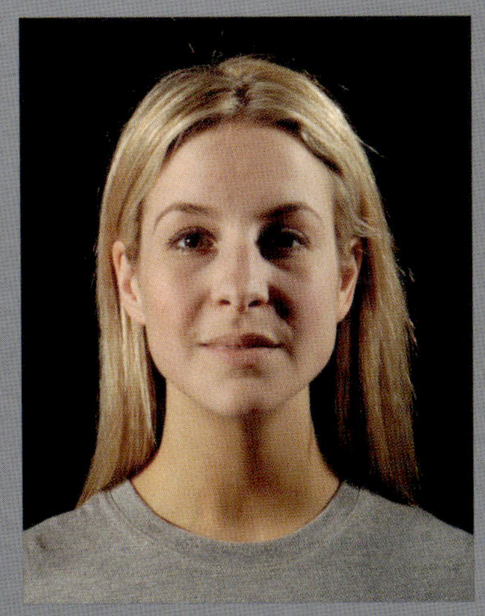
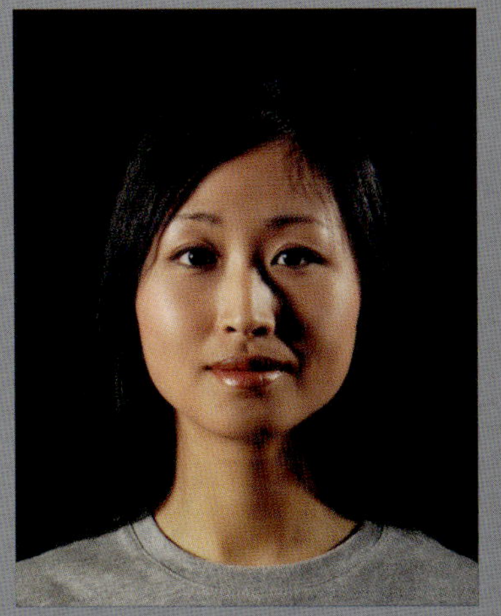
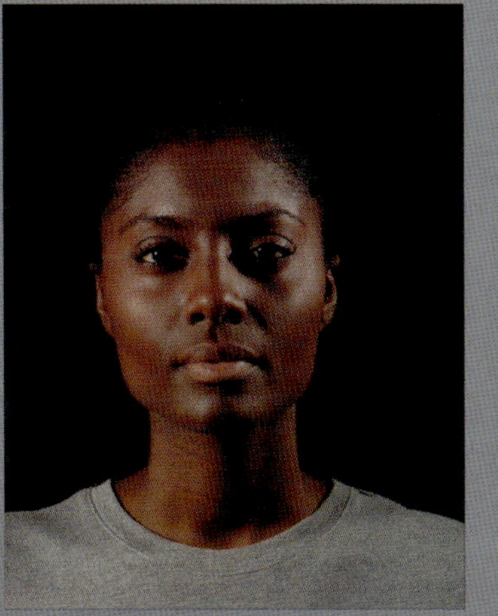
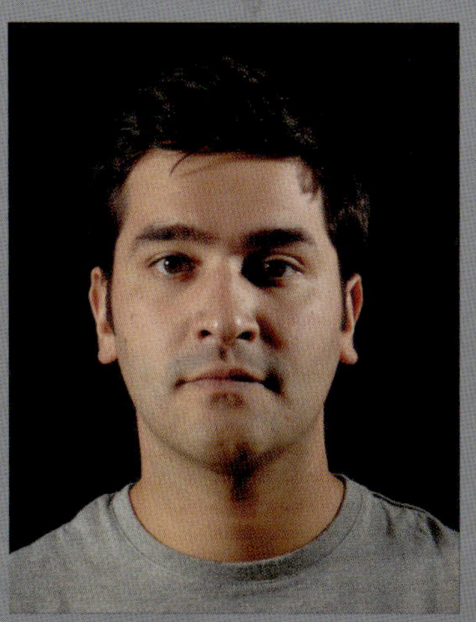

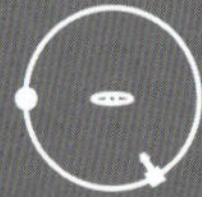

SOFTBOX & SNOOT

LIGHT 1 (SOFTBOX): FROM 90° LEFT

LIGHT 2 (SNOOT): FROM 30° RIGHT

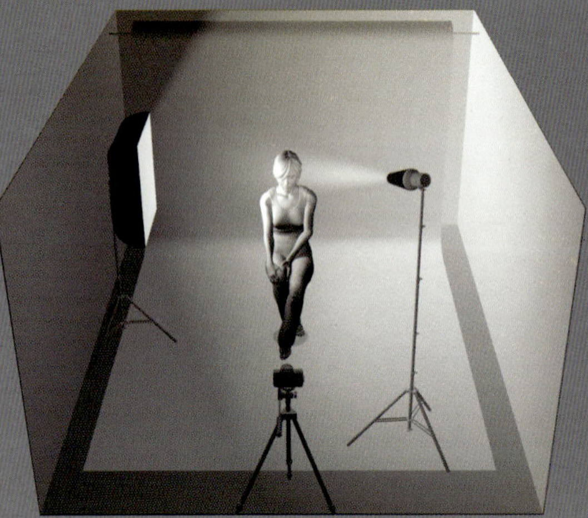

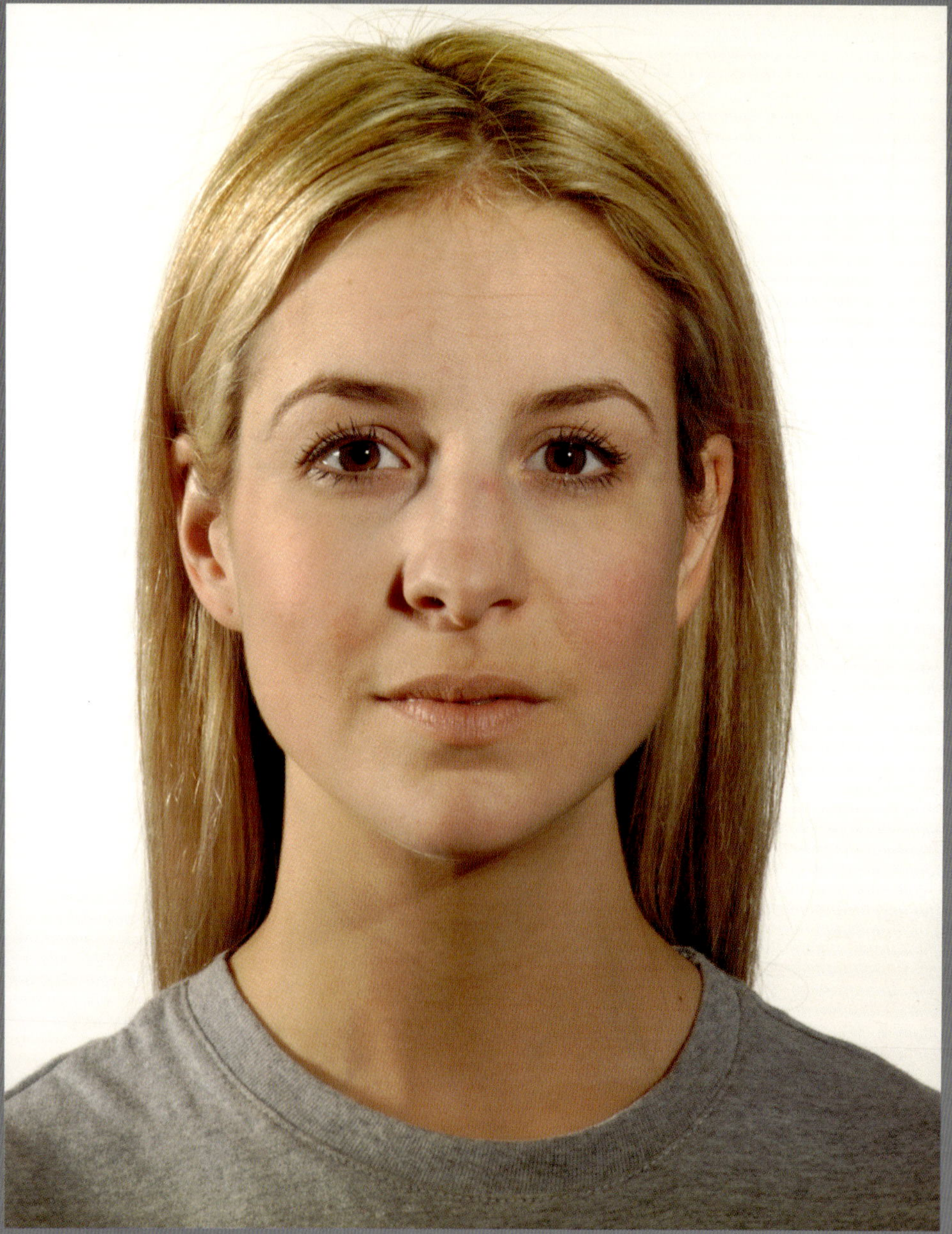

The softbox has been moved further around the subject, so it is now striking the model from a 90-degree angle. The snoot is directed from the opposite side, filling in the shadows that would otherwise be created by a single light. The result is a near evenly-lit portrait, with a subtle shadow line down the center of the face and neck.

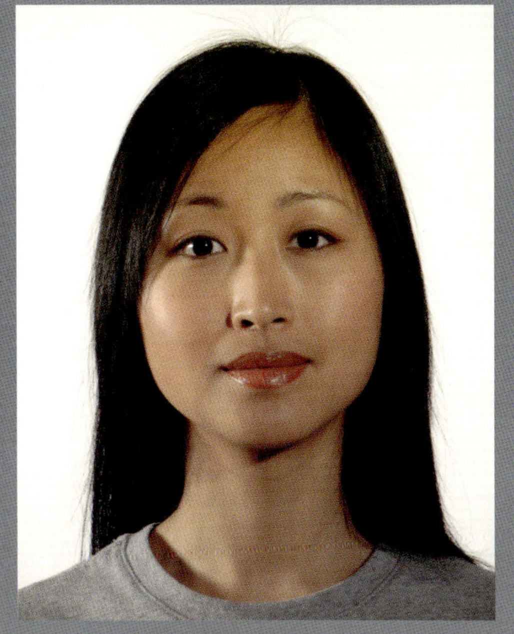

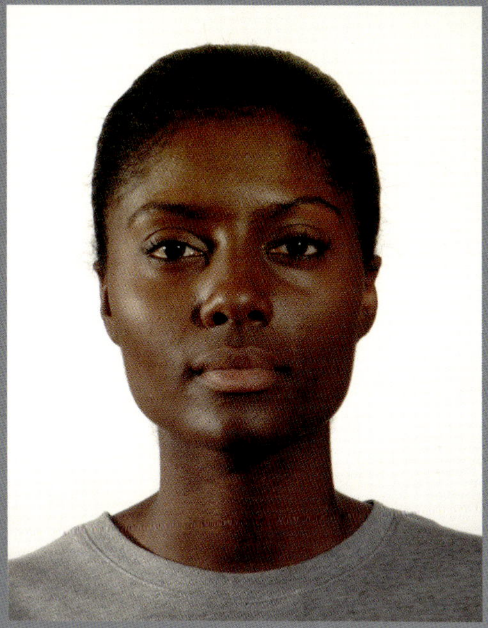

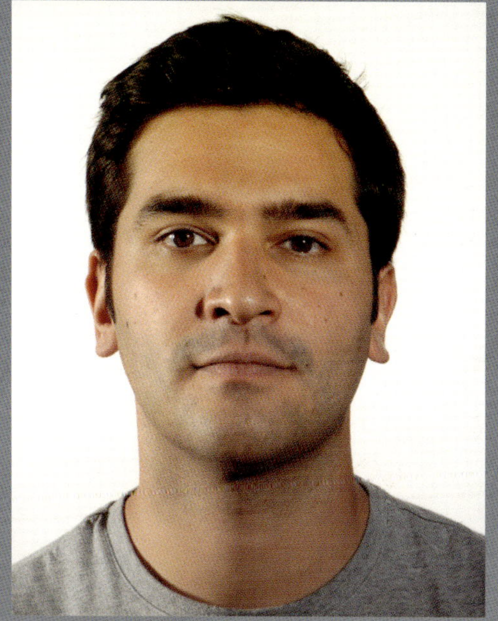

DARK BACKGROUND

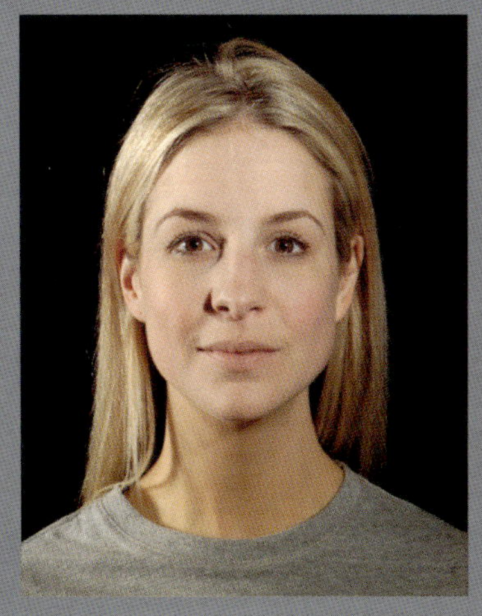

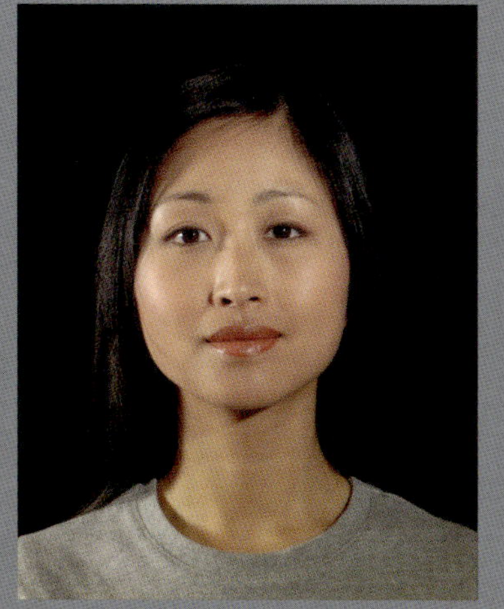

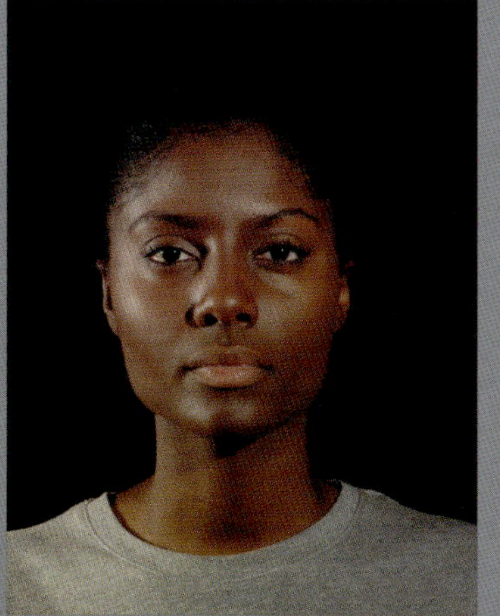

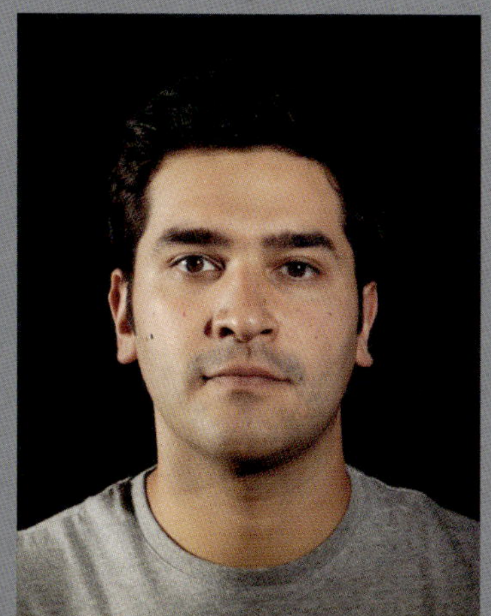

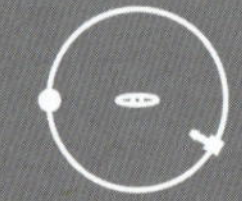

SOFTBOX & SNOOT

LIGHT 1 (SOFTBOX): FROM 90° LEFT

LIGHT 2 (SNOOT): FROM 60° RIGHT

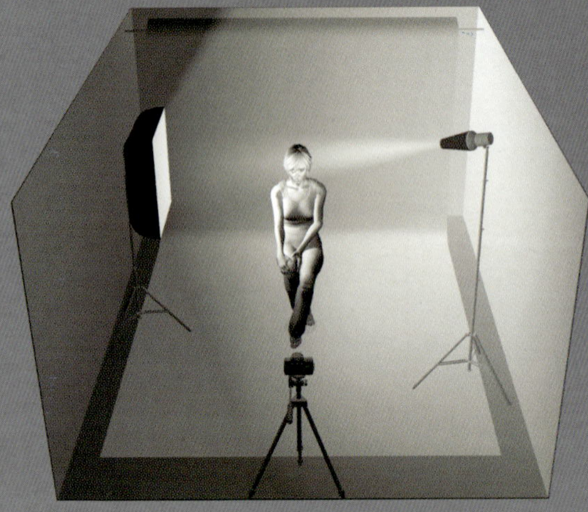

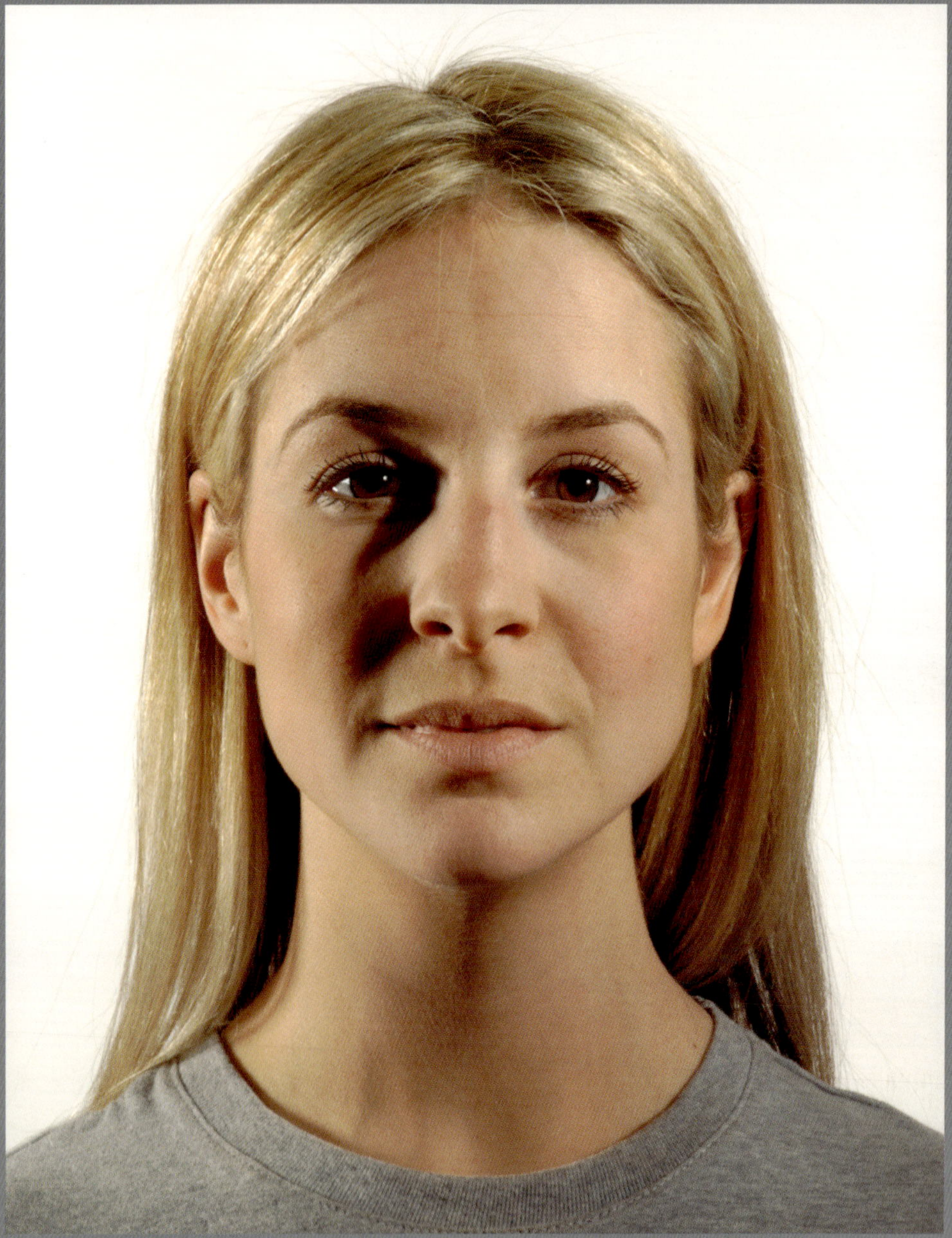

With the softbox remaining at a right angle to the camera, and the snooted light moved further to the left of the subject, deep shadows are introduced along the model's left eye socket and the bottom of their nose. This is most apparent on subjects with lighter skin tones where the contrast between the skin and the shadows is high.

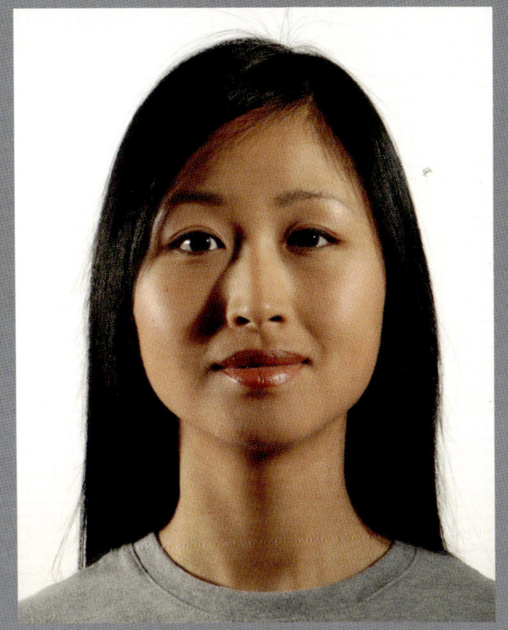

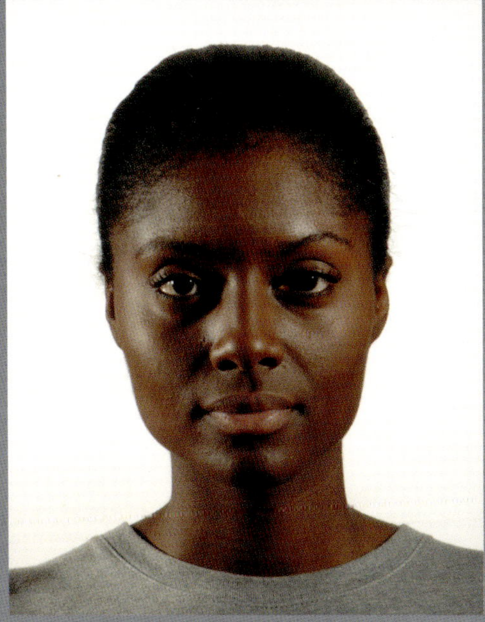

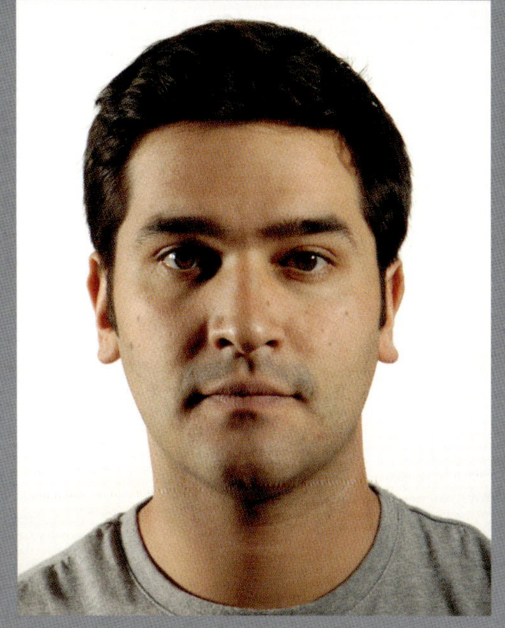

DARK BACKGROUND

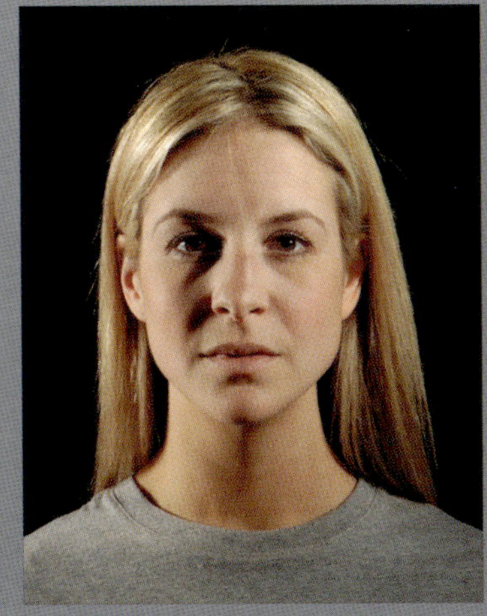

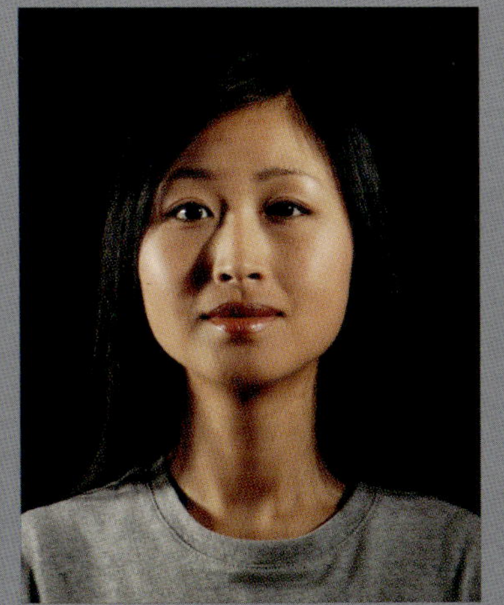

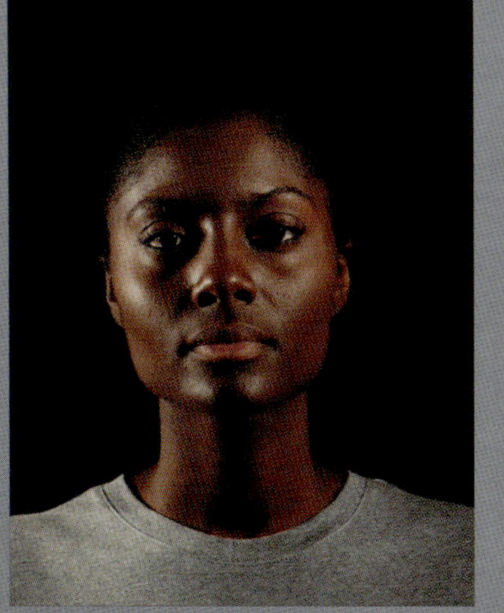

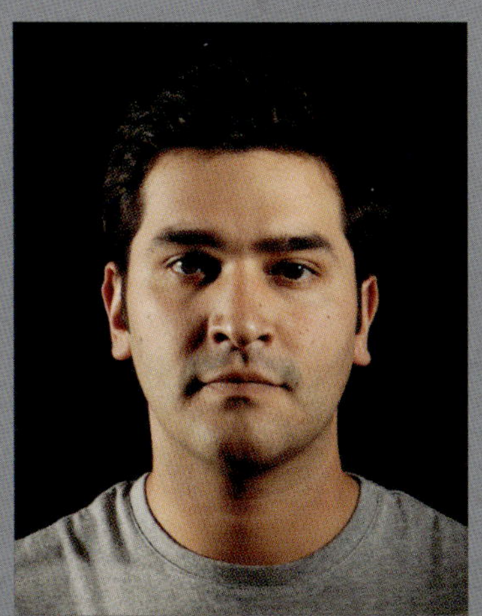

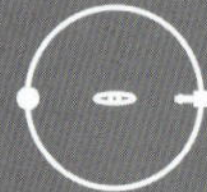

SOFTBOX & SNOOT

LIGHT 1 (SOFTBOX): FROM 90° LEFT

LIGHT 2 (SNOOT): FROM 90° RIGHT

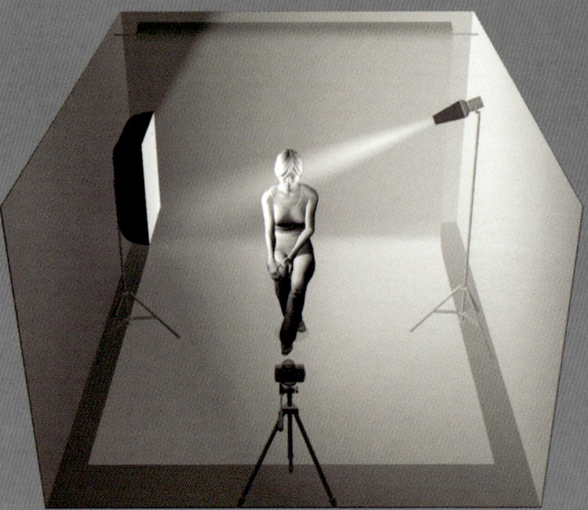

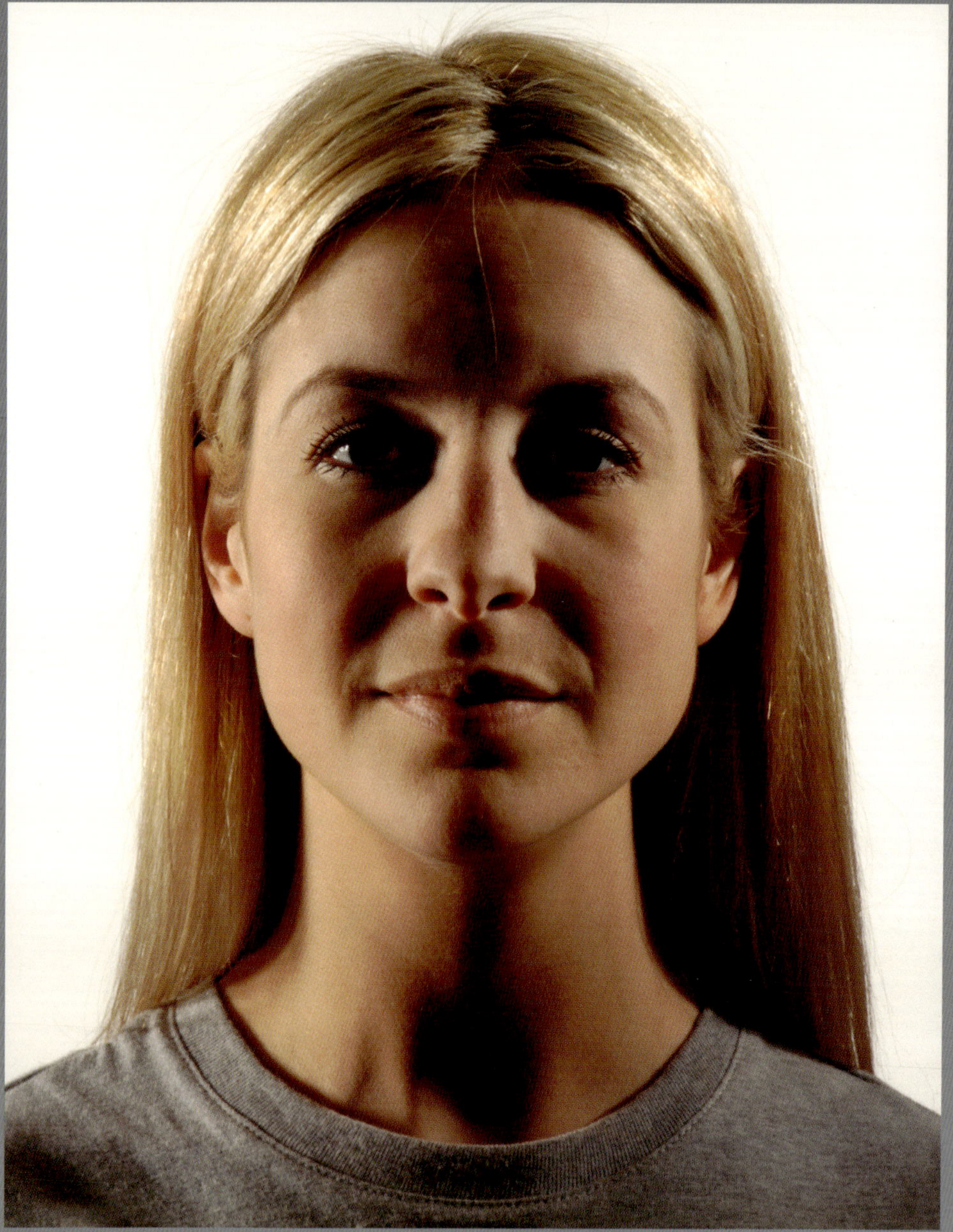

When the softbox and snoot both point at the subject from a 90-degree angle to the camera they introduce deep shadows on the opposing side of the face. However, due to the diffusion of the softbox, the side of the face lit by the softbox appears slightly lighter, even though both lamps are set at the same distance and power.

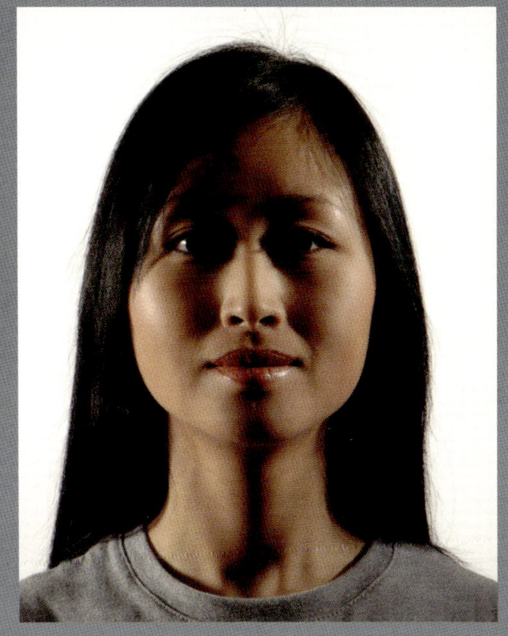

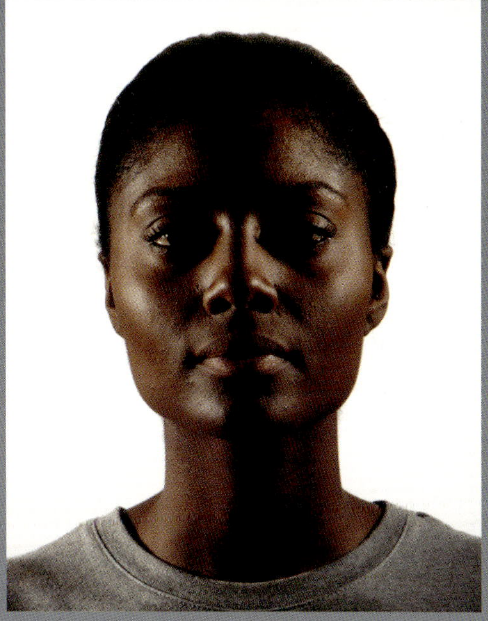

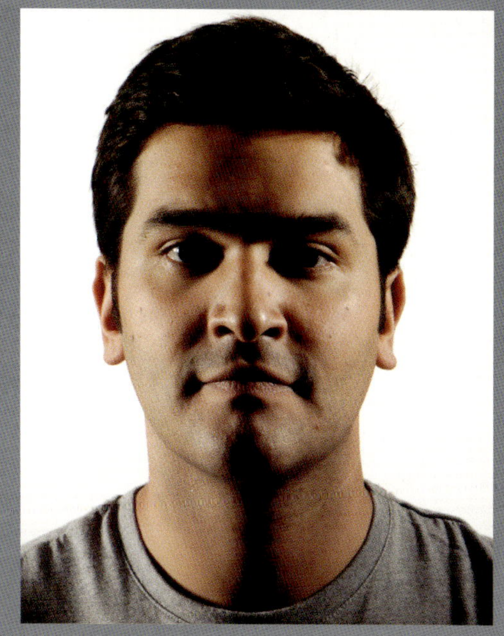

DARK BACKGROUND

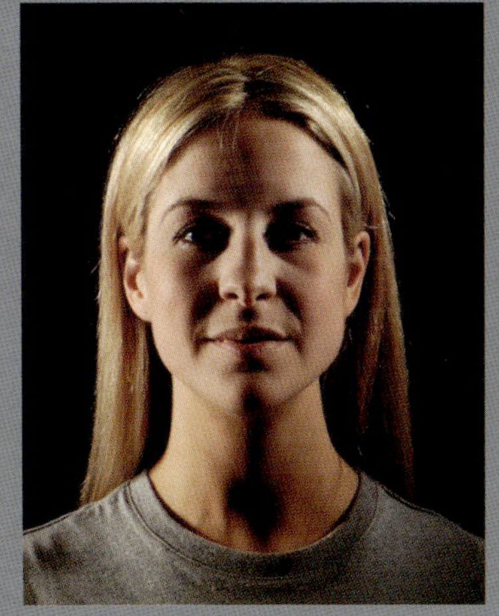

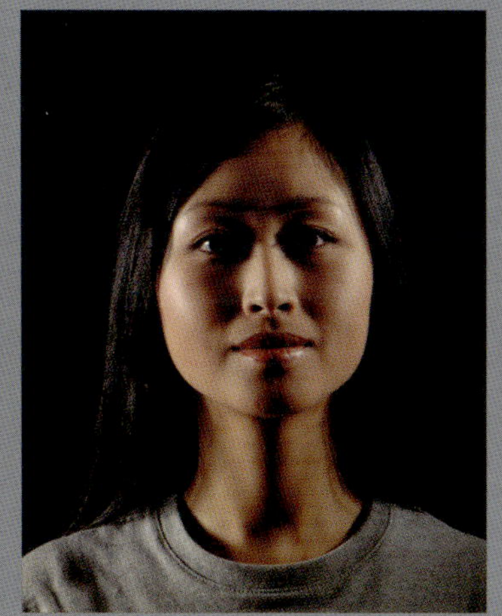

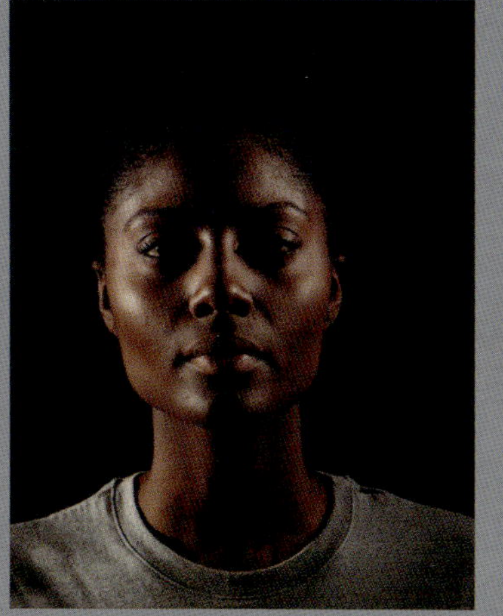

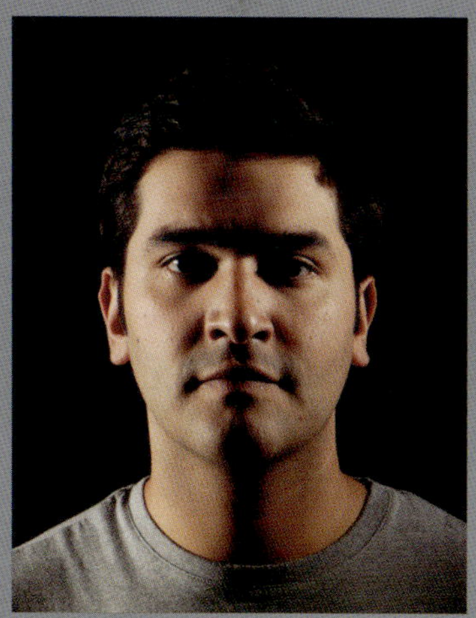

CHAPTER 8

REFLECTORS

For the majority of your portrait work, two lights will provide you with everything you need in terms of choosing precisely how and where you want the light to fall on your subject. However, photographic lighting can be expensive, especially when you start looking at pro-spec flash units and their associated light modifiers. Quite often this can mean making a compromise, but opting for lower-priced equipment can be a false economy—it's likely to be less widely supported by accessory manufacturers and getting spare parts may also be less straightforward.

Instead, consider investing in a single, high-quality light and a good-sized softbox in the first instance, and then add a second light and further accessories as and when your budget allows.

Now, you might think that a single light means you're going to be limited to the type of high contrast portraits we saw at the start of this book, but this isn't true—simply use a reflector. As you will see in this section, a reflector—which doesn't need to be anything more than a large sheet of cardstock—can help create striking portrait lighting effects, without the expense of a second light.

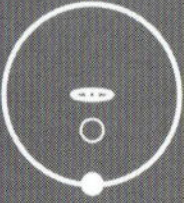

REFLECTORS

LIGHT 1: FROM 0º

REFLECTOR: UNDER CHIN

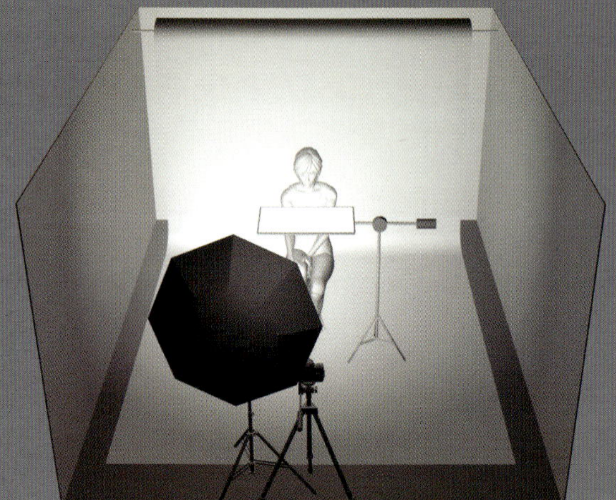

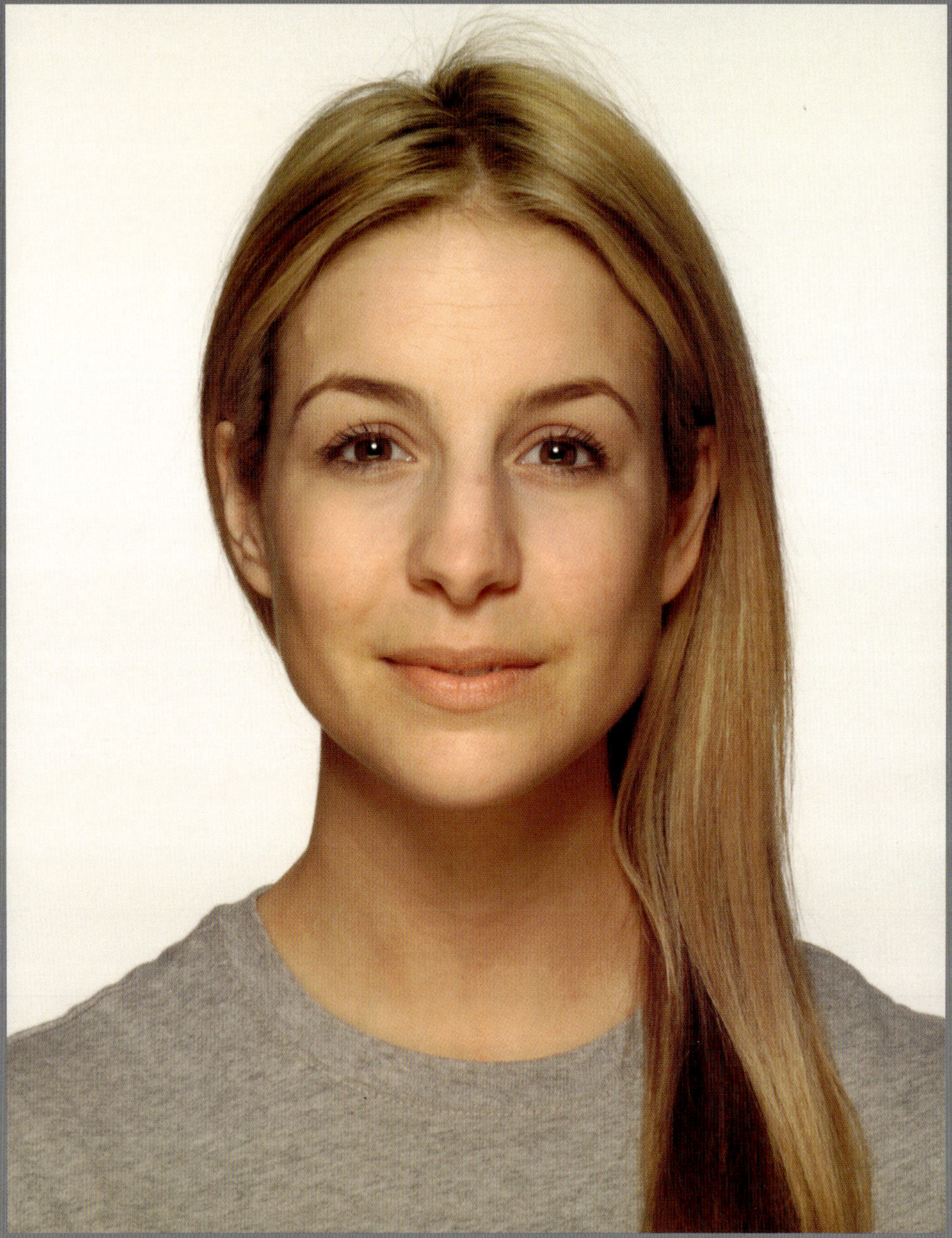

The effect of using a single light from the camera position can be seen on pages 36–37, and it's noticeable that using such a light can introduce fairly obvious shadows beneath your subject's jawline. Here, a reflector is positioned out of shot, which is bouncing the light back under the chin, helping to lighten the underside of the jaw.

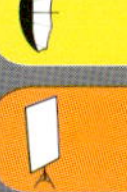

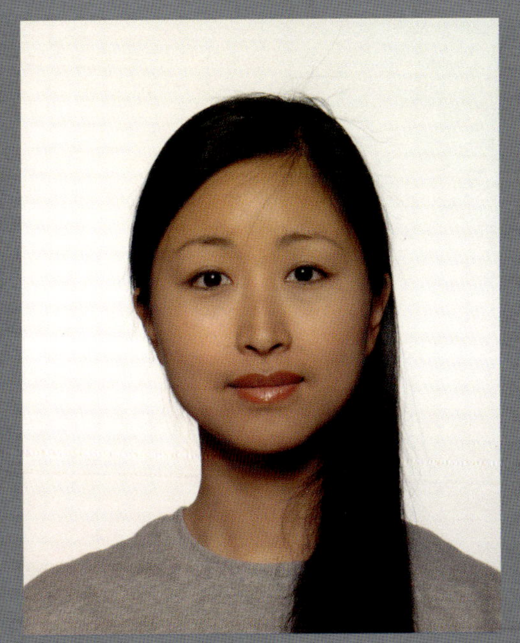
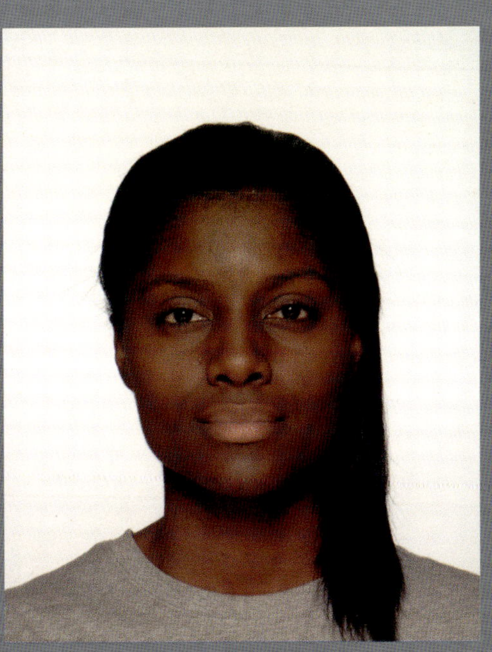
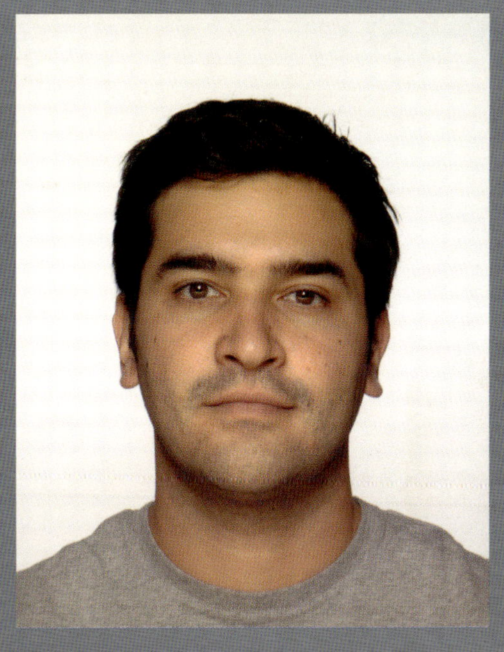

DARK BACKGROUND

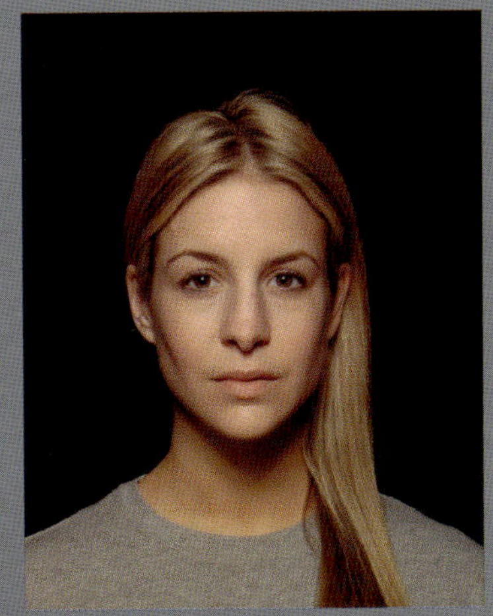
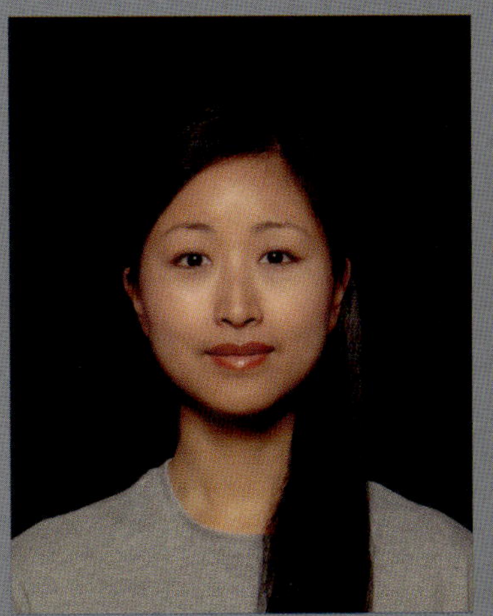
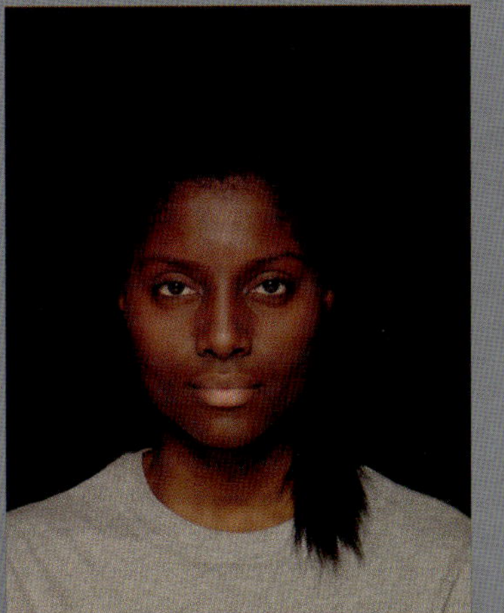
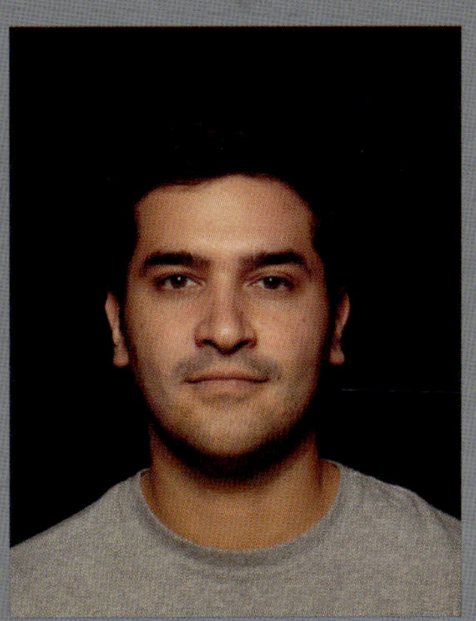

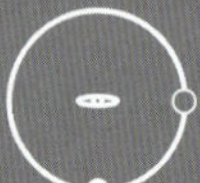

REFLECTORS

LIGHT 1: FROM 0°

REFLECTOR: FROM 90° RIGHT

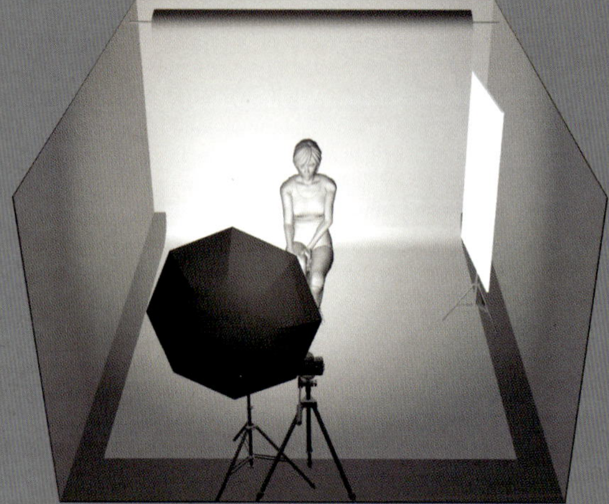

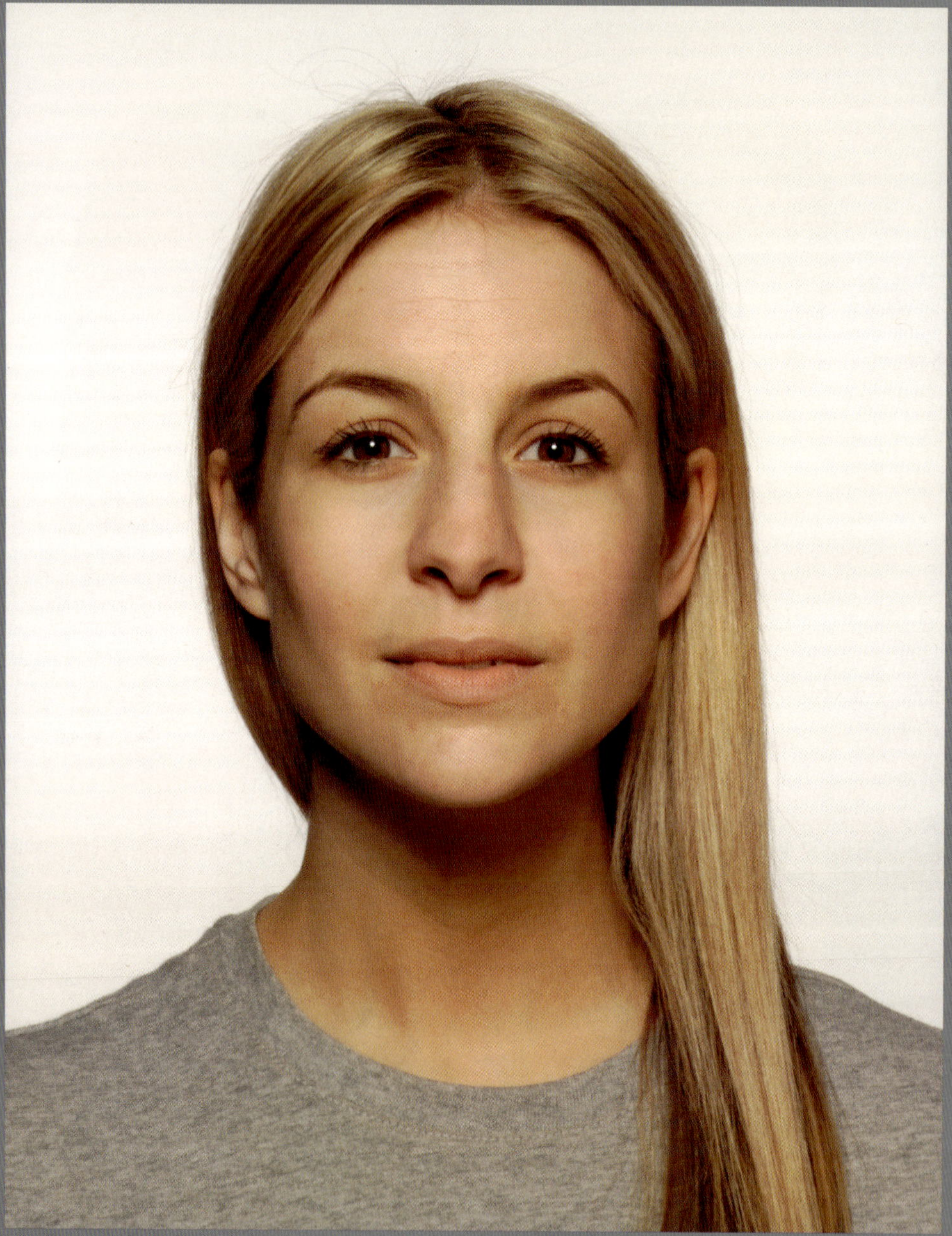

In a way, a reflector can be thought of as a second light. As it is reflecting the main light, it will always be a "soft" light, although how "bright" it is can be controlled by the distance it is positioned from the subject—the closer the reflector is to your model, the "brighter" and more obvious it will appear.

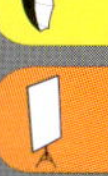

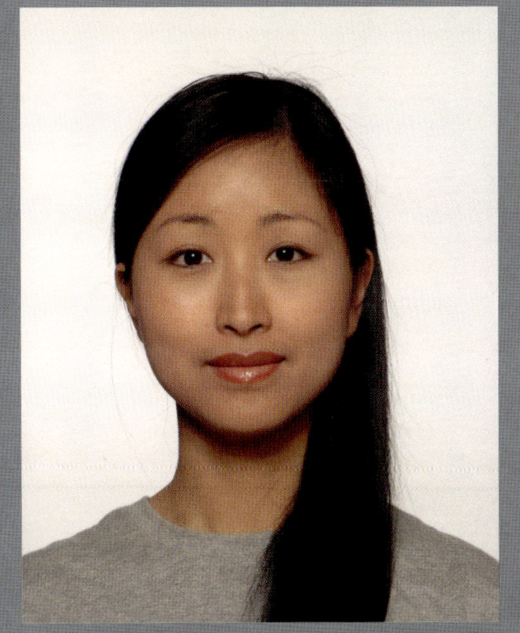

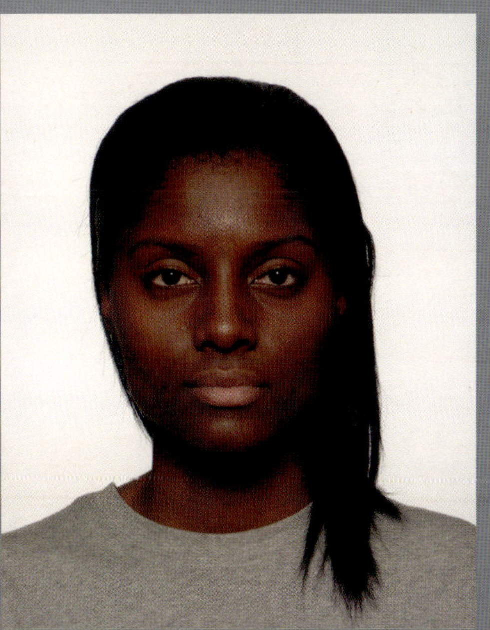

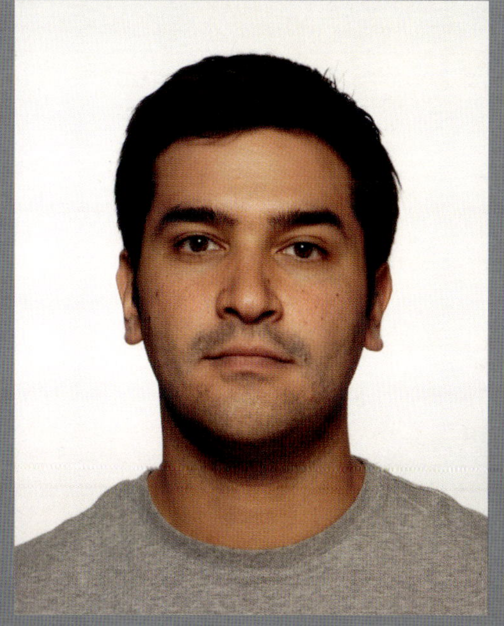

DARK BACKGROUND

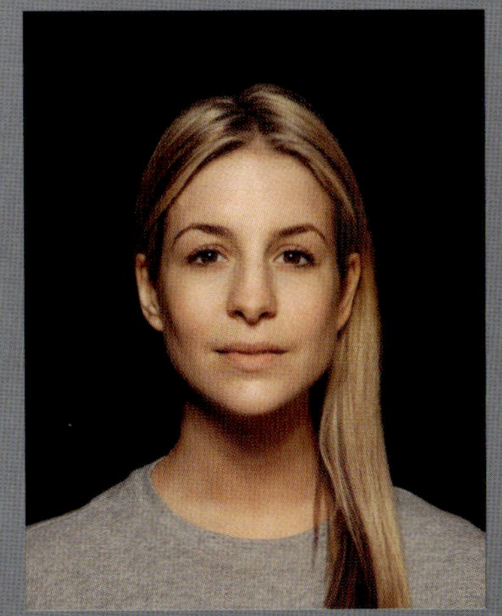

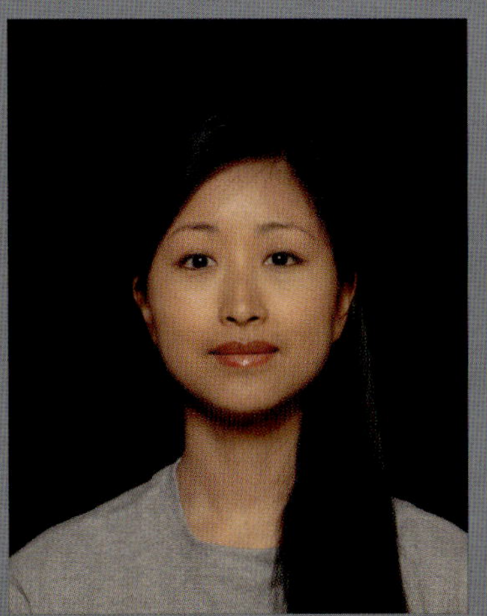

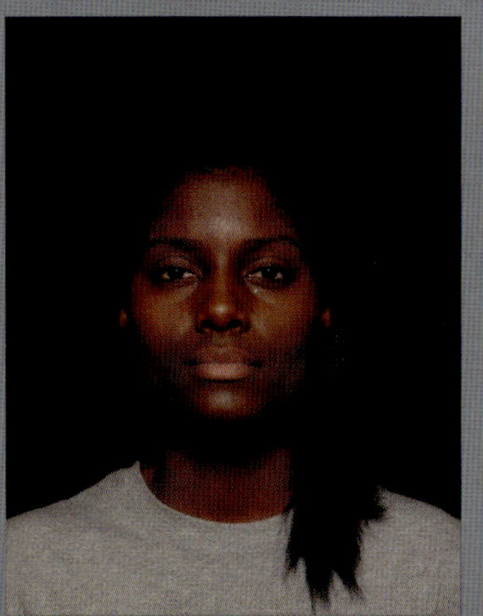

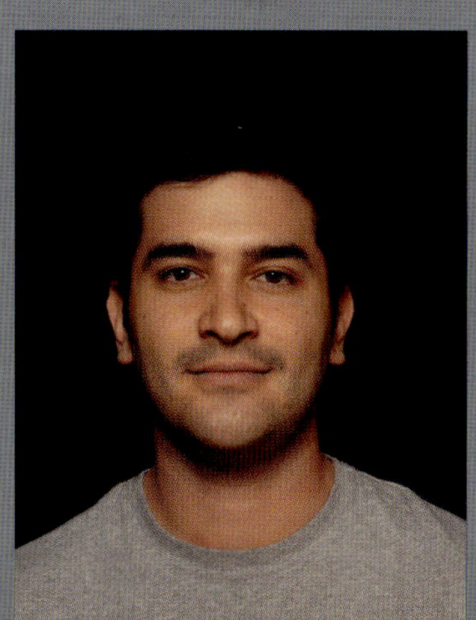

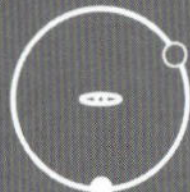

REFLECTORS

LIGHT 1: FROM 0°

REFLECTOR: FROM 120° RIGHT

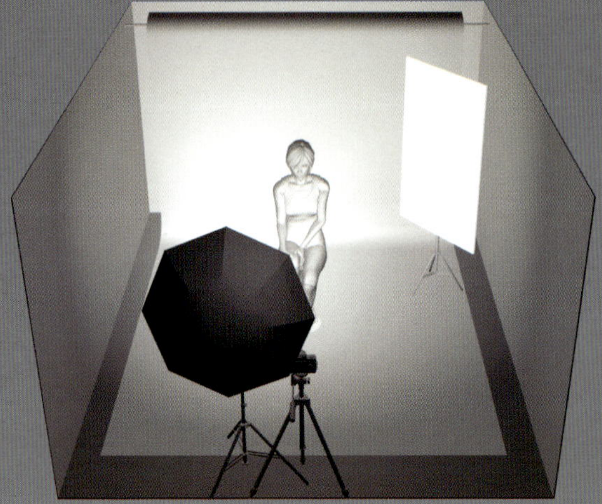

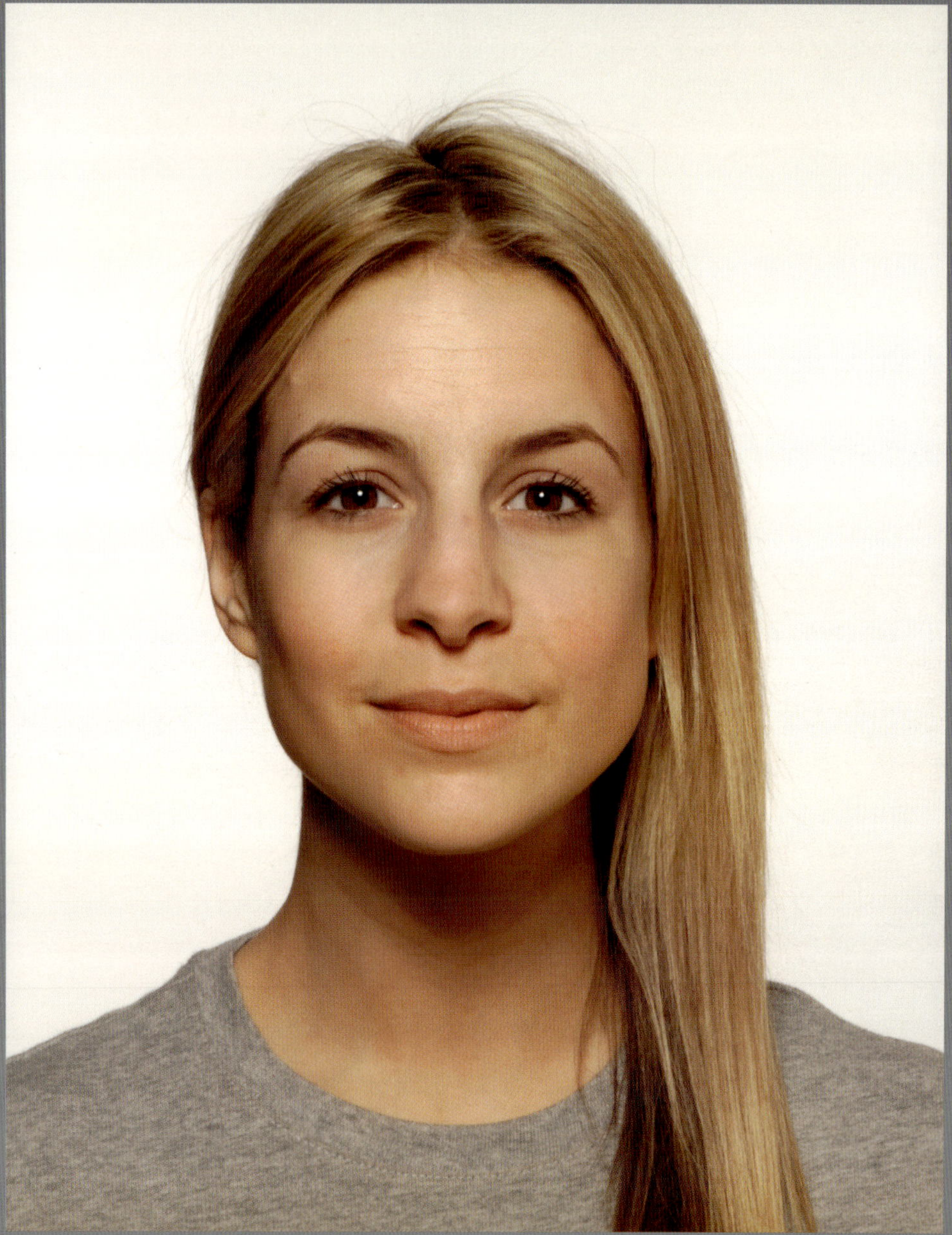

When you're photographing a dark-haired subject against a dark background, positioning a reflector slightly behind and to one side of the model can help lighten their hair slightly and help it stand out against the background. Using a silver reflector will increase the intensity of the reflected light, and heighten the effect.

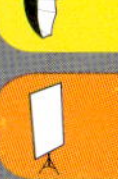

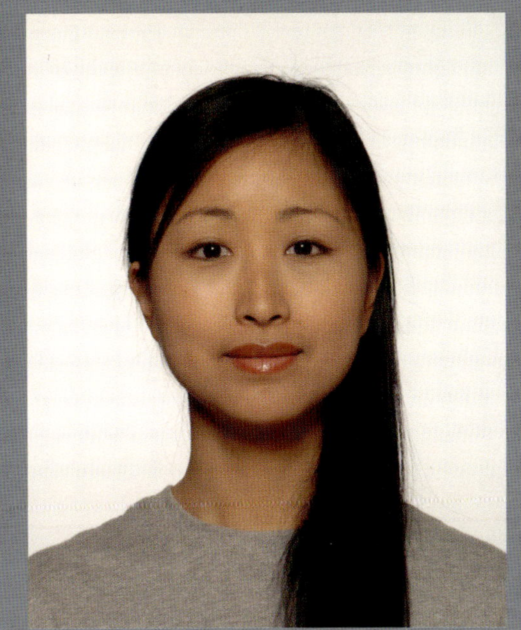

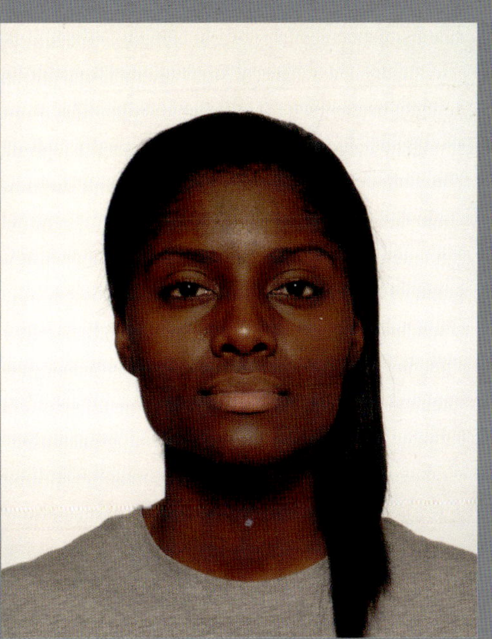

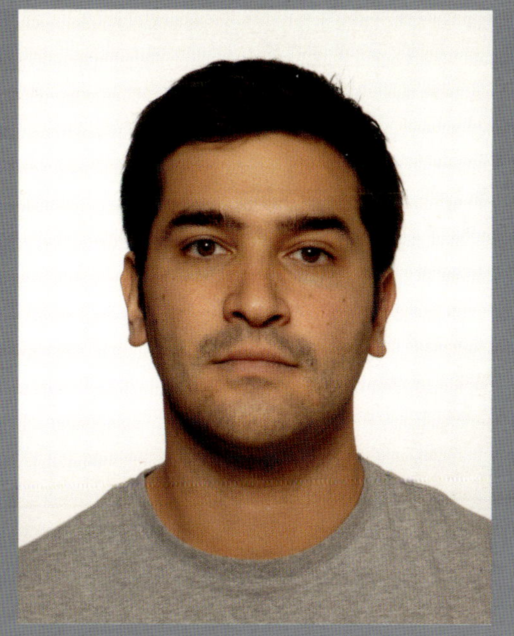

DARK BACKGROUND

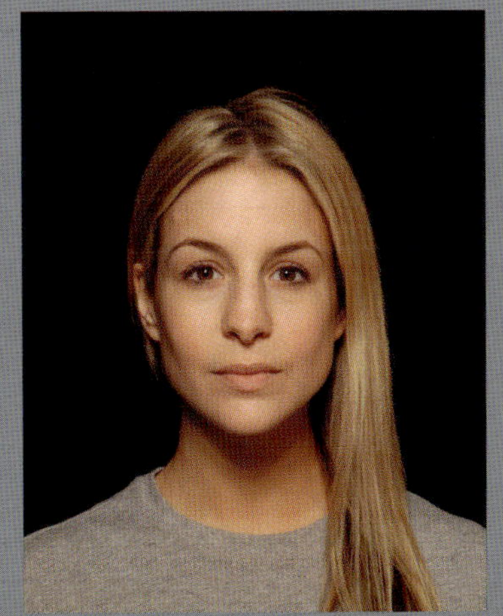

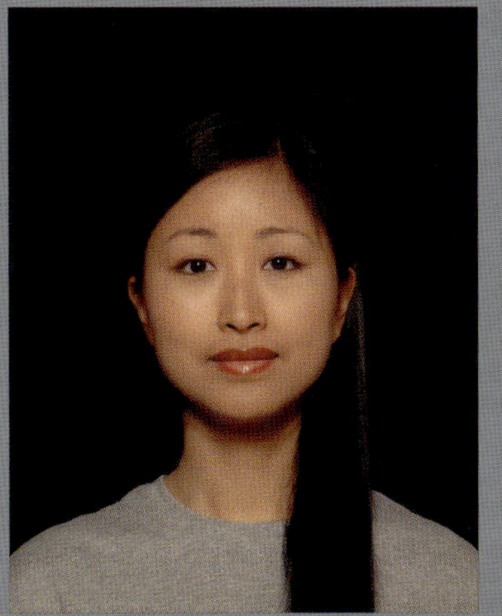

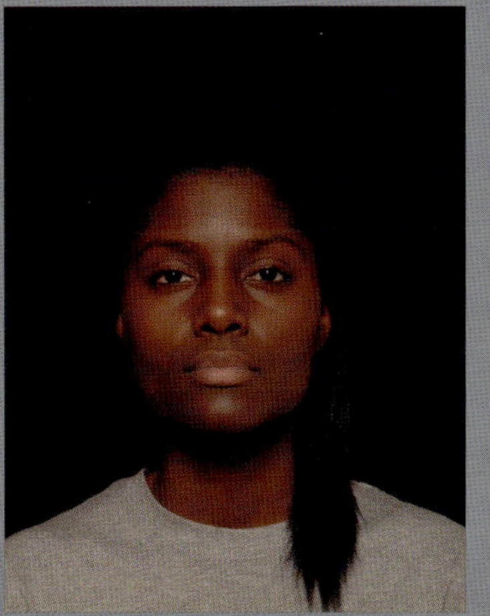

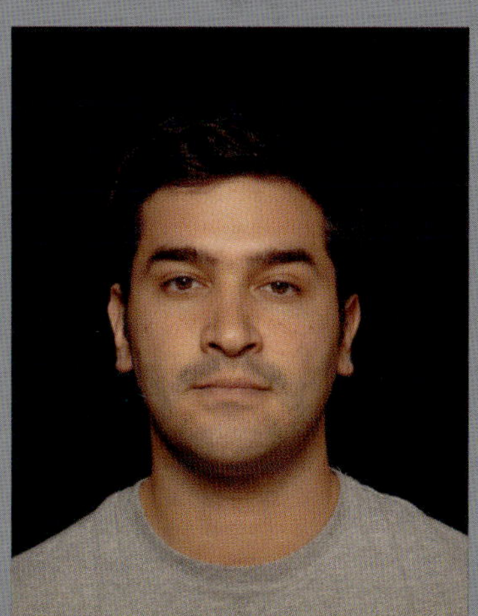

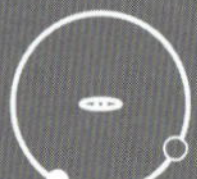

REFLECTORS

LIGHT 1: FROM 30° LEFT

REFLECTOR: FROM 60° RIGHT

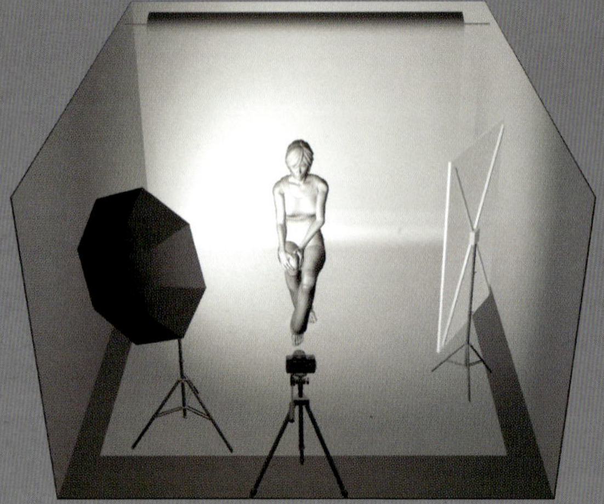

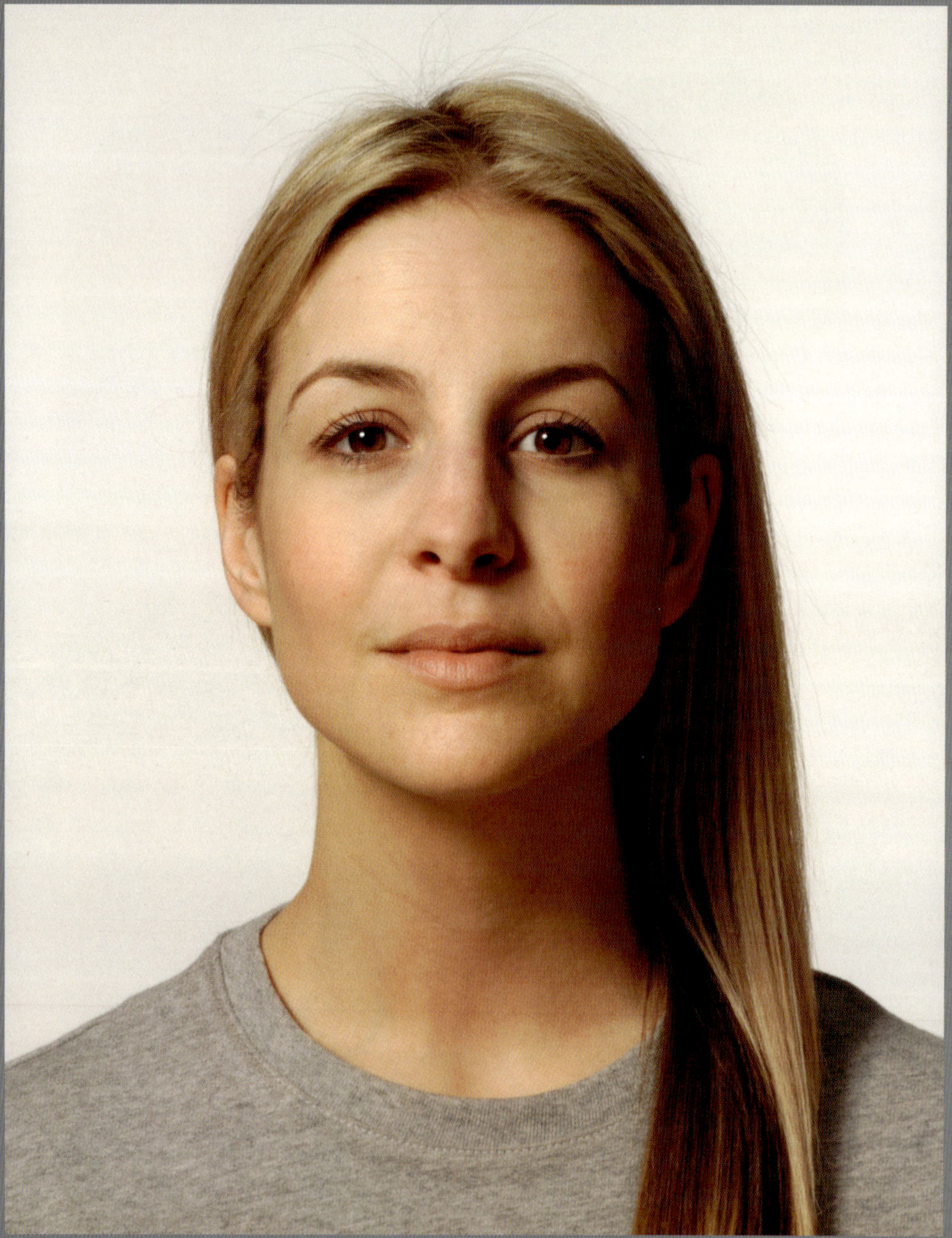

Compare the sequence of shots here to those on pages 34–35 and you can see the effect a reflector has. While a single light on its own creates deep, featureless shadows on the left side of the model's face, the addition of a reflector reveals the detail in the shaded side of the face.

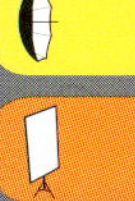

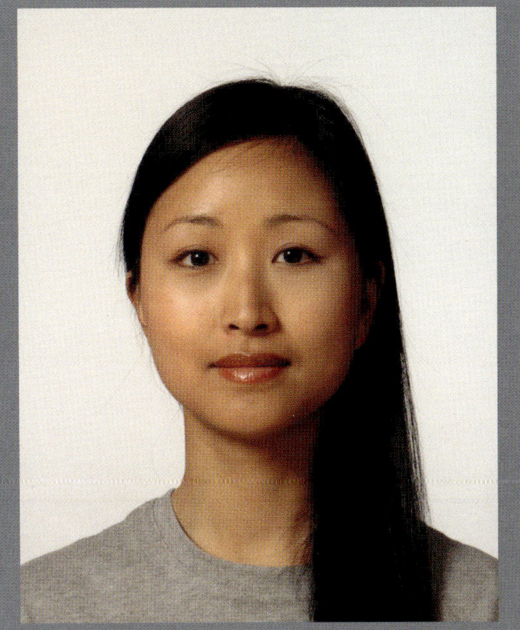

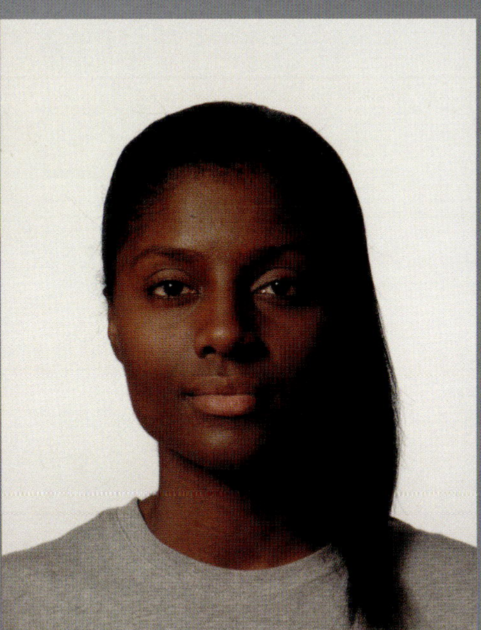

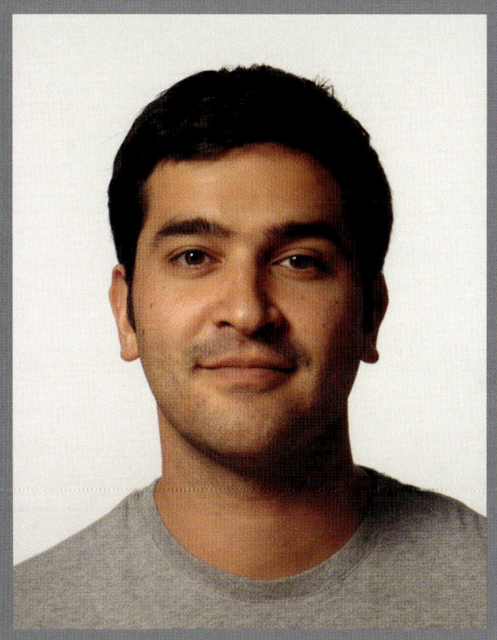

DARK BACKGROUND

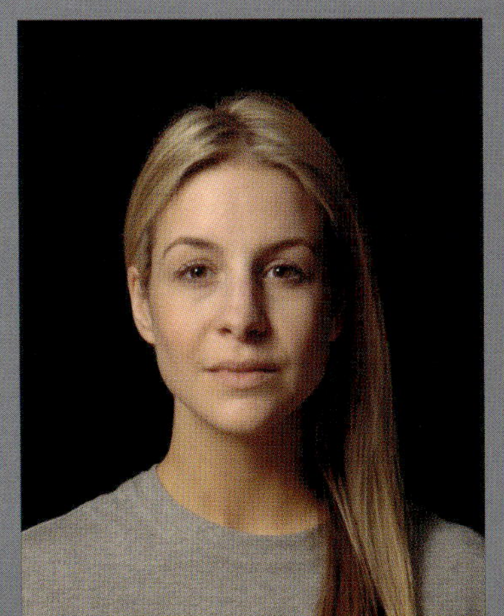

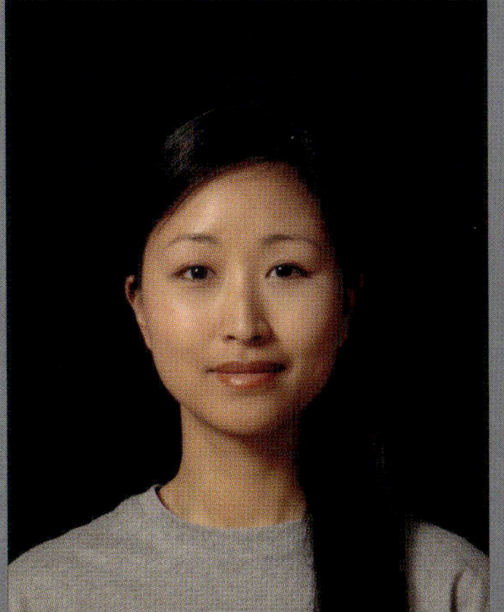

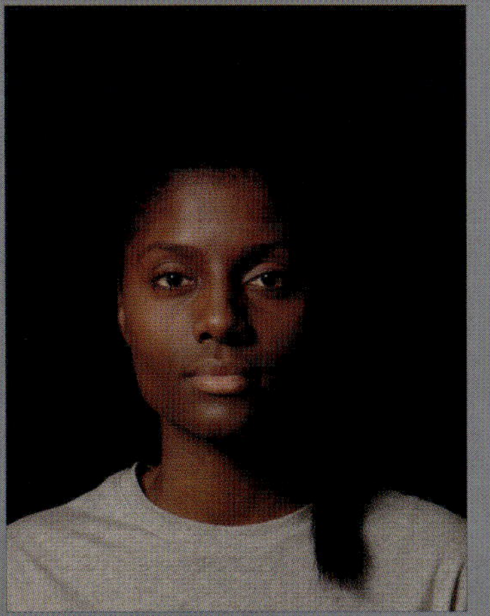

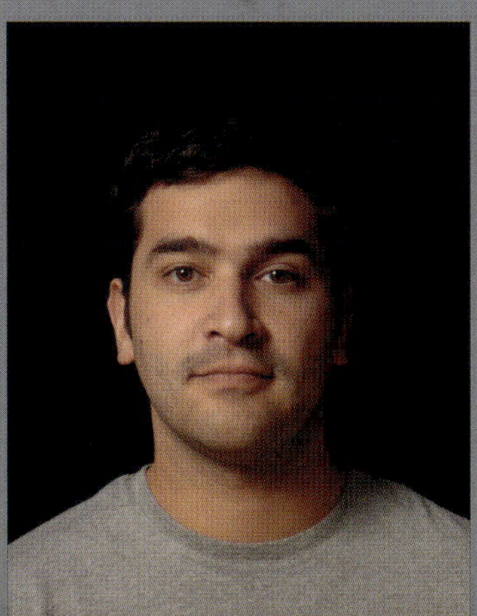

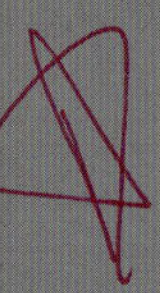

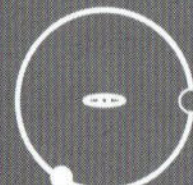

REFLECTORS

LIGHT 1: FROM 30° LEFT

REFLECTOR: FROM 90° RIGHT

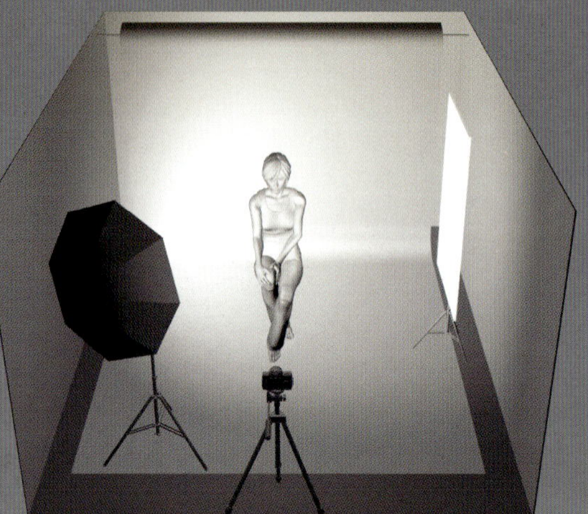

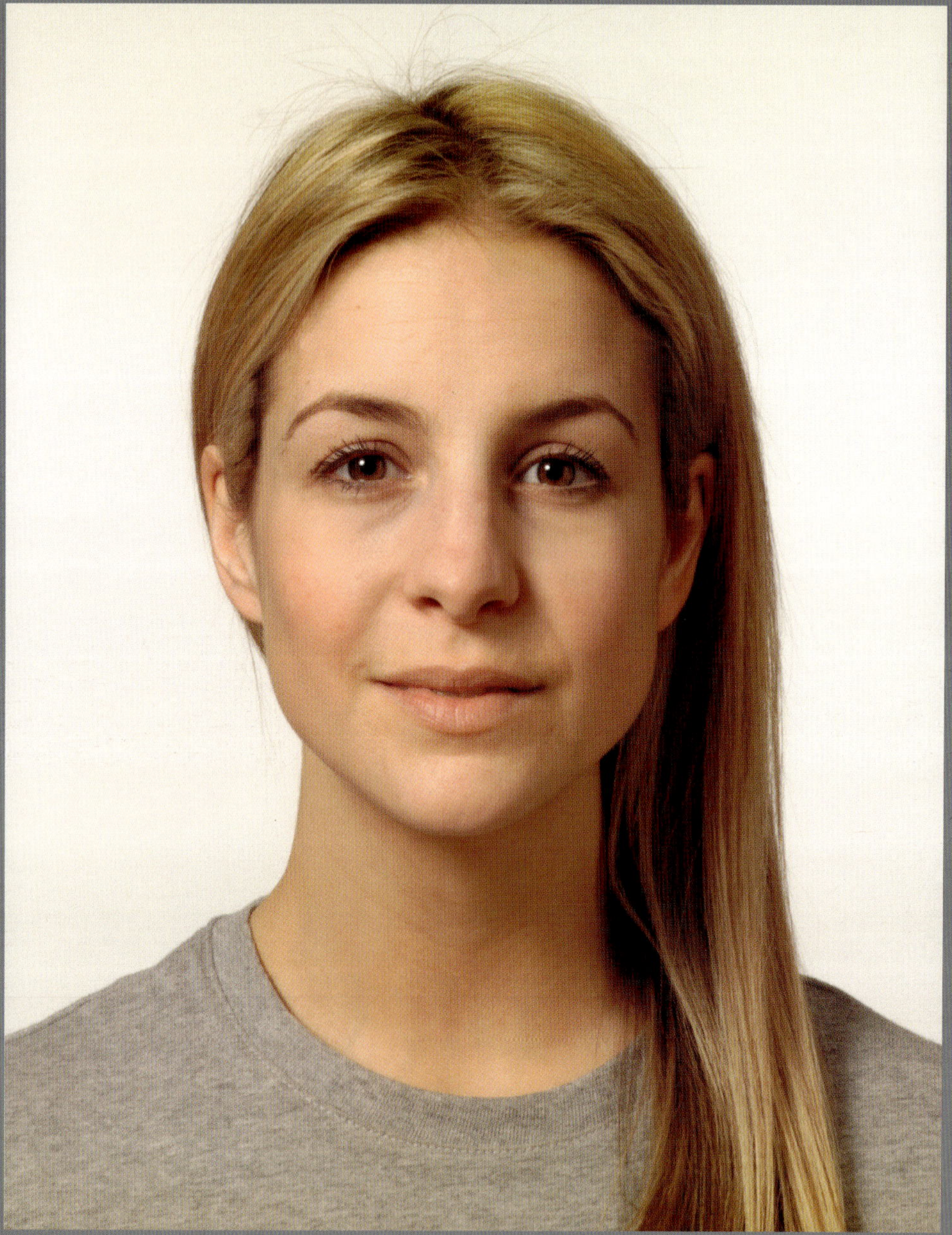

A "classic" photographic portrait does not usually feature shadow areas that lack detail, however, there really needs to be some contrast to avoid the shot looking flat and lifeless. This simple setup provides precisely that, with the catchlights in both eyes adding "life" to the model.

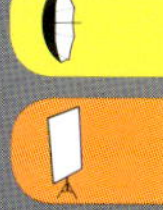

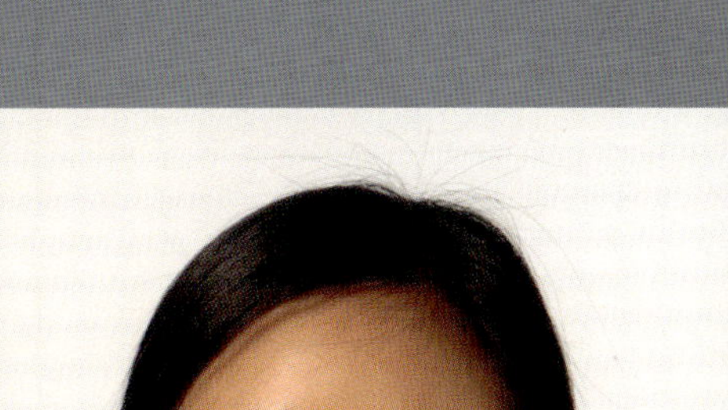

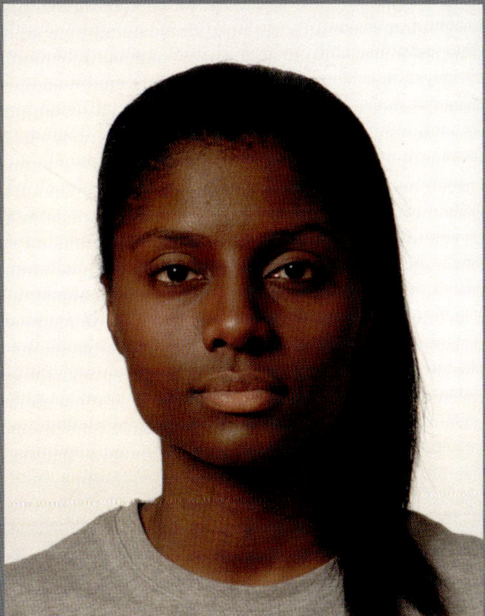

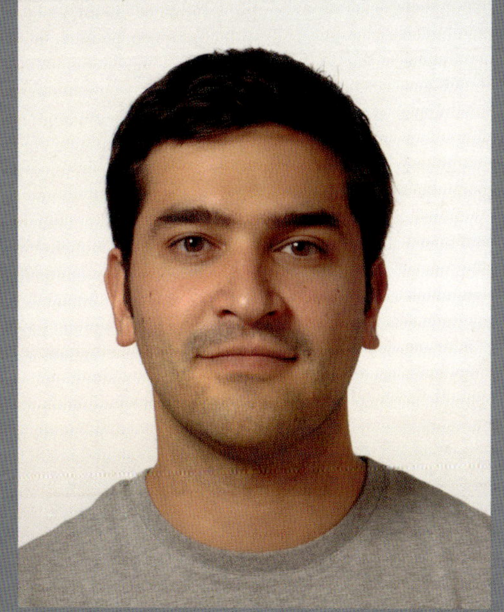

DARK BACKGROUND

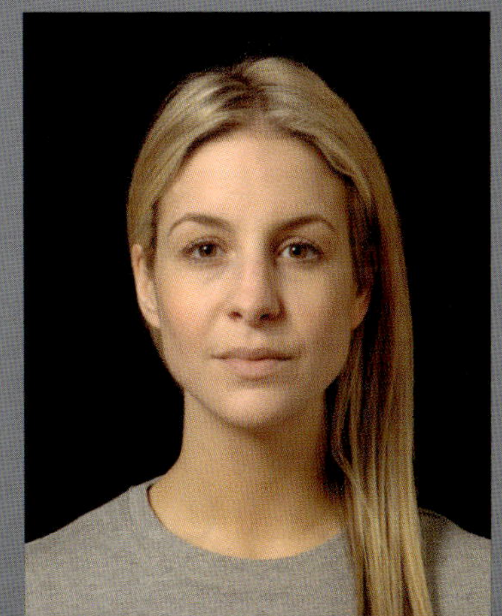

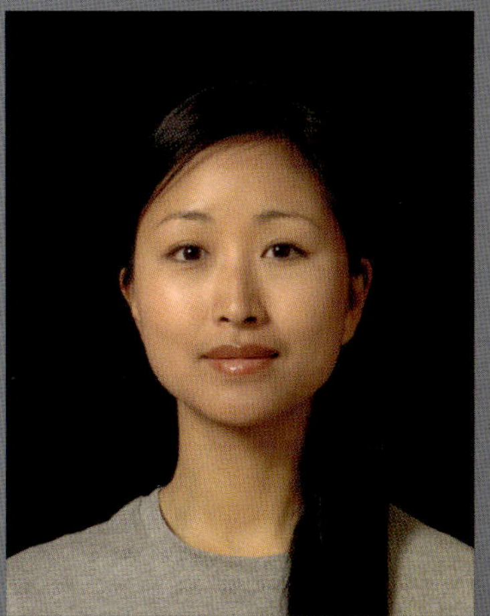

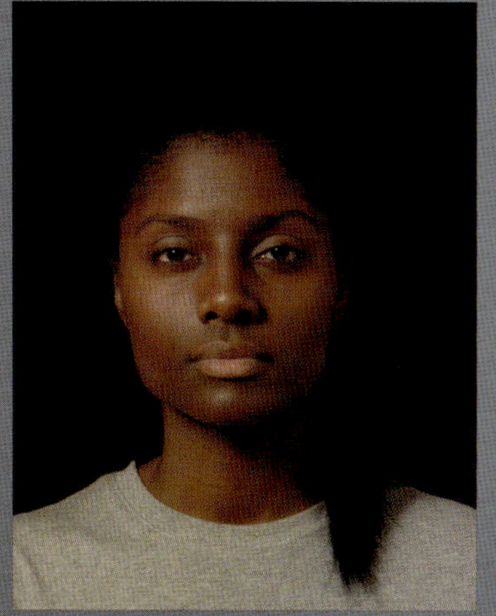

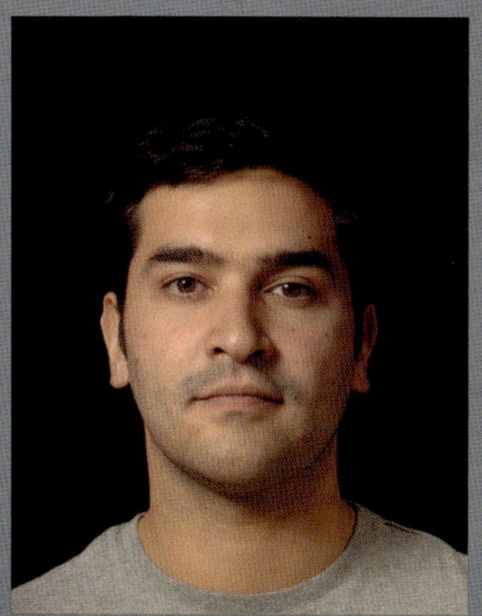

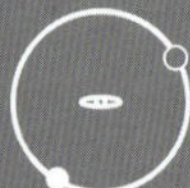

REFLECTORS

LIGHT 1: FROM 30° LEFT

REFLECTOR: FROM 120° RIGHT

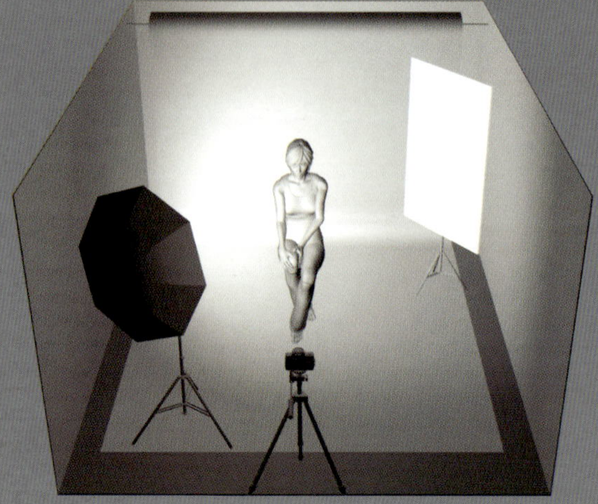

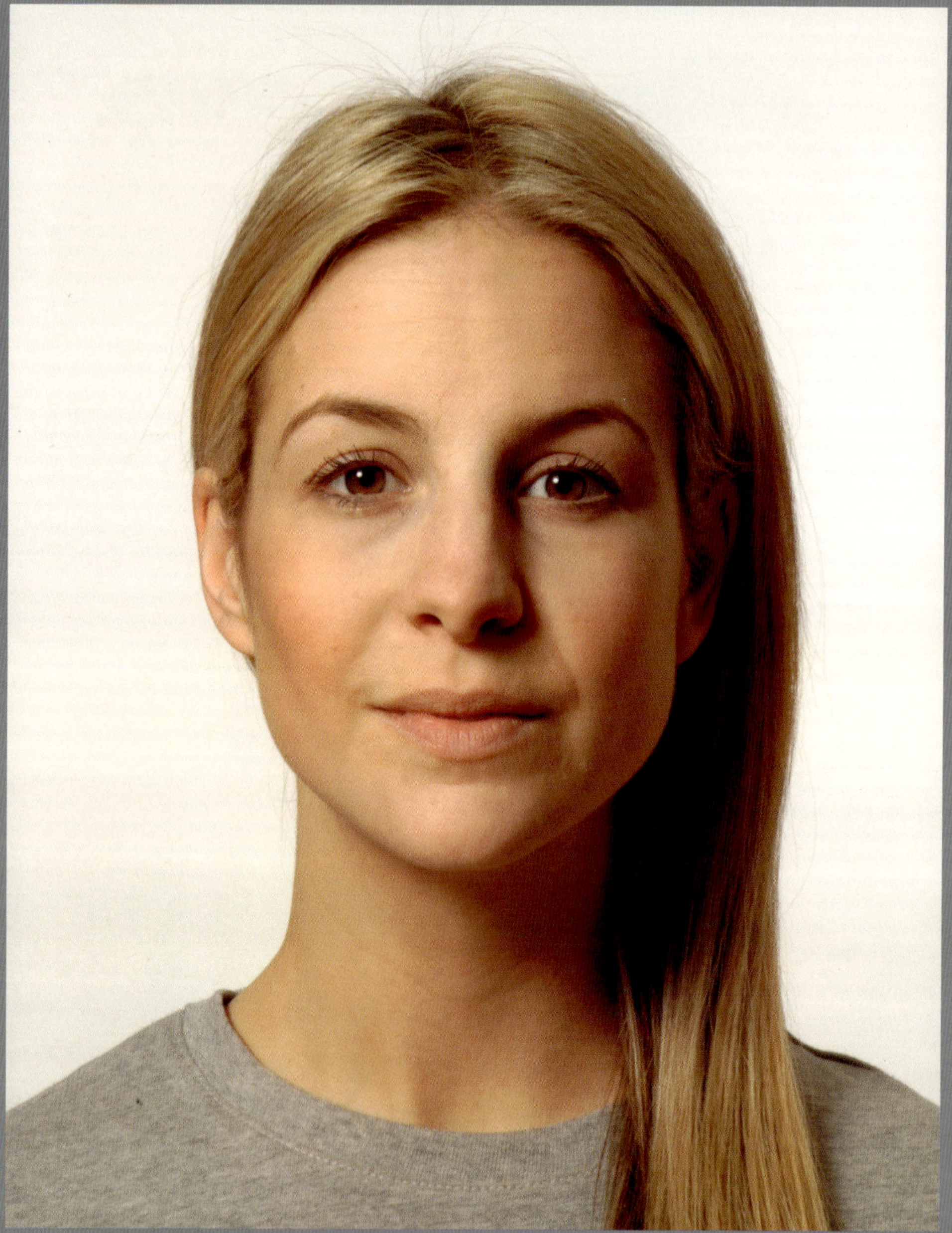

With the light still at a 30-degree angle, but the reflector moved slightly behind the subject, the shadows on the left side of the face are darkened. However, the reflector is still bouncing back enough light to prevent the shadows blocking-up and creates a simple lighting setup that is suitable for most subject and background combinations.

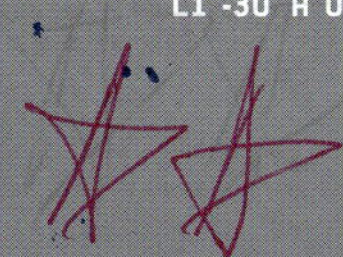
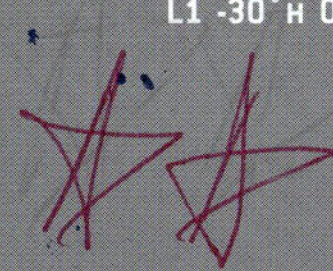

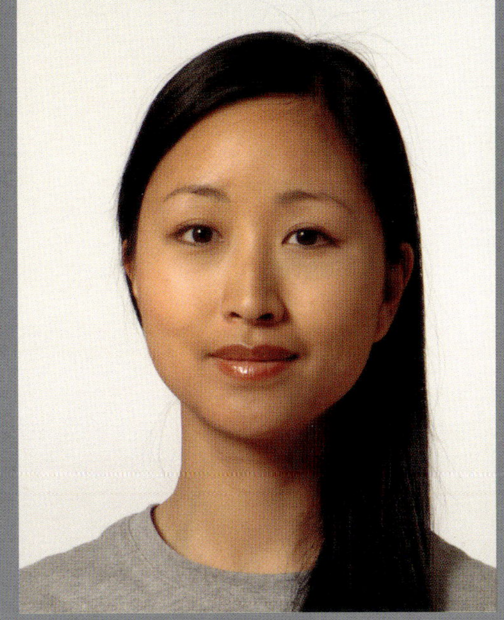
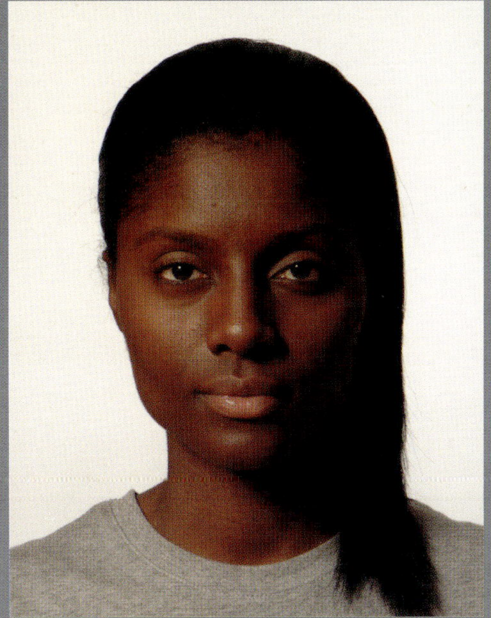
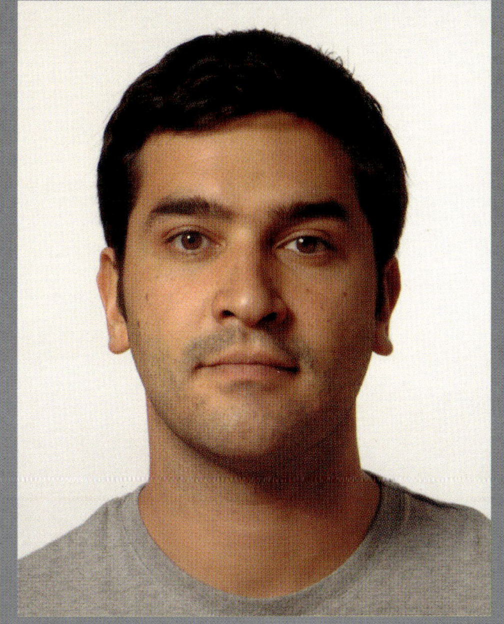

DARK BACKGROUND

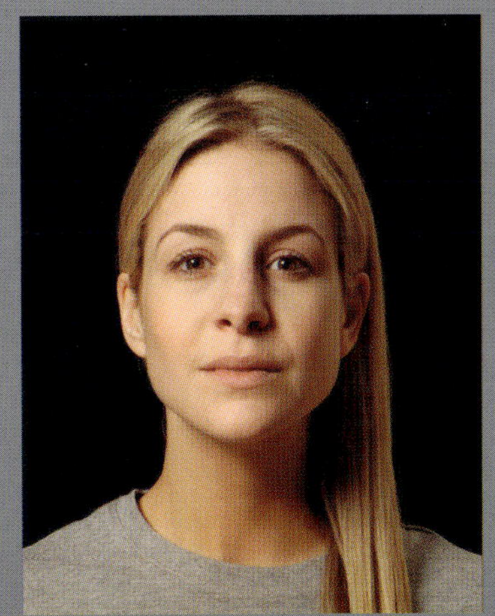
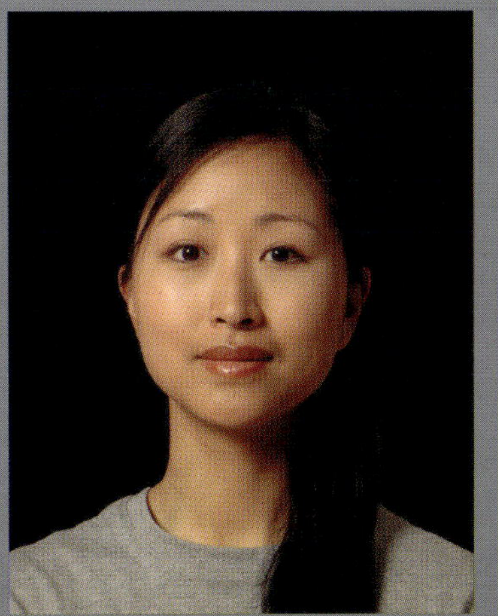
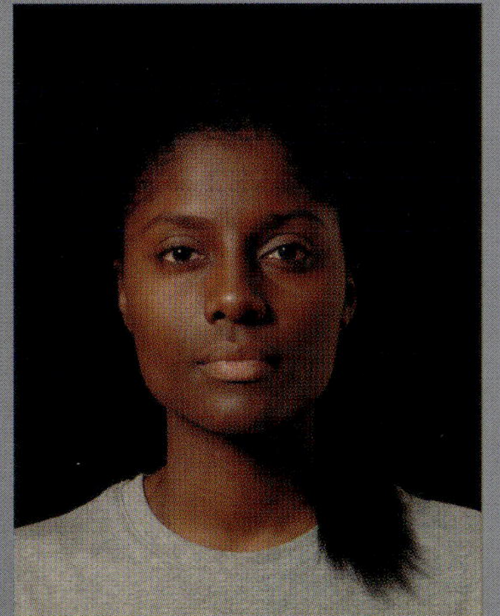
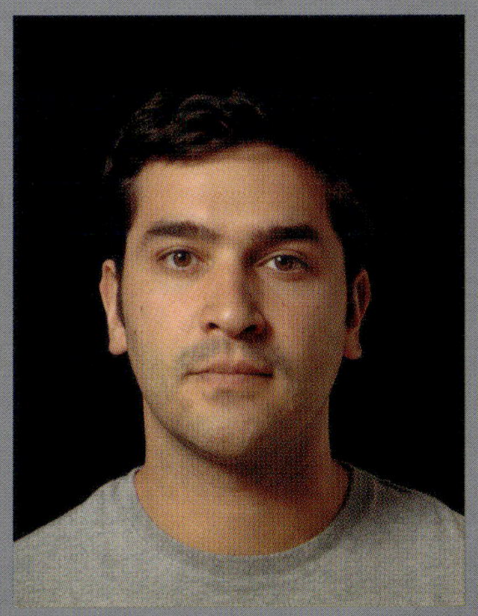

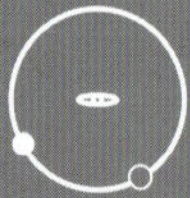

REFLECTORS

LIGHT 1: FROM 60° LEFT

REFLECTOR: FROM 30° RIGHT

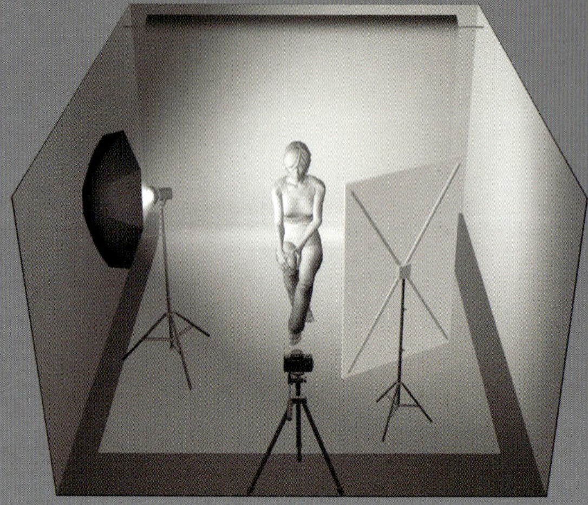

The closer the light and the reflector are to each other, the less effect the reflector has. In this example, the light is at a 60-degree angle to the subject, while the reflector is at 30 degrees to the opposite side. Although the reflector is having some effect (see pages 32–33 to compare it to a single light), the shadows are still heavy.

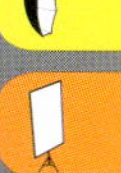

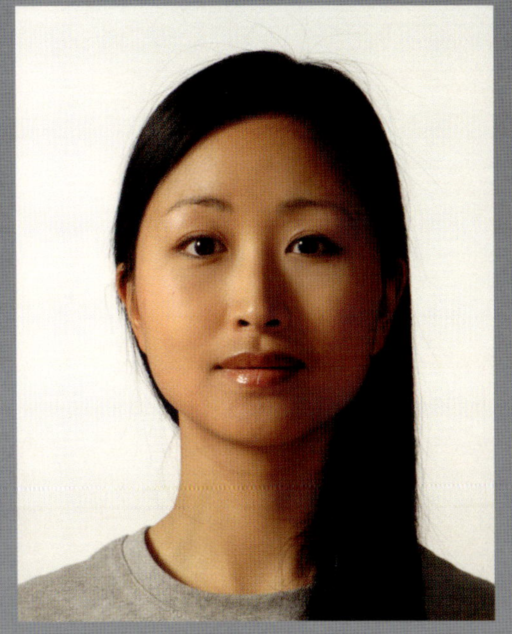

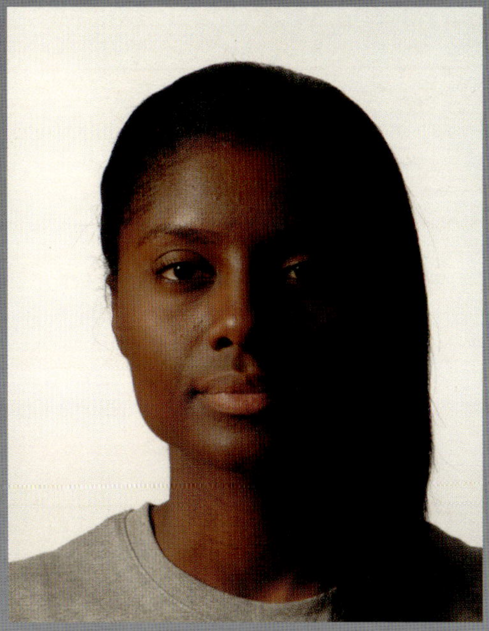

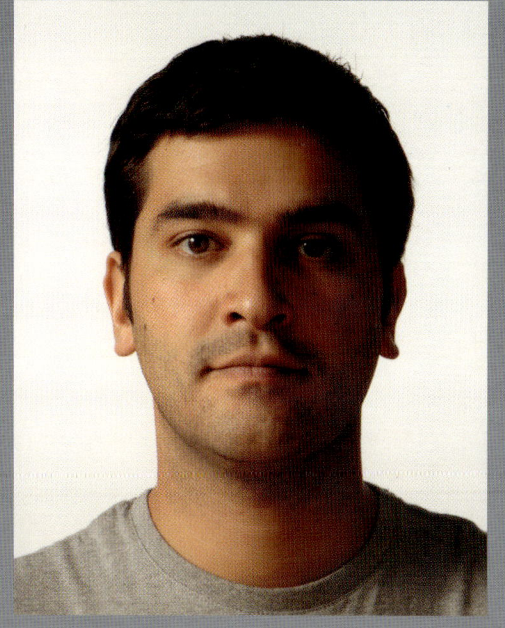

DARK BACKGROUND

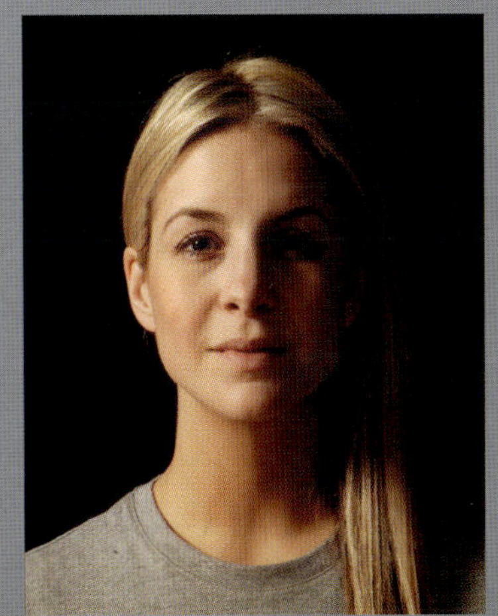

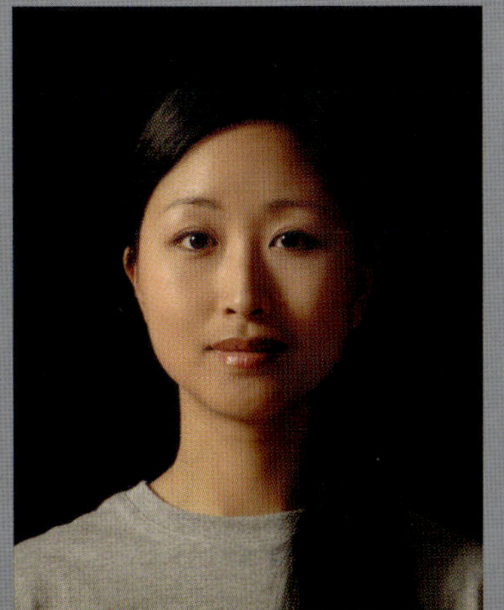

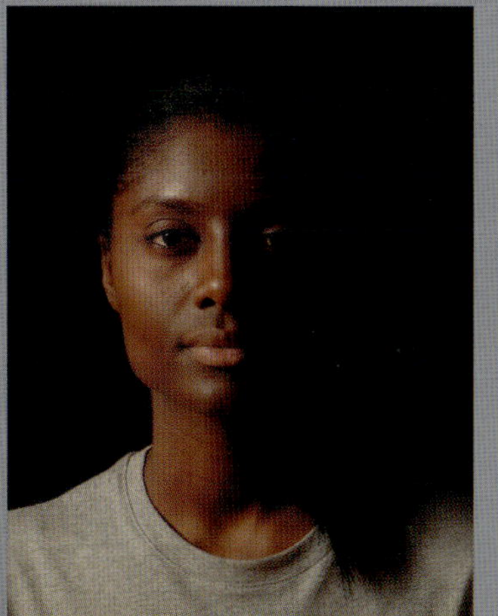

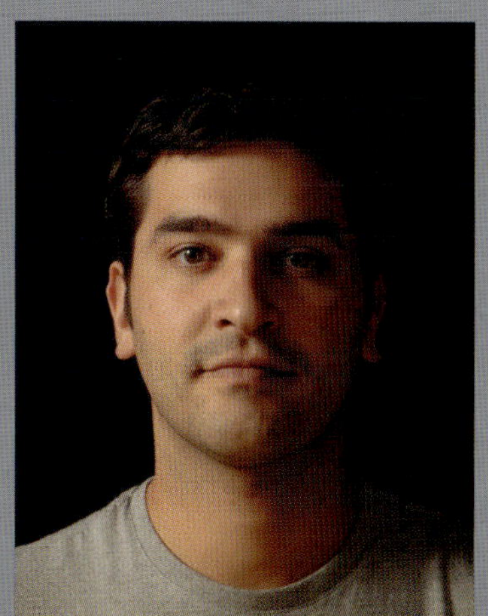

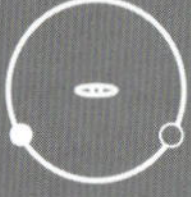

REFLECTORS

LIGHT 1: FROM 60° LEFT

REFLECTOR: FROM 60° RIGHT

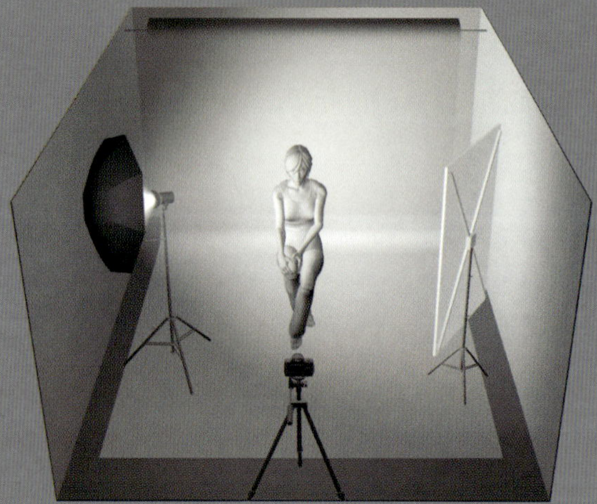

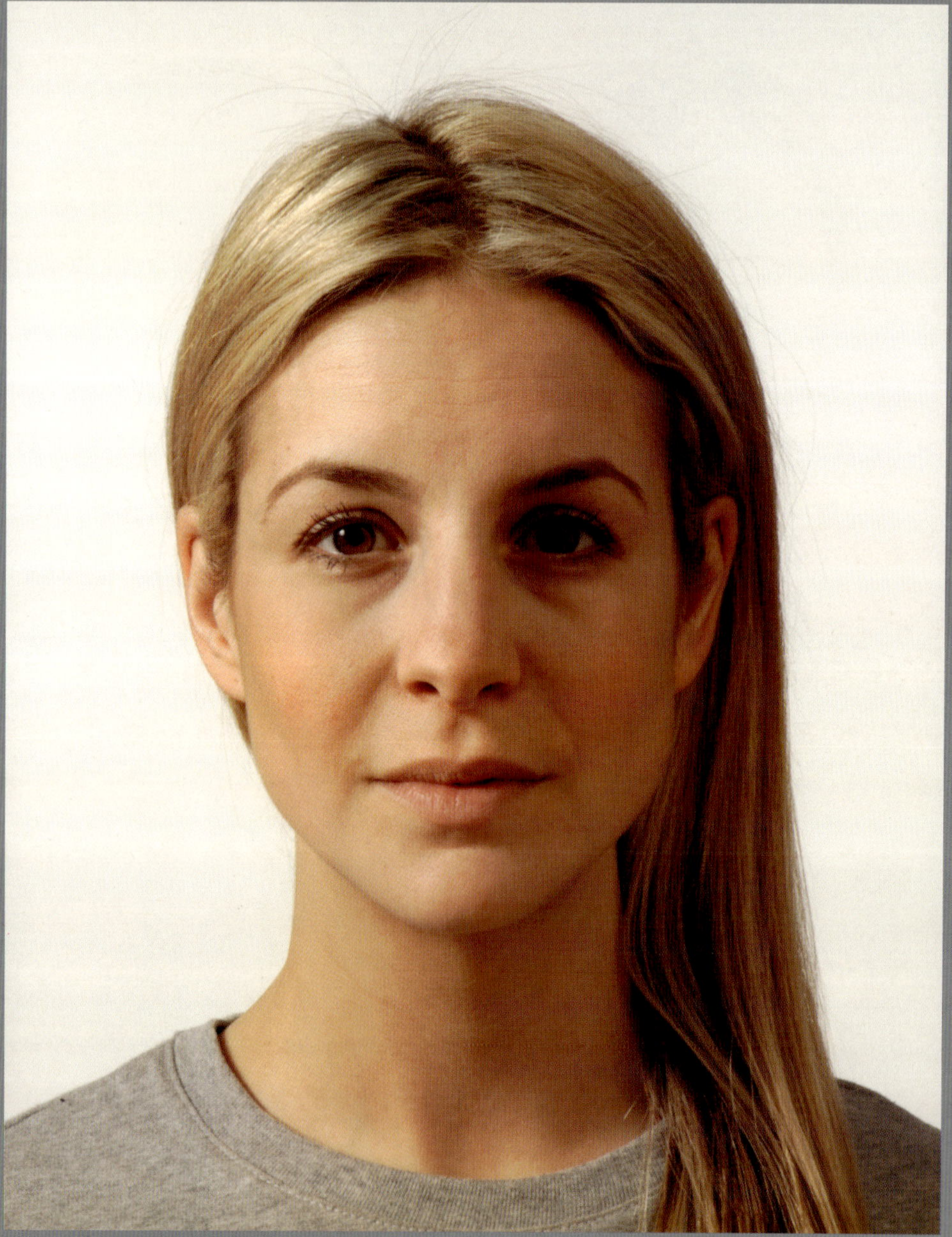

The angle between the light and the reflector has been opened up in this sequence, which means more light is striking the reflector, and more light is therefore being bounced back onto the subject. Compared to the previous setup, detail in the shaded side of the face is much clearer.

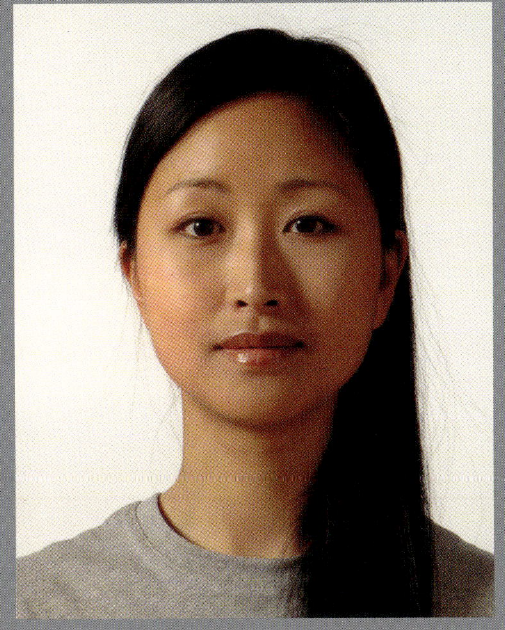

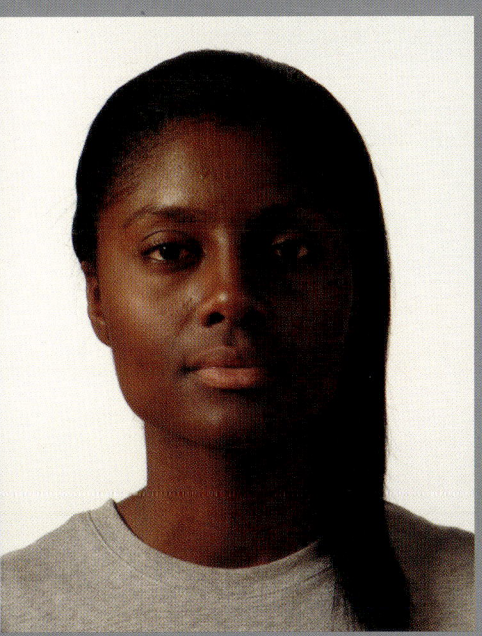

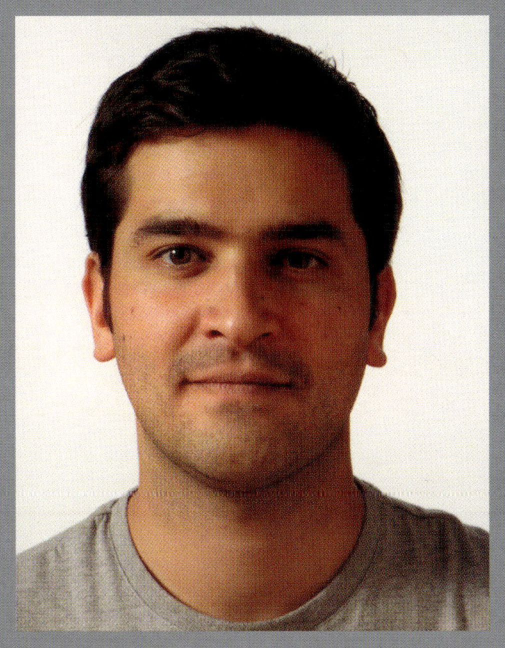

DARK BACKGROUND

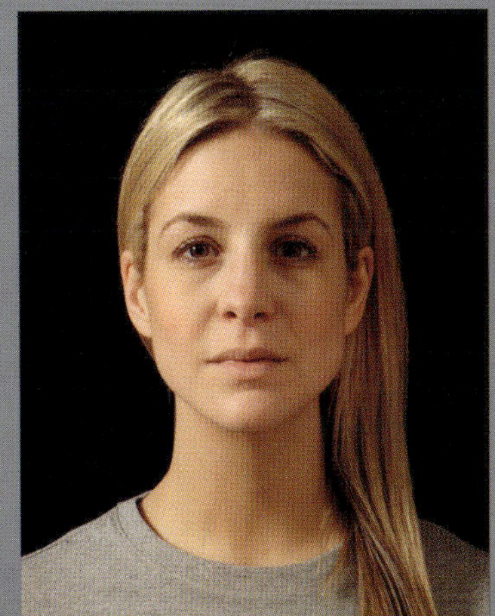

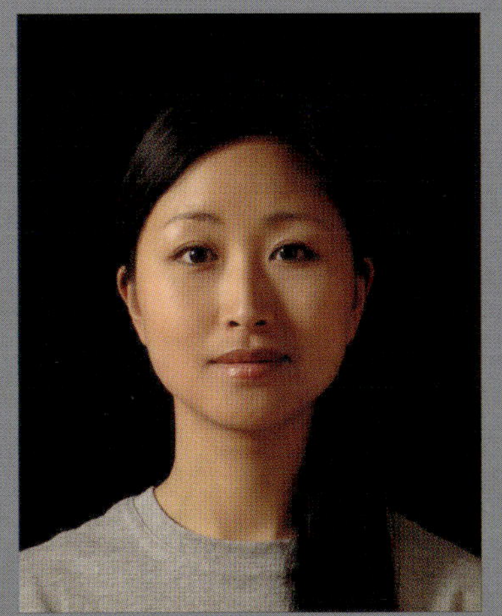

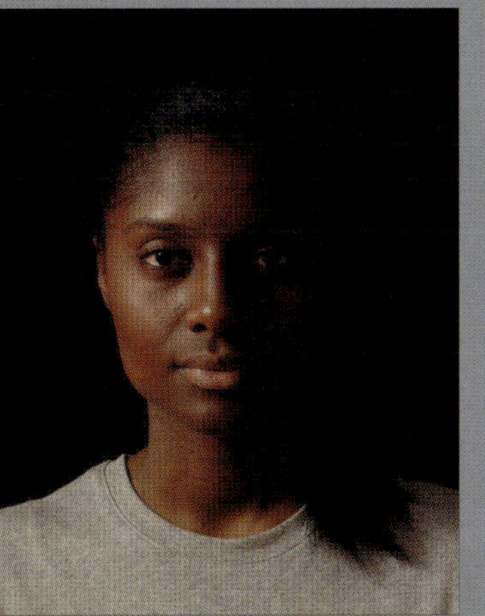

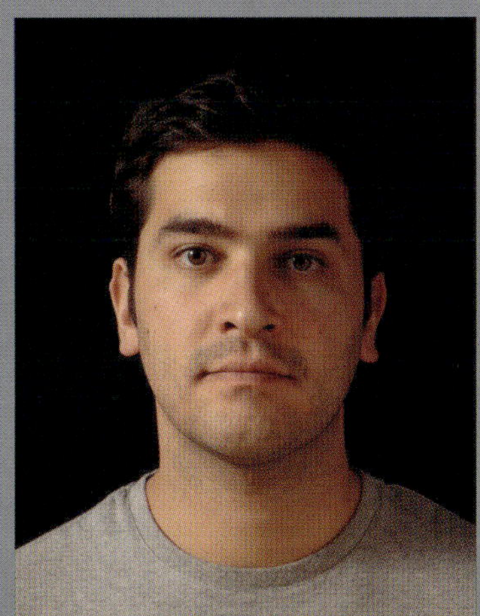

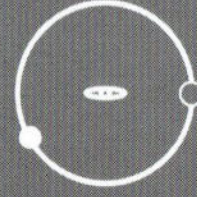

REFLECTORS

LIGHT 1: FROM 60° LEFT

REFLECTOR: FROM 90° RIGHT

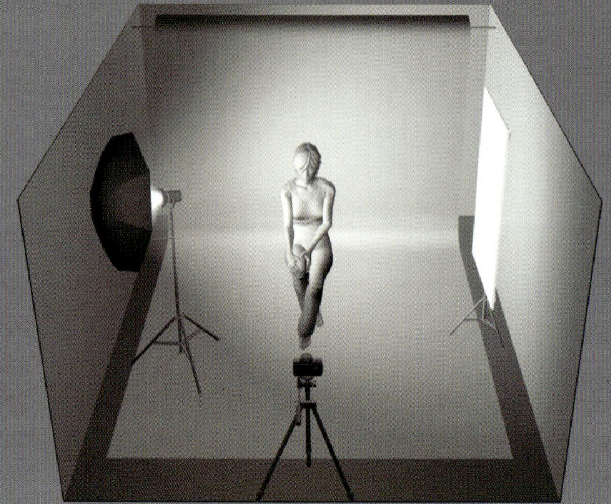

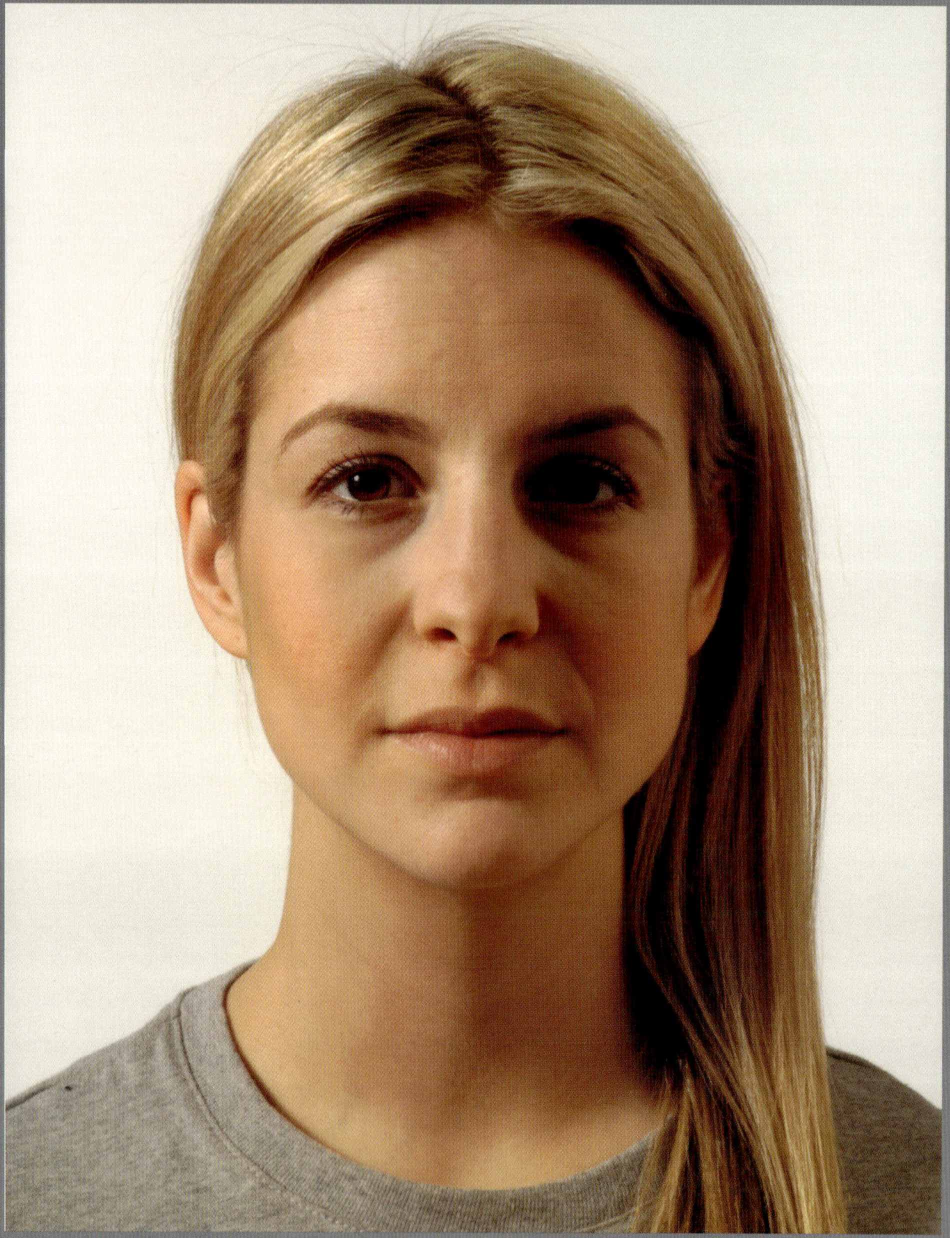

With the reflector set at a 90-degree angle to the camera, and the light at 60 degrees, the right side of the subject's face is well lit, with the reflector highlighting the opposite side. The broad band of shadow down the left side is soft, but adds three-dimensional modeling to the shot.

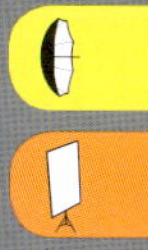

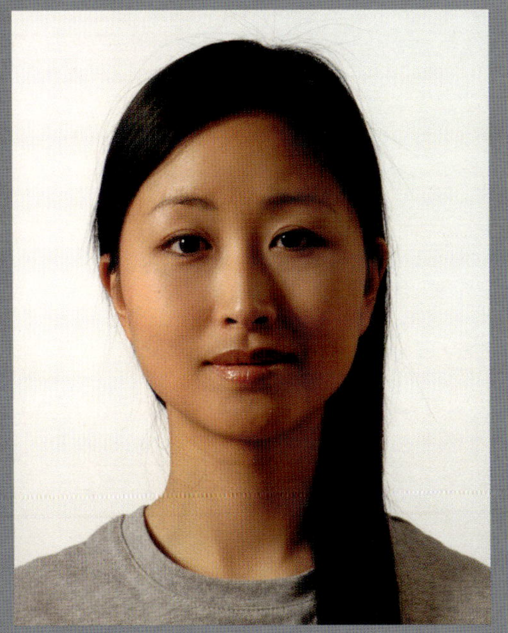

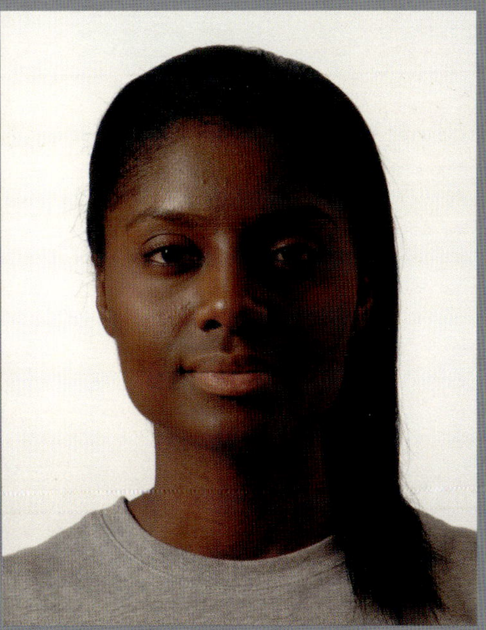

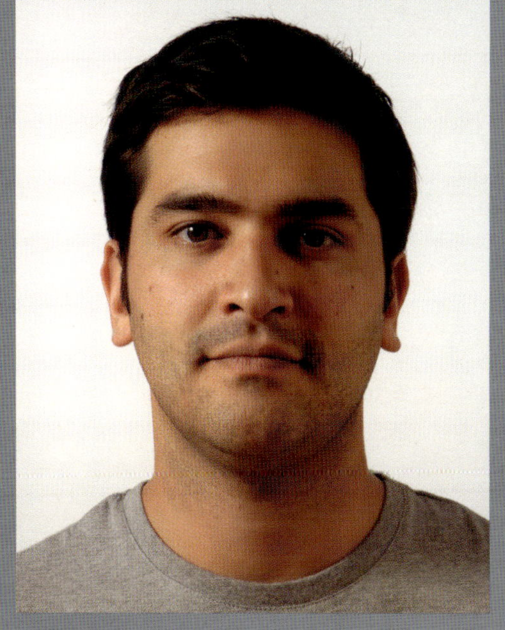

DARK BACKGROUND

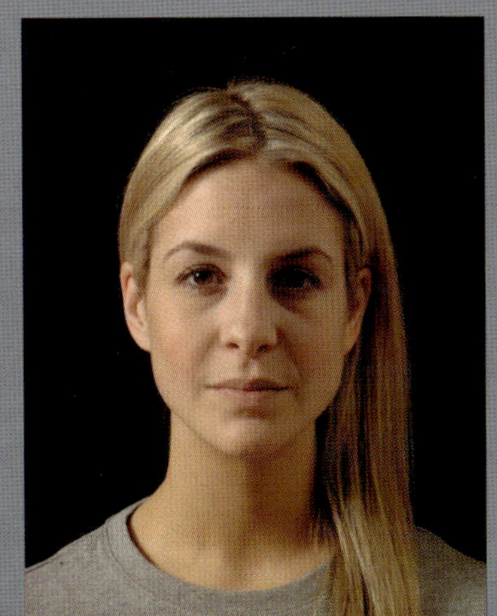

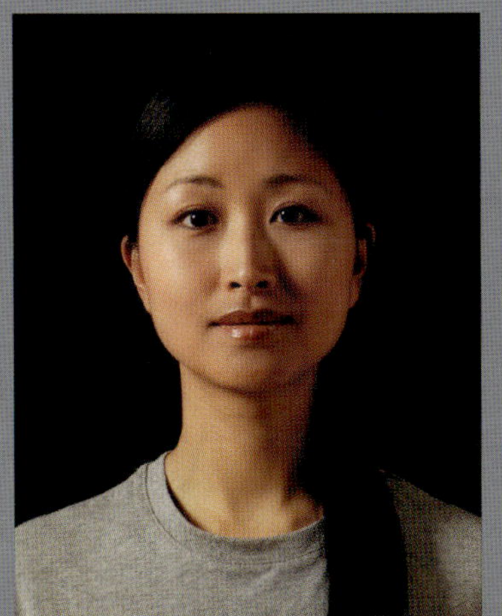

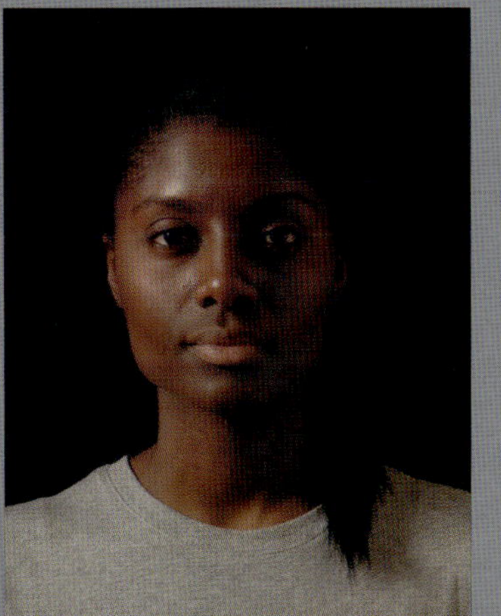

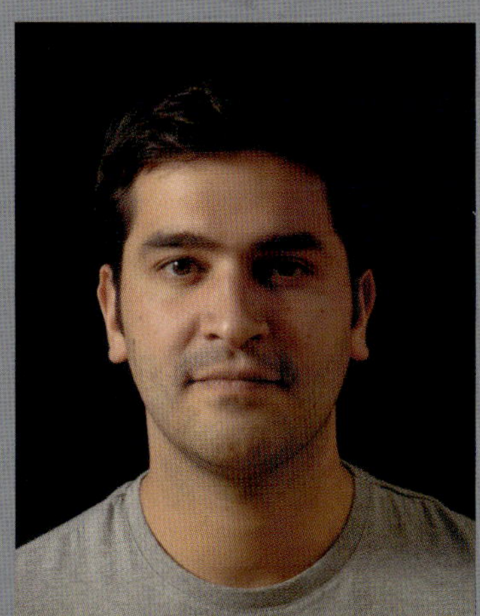

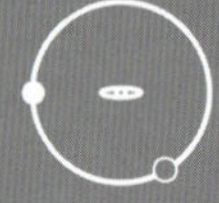

REFLECTORS

LIGHT 1: FROM 90° LEFT

REFLECTOR: FROM 30° RIGHT

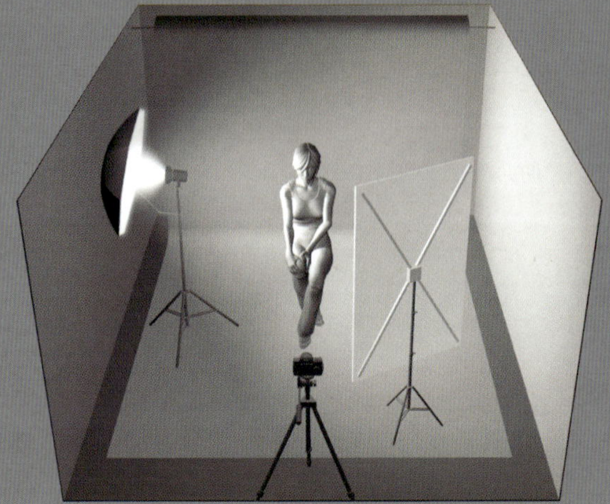

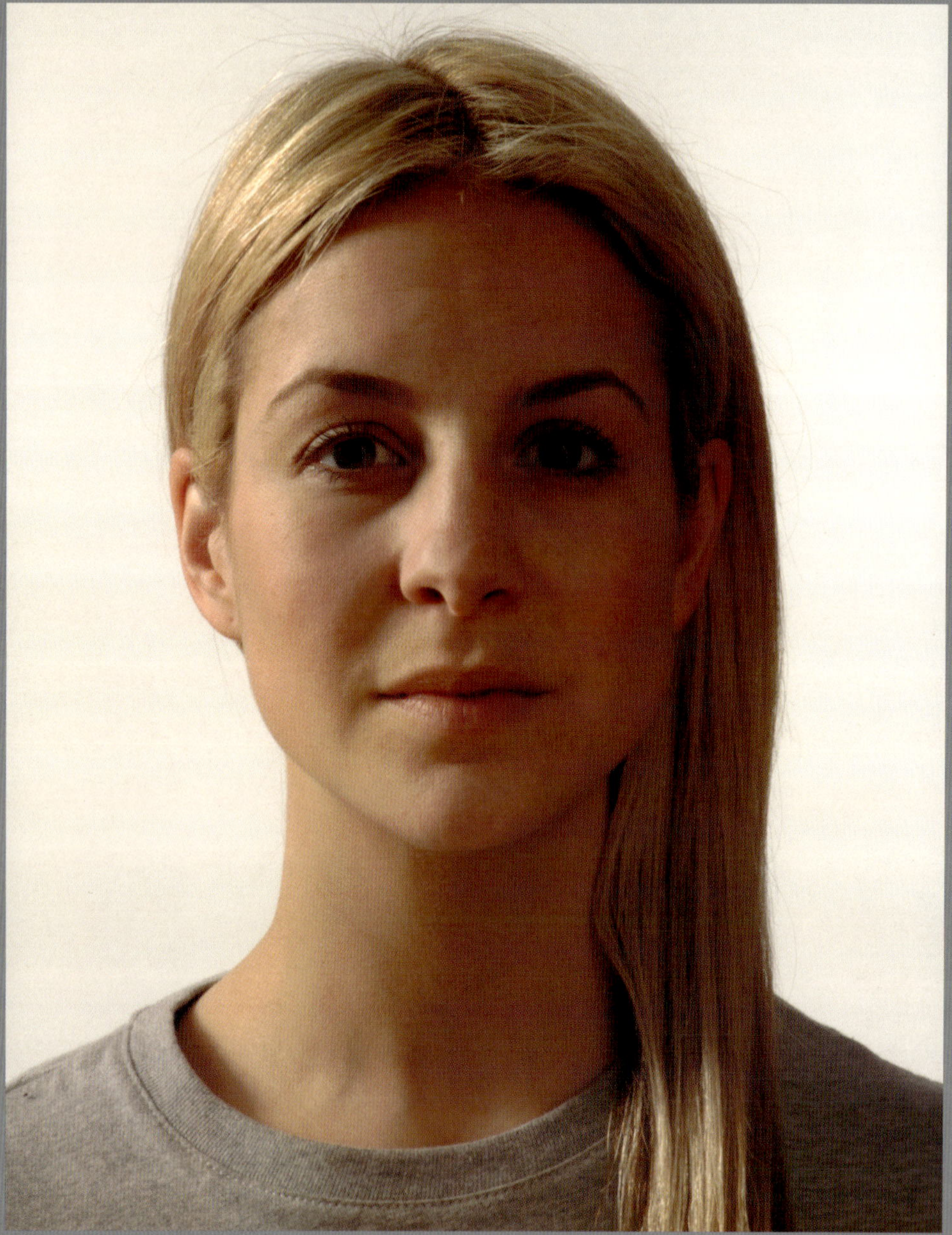

Here, the light is coming from the side, while the reflector sits in front of the subject. This effectively means that the reflector is providing most of the light to the front of the face. Even though the reflected light is weak compared to the strobe, it is still enough to make a model stand out against a dark background.

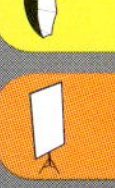

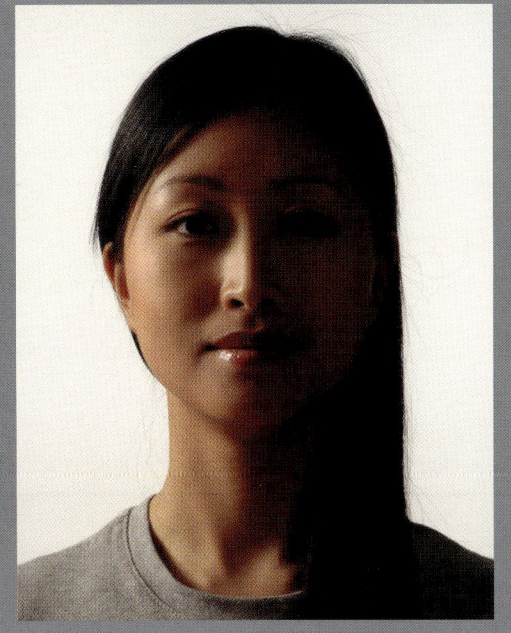

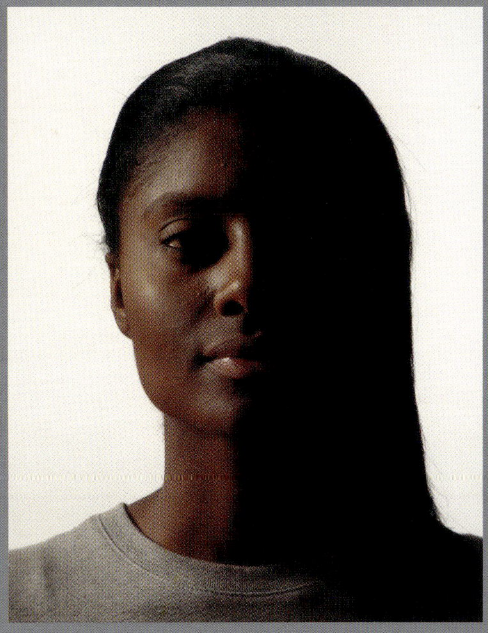

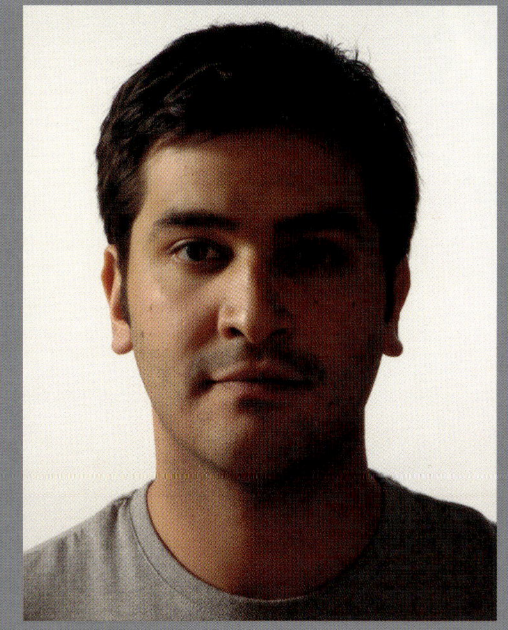

DARK BACKGROUND

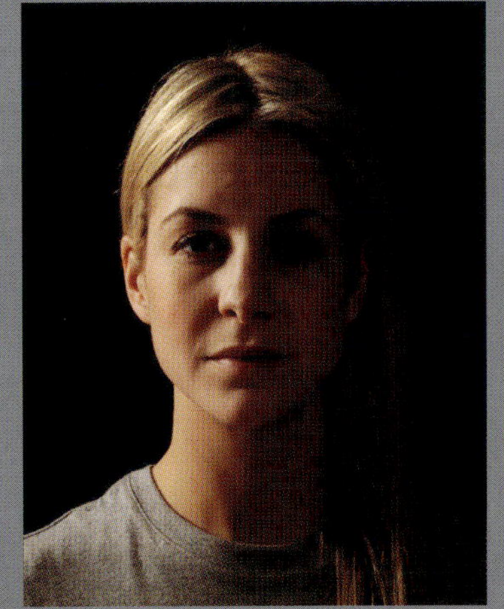

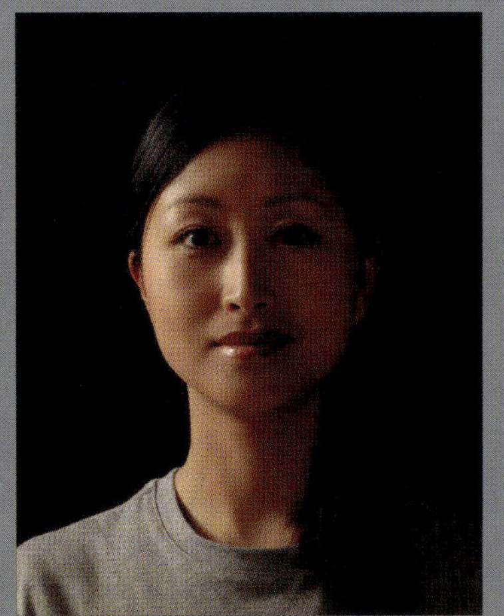

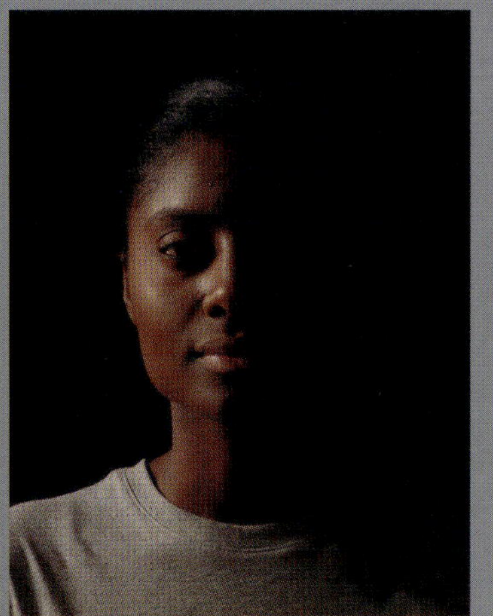

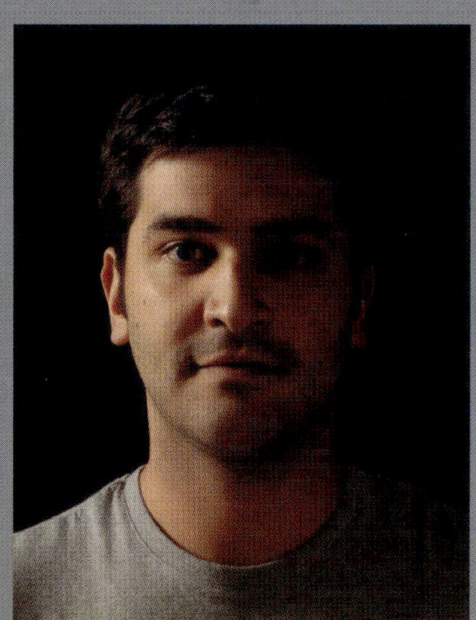

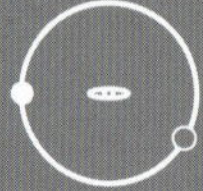

REFLECTORS

LIGHT 1: FROM 90° LEFT

REFLECTOR: FROM 60° RIGHT

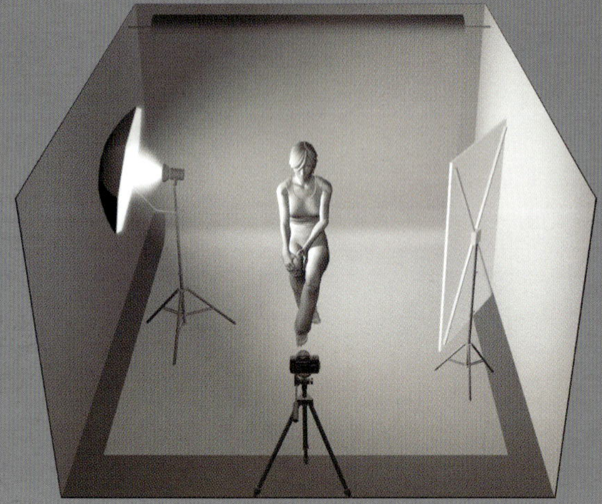

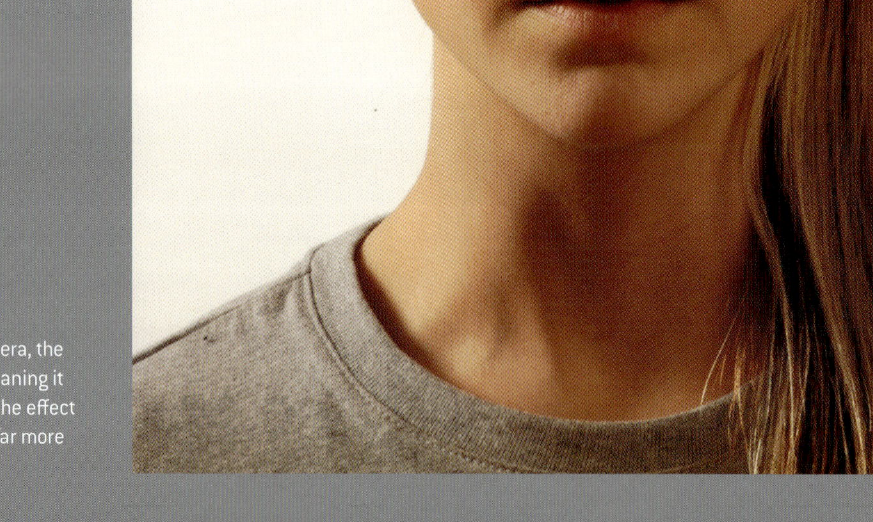

While the light remains at 90 degrees to the camera, the reflector has been moved further to the right, meaning it is now almost opposite the light. This increases the effect it has—more light is being reflected, so there is far more light falling on the left side of the model's face.

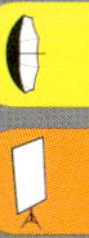

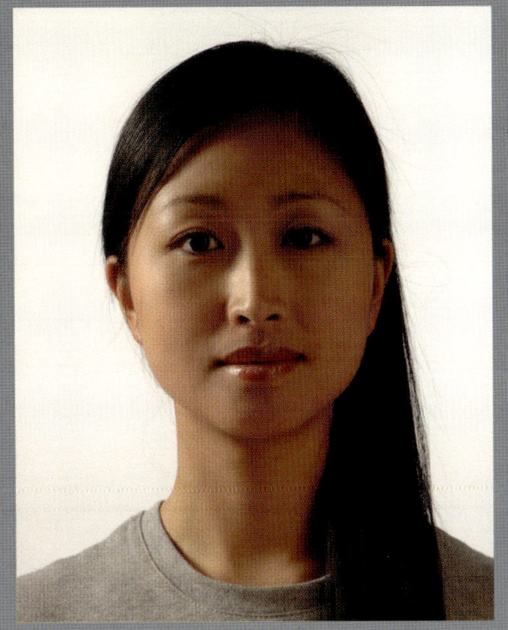

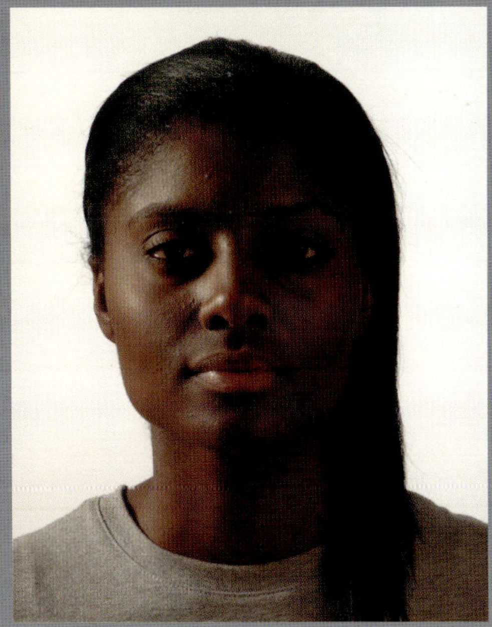

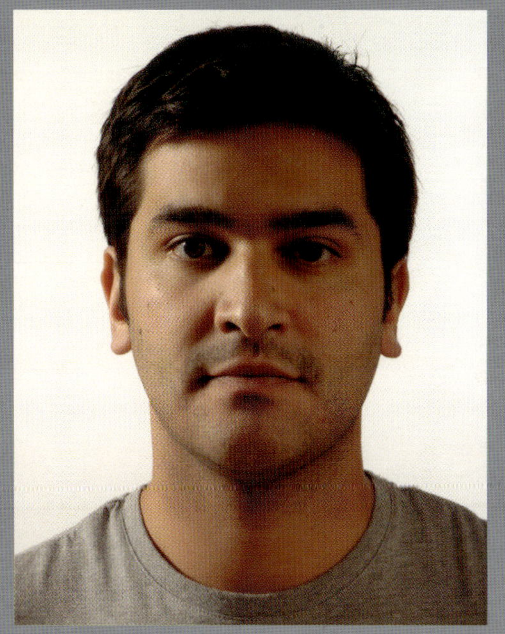

DARK BACKGROUND

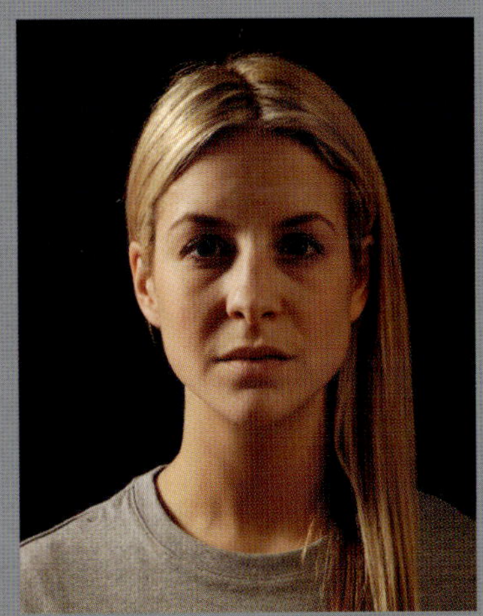

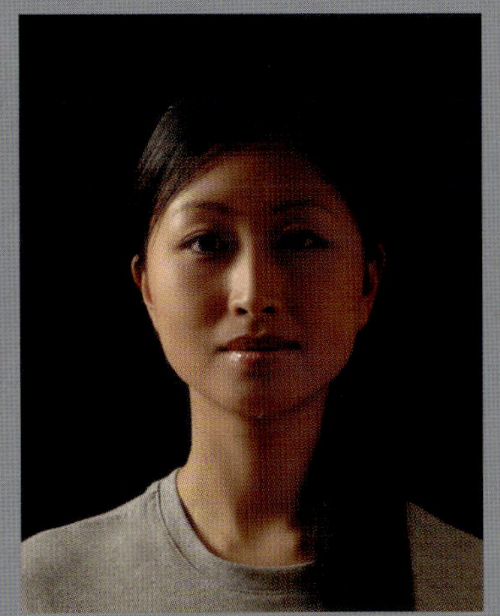

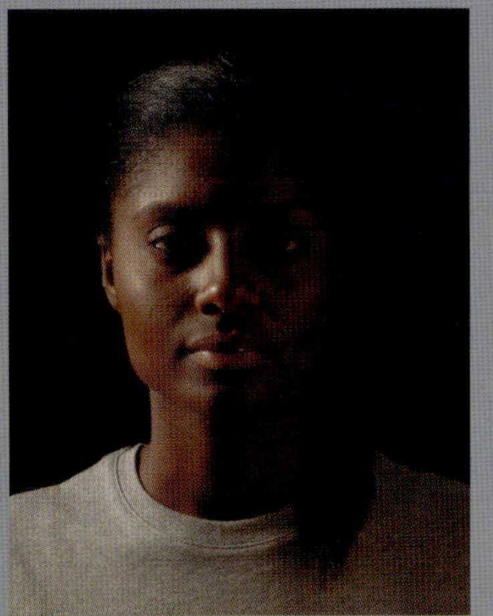

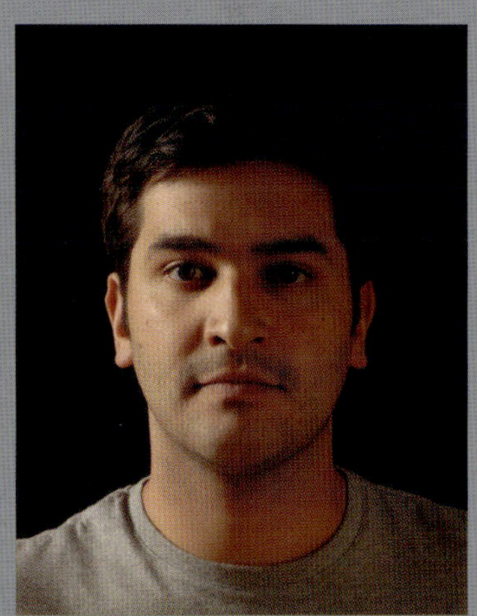

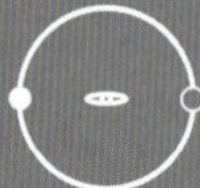

REFLECTORS

LIGHT 1: FROM 90° LEFT

REFLECTOR: FROM 90° RIGHT

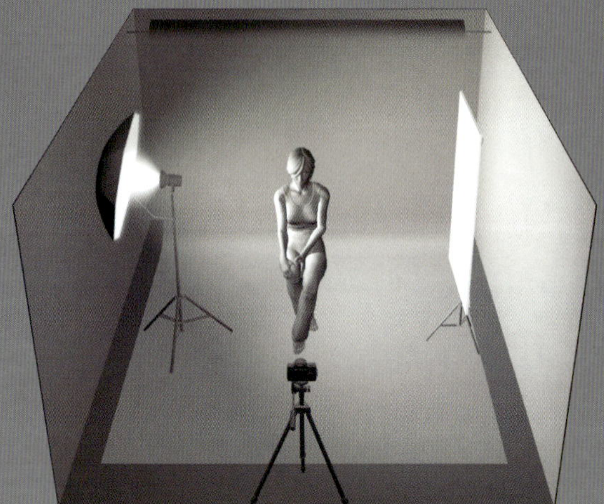

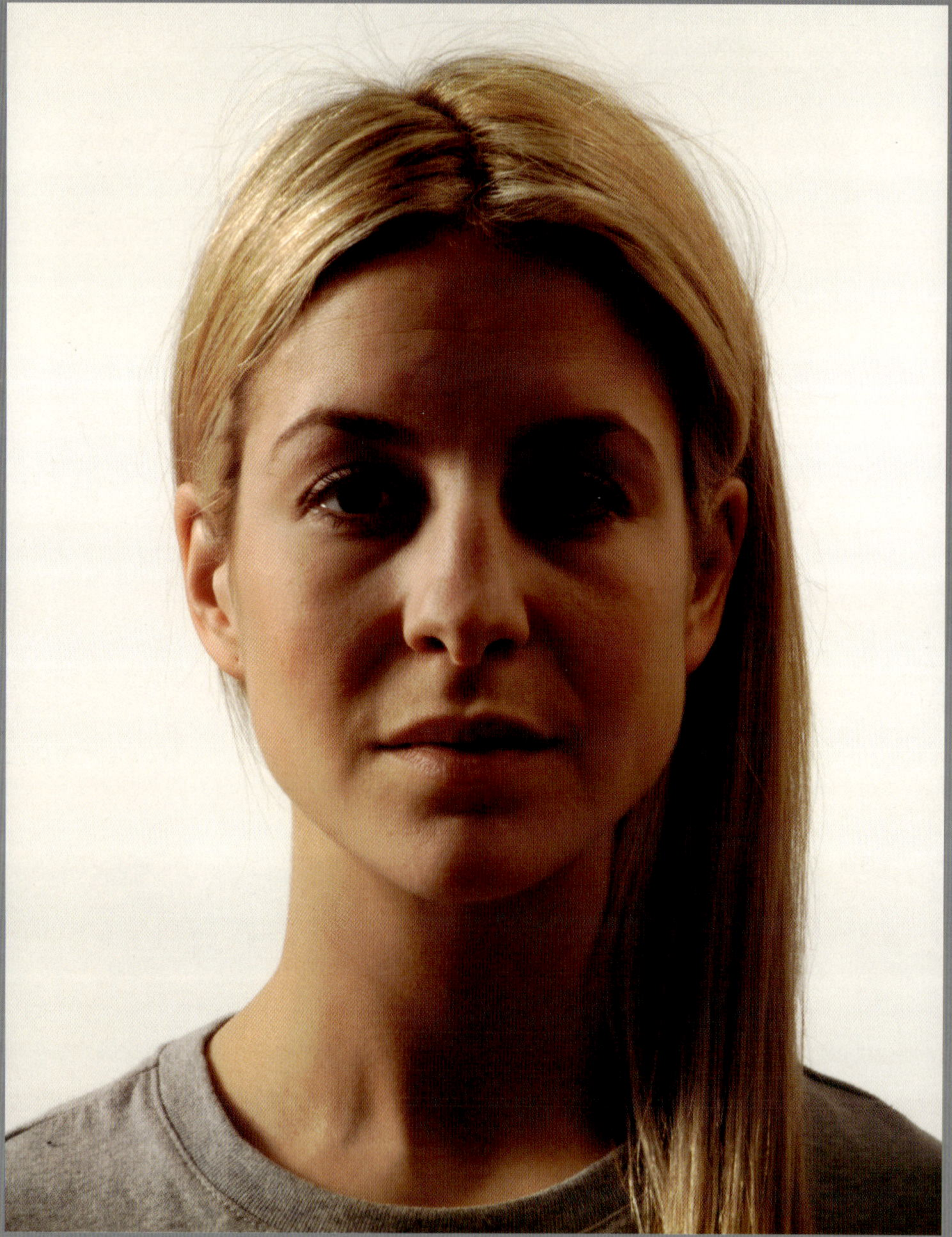

This setup clearly demonstrates the effect of a reflector compared to a "proper" light. While the right side of the models' faces are well lit by the light, the left side (illuminated by the reflected light) is significantly darker. The reflected light is noticeably softer, also.

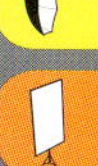

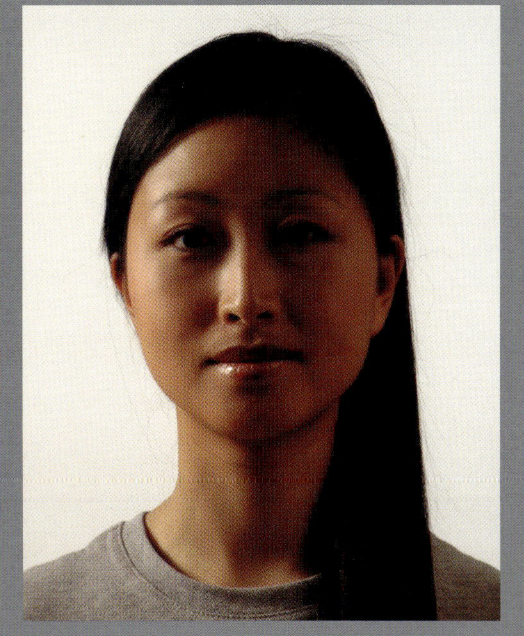

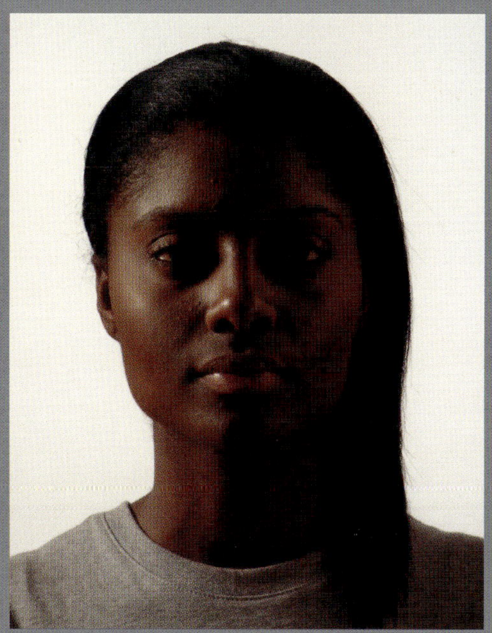

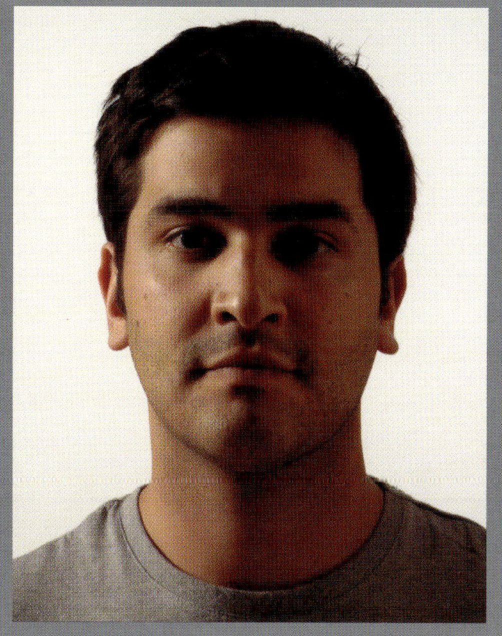

DARK BACKGROUND

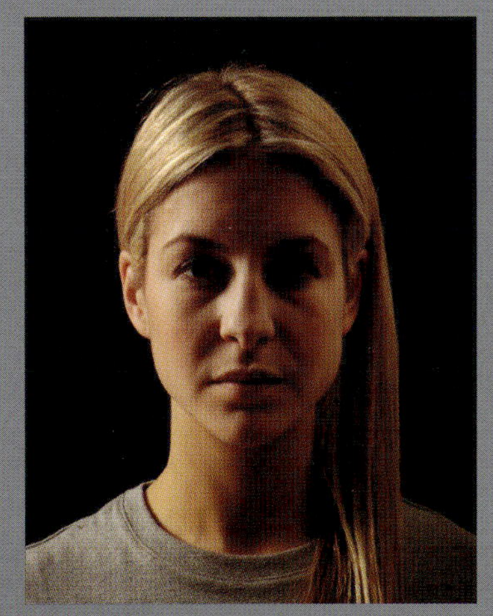

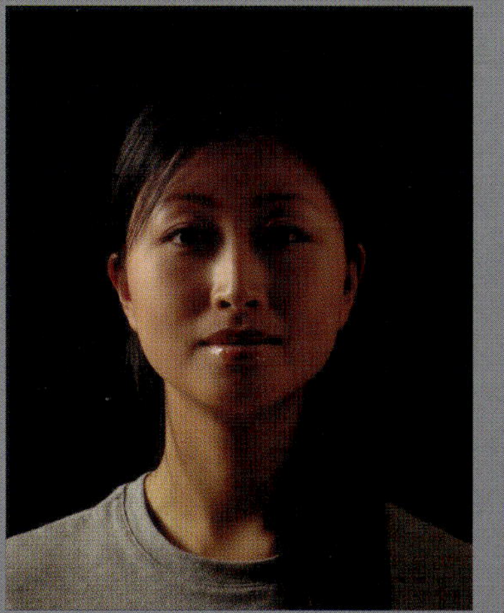

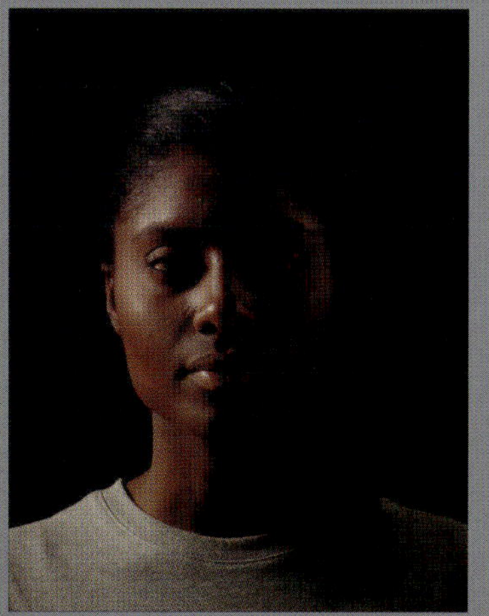

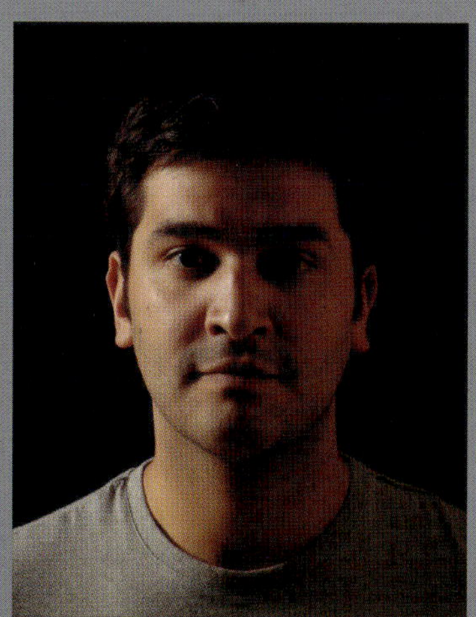

CHAPTER 9

TWO COLORED LIGHTS

If you're shooting portraits using incandescent (tungsten) lights, or one of the many different fluorescent light sources that are available for digital photography, continuous lighting makes it easy to see what effect your lights are having. However, this isn't always possible when you're using flash. While some studio strobes have a modeling light to help show where, and how, the flash will fall, not all of them are proportional to the flash, meaning there is still a certain amount of "guesswork" involved. This is even more of an issue when you take hotshoe-mounted units off-camera—most will not provide a modeling light, and those that do use a brief, power-draining strobe effect that isn't necessarily helpful.

The following section uses colored gels—one red and one blue—on two lights, to show precisely how the light from each falls on the subject. This is a good way of experimenting with lighting setups of your own—simply gel your lights to reveal precisely how they are interacting and, when you have created the look you are after, remove the gels to shoot for real or simply keep the colored shot as a reference for later use.

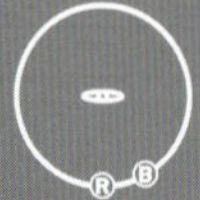

TWO COLORED LIGHTS

LIGHT 1 (RED): FROM 0°

LIGHT 2 (BLUE): FROM 30° RIGHT

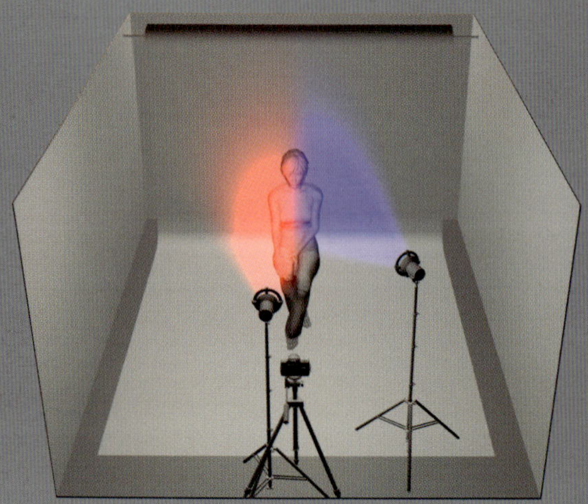

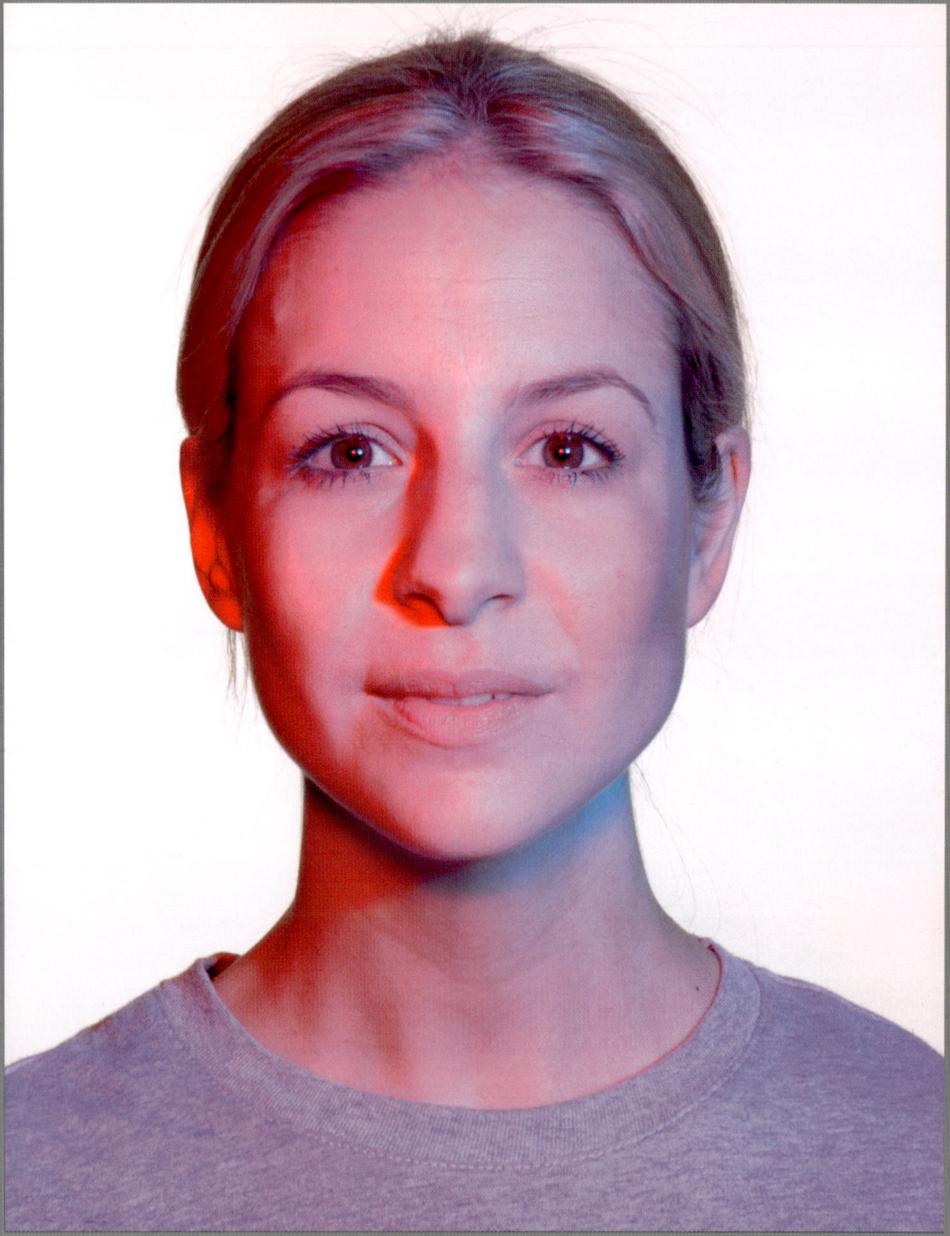

The red lamp is providing full-frontal illumination of the subject, with a blue light coming in from a 30-degree angle. Overall, the colors are mixing in most areas, with the exception of the right side of the model's face and nose. The deep red shadows show the areas the blue light does not reach.

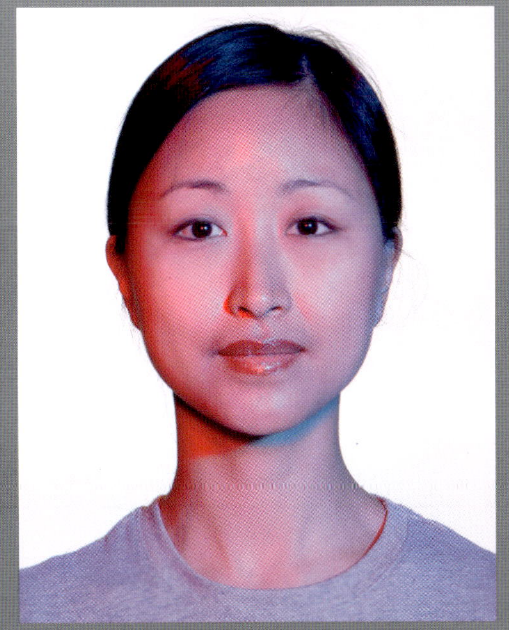
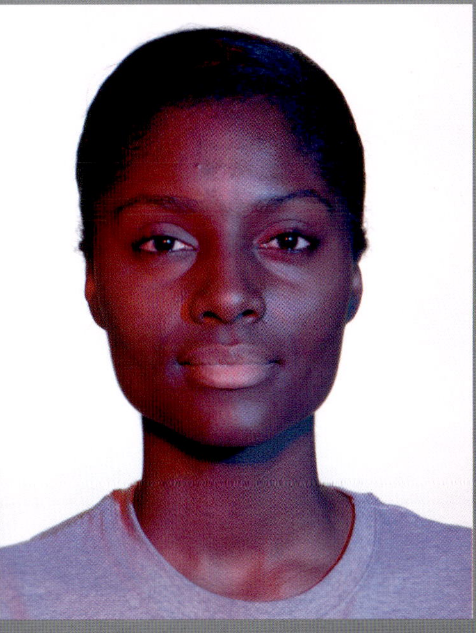
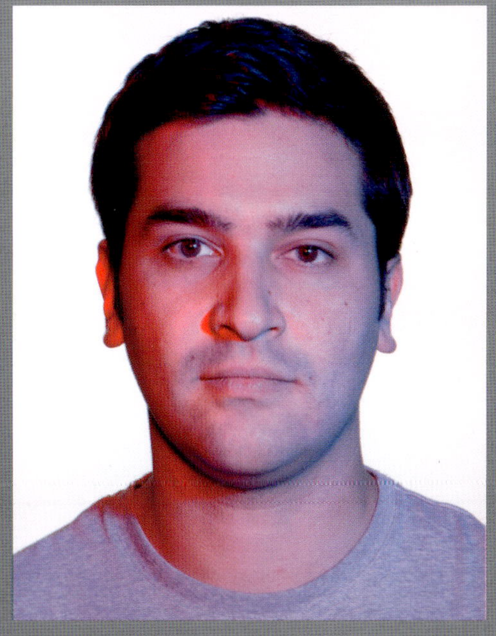

DARK BACKGROUND

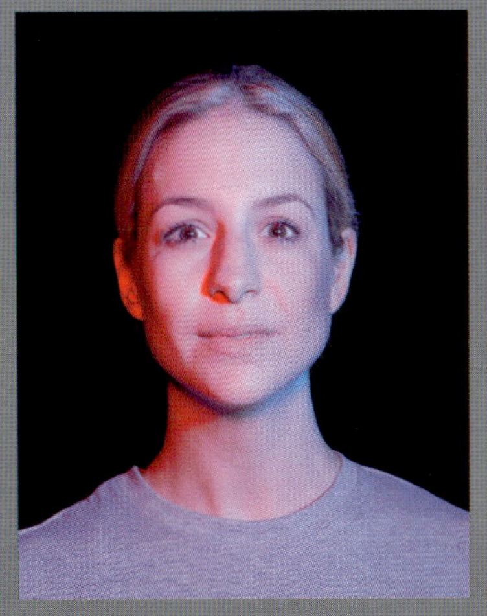
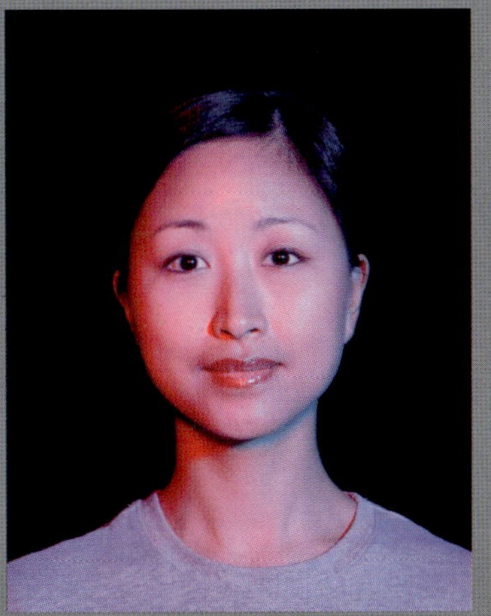
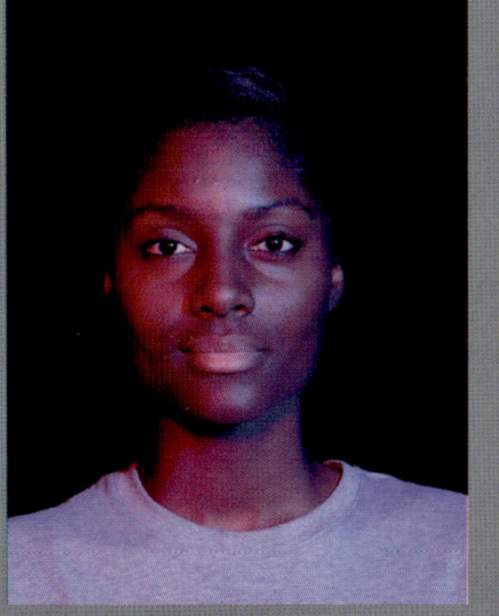
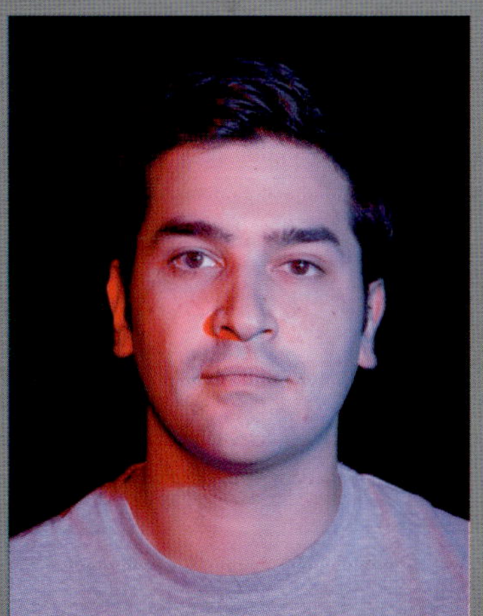

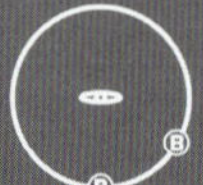

TWO COLORED LIGHTS

LIGHT 1 (RED): FROM 0°

LIGHT 2 (BLUE): FROM 60° RIGHT

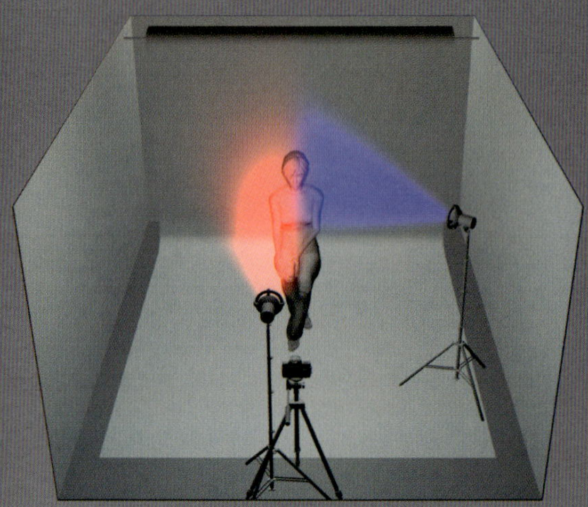

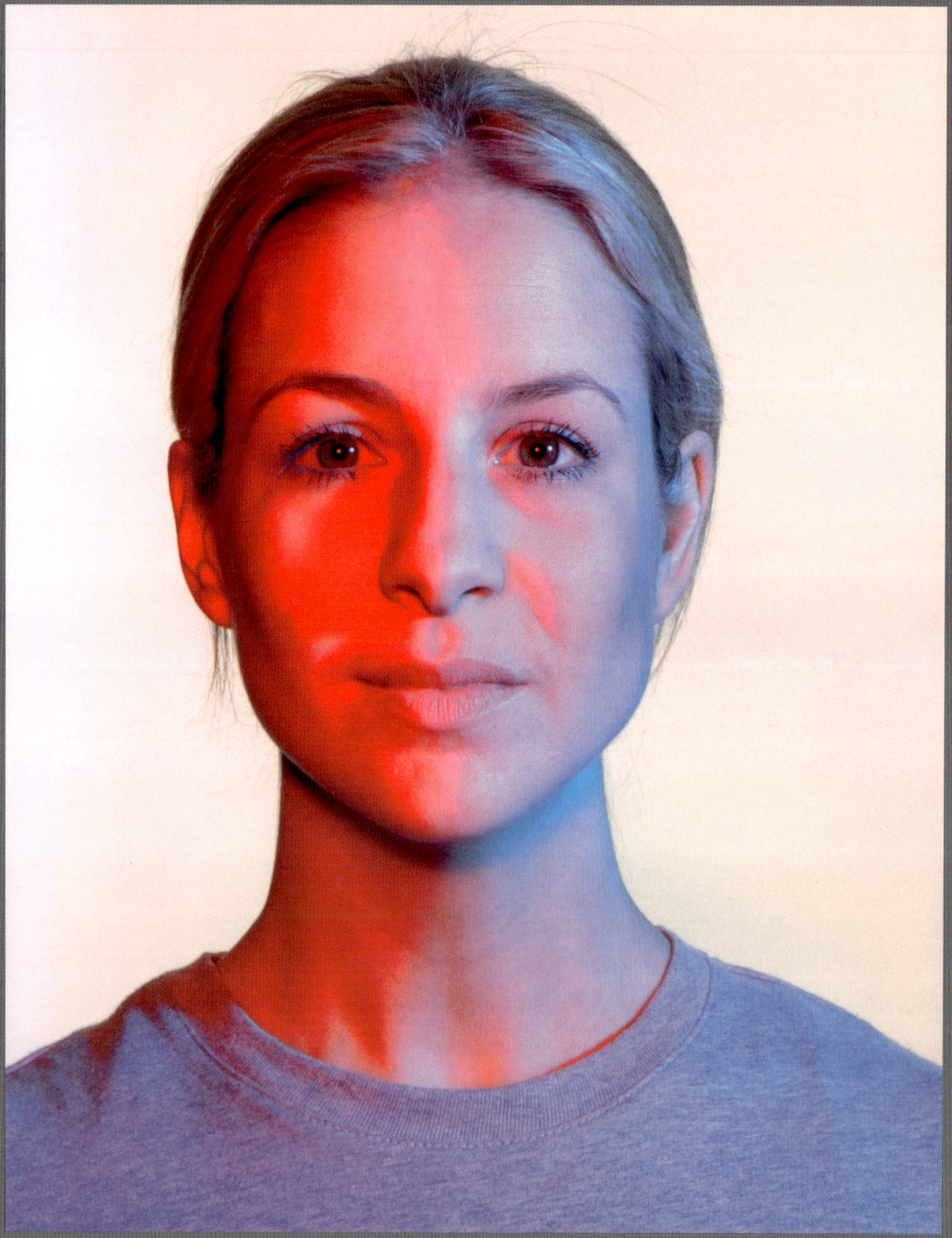

As the blue light is moved further to the left of the subject (to the right of the camera), its effect on the right side of the face is noticeably reduced—the strong red coloring on the right of the model's face reveals the areas that are lit only by the light from the front.

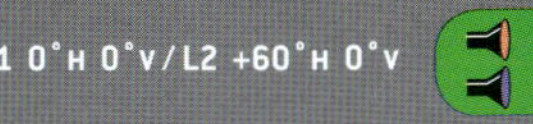

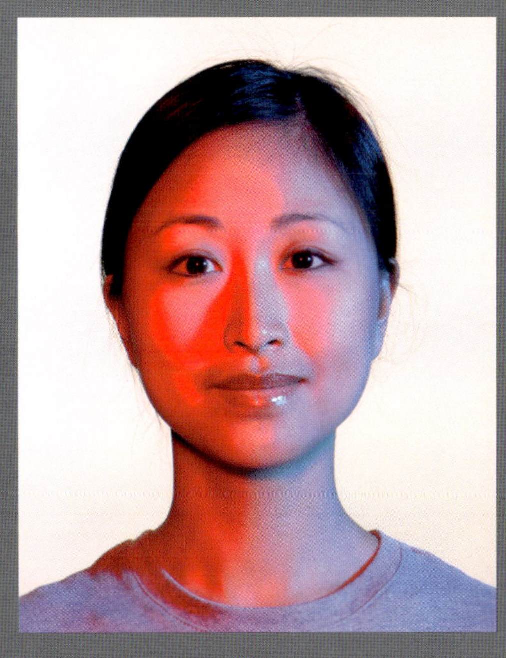

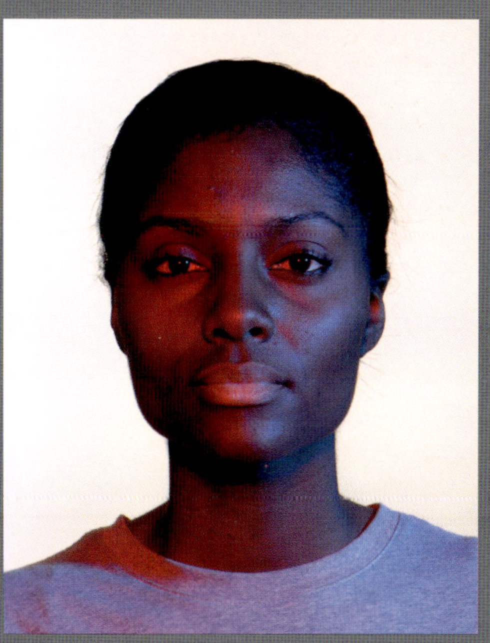

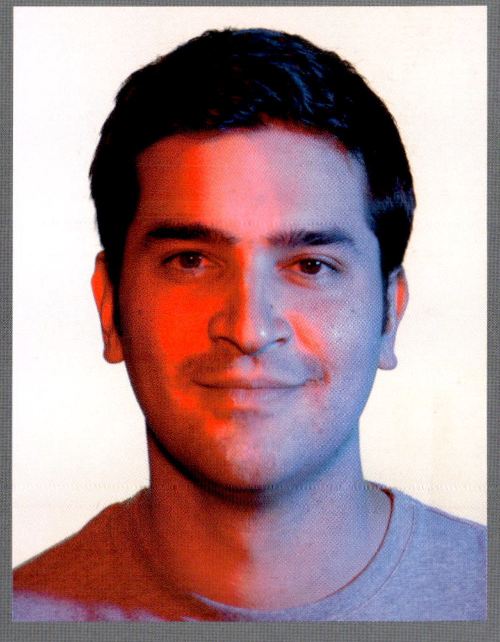

DARK BACKGROUND

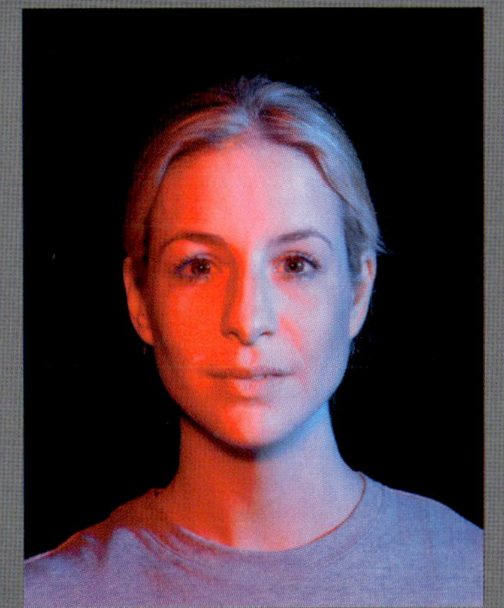

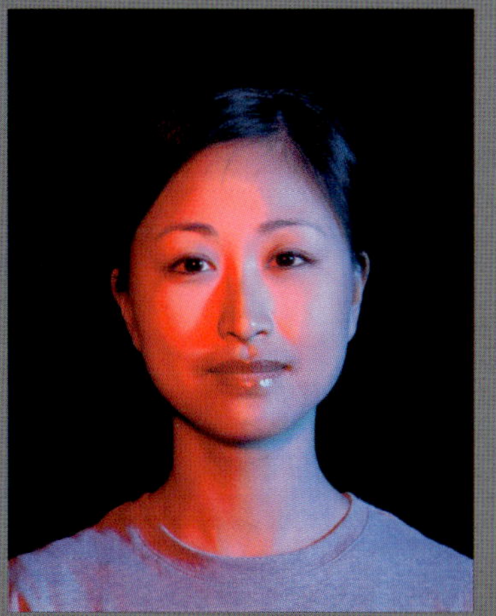

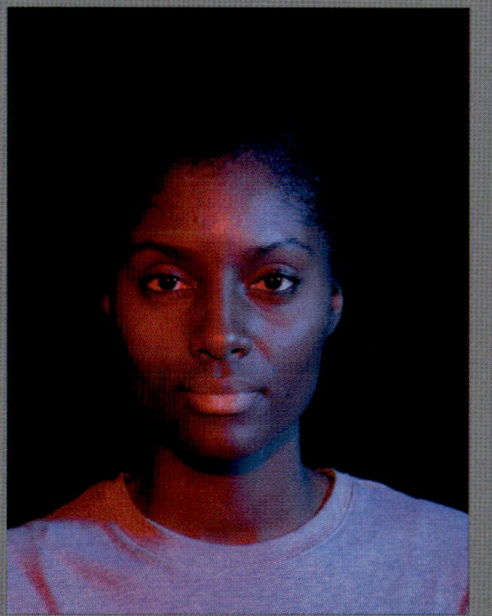

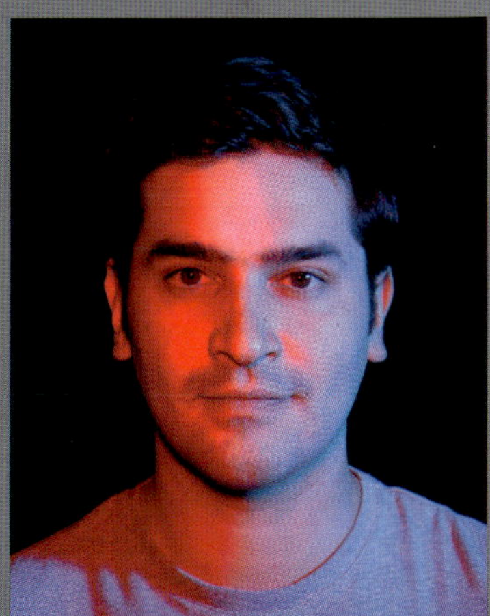

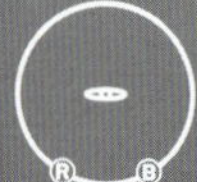

TWO COLORED LIGHTS

LIGHT 1 (RED): FROM 30° LEFT

LIGHT 2 (BLUE): FROM 30° RIGHT

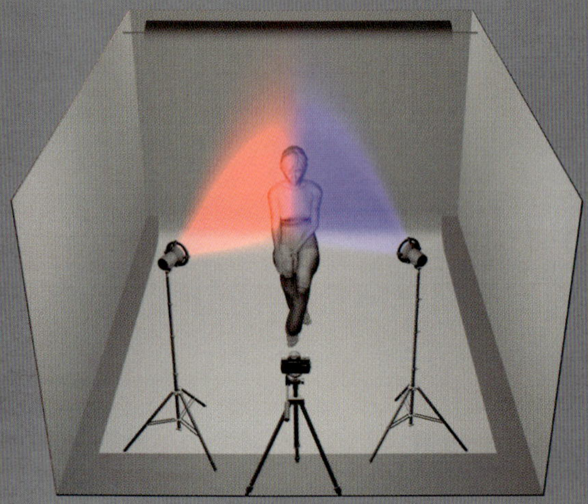

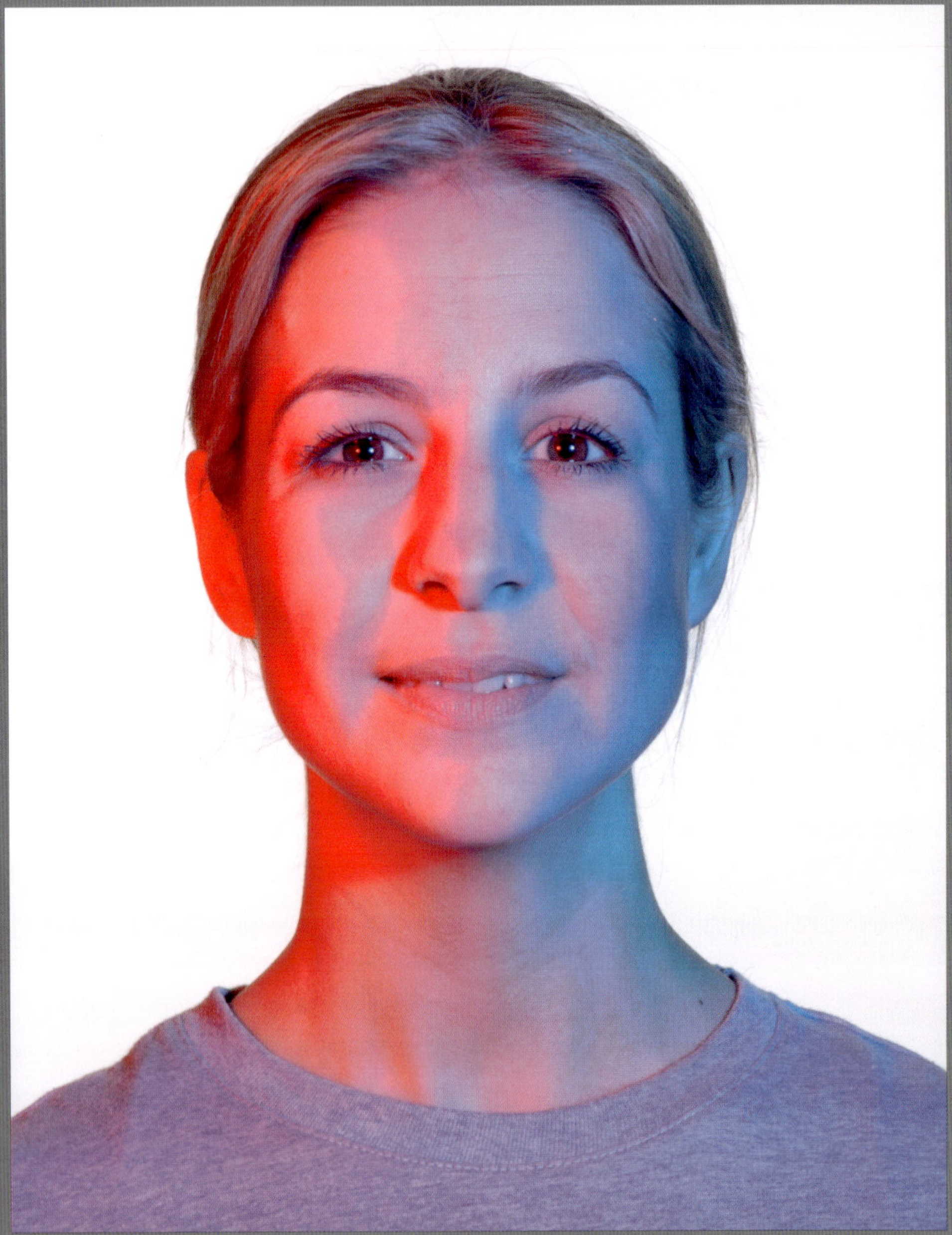

With both the red- and the blue-gelled lights aimed at the subject from the same angle, it's clear to see that the effect of one on the model is mirrored by the other: the red light is primarily illuminating the right side of the face, while the blue light illuminates the left side.

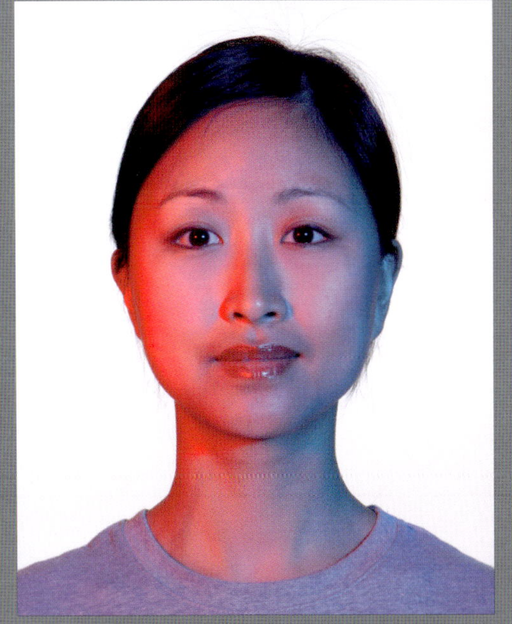

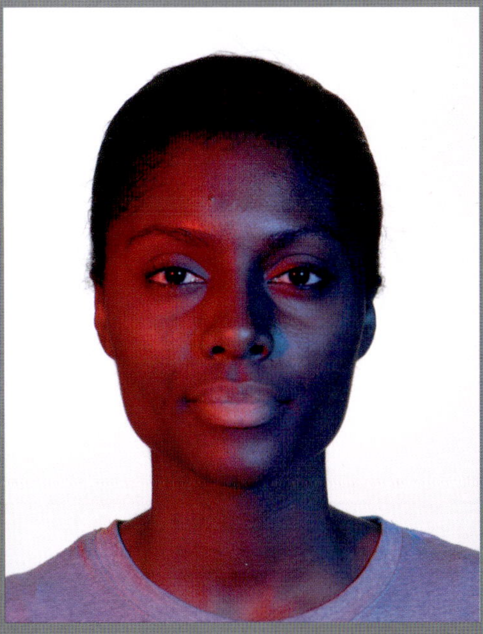

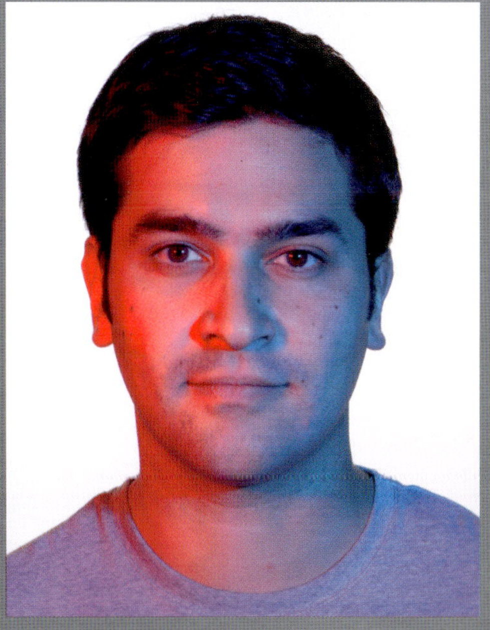

DARK BACKGROUND

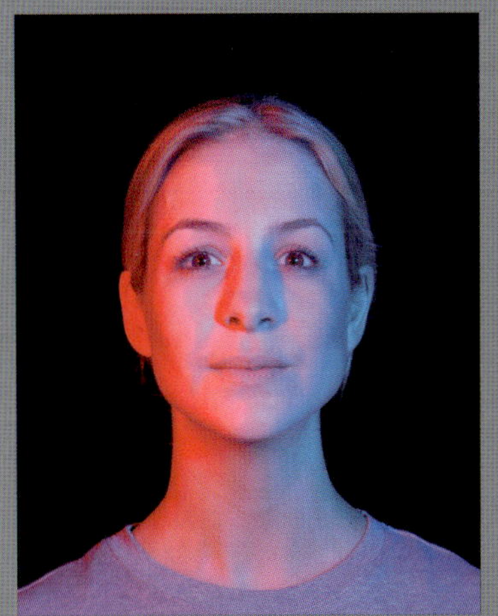

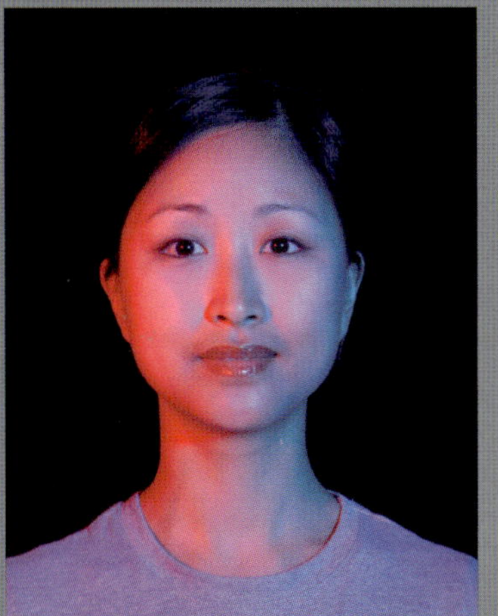

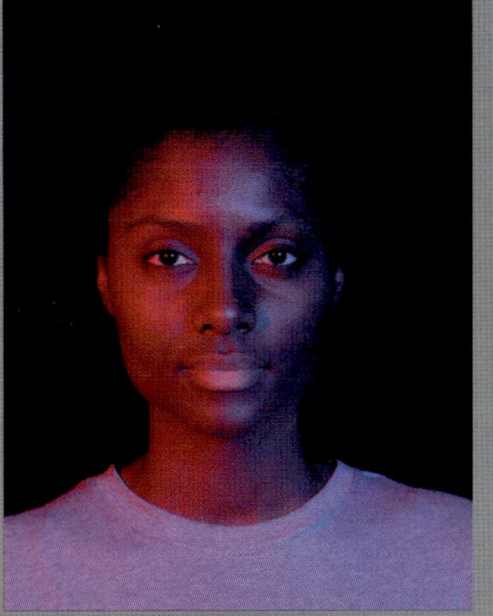

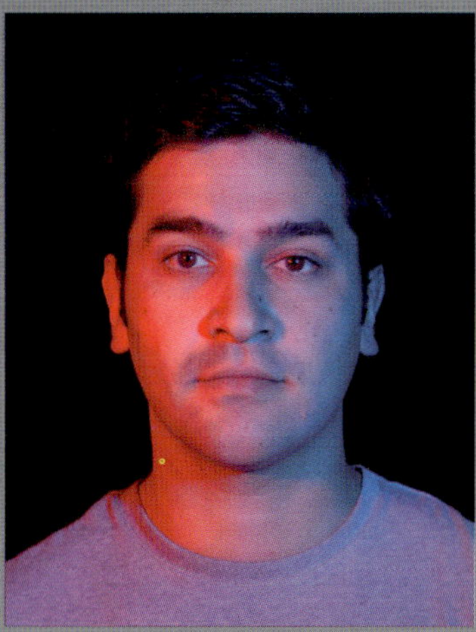

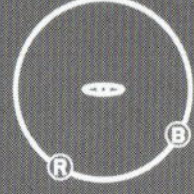

TWO COLORED LIGHTS

LIGHT 1 (RED): FROM 30° LEFT

LIGHT 2 (BLUE): FROM 60° RIGHT

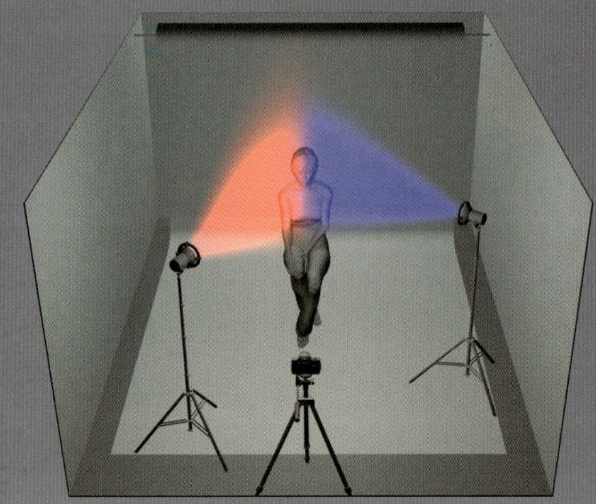

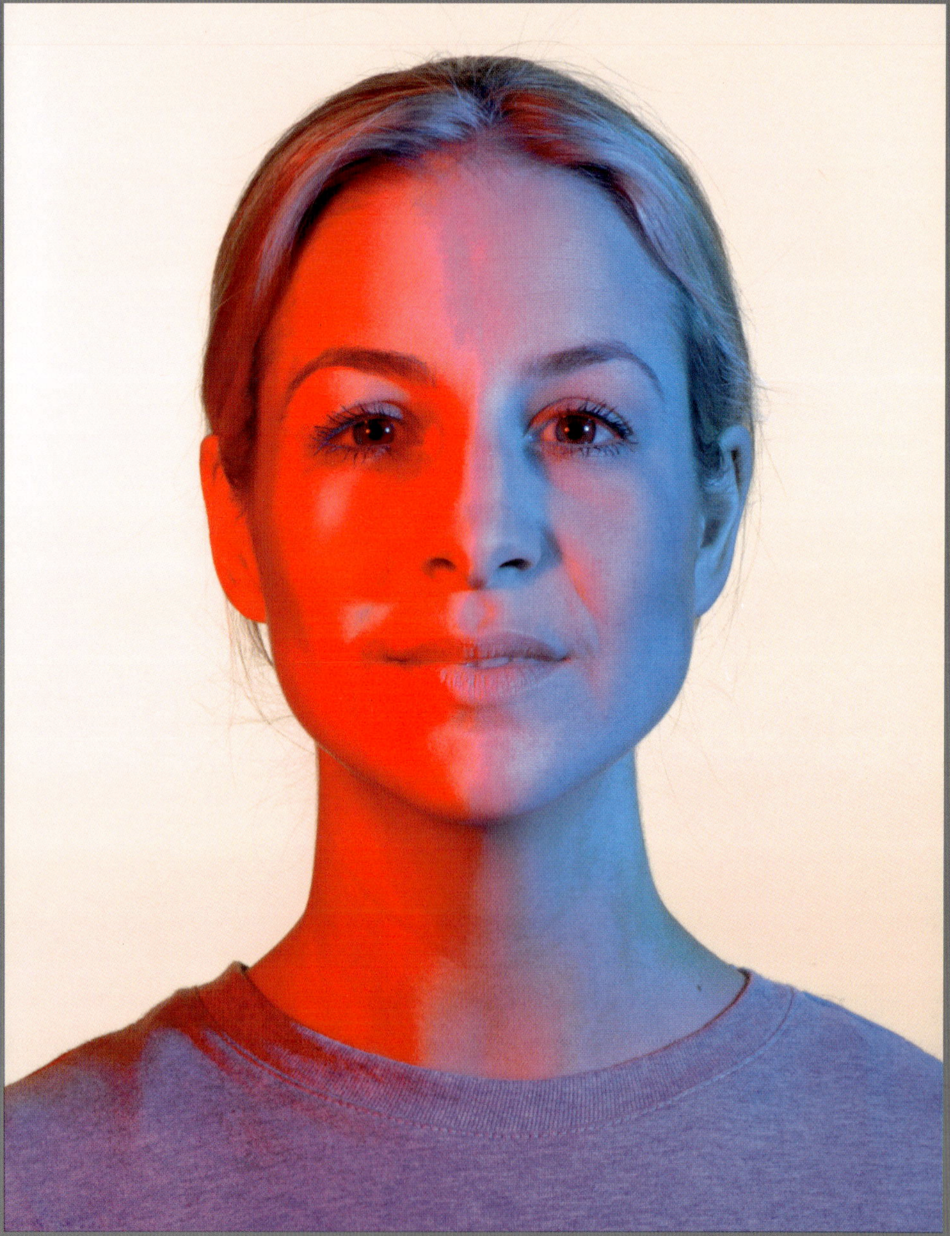

With the red light at a more acute angle than the blue-gelled lamp, it is the red light that is having the greatest effect in this setup, lighting almost the entire right side of the face. The area where the lights mix is limited to a band down the left side, across the eye, cheek, and chin.

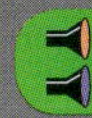

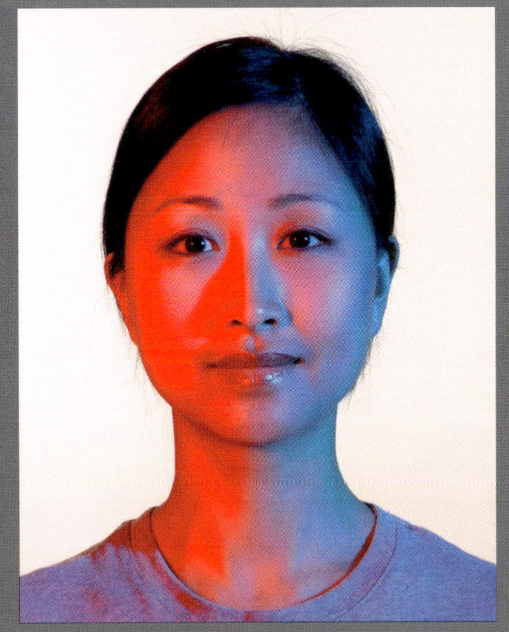

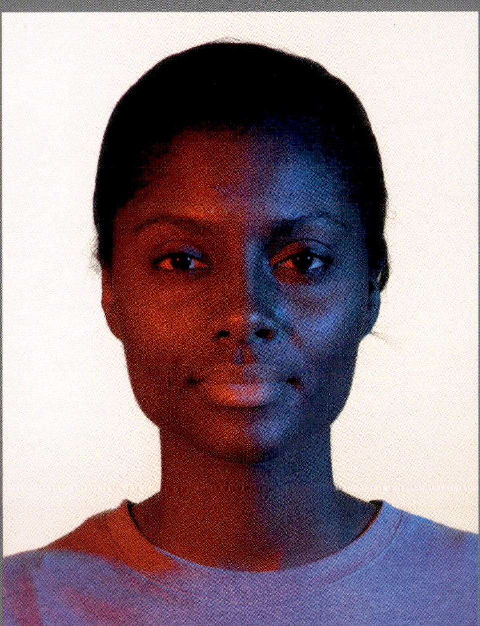

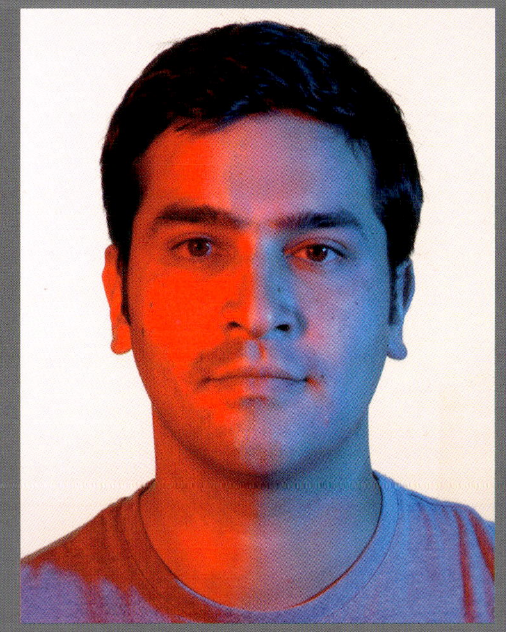

DARK BACKGROUND

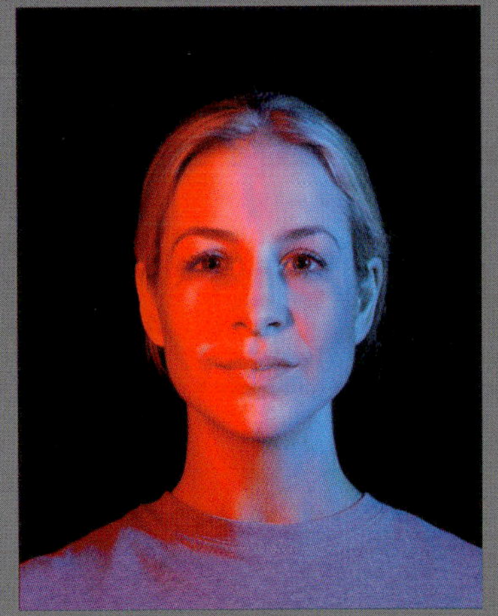

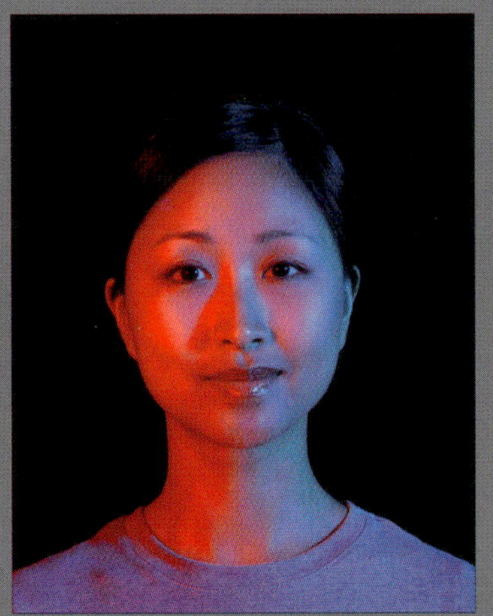

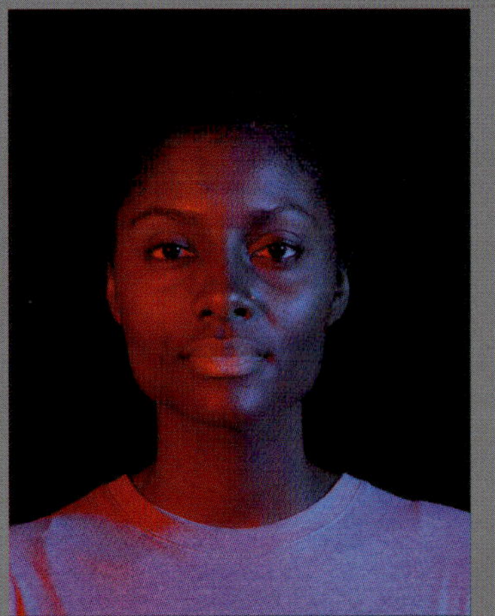

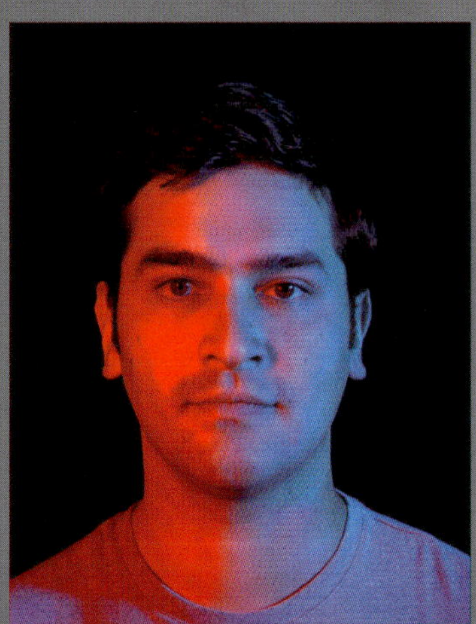

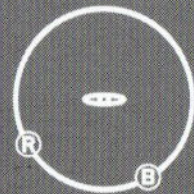

TWO COLORED LIGHTS

LIGHT 1 (RED): FROM 60° LEFT

LIGHT 2 (BLUE): FROM 30° RIGHT

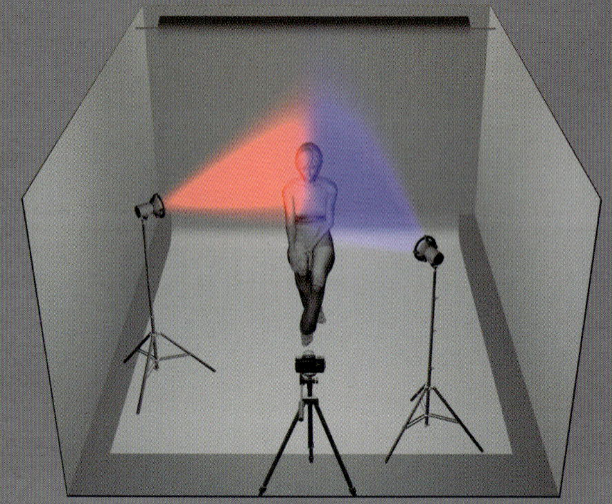

Positioning the blue-gelled light closer to the camera, and moving the red light at a 60-degree angle to the camera reverses the previous setup. Now, it is the blue light that is illuminating the majority of the face with the red light filling in the right side.

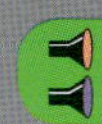

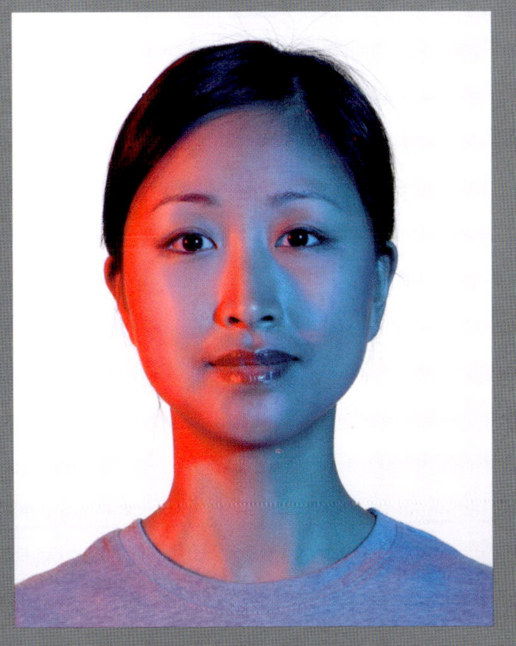

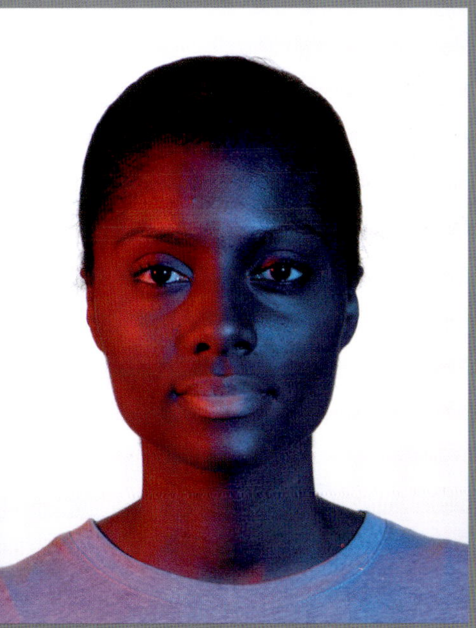

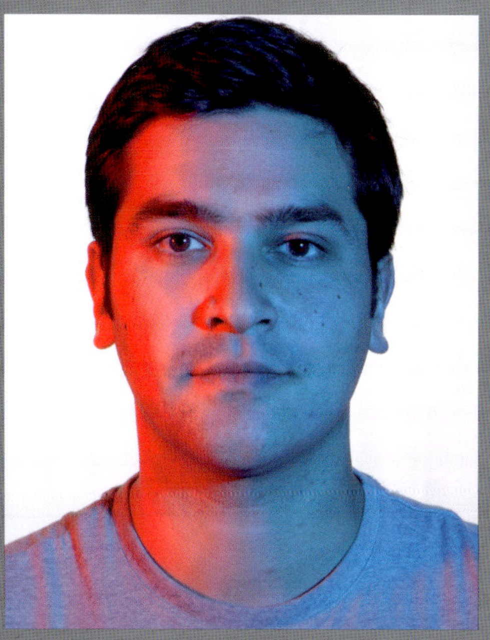

DARK BACKGROUND

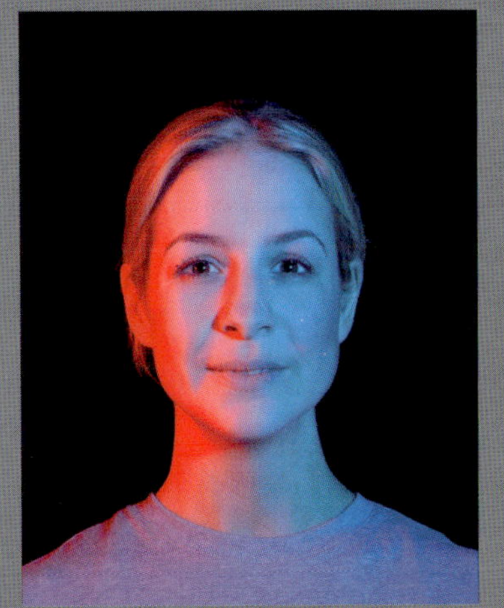

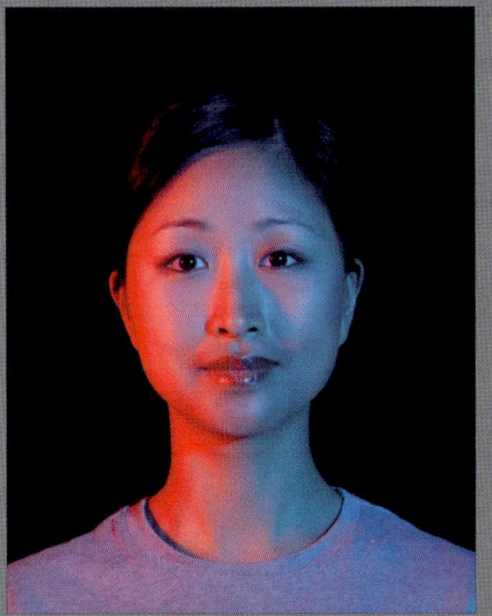

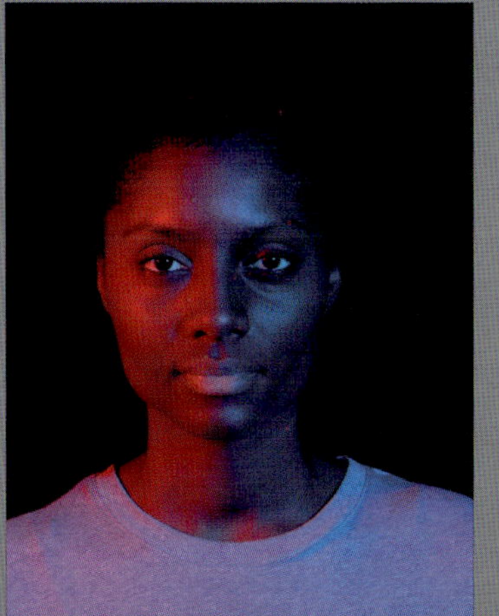

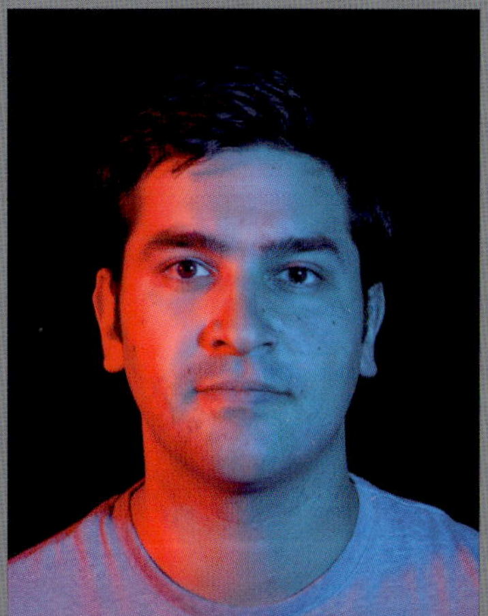

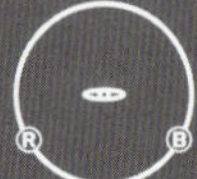

TWO COLORED LIGHTS

LIGHT 1 (RED): FROM 60° LEFT

LIGHT 2 (BLUE): FROM 60° RIGHT

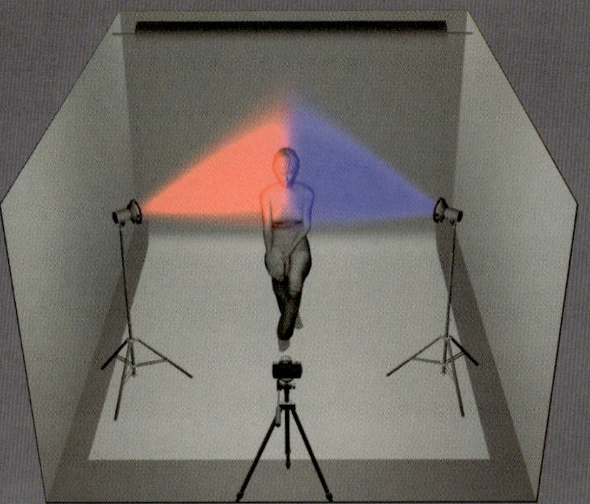

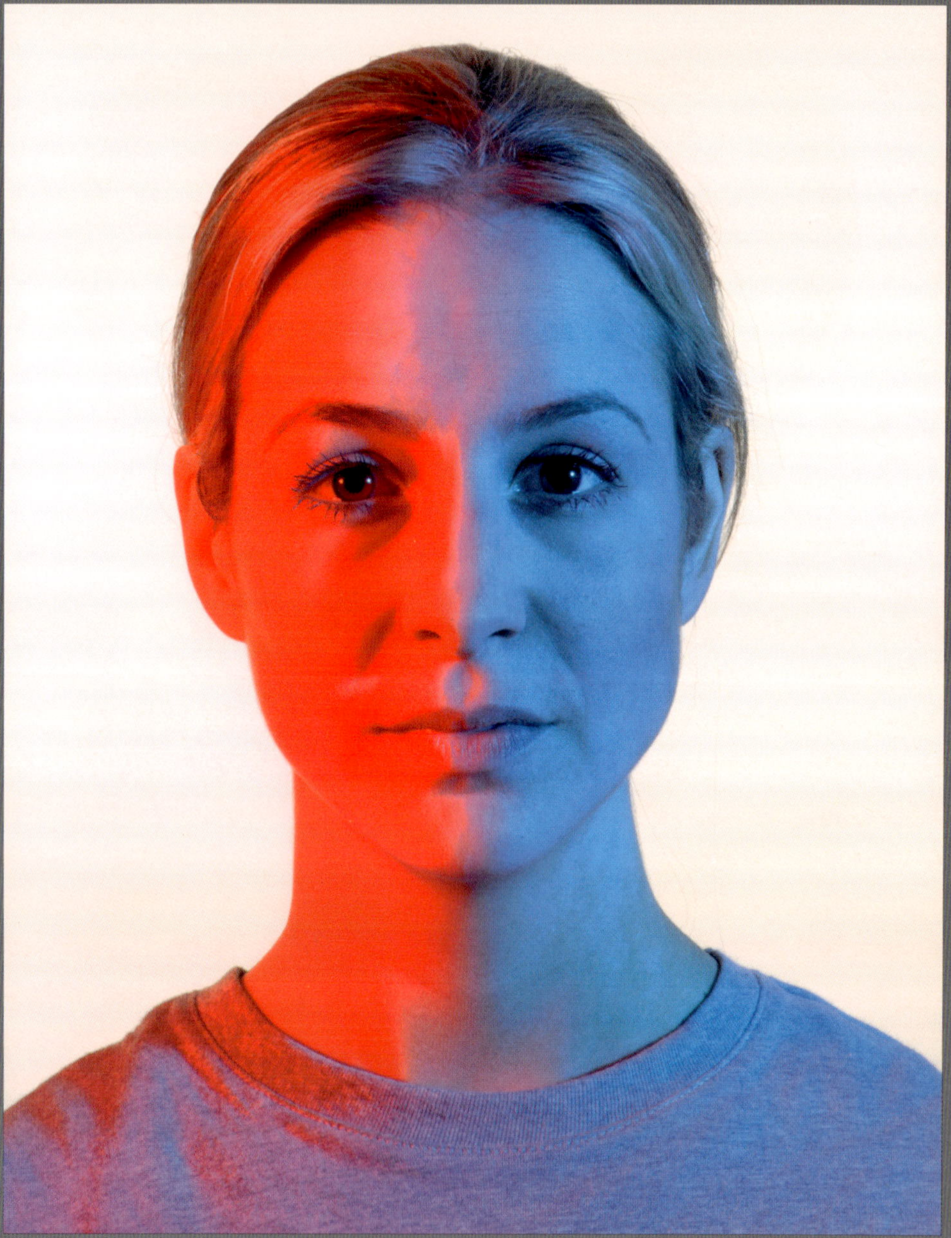

As with the setup shown on pages 198–199, both lights are set at the same angle to the subject, on opposing sides of the camera. However, unlike that setup, where the lights were at a 30-degree angle, moving them so they are at 60 degrees to the camera reduces the area where they overlap to a thin sliver strip down the center of the face.

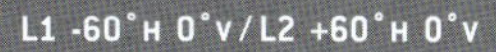

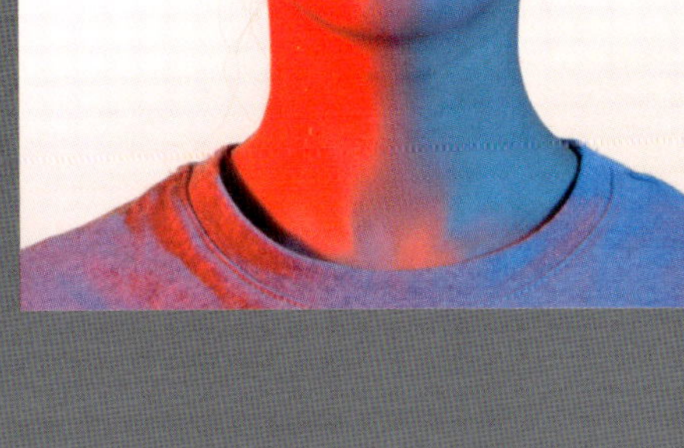

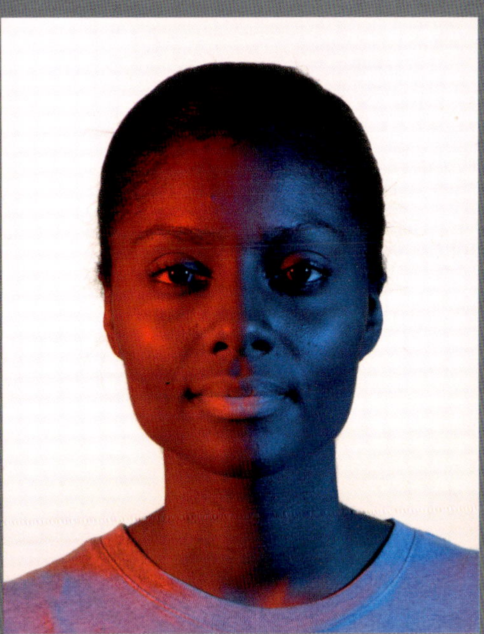

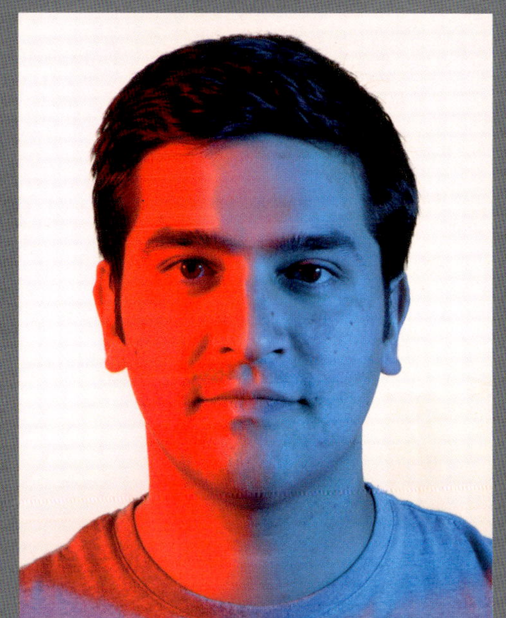

DARK BACKGROUND

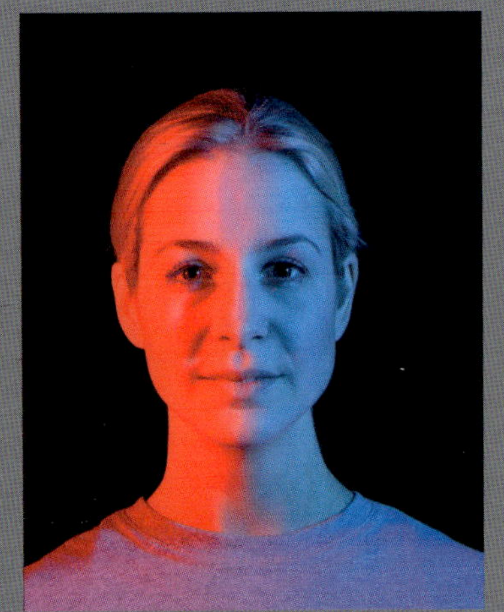

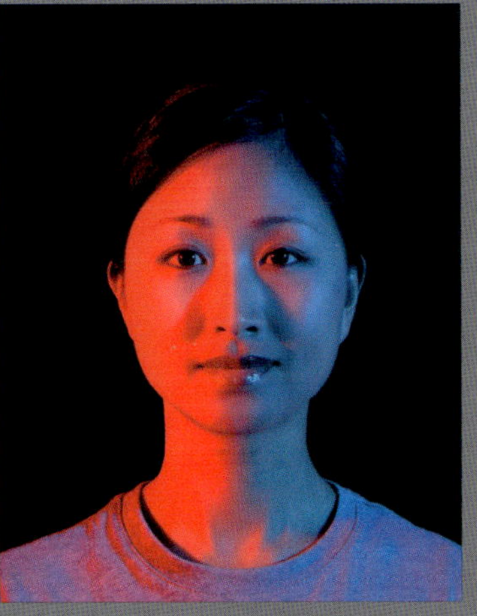

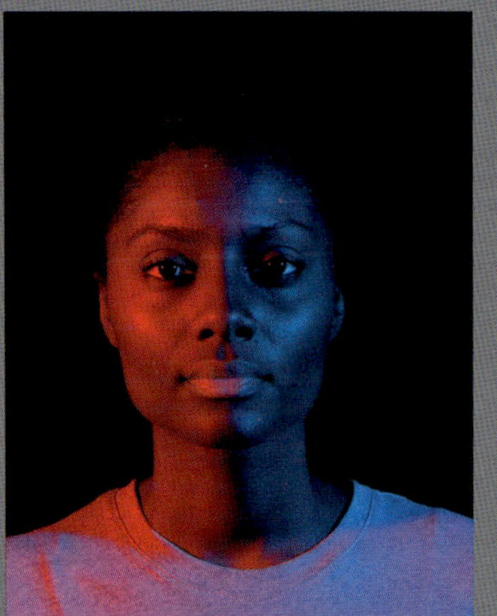

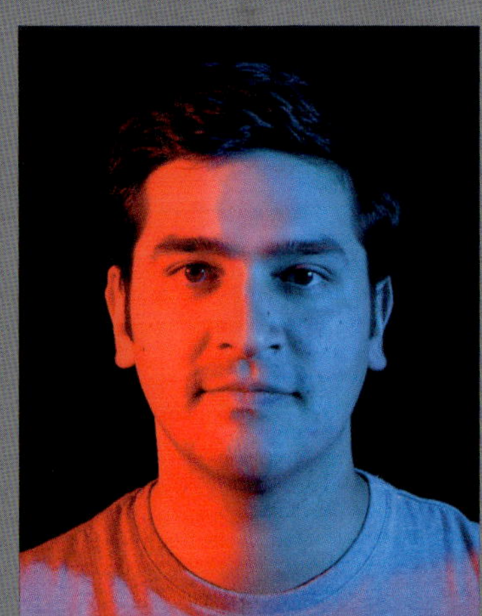

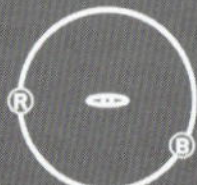

TWO COLORED LIGHTS

LIGHT 1 (RED): FROM 90° LEFT

LIGHT 2 (BLUE): FROM 30° RIGHT

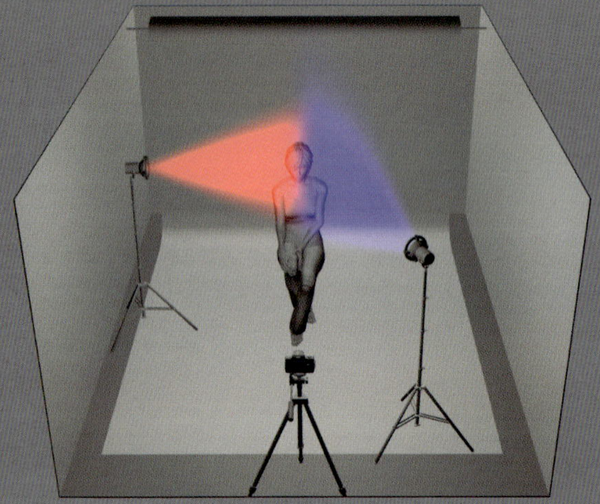

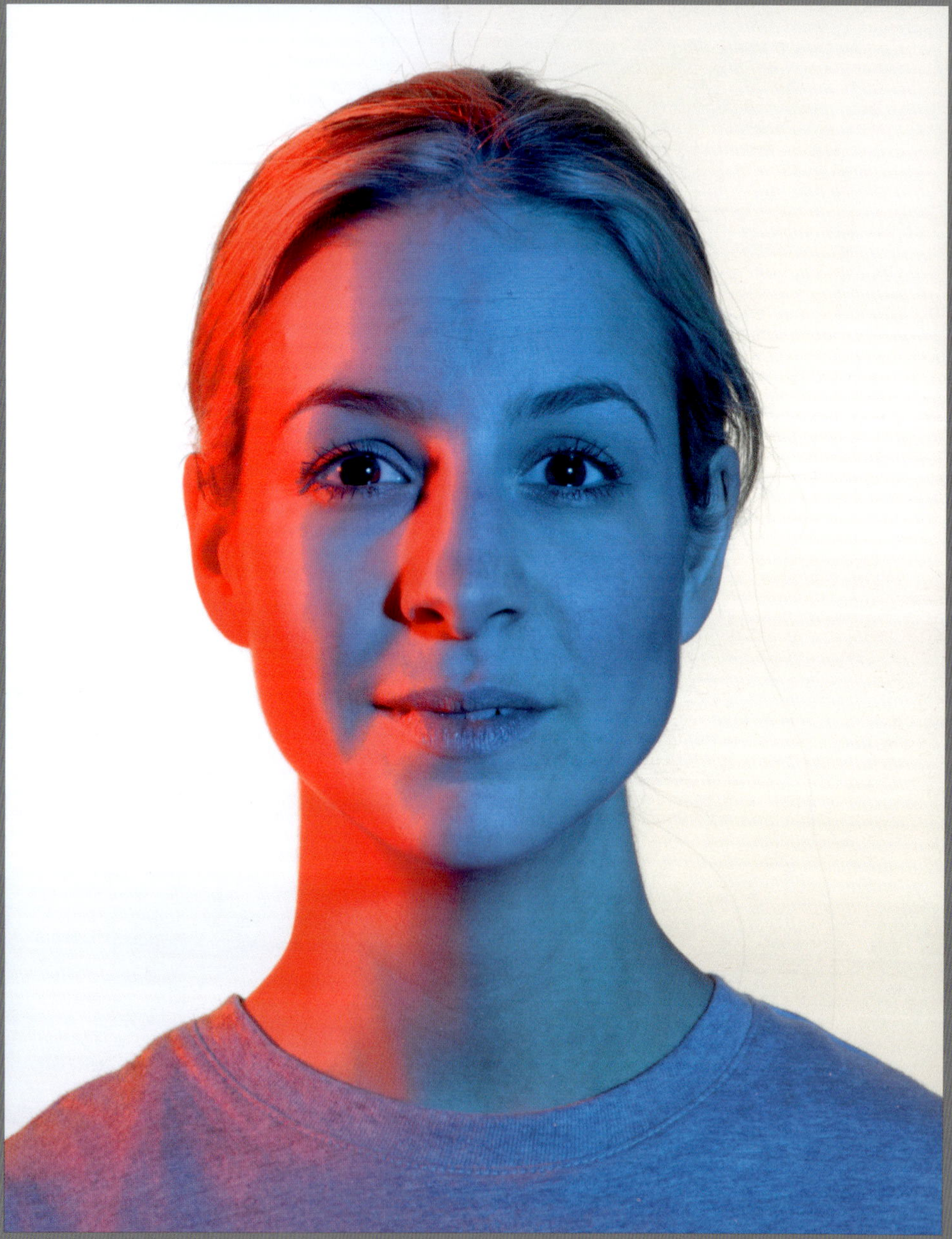

When the red-gelled light is set at a 90-degree angle, and the blue-gelled light is much closer to the camera, the overlap between the two is almost nonexistent. Apart from a small patch on the nose and the lips, each light affects a specific area of the subject.

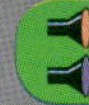

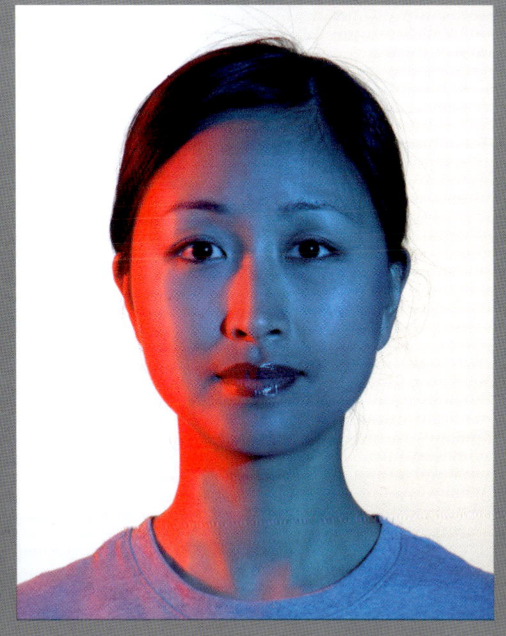

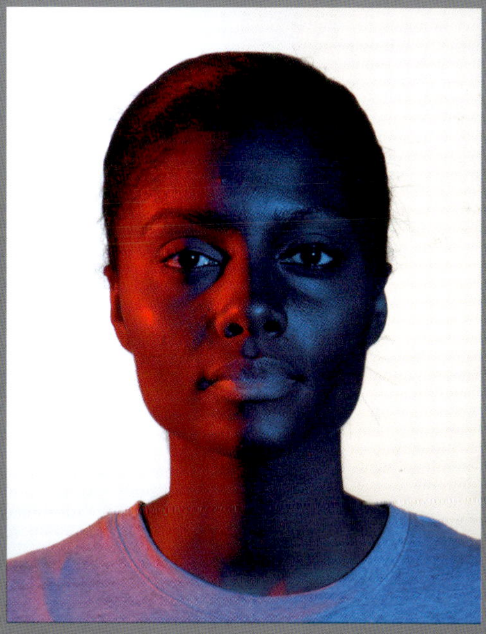

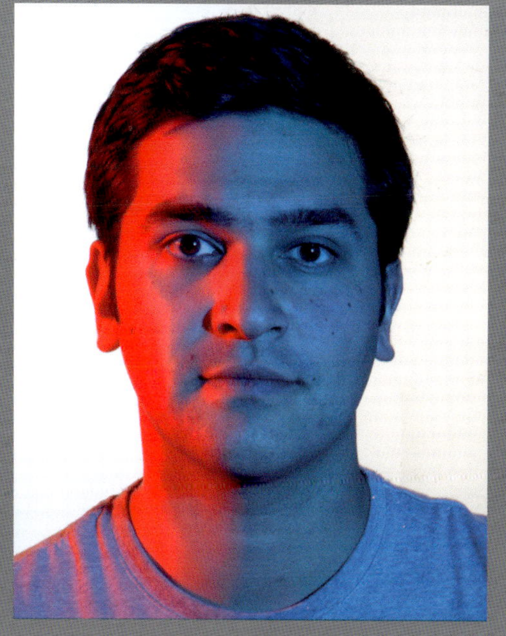

DARK BACKGROUND

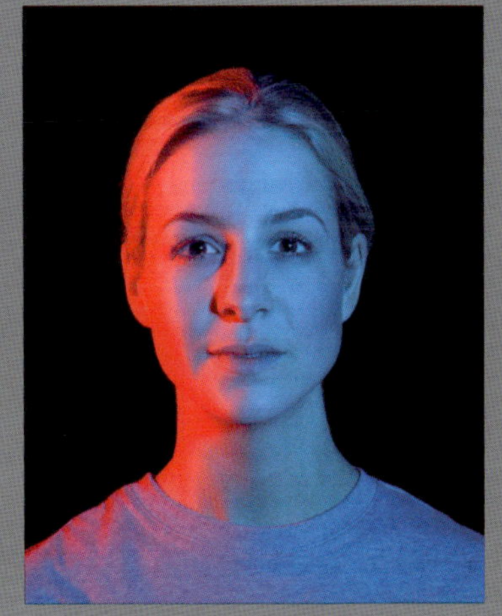

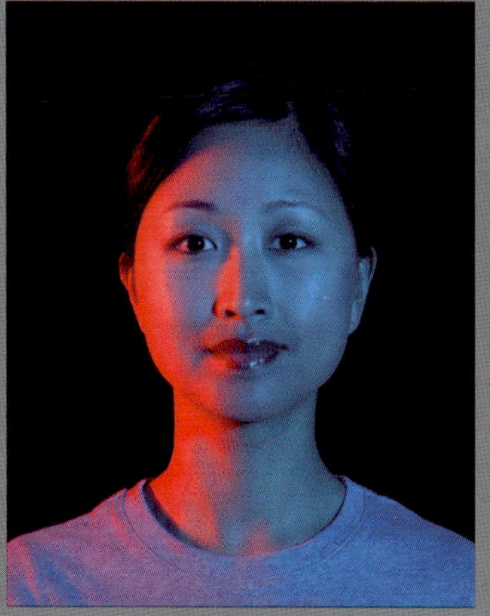

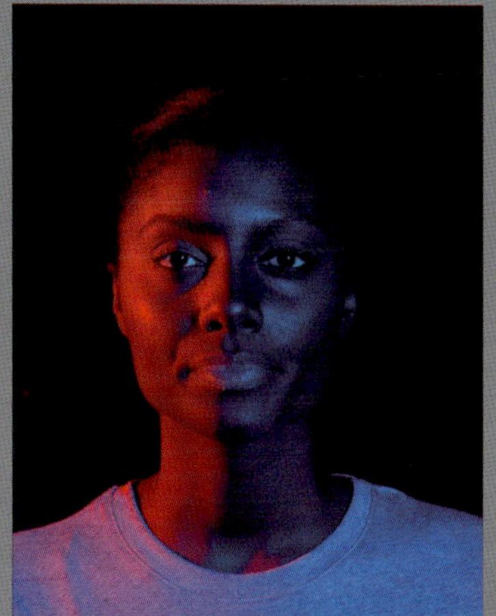

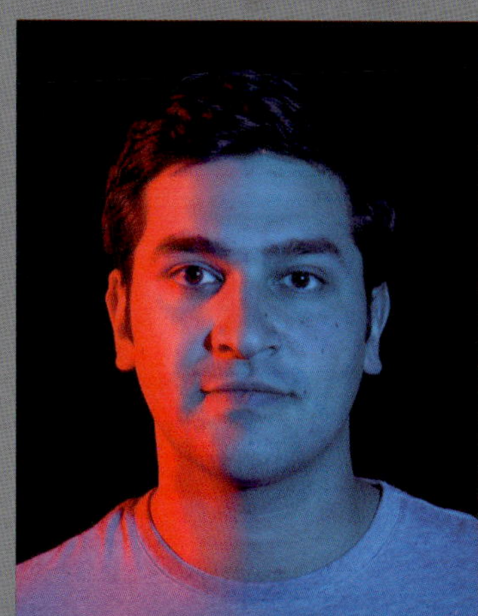

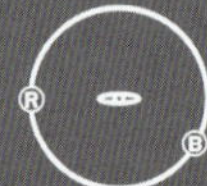

TWO COLORED LIGHTS

LIGHT 1 (RED): FROM 90° LEFT

LIGHT 2 (BLUE): FROM 60° RIGHT

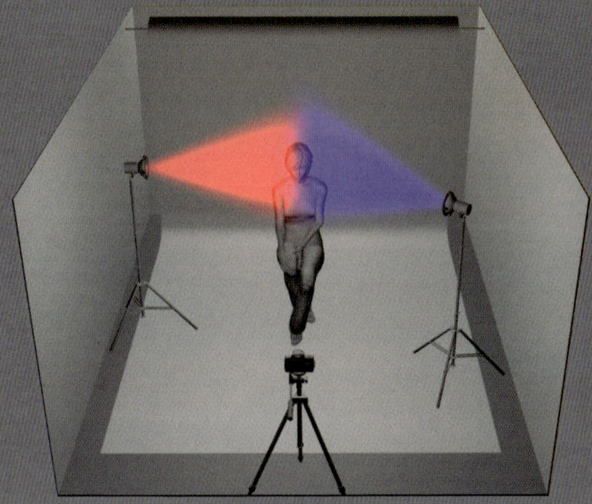

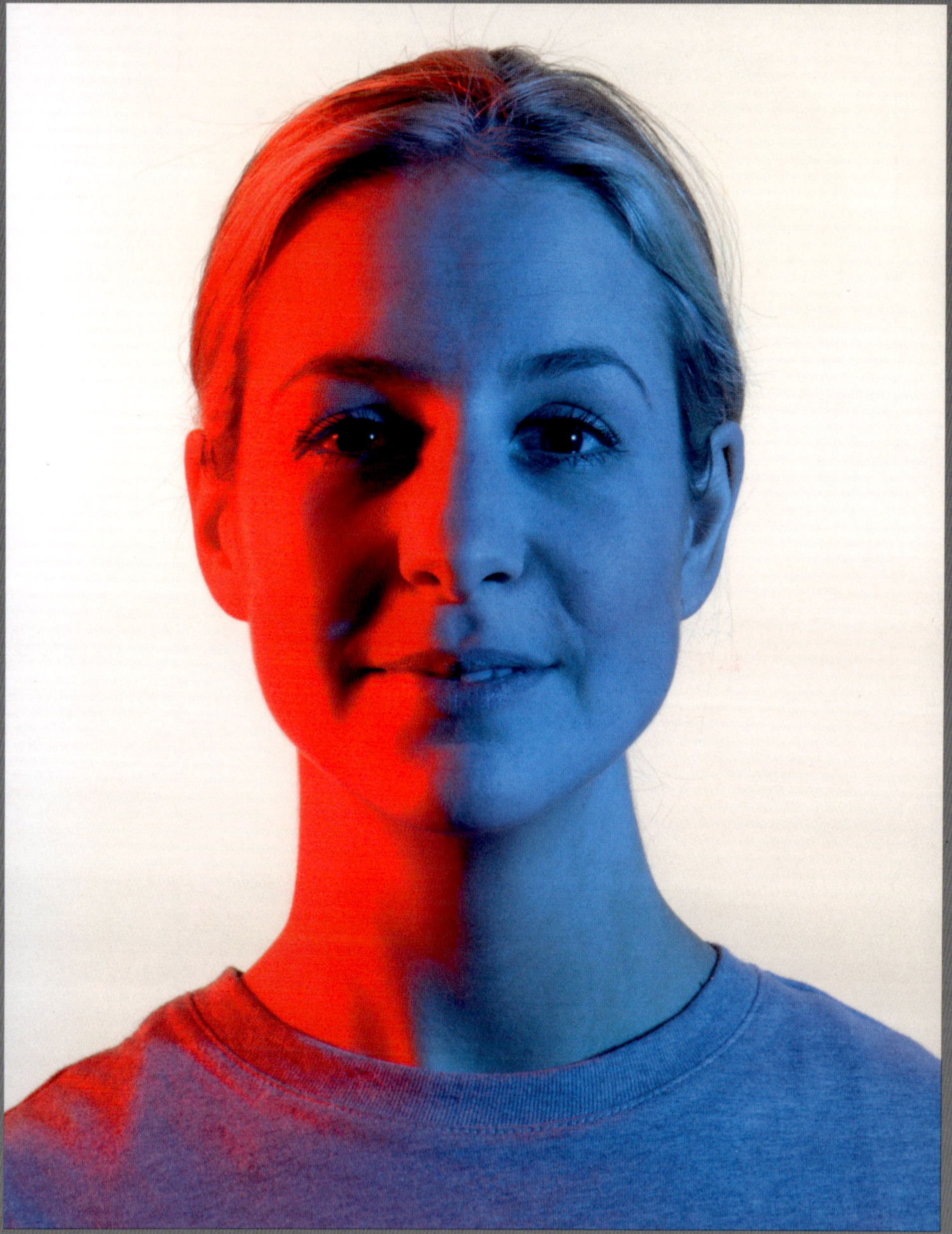

In this setup, with both lights set at a broad angle to the camera, distinct unlit patches appear—the deep black shadows where neither light is having an effect. Note, however, that the blue-gelled lamp is adding a splash of light to the model's right eyelid area.

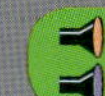

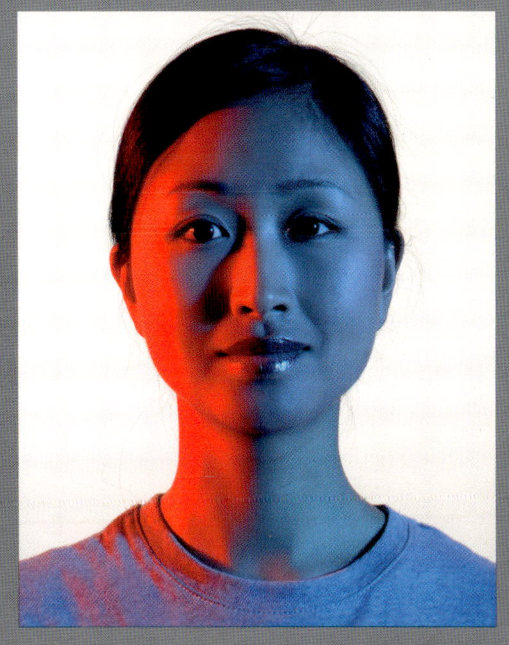

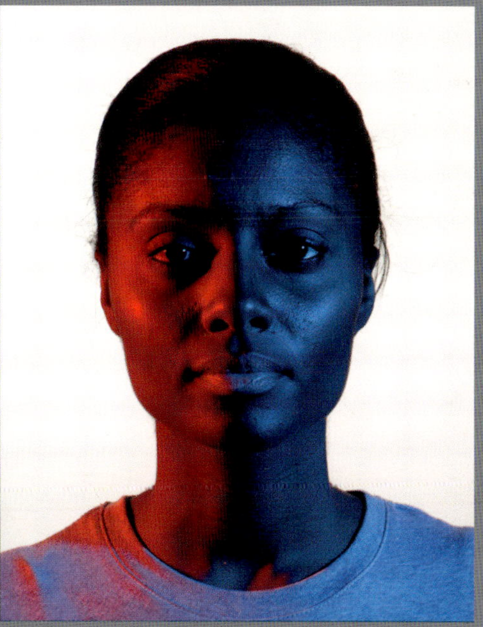

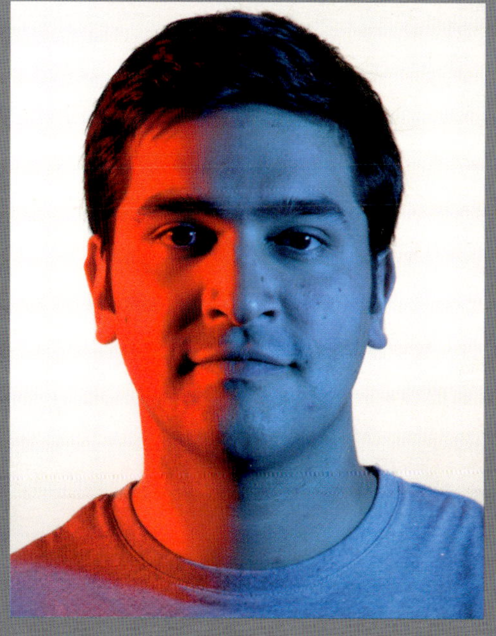

DARK BACKGROUND

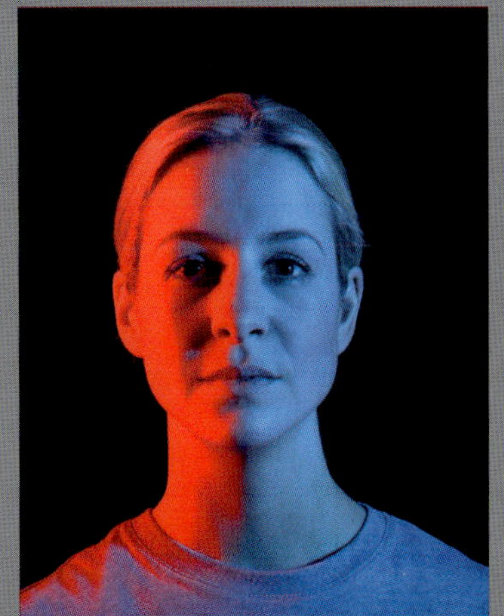

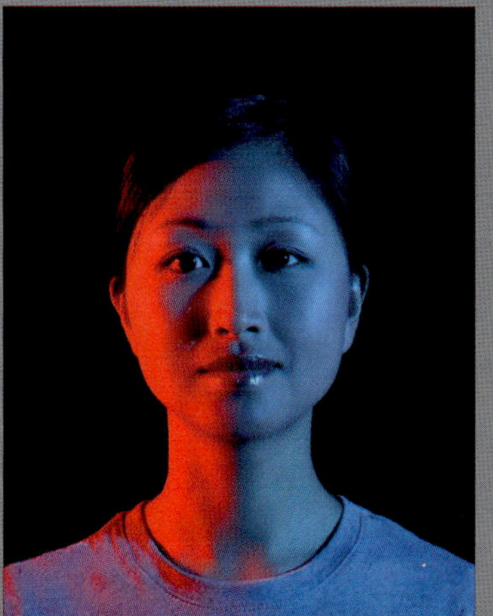

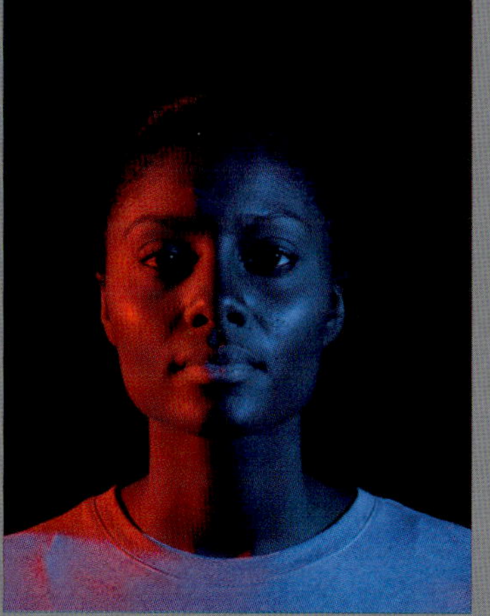

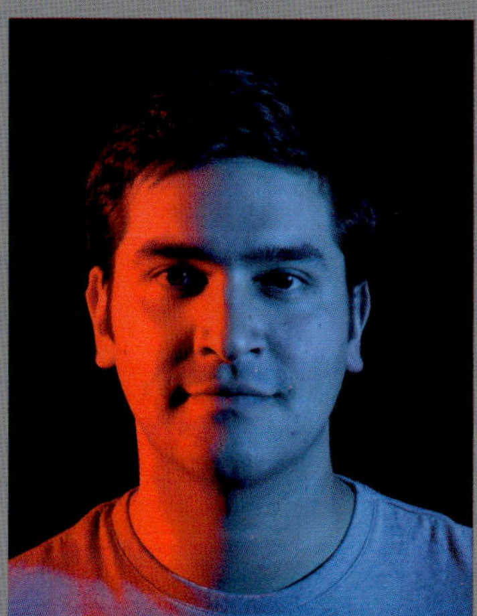

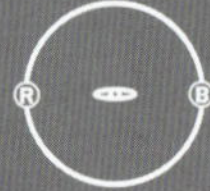

TWO COLORED LIGHTS

LIGHT 1 (RED): FROM 90° LEFT

LIGHT 2 (BLUE): FROM 90° RIGHT

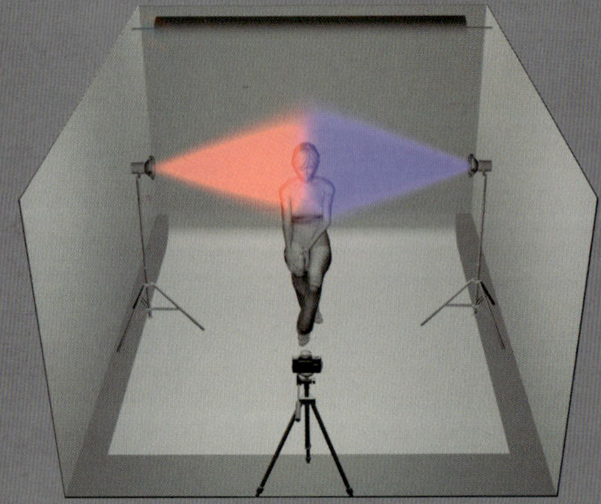

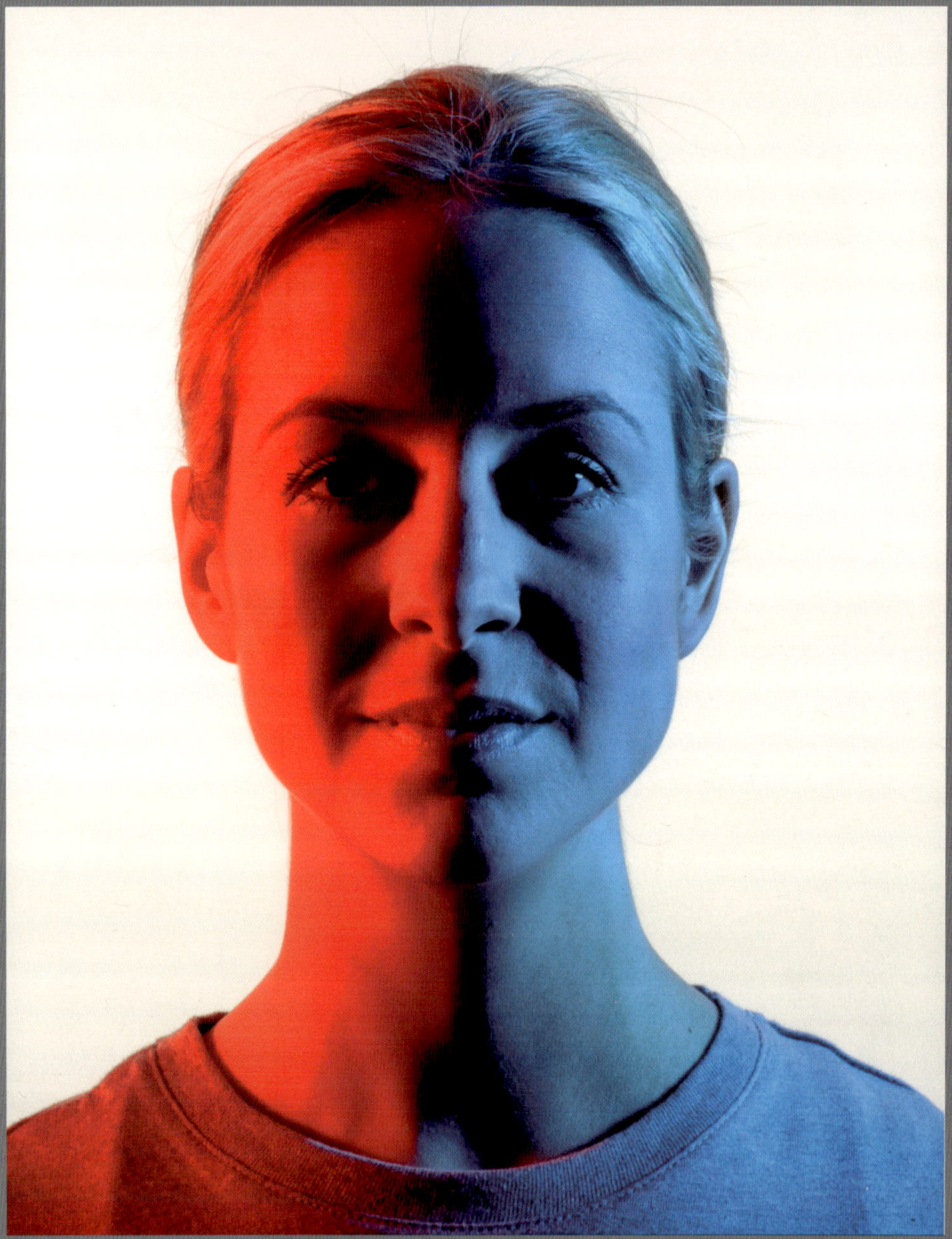

With the lamps set directly opposite each other, aiming at the subject from either side, there is no mixing of light. The dark, perfectly symmetrical shaded area down the center of the face shows where neither light is falling, and the eyes have also fallen largely into shadow.

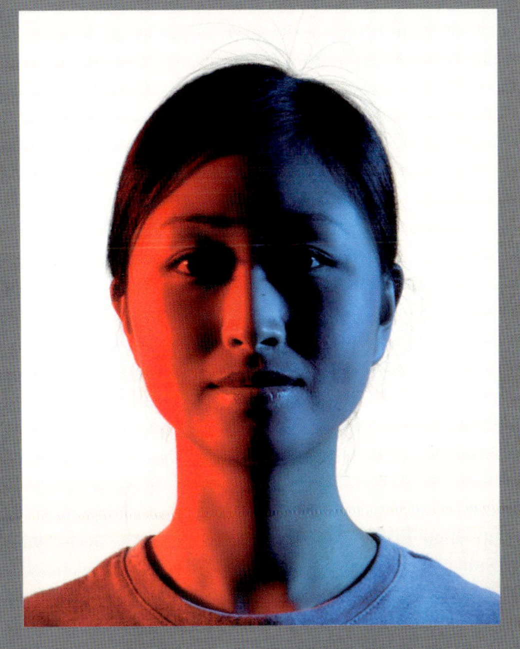

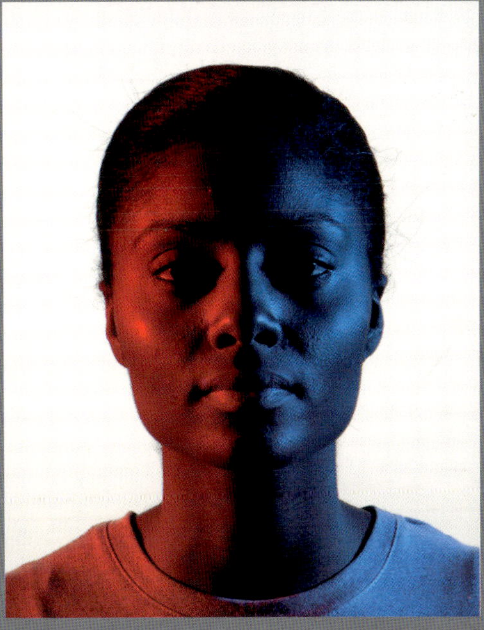

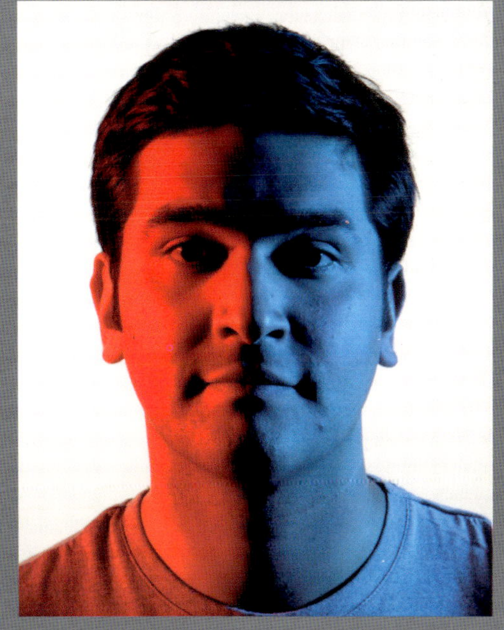

DARK BACKGROUND

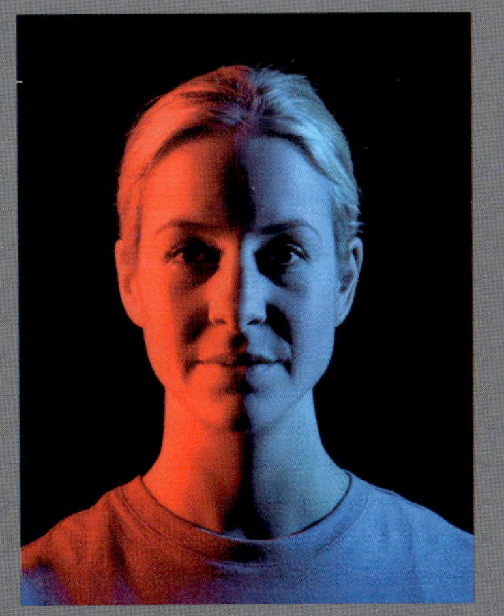

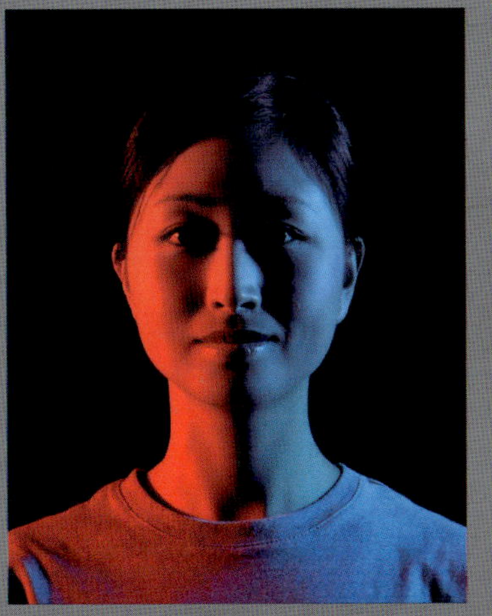

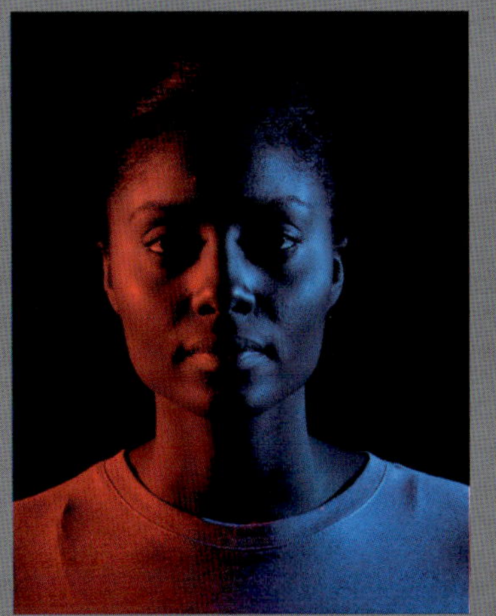

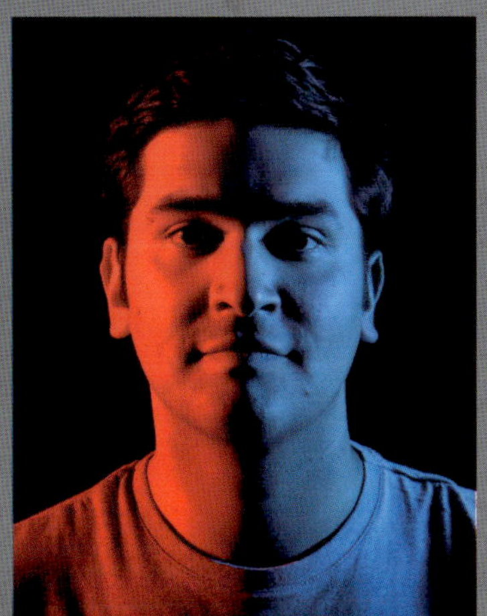

CHAPTER 10

MIXED LIGHT LEVELS

If you're using continuous light sources for your portrait photographs—tungsten lighting, or daylight-balanced fluorescent lights, for example—then controlling how much power they output will depend entirely on the specific lighting model. Some will allow you to vary the output, perhaps by illuminating fewer tubes in a fluorescent light-bank to reduce the intensity, while others might not have any control, so moving them closer to, or further from the subject will be the only way that you can control the light.

With flash lighting, however, there is often much greater control over the power output. Studio strobes may offer a range from full power down to an output of 1/32 (or lower) of their maximum strength. In a confined studio space, being able to control the flash output in this way is particularly beneficial, as it means you can get the look you want from your lights, as well as the intensity of light you need to shoot at your chosen aperture. In this section we'll look at just how simply changing the output of your lights can transform your lighting setups.

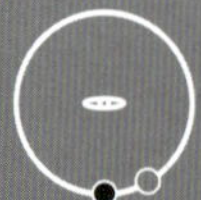

MIXED LIGHT LEVELS

LIGHT 1 (FULL): FROM 0°

LIGHT 2 (2 BELOW): FROM 30° RIGHT

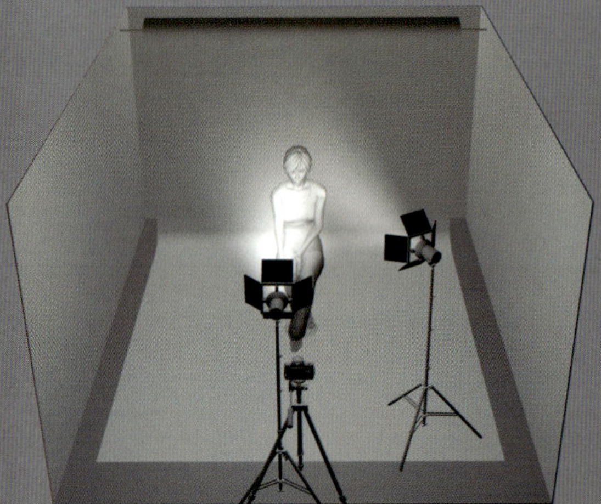

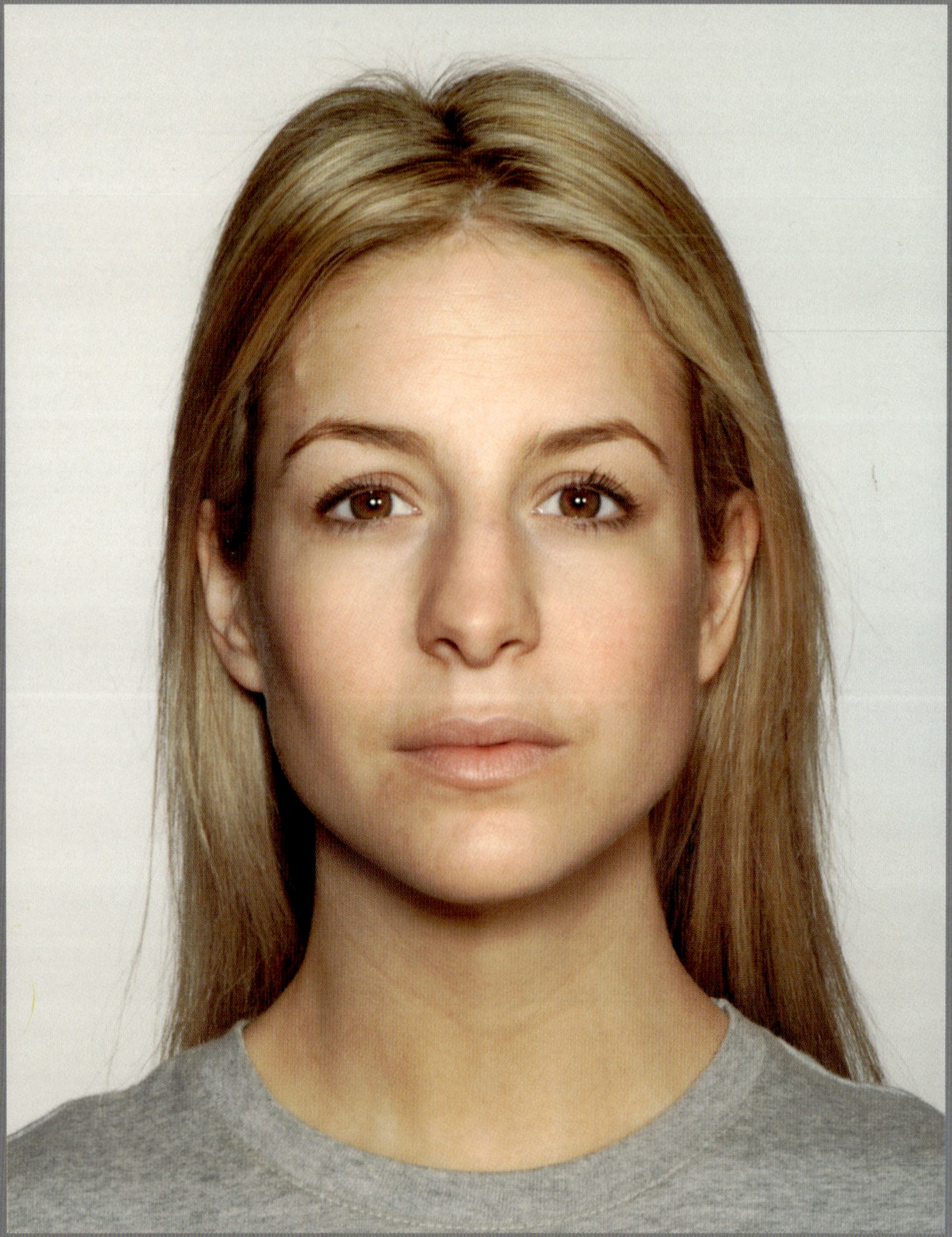

When you are using two lights at different power settings, you basically have one main light source (your "key" light) that is providing the overall illumination, and a second ("fill") light that is there to lighten shadows. As you saw earlier, a low-cost alternative to a fill light is a reflector.

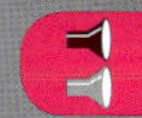

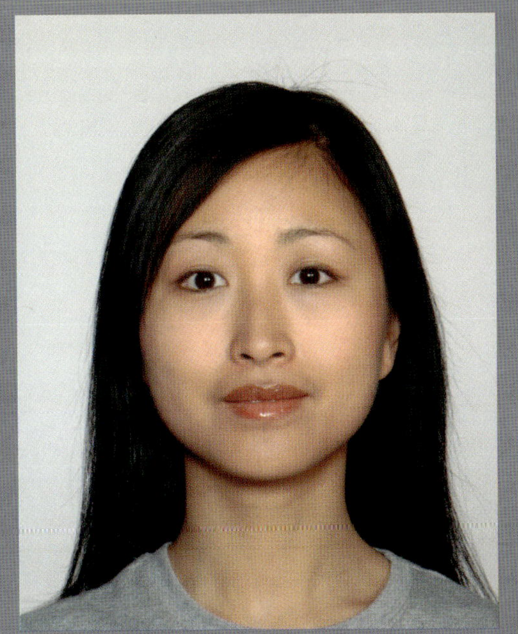

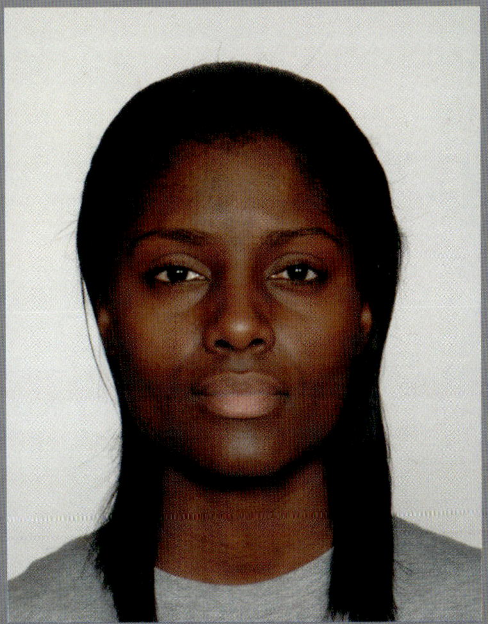

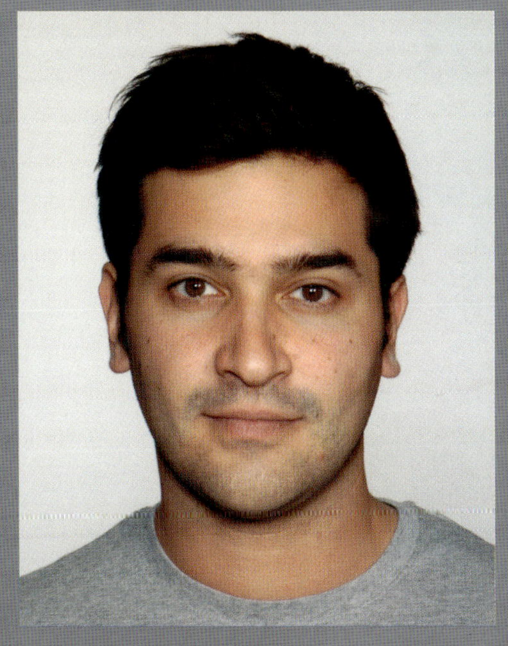

DARK BACKGROUND

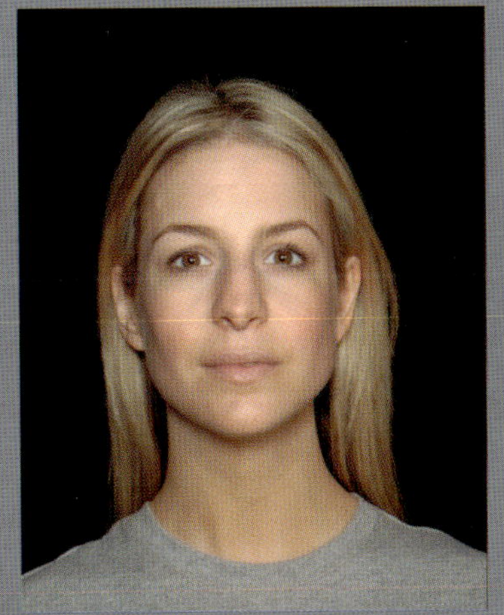

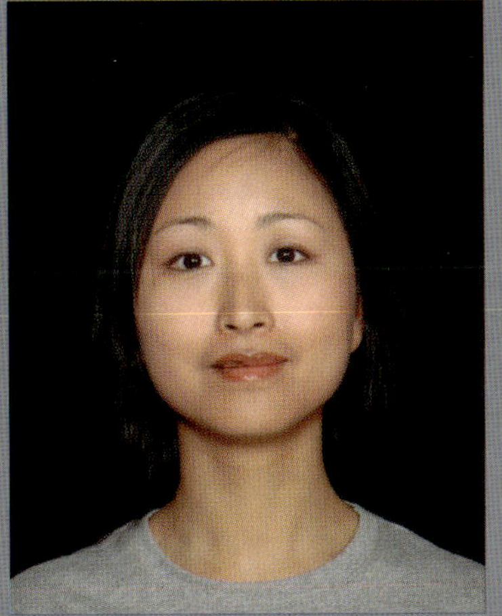

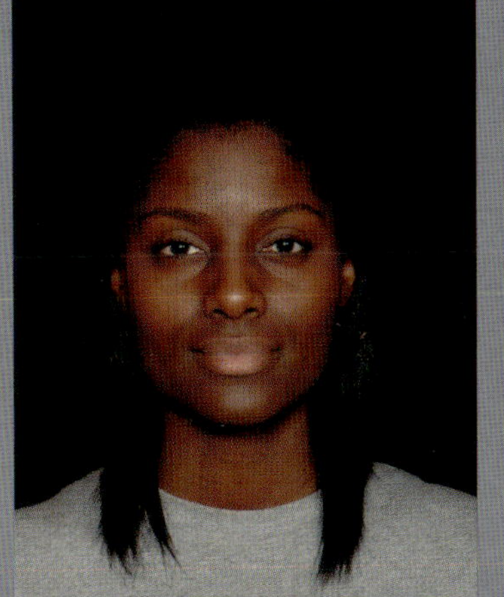

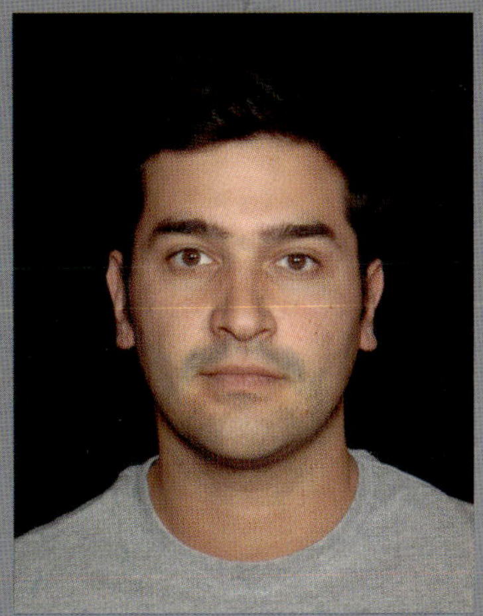

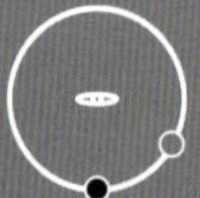

MIXED LIGHT LEVELS

LIGHT 1 (FULL): FROM 0°

LIGHT 2 (2 BELOW): FROM 60° RIGHT

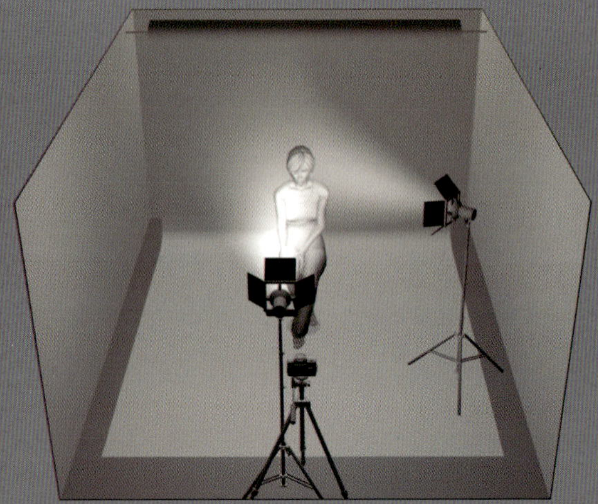

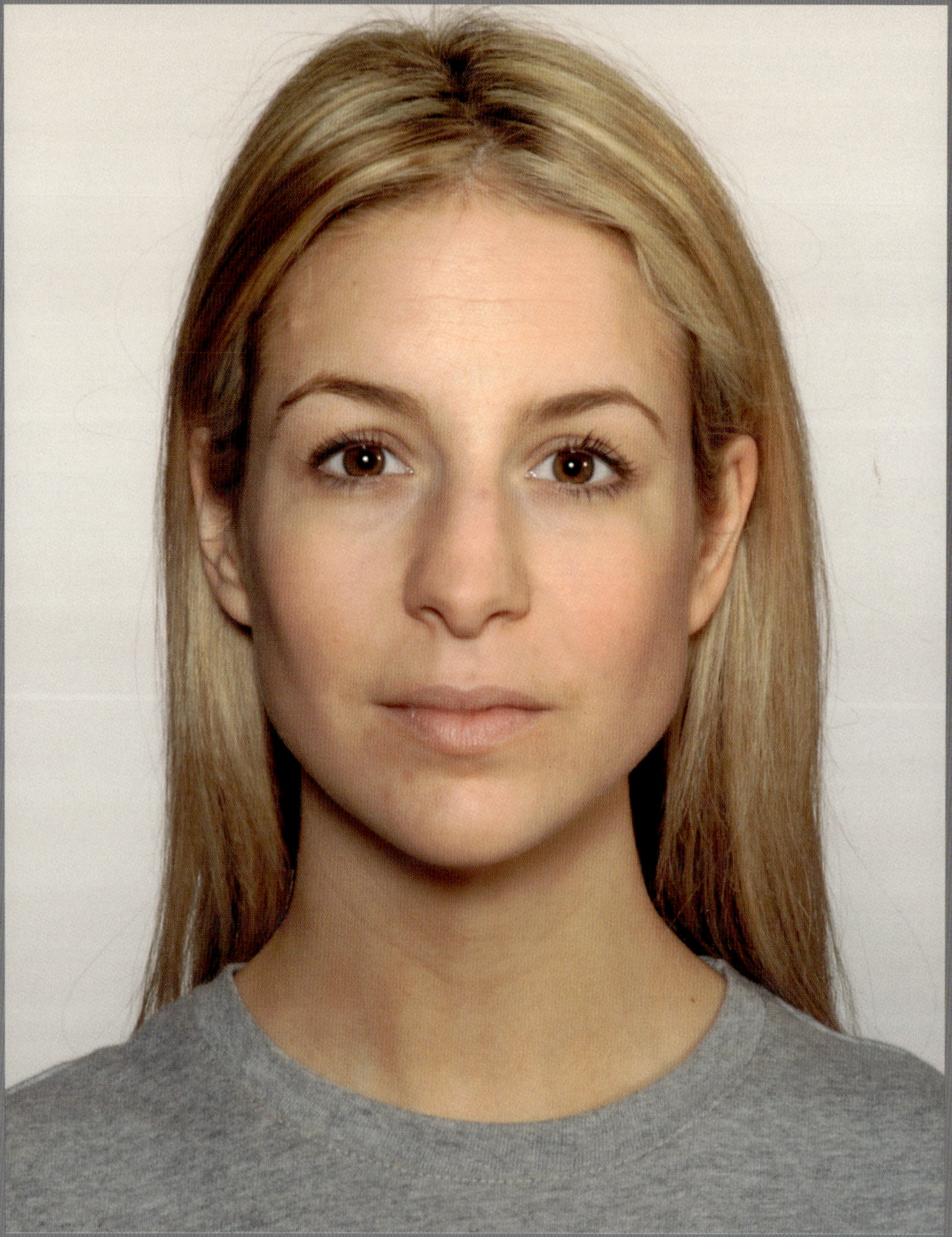

With the main light set at full power, directly in front of the subject, and the fill light at a 60-degree angle, outputting one stop less light, the left side of the model's face is subtly lighter than the right side, preventing the portrait from looking overly flat.

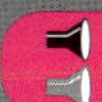

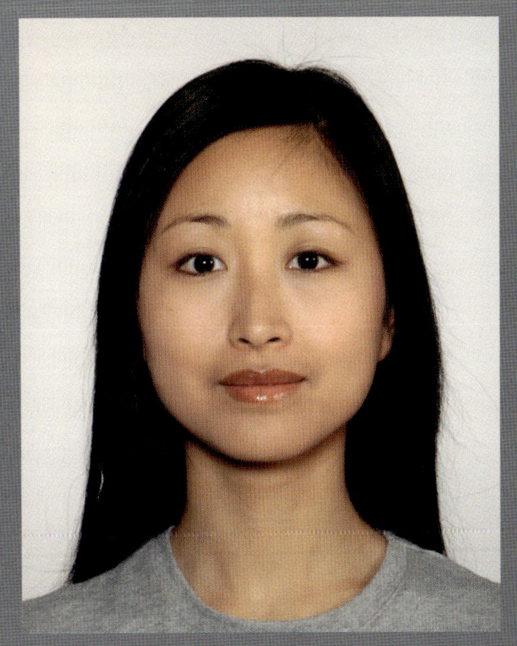

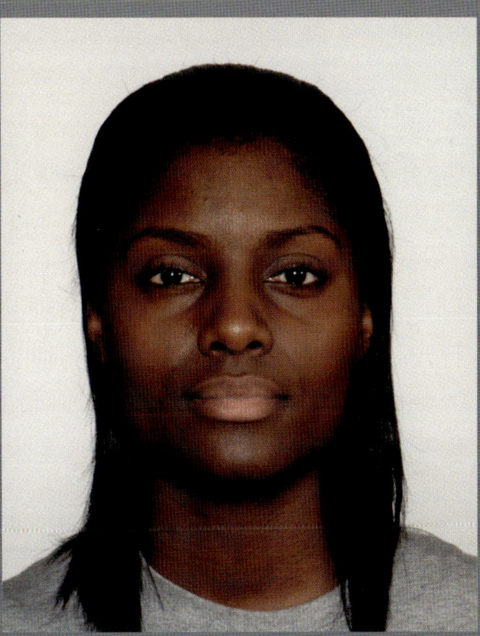

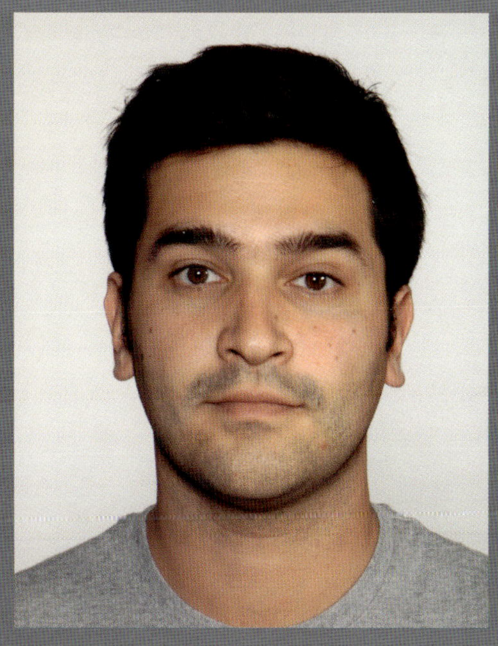

DARK BACKGROUND

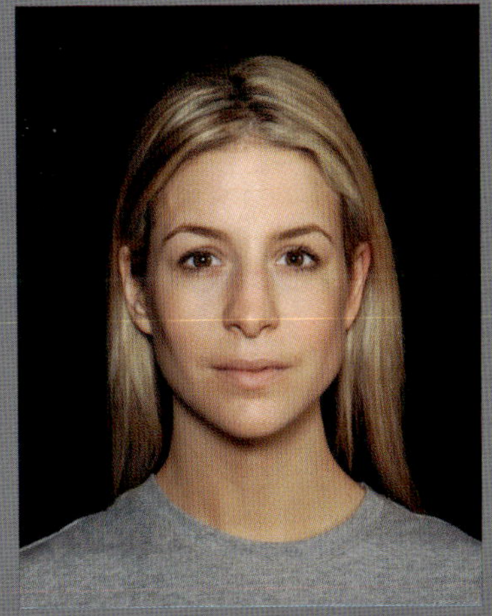

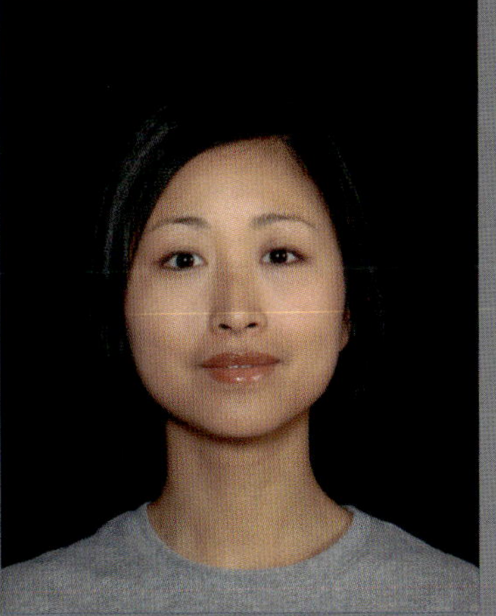

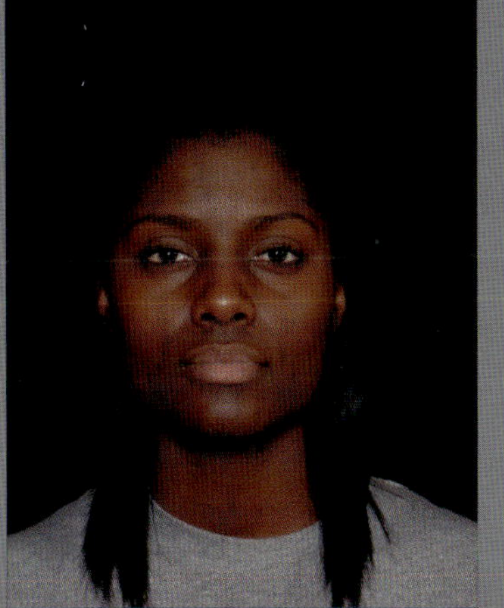

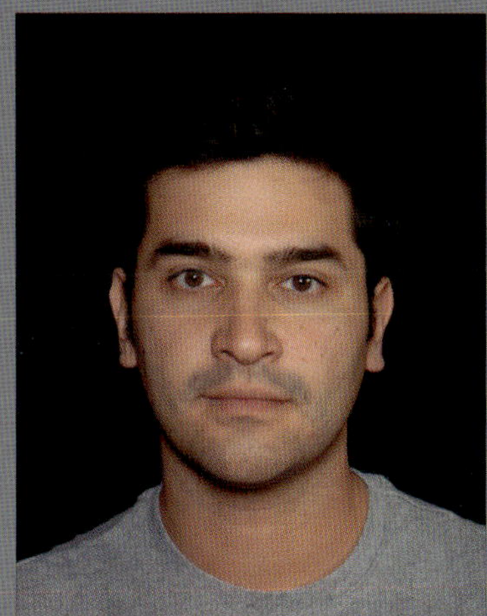

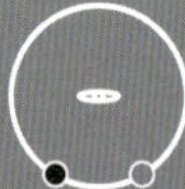

MIXED LIGHT LEVELS

LIGHT 1 (FULL): FROM 30° LEFT

LIGHT 2 (2 BELOW): FROM 30° RIGHT

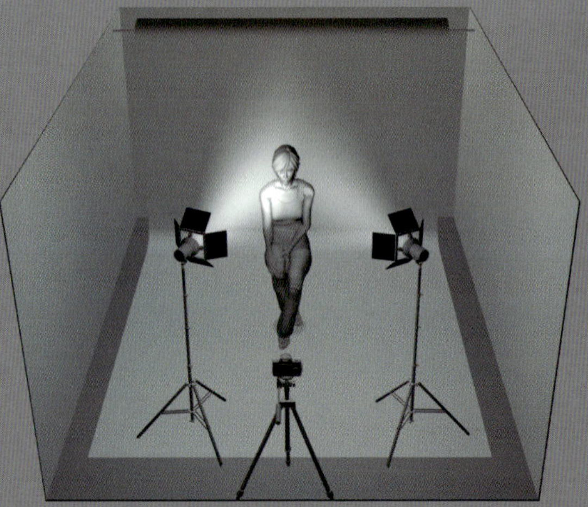

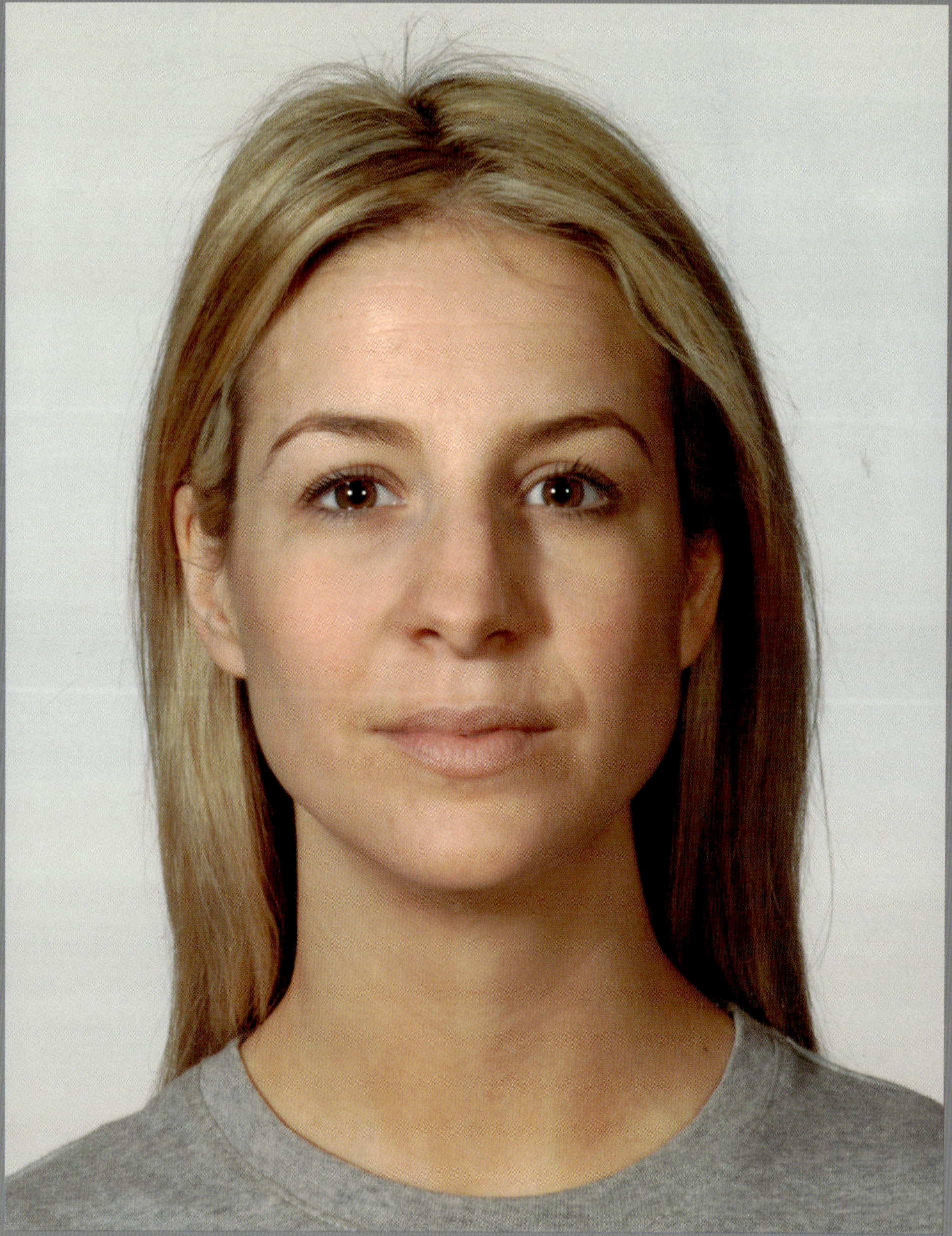

Both lights have been positioned at a 30-degree angle, but the main light to the left of the camera is two stops brighter than the fill light to the right. Unlike the similarly symmetrical setup on pages 92–93, the different power settings avoid the face being evenly lit.

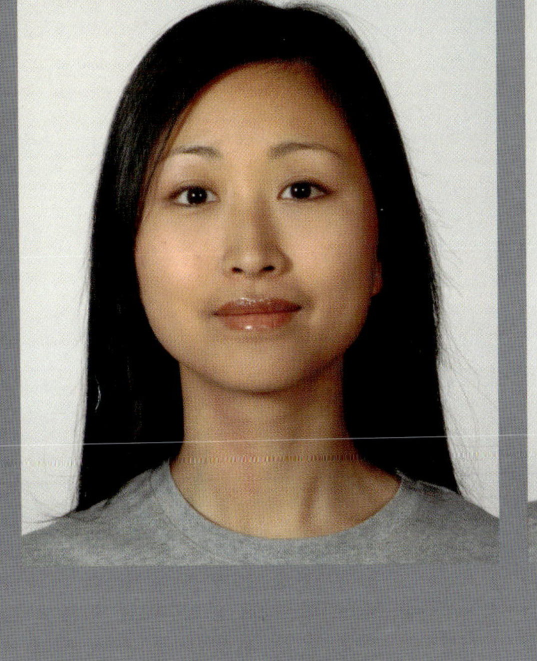

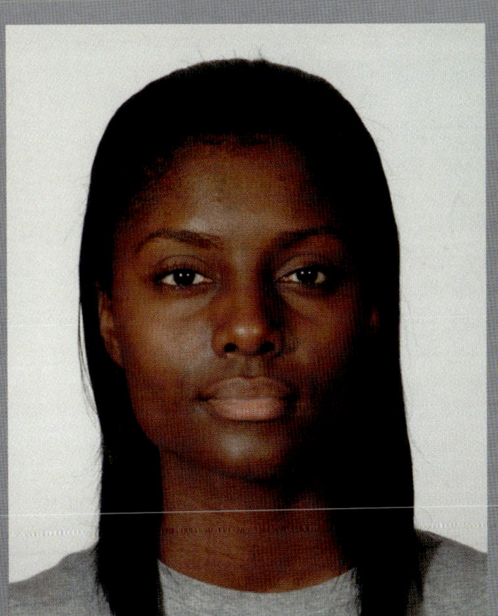

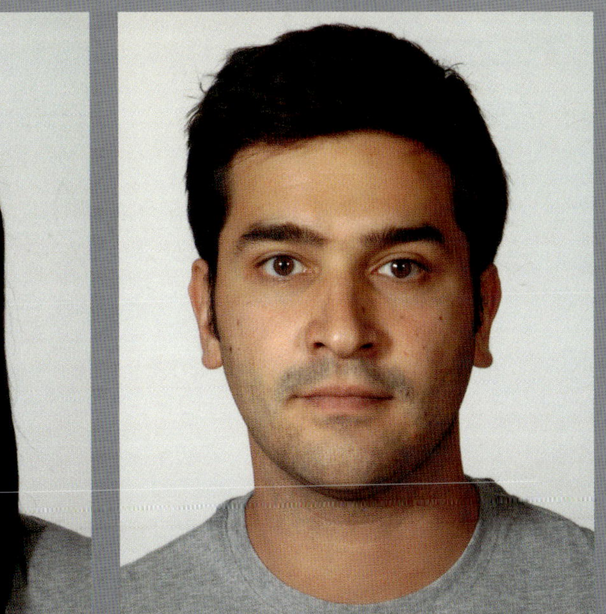

DARK BACKGROUND

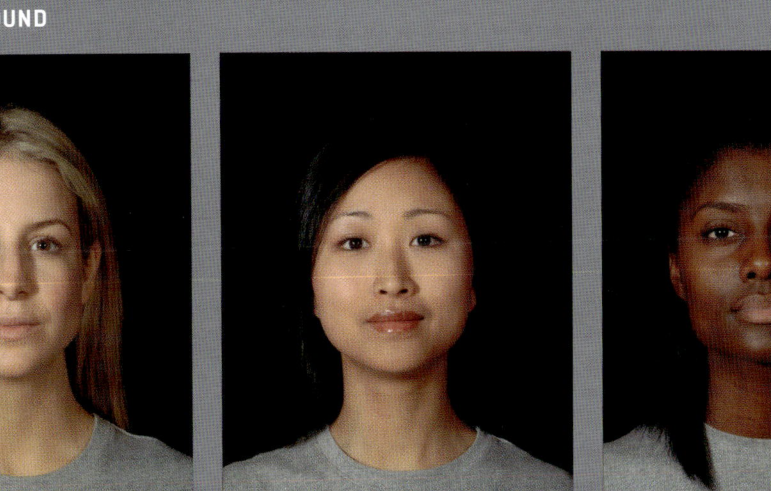

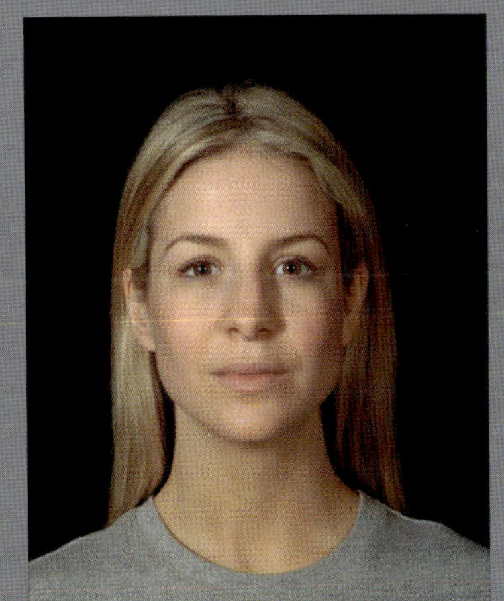

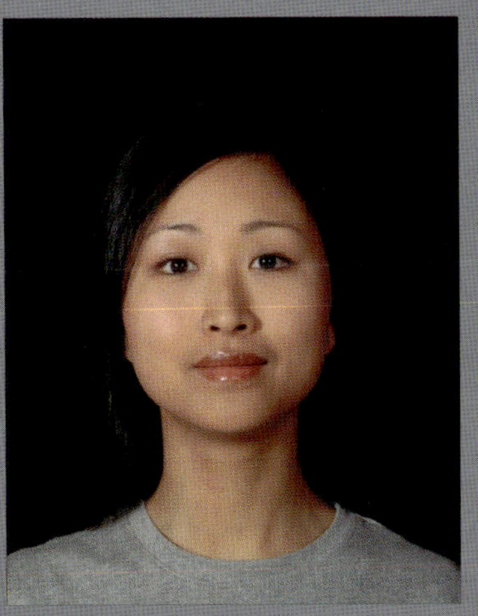

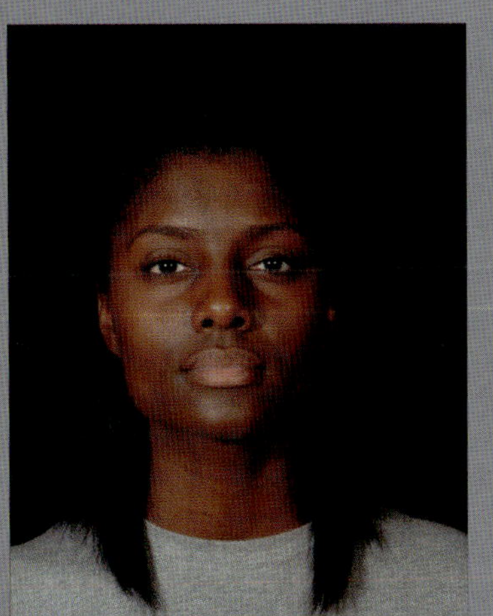

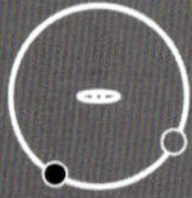

MIXED LIGHT LEVELS

LIGHT 1 (FULL): FROM 30° LEFT

LIGHT 2 (2 BELOW): FROM 60° RIGHT

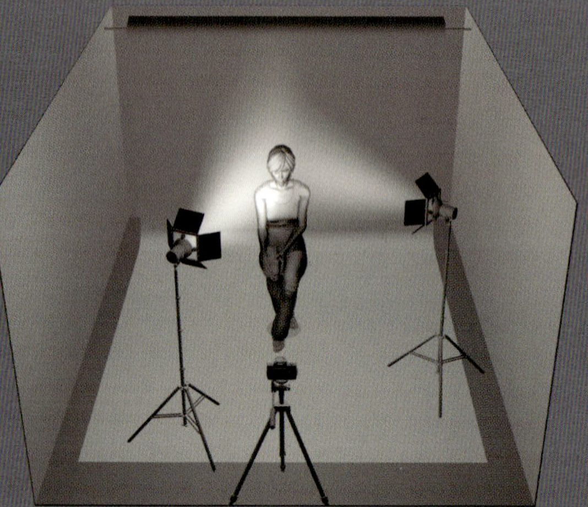

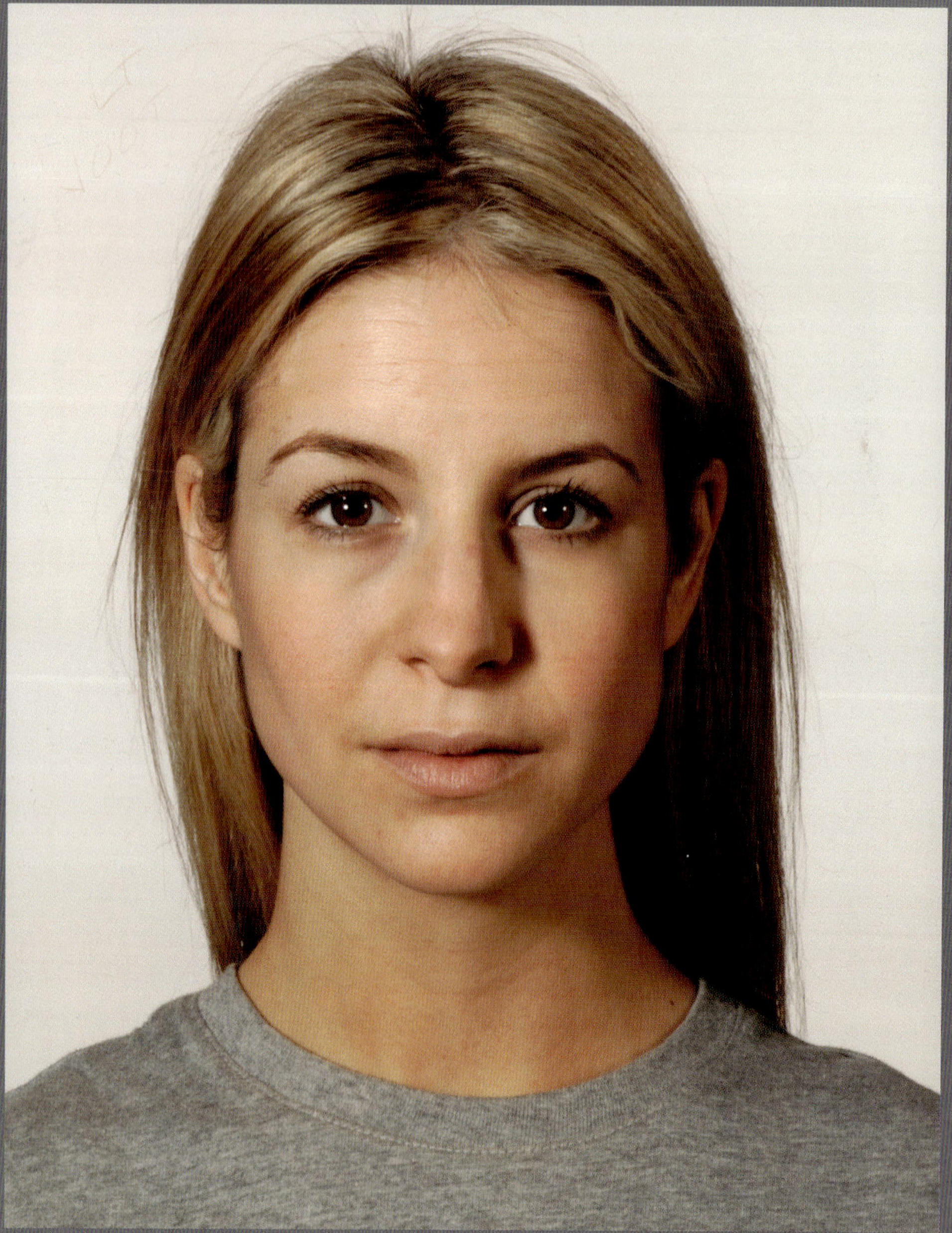

In this setup, the main light is close to the camera, with the fill light coming in from a 60-degree angle. This gently lightens the shadows that would otherwise be caused if you were using a single light (see pages 34–35 for the effect of a single light).

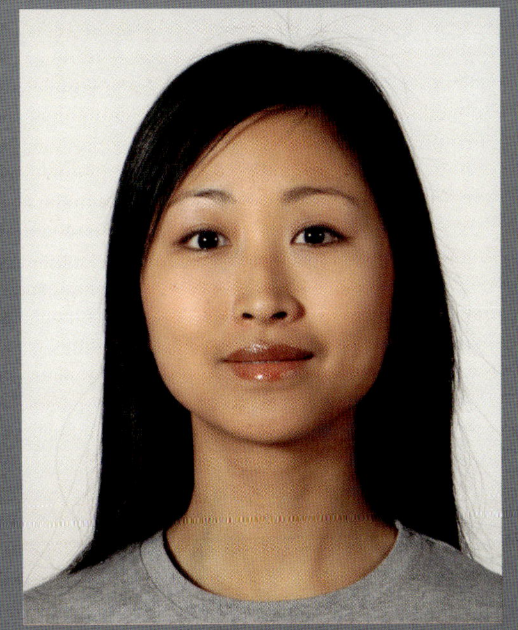

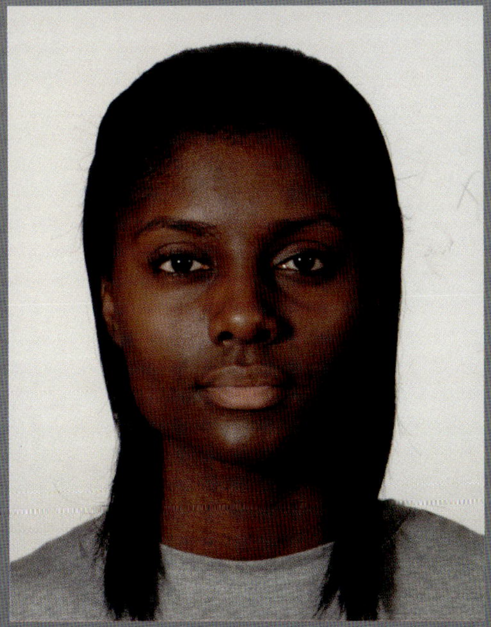

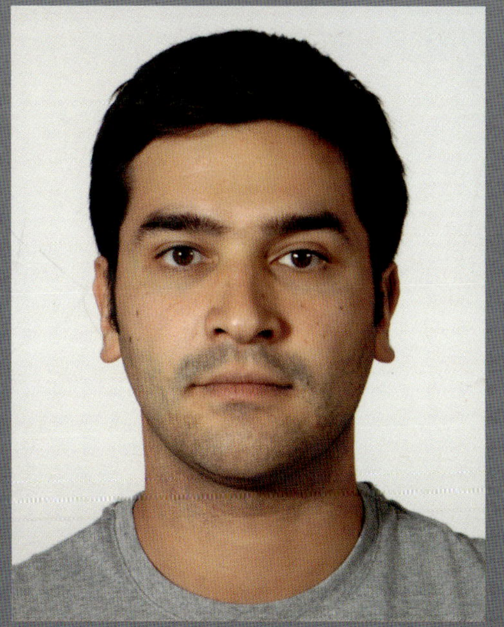

DARK BACKGROUND

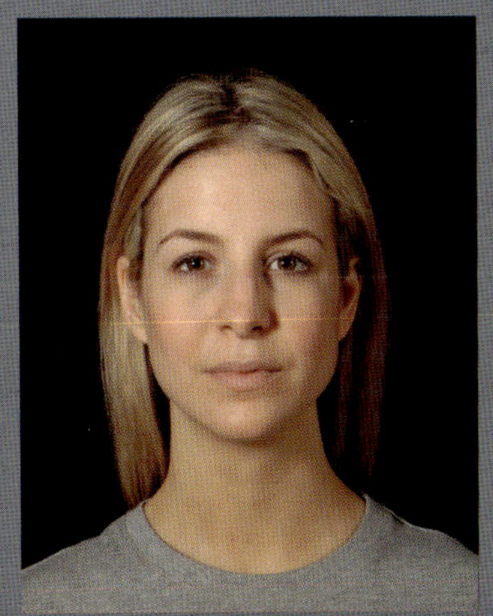

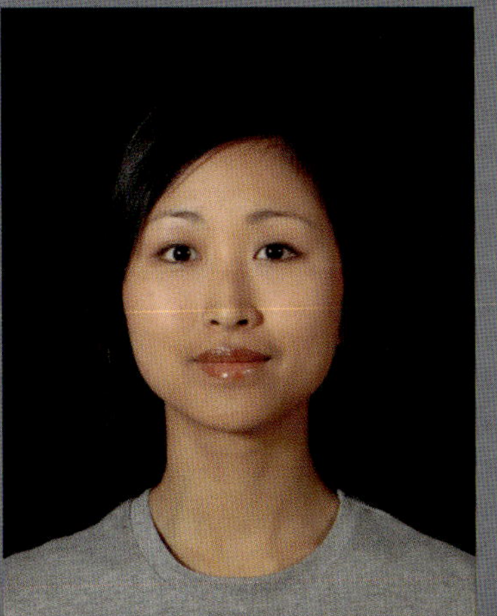

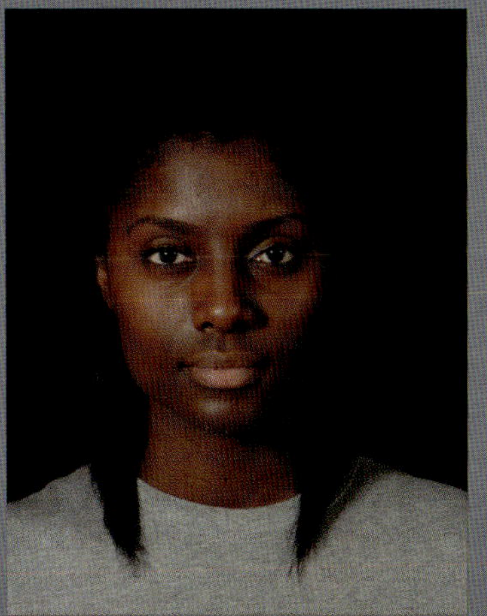

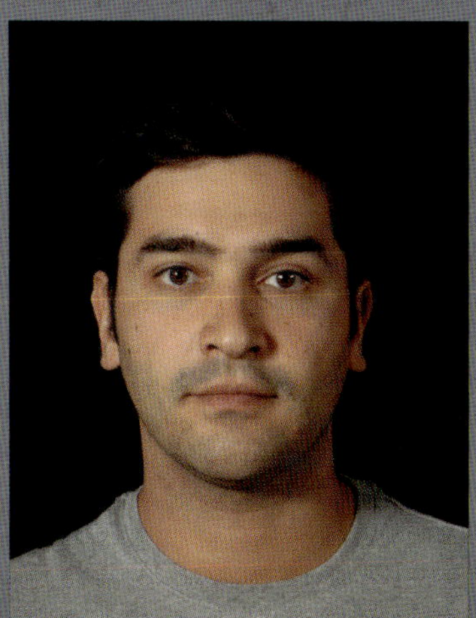

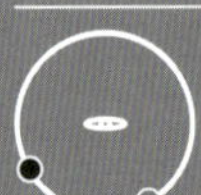

MIXED LIGHT LEVELS

LIGHT 1 (FULL): FROM 60° LEFT

LIGHT 2 (2 BELOW): FROM 30° RIGHT

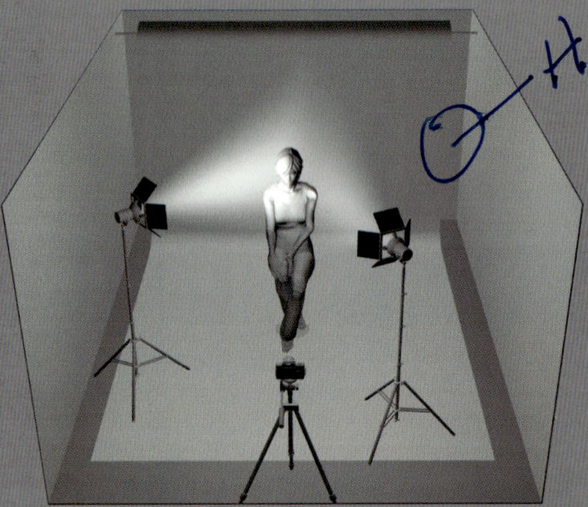

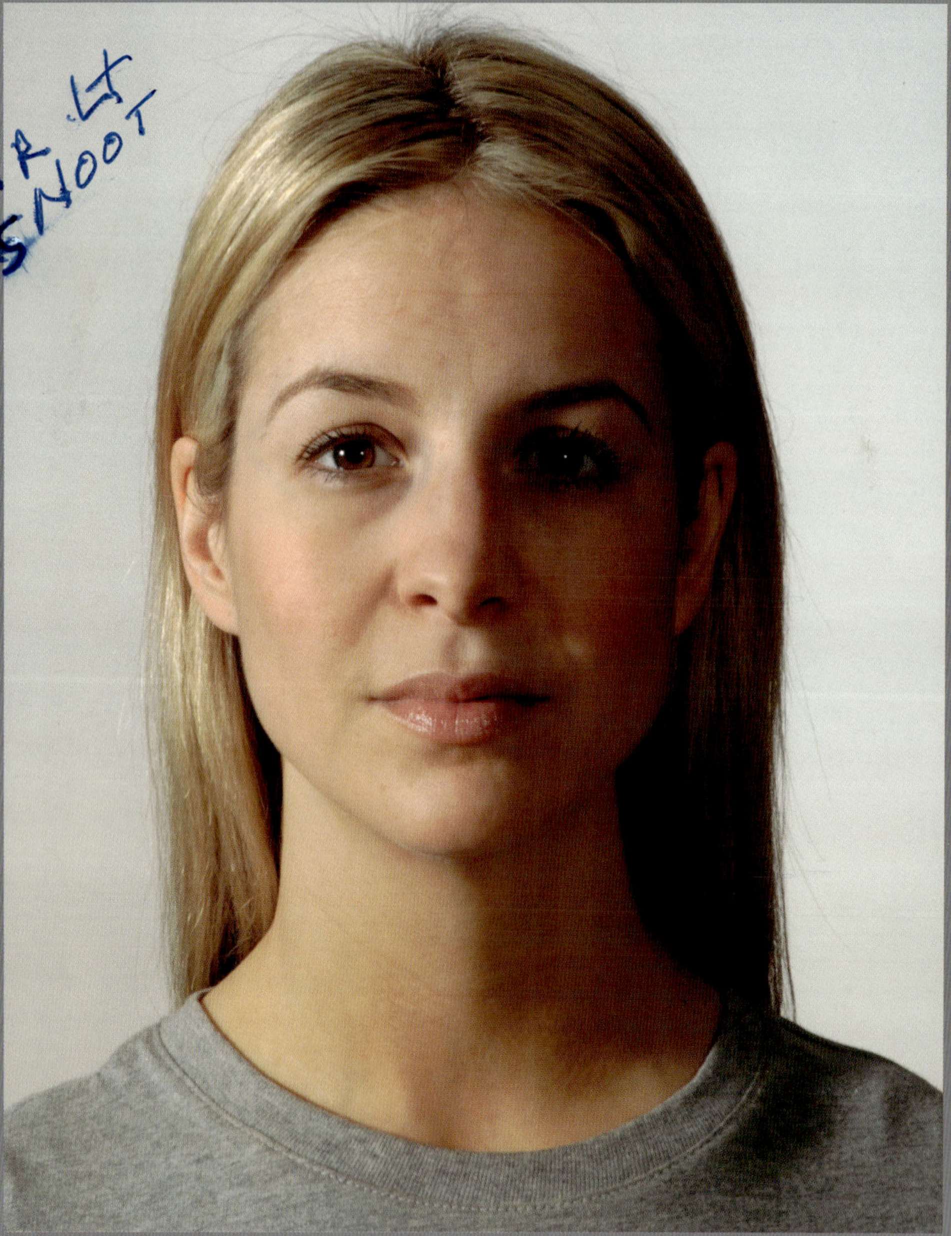

As the main light is moved further away from the camera, the effect of the fill light is made more apparent as it illuminates the left side of the model's face and prevents it falling into heavy shadow. This is especially effective when the subject is against a dark background.

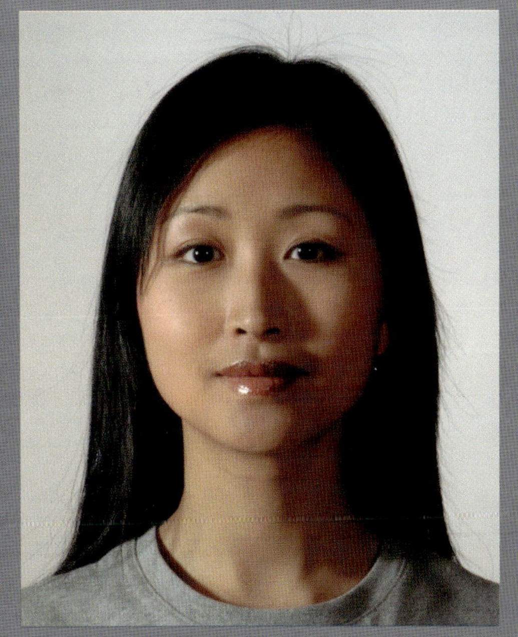

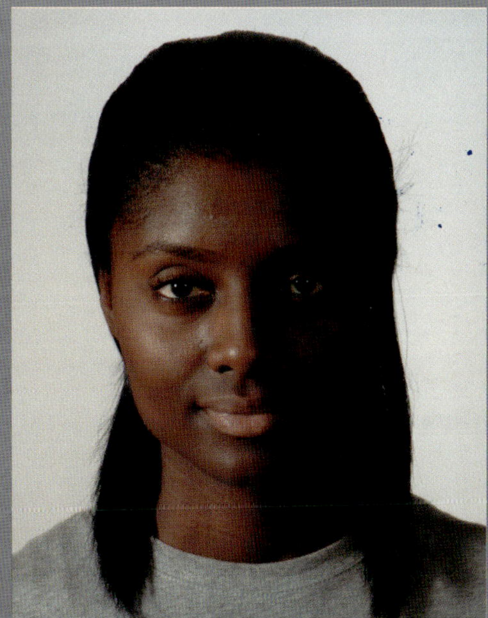

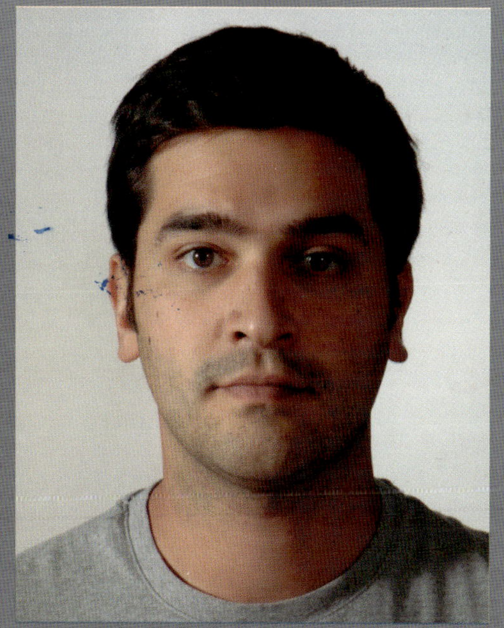

DARK BACKGROUND

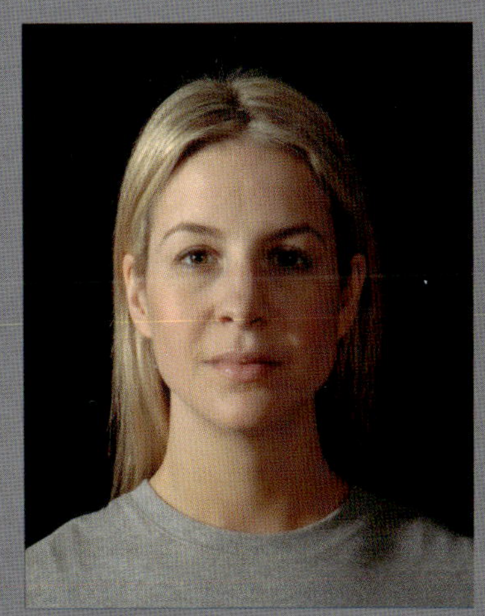

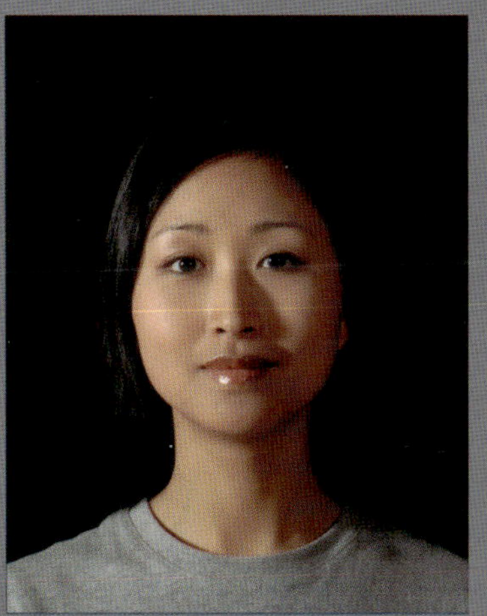

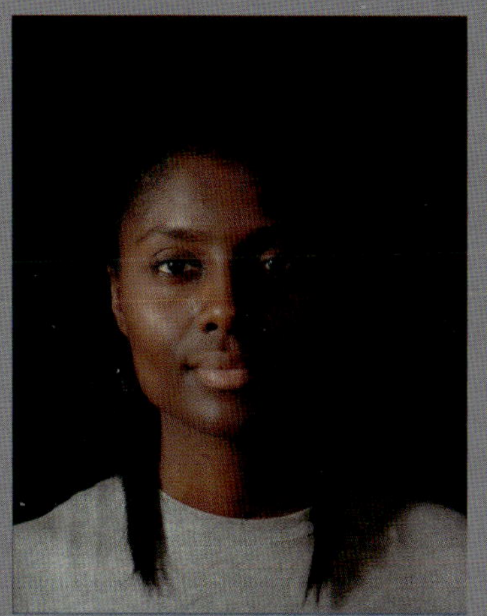

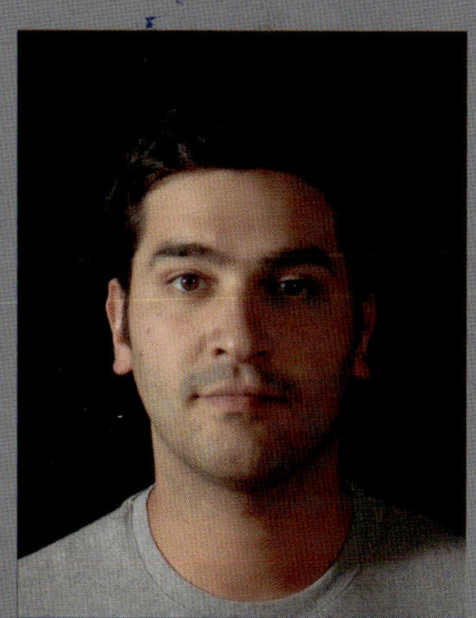

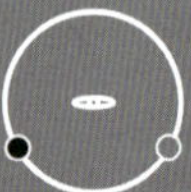

MIXED LIGHT LEVELS

LIGHT 1 (FULL): FROM 60° LEFT

LIGHT 2 (2 BELOW): FROM 60° RIGHT

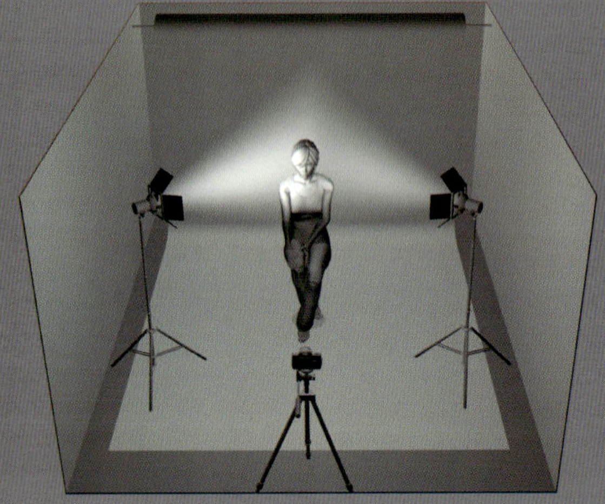

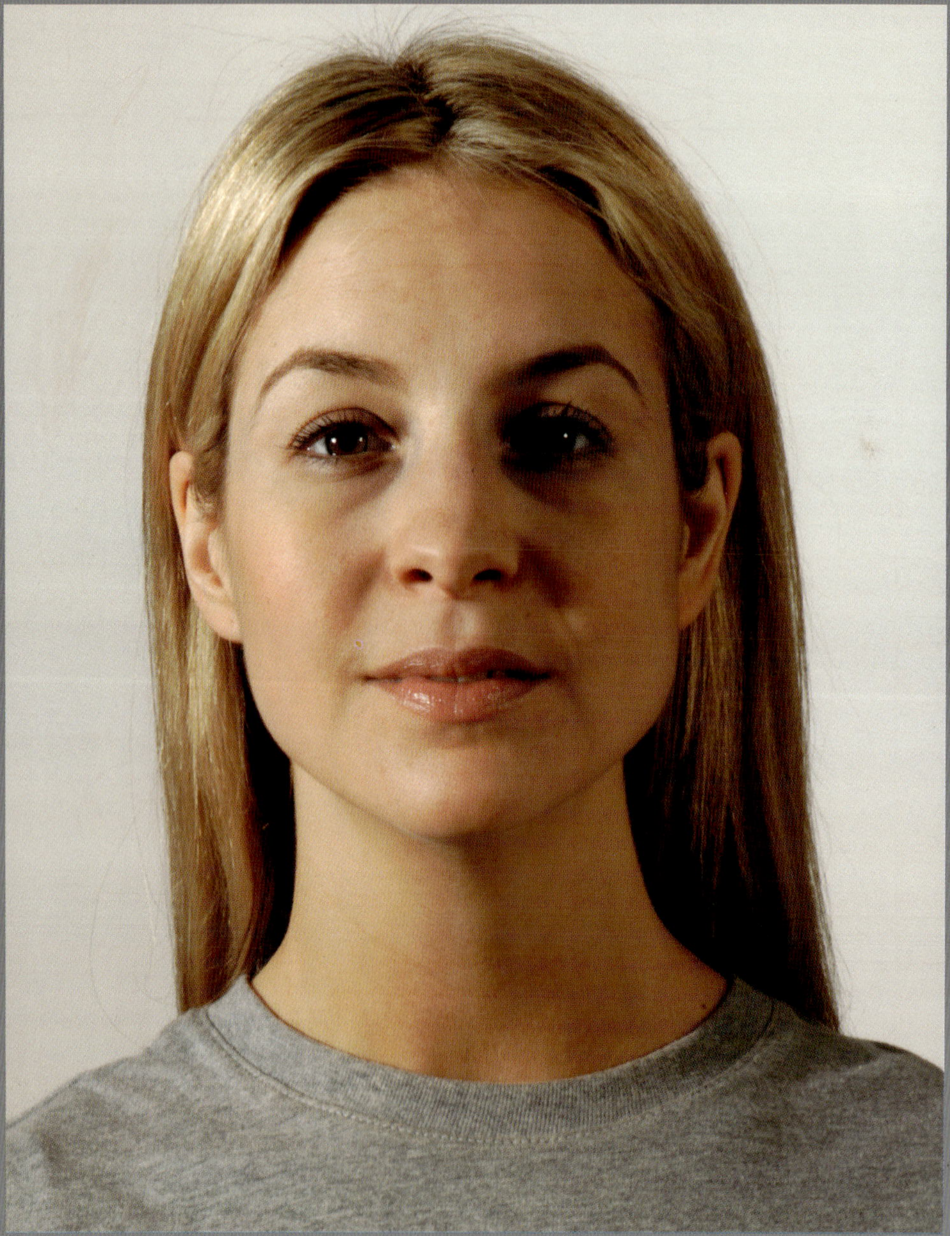

In this symmetrical setup, both lights are coming from a 60-degree angle, but the weaker output of the fill prevents the lighting arrangement from creating an overtly flat image. The contrast between the two sides of the face creates a distinct three-dimensional look.

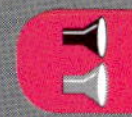

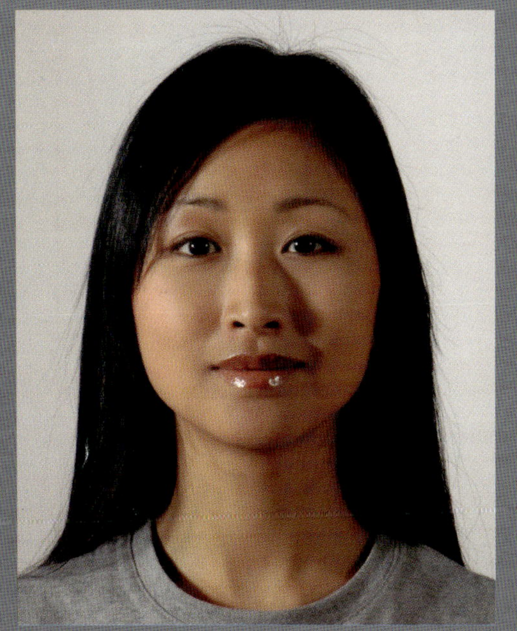

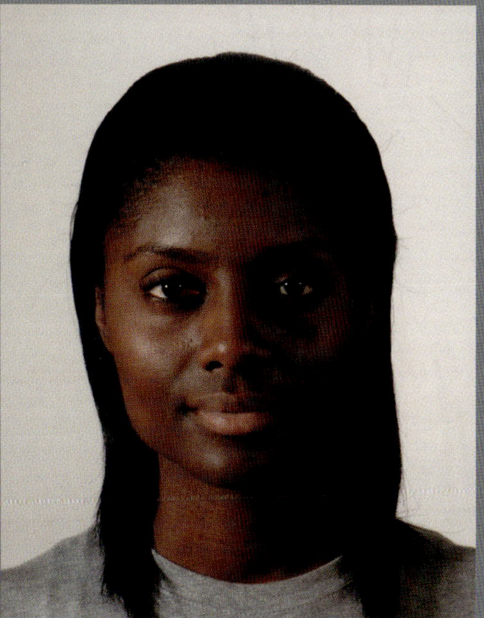

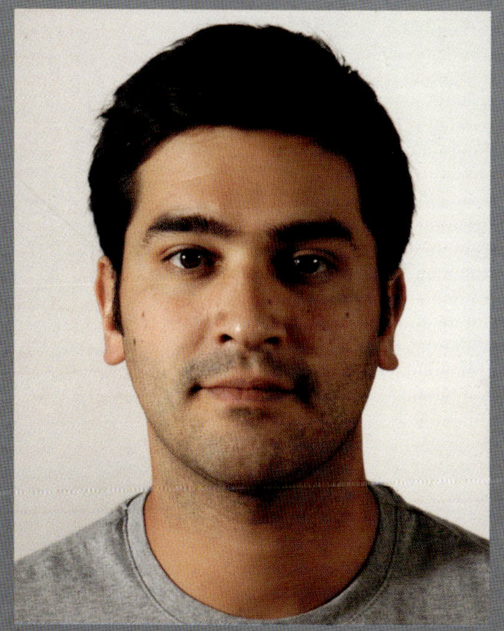

DARK BACKGROUND

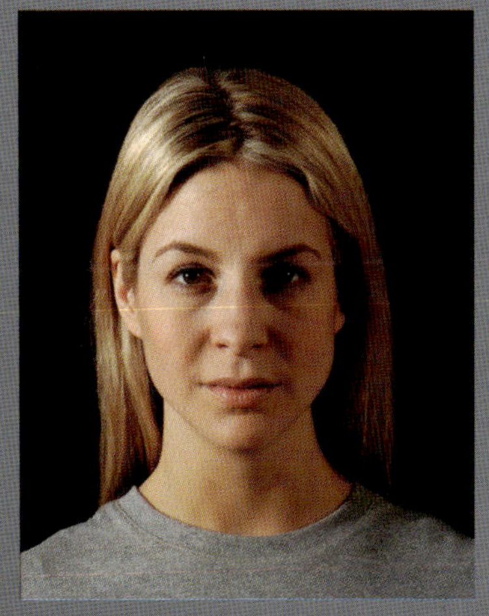

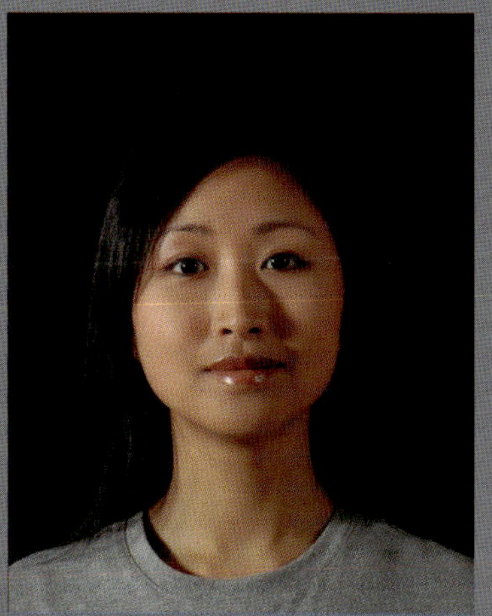

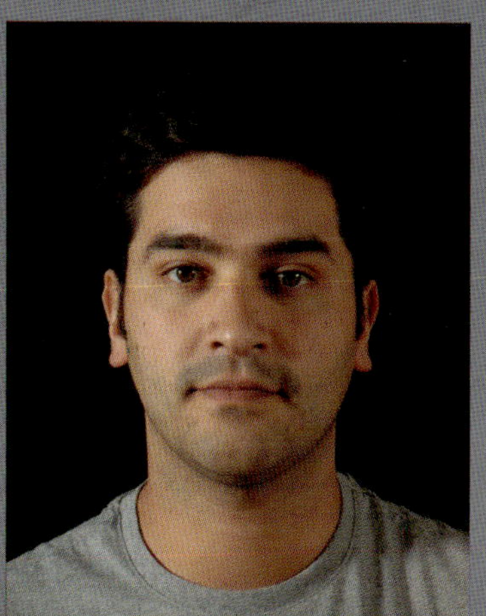

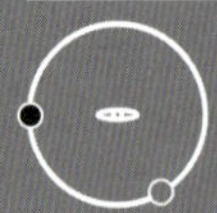

MIXED LIGHT LEVELS

LIGHT 1 (FULL): FROM 90° LEFT

LIGHT 2 (2 BELOW): FROM 30° RIGHT

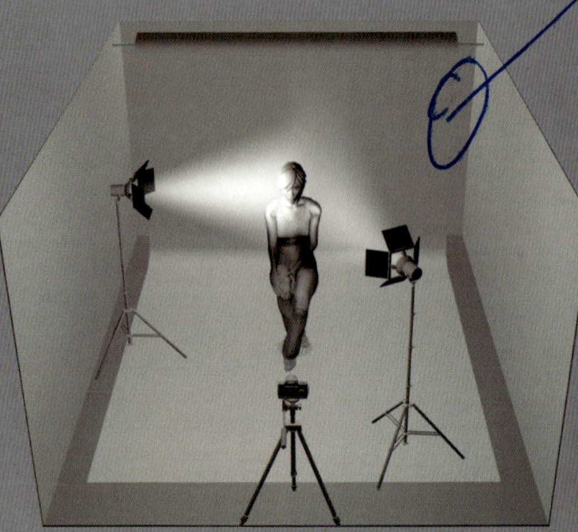

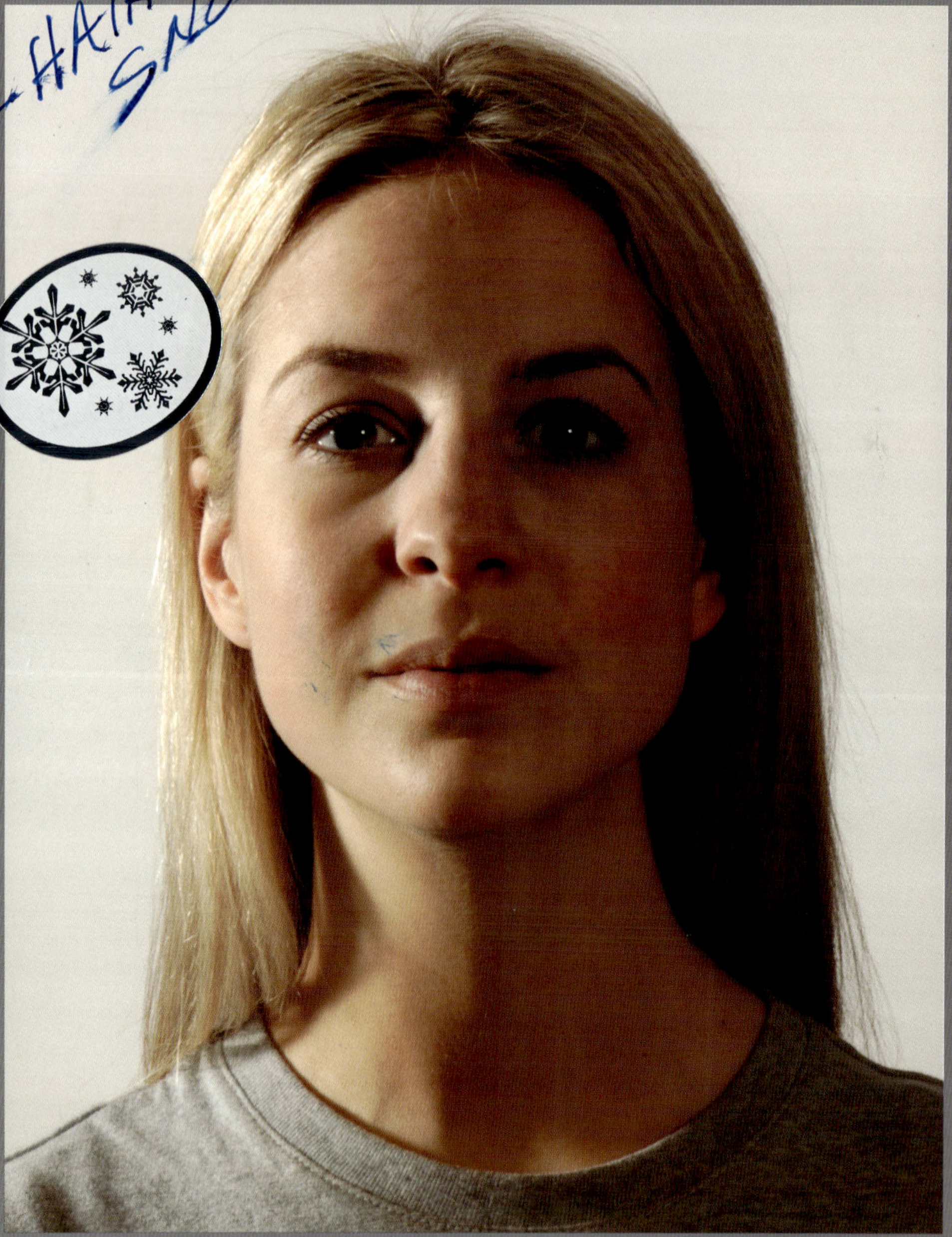

With the main light at a 90-degree angle to the camera, it largely illuminates the side of the model's face and nose. The weaker fill light (set at two stops less power than the main light) lifts the shadows sufficiently to reveal the subject's facial features, even against a dark background.

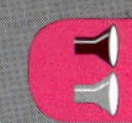

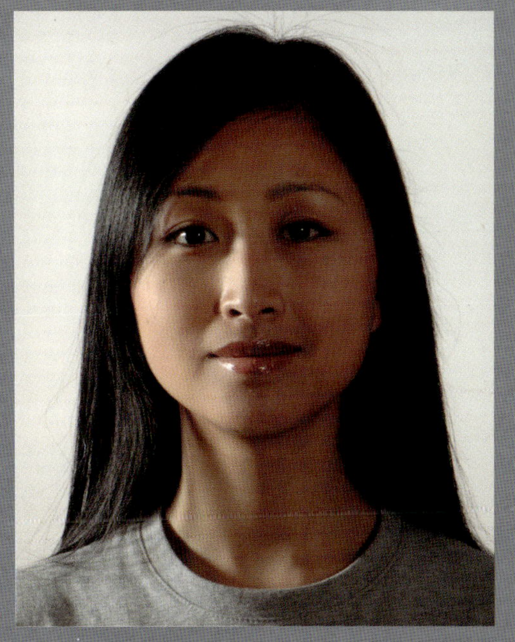

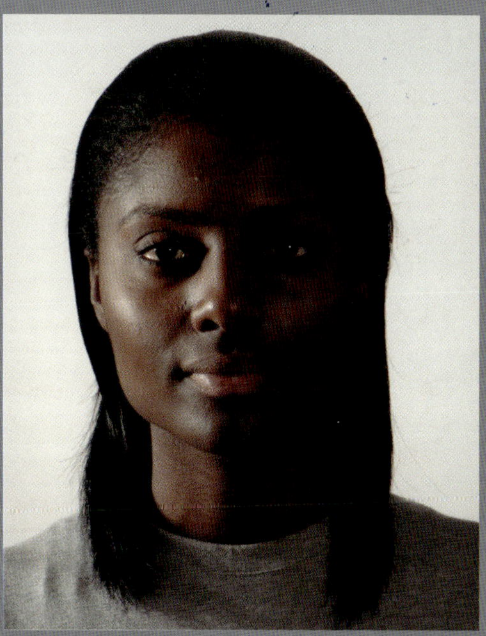

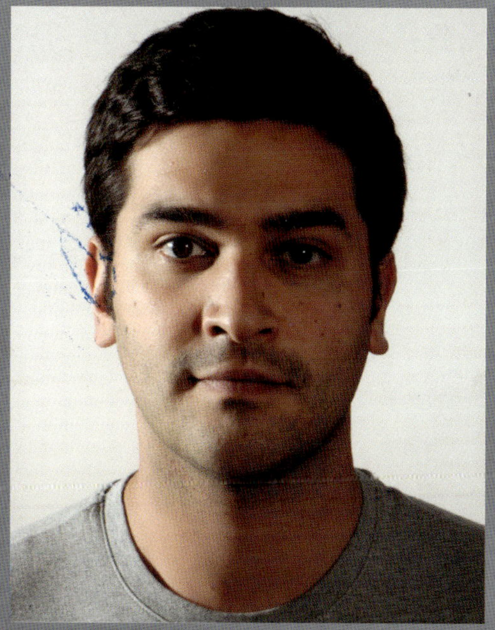

DARK BACKGROUND

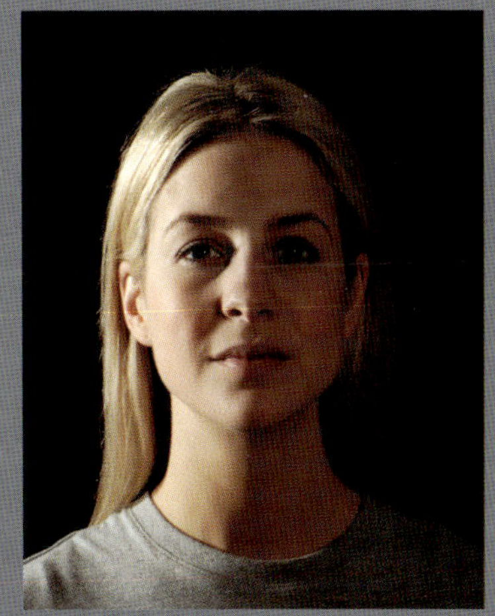

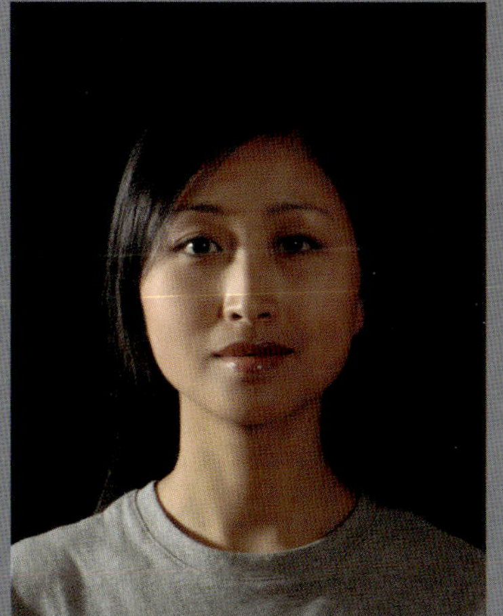

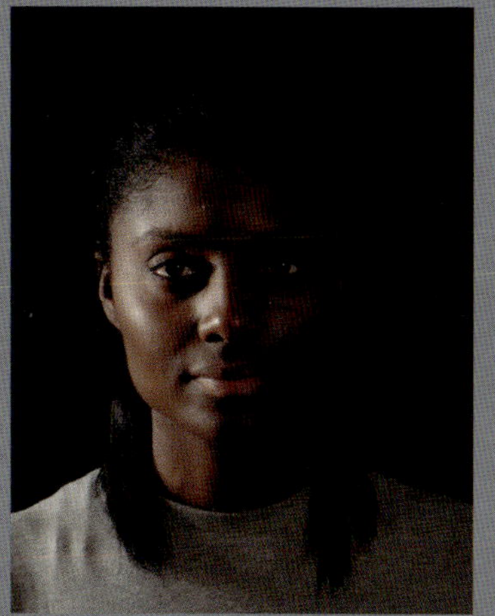

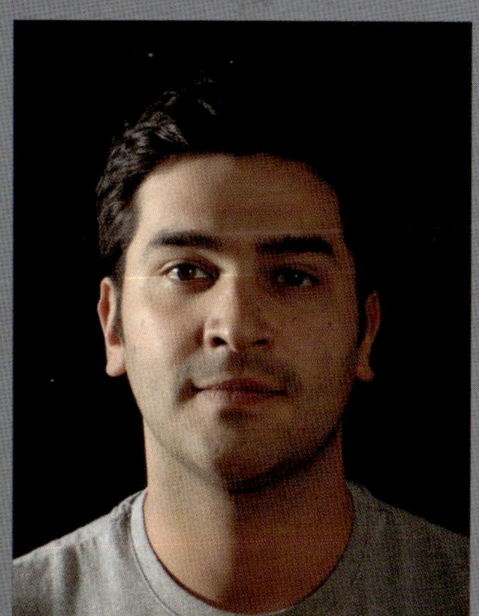

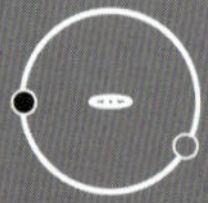

MIXED LIGHT LEVELS

LIGHT 1 (FULL): FROM 90° LEFT

LIGHT 2 (2 BELOW): FROM 60° RIGHT

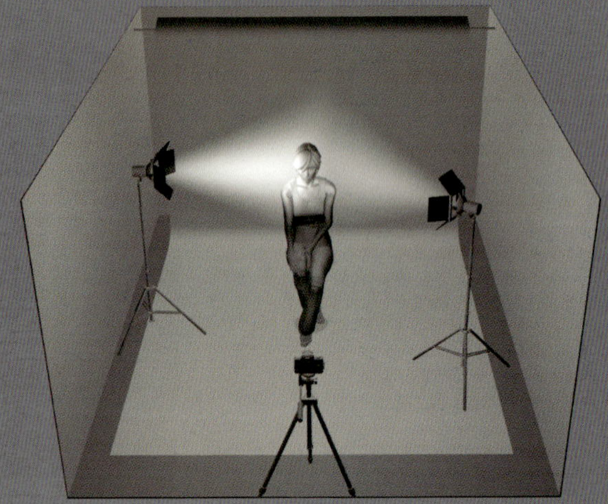

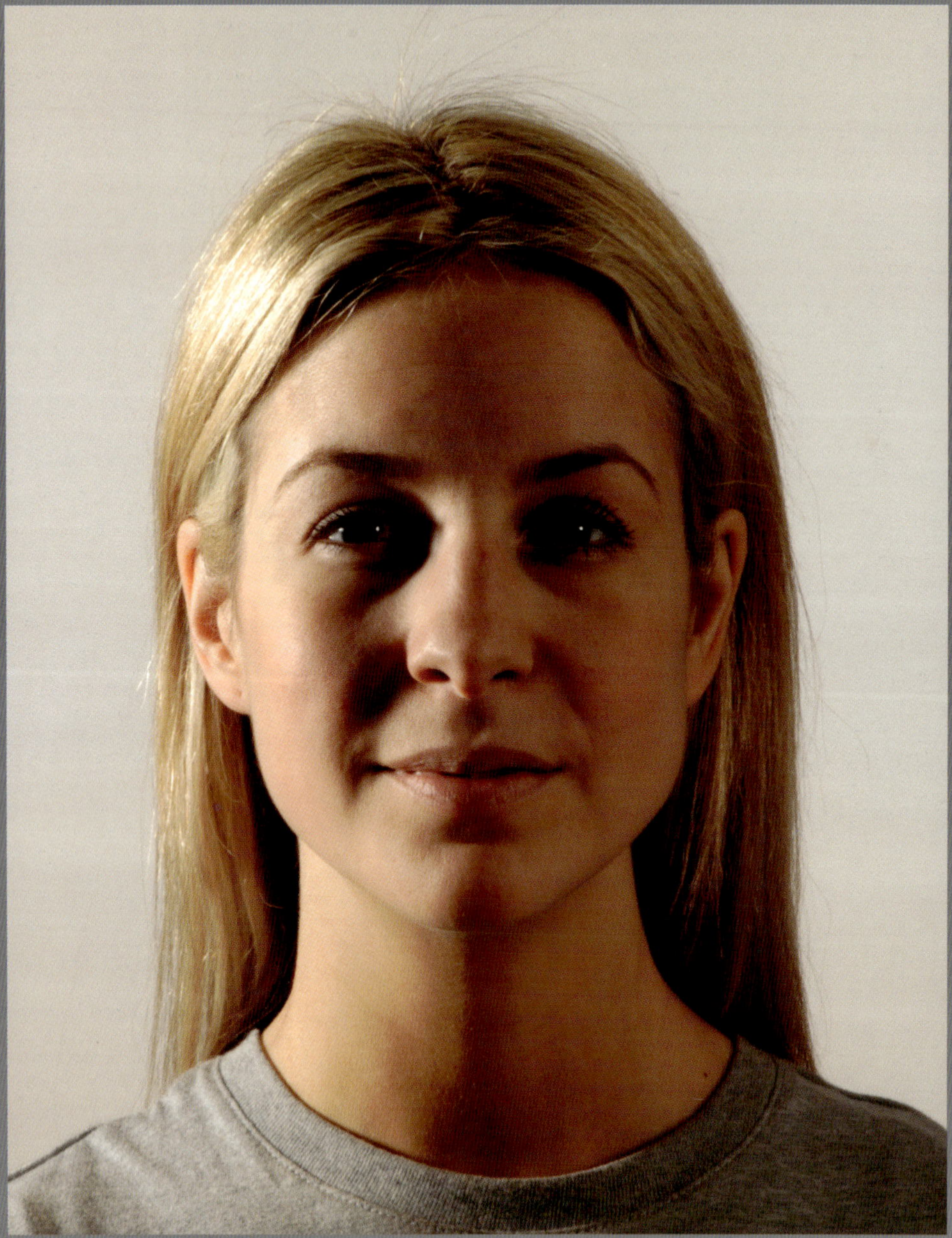

If you compare this setup to that on page 112–113 (where the lights are in identical positions), you can see how using two lights at different strengths can create an entirely different look: where the previous setup delivers a bright, relatively evenly-lit portrait, here the look is more sculptural.

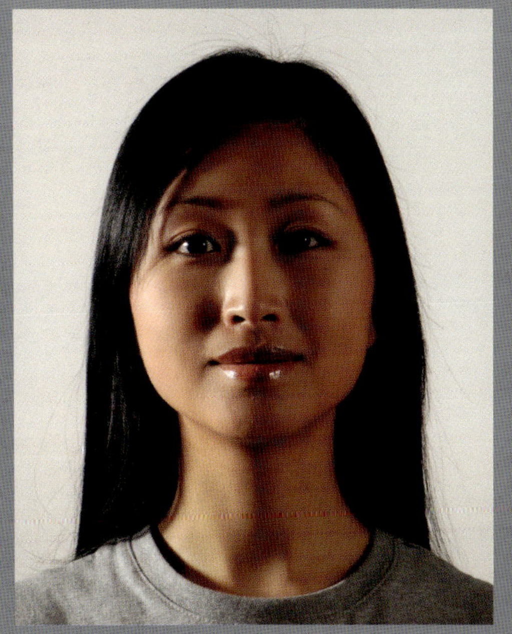

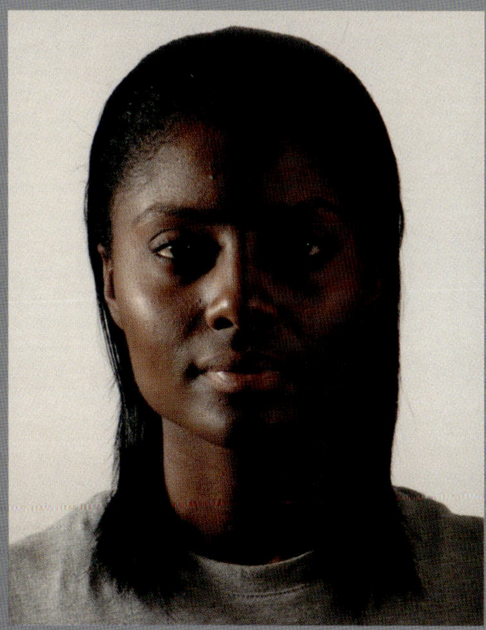

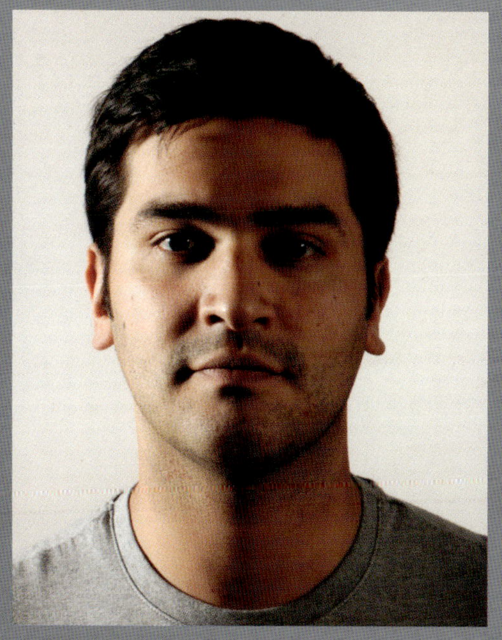

DARK BACKGROUND

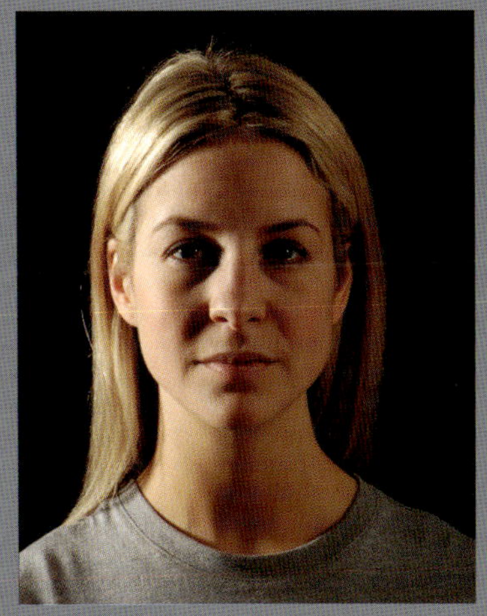

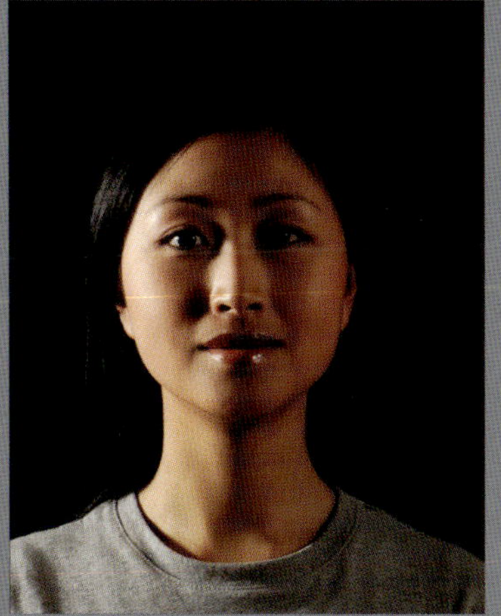

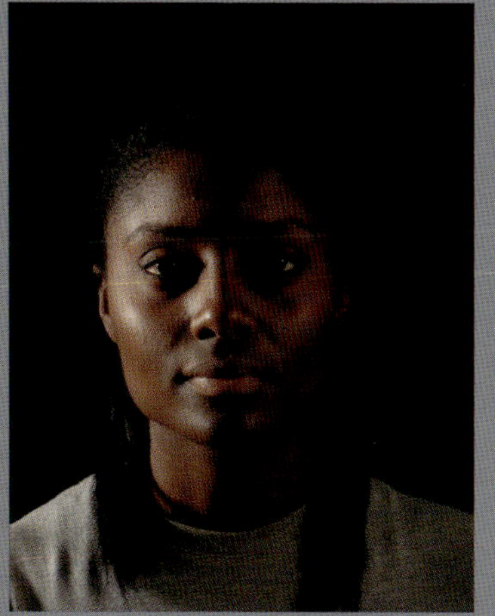

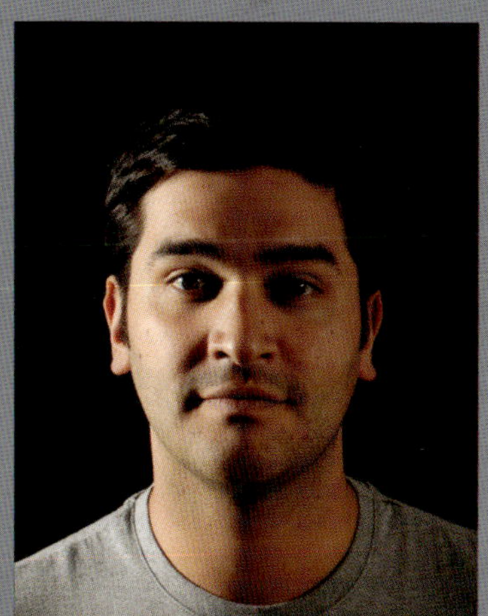

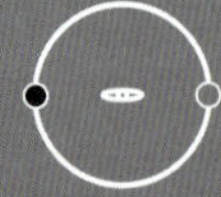

MIXED LIGHT LEVELS

LIGHT 1 (FULL): FROM 90° LEFT

LIGHT 2 (2 BELOW): FROM 90° RIGHT

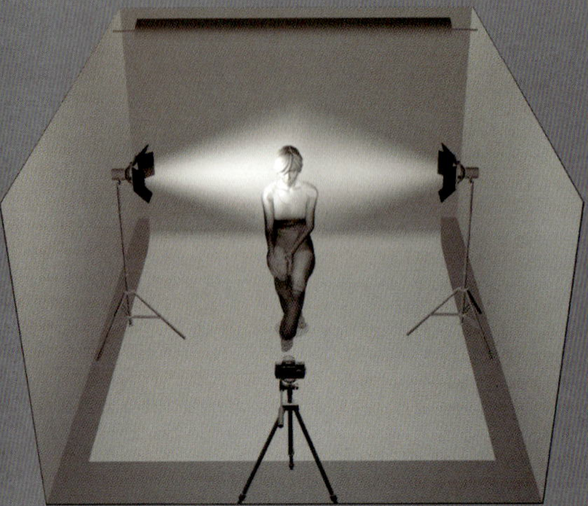

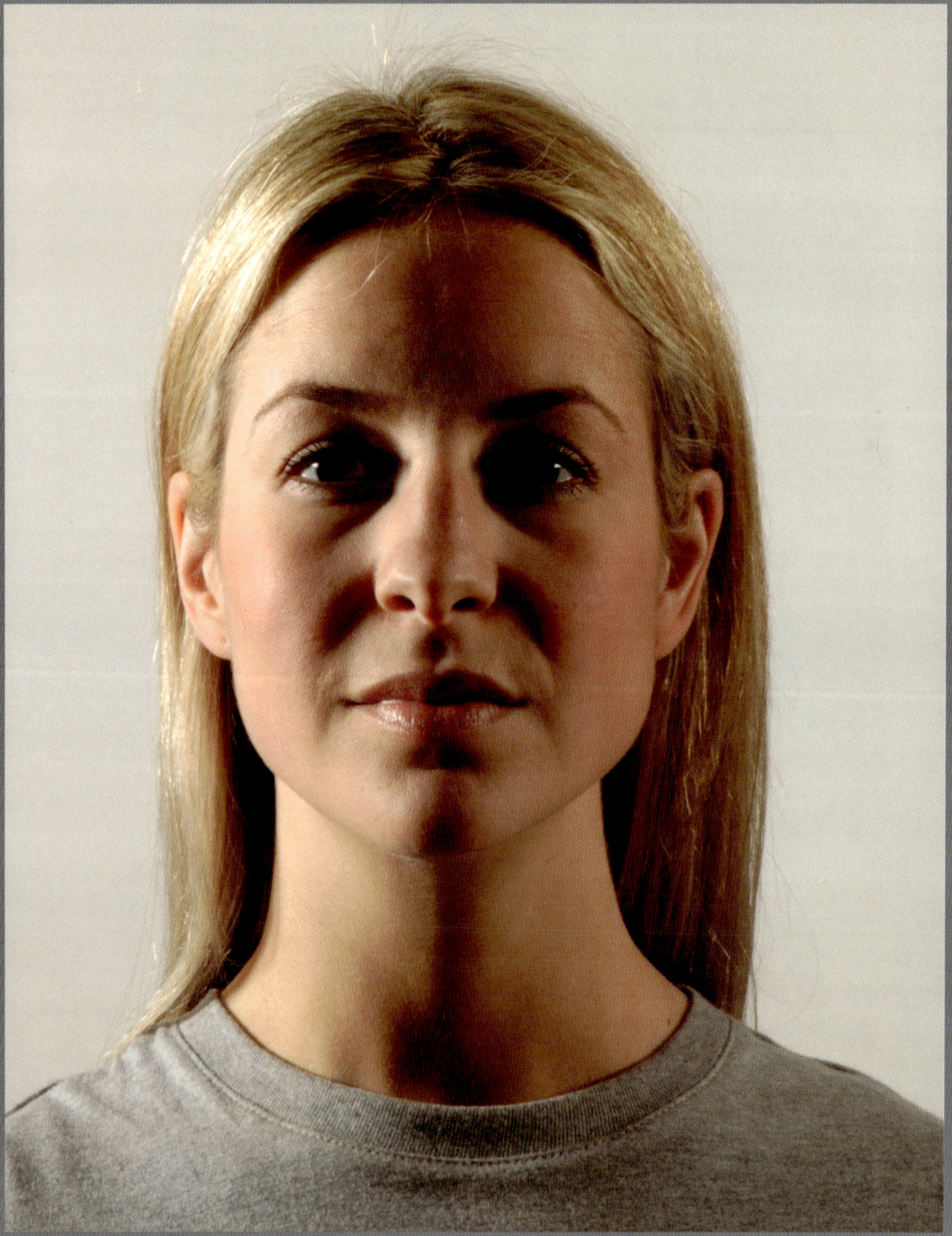

As you have seen previously, two opposing lights set either side of the subject will invariably produce a shaded band down the center of your subject's face. Limiting the power of one of the lamps also darkens one side of the face, reducing the symmetry of the lighting.

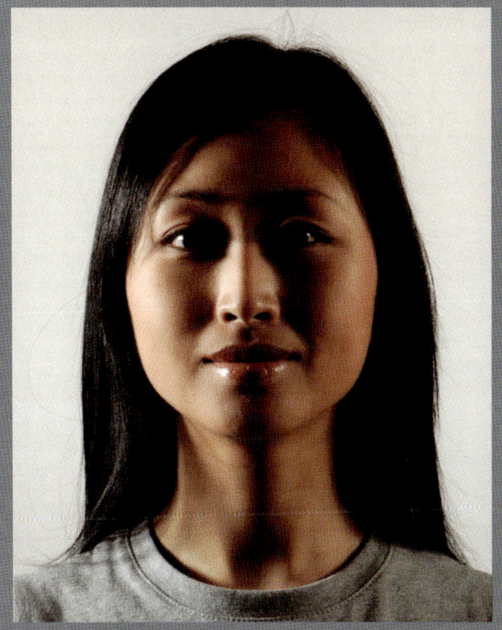

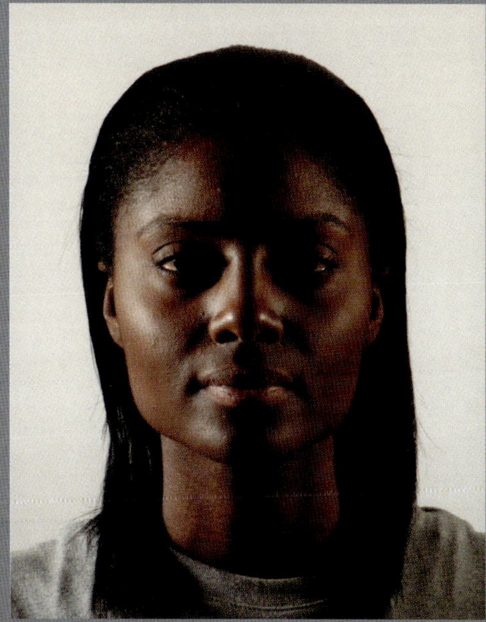

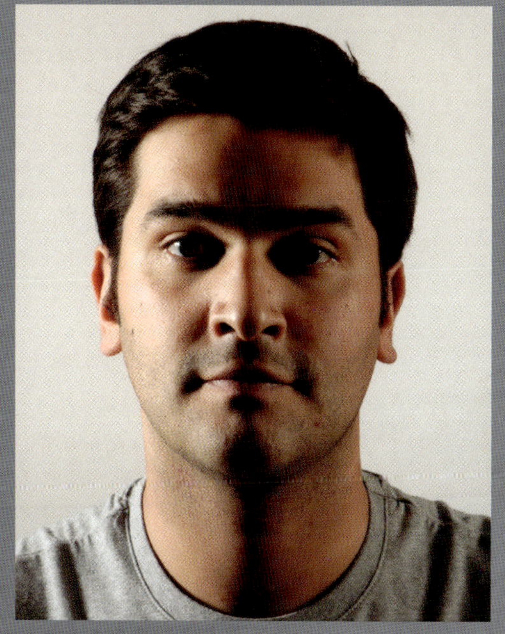

DARK BACKGROUND

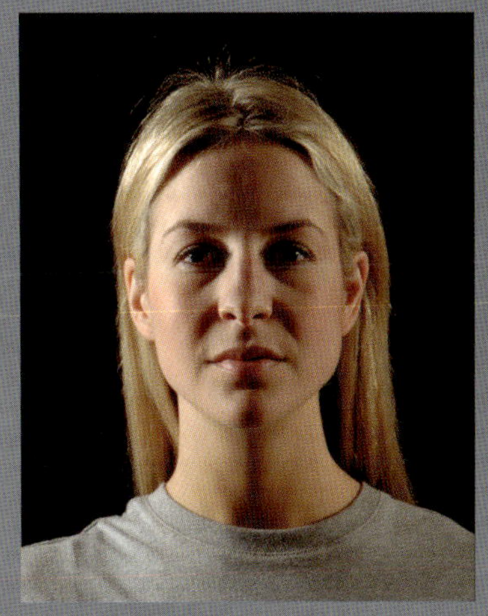

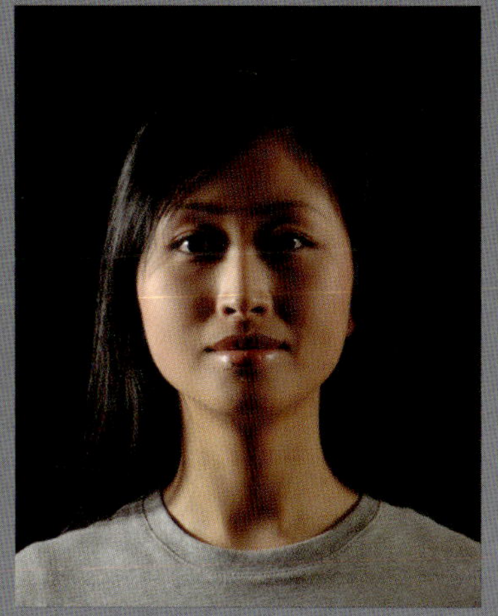

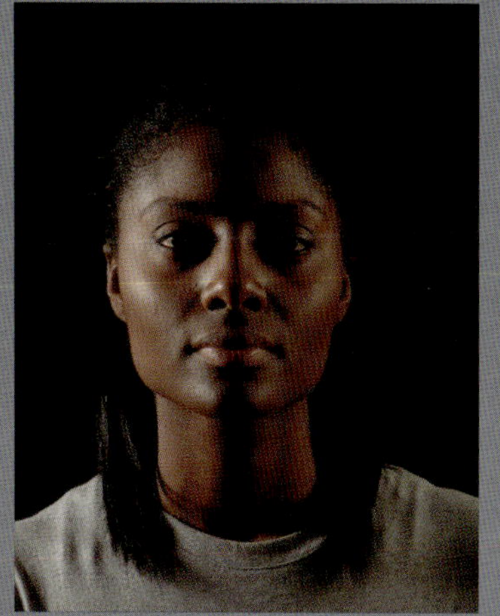

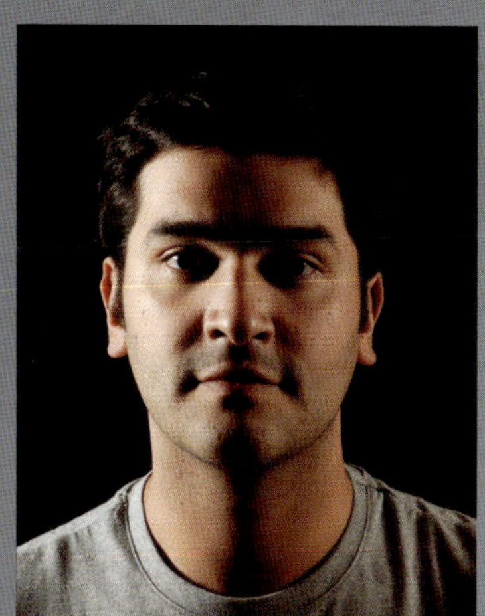

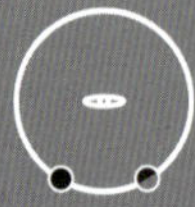

MIXED LIGHT LEVELS

LIGHT 1 (FULL): FROM 30° LEFT

LIGHT 2 (4 BELOW): FROM 30° RIGHT

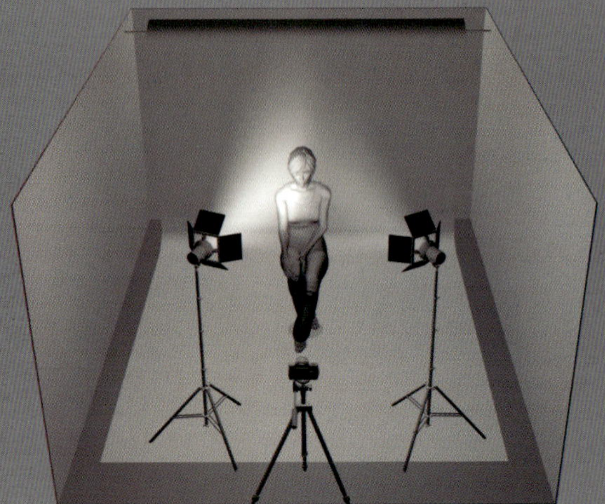

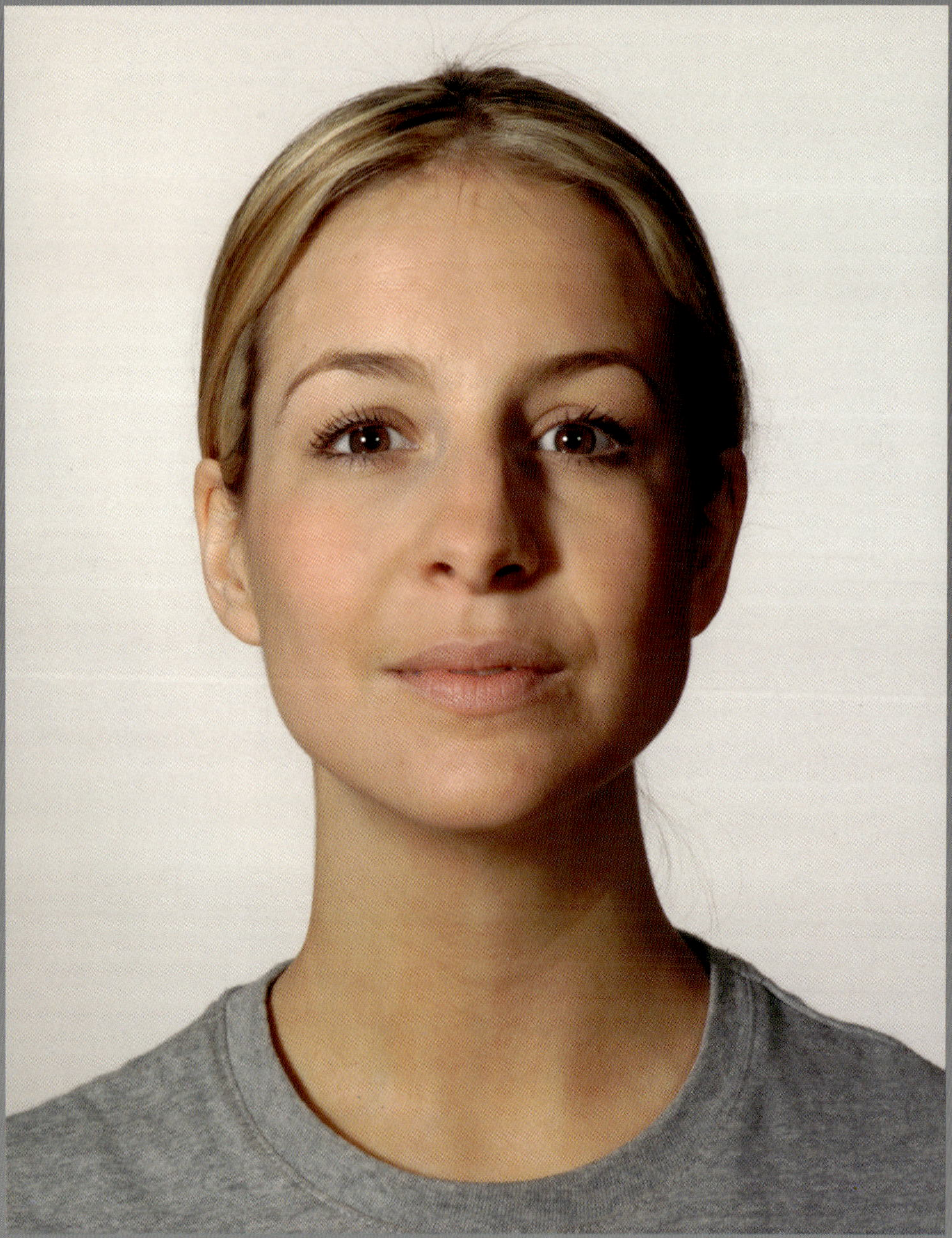

Compare this setup to that shown on pages 218–219. The lights are in identical positions, but in this arrangement the power of the fill light has been reduced, so it is now four stops lower than the main light. The shadows are still lifted, but the overall contrast in the face is heightened.

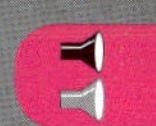

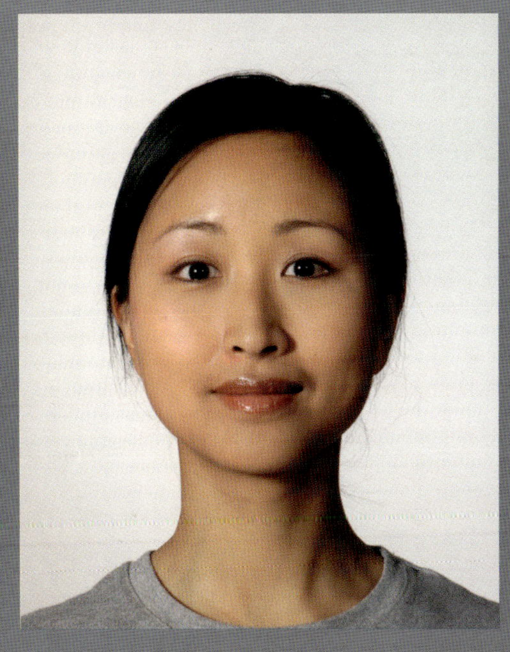

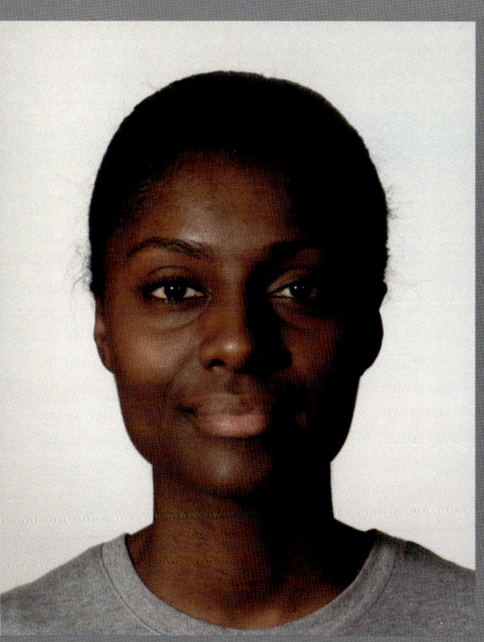

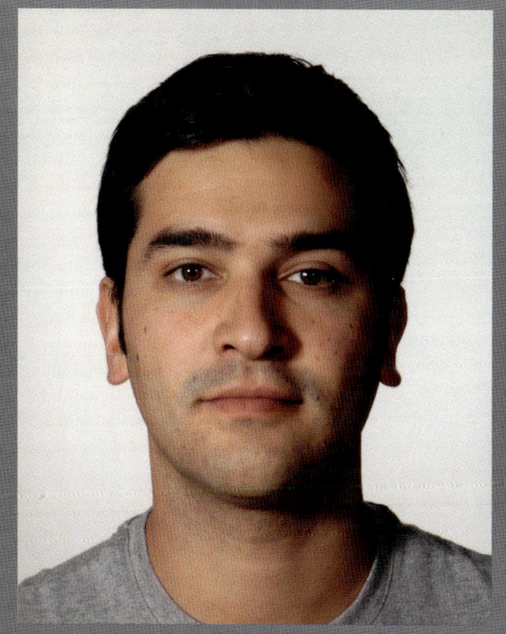

DARK BACKGROUND

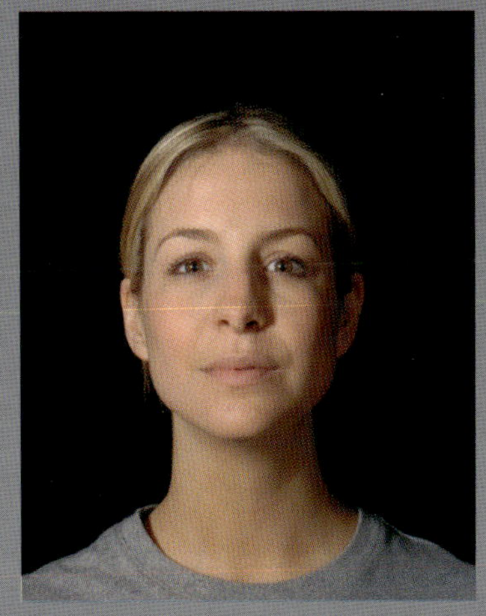

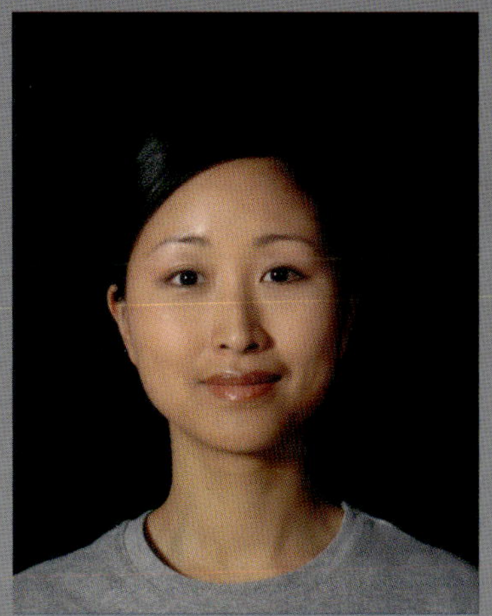

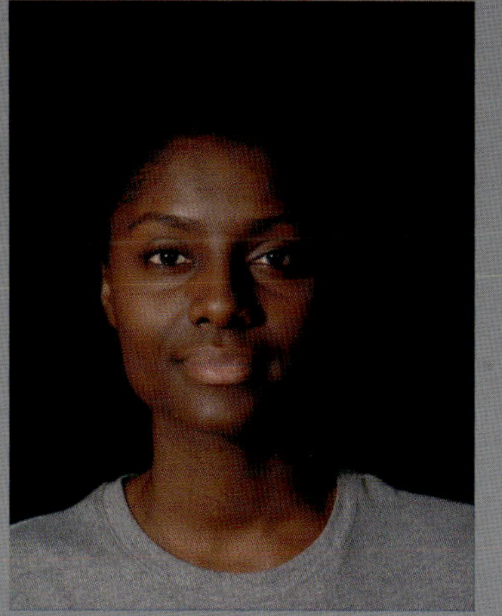

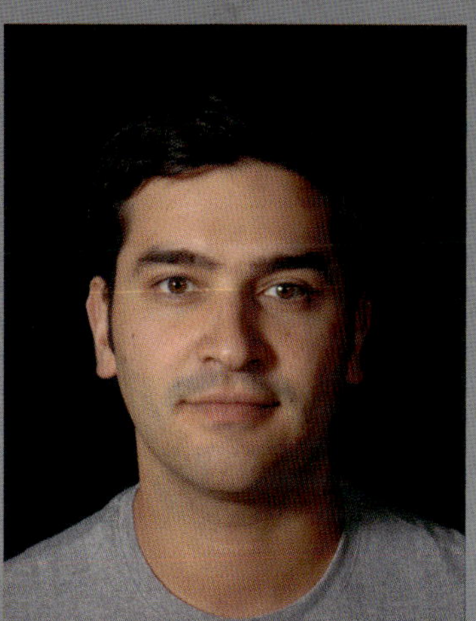

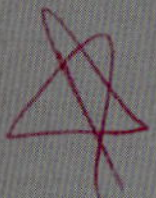

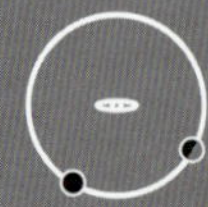

MIXED LIGHT LEVELS

LIGHT 1 (FULL): FROM 30° LEFT

LIGHT 2 (4 BELOW): FROM 60° RIGHT

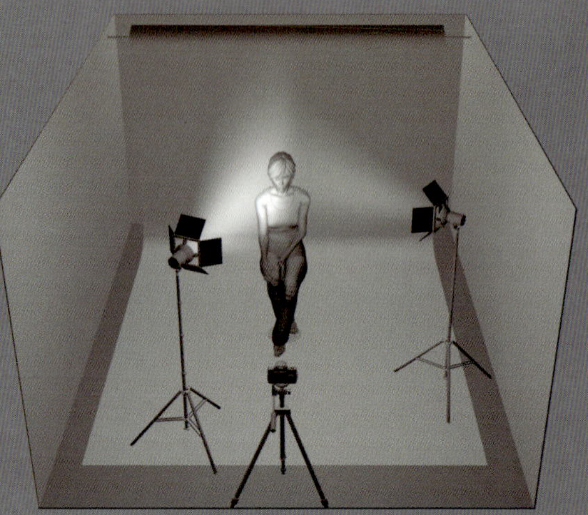

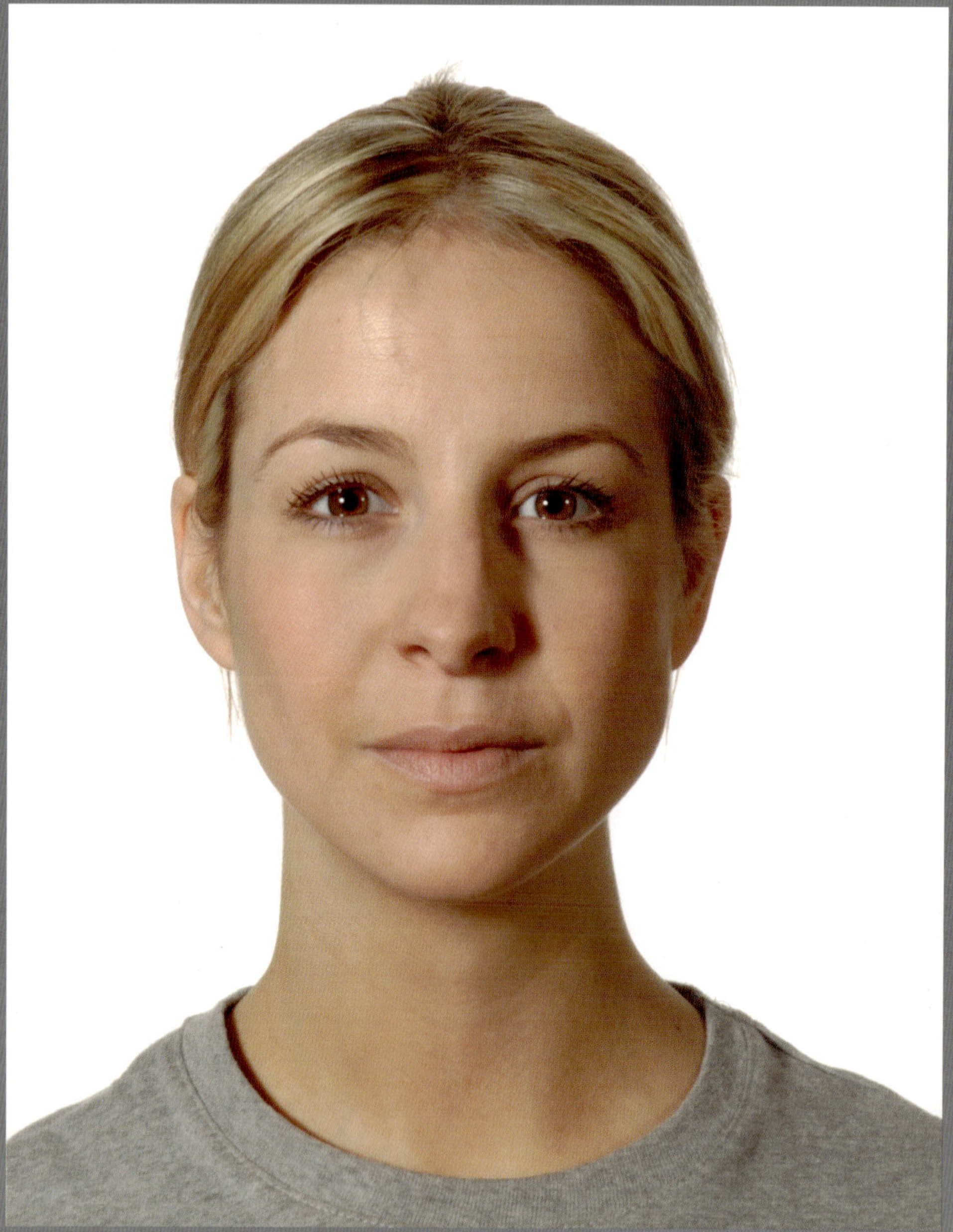

Again, the fill light is set at four stops less than the main light, meaning the shadow areas created by the main light, although filled, remain fairly dark. Increasing the contrast between the two lights is especially effective when you're shooting black and white.

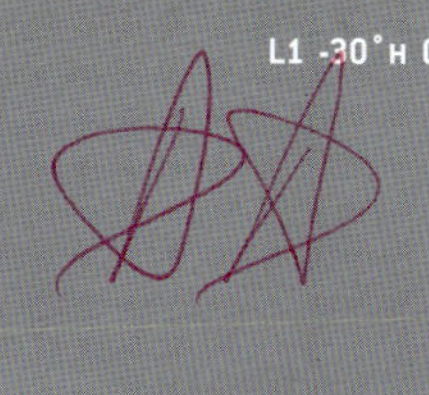

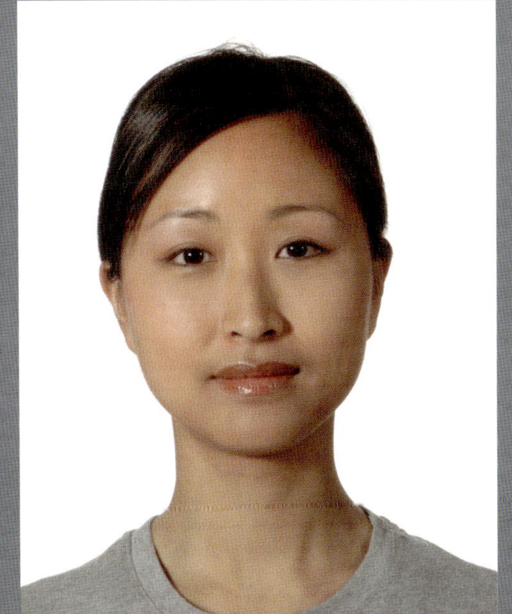

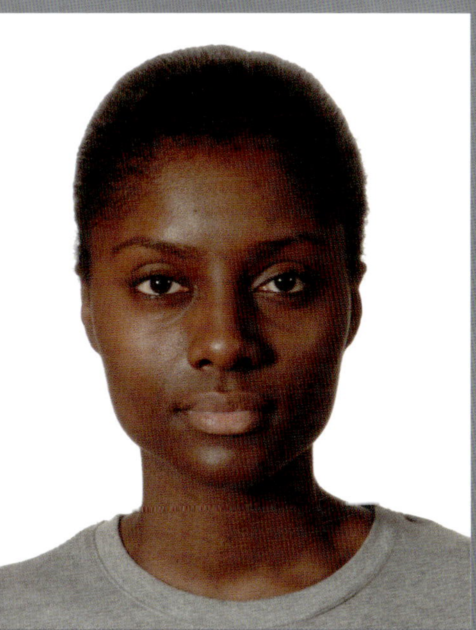

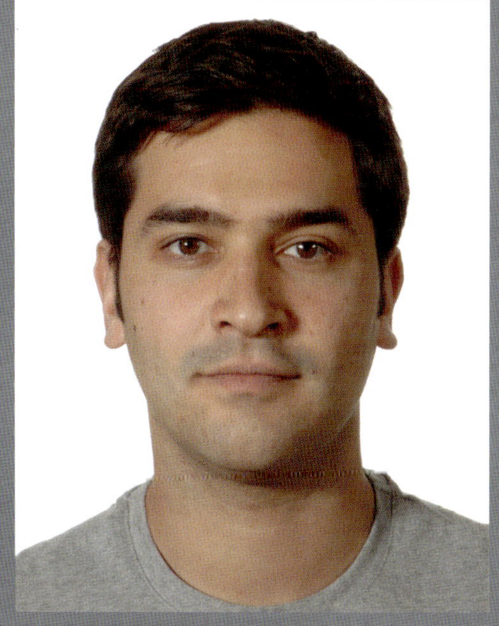

DARK BACKGROUND

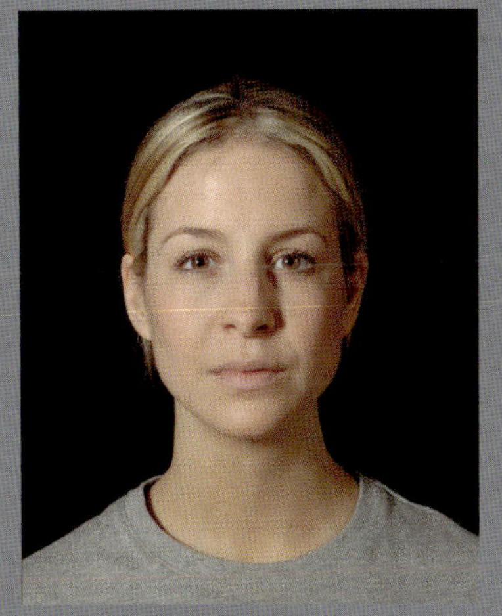

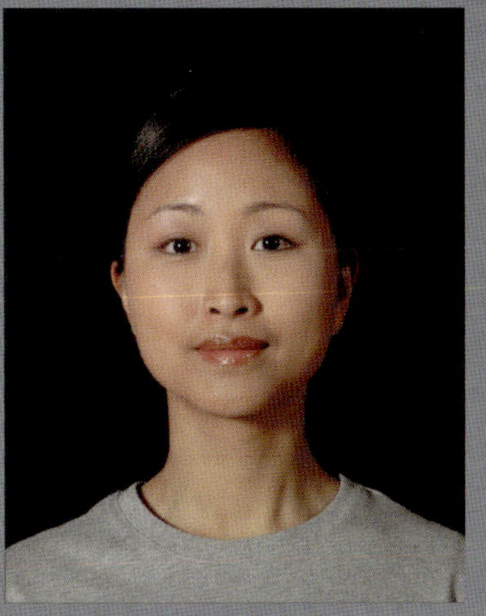

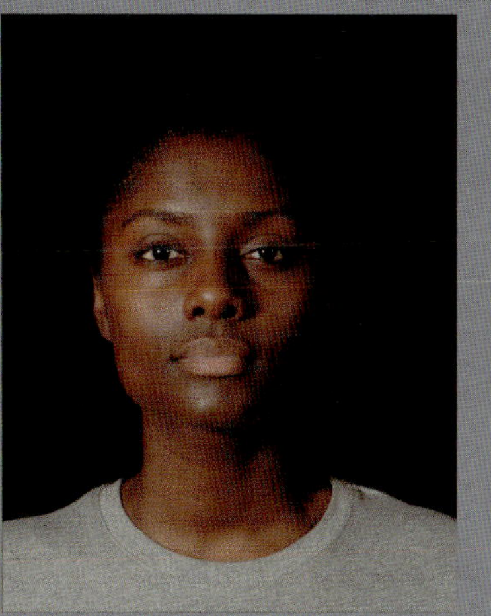

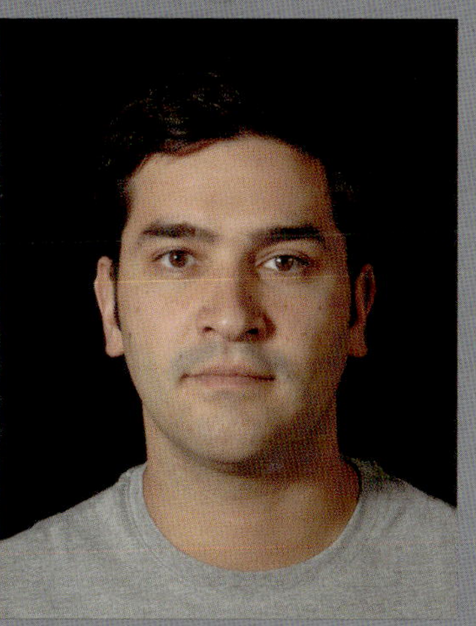

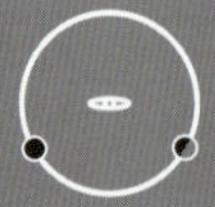

MIXED LIGHT LEVELS

LIGHT 1 (FULL): FROM 60° LEFT

LIGHT 2 (4 BELOW): FROM 60° RIGHT

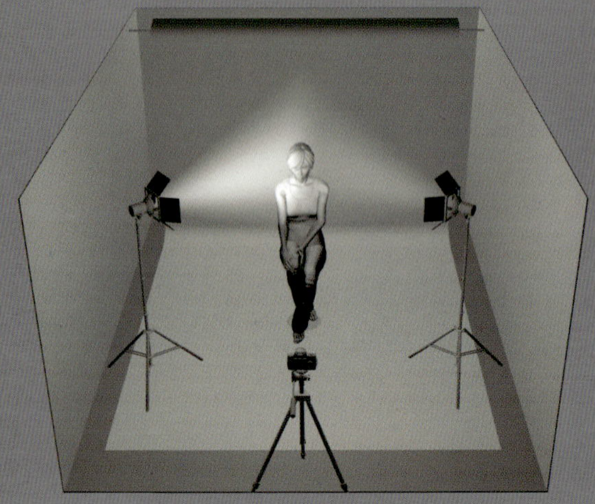

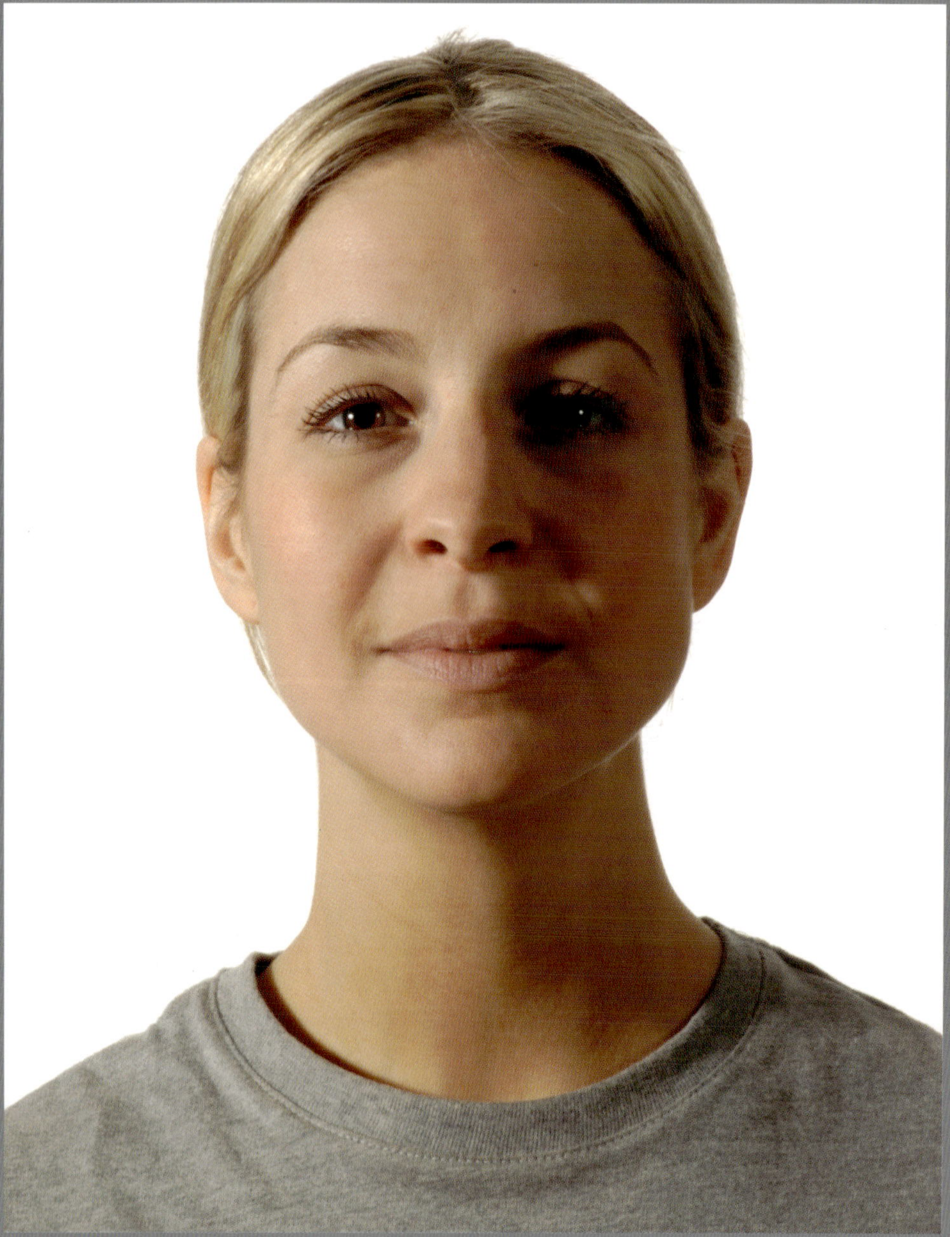

Although the fill light is set four stops lower than the main light, its angle to the subject still produces a bright catchlight in the model's darker (left) eye. The less-powerful fill also creates some much-needed contrast in what would otherwise be an evenly-lit portrait.

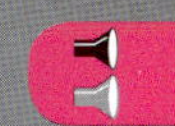

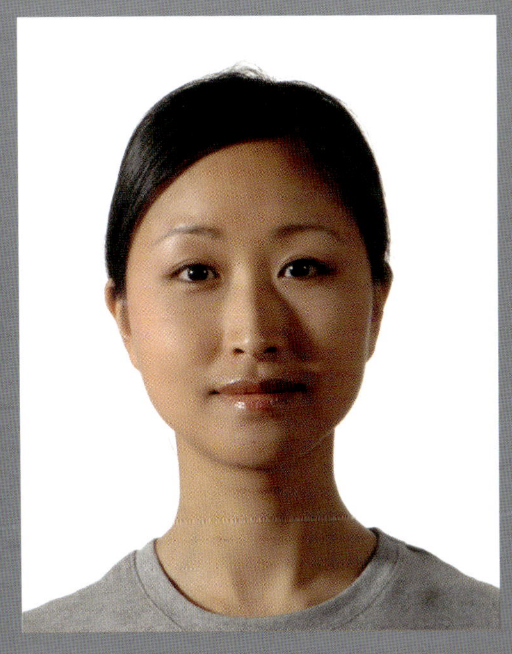

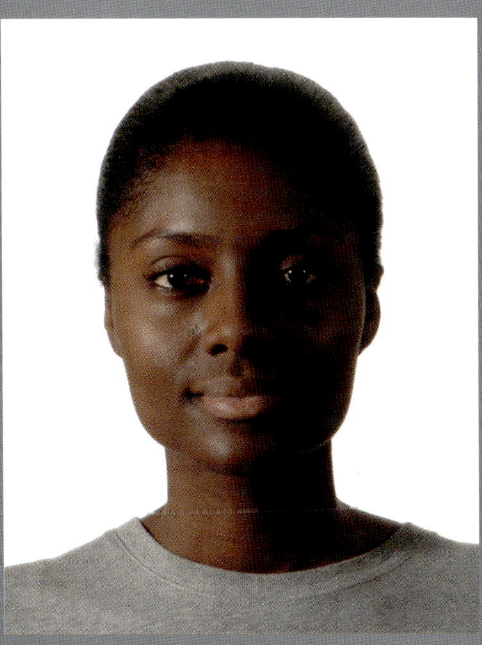

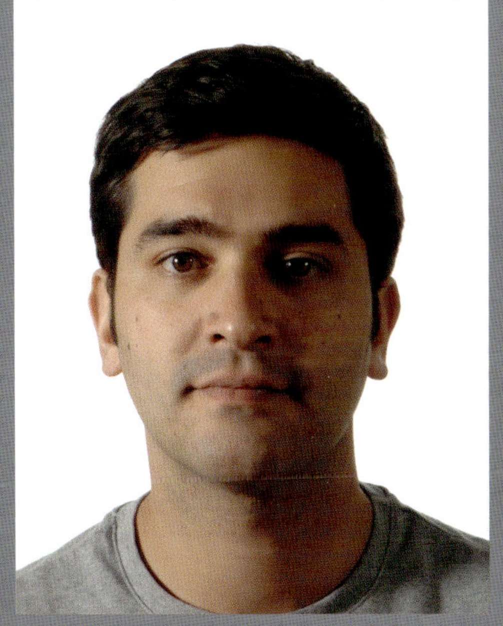

DARK BACKGROUND

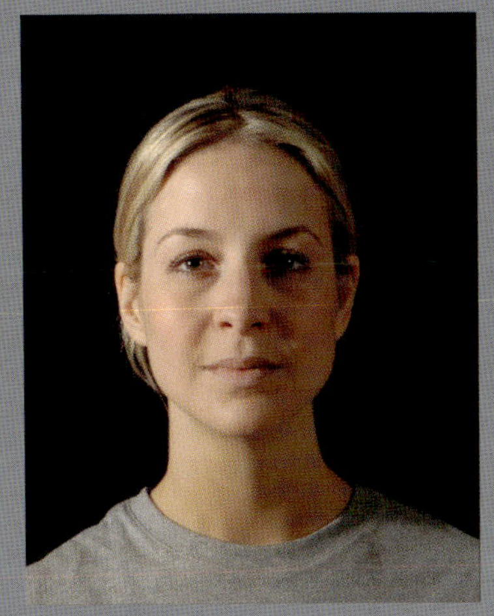

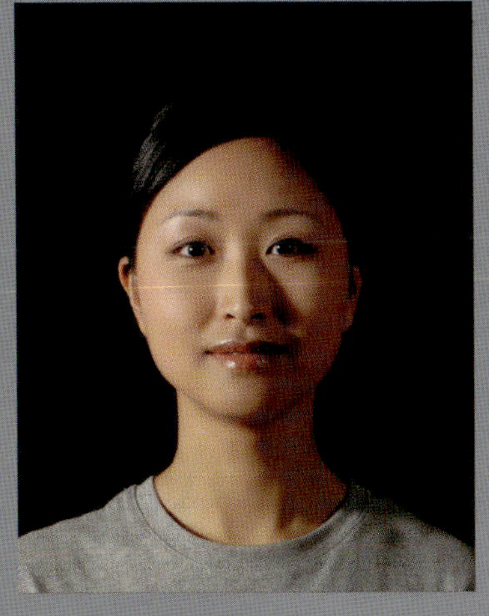

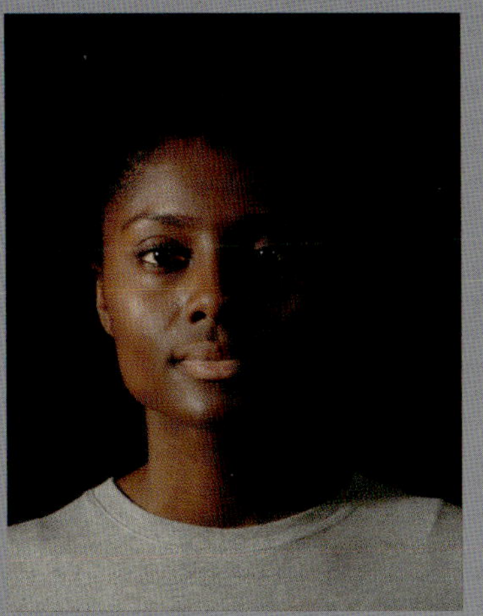

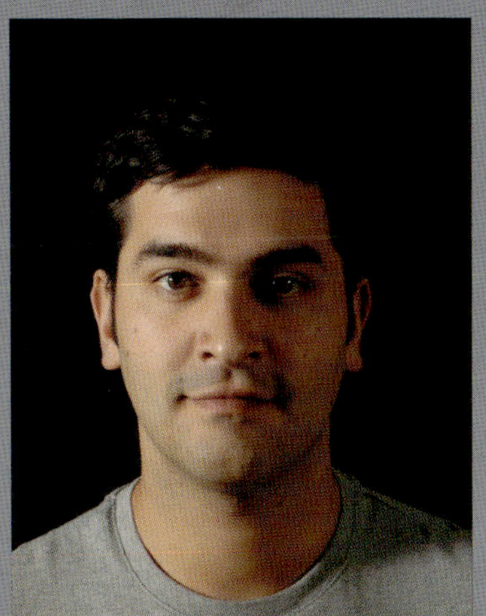

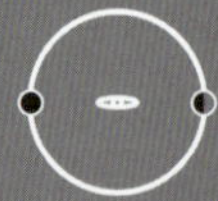

MIXED LIGHT LEVELS

LIGHT 1 (FULL): FROM 90° LEFT

LIGHT 2 (4 BELOW): FROM 90° RIGHT

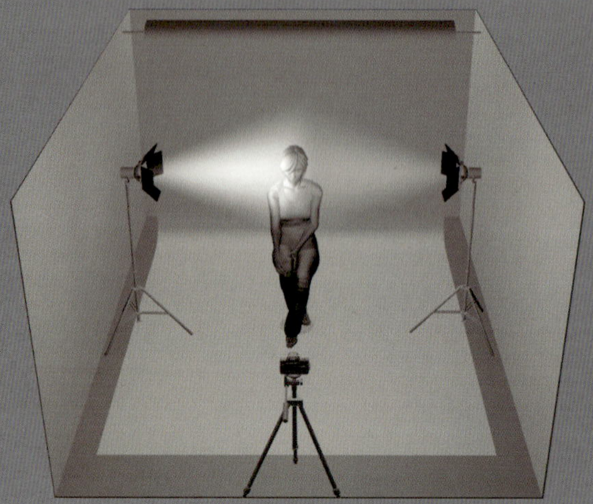

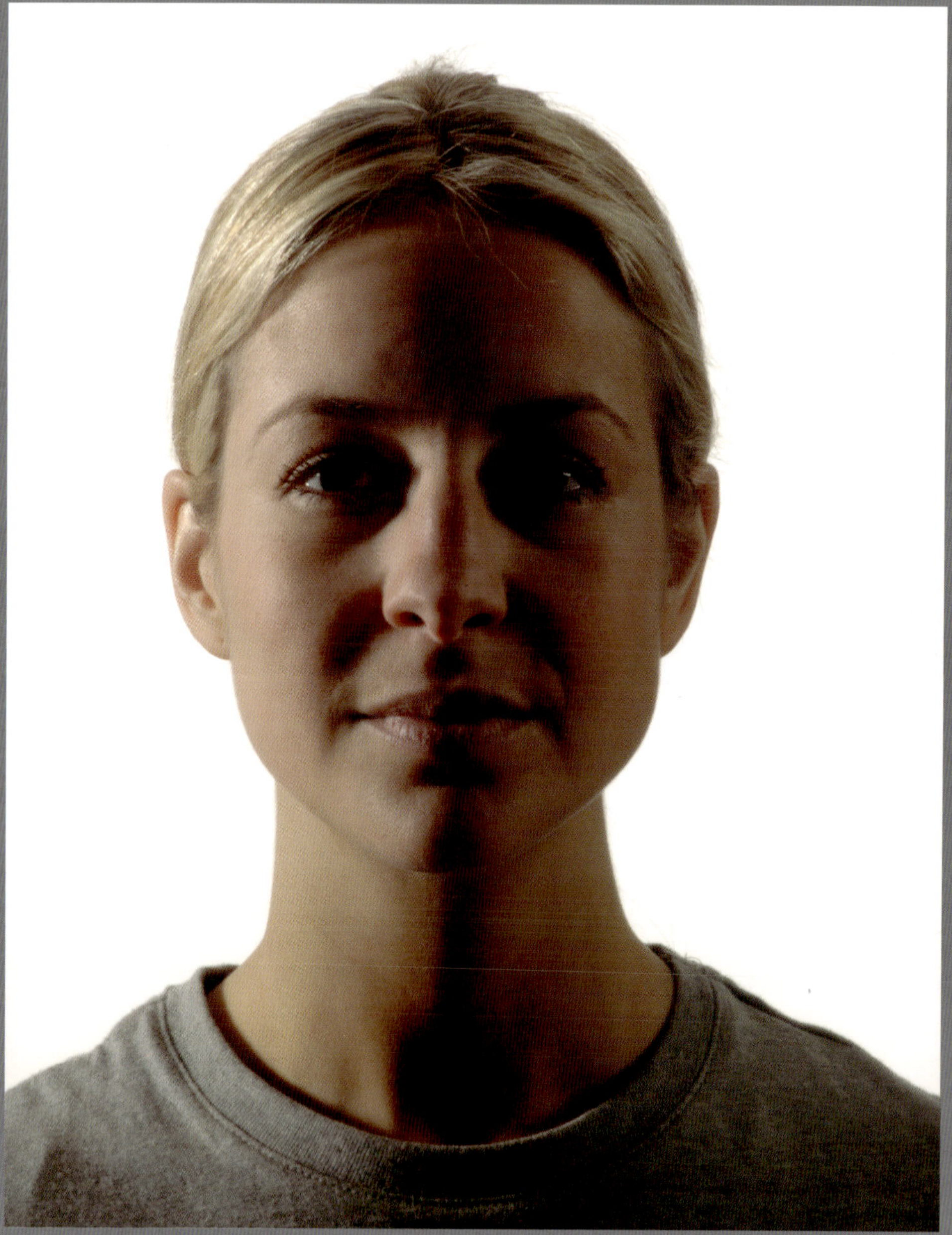

Another symmetrical lighting setup, but two lights set to output different power settings avoid the mirrored lighting effect seen on pages 114–115. However, the distinct shadows around the eyes and cheeks created by the opposed lights remains, as does the dark central "stripe."

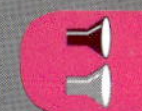

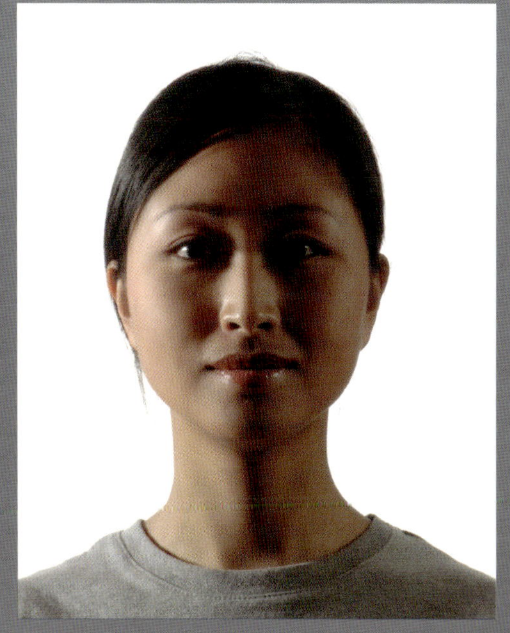

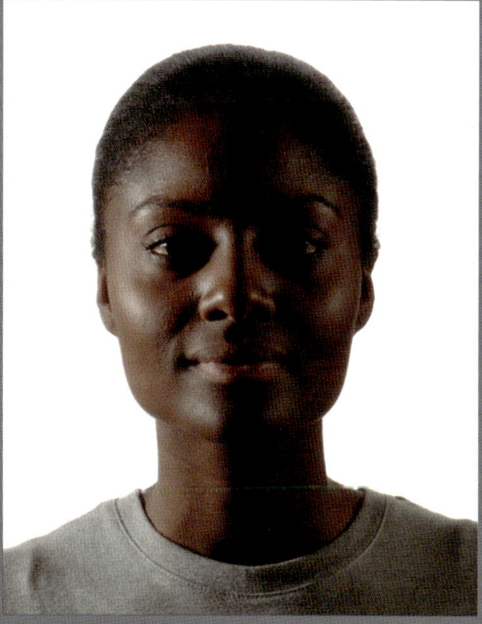

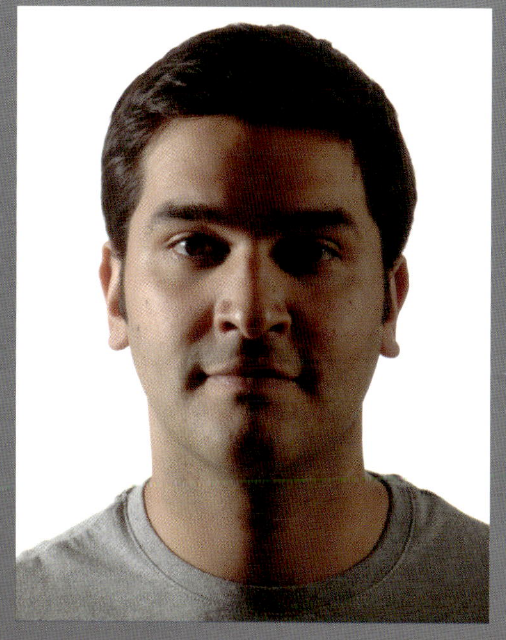

DARK BACKGROUND

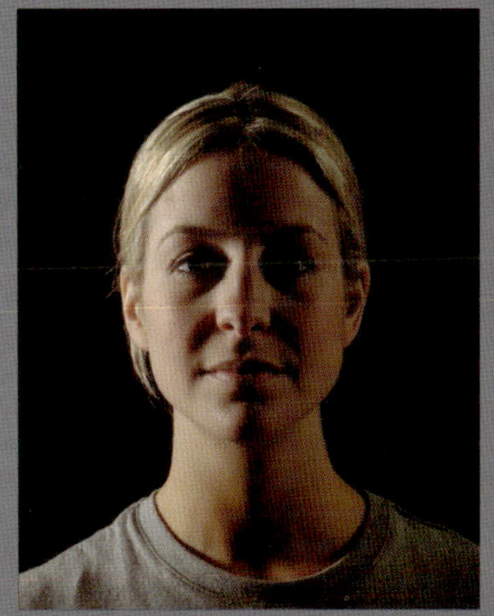

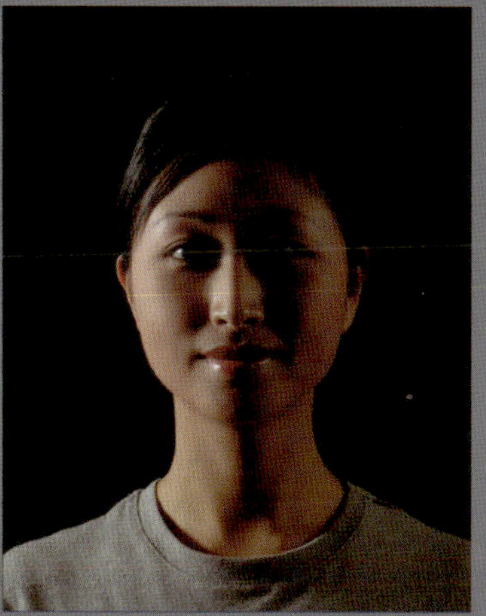

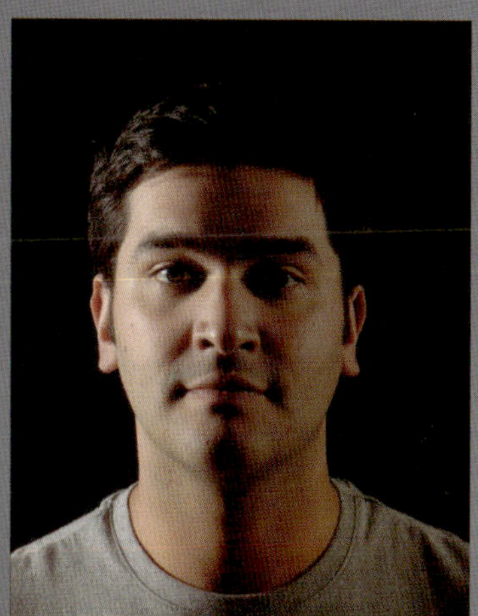

CHAPTER 11

RAISED CAMERA

The potential combinations of lights in terms of the quantity, direction, and power output, plus the many and varied camera angles and heights, means there are near-infinite possibilities for your portrait photography. So far, everything we have done has been based on the camera looking at the subject at eye level—the most common position for portraiture.

In this final section of the book, the camera has been raised above the subject, to give a mild "bird's-eye" perspective. As soon as this happens, your lighting setup is transformed as new shadow and highlight areas are revealed (or concealed), changing once again how your subject appears to the camera.

Of course, this only scratches the surface of the myriad camera positions available to you, so take the time to experiment with where you shoot from, and where you set your lights. Remember, there are no fixed rules—it's all about what works for you and what you are trying to achieve with your portrait photography.

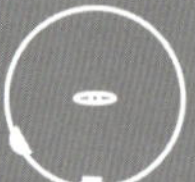

CAMERA RAISED ABOVE SUBJECT

LIGHT 1: FROM 60° LEFT

CAMERA: FROM 0°, 30° ABOVE

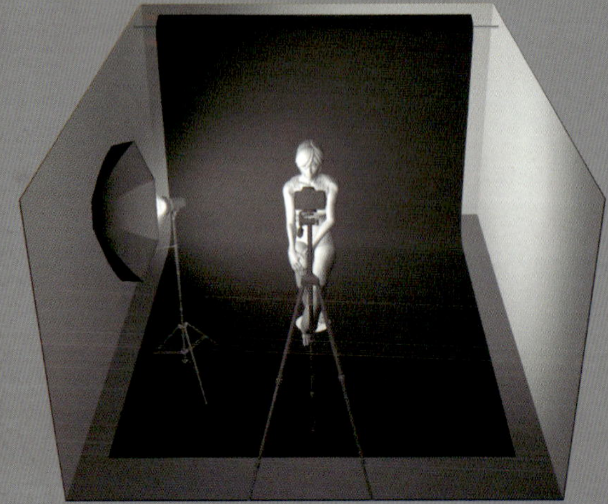

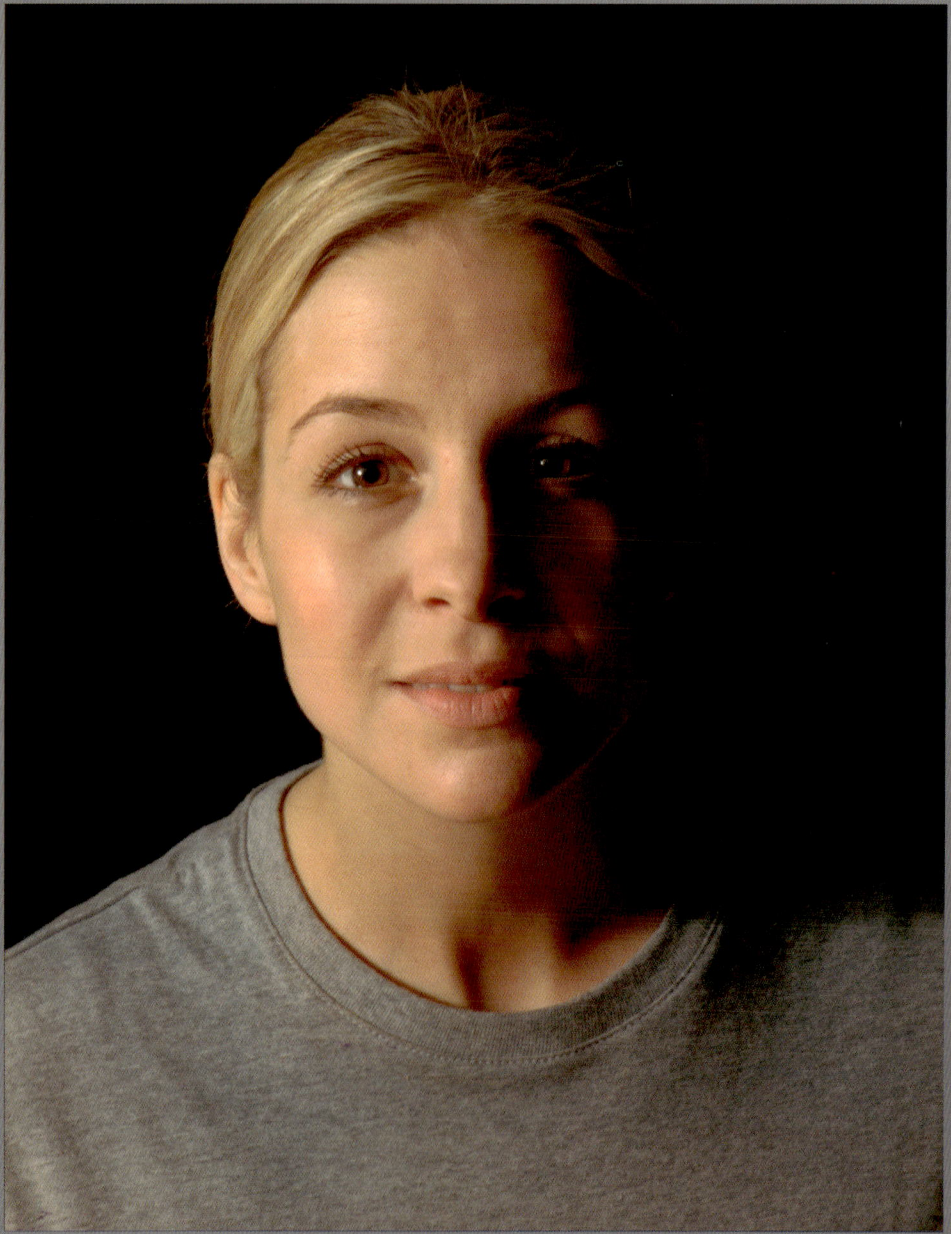

The lighting setup used for these shots may be identical to one of the first shown in the book (see pages 32–33), but the change in the camera angle has created a very different look. Shooting from above appears to shorten the subject's neck, while the left side of the face isn't as dark.

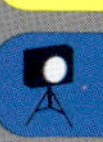

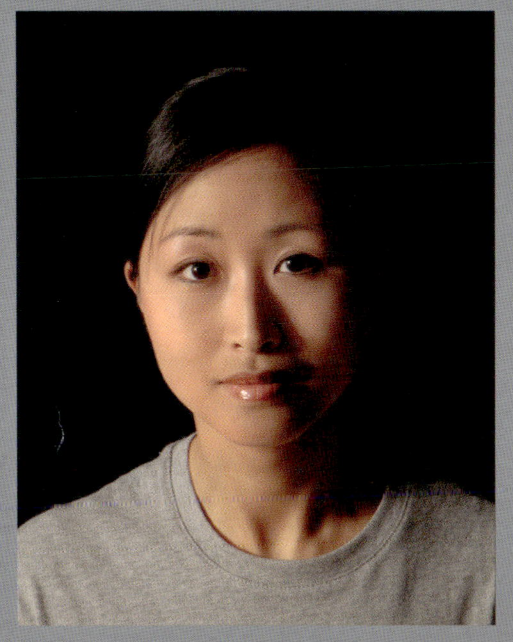

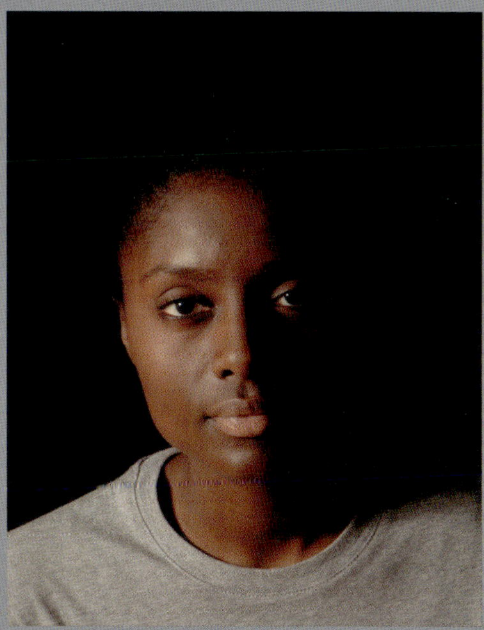

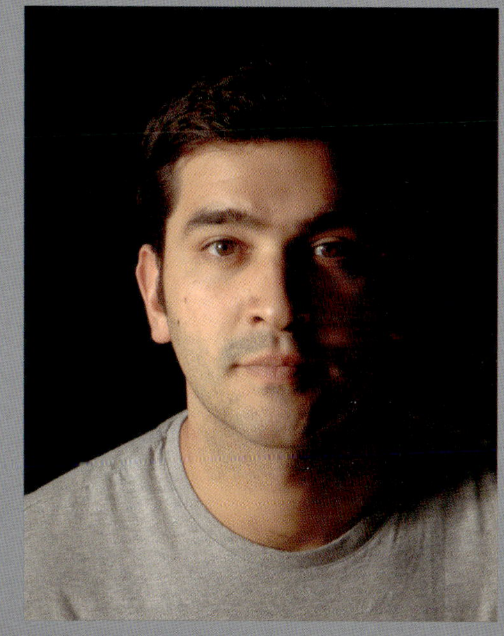

EYES LEVEL

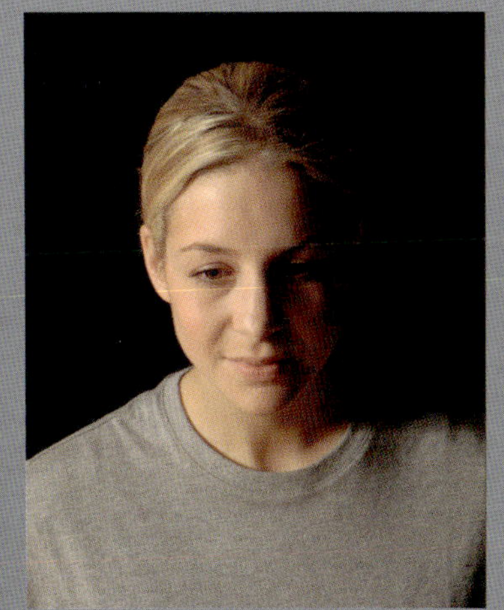

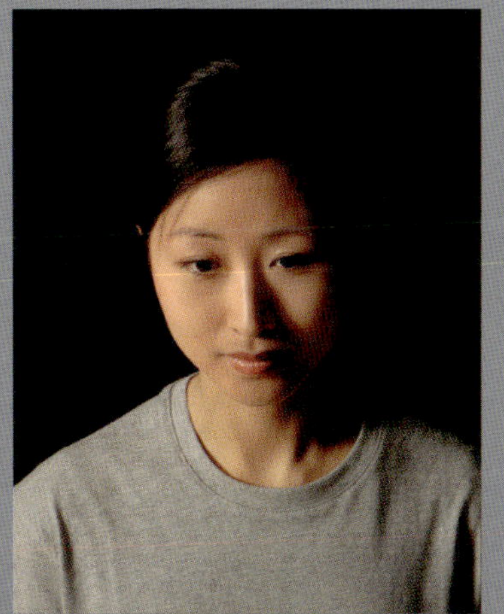

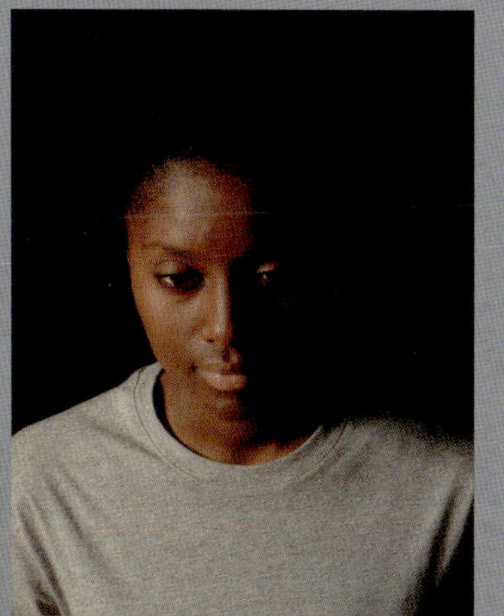

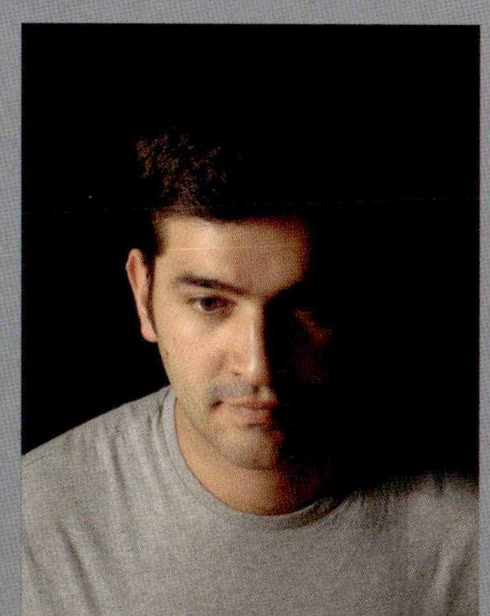

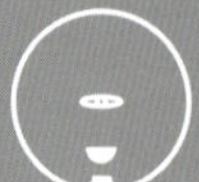

CAMERA RAISED ABOVE SUBJECT

LIGHT 1: FROM 0°

CAMERA: FROM 0°, 30° ABOVE

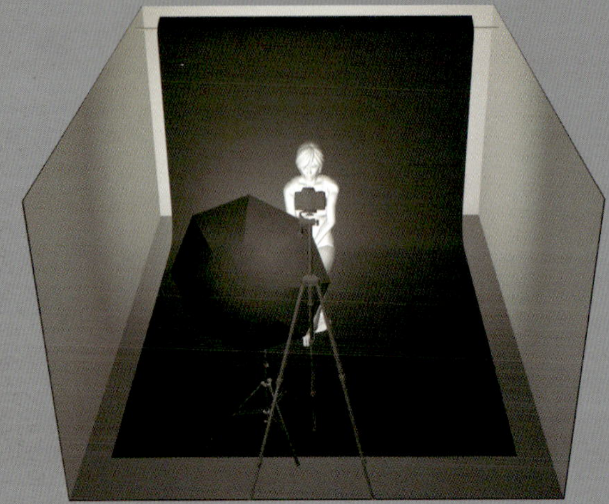

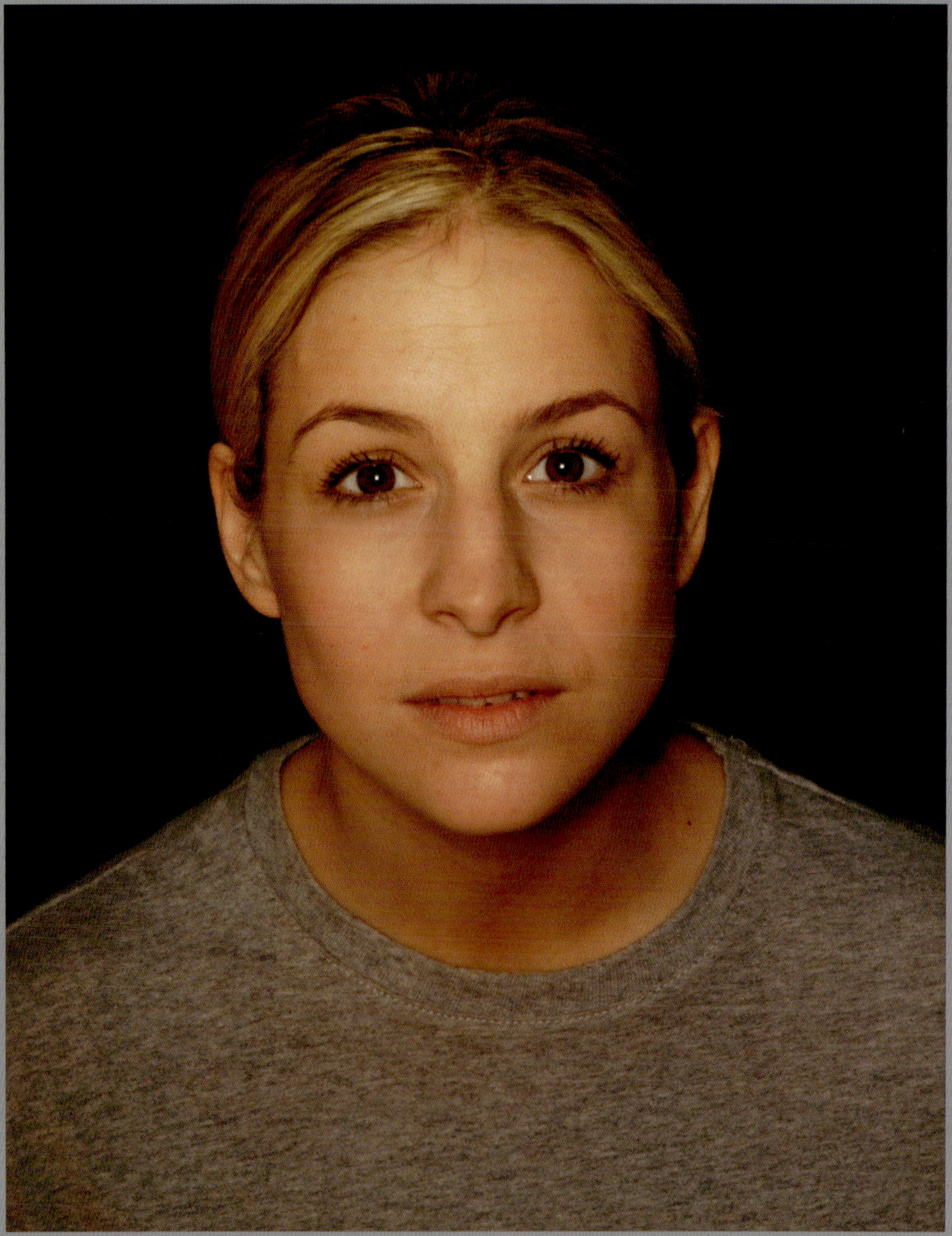

With the camera and a single light set at the same angle, from above the subject, the lighting is flat and even as you would expect. However, the shadow created by the model's chin is larger and softer than it is when the camera is at eye level (see pages 36–37), which subtly draws greater attention to the face.

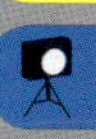

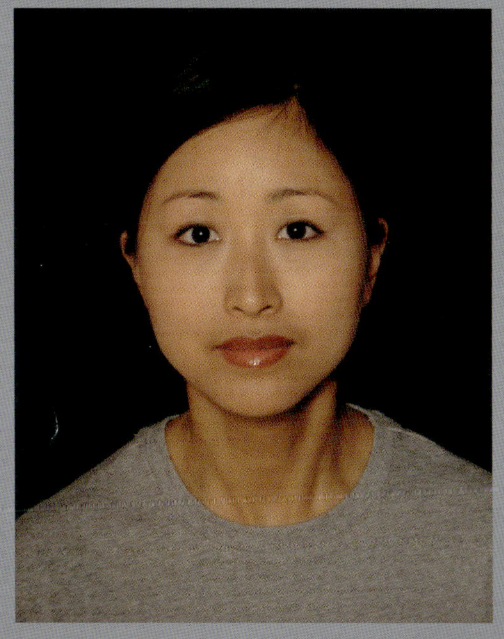

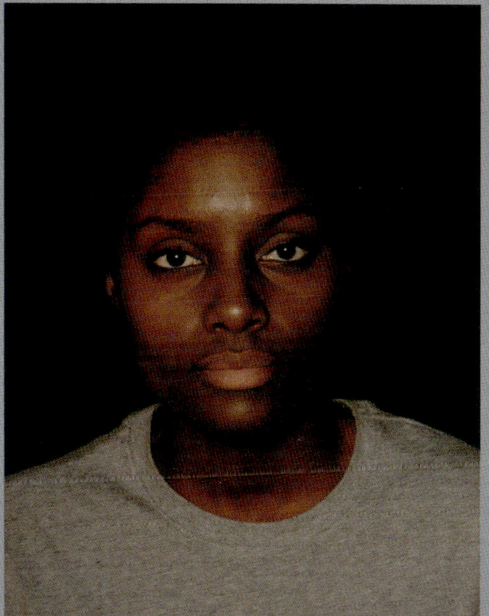

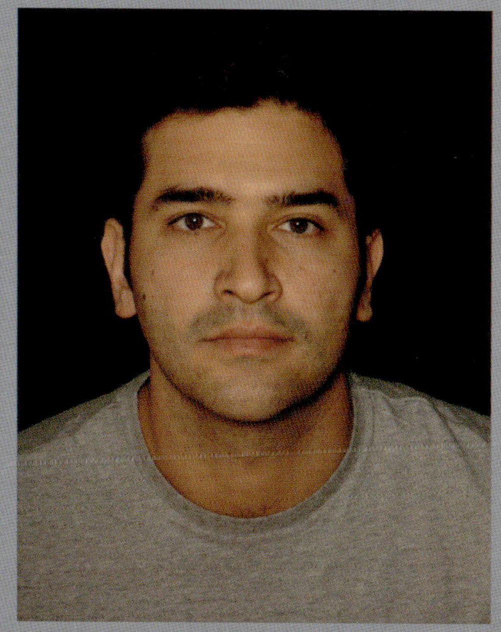

EYES LEVEL

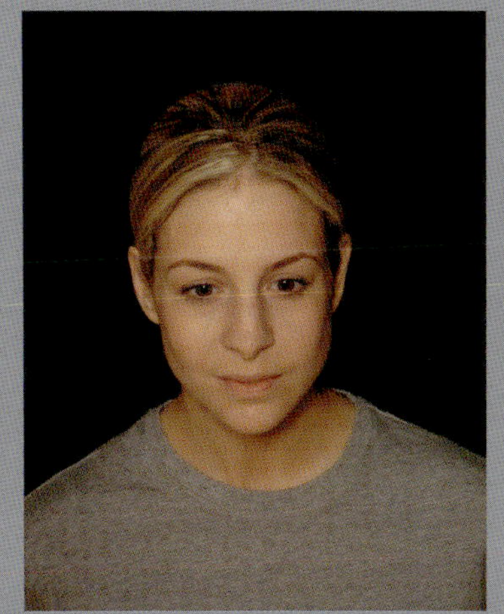

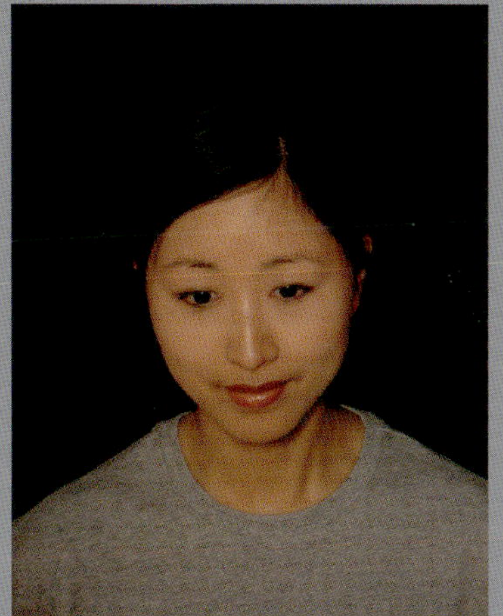

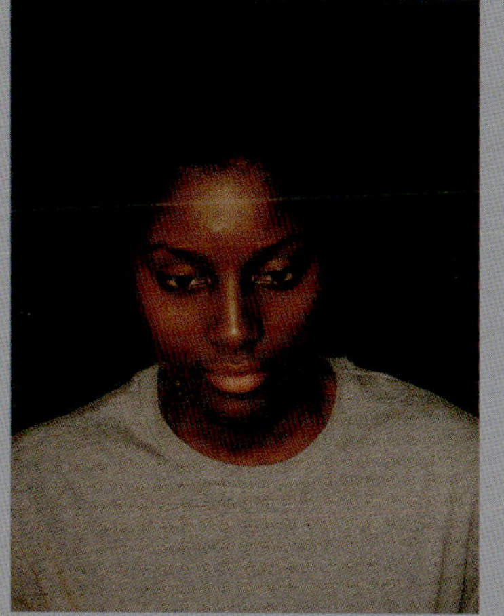

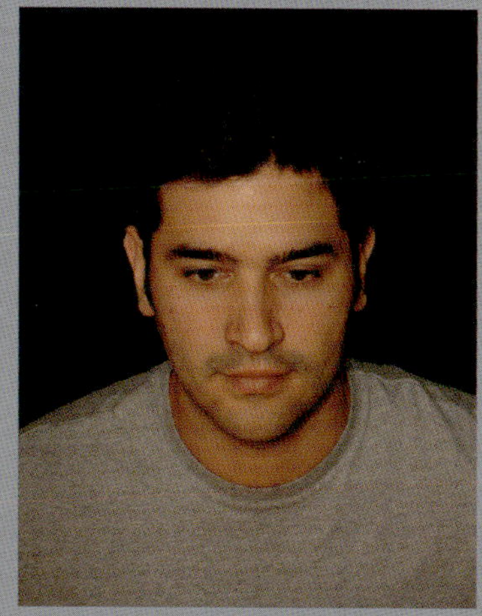

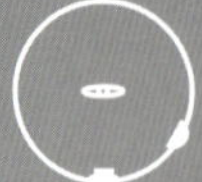

CAMERA RAISED ABOVE SUBJECT

LIGHT 1: FROM 60° RIGHT, 30° ABOVE

CAMERA: FROM 0°, 30° ABOVE

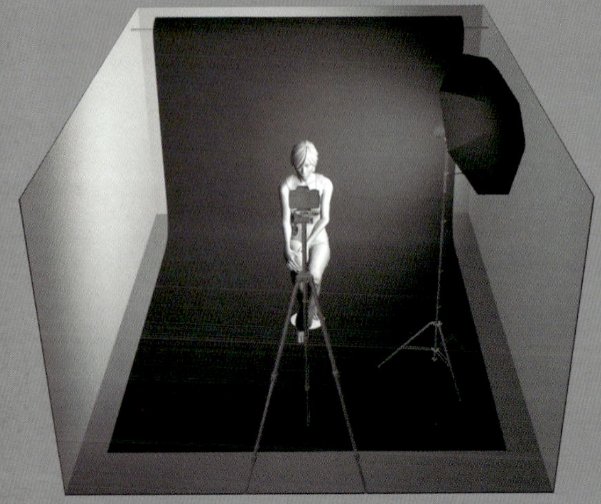

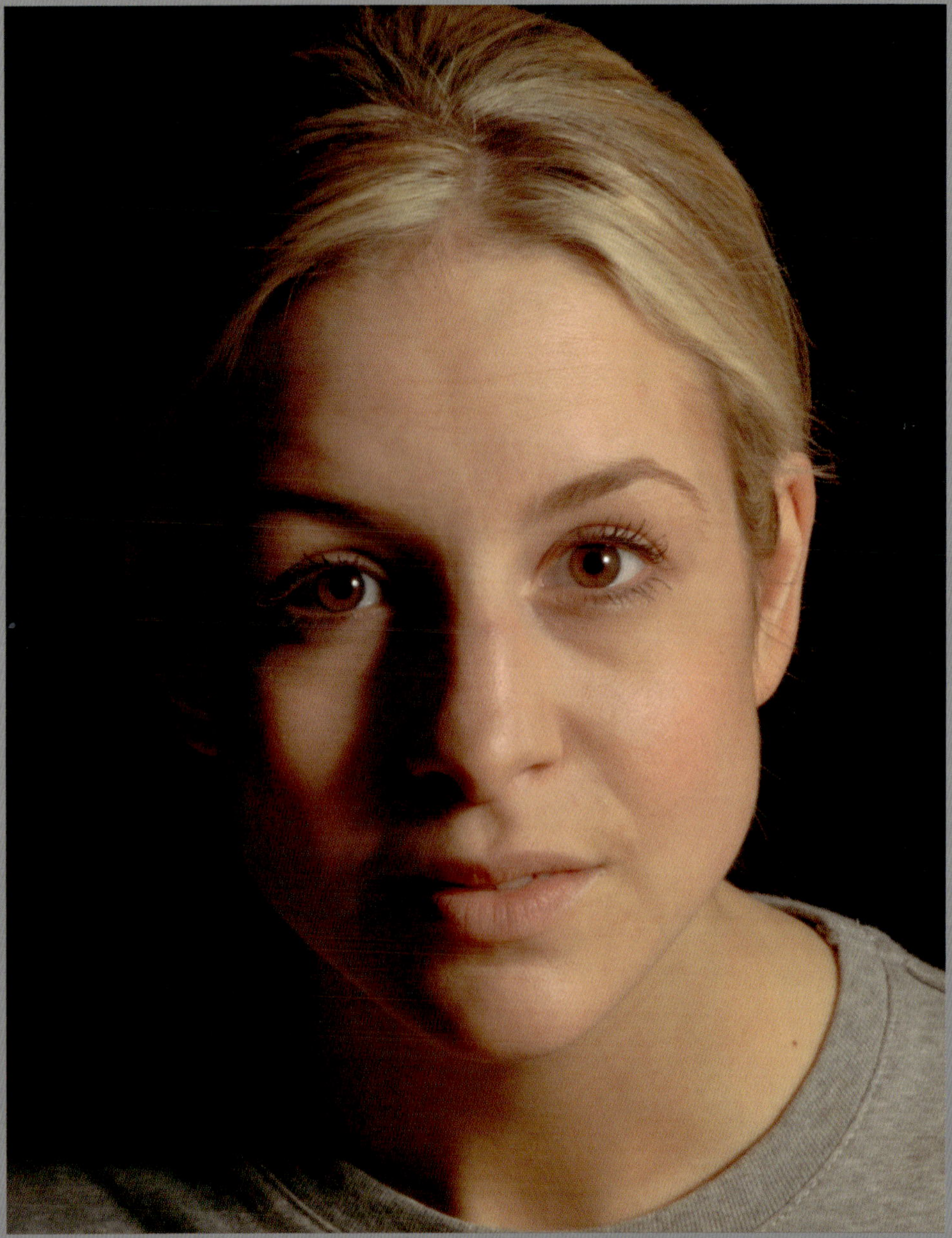

Both the light and the camera are above the subject, with the light set at a 60-degree angle. Even without a reflector to fill in the shadows, the result is flattering, especially when the model is looking up at the camera: both eyes are visible and contain catchlights that help prevent the portrait looking lifeless.

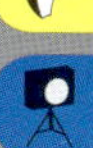

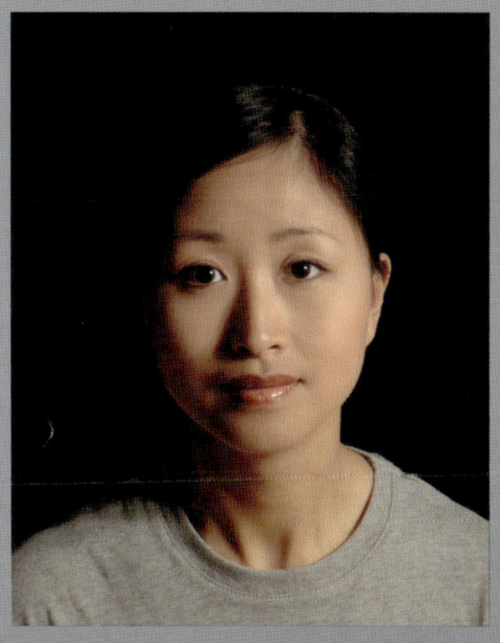

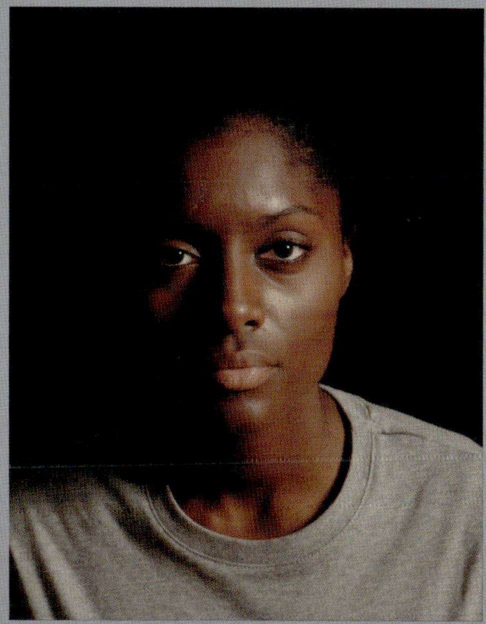

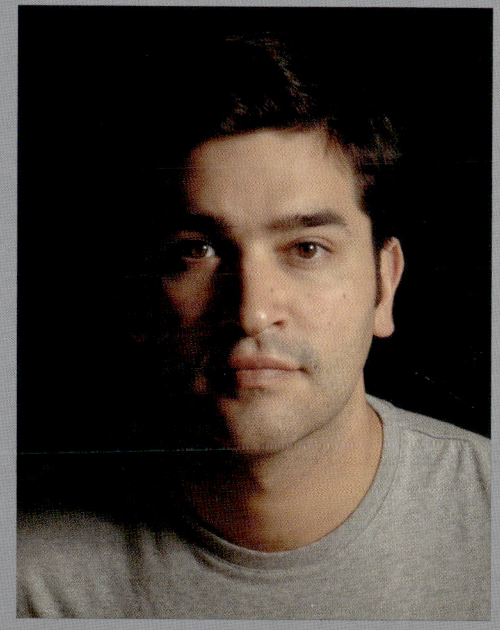

EYES LEVEL

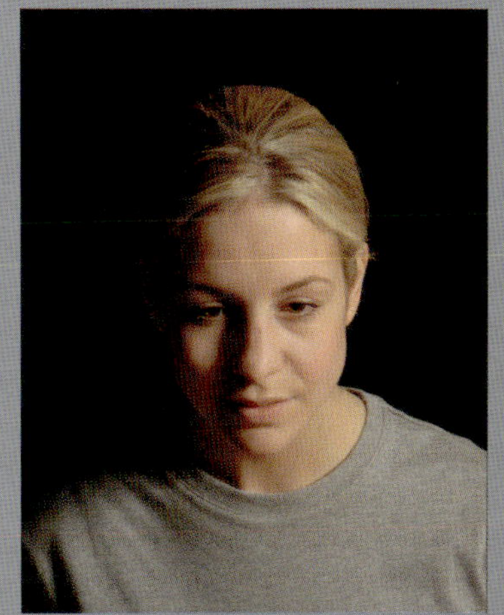

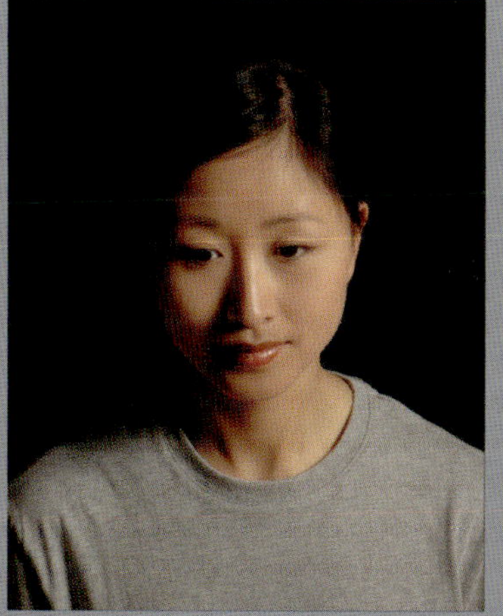

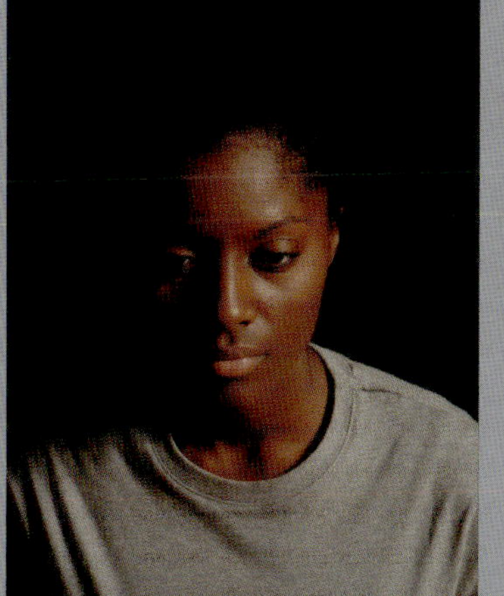

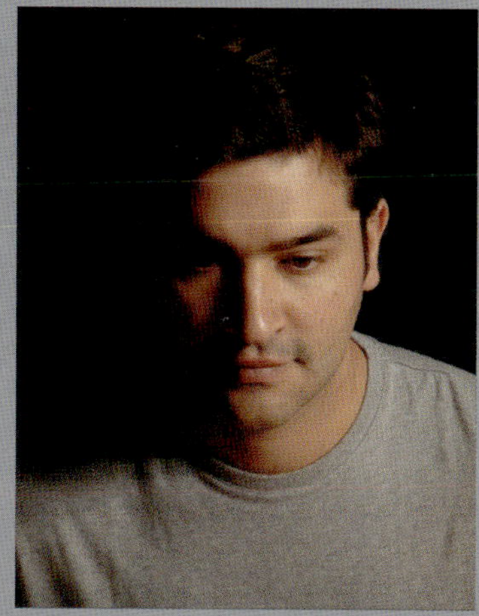

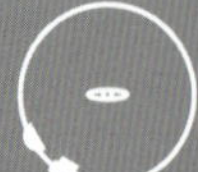

CAMERA RAISED ABOVE SUBJECT

LIGHT 1: FROM 60° LEFT

CAMERA: FROM 30° LEFT, 30° ABOVE

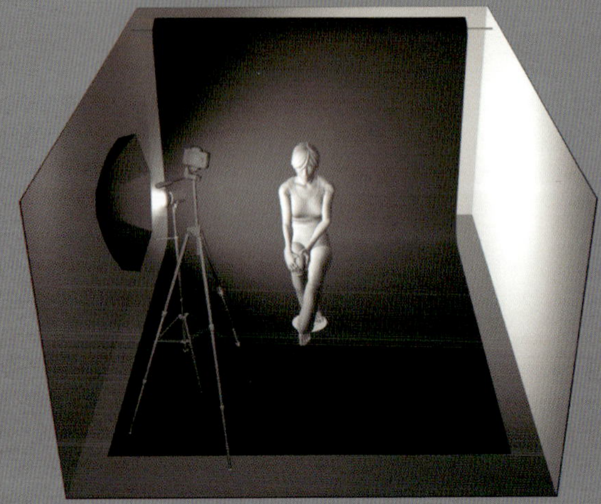

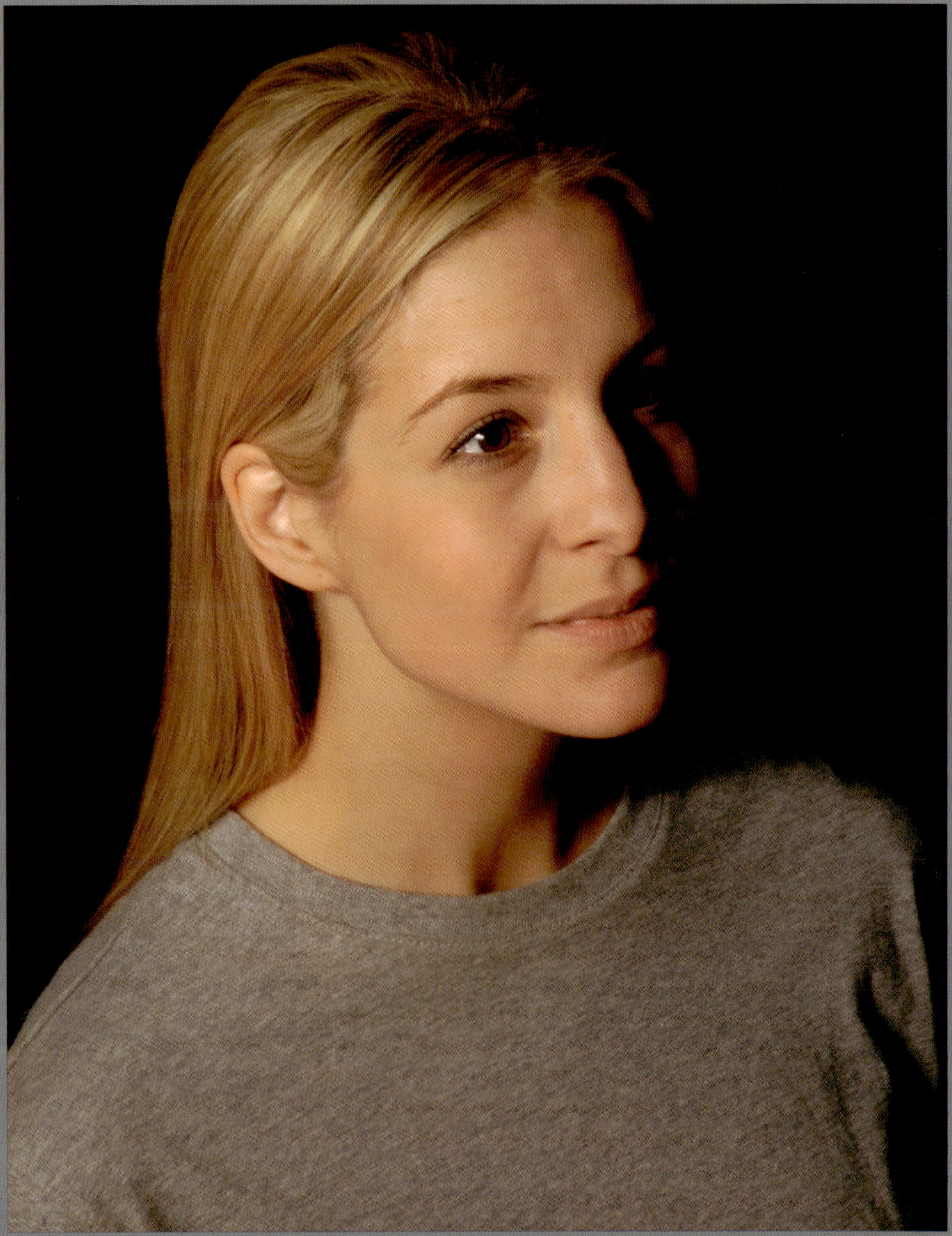

Portraits don't have to be taken from directly in front of the subject, and having your model turn away from the camera slightly, or moving the camera, is another way of changing the dynamic of the shot. You will most likely lose eye contact with your model, but this isn't always necessary.

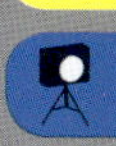

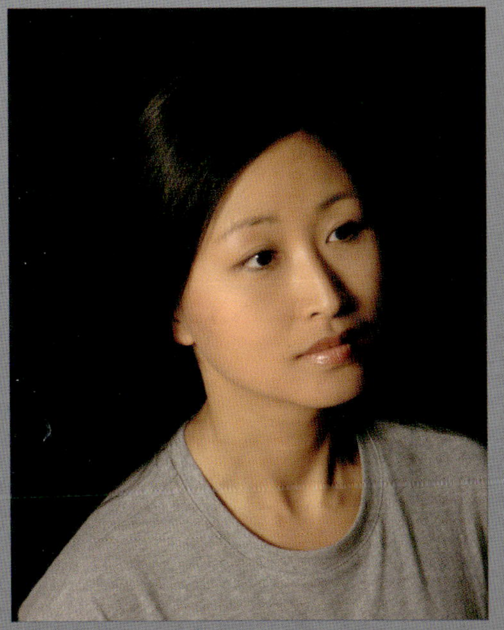

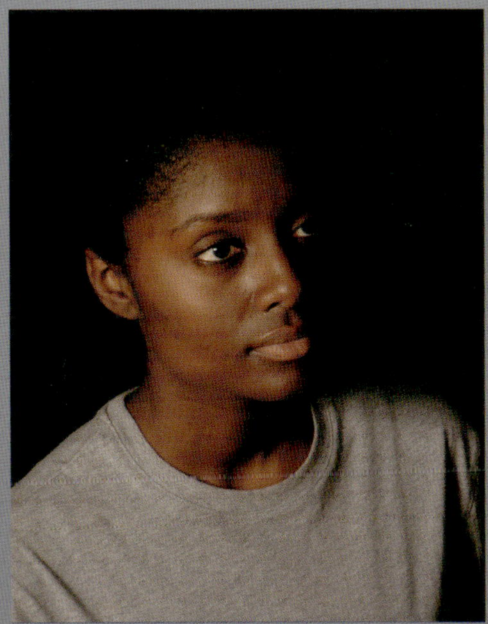

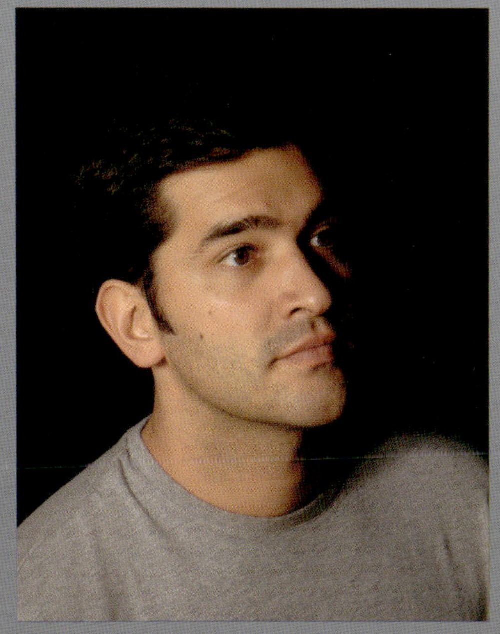

EYES LEVEL

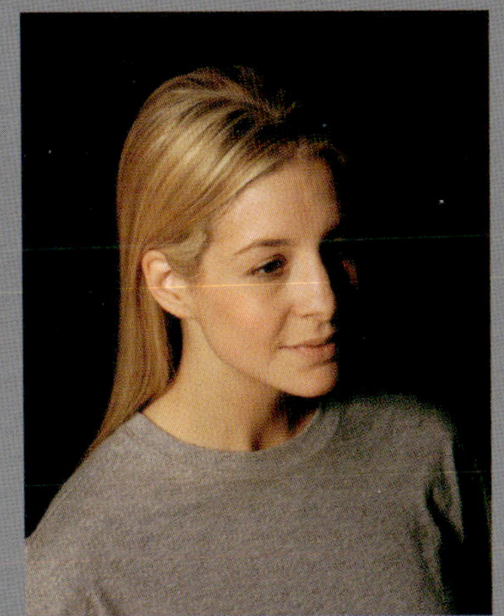

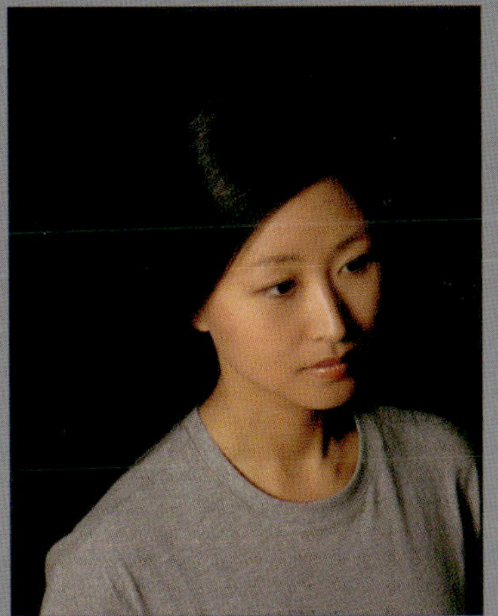

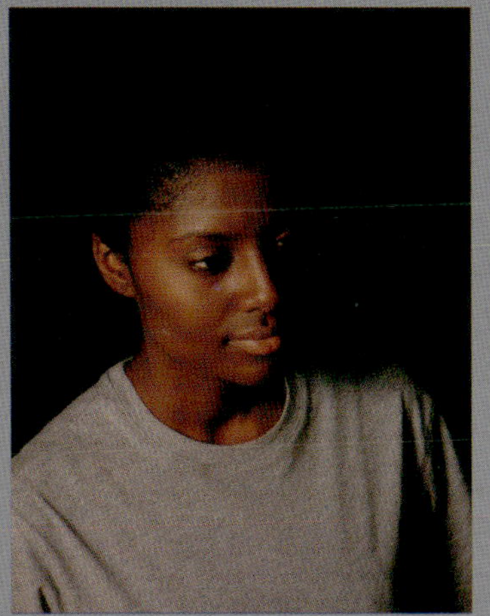

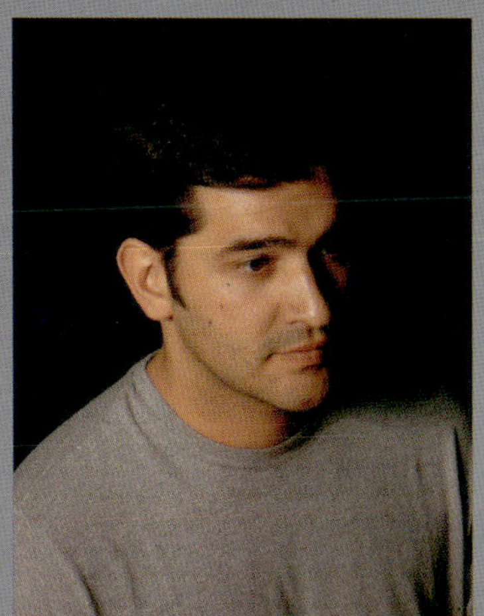

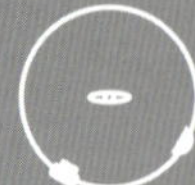

CAMERA RAISED ABOVE SUBJECT

LIGHT 1: FROM 60° RIGHT

CAMERA: FROM 30° LEFT, 30° ABOVE

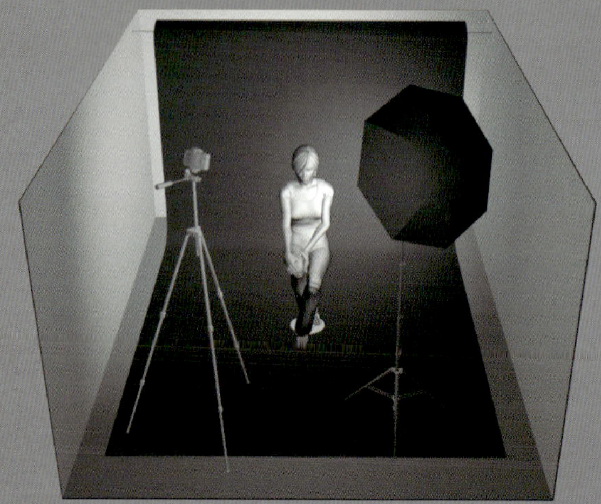

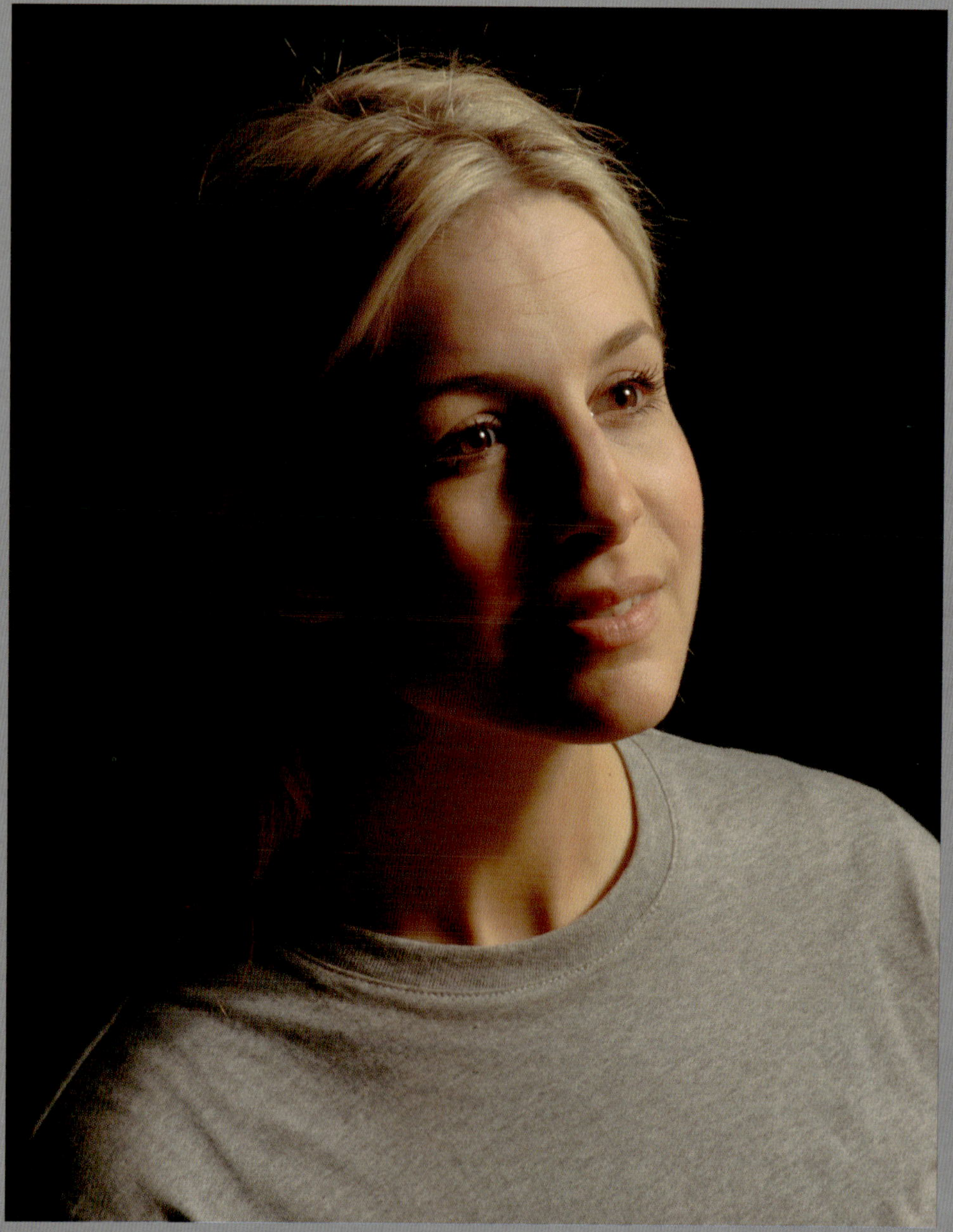

In this final setup, the camera is effectively photographing the shaded side of the model's face, which creates an interesting portrait. A triangle of light beneath the eye closest to the camera defines the subjects facial features, and although much of the subject is in shadow, catchlights appear in the eyes when the model tilts their head upward.

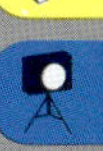

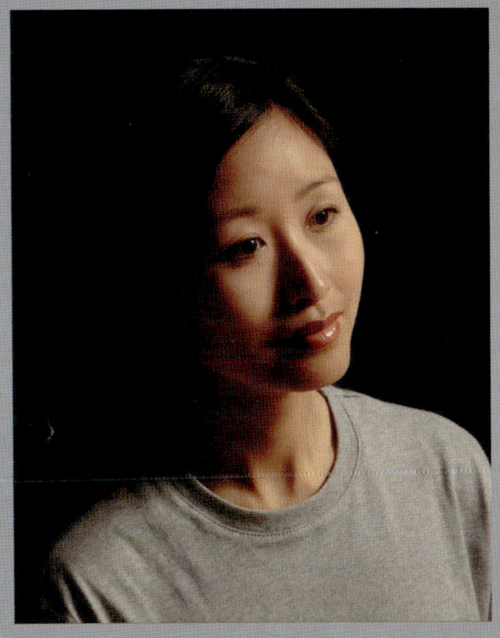

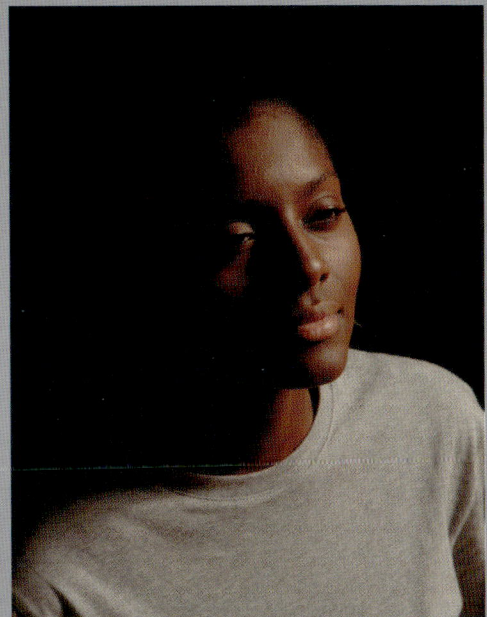

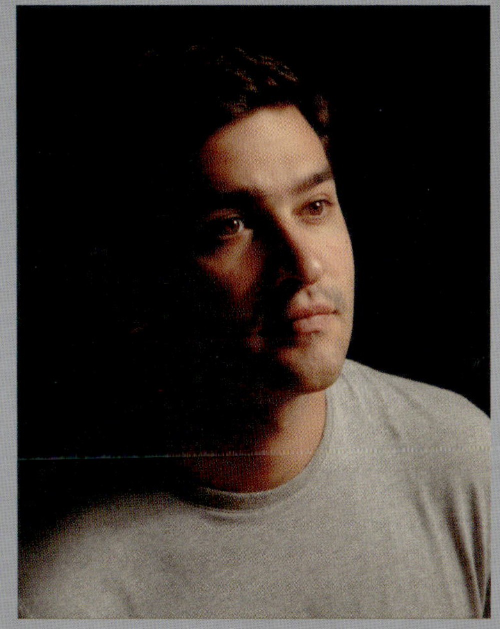

EYES LEVEL

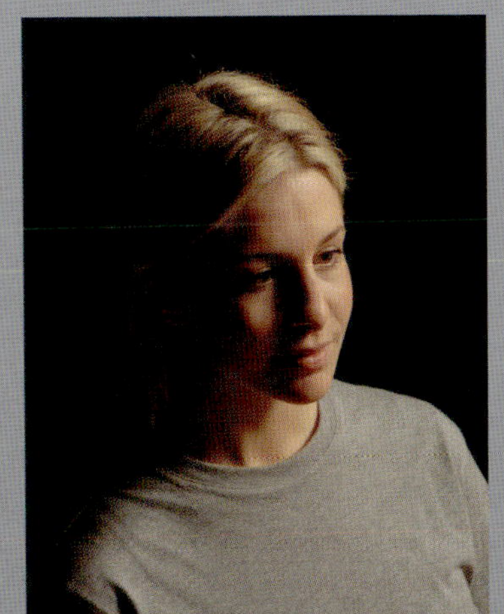

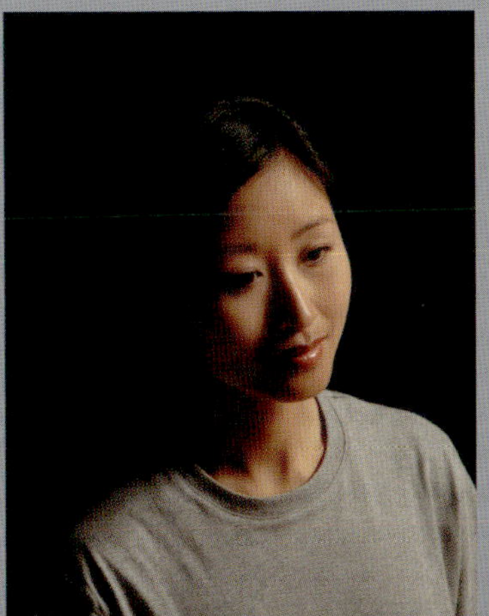

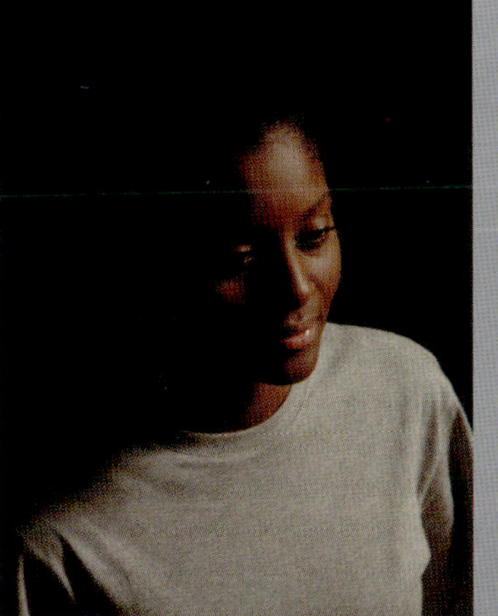

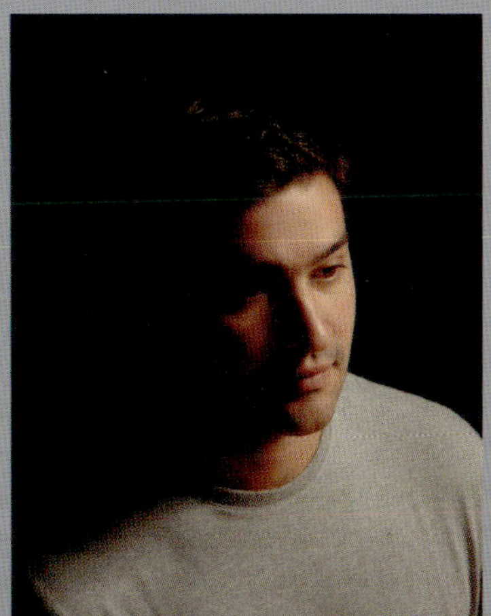

GLOSSARY

Ambient light: The light that already exists in the location you are shooting in before you add flash or other light sources. Outdoors, the ambient light is likely to be daylight, while indoors it could be incandescent, fluorescent, daylight, or a mix of these. The strength and color temperature of the ambient light needs to be considered if you want to add to it, or mix it with photographic lighting.

Aperture: The opening behind the camera lens that controls the amount of light reaching the imaging sensor or film. The aperture is given as an *f*-number, or *f*-stop, a fraction representing the focal length of the lens divided by the diameter of the aperture opening (a 10mm aperture in an 80mm lens is an *f*-stop of *f*/8, for example, while an *f*-stop of *f*/16 on the same lens would denote an aperture of 5mm). The wider the aperture (larger hole / lower *f*-stop number), the shallower the depth of field in an image. The smaller the aperture (smaller hole / higher *f*-stop), the greater the depth of field.

Barn doors: A light modifier that attaches to the front of a lamp, typically comprising of four adjustable flaps ("doors") that are set at right angles to each other and can be opened and closed to regulate where the light falls. Common on incandescent and other continuous light sources used in movie and television production, but less commonly used on flash units.

Beauty dish: A form of reflector dish that utilizes a small panel immediately in front of the light source to bounce the light back into the dish before it strikes the subject. This produces a diffuse, shadow-free light that is ideal for soft, "beauty" style portraits.

Boom arm: A rigid, lightweight pole used in conjunction with a light stand to offer greater flexibility in positioning a light. Can be used laterally, allowing a light to be above the subject without the stand appearing in shot. Needs to be carefully counterweighted so the light is balanced.

Bounced light: Light that is reflected back on to the subject or scene, rather than being used directly. Bouncing a light increases its diffusion, creating a softer light and less harsh shadows than direct light. With a hotshoe flash, a common practice is to bounce the flash off a ceiling or wall. With studio lighting, the same can be achieved, although if the area you are shooting in is large, a reflector can be used instead. Shooting with an umbrella is also a form of bounced light.

Bracketing: Refers to making a number of exposures above and below the recommended setting to be certain that one photograph is correctly exposed. For example, if the metered exposure is 1/125 sec at *f*/8, two further exposures at *f*/11 and *f*/5.6 might be made at 1/125 sec. Bracketing can also be achieved with the shutter speed, although only with continuous light sources—with flash, you should always bracket using the aperture.

Colormeter: A meter that provides a precise measurement of the color temperature of light, often in degrees Kelvin. Handheld colormeters offer the greatest precision. The automatic white balance system in a digital camera uses a colormeter to determine and correct for the color of ambient light.

Color temperature: The color of a light source, measured in (degrees) Kelvin. All light has a different color temperature, from dull red (1900K) through orange, to yellow, white, and blue (10,000K), with the most encountered by photographers being daylight (5500–5600K) and incandescent (3200K). With a digital camera the color temperature is taken into account by the camera's automatic white balance system, or by choosing a predetermined value (daylight, cloudy, shade, incandescent, and so on). In film photography, a colormeter is needed to determine the color temperature, with color correction filters used on the lens to match the light to the color film being used (typically daylight-balanced).

Contrast: The range of tones across an image from dark to light. High contrast images will have strong, black shadow areas and pure white highlights. Contrast ratio: The ratio between the brightest and darkest parts of an image, often measured in *f*-stops. If the contrast ratio exceeds the dynamic range of the camera, then the shadows or highlights (or both) will not record any detail, depending on the exposure used.

Depth of field: The distance in front of, and behind, the point of focus that appears sharp in an image. Depth of field is not equidistant from the focus point, instead extending approximately 1/3 in front of the focus point and 2/3 behind it. A wide aperture results in a shallow depth of field, while small apertures produce a deeper depth of field.

Dichroic filter: A specialist filter used on incandescent lights to convert the color temperature from 3200k to 5600k, or daylight. These glass-like filters are designed to withstand the heat created by tungsten lighting and also contain protective UV filtration. More robust than a gel.

Diffuse light: A softened light that typically gives more even coverage and less shadows. Softboxes, umbrellas, beauty dishes, and reflectors all help diffuse a light, as will shooting through a gauze or mesh scrim.

Dynamic range: In a camera, this is a measurement of the range from light to dark that the sensor (or film) can record detail in with a single exposure. Often given as a range of stops, where the number refers to the number of stops between the highlight and shadow areas. For example, a camera with a 9-stop dynamic range can record detail in highlights that are 9-stops brighter than the shadows (or vice versa). The greater the camera's dynamic range, the better-suited it is to recording detail in high contrast scenes.

Fill light: In a lighting setup, a fill light is a light used to "fill in" shadows rather than provide the overall illumination. The fill light can be a lamp, or simply a reflector that is used to lighten shadow areas. *See also* Key light.

Flag: In photography, a board or panel that is used to prevent light falling on a certain area of the subject or set by physically blocking its path.

Flashmeter: A handheld lightmeter that is capable of taking an exposure reading from a flash, often in addition to taking ambient light readings.

Flash duration: The length of time that a flash fires for. Typically, this is far shorter than the shutter speed used on the camera—a flash duration can be as brief as 1/10,000 sec, or faster. A short flash duration is useful for freezing movement, and the duration is shorter as flash power is reduced.

Fluorescent: A continuous light source that uses electricity to excite mercury vapor to produce light. Once notorious for operating across a wide range of (often inconsistent) color temperatures, fluorescent lights are increasingly being used in photographic lighting.

f/stop: The camera's aperture setting; i.e. f/8, f/11, f/16, and so on.

Gel: A thin sheet of gelatin (or acetate) that is positioned in front of a light to adjust its color. This can be for technical reasons—converting the color temperature of tungsten lights to daylight, for example—or for creative effect.

Grid: A grid, or honeycomb, attaches to the front of a reflector dish to help direct the light in a more linear fashion toward the subject, preventing it from spilling out into other parts of the scene.

Head: Common shortening of "flash head," whether referring to a flash unit from a power pack-based system or a monolight.

HMI light: Abbreviation of Hydrargyrum Medium-arc Iodide, an HMI uses an arc lamp instead of an incandescent bulb to produce light. This makes it cooler running than incandescent lamps and more energy efficient. Runs at 5600K, so daylight balanced.

Honeycomb: *See* Grid

Hot light: Colloquial term for incandescent lights due to the high temperatures they produce.

Hotshoe: An accessory fitting found on most digital and film SLRs and some high-end point-and-shoot models, normally used to attach and control a flash unit. Depending on the camera model, it may also pass information to the flash such as the focus distance, to help produce the correct exposure.

Incandescent light: A type of light that uses a tungsten bulb to produce light. The tungsten filament in the bulb is heated, creating both light and heat with a warm color temperature of 3200K. *See also* Blonde and Redhead.

ISO: An international standard rating for film speed, now transferred to digital cameras. Refers to the sensitivity of the sensor or film to light; a low ISO setting (100) requires more light, while higher ISO settings (400) require less light. High ISO settings also produce digital images with more noise (digital interference that is revealed as a texture), or film-based images with increased grain.

Joules: A unit of energy, used in the measurement of flash output. Effectively, the work needed to produce one watt of power for one second (one watt second). *See also* Watt second.

Kelvin (K): A unit of temperature measurement that is used in photography to indicate the color balance of a lightsource: 3200K for tungsten lighting, and 5500K for daylight, for example. *See also* Color temperature.

Key light: The primary light in a lighting setup, which is providing the overall, or "key" illumination on the subject and usually creating the most distinct shadows. *See also* Fill light.

Lens flare: Light striking or refracting into the camera lens will create "flare," resulting in lowered contrast across the shot or, in extreme cases, distinct mulitcolored and multi-sized artifacts the shape of the aperture as the light strikes individual glass elements within the lens. Usually avoided by using a lens hood, flagging the camera so light is not falling on the lens, and by making sure no lights are pointing directly into the lens. Can also be used intentionally for creative effect.

Lightmeter: A measurement device used to measure the intensity of light and convert it into a photographic exposure comprising an ISO, aperture, and shutter speed value. Every digital SLR has a lightmeter built in, which takes reflected readings from the subject, typically through-the-lens. Handheld lightmeters allow incident light readings to be made, which measures the light falling on the subject, not the light reflected from it. This avoids any potentially misleading results from overly dark or overly light subjects. *See also* Flashmeter.

Main light: *See* Key light.

Modeling light: In a flash head, this is a secondary, continuous lamp that is used to provide a "preview" of the effect the flash will have. Can be proportional to the flash power, allowing you to see the effect each light in a multi-light setup is having, or set to full power to provide an overall illumination, irrespective of the flash output setting.

Monolight: A flash head that contains all the necessary power and flash controls in a single casing, without the need for an auxiliary power pack.

Octobox: A variation of the traditional rectangular or square softbox that uses an octagonal design. Preferred by many portrait and fashion photographers as the catchlights produced in the model's eyes appear more rounded.

Pack: In studio lighting, the auxiliary power pack required in a "pack-and-head" flash system. Available in different power settings, the total of which is distributed between the flash heads plugged into the pack, the pack forms the "control center" for all of the flashes.

Radio trigger: A method of triggering flash units wirelessy using a radio signal, rather than an optical slave cell. Each flash is equipped with a radio receiver and a radio transmitter is attached to the camera (usually via the camera's hotshoe). When the camera is fired, the transmitter sends a signal that is picked up by the flash-mounted receivers, triggering the flash.

Recycling time: In flash photography, the time taken for a flash head to build up the energy in its capacitors before it is ready to fire again. The shorter the recycling time, the quicker the flash will be ready, which is important for fast shooting. Reducing the power of a flash will typically shorten the recycling time.

Reflector: 1) A dish fitted to the front of a lamp to regulate the spread of light. 2) A board or other reflective surface designed to bounce light back onto a subject, normally used to lighten shadows.

Ringflash: A circular flash design that is mounted around the camera lens. Creates shadowless lighting as a result, with distinctive "donut"-shaped catchlights in the eyes. Primarily available for use with pack systems, but some monolight designs and smaller, battery-operated flashes exist. Also available as a continuous light source —a ring light.

Shutter speed: The length of time that the camera's shutter is open, exposing the digital sensor or film to light.

Slave cell: An optical cell that is attached or built in to a flash. When it detects the flash from another light, the slave cell triggers the flash it is connected to. This allows multiple lights to be triggered by one "master" flash that is connected to the camera.

Snoot: A conical light attachment that narrows the light emitted from a lamp to concentrate it on a small area.

Softbox: A light modifier designed to produce a diffuse light from a direct light source, allowing the power of the flash to be retained better than if it is bounced or reflected. Available in a wide range of sizes and shapes, with both silver and white reflective material on the inside, as well as internal baffles to further diffuse the light. A standard portrait accessory.

Striplight: 1) A fluorescent light using long tubes to create an elongated light that delivers a distinctly narrow beam of light. 2) A softbox designed to recreate the look of a fluorescent striplight.

Tungsten light: *See* Incandescent light.

Umbrella: A light attachment used to bounce light back onto the subject, and so soften its effect. Available in white, silver, and gold, and also as semi-translucent "shoot through" designs that work in a similar fashion to a softbox, although the softening effect is not as pronounced.

Watt second: In flash systems, watt seconds (w/s or w-s) are used to indicate the power of the flash unit. This is the input power of the flash, not its output power, and as it doesn't consider the efficiency of the flash components themselves there can be a significant difference in the output of two different models of flash unit, even if they both claim to have the same power rating.

ACKNOWLEDGMENTS

With many thanks to the following: Alastair Campbell and Adam Juniper of Ilex Press for their faith, direction and enthusiasm. Lucy, Rachael, Julia and Gabeen, the models for professionalism, assistance and laughing at my jokes. Thank you to Alan Marsh for studio facilities and sustaining supplies of tea and coffee, and Chris Mills for his coordination. This shoot would not have been possible without black gaffer tape and white string. Everybody involved in this project has learned much from the experience. Let there be light. This book is for photographers who want to keep seeing in different ways.

PICTURE CREDITS

All images in this book unless otherwise indicated were taken by Peter Hince. Courtesy of iStockphoto (www.istockphoto.com): p6, p10, p11 (left and bottom), p12 (top), p13, p14, p17, p18 (right), p19 (bottom), p20 (top), p21, p25 (bottom left and right); Courtesy of Profoto (www.profoto.com): p12 (bottom), p15 (top), p20 (bottom), p23, p24, p25; Courtesy of Fotolia (www.fotolia.com): p2, p7, p11 (top right), p15 (bottom left), p16, p18 (bottom left), p19 (top right).